The Buildings of Charleston

THE BUILDINGS
of CHARLESTON

A Guide to the City's Architecture

JONATHAN H. POSTON
for
Historic Charleston Foundation

University of South Carolina Press

© 1997 University of South Carolina

Published in Columbia, South Carolina, by the
University of South Carolina Press

Manufactured in the United States of America

01   00   99   5   4   3   2

Library of Congress Cataloging-in-Publication Data

Poston, Jonathan, 1954–
    The Buildings of Charleston: a guide to the city's
architecture / Jonathan H. Poston
        p.   cm.
    "In cooperation with Historic Charleston Foundation."
    Includes bibliographical references and index.
    ISBN 1-57003-202-5
    1. Architecture–South Carolina–Charleston. 2. Charleston
(S.C.)–Buildings, structures, etc. I. Historic Charleston Foundation
(Charleston, S.C.) II. Title.
    NA735.C35P67 1997
    720'.9757'915–dc21   96-37990

CONTENTS

PREFACE

Guidebooks have been part of published literature available to Charleston's visitors since the antebellum period. Articles in *Leslie's Illustrated Newspaper, Harper's Weekly,* and *Harper's New Monthly Magazine* chronicled the city's historic charm in the mid-nineteenth century, and after the Civil War work such as Arthur Mazyck's 1875 *Guide to Charleston Illustrated* and his better-known *Charleston, South Carolina* appeared, the latter with heliotype photographs. These pioneering efforts and subsequent guides by postcard companies, such as *Charleston, S.C.,* published in 1890 by the Albertype Company, gave visitors tangible reminders of Charleston's churches, public buildings, residences, parks, and monuments.

The first major book produced on Charleston architecture, *The Dwelling Houses of Charleston, South Carolina* (1917), co-authored by Alice Ravenel Huger Smith with her father Daniel Elliott Huger Smith, inspired architectural historians such as Fiske Kimball, who praised its scholarship and "picturesque atmosphere sketches with beautiful photographs and exact plans and details." Miss Smith's work included measured plans by the young architectural historian Albert Simons, who along with architect Samuel S. Lapham produced the next stage of documenting Charleston's architectural past with their Octagon Library volume *Charleston, South Carolina* (1927) and provided drawings for their colleague Samuel Gaillard Stoney's *Plantations of the Carolina Low Country* (1938).

These authors joined New York architectural historian John Mead Howells (better known for his work on Portsmouth, N.H.) and museum professional Helen McCormick in 1940 to prepare America's first citywide architectural survey, a project under the aegis of the Carolina Art Association and its innovative, preservation-minded director, Robert N. S. Whitelaw. In 1944 the Carolina Art Association began the issuance of *This Is Charleston,* the published version of the survey, with addresses, thumbnail photos, dates, ratings, and pithy descriptions of the city's most historic buildings. For the serious historian and the educated traveler, this book became the sine qua non for any walk through the historic areas of peninsular Charleston, as well as a handy reference for future preservationists and city officials. Those who were interested in more detailed information could find chains of title and architectural facts on individual buildings nearly every week in the pages of Charleston's *News and Courier* and *Evening Post* newspapers in a column entitled "Do You Know Your Charleston," authored by various individuals including, in more recent decades, W. H. Johnson Thomas, Isabella Leland, Jack Leland, Robert Stockton, and Jane Allen. Stockton edited this considerable volume of material and his own notes for use by the City of Charleston as the text for all city guides.

The roots of the present volume, however, lie in the first publication in 1965 of *Across the Cobblestones,* a 106-page guidebook produced by the Junior League of Charleston to benefit Historic Charleston Foundation's Revolving Fund. This small paperback, including historical and architectural highlights of the peninsula below Charlotte Street and notes on other areas of interest (including "Local Fauna" and "Charleston Furniture"), went through numerous printings by the late-1970s.

In the fall of 1994, following Historic Charleston Foundation's sponsorship of a successful conference of the Vernacular Architectural Forum (VAF) and production of a large guide for the meeting's customary tours, the Foundation's trustees and executive director Carter L. Hudgins asked Jonathan Poston, director of preservation, to produce a new work. This book is an attempt to build on all of its predecessors. The intent of this volume is to offer the interested traveler a comprehensive sourcebook when planning a visit to Charleston and when walking its streets. The book also may provide an additional source for homeowners, preservationists, and planners who rely on *This Is Charleston* and other early works for quick reference. Historical information on builders and notable facts about many of the sites synthesize the scholarship drawn from published histories available from the "Do You Know" columns of the Charleston newspapers, other guides and books about Charleston architecture, and the significant files of Historic Charleston Foundation for Broad Street, Ansonborough, and individual houses throughout the city. These files contain notes largely prepared for Historic Charleston Foundation by scholars of Charleston's history and buildings including the late Louis Green, Samuel Gaillard Stoney, Elias Ball Bull, and, more recently, Harlan Green, Robert Stockton, Ruth Williams Cupp, Alice F. Levkoff, Louis Nelson, and the author. A considerable part of this book, however, comes from new research by staff and interns of Historic Charleston Foundation, as well as friendly colleagues from other institutions.

This book focuses on the official "Old and Historic District of Charleston, S.C.," most of which is listed on the National Register of Historic Places and a large portion of which is designated as a National Historic Landmark District. This by no means indicates lesser importance for the significant boroughs in the upper peninsula contained within the locally designated "Old City District" or for sites within and adjacent to the city across the rivers. These neighborhoods will require further study for inclusion in a future edition of this book, while the outlying sites will be the focus of a separate publication. Attempts have been made to include as many buildings and streets of note as possible.

It might be risky to assert that new understandings of Charleston's architecture can emerge from a book such as this. Many important scholars of American architectural and social history have recently begun to examine the Lowcountry, and architectural documentation projects have only lately resurfaced in the city after a nearly fifty-year hiatus of such work. Consider, for example, the sheer volume of older structures in Charleston built by German immigrants and other ethnic groups. In a city with a reputation for pervasive English and to some degree French origins, the discovery of Charleston's architectural diversity calls into question long-held assumptions about the city's buildings and its social history. So, too, this book challenges the assertion in Samuel and Narcissa Chamberlain's splendid photographic essay, *Southern Interiors* (1956), that Charleston was spared from "the scourge of Victorian architecture." On the contrary, Charleston's historic neighborhoods, save Ansonborough, have an enormous stock of Queen Anne style residences built between 1870 and 1915.

Through all its vicissitudes, Charleston architectural style has remained dynamic. Each visitor should look at the way layers of history have created a unique mix of styles. A walk down any street highlighted in this guide will undoubtedly provide visual delight and remarkable adventure.

ACKNOWLEDGMENTS

The production of this book has been an overwhelmingly collaborative effort. The greatest contributions have come from Katherine Saunders, who joined Historic Charleston Foundation as preservation planning coordinator in May 1996 and charged into the existing project with extraordinary talent and energy. Katherine directed a stock of excellent interns, notably Dana Addison of Mary Washington College and Debbie Bordeau, a graduate of Randolph-Macon Woman's College, in using the Register of Mesne Conveyance Office and other repositories. Katherine, Debbie, and Dana, with help from intern Elizabeth Guckenberger from Boston University, produced an enormous stock of new house histories, especially for chapters 4, 7, 8, and 9. All of them worked with the author through evening writing sessions preparing the manuscript, as did Foundation media relations coordinator Carroll Ann Bowers. As deadlines approached, Katherine, Debbie, who was by then a full-time HCF staff member in the development division, and Carroll Ann again pitched in their writing, editing, and photography talents to insure that the book was completed successfully. Thus the author and the Foundation owe the creation of this book to many individuals but are especially in the debt of Katherine Saunders, Debbie Bordeau, and Carroll Ann Bowers. This book bears the imprint of skills, patiently applied, by the staff of the University of South Carolina Press in editing and designing this book, and to them, particularly Rebecca Blakeney and Margaret V. Hill, and Catherine Fry, the director of the Press, I express my most sincere thanks.

Gratitude for early work on this project is extended for assistance in the summer of 1995 by interns Gina Haney, then an M.A. candidate at the University of Virginia; Louis Nelson, a former HCF preservation staff member and a Ph.D. candidate at the University of Delaware; and Carol Borchert, then a Winterthur fellow. They helped begin the process of converting the VAF guide into a more comprehensive book and helped lay the groundwork for the first three chapters of *The Buildings of Charleston*.

Photography of many sites stemmed from work begun in 1978 by William Struhs. Some photographs have resulted from the excellent Historic American Buildings Survey work of Jack Boucher, especially on projects with the Foundation including Hurricane Hugo recovery, the Battery Documentation Project, and the Charleston District Jail Project. Photography of additional buildings was completed in 1996 by Struhs, as well as Katherine Saunders, her father, Wayne Saunders, and Carroll Ann Bowers.

Carroll Ann Bowers also joined in the evening writing sessions, as did intern Chris Frey and *Post and Courier* city editor John Burbage, who provided important help and assistance in the completion of the manuscript. Appreciation is further extended to Connie Wyrick and Elise Pinckney and to the numerous individuals who completed the initial VAF guide and contributed important research now included within these pages, especially Carl Lounsbury, Maurie McInnis, Robert Leath, Michael Robertson, Alice F. Levkoff, Sarah Fick, Bernard L. Herman, and Richard Marks III. The author is also grateful for previous research or more recent information provided by Christine Trebellas, Stephen Davis, Laura Snider, Glenn Keyes, John Bivins, Joseph K. Oppermann, David Shields, Denise Stone, Spencer Tolley, Max L. Hill III, Simons Young, William Pettus V, Matthew Strong, Keith Eggener, and Ernest Shealy.

Important research direction, information, and early images for the illustration of the book came from the staffs of The Charleston Museum, particularly Mary Giles and Sharon Bennett; the S.C. Historical Society, especially Alex Moore, Pete Rerig, Steven Hoffius, and Pat Hash; the Charleston County Register of Mesne Conveyance; the Charleston Library Society, particularly Pat Bennett; the *Post and Courier* newspaper; the Gibbes Museum of Art, notably Angela Mack, Jennifer Haynesworth, and Paul Figueroa; Preservation Consultants, chiefly Sarah Fick and John Laurens; the Middleton Place Foundation, especially Barbara Doyle, Kris Kepford-Young, and Charles Duell; Drayton Hall, chiefly George McDaniel, Meggett Lavin, Tracy Hayes, and Bob Barker; the Museum of Early Southern Decorative Arts, mainly Sally Gant; the Colonial Williamsburg Foundation; the City of Charleston, especially city hall curator Linda Heffley; the Preservation Society of Charleston, especially Robert Gurley and Cynthia Jenkins; and the Charleston County Library. The College of Charleston's Avery Institute, the Valentine Museum, the American Institute of Architects, and the Yale University Art Gallery graciously granted the use of images in their collections as well. Several local architects and firms assisted with material on their commissions, including Glenn Keyes Architects, Thomson Penney of LS3P Architects, Jeffrey Rosenblum of Rosenblum Associates, Dan Beaman of Cummings and McCrady, Ray Huff of Huff, Reisberg, and Lunn, Evans and Schmidt Architects, and Mitchell, Small and Donahue Architects. Foundation trustees and friends provided older images as well, and I am particularly grateful to Jane Hanahan, Dr. G. Fraser Wilson, the Reverend Frank McClain,

Sallie Simons, Robert Prenner, LaVonne Phillips, Dorothy Kerrison, Dianne Avlon, and Vereen Coen for images or detailed information and for the patience of all of those Charlestonians, too numerous to mention, who allowed their houses to be exhaustively examined. Additional photographs and image copywork were principally produced by Ron Anton Rocz, Terry Richardson and Rich-Steel ProLabs, Alterman Studios, and King Street Photo.

Significant contributions to this work, as with all HCF architectural history endeavors, can be traced to the Architectural Research Department at Colonial Williamsburg, essentially Dr. Carl Lounsbury, Willie Graham, Ed Chappell, and Mark Wenger; the Center for Historic Architecture and Engineering at the University of Delaware, especially Dr. Bernard Herman, Gabrielle Lanier, and David Ames; and the Center for Historic Preservation at Mary Washington College, with particular thanks to Dr. Gary Stanton and W. Brown Morton. I am most appreciative of Bernie Herman's contribution of an essay on the Charleston single house and George Washington University professor John Vlach's summation of the development of Charleston ironwork. Assistance and guidance were also provided on numerous occasions to the author by the late Paul Buchanan of Williamsburg, Orlando Ridout V of Annapolis, Richard Marks III, Louis P. Nelson, Rae Ann Blyth, M. E. Van Dyke, Amanda Griffith Herbert, Benjamin H. Wilson, Chris Frey, Mary Pope Waring, and Carter L. Hudgins. The latter two individuals guided the selection of the sites included in this book and its overall emphasis. Furthermore, I could never replace the splendid education provided by working with Buchanan, Lounsbury, Graham, Ridout, Wenger, Chappell, Herman, Morton, Herbert, and Marks on the examination of numerous buildings around Charleston and having the benefit of their keen observations and research.

Measured drawings used in this guide include many elevations and plans from the Historic American Buildings Survey, especially from those undertaken with Foundation assistance, plans completed by International Council of Monuments and Sites fellow Nicholas Affidzi, and documentation drawings produced for the VAF guide. The individuals working on these drawings included David Craig, Emily Curtis, Virginia Dore, Laura Edwards, Shelley Ekermeyer, Allyson Eubank, Claudette Gamache, Elizabeth Keane, Cynthia Liccese, William Sherman, Jennifer MacGowan, Anita Dodd, Bobbie Kerr, and particularly Willie Graham, Steve Bauer, Mark Wenger, Carter Hudgins, Ed Chappell, Gary Stanton, Gabrielle Lanier, Bernard Herman, and Gina Haney.

As deadlines neared for final completion of this work, all of Historic Charleston Foundation's staff pitched in to help with editing and checking the manuscript. I am indebted beyond measure to Katherine Saunders, Debbie Bordeau, and Carroll Ann Bowers for continuing their commitment and also to Robert Leath, Sean Houlihan, Annette

Chamberlain, Carter Hudgins, Betty Guerard, Lee Manigault, Judy Purches, Tom Savage, Carol Borchert, Renee LaHue, and Jason Neville for making the last week's work a success. Immeasurable assistance also came from individuals who offered final comments on various parts chapters of the manuscript, including Joseph H. McGee, Maurie McInnis, Sarah Fick, Tom Savage, Richard Marks III, Carl Lounsbury, Elise Pinckney, Martha Zierden, John Burbage, and Robert Rosen. Dr. Lounsbury's *Illustrated Glossary of Early Southern Architecture and Landscape* was a welcome and useful source in compiling the glossary for this book. The secretary of the preservation division, Therese Munroe, not only started the index work but also handled numerous details of final manuscript preparation, including entering corrections with Betty Guerard. I especially thank Therese for keeping the preservation division running smoothly while all other eyes were on the manuscript. Appreciation is extended to Carter Hudgins, Donna Hudgins, and Debbie Bordeau for their completion of the indexes.

The author expresses the greatest acknowledgment to Steven Bauer for completion of the splendid bird's-eye drawing that serves as the base graphic for the neighborhoods in this volume. Credit also goes to Paul Rossmann for his elegent design of the base map. My thanks finally to the trustees of Historic Charleston Foundation for their support and inspiration.

Jonathan H. Poston
Charleston
February 1997

HOW TO USE THIS BOOK

The entries in this book are divided by chapters according to area, delineated either through the historical boundaries of a single neighborhood or by historical factors defining that section of Charleston. Within each chapter an introductory essay provides a starting point for understanding the history and development of that portion of the city, followed by individual streets set out alphabetically and houses numbered in ascending order. A portion of an axiometric drawing of the peninsula precedes each section to provide handy orientation to the location of the entries. Modern photographs accompany some entries while others are illustrated by early photographs, plats, drawings, or measured plans that serve to offer significant understanding or interest to the text.

Some streets are essays in themselves with dates of development, former names, and information on important structures. Most buildings, however, are individually listed with captions including official street addresses; names for buildings (based either on Charleston tradition or on the name of the builder and occasionally joined with the name of a family that lived in the building for a significant length of time); dates of construction (based on research and stylistic estimation); dates of important known restorations, rehabilitations, reconstructions, additions, or alterations; and names of known or attributed architects and craftsmen. Restoration indicates the distinct attempt to return a building to its earlier or original character; rehabilitation indicates the updating of a structure, often to a new or compatible use while retaining most of its historic character; and reconstruction (rarely seen in Charleston) involves the re-creation of vanished buildings. Alteration can describe changes to buildings without regard to original character, while renovation usually denotes changes and repairs that involve maintenance or modernization, not necessarily restoration, of the historic appearance of a given structure.

The text of each building entry usually provides descriptive architectural information, authentic historical data, and some statement of the significance of the site. Related buildings in the block or across the street that are not the subjects of individual entries or buildings of related history described elsewhere are designated in italics within the given entries. Interior descriptions are rarely provided for individual dwellings, as these are not visible to the touring public; but such information is usually given for house museums, public buildings, churches, some commercial structures, and occasionally private houses when their interiors are of particular importance. An 🅝 symbol adjacent to an entry denotes its individual inclusion on the National Register of Historic Places; while an 🅛 symbol identifies those structures additionally designated as National Historic Landmarks by the United States Department of the Interior. A comprehensive index at the back provides listings by street and number as well as cross-referencing for the names of individual houses. Historic house museums and other public sites are given special emphasis. They have set hours of operation.

The vast majority of houses included in this volume are privately owned and are to be viewed from the street or sidewalk only, excepting those opened by ticket for seasonal tours. Historic churches are sometimes open depending on individual schedules. Research on each building reflects current available scholarship, and the author welcomes new information. Even in Charleston with its abundance of historic resources and historic preservation codes, dynamic change may alter the buildings described in this book. It is expected that new versions of this volume will appear in the future to address such modifications.

A BRIEF CHARLESTON CHRONOLOGY

1663 King Charles II of England grants the territory known as Carolana, later Carolina, to eight loyal supporters, the Lords Proprietors: John Berkeley (Baron Berkeley of Stratton), Sir William Berkeley, Sir George Carteret, Sir John Colleton, Anthony Ashley Cooper (later Earl of Shaftesbury), William Craven (Earl of Craven), Edward Hyde (Earl of Clarendon), and George Monck (Duke of Albemarle).

1669 Lord Anthony Ashley Cooper, who is honored by having Charleston's principal rivers named for him, issues the Fundamental Constitutions with the help of his secretary, John Locke. These constitutions, readily accepted by the colonists, provide a framework for government, initially allowing for a landed gentry and religious tolerance. The first colonists set sail from England.

1670 The first permanent English settlement south of Virginia is established at Albemarle Point on the west bank of the Ashley River, several miles inland of the current city of Charleston.

1672 Oyster Point, the lower part of the peninsula between the Ashley and Cooper Rivers, is surveyed as a future town site due to its defensive capabilities and potential as a port.

1679 The Lords Proprietors direct Gov. Joseph West to complete the settlement's move to Oyster Point within the year. They further order that the new settlement be called Charles Town in honor of their king.

1680 Charles Town is officially moved to its new location and laid out according to the "Grand Modell," a plan that included gridded streets and a central public square.

The first Huguenots arrive in the ship *Richmond.*

1681 Dissenters of the Anglican Church form an independent meeting or congregational church on present-day Meeting Street.

1682 The congregation of St. Philip's Church is organized as the colony's first Anglican parish (the first St. Philip's Church was on the site of the present St. Michael's Church and at the center of the public square of the Grand Modell).

1695 The first Jewish settler is recorded in Charles Town.

1696 South Carolina's first slave legislation, borrowed heavily from Barbadian codes, is enacted.

1698 Charles Town's first earthquake occurs in February while the town is recovering from its initial smallpox epidemic, and a few weeks later a major fire destroys one fourth of the town.

1699 A yellow fever epidemic, the first of many, is responsible for nearly 200 deaths, and a major hurricane sweeps into town during the same period.

1700 Charles Town's library, a parochial institution founded by Anglican missionaries three years earlier, is funded by the Assembly and becomes America's first public library.

1704 Walled fortifications surrounding the town are completed as shown on the Crisp map of 1704; designed to ward off a Spanish attack by sea, these walls remain essentially in place until after 1719.

1706 The Assembly passes the Church Act under the influence of the Goose Creek Men, a political party of planters primarily of Barbadian origin; the act establishes the Anglican Church in the colony and directs the creation of ten parishes with churches to be constructed at the colony's expense.

1708 A majority-black population in South Carolina is recorded for the first time.

1712 The province of Carolina is divided and governed as two colonies: North Carolina and South Carolina.

1715 The Yemassee Indian War begins when 100 settlers are massacred by members of the Yemassee tribe in St. Helena (Beaufort); refugees flee to Charles Town.

1718 Col. William Rhett defeats pirates in a naval battle in the Cape Fear River; the so-called "Gentleman Pirate," Stede Bonnet, is captured, tried, and hanged at Oyster Point.

1719 Dissatisfied with the rule of the Lords Proprietors, the S.C. House of Assembly forms a convention and petitions to become a crown colony.

1730 The population of the colony, excluding tribal Indians, has grown to nearly 30,000. Of these, more than 20,000 are slaves.

1732 The *South Carolina Gazette* begins publication in Charles Town as the first newspaper south of Virginia.

1735 The first opera performed in America, Colley Cibber's *Flora, or Hob in the Well*, is produced in the public room of Shepheard's Tavern in Charles Town.

1736 The Charles Town (Dock Street) Theatre, one of the first theaters built in America specifically for the production of plays, opens with a performance of *The Recruiting Officer.*

1739 A slave insurrection on the plantations along the Stono River southeast of the city results in America's bloodiest and one of its only successful slave rebellions.

1740 The fire of 1740, the worst fire yet, burns nearly half the city, including Elliott, Broad, Union (State), parts of Church, and other streets.

1744 The first successful production and processing of indigo is completed; Eliza Lucas Pinckney is credited with its initial success and with her husband Charles Pinckney for its promotion as the colony's second most important staple crop.

1748 The Charles Town Library Society is organized.

1752 An extremely destructive hurricane washes across the city; another follows two weeks later.

1753 At the corners of Broad and Meeting Streets, Charles Town's planned civic square is finally a reality, with construction beginning on both the Statehouse and St. Michael's Church through authorization of the Assembly two years earlier.

1762 The St. Cecilia Society, America's first musical organization, is established in Charles Town.

1764 The Stamp Act and the Sugar Act arouse local opposition.

1765 By this date Charles Town has become known as Charlestown.

1772 Charlestown, nearing a population of 12,000, is the fourth largest city in British North America.

1773 A committee of the Charlestown Library Society begins collecting materials to start the first museum in America, later called the Charleston Museum, while merchants organize the nation's first Chamber of Commerce.

1774 South Carolina delegates go to the First Continental Congress in Philadelphia, and Henry Middleton becomes its second president.

1775 The Revolution begins; South Carolina's last royal governor, Lord William Campbell, flees.

1776 South Carolina adopts its own constitution in March and sets up an independent government, with John Rutledge as president and Henry Laurens as vice president.

On June 28 William Moultrie and a small band of patriots protect Charlestown Harbor by repulsing the English fleet led by Sir Peter Parker; Fort Moultrie, a palmetto log fort, becomes the site of the first decisive victory over the British; the palmetto tree later becomes the state symbol on its flag.

Four of Charlestown's native sons: Thomas Heyward Jr., Thomas Lynch Jr., Arthur Middleton, and Edward Rutledge, sign the Declaration of Independence in Philadelphia.

1778 Another great fire destroys several blocks of the city.

1780 Charlestown falls to the British on May 12. The occupation lasts for two years.

1782 The British evacuate, taking with them the bells of St. Michael's, much of the town's silver, 3,000 loyalists, and 5,000 slaves.

1783 The city is incorporated and is henceforth known as Charleston, with Richard Hutson as its first intendant (mayor), elected with a board of wardens.

1785 The College of Charleston is incorporated.

1786 An affirmative vote by the Assembly sets plans to move the capital from Charleston to a new site, including Taylor's Plantation, renamed Columbia.

1787 Charlestonians John Rutledge, Charles Cotesworth Pinckney, Charles Pinckney, and Pierce Butler represent South Carolina at the Constitutional Convention in Philadelphia.

Members of America's first golf club, founded in Charleston by Scottish merchants, begin to play the game on a green or open square in the Village of Harleston neighborhood.

1788 The South Carolina Statehouse in Charleston is gutted in a suspicious fire; South Carolina ratifies the U.S. Constitution in the Exchange Building.

1791 President George Washington visits the city; he is lavishly entertained and stays at the home of Thomas Heyward Jr. on Church Street, now known as the Heyward-Washington House.

1796 A disastrous fire spreads west from East Bay to Meeting Street; the area between Broad and Cumberland Streets is chiefly damaged.

1803 The foreign slave trade reopens in South Carolina for the first time since 1787; more than 40,000 African slaves are imported in the next five years before the practice is brought to an end under the U.S. Constitution in 1808.

1811 A great "cyclone" strikes the city and damages many buildings.

1813 Another fierce hurricane comes ashore in the Lowcountry surrounding Charleston.

1822 The Denmark Vesey slave insurrection plot is uncovered; conspirators are hanged or sent from the state, and stricter slave laws are enacted as a result.

1824 John C. Calhoun, former secretary of war, is elected vice president of the United States under President John Quincy Adams.

Members of K.K. Beth Elohim synagogue organize the Reformed Society of Israelites beginning Reform Judaism in America.

1827 Edgar Allan Poe is stationed at Fort Moultrie on Sullivan's Island; his short story "The Gold Bug" draws heavily upon this experience.

1828 A banner economic year for Charleston commences with the shipment of its largest Sea Island cotton crop and its second greatest rice crop.

1832 The Nullification controversy begins as a response to the tariff of 1832, an enactment unfavorable to the southern states.

1833 The completion of a railway stretching from Charleston to Hamburg at a distance of 136 miles results in the longest railroad in the world at this time.

1835 St. Philip's Episcopal Church is destroyed by fire.

1838 Fire rages across 145 acres of the city, destroying nearly 1,000 buildings eastward from King Street to Ansonborough.

1839 With the beginning of an annual appropriation from the city, the College of Charleston becomes the first municipally supported college in the United States.

1842 The Citadel, The Military College of South Carolina, is established in Charleston.

1860 South Carolinians sign the Ordinance of Secession on December 20 at Institute Hall in Charleston. Six days later U.S. Army Maj. Robert Anderson moves his troops from Fort Moultrie to Fort Sumter.

1861 On April 12 the firing on Federal forces at Fort Sumter initiates the War Between the States; perhaps the worst fire in Charleston's history occurs on December 11, with the path of the blaze extending in a diagonal direction from the Cooper to the Ashley Rivers.

1863 The 54th Massachusetts, an African American regiment under the command of Col. Robert Gould Shaw, leads an assault on Battery Wagner off Charleston Harbor on Morris Island; the regiment sustains heavy casualties.

The federal bombardment of Charleston, which will last nearly eighteen months, begins in August; shells fall as far north as Calhoun Street.

The president of the Confederacy, Jefferson Davis, visits Charleston near the end of the year; he stays in Gov. William Aiken's house on Elizabeth Street.

1864 The Confederate submarine *Hunley* sinks the Union ship *Housatonic* off Sullivans Island, but it is also lost, with no survivors; the action marks the first successful sinking of a ship during warfare by a submarine.

1865 Federal troops occupy the city in February, after 587 days of siege.

1867 Phosphates are discovered on former plantation lands outside the city, precipitating a booming new industry.

1879 William Ashmead Courtenay is elected mayor and during his eight-year administration greatly expands the city's parks and other public services and improvements.

1885 Another great "cyclone" rakes the city.

1886 A devastating earthquake strikes Charleston in August, destroying and damaging countless properties and killing ninety-two people.

1893 Another severe hurricane batters the Charleston area.

1901 The Navy Yard at Port Royal is relocated to a Cooper River site, a few miles above Charleston's city limits.

1902 The Interstate and West Indian Exposition, a world's fair, opens at Hampton Park, bringing international attention to the city.

1911 A hurricane hits the city and environs in August with recorded wind speeds between 94 and 106 mph and brings to an end the rice industry in South Carolina.

1917 The boll weevil is first detected; the insects destroy the Sea Island cotton industry by 1919.

1920 The Society for the Preservation of Old Dwellings, now the Preservation Society of Charleston, is founded by Susan Pringle Frost.

1929 The Cooper River Bridge opens, connecting Charleston and Mount Pleasant.

1931 A pioneering zoning ordinance is passed by Charleston City Council, creating the nation's first official historic district and Board of Architectural Review.

1935 The opera *Porgy and Bess,* based on Charlestonian DuBose Heyward's novel *Porgy* and composed by George Gershwin, opens in New York City.

1938 Two tornadoes strike the city within fifteen minutes; the second devastates the City Market.

1940 A hurricane, the worst in nearly thirty years, hammers the city.

1941 With the beginning of World War II, the Charleston area swells with additional population and the Navy Yard becomes the third largest industry in the state.

1947 Judge J. Waites Waring rules in Charleston that South Carolina primary elections must be opened to African Americans, thus introducing the city to the civil rights era.

The civic services committee of the Carolina Art Association establishes Historic Charleston Foundation (HCF).

1959 The HCF Ansonborough Rehabilitation Project begins, using an innovative method of financing—a revolving fund for restoration.

J. Palmer Gaillard becomes mayor of Charleston and within a year opens the first municipal facility to blacks in South Carolina.

1966 The city's historic district is expanded to include the neighborhoods of Ansonborough and Harleston, and the preservation zoning ordinance is significantly updated.

1969 The hospital strike in Charleston becomes one of the nation's leading civil rights struggles.

1975 Joseph P. Riley Jr. is first elected mayor of Charleston.

1977 The arts festival "Spoleto USA" begins.

1989 Hurricane Hugo causes extensive damage to the Charleston area.

1990 Charleston's Waterfront Park opens to the public.

1995 The Navy Yard and Naval Base close; tourism has become Charleston's largest industry.

INTRODUCTION TO
CHARLESTON ARCHITECTURE

*I*n 1838 the noted English actress and future abolitionist Fanny Kemble visited Charleston and said:

> *This city is the oldest I have yet seen in America. . . . The appearance of the city is highly picturesque, a word which can apply to none other of the American towns. . . . It is in this respect a far more aristocratic (should I not say democratic?) city than any I have yet seen in America, inasmuch as every house seems built to the owner's particular taste; and in one street you seem to be in an old English town, and in another in some continental city of France or Italy. This variety is extremely pleasing to the eye.*

View of Meeting Street, looking north. Engraved by S. Trier, circa 1840

Similar observations of the city's beauty and distinct architectural character are repeated over and over in early travelers' accounts. Unlike most American cities, Charleston has an urban landscape that still largely reflects its individual history and development.

The colony of Carolina, originally named Carolana in honor of Charles I, was granted by his son, Charles II, to eight courtiers who had helped him recover the throne of England. These Lords Proprietors were led by Anthony Ashley Cooper, Earl of Shaftesbury. Aided by his secretary, the political philosopher John Locke, Shaftesbury developed a unique plan for rule of the colony. This document, the Fundamental Constitutions of Carolina, set up a landed aristocracy, later to be abandoned, and also mandated religious toleration.

Broad at Church Street looking east toward St. Michael's steeple

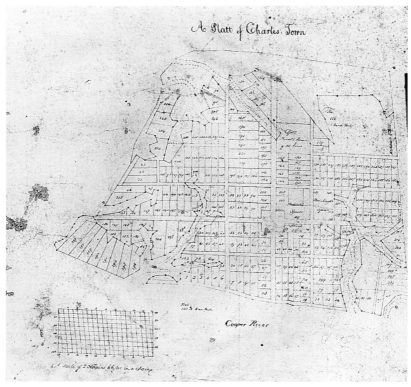

Redrawn plat of the original Grand Modell

Arriving in 1670, the first colonist originally sited their settlement across the Ashley River. This first Charles Town was well established by 1680, when it was decided that the proprietary colony of Carolina would erect a new town on the site formerly called Oyster Point. By the 1690s the town had more than a hundred houses, and by the end of the decade it was surrounded, partially or completely, by a large brick and possibly tabby wall with corner bastions and a drawbridge where Broad and Meeting Streets intersect today.

The wall dictated the earliest architectural development of the urban core, circumventing the original plans of the Lords Proprietors for a baroque grid plan with a great central square. A 1739 engraving by Bishop Roberts indicates it was an earlier sort of English architecture: late-seventeenth-century postmedieval and Jacobean, with curvilinear gables and steeply pitched roofs, characteristics borrowed by the English from the low countries of Europe. Some buildings were half-timbered or of Burmuda stone, although the Lords Proprietors encouraged brick.

A number of late-seventeenth- and early-eighteenth-century fires destroyed this construction, except for a few buildings such as the Old Powder Magazine and the John Lining House. The population of Charles Town at this time was fairly diverse, and the society was characterized by openness and fluidity. English Anglican immigrants, sometimes the younger sons of Barbadian sugar planters, vied for control with English Dissenter families. Hundreds of French Huguenot refugees arrived in the 1680s, and many soon achieved wealth and position. Other groups such as Scots, German Palatines, and Sephardic Jews came as well. African slaves brought in at the initial behest of the Barbadians arrived in vast numbers, especially between 1700 and 1740. During this period more than 40 percent of all slaves imported to the mainland of North America came through the port of Charles Town via Sullivan's Island. Their creole language, known as Gullah, and their African cultural traditions were preserved on isolated plantations and influenced the dominant culture as well.

The completion of St. Philip's Episcopal Church in 1722 marked the beginning of a new elegance for Charles Town. In the surrounding countryside, where the earliest plantation houses were of simple construction, great Georgian dwellings were being built by the 1720s. These included Archdale Hall, The Oaks, and Ashley Hall—now destroyed; and Drayton Hall (1742), still extant and considered the finest example of Georgian Palladian architecture in America.

Detail of the Half-Moon Battery and Court of Guard from Bishop Roberts's Charles Town Harbor, *circa 1738*

View of Drayton Hall, circa 1742, before it was purchased by the National Trust

View of Charles-Town *by Thomas Leitch, 1774*

After a major fire in 1740, a great period of rebuilding began, fully developing Charleston's traditional version of Georgian architecture. The "Charleston single house," a typical single-pile Georgian house turned on its end to fit city lots so inhabitants could take advantage of prevailing breezes, became the rule. Later these were embellished with porches, or piazzas, often several tiers high, on the southern or western elevation. Charleston's most opulent colonial buildings were built after 1760 as the boom in rice and indigo exports made the city the fourth largest in British North America and, by all accounts, the wealthiest. One writer noted that three hundred houses were built between 1760 and 1770, "many of them very elegant." St. Michael's Church, the State-house (rebuilt in 1792 as the Courthouse), and the Exchange building were public manifestations of this wealth. The work of artisans, including painters, silversmiths, carvers, and cabinetmakers, flourished to serve rich consumers, who also imported many luxuries from London. Theater and music advanced to a degree unusual for the American colonies.

The Revolutionary War and years of British occupation took a severe toll on the buildings of Charleston. After the war "mechanics" experienced in construction trades slowly began to repopulate the city. The Adamesque style, or Neoclassicism, adapted to local tastes and climate, took hold in the newly incorporated city of Charleston, as it did in much of the rest of the new nation.

The great "gentleman architect" of the city in this period was Gabriel Manigault (1758–1809), designer of the South Carolina Society Hall, the Joseph Manigault House, the Orphan House Chapel, and the Bank of the United States, later Charleston City Hall. Unidentified architects designed such imposing mansions as the Nathaniel Russell House. A few English Regency style buildings often attributed to the brief sojourn of English architect William Jay, such as the Duncan House (Ashley Hall School) and more assuredly the William Mason Smith House, were also of this early national period when Charleston experienced renewed wealth from exports of rice and Sea Island cotton.

Charleston's most famous native architect, Robert Mills, indicated the prevailing Classical Revival style with his design for a new Independent (Congregational) Church, lost in the fire of 1861, and foreshadowed the coming dominance of the Greek Revival with his designs for the First Baptist Church (1822) and the Fireproof Building (1826). Countless buildings in the Greek Revival style followed, including residences such as the Roper House and religious buildings such as Temple Beth Elohim.

Gabriel Manigault's Orphan House Chapel of 1807, under demolition in the 1950s

Edward Brickell White was the most important architect of the city after 1830 working in associational styles. He designed the Market Hall in Greek Revival style, the portico for the College of Charleston in Roman Ionic, and a new Huguenot Church in Gothic Revival. Romantic styles, especially Italianate, were often used for new structures and for remodeling older buildings before the War Between the States.

Charleston in the three decades before the war was a rather closed city, characterized by some economic decline and fearful of its slaves since the discovery of the Vesey Plot in 1822. Bent on protecting its system, fiercely proud of its architectural

Greek Revival style column

Panorama of Charleston *by John William Hill, 1850*

William Aiken Walker's painting of Fort Sumter during the Union ironclad attack, 1864

The Northeast Railway Depot, a casualty of the 1865 fire

Interior of S.C. Institute Hall

beauty and opulent lifestyle, and inflamed by the rhetoric of fire-eating politicians, a convention in Charleston in December 1860 voted to secede from the Union. The war began in April 1861 with the attack on Fort Sumter, the U.S. military stronghold on an island at the entrance to the harbor.

The blockade and bombardment of the city during the war, a fire in 1861, and another around the railroad depot in the evacuation of 1865 took a heavy toll on the city's architectural ensemble. The city's recovery began in the 1870s with the discovery of phosphate deposits on the Ashley River plantations and some resumption of the planting of cotton and rice. But a hurricane in 1885 and a major earthquake in 1886 stymied the expression of the city's renewed wealth. Nevertheless, even these disasters did not eradicate the city's architectural tradition. Many new buildings were built in Victorian styles but usually with piazzas and some attention to Charleston traditions. Even new public buildings, such as the Second Empire style Federal Courthouse and Post Office of 1896 at the intersection of Meeting and Broad Streets, were sited and detailed so as to give deference to their colonial neighbors. By and large, however, Charlestonians did not build anew: they shored up and repaired the old structures. A debt is owed to the mingled poverty and pride that led to the city's preservation up to World War I.

In the years after 1918, with progress coming in the form of the motor car, industry, and expanding naval facilities and military operations, Charlestonians, then experiencing a cultural renaissance in art and literature, became concerned about change. Venerable houses were being demolished for gasoline stations, and wealthy collectors came south to buy Georgian and Federal woodwork and antiques and take them home. Concerned citizens banded together in 1920 when the Joseph Manigault House, now a museum, was threatened with demolition, and they formed the Preservation Society. But more losses in 1929 and 1930 prompted City Council to pass a historic zoning ordinance a year later, creating the first Board of Architectural Review and the first historic district in America. In the late-1930s the Carolina Art Association received funds to conduct America's first citywide survey, which determined the significance of thousands of pre-1860 buildings. The lack of funds for protection of the majority of these structures prompted the founding of Historic Charleston Foundation in 1947 to preserve and protect the architectural and historic character of Charleston and its environs.

In pursuit of its commitment, the Foundation provided, as it does today, an aggressive program of urban planning and advocacy, acquisition and rehabilitation of buildings through a revolving fund, and technical assistance for the more than 3,500 historic structures in the peninsula city, while also operating three museum sites and the city's famous Spring Festival of Houses and Gardens.

Rear view of Rainbow Row in the 1930s

29

Charleston today is a city of more than 90,000 people in a metropolitan area of nearly half a million. The city is economically strong from numerous industries but especially from shipping, military bases, and tourism. The expanding role of preservation as a factor in the city's political life and growth is emphasized by construction of the Waterfront Park along the Cooper River and the Visitor Reception and Transportation Center, built in the old 1850s railroad complex at the center of the peninsula. The city's rich cultural past is now augmented by attractions such as the Spoleto Festival USA, the nation's most comprehensive performing arts festival.

Growth, however, has brought concerns about density and new construction and the accumulation of suburban sprawl and overdevelopment to nearby coastal islands and marshes. Preservationists, now closely allied with conservation groups, work together to advocate planning protection before state and local commissions and to seek easements and other protection for Charleston's fragile environment. These groups and others are also concerned about the preservation of local Gullah culture, including traditions in crafts such as sweetgrass basket making, the protection of historic plantations and nearby rural sites from sprawl, and the pressure of tourism on Charleston's fragile historic district. The aftermath of Hurricane Hugo has accentuated these conservation concerns and prompted preservationists to work harder to promote better conservation strategies and improved building restoration and craftsmanship. Charleston's unequaled architectural array continues to excite and impress visitors and to inspire Charlestonians to protect America's best-preserved city vigilantly.

Rooftops of South Battery

INTRODUCTION TO THE CITY'S IRONWORK, SINGLE HOUSES, AND BURIAL GROUNDS

CHARLESTON'S IRONWORK TRADITIONS
John M. Vlach

As early as 1739 Charleston houses featured wrought-iron balconies. These seem to have been architectural afterthoughts added to help make British houses more pleasant in the subtropical Carolina climate. Balconies were the major form of decorative ironwork made in the city before the Revolutionary War. However, the first colonial blacksmith to advertise his ornamental abilities, James Lingard, claimed in 1753 to "make all kinds of scroll work for gates and stair cases." We can conclude then that local smiths were trying their hands at a variety of forms in order to satisfy the demands of wealthy planters and merchants for elaborate mansions and gardens.

Their designs were mainly imitations of British works or derivations from published plan books. The altar gates and railing at St. Michael's (80 Meeting Street) were imported from England in 1772 and provided inspiration for at least a dozen window grilles, a balcony, and the portal gate at St. Philip's. A 1765 pamphlet entitled *The Smith's Right Hand; or a Complete Guide to the Various Brunches of All Sorts of Iron-work Divided into Three Parts* is mainly a collection of plates depicting many gates,

Decorative ironwork, south gates, St. Philip's Episcopal Church

Wrought-iron railing and lamp standards, 64 South Battery

fences, railings, and balconies. Pattern books like this one found their way into Charleston smithies and no doubt had considerable influence. Indeed the book just mentioned has several plans for fences and gates found in Charleston. While South Carolina remained a British colony, its art forms were decidedly English, and London styles set the tone for Charleston. Even into the late eighteenth century British patterns shaped the local preferences in wrought-iron decoration.

When new designs were attempted, they were often mixed with older patterns. The railing on the William Gibbes House at 64 South Battery Street has a distinctive center panel, but the support panels under the lamp standards are derived from St. Michael's altar rail. Early Charleston ironwork has been criticized as lacking the ornamental virtuosity of its British antecedents. The smiths have usually been excused, however, because of their lack of training or poorly equipped shops. But the mixture of forms as found at the Gibbes House suggests that a new regional style was being developed, that Charleston's ironworkers were searching for a unique set of artistic expressions. Their new repertoire of forms would be based on historic precedents, while new motifs were combined with them in unexpected ways. Charleston blacksmiths may not have been trying to replicate British ironwork as much as they were trying to modify it. It would be best to consider their efforts the creative adventure of a transitional society. As Britons became Americans, their arts changed. The wrought iron produced during the early national period mirrors those changes. Rather than criticize the simplicity and plainness of these works, we should read them as metaphors of their age and as cautious experiments with novelty.

The nineteenth century brought more changes, particularly after the arrival of three German blacksmiths, J. A. W. Iusti, Christopher Werner, and Frederic Julius Ortmann. Much of the old Charleston wrought iron that survives today is by these men. Indeed, the two most famous gates in the city, St. Michael's cemetery gate (circa 1840; 80 Meeting Street) and the Sword Gate (circa 1848; 32 Legare Street), are by Iusti and Werner, respectively.

Often when wrought-iron decoration was designed, contracts for its fabrication were sent out for bid. Such was the case with the gates at St. John's Lutheran Church at 10 Archdale Street. A. P. Reaves worked up the plan, while Jacob Frederick Roh and his eight helpers built them. Robert Mills is thought to have designed the gates and fence at the First Baptist Church at 61 Church Street. The City Hall at 80 Broad Street and the South Carolina Society Hall at 72 Meeting Street, designed by Robert Mills and Gabriel Manigault, respectively, have elaborate stair railings and grilles. Nineteenth-century wrought iron is generally ornate, employing numerous scroll forms and floral motifs. The gates at City Hall Park and those at St. Philip's at 146 Church Street are excellent examples of nineteenth-century decorative trends. Both works have large S's, lyres, and anthemion leaves. This last motif,

St. Michael's churchyard gates

*Cast-iron panel,
50 Hasell Street*

33

commonly used in Greek Revival buildings, is emblematic of the period; its presence proves that Charleston artisans kept abreast of the latest national trends in architecture. Charleston ironwork reflects several social changes that occurred in the early nineteenth century: the melding of diverse ethnic stocks, the elaboration of personal talent and enterprise, and the localization of national styles.

Toward the middle of the nineteenth century, cast-iron ornament became commonplace in Charleston. It was mass-produced, usually in northern cities, and shipped to all parts of the country. Mail-order catalogs featured elaborate drawings and perspective views of intricate grilles, benches, gazebos, and the like. Some of these standard items were imported into Charleston, but the John F. Riley company did some local casting following the accepted patterns. Cast-iron grilles and gates were much more elaborate than those made with wrought iron. Leaves, stems, and flowers could be fashioned with extreme realism. The intricacy of such ornaments was appropriate for the late-nineteenth-century Victorian modes of architectural adornment, and consequently there was a decline in the demand for decorative wrought iron. Civil War bombardments and an insensitive occupation by Northern troops took a toll on the city and caused the destruction of much of the older wrought iron. In the postwar period, wooden fences were often used as replacements. Many of these imitated scrollwork with carpenter's joinery.

The taste for hand-forged ironwork was, however, firmly implanted in Charleston, and requests for it continued to occupy local blacksmiths. Werner worked until 1870 and Iusti until 1882. Ortmann's sons carried his business on until the 1930s. Both Philip Simmons and James Kidd remember the Ortmanns as the local specialists in ironwork during the first decades of the twentieth century. Kidd recalls, "Ortmann done a lot of this work. He iron off all these part of Charleston. Ortmann done all of Charleston's ironworks, the steprails up on City Hall. Yea, he done that old-time work a long time. Nobody else would fool with it." As work opportunities for general blacksmiths became fewer during the 1920s, they turned more extensively to decorative iron. Peter Simmons did some repair work on gates late in his career, after he was eighty years old. James Kidd, primarily a farrier, made fences and stair rails when he sensed that "the game was running out." Philip Simmons also turned to decorative wrought iron and thus fully entered into a tradition that had begun in the 1730s.

Most of Simmons's designs derive directly from local Charleston precedents—for example, his gates at St. Andrew's Lutheran, 43 Wentworth Street, and at the First Baptist Church, 61 Church Street. Indeed, in every case at least one motif or decorative unit can be traced to earlier works. Simmons wants his work to look old, so he selects old patterns as models. The various kinds of scrolls, the spears, the fleurs-de-lis, the iron rings, the leaves, the wiggletails, and the flowers are all elements repeated from eighteenth- and nineteenth-century examples.

The Snake Gate,
329 East Bay Street

The lunette panels found at 100 Tradd Street and in the Snake Gate at 329 East Bay Street repeat the lunette shape of St. Philip's cemetery gate. The overthrow at 67 Broad Street, with its interlinked C scrolls, is similar to an arrangement in a nineteenth-century window grille on East Bay Street. The ventilator grilles at the same address feature the broken scroll design used in the gate at the Miles Brewton House at 27 King Street in the 1760s. The accidental turns of history have placed Simmons at the end of a long line of decorative ironworkers, but inheritance alone has provided a potential role to fill. Simmons's deliberate efforts to learn the old-fashioned forms and execute them well have made him the custodian of the traditions for Charleston ironwork, a position acquired by intention, not accident. In this role, he is both historian and artisan, for he tells his customers what designs are appropriate as well as providing the finished products. His wrought-iron sculptures—snake, bird, and fish—are his most unusual additions to the local ironwork. They are without precedent and stem from his active imagination. But many of the other gates and grilles are also unique, even though their content is not new. Creativity is possible within the limits of a tradition, even the rigorously conservative one found in Charleston. New compositions of the usual motifs bring novelty to the 250-year-old tradition. With seemingly standardized fences, balconies, railings, and gates Simmons expresses many of his own ideas about what he considers impressive, "fancy," and "nice." During his fifty-five years of ornamental ironwork he has developed a well-reasoned aesthetic sense that not only directs his hands but also determines to some degree the communal taste in ironwork. At the outset of his career he took orders; now he gives them. Simmons explains: "They say, 'My neighbor got a porch over there and they got wrought iron all over it, but I don't want it like that.' And we sit down and we talk and I come up with something. That's what I like about the blacksmith trade; doing it from scratch and arriving at the idea from my own mind, my own thoughts. That's the part I enjoy." In the midst of his time-bound trade and even while preserving the historic appearance of Charleston, he remains his own man. He has found self-expression in the communal tradition.

SIGNIFICANT DECORATIVE WROUGHT-IRON
SITES IN CHARLESTON

10 Archdale Street St. John's Lutheran Church	Gate, 1822	Frederick Jacob Roh
60–64 Broad Street	Balcony	
39 Church Street	Gate, 1890s	Ortmann Brothers
146 Church Street St. Philip's Cemetery St. Philip's Entrance	Gate, circa 1770 Gate and Fence, circa 1825	
329 East Bay Street Gadsden House	Snake Gate, circa 1965	Philip Simmons
90 Hasell Street Beth Elohim Synagogue	Gate, circa 1841	C. Werner
27 King Street Miles Brewton House	Gate and Fences, 1760 and 1822	
14 Legare Street Simmons-Edwards House	Fence, early-nineteenth century	
32 Legare Street	Sword Gate, circa 1848	C. Werner
45 Meeting Street Hollings House	Railings and Window Grilles, circa 1967	Philip Simmons
72 Meeting Street S.C. Society Hall	Lamp Standards, circa 1750 Balustrade, circa 1804	Possibly from London London
80 Meeting Street St. Michael's Church	Communion Railing, 1772 Graveyard Gate, 1848	Imported from London J. A. W. Iusti
105 Meeting Street Hibernian Hall	Gate, 1840	C. Werner
188 Meeting Street Market Hall	Railings, 1841	
Meeting Street Transportation Center	Gate, 1991	Philip Simmons
2 St. Michael's Alley	Gate, 1970s	Philip Simmons
64 South Battery William Gibbes House	Railings, circa 1785	
Stoll's Alley Nos. 9, 2, 5	Gates, 1939–40	Philip Simmons
Waterfront Park	Gates, 1990s	Philip Simmons Shop

THE CHARLESTON SINGLE HOUSE

Bernard Herman

The urban house form most closely associated with the historic fabric of Charleston from the mid-eighteenth century is the single house. The essential characteristics of the single house, according to its most meticulous student, Gene Waddell (author of "The Charleston Single House . . . ," *Preservation Progress* 22 [March 1977]: 4–8), are "two or more stories of the same plan with a central stair hall between two rooms on each floor and an entrance opening directly into the hall." Waddell continues: "A Charleston Single House is a separate, multi-story dwelling one room wide and three across including a central entrance and stair hall. It also typically, but not necessarily, has its narrow end to the street, a piazza along one of its longer sides, and back wall chimneys." Ken Severens (author of *Charleston Antebellum Architecture and Civic Destiny* [Knoxville: University of Tennessee Press, 1988]) offers the most commonly cited rationalization for

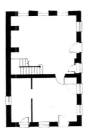

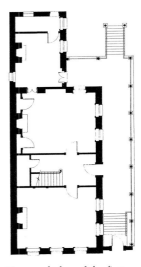

Measured plan of the first floor, 14 Legare Street

Large-scale Charleston single house, 14 Legare Street

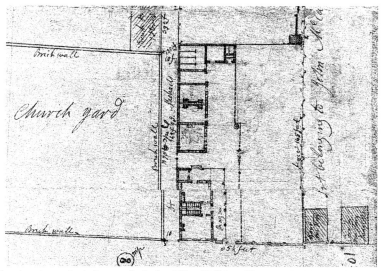

Plat showing a single house, the Judge Elihu Hall Bay House at 76 Meeting Street, in context, circa 1800

the single house: "The single house was a creative response to the increasing scarcity of space in the city and was designed to mitigate the unpleasantness of hot, humid summers. With its narrow side directly on the street, the rectangular house with two rooms in each story grew tall to raise the main entertaining room to the level of the prevailing breeze which passed through a side piazza. As a free-standing house communicating more with a side garden than with the street the single house offered a masterful but still vernacular solution to the residential problems of achieving comfort, privacy and propriety."

The single house emerged in the third quarter of the eighteenth century as one of Charleston's most favored dwelling forms. In the colonial period, however, the domestic fabric of the city's architecture had been considerably more diverse and more in keeping with a broader transatlantic English tradition of provincial ports and market towns. The row houses and large Georgian town houses of early Charleston had their particular equivalents in provincial streetscapes throughout the Anglo-American world. A key design consideration within the diverse repertoire of urban dwelling options was a common need for buildings combining commerce and residence. The most common solution possessed a street-level one-room shop with a general living space or dining area behind and "best" room and chambers above.

One key to understanding the Charleston single house is learning how the general pattern of combined commercial and residential functions worked in and was modified by the changing economic and social contexts of a particular city situated on the border between the plantation South and the cosmopolitan world of Atlantic mercantilism. In urban circumstances throughout the Atlantic world city dwellers and builders confronted the problem of creating a traffic pattern admitting business into the front room while screening domestic access into the back room. In postmedieval English town house premises, the solution lay in providing dual entries and segregated access. Thus, entry from the public street was provided directly into the shop as well as into a passage running past the commercial rooms, yielding access into the back domestic quarters and terminating in a narrow yard or court.

By the close of the eighteenth century the single house had triumphed as the preferred form for Charleston's urban housing. Most often documented was an arrangement composed of a fully detached house situated at right angles to the street with a rear wall against the side property line, and possessing a narrow passage or drive leading to a backyard ringed with service buildings. Semidetached single houses were also constructed—such as Sylvia Depeau's double tenements and backbuildings. Rarer were arrangements in which long, narrow single house lots were subdeveloped with additional tenements, as in the case of Matthew Webb's King Street property, which extended 233 feet back from its 27-foot street frontage. A lot plan was devised to incorporate an "Alley or Passage in common" connecting all the householders to the public street.

Another key to interpreting the single house is to look at the house, its outbuildings, and lot organization as an integrated domestic unit.

A classic version of the Charleston single house, 75 Anson Street

Eighteenth- and early-nineteenth-century Charleston can be fairly characterized as a plantation city. The city both informed and was informed by the physical, social, and economic organization of the plantation landscapes and architecture of the Cooper and Ashley Rivers. Most discussions of the Charleston single house focus on the principal dwelling. Examination of existing sites and primary documentary evidence, however, clearly reveal the single house's social and symbolic stature as that of the plantation "big house." The environment associated with the Charleston single house, like the plantation "big house," cannot be fully understood without regard for the whole architectural setting. Simply put, the Charleston single house is defined as much by its dependencies and lot organization as it is by its structure.

In plan, the extended single house consisted of a series of interconnected functional zones that communicated with each other and the street via a number of routes. The main house abutted but did not front the street. Access from the street followed one of two routes: from the sidewalk onto the piazza or from the sidewalk or street and down the carriageway. The piazza route led to the main and most formal entry into the stair passage, to a secondary entry into the breakfast room, or to a set of steps at the far end of the piazza that led to the dooryards of the back buildings. The last of the three options, however, was made redundant by the carriageway, while the first two directed traffic of varying levels of formality and familiarity. The carriageway led into the single house compound at street level admitting both wheeled and pedestrian traffic. Pedestrians entering by the carriageway literally passed beneath the gaze of the occupants of the main house as they went about their business at the back of the house or among the back buildings. Wheeled traffic, primarily carriages, would have entered nearly at eye level with the piazza and stopped at the rear steps onto the piazza which led back toward the main entry. This mode of entry was only slightly less formal than entry from the sidewalk. In all instances, the organization of the single house ran from street to backyard wall in a pattern of decreasing formality and increasing dirtiness. We are able also to see in the single house a functional shift from predominantly social to predominantly utilitarian spaces. But it is also important to bear in mind that these linked domestic spaces exist in and define a highly stratified and processional urban plantation landscape not unlike that described by Dell Upton in the countryside of eighteenth-century Virginia ("White and Black Landscapes in Eighteenth-Century Virginia," *Places* 2, no. 2 [1985]: 66).

When we examine the urban landscape of the single house compound in the aggregate we find that it is further distinguished by the qualities of constriction and segmentation. Access in and out of the single house yard was either via the piazza or the carriageway—both beneath the gaze of the controlling and authoritative occupants. The threshold where the lot met the street was also the narrowest point of open space in the single house yard. The greatest physical constriction

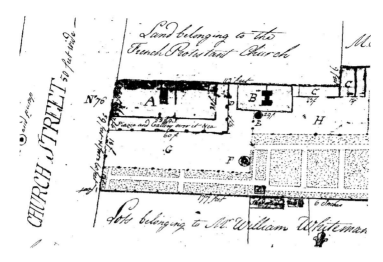

Plat of a single house with its dependencies on the east side of Church Street, 1802

of the yard at its most public (and, in some ways, socially vulnerable) point signified a symbolic tightening, monitoring, and regulation of movement in and out of the single house yard. Domestic space within the confines of the single house microcosm and the city as a whole became increasingly segmented in the sense that it was partitioned into discrete areas delimiting complex social hierarchies.

The segmentation of the aggregate single house streetscape served reciprocally to emphasize the constricted contours of the individual compounds. These qualities in the mid-nineteenth-century Charleston landscape were furthered by the construction of brick partition walls between lots. Eighteenth- and nineteenth-century plats reveal that private property had been extensively fenced but not visually enclosed. Historical archaeology and construction evidence further indicates that post-and-rail fences were being replaced with brick walls after about 1820. In the same period slave quarters were being uniformly built without windows overlooking neighboring properties and public streets. Both phenomena were occurring in the time of greater fear generated by the threat of a slave insurrection in a city with an African American majority.

The processes of segmentation and constriction in Charleston's urban landscape required substantial building lots that could accommodate house, drive, yard, and back buildings. The explanation that the single house resulted from urban congestion is belied by the buildings themselves. Single houses actually squandered street frontage in a manner consistent with their image as the "big houses" of urban plantations. Similarly, the contention that the orientation and design of the single house reflected a specific response to subtropical climatic conditions may be based more on historical rationalization than on the careful documentation of material and social realities.

CHARLESTON BURIAL GROUNDS
Jonathan H. Poston

James Deetz's view that the mortuary art of Colonial Anglo-America represents a significant body of material culture and an important opportunity to understand its social history is nowhere more applicable than with the stones in the burial grounds of Charleston. Few cities have retained the number of in situ early gravestones, and in few places is there such a variety of markers. Although some recent work has focused on the fascinating "funeral business" in early Charleston and one excellent recent book has examined the gravestones of South Carolina and Georgia from an essentially art-historical perspective, no work to date has examined the material and cultural implications of the grave markers of Charleston. These markers well represent the trade, social structure, and demography of the area. The city's earliest graveyards such as the Circular Congregational, Huguenot, Baptist, and Anglican are important repositories for this information. Lost burial grounds such as the Quaker and Brown Fellowship graveyards and potters' fields appearing on early maps are equally important to this understanding.

A key to understanding lies in the fact that the Lowcountry of South Carolina had no original resources for the quarrying of stone of any

Circular Congregational Churchyard

variety. Until the late-eighteenth century even upstate supplies of granite and veins of mineable Georgia marble were unknown. From the beginning Charlestonians had to rely on imports of stone for any purpose. Thus, even for high-status individuals, the earliest Charleston grave markers were made of wood. In 1809 Dr. David Ramsay noted the survival on Thomas Drayton's eighteenth-century plantation of a red cedar grave marker to Stephen Fox, who died in 1706. These markers often took the form of rails (or what some have mistakenly called "bedboards"), and the early view of St. John's Lutheran Church in the nineteenth century by John William Hill confirms the profusion of wooden grave boards that have since disappeared. Charleston has some of the only survivors in America of this type: the in situ board, somewhat repaired, to Mary Ann Luyten at St. Michael's; and a grave board recently removed from St. Stephen's Church on the Santee to the Charleston Museum. Wood stelae markers from the late eighteenth century with traces of original paint also survive at St. James' Church on James Island, as does a slave marker dated 1860 at Hyde Park Plantation on the Cooper River.

Ledger stone, 1694, for Landgrave Thomas Smith, Medway Plantation

The graves of some Charlestonians of wealth are marked by slabs or ledger stones. A local stonecutter probably lettered the 1694 ledger for Landgrave Smith at Medway. In similar style, the same cutter may have executed the stone for Thomas Nairn at Old St. Andrews Church in 1704. As soon as they could afford it, however, South Carolina's wealthy planters and merchants of British extraction in this period began to order from England more elaborate flat stones and chest tombs. These were placed as markers for family members buried in parish churchyards, on the plantations, or even in town. Armorial bearings can be found on the elaborate marble chest tomb

"Death's Head" stone of Martha Peronneau, Circular Congregational Churchyard

First Scots Presbyterian Churchyard

Unitarian Church Cemetery

for dissenting English merchant Anthony Matthews in the Congregational Churchyard, dating to 1735. Some chest tombs marked family vaults in which planters, imitating English gentry customs, built structures to receive several generations of burials. Many Charleston churchyard vaults, like those southward to Savannah, stand only partially above ground, and occasionally they are true barrel-vaulted brick and stuccoed structures. The Simons vault at the Circular Churchyard is dated by tradition at 1698–1699 and may be the oldest grave marker or structure in the city. A larger vault for the Manigault family in the Huguenot churchyard is perhaps the most baronial, containing more than thirty family members interred between 1729 and 1870. The Hutson-Peronneau vault in the Circular Churchyard is from the late-eighteenth century, but it was surmounted by a new aboveground mausoleum in about 1840.

Most well-to-do Charleston merchants, particularly those of New England extraction, began to import slate gravestones from New England at an early date. The earliest of these are stones with the "death's head" symbol dated as early as 1711. Stones with similar motifs, carved by the Lamson family of Charlestowne, Massachusetts, are found in the Circular Churchyard. Although examples of such forbidding mortuary symbols are spread through the early graveyards, the most common motifs found on imported stones are cherubs (also called winged soul figures) and portraits. Carvers such as John Stevens and John Bull of Newport, Henry Emmes of Boston, and Lemuel Savery of Plymouth sent signed stones to Charleston from the 1740s to the 1780s. The Charleston portraits, generally carved (and in one case signed) by William Codner of Boston and by his relative Henry Emmes, are apparently representational. This constitutes the largest concentration of such stones outside of Boston.

In the decades prior to the Revolution some English and Scottish stonecutters came to Charleston for brief periods, leaving behind high-style cherub motifs. Occasionally New England carvers such as John Bull of Newport spent brief periods in the city promising "with encouragement" to continue in the stonecarving trade. The most elaborate stonework, however, was still imported from England. Josiah Quincy of Boston pointed out "the taste for marble monuments" in churches as prevailing in Charleston to a greater degree than in the North. St. Philip's Church and even dissenting congregations became repositories for elaborately carved plaques, often sent from English sculptors and marking the burial of those prominent individuals beneath the floor or in church vaults. With the destruction of so many of the earliest church buildings, only the plaque of Lady Anne Murray in First Scots Presbyterian Church, carved locally of wood, serves as a reminder of the colonial phase of this practice.

Immediately after the American Revolution, the Neoclassical urn and willow motif became a favorite in the city. Some examples were imported from Providence or Newport carving shops, but immigrant stonecarvers from England and Scotland eventually took over the trade. Thomas Walker, who came to Charleston from Edinburgh around 1790, established a family dynasty in carving. In his work the old-fashioned Scottish motifs of death's heads and cherubs were eventually supplanted with delicate Neoclassical urns. Walker's products became the favorite stones for Charleston's graveyards of all religious groups including Roman Catholic, Lutheran, and Jewish. By the mid-nineteenth century large local firms such as W. T. White and Philadelphia stonecutting operations were supplying large obelisks, broken columns, crosses, and other monuments in marble for Charleston graveyards.

With new attention to the city's sanitation in the 1840s, Charleston followed the lead of Boston and Philadelphia in establishing new park cemeteries outside the city. Magnolia Cemetery, 1850, on the Cooper River north of the city limits was soon followed by new cemeteries for the Lutheran, Catholic, Jewish, and African American communities of the late-nineteenth century. Marble mausoleums designed by local architects vied with monuments and smaller stones placed in fenced and family plots in landscaped settings.

Charleston's churchyards and burial grounds remain in a remarkable state of preservation despite urban change and natural disasters. Several congregations, such as the Circular Church, have completed large-scale restorations, while others, including St. Michael's Church and the Episcopal Cathedral of St. Luke and St. Paul, are finishing long-range conservation and restoration plans with the technical assistance of Historic Charleston Foundation. Most of these graveyards are open to the public during regular weekdays.

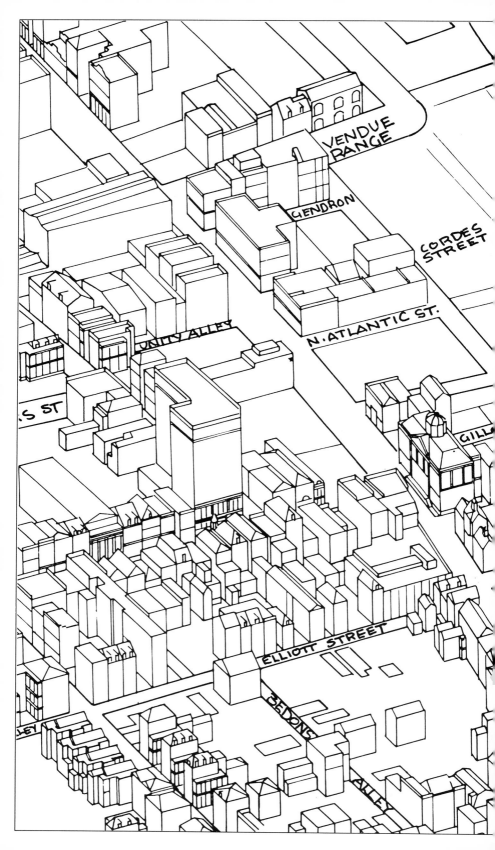

VENDUE
RANGE

GENDRON

CORDES
STREET

UNITY ALLEY

N. ATLANTIC ST.

.S ST

GILL

ELLIOTT STREET

BEDONS

ALLEY

LEY

I

THE WALLED CITY

Charleston's Architectural Beginnings

*F*or most of its first half century the growth and development of
Charleston was shaped by a fort and its walls. Initially thought
necessary for defense against invading Spanish from Florida or ma-
rauding pirates, the wall was a reminder that Charleston sat during its
infancy at the outermost fringes of the English empire. Early Charleston's
walls gave the city something of the look of a European outpost, but
they also shaped how the town grew and what its early architecture
would be. The necessity of the walls faded as the city prospered and the
once-real threats from Spaniards and pirates ebbed, but the influence
of the fortifications continued to shape the early city's street plan and
its streetscapes. Charleston's earliest precincts lay within these bounds,
and while almost all of the earliest buildings have disappeared, understanding the role of Charleston's walls is a good way to understand the
architecture of the area they once protected.

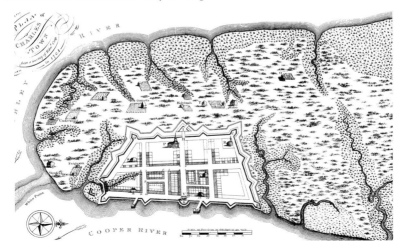

*Engraving from Edward Crisp's 1704 map of Carolina showing the fortifications of
Charles Town*

Bronze marker at the site of the Carteret Bastion showing detail of the walled city from the 1704 Crisp map

In 1672 a committee of the Grand Council of the Carolina colony surveyed the Cooper River area for the most convenient places for towns. Lands belonging to original settlers were voluntarily surrendered to provide twelve thousand acres of land for "a Colony in A Square as much as Navigable Rivers will Permit." The "Grand Modell," probably sent from England, served until the second quarter of the eighteenth century as the original plan of the city's lots. Each grantee of these first lots was required to build a house of two stories in height and at least 30 feet by 16 feet in dimension.

Only a few years later Thomas Ashe visited Charles Town and described the area as follows:

> It's very commodiously scituated from many other Navigable Rivers that lie near it. . . . The Town is regularly laid out into large and capacious Streets, which to Buildings is a great Ornament and Beauty. In it they have reserved convenient places for Building of a Church, Town-House and other Publick Structures, an Artillery Ground for the Exercise of their Militia, and Wharves for the Convenience of their Trade and Shipping.

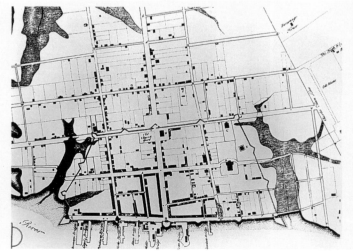

Bishop Roberts and W. H. Toms's Ichnography of Charles-Town at High Water, *1739*

Threats of attack by Spanish Florida and from the French necessitated construction of a continuous fortification around the intensely developed sections of the town. The southern edge of the peninsula, a low beach called "Oyster Point," was fortified, and by 1704 plans were made for construction of gates and a drawbridge at Broad Street and a seawall along the Cooper River waterfront. Removal of the fortifications began in the 1720s when the western wall was taken down; the process was probably completed before 1740.

Inside the walls residents lived in houses constructed of a variety of materials: they were half-timbered, tabby (an oyster shell mortar), imported Bermuda stone, and brick. Following various fires, particularly that of 1740 in which more than 40 percent of the city was destroyed, various statutes proscribed masonry for construction within the original boundaries. There were many exceptions to this law, however, and it seems seldom to have been enforced. Certainly houses beyond the city continued to be overwhelmingly of wood. The earliest view of Charles Town, painted by the drawing teacher Bishop Roberts in 1738 and subsequently engraved in London, shows a row of densely spaced masonry buildings with columned porches or elaborate second-floor balconies on turned posts lining the Bay Street waterfront. These balconies were encouraged by statute and served as the forerunners of Charleston's legendary iron balconies and wood piazzas.

The earliest surviving dwellings were often of two rooms per floor or of some other asymmetrical plan. Some evidence of the form remains in those blocks of Tradd Street between Meeting and East Bay Streets and in certain areas of Church and King Streets. Most such structures were destroyed in the fire of 1740. Larger dwellings on Church, Broad, and East Bay Streets were of asymmetrical floor plan with chambered rear staircases and four rooms per floor. Buildings for public use and market functions were dispersed among various locations, including the Guardhouse and Council Chamber over the fortification, the Half-Moon Battery; a courts building one block south; the Powder Magazine at the northern edge of the walled city, and various other buildings used by the Assembly. Merchants built substantial structures, each serving as a

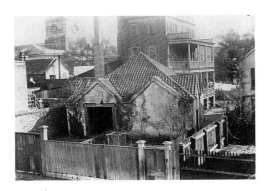

The Old Powder Magazine, circa 1900, before restoration

countinghouse on the ground floor and a dwelling above, along the Bay Street waterfront, as well as on Elliott Street, the principal shopping thoroughfare. Along the wharves warehouse structures for naval stores, deerskin tanneries, cooperages, and rice granaries crowded in with stores and quarters for workers. Churches and meetinghouses were well established on their present sites by the end of the seventeenth century: the Dissenters on Meeting Street just within the walls, the French Huguenots at Church and Queen Streets, the Anabaptists on Church Street, the Quakers outside the walls on King Street, and the predominating Anglicans first at Meeting and Broad Streets and later at the northern edge of Church Street. The construction of the latter building of St. Philip's by 1722 was perhaps the first architectural high point of the eighteenth century in Charles Town.

In the fire of November 1740 most of the town, including nearly three hundred dwellings, was destroyed. Additional damage came from the hurricane of 1752. The redevelopment of East Bay Street was largely along earlier lines, but other areas including Church Street and Tradd Street became sites for the emerging single house form and eventually for the construction of a few double-pile Georgian houses by wealthier individuals. The completion of the elegant Georgian style Exchange over the foundation of the Half-Moon Battery marked the emergence of Charleston's pre-Revolutionary golden age and its brief stance as the wealthiest city in British North America.

Rebuilding became necessary in certain areas after the fire of 1778, which had consumed many of the same blocks as had the fire of 1740, including East Bay Street, Elliott Street, and the eastern end of Broad

An eighteenth-century single house at 47 East Bay Street

View of Vendue Range looking west in 1865

Street. And more reconstruction was needed in 1796 after a fire burned areas south of Cumberland Street to Broad Street and the area of Church Street just below St. Philip's Church. Single houses and public buildings of the Neoclassical (Federal) style and occasionally Greek Revival double parlor dwellings were added to the ensemble. Broad Street became a street of shops with dwellings above and, increasingly, the locus for new banks and offices. During the War Between the States this section, the old walled city, received the heaviest bombardment in the siege of 567 days and was virtually abandoned for the last two years of the conflict. St. Philip's was struck by ten shells, and one sailed over the roof during services, exploding in the graveyard. Mrs. St. Julien Ravenel described the lower part of town:

> *Everything was overgrown with rank, untrimmed vegetation. Not grass merely, but bushes, grew in the streets. The gardens looked as if the Sleeping Beauty might be within. The houses were indescribable: the gable was out of one, the chimneys fallen from the next; here a roof was shattered, there a piazza half gone; not a window remained. The streets looked as if piled with diamonds, the glass lay shivered so thick on the ground.*

In the late-nineteenth century this area remained a primary residential location for native whites as well as blacks, who lived in tenements in large dwellings and crowded in rear outbuildings and in alleys, a residential situation well described in contemporary literature such as DuBose Heyward's *Mamba's Daughters: A Novel of Charleston* (1929). Interspersed among the dwellings were stores and industrial sites.

The restoration movement of the 1920s through the 1950s centered on the earliest streets such as Tradd and East Bay, where individuals such as Susan Pringle Frost personally purchased houses and resold

Detail of C. Drie's Bird's Eye View of the City of Charleston, South Carolina, 1872

101 East Bay Street and Rainbow Row in the 1950s

them to restoration-minded people. Dorothy Porcher Legge, beginning with the purchase of her residence at 99–101 East Bay Street, pioneered the restoration of that line of eighteenth-century structures today called "Rainbow Row" after her 1930s concept of a Colonial Caribbean color scheme. The occasional Victorian dwelling or the Craftsman style house of the early-twentieth century vies with the interspersed Colonial Revival style residences to complete the ensemble of the original walled city. Owing to its exclusive protection in the first Charleston preservation ordinance of 1931, the area of the original walled city (with some exceptions) experienced the fewest post–World War I demolitions of any historic area in the city.

ADGER'S WHARF
(NORTH AND SOUTH)

Originally developed circa 1735

Named after the nineteenth-century shipping magnate James Adger, these streets, still mostly paved in cobblestone, comprise the eighteenth-century location of Ancrum's and Motte's Wharf and later Greenwood's Wharf, which lay adjacent to a public fish market immediately to the south (now a parking lot). Motte's Wharf and Greenwood's Wharf were first united by William Crafts and Nathaniel Russell around 1800 and were sold to the ambitious, northern Ireland–born merchant James Adger in 1842. The house at *90 East Bay Street* is a rare eighteenth-century survival of these wharf buildings, despite notable changes to its windows and first-floor storefront in the nineteenth century. Its neighbors at 18 and 20 South Adger's Wharf achieved their present forms by the mid-1830s.

Between 1834 and 1861 the buildings at 4–16 South Adger's Wharf and 1–15 North Adger's Wharf contained cotton warehouses and factors' offices, and from here Adger's steamship lines provided weekly passenger transport to New York. Converted into residences and some offices beginning in the 1940s, the buildings retain their original masonry warehouse

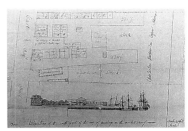

Plat showing buildings and wharves at the end of Tradd Street, circa 1793

Adger's Wharf today

Early-twentieth-century view of Adger's Wharf

openings, now infilled with Colonial Revival style windows and doors. The former warehouse and factor space at 2–18 North Adger's Wharf served as cotton sample storage and offices as late as 1951.

The granite foundations of Adger's Wharf are incorporated in that portion of Waterfront Park lying at the foot of these streets adjacent to the Charleston Harbor Pilots Headquarters.

BEDON'S ALLEY
Developed 1704–88

By 1739 this small street, then called Middle Lane, contained a mix of mercantile stores and ship chandleries, but its development was stymied by heavy damage in the fires of 1740 and 1778. After the latter fire the wealthy contractor Humphrey Sommers built the three-story stucco building at 2 Bedon's Alley as a tenement with shops on the first floor and a residence above. Merchant James Cunnington's narrow structure erected some years earlier at 5 Bedon's Alley had similar usage with a counting-house on the first floor and elegant residence above. The three-story south wing was added in 1794. Tradition holds that America's oldest musical organization, the St. Cecilia Society, was founded in this building.

Most of the small brick houses on the east side of the street were built as outbuildings for the large establishments in Rainbow Row; 8 and 10 Bedon's Alley, for example, provided service functions for Scottish merchant Adam Tunno's large office and residence at *89 East Bay Street*. These structures were rescued in the 1920s and 1930s by Susan Pringle Frost and renovated as individual dwellings with detailing and landscape treatments in the Colonial Revival style.

Etching by Alfred Hutty showing the rear of 99–103 East Bay Street from Bedon's Alley in 1921

5 Bedon's Alley

1 BROAD STREET, STATE BANK OF SOUTH CAROLINA BUILDING

Constructed 1853; restored 1978

Edward C. Jones and Francis Lee, architects

Jones and Lee, Charleston's most notable antebellum architectural partnership, designed this three-story brownstone building in the Renaissance Revival style. Damaged by shelling in the Civil War, it was reopened in 1868 for the company of the former blockade runner and Confederate treasurer George Trenholm. The edifice was purchased in 1875 for the Carolina Savings Bank owned by George Williams, builder of the imposing house at *16 Meeting Street*. Important exterior features include the curvilinear bay with entry door and engaged portico, and the dissimilar lion-headed keystones above each first-floor window. The interior lobby was restored when the building returned to bank usage in 1978 and still contains its Rococo Revival style plaster cornice and frieze.

1 Broad Street, doorway

Engraving of 1 Broad Street from Harper's Weekly, *1857*

3 BROAD STREET, WALKER, EVANS & COGSWELL BUILDING

Constructed 1853–54; rehabilitated 1983–84

Edward C. Jones and Francis Lee, architects

This is an Italianate, Flemish-bonded brick structure with brownstone window heads and sills. It became the principal store of Walker, Evans & Co., stationers, engravers, and bookbinders, within two years of its construction by Edward Sebring, president of the State Bank next door. In 1856 it was joined at the rear to the firm's earlier headquarters at *117 East Bay Street*. Both structures remained in use by the successor company, Walker, Evans & Cogswell, until 1982. The East Bay Street building, formerly of four full stories, boasts a post-earthquake

3 Broad Street, the Walker, Evans & Co. Building, from a nineteenth-century invoice

deep pressed metal cornice and mansard roof. The structure at 3 Broad also lost its original brownstone cornice in the earthquake of 1886, after which a pressed tin cornice was added. From 1861 to 1865, the company relocated to Columbia and served as Confederate government printers.

11 BROAD STREET, S. G. COURTENAY & CO. BOOKSTORE BUILDING

Constructed 1856; altered early-1900s; rehabilitated 1985

Edward Brickell White, architect; David Lopez, contractor

11 Broad Street, from the Courier, 1856

Designed in the Italianate style by Edward B. White for Samuel Courtenay's large bookstore, the curvilinear parapet still bears a carved brownstone relief of globe, scroll, and books. The first-floor facade was altered in the early-twentieth century, and the building served for many years as a popular dining establishment for Broad Street lawyers. In a 1985 rehabilitation the original doorways and arches with surmounting console brackets were restored in cast brownstone.

The two smaller buildings to the east are also products of the mid-1850s and are similar in style and materials. They also retain second-floor offices with original woodwork and other Victorian decorations. *7 Broad Street* was probably an earlier building that was renovated for the brokers William M. Martin and John C. Martin. *9 Broad Street*, a narrow one-bay, two-story structure, was built by William Pinckney Shingler and his brother, "exchange brokers" in cotton. Edward B. White designed this building in the Italianate style; it has a brownstone facade executed by W. G. Chave and is anchored to the brick walls of adjacent structures. Shingler built the houses at *9* and *10 Limehouse Street* in 1857 and 1858, respectively.

The small structure immediately to the west, *13 Broad Street*, may once have related to the rest of these structures, but its facade was altered to red pressed brick in the Victorian, Queen Anne style in the 1890s for the office of attorney Henry Conner.

15 BROAD STREET, SMITH BUILDING

Constructed circa 1801–15; altered mid-1850s; rehabilitated 1983

Hugh Smith, architect

Built as a residence with a commercial ground floor by the amateur architect and merchant Hugh Smith or his mother, Agnes, the structure was altered in the 1850s with the application of cast terra cotta ornaments, including second-story window heads with broken pediments and shell motifs and plain third-story pedimented window heads, along with a cornice in the Italianate style. Second-floor, cast-iron balconies were added at this date as well. Serving as a succession of stores and offices, 15 Broad became the site of the People's Bank in 1854.

16 BROAD STREET, SECOND BANK OF THE UNITED STATES BUILDING

Constructed 1817; addition 1850

This two-story stucco building was erected to house the Second Bank of the United States, but after that institution's closure in 1834, it was acquired by the Bank of Charleston. The simple Neoclassical facade is accented by a pediment with its original carved and gilded oak eagle. On its interior the main banking room retains

Pediment of 16 Broad Street with gilded eagle

its elaborate Rococo Revival plaster cornice. The north wing, designed by Edward C. Jones in 1850, still houses the building's old boardroom, a splendid space with Italianate and Rococo Revival detailing, including marbleized pilasters supporting an arcaded cove and ceiling. The present bank complex also incorporates several other important buildings including *2 State Street*, *14 Broad Street*, built in 1799 but twice remodeled; and *12 Broad Street*, a circa 1783 structure with a granite, pilastered facade in the Greek Revival style added in 1839.

17 BROAD STREET, SOUTH CAROLINA LOAN AND TRUST CO. BUILDING

Constructed circa 1848; facade and interior remodeled circa 1870–71

Thomas Abrahams and John Seyle, architects; George W. Egan, contractor

Claudian Northrop, a prominent antebellum attorney, Confederate soldier, and later a leading Catholic priest, built this two-story masonry commercial structure shortly after acquiring the property. After the Civil War the South Carolina Loan and Trust remodeled it as their headquarters with the addition of the fashionable cast-iron Italianate detailing to the new facade. An arched loggia with Corinthian columns ornaments the entry, while arched windows and a curvilinear gable accent the upper portion of the building. On the interior, the former banking room retains its cove ceiling with central plaster medallion and notable dentiled cornice.

18–22 BROAD STREET, PEOPLE'S BUILDING

Constructed 1910–11

Victor Frohling, architect

Mayor R. Goodwyn Rhett, while president of the People's Bank, spearheaded the construction of the People's Building as Charleston's first skyscraper. It stands on the site of a late-eighteenth-century brick double tenement, an indication of the city's early-twentieth-century progress. Critics then, as now, debated the effect of the eight-story structure on the skyline of the original city. Designed by the New York architect Victor Frohling, the largely yellow brick building has granite rustication on the ground and mezzanine stories and terra cotta ornamentation, now painted with a metallic finish, at the top floor, although a later owner removed the surmounting entablature. The columned portico and shuttered groundstory window openings of the People's Building retain a Charleston flavor, while the rest of the structure hints at the contemporary national influences. The marble lions flanking the entry, brought from an estate in Massachusetts in the 1950s, are considered landmarks in their own right and were saved from removal by the city's Board of Architectural Review in 1990.

18–22 Broad, circa 1930s, before the removal of the overhanging soffit

19 BROAD STREET, OLD *NEWS AND COURIER* (JACOBSON) BUILDING

Constructed circa 1817; remodeled with new facade circa 1840

The site of several banks between 1817 and 1861, this structure became the office of the newly merged newspapers *The News* and *Courier* and served as their offices until 1902. The lower portion of the Greek Revival facade of this building still survives, while the granite entablature was destroyed in the earthquake of 1886. The engaged pedimented portico with laurel wreath frieze and the side pilasters are of granite, while the rest of the building is a severe stuccoed brick.

Mid-nineteenth-century photo of the Old News and Courier Building, 19 Broad Street

59

21–31 BROAD STREET

Variously constructed between 1786 and 1839; remodeled facades circa 1887–1900

Originally built in the early-nineteenth century, the buildings at 21 and 25–27 Broad received their Victorian pressed tin details after the earthquake of 1886. An even more elaborate metal door surround and bracketed cornice were added to 31 Broad Street, which had been constructed before 1792 by Charleston's leading colonial clock- and watchmaker, William Lee. Victorian changes to its contemporary neighbor at 29 Broad Street include a bracketed cornice and slate mansard roof with surmounting balustrade. Of this group, only 23 Broad Street, built by tailor Edgar Wells after the Revolution, retains many elements of its pre–Civil War facade, especially the fenestration of its upper two stories.

Watchmaker William Lee's late-eighteenth-century building displays late-nineteenth-century facade details

28 BROAD STREET, JAMES GREGORIE HOUSE

Constructed 1791; various nineteenth- and twentieth-century renovations

This eighteenth-century merchant's residence originally possessed a countinghouse and store on the first floor, family quarters above, and anterior dependencies for both domestic and commercial use. The building retains the original arched brick windows on the second story, indicating the former location of the family's drawing rooms. A lost formal garden at the rear of Gregorie's property along Chalmers Street was once the domain of Mary Christiana Hopton Gregorie, whose mother, Sarah Hopton, was one of Charleston's leading early gardeners. Except for the fine upper brick facade, the property now bears little resemblance to its 1797 appearance. Becoming law offices by the mid-nineteenth century, it is now headquarters for one of South Carolina's oldest law firms. The exterior brick cornice and first-floor granite storefront represent nineteenth-century changes to the building. The original kitchen and washhouse have been incorporated into the current legal office complex at the rear, as has the circa 1791 William Rouse building at *26 Broad Street*, with its later Italianate style facade.

33 BROAD STREET, JOHN SMITH HOUSE AND OFFICE

Constructed circa 1787; storefront circa 1830; restored 1970s

John Smith's house and office remains Broad Street's best example of an early-nineteenth-century wood storefront. Fluted pilasters between the windows supporting an entablature and similar details flanking the principal door architrave punctuate the first floor. An early wrought-iron balcony with interlocking guilloche patterns orna-

ments the second floor. Restored in the 1970s, the building, with its early store-front facade as well as surviving architectural details of its upper-story residence, illustrates the mixed use of the buildings in this area prior to the mid-nineteenth century. Although its storefront has been lost, the neighboring contemporary building at *35 Broad Street* retains its original residential upper floors with a surmounting Palladian windowed dormer projecting from the hip roof. Similar fenestration at the circa 1792 building at *37 Broad Street* was altered after the Civil War with scored stucco treatment and metal cornices and window surrounds.

36–42 BROAD STREET

Variously constructed between 1780 and 1806; late-nineteenth-century facade renovations

These four structures were constructed in the Federal period and retain their later-nineteenth-century facades with metal window surrounds and bracketed entablatures of similar material. While the structure at 38 Broad is the most important historically, having been erected as a shop and residence and later housing the first State Bank of South Carolina, the most outstanding edifice architecturally is 42 Broad Street, built by the merchant tailor William Inglesby. Dr. Joseph Inglesby, the 1850s owner, apparently added the cast-iron facade in the Italianate style.

39 BROAD STREET, EXCHANGE BANK AND TRUST COMPANY BUILDING

Constructed circa 1891

This bank building of heavily rusticated sandstone and granite marks the stylistic evolution from the Romanesque Revival architecture, pioneered by H. H. Richardson, to the characteristics of the skyscraper style emerging in large cities.

The marked verticality of the windows seems a precursor to the "banding" that was important to the latter style. Otto Witte, founder and president, orchestrated the construction of this modish structure. A native of Germany who immigrated to Charleston in 1840, Witte rose to wealth and position, serving as consul for various German, Swedish, and Austro-Hungarian governments, and by the mid-nineteenth century he became a real estate baron, owning numerous rental properties throughout the city. He purchased *172 Rutledge Avenue* (now Ashley Hall School) as his residence during the heyday of this bank.

Engraving of the Exchange Bank and Trust Company Building, 39 Broad Street

43–47 BROAD STREET, PLENGE HABERDASHERY

Constructed circa 1855; renovated circa 1870

Although built in the antebellum period as the shop of the saddler and harness makers Charles Love and Conrad M. Wienges, this large structure was thoroughly altered in about 1870 by its subsequent owner, haberdasher Charles Plenge, with the addition of a pressed metal cornice and Italianate facade treatments in stucco. One of the enduring characteristics of the building is the late-nineteenth-century painting *The Hatter* on the west facade that formerly served as signage and a popular trademark. William Waller, a saddler, built the structure next door at *41 Broad Street*. A subsequent owner added a new facade to this building with an Italianate cornice and window heads within a few years after the War Between the States.

The original trade card, Plenge the Hatter

46 BROAD STREET, CITIZENS AND SOUTHERN BANK BUILDING

Constructed circa 1929

Otto Olaf, architect

The present building with its monumental portico, supported by fluted Ionic col-

umns and with bracketed window surrounds, still serves as a bank and is one of Charleston's few Neoclassical Revival style public edifices. Otto Olaf, the architect, was also a civil engineer and designer of the Savannah River Bridge. The real importance for this location lies with the bank's predecessors, the last of which was demolished in 1928. From the 1730s the northeast corner of Church and Broad Streets had been occupied by a succession of important taverns: Shepheard's, Swallow's, Gordon's, and the City Tavern. The long room, stretching north along Church Street, served various purposes for the colonial government, as well as providing the setting for Charleston's (and America's) first full theatrical season in 1735 and as the location of the establishment in the United States of the Scottish Rite of Free Masonry in 1801. This last tavern building on the site became a nineteenth-century grocery store, Klinck and Wickenburg.

6 CHALMERS STREET, OLD SLAVE MART

Constructed circa 1859
Rebuilt in its present form 1870s

The Old Slave Mart as a museum from 1937 to the mid-1980s

Through the 1850s, the city passed ordinances to attempt to centralize and regulate slave sales, and various privatized sales areas sprung up along Chalmers, State, and Queen Streets. Ryan's Mart on Queen Street, converting a four-story brick double tenement into a barracoon, extended to this Chalmers Street site with an area for auctions. Z. B. Oakes, a transplanted New Englander, purchased the site in 1859 and created a shed for sales with a roof trussed to the building next door and supported by octagonal pillars. In the 1870s the structure was refitted as a tenement. In 1938 the property was established as a privately owned museum of African and African American art and history by Charlestonian Miriam B. Wilson. Today the city of Charleston owns the structure and with the South Carolina African American History Council is developing long-range plans for establishment of a museum on this site.

8 CHALMERS STREET, GERMAN FIRE STEAM ENGINE COMPANY

Constructed 1851; rehabilitated 1981

Edward C. Jones, architect

Built in a mix of the Gothic Revival and a style called "Norman" or Romanesque Revival, this engine house served as headquarters for the seventy-member Deutschen Feuer Kompagnie, one of the many ethnic fire companies established in Charleston in the early-nineteenth century. The private engine companies eventually merged with the city fire department, and this site became Engine House no. 1 by 1881. The engine house use was discontinued at 8 Chalmers when the new city fire stations were built by 1888. The building served as the Carolina Light Infantry's armory until 1907 and as the site of African American charitable organizations, "Good Samaritan Hall" and the Embry Mission, until 1937. An early coat of stucco still covers the three-bay building with corner turrets, arched windows, a Gothic pavilion, and stepped parapet. Adapted as an office in 1981, the structure contains one of Charleston's most interesting working spaces.

17 CHALMERS STREET, PINK HOUSE

Constructed circa 1712; restored 1930s

The Pink House, constructed of pinkish Bermuda stone, is the sole surviving alehouse from the bawdy colonial district that ran along Union or Chalmers Alley (as the eastern end of Chalmers Street was known until 1818). The gambrel roof, covered in pantiles, dating from the mid-eighteenth century, appears to have been constructed while the chimney was being upgraded;

the original roofline probably mirrored the gable roof of the small building to the west.

A taverner owned the site in the 1750s, and by the 1780s it had passed to James Gordon. The wealthy Baltimoreans Mr. and Mrs. Victor Morawetz restored the building in the 1930s.

50 CHURCH STREET, E. J. F. FISCHER HOUSE
Constructed circa 1888–89

This Queen Anne style house, like its single house neighbors at *46* and *48 Church Street*, was constructed after the earthquake of 1886. Built by E. J. H. Fischer by 1889, the dwelling replaced an early-eighteenth-century brick Baptist meetinghouse that had become a chapel for seamen called the Mariners Church. The church incurred heavy damage in the earthquake and its trustees sold this property to Fischer. The two-story wood house follows the side-hall plan and has detailing such as heavy bracketed cornice and balustrade bay window more often found on houses in the area west of Legare Street.

53 CHURCH STREET, JULIUS LEE HOUSE
Constructed by 1881

This site was owned by the Joseph Ball family for nearly 100 years. His widow's estate was finally settled in the late-1870s. Property tax records and deeds indicate that the purchaser, a stevedore, apparently built a typical example of a masonry Charleston single house with a pilastered, closed gable end and Tuscan-columned piazzas. It has served for many years as the parsonage for the First Baptist Church.

55 CHURCH STREET, BENJAMIN PHILLIPS HOUSE

Constructed circa 1818; converted to apartments circa 1952; restored to residence 1987

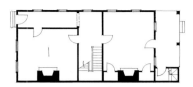

Measured plan of the first floor, 55 Church Street

This is a three-and-a-half-story weatherboarded frame house built by a Charleston merchant in the late-Neoclassical style on the site of the eighteenth-century town house of an Ashley River planter. It is notable for its unusual plan, which is an early divergence from the Charleston single house. The arched and fanlighted front door leads to a side passage that provides access to a front room, probably originally for business, and thence to the rest of the building with its residential spaces. Although passing through a succession of prominent resident owners including the physician and scientist Dr. Thomas Y. Simons from 1835 to 1847, the building became a boardinghouse and then apartments before a recent restoration. The garden at the rear has received acclaim as a modern interpretation of the classic town garden of eighteenth-century Charleston.

58–60 CHURCH STREET, JAMES VEREE HOUSES

Constructed 1754–90; restored 1930s–40s

James Veree, a French Huguenot carpenter, purchased a parcel containing these lots in 1754 and probably constructed the house at 58 Church Street immediately and the dwelling to the north a decade later. The property at 58 Church has the largest of the original houses but contains simple woodwork. James Veree Jr. sold the house to a signer of the Declaration of Independence, Thomas Heyward, who apparently used it as a rental property.

A single house with three front bays, it has been noted for its rear garden, designed by the owners with the assistance of Loutrel Briggs in 1942.

The west first-floor room is the outstanding feature of 60 Church, having pre-Revolutionary mahogany paneling with fretwork inlay, possibly attributable to Martin Pfeninger, a German cabinetmaker living in Charleston in the 1770s. After Veree moved to Burlington, New Jersey, he sold 60 Church to Stephen Duvall, a harbor pilot, who furnished it elaborately, according to his estate inventory. An officer in the S.C. navy in the Revolution, Duvall died of a fever while imprisoned by the British under the Exchange Building in 1780.

Veree also owned the lot at *56 Church Street*. In 1792 James Veree Jr. sold the lot to the widow Margaret Daniel, who built a house on the site between 1794 and 1796.

This house retains its early piazza containing a notable door architrave with engaged and fluted Tuscsan columns supporting a Neoclassical frieze.

59 CHURCH STREET, THOMAS ROSE HOUSE

N *Constructed circa 1735; restored 1929, 1939*

Indicative of the merchant house plan in American and English port cities, the Thomas Rose House reflects the asymmetrical plan used for larger dwellings in Charleston during the second quarter of the eighteenth century. The Rose House stands two and a half stories high with five bays on the front facade, topped by a brick cornice, and capped by a hipped slate roof. The second-floor drawing room or dining parlor extends across the entire floor, constituting one of the earliest surviving examples of this plan in the city. An exterior central doorway once led directly to a first-floor counting room. This door was walled up when piazzas were added in the nineteenth century.

Thomas Rose constructed the house on original Charles Town lot no. 61, inherited

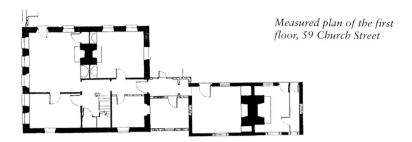

Measured plan of the first floor, 59 Church Street

by his wife Beauler Elliott, replacing an earlier dwelling. A 1734 letter to Thomas's brother Richard Rose in England requesting that bricklayers be sent to Charleston appears related to the construction of the house. It was sold by Rose shortly after completion to the Savage family, who owned it for the next ninety years, keeping twelve slaves on the property.

Sympathetic northern owners, the Frank Whitmans, restored the house in 1929, using local restoration architect Albert Simons. The Victorian piazza details were removed and replaced by woodwork imitating Neoclassical moldings. The structure was later purchased by the Connecticut architectural historian Henry Philip Staats, and further restoration work was undertaken. Staats was a founder of Historic Charleston Foundation and with his wife, Juliette Wiles Staats, bolstered preservation and artistic endeavors in Charleston.

The original kitchen and laundry outbuildings survive and were incorporated into the present house plan via a twentieth-century addition. The property is held by the Church Street Historic Foundation, which the Staats family established to preserve this area of the city. It is privately occupied.

62 CHURCH STREET, MARY W. FIFE HOUSE

Constructed circa 1817; altered circa 1840, 1972

Although this site was part of original Charles Town lot no. 78, earlier houses here had disappeared by 1815. Combined at this period with property on East Bay Street and holding "a drain" and well, the owner, John Woddrop, the lot was conveyed by the widow Mary W. Fife, who probably built the current house. Fife's son sold the property to druggist James Heilbrun, owner of several other sites along Church Street. Heilbrun operated "sulfur baths" in mid-nineteenth-century Charleston, and some have speculated that the reference to the well on this site, under the present house, may hold significance. Much of the interior of the house relates to the late–Greek Revival period, indicating substantial renovations during the ownership of Heilbrun or after his sale of the house in 1863.

61–63 CHURCH STREET, FIRST BAPTIST CHURCH

Constructed 1819–22; restored 1990

Robert Mills, architect

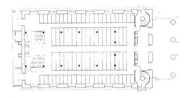

Measured plan, First Baptist Church, 61 Church Street

Early-twentieth-century view of First Baptist Church

Site of the original "Anabaptist" Meeting House, the lot had been given by the prominent Elliott family in 1699 to provide a place of worship for a fledgling congregation begun by immigrants from Kittery, Maine, some fifteen years earlier. The earlier wooden structure held the pulpit of the fiery Reverend Richard Furman, a revolutionary patriot and co-author of South Carolina's move to disestablish the Anglican Church. The British occupying commander used the meetinghouse for storage of provisions from 1780 to 1782.

The Charleston-born architect Robert Mills designed the present edifice (the third on the site) by 1819, when the cornerstone was laid. Mills worked extensively in his native city at this juncture, following his studies with Thomas Jefferson and then Benjamin Latrobe, and successful commissions in Baltimore, Philadelphia, and Richmond. This was, however, prior to his important work in Washington planning the Treasury and Patent Buildings and the Washington Monument. As with the numerous courthouses he designed throughout South Carolina, he considered the new First Baptist Church with its temple form plan to be "purely Greek in its style," calling it the "best specimen of correct taste in architecture of the modern buildings of this city." Actually a Roman Doric or Tuscan colonnade supports the front pedimented portico. The simple parapet was originally designed with a laurel wreath frieze and surmounted by a roof lantern, but neither of these features survives. On the interior a double colonnade supports the galleries on three sides with both Ionic and Doric orders. A portion of the original graveyard was removed in the 1950s for the construction of the educational building. Important stones, however, line the south walkway, including that of Dr. Furman and the Abigail Barker stone carved in Newport, Rhode Island.

66 CHURCH STREET, JOHN MCCALL HOUSE

Constructed circa 1784; altered 1940s

John McCall, the city treasurer, acquired a site that probably was burned over in the fire of 1778. The lot once contained a brick house owned successively by Thomas Rose Sr. (father of the builder of *59 Church Street*) and by the wealthy merchant Anthony Matthews. McCall's house began as a single house on a raised brick basement, capped by a hipped roof with projecting dormers. Alterations producing apartments in the mid-twentieth century included enclosures on the street side that harm the effect of the multi-tiered, Greek Revival style piazzas.

69 CHURCH STREET, CAPERS-MOTTE HOUSE

Constructed circa 1750; altered early-nineteenth century; additional restorations 1971

One of the largest pre-Revolutionary houses in the city, this dwelling has been the home of several notable South Carolinians. Both Richard Capers and Jordan

69 Church Street before restoration in the 1970s

Roche owned the property successively, and one of them was responsible for the mid-eighteenth-century construction on the site. Roche's niece, Rebecca Brewton Motte, with her husband, the public treasurer Jacob Motte, leased the house from 1761 until the death of the latter in 1770. The structure is an unusually large form of the pre-Revolutionary double house with three full floors, excavated cellar, and spacious garret.

In the early-1800s a subsequent owner closed the front door, converted the front rooms to a nineteenth-century double parlor, and added piazzas on the south elevation. Later the surviving outbuildings were renovated in the Gothic Revival style. In 1869 the widow Eliza Middleton Huger Smith (Mrs. William Mason Smith) purchased the property. A daughter of Sen. Daniel Elliott Huger of *34 Meeting Street*, Mrs. Smith's plantation house at Smithfield, in St. Bartholomew's Parish south of the city, was burned by Sherman's troops in 1865. Her son D. E. H. Smith and her granddaughter Alice Ravenel Huger Smith became Charleston's first chroniclers of the city's architecture, and Miss Smith is one of the most celebrated artists of the early-twentieth-century Charleston Renaissance. After her death in 1958, 69 Church Street passed out of the Smith family. A subsequent owner removed the piazzas and restored a conjectural central entrance door to the street elevation in 1971.

71 CHURCH STREET, COL. ROBERT BREWTON HOUSE

🅛 *Constructed circa 1721–41; various twentieth-century renovations*

This Brewton family dwelling has long been cited as the oldest surviving single house in Charleston, but it may have been rebuilt after the fire of 1740. Col. Robert Brewton, wealthy politician, merchant, and powder receiver, constructed it and lived here until selling the property to his

brother-in-law, Jordan Roche. The three-bay structure, with its fine quoins and molded brick cornice, has undergone some change in the late-twentieth century, including the removal of late-nineteenth-century piazzas and the addition of a modern masonry coating over the old stucco surface.

73 CHURCH STREET, THOMAS DALE HOUSE

Constructed 1733; altered circa 1920

Exemplary of eighteenth-century construction techniques used within the walled city, this building formerly had a third story, now removed. Although altered early in this century, its small scale and rear work yard suggest an original floor plan consisting of two rooms topped by either one or two stories. Most notable is the presence of an early central chimney, a construction feature replaced by party wall chimneys in late-eighteenth- and nineteenth-century Charleston single houses. Dr. Thomas Dale was a physician particularly noted for his literary achievements in early colonial Charleston. Upon his marriage to Mary Brewton this house was given as a gift by her father, Miles Brewton I.

74 CHURCH STREET, RUSSELL-DEHON TENEMENT

Constructed circa 1782–88; various twentieth-century renovations

This simple two-story wooden single house with a closed gable roof served as a replacement for an earlier building that burned in the fire of 1778. Although the builder is unclear, the heirs of Sarah Russell Dehon, then living in the Russell House at *51 Meeting Street*, sold this rental dwelling in 1852 from the group of properties held by the intermarried Hopton and Russell families on Tradd Street and Longitude Lane. Apparently the Russell-Dehon

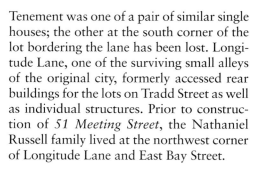

Tenement was one of a pair of similar single houses; the other at the south corner of the lot bordering the lane has been lost. Longitude Lane, one of the surviving small alleys of the original city, formerly accessed rear buildings for the lots on Tradd Street as well as individual structures. Prior to construction of *51 Meeting Street*, the Nathaniel Russell family lived at the northwest corner of Longitude Lane and East Bay Street.

76–78 CHURCH STREET

L *Constructed circa 1785; various nineteenth-century renovations*

Two post-Revolutionary dwellings have been combined in recent years as one residence. Both are brick with early stucco coatings. While the house at 76 Church has a significant clay pantile roof, its neighbor has long been noted for its unusually old-fashioned steep roofline (called "medieval" by Albert Simons and Samuel Lapham) and bulky early chimneys. The cast-iron balcony at 78 Church probably dates from the 1820s. The house at 76 Church is a designated National Historic Landmark, as DuBose Heyward wrote the novel *Porgy* here.

77 CHURCH STREET, LOUIS DANJOU HOUSE (BREWTON'S CORNER)

Constructed circa 1810; renovated circa 1925; some subsequent restoration

Built by the grocer Louis Danjou, an immigrant born in Cluny, France, on the site of a wooden house erected by the Brewton family and on a spot usually called Brewton's Corner, this building functioned as both a commercial and residential space from the early-nineteenth century to the mid-twentieth century. The ground-floor rooms functioned successively as a grocery, a doctor's receiving room (for the antebel-

lum physician Dr. Peter Porcher), a school (the Gaud School, forerunner of today's Porter-Gaud School), and a series of antique shops. The Church Street entrance of the three-and-a-half-story, Flemish bond brick building consists of a finely crafted doorway lit by a transom with curved wooden muntins, one of the oldest intact commercial entrances in the city. Rented as a winter residence in 1928 by Loutrel Briggs, the noted landscape architect, and his wife, the house and adjacent properties on Tradd and Church Streets were subsequently renovated as an inn, for decades a popular hostelry for spring visitors. In the 1920s the street end of the piazza was closed off and Loutrel Briggs designed the plan for the courtyard garden. The original carriage house at *75 Church Street* retains its arched door openings, and though still part of the property, it has been renovated as a separate residence.

75 Church Street, outbuilding to 77 Church Street

82 CHURCH STREET, WILLIAM MILLS HOUSE

Constructed circa 1782; altered late-nineteenth century

The Scottish Presbyterian merchant William Mills gave this property to his son Thomas in 1799. City directories indicate that the elder Mills lived on this or a neighboring site at least a decade prior to the transfer from father to son; thus it is possible that the younger sibling, the famous architect Robert Mills, spent a portion of his youth in this house. A recently discovered drawing shows this building originally standing as a Charleston single house with a ground-story shop on the Church Street side; a second-story, covered, wrought-iron balcony; a hipped roof; and a rear wall and kitchen divided by a yard from the small three-story building at *84 Church Street*. A late- nineteenth-century renovation cre-

ated an addition to the north, incorporating the dependency and work yard; this resulted in the removal of much of the original detailing.

83–85 CHURCH STREET, CABBAGE ROW (WILLIAM HENDRICKS TENEMENTS)
Constructed 1749–50; rehabilitated 1936

Similar to other paired houses in early Charleston, this two-story, stuccoed double tenement with a central archway to the rear courtyard was originally constructed as a speculative venture by Christ Church planter William Hendricks. Hendricks directed his executors in his 1749 will to complete his two brick tenements on Church Street and "also the back buildings thereto." Old nine-over-nine window sashes remain on the north tenement, but the six-over-six and two-over-two windows on the south tenement reflect later alterations. Visible through the archway, the original paired kitchen building with its massive central chimney was rehabilitated in 1936 with a substantial addition for use as a winter residence by Mr. and Mrs. Reynolds Brown. The landscaping of the paved courtyard was completed at the same time. The Browns' rehabilitation of the kitchen building, furnished with family antiques, marked the beginning of a trend of renovating former dependencies in the city as showplace residences.

86 CHURCH STREET, ISAAC MAZYCK HOUSE
Constructed circa 1783; restored 1950

Built by Isaac Mazyck III after the fire of 1778, this three-story stucco house has a wide fanlighted entry on the south end of the front facade that accesses a side passage running the length of the dwelling, an unusual feature for this period. A second-floor drawing room follows the lead of earlier merchant houses on Church Street and stretches across the entire front of the building. Mazyck, grandson of a Huguenot immigrant, died soon after its completion and bequeathed the house to his daughter, Mrs. Robert Wilson. She and her descendants rented the property as an office and residence to a series of tenants for more than a century. A small house to the north was demolished in the early-nineteenth century, and the property was divided with *90 Church Street*, thus permitting the large gates and drive. Two brick kitchen buildings, of differing periods, flank a rear paved courtyard. A missing section of the later stucco on the northwest corner of the house reveals the original Flemish-bonded brick with finely tooled lime mortar.

87 CHURCH STREET, HEYWARD-WASHINGTON HOUSE

L *Outbuildings constructed circa 1740; house constructed circa 1771; altered late-nineteenth century; restored 1929–30 and subsequent dates*

This property was granted to Joseph Ellicott in 1694. A subsequent owner, a well-to-do gunsmith, built a two-story brick single house here in about 1740. The rice planter Col. Daniel Heyward purchased the site in 1770, and his son, Thomas, began construction on the present house in 1771. Heyward razed the previous single house yet kept the former two-story kitchen and one-story stable dependencies that still exist in the rear courtyard.

The Heyward dwelling stands as a well-developed example of a brick double house with a central hall and two rooms on each side. On the second floor a large front drawing room and smaller withdrawing room extend across the front elevation, the former retaining its original paneled woodwork. On the exterior brick jack arches over the windows and the conjectural doorway provide the only decoration to a facade that supports a low hipped roof with a single front dormer. Thomas Heyward, using this as his Charleston town house, became a signer of the Declaration of Independence in 1776. After the fall of Charleston, the British imprisoned Heyward and his brother-in-law George Abbot Hall in St. Augustine. Tradition holds that their wives stayed on in the house. When the women refused a British order to illuminate their windows, a mob stormed the house, which led to a miscarriage by Mrs. Hall and her ensuing death. Residing more often on his plantations after the war, Heyward rented the house to the city for the lodging of President George Washington during his week-long stay in Charleston in 1791. Washington wrote of his visit in his diary, "The lodging provided for me in this place, was very good, being the furnished house of a gentleman at present in the country." Selling the house three years later, Heyward bought another town house down the street. By the late-nineteenth century the residence became a bakery on the ground floor and the owner installed a storefront on the southern half of the front elevation while lowering the windows and installing a door on the three southernmost bays.

The Charleston Museum purchased the property in 1929 with assistance from the Society for the Preservation of Old Dwellings, although this transaction was not completed until the 1950s with some help from the Society and from Historic Charleston Foundation. The architectural firm of Simons and Lapham carried forth a splendid investigation of the altered first floor, discovering the layout of the narrow front hall and finding lost mantels in the fowl house in the back. After restoration of the front door architrave and first-floor rooms, the building opened as the first historic house museum in Charleston. Garden precedents from the third quarter of the eighteenth century guided the creation of a parterre, planted only with flowers and shrubs known in the city in 1791.

89–91 CHURCH STREET, CATFISH ROW

Constructed circa 1783; restoration 1928–30

A larger, three-story version of the Hendricks tenements, this stucco building achieved fame as the setting for DuBose Heyward's famous novel *Porgy* and the subsequent libretto. Heyward knew the building well, not only because he lived in the next block but because he had previously rented the dependency across the street at *90 Church Street*. Along with the Hendricks tenements, this structure was formerly known as Cabbage Row, but Heyward dubbed it "Catfish Row," its appellation thereafter. Retaining its original fenestration, particularly its early-nineteenth-century shop fronts, the central passageway arch still boasts a late-eighteenth-century wrought-iron lunette with scrollwork and central pendant.

Occupied for decades after the Civil War as a dense rooming house for as many as one hundred African Americans, the building was purchased in 1928 by the wife of

Catfish Row, the setting for DuBose Heyward's novel Porgy, *after restoration*

Rear view of Catfish Row before restoration in the late 1920s

79

landscape architect Loutrel Briggs. Briggs restored the exterior, adding old woodwork to the upper interiors for rental apartments and renovating the gutted shells of the flanking rear outbuildings as new units.

90 Church Street

90 CHURCH STREET, PETER LEGER HOUSE

Constructed circa 1759–60; restored 1927

92 CHURCH STREET, ALEXANDER CHRISTIE HOUSE

Constructed circa 1805; renovated 1908, late-1980s

94 CHURCH STREET, COOPER-BEE HOUSE

Constructed 1760–65; various twentieth-century restorations

Called by the late architectural historian Samuel G. Stoney "three variations on the theme of the Charleston 'single house,'" numbers 90, 92, and 94 Church Street reflect the development of the single house from the mid-eighteenth century. The clients who contracted for the three three-story brick houses—Leger, Christie, and Cooper—were all wealthy and socially prominent individuals whose architectural aspirations, according to one architectural historian, defined Charleston's early town houses as "a union of cosmopolitan and vernacular building traditions." 90 and 94

Measured plan of the first floor, 92 Church Street

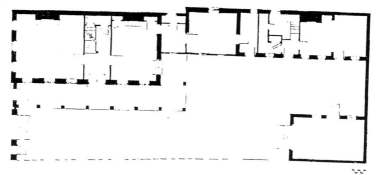

Church Street were constructed in the 1760s as three-story, hipped roof, center-passage plan dwellings with ground-floor front commercial rooms or offices; while the taller 92 Church Street was built solely as a residence for a Scottish merchant in the early-nineteenth century. The site at 90 Church contains a two-story slave quarters-kitchen, while 94 Church includes a narrow passage behind the house providing access to the neighbors' back buildings on the interior of the block. All three edifices, particularly 90 Church, retain splendid original woodwork.

During the early- to mid-nineteenth century these buildings were altered. The Cooper-Bee House received all new out-buildings, and the owner of the Leger House completed both a new garden and outbuildings. Both houses gained two-story piazzas as well. All three houses underwent the removal of their commercial usage, and the houses were physically connected to their back buildings, showing a segregation between work space and domestic space and reflecting a topographically redefined central business district. The latter change in which individual buildings on the lot were connected with infill wings represented a two-part shift in lot planning toward, first, the consolidation of household functions under a single roof and, second, a growing sense of room specialization. All three buildings were returned to single family usage in the present century: 90 Church Street was restored by W. Lucas Simons, the brother of architect Albert Simons; 92 Church Street became the rectory of St. Philip's Church; and 94 Church Street served briefly as the spring tours headquarters for Historic Charleston Foundation. The latter has been extensively restored by its owner in recent years with a contemporary renovation of its rear hyphen.

94 Church Street

93–99 CHURCH STREET, CHARLESTON IMPROVEMENT CORPORATION HOUSES

Constructed 1906–07

Although residential throughout the twentieth century, the parcel now known as 93–101 Church Street was formerly owned by the Charleston Hydraulic Press Company, and during the second half of the nineteenth century it encompassed a large industrial complex. In 1906 the Charleston Improvement Corporation purchased the property. This entity, led by businessman Tristram T. Hyde (later mayor of Charleston), was responsible for the construction of many mid-sized houses throughout Charleston between 1906 and 1930, including those nearby at *52 Tradd Street* and *9 St. Michael's Alley*. The company produced these structures, their most extensive development, with similar Queen Anne style gable ends and front piazzas and varied them slightly with double-tiered porches at 93 (now gone) and 97 Church and pedimented entries and side piazzas at 95 and 99 Church. A fifth dwelling at 101 Church Street, used as a restaurant on the ground floor, burned and was replaced by the current parking lot.

100 CHURCH STREET, BANK OF THE UNITED STATES BUILDING

Constructed circa 1785–90

When the Charleston branch of the Bank of the United States was chartered in 1790, this simple three-story stuccoed building served as its first headquarters before its move to *80 Broad Street*. In keeping with Charleston's commercial traditions, an arched opening provides access to the first floor, while residential spaces are accessed through the door on the opposite end of the front facade. The building was owned through most of the antebellum period by

Mary A. S. Marion, a member of a prominent Berkeley County plantation family
that included Gen. Francis Marion, the
famed "Swamp Fox."

116 CHURCH STREET, CANNON-KIRKLAND HOUSE

*Constructed circa 1790–1810; altered
circa 1840–50; rehabilitated 1986*

The wealthy lumberman and contractor Daniel Cannon or his daughter Martha
apparently built this fairly typical masonry
Charleston single house as rental property
before or after the fire of 1796. Miss Cannon at her death in 1815 directed the sale
of her "house and Lot in Church Street"
for the benefit of her estate. Dr. Joseph
Kirkland, who had apparently been a tenant on the property since 1813, purchased
the house and lot. Kirkland, a prominent
physician, was noted for his innovative
treatments using "electricity," but he was
also a member of the South Carolina House
of Representatives from this parish from
1810 to 1815 and an advocate of public
improvements and education. Kirkland's
widow, Marianne Kennan Guerard
Kirkland, and his son Dr. William Kirkland
continued to live in the house and use it
for the latter's medical practice as well. The
younger Kirkland sold the house in 1850
to John Klinck, proprietor of the adjacent
Klinck, Wickenberg, and Company grocers.

Although a number of Federal features
survive, including the notable wrought-iron
balcony on the second story, the piazza and
principal entry doors date from the Greek
Revival period and were added in 1840–
50. The attached rear dependency of English bond brickwork may be earlier. The
most distinctive feature of the building is
the wall with high balustrade separating
the first story of the piazza from the carriage drive.

128 CHURCH STREET, KEENAN-O'REILLY HOUSES

North section constructed circa 1802–15, south section circa 1820; renovated 1970s, 1990s

Constructed as two separate buildings, these were first joined together in a renovation in the 1970s. The small two-and-one-half story house to the north, with its recently restored brickwork and hipped, pantile roof, was built after 1802 by shopkeeper George Keenan and sold in 1815 to Joshua Brown. To the south, the flat-roofed, parapeted building was constructed by James O'Reilly after 1820.

132 CHURCH STREET, DOUXSAINT-MACAULAY HOUSE

Constructed circa 1796-1800

Although this dwelling has a plaque denoting its construction by the French Huguenot Paul Douxsaint in about 1726, that structure apparently burned in the fire of 1796. The exterior of the building, with its beaded weatherboarding, nine-over-nine windows with narrow muntins, and dormered hipped roof, follows the molding patterns of the early-Federal period. Most of the interior retains late-eighteenth-century wainscoting and mantels, although several rooms have late-nineteenth-century alterations. The property retains an original, separated kitchen-laundry dependency at the rear, and brickwork on this structure with dogtooth cornicing relates to the post-Revolutionary period as well. In the nineteenth century Daniel Macaulay, a member of one of Charleston's leading Scottish merchant families, owned and occupied the dwelling.

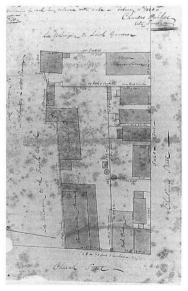

Plat of 1828 showing 132 Church Street

136 CHURCH STREET, FRENCH PROTESTANT (HUGUENOT) CHURCH RECTORY

L *Constructed before 1800; altered circa 1850; renovated 1983*

The date of this building remains unclear, but it seems that this is a post-Revolutionary dwelling and may replace one burned in the fire of 1796. The property remained in the possession of the French Huguenot Church from the early-eighteenth century until 1871. The dwelling was heavily modified in the 1850s and retains its Italianate style door architrave.

140 CHURCH STREET, FRENCH PROTESTANT (HUGUENOT) CHURCH

Congregation organized at this site 1687; present structure built 1844–45; restored 1888, 1987, 1996

Edward Brickell White, architect; Ephraim Curtis, builder

After organizing in 1687 as an official outgrowth of a French Protestant church at Pons in France, the congregation members left the fledgling Congregational meeting house nearby and constructed a church on land at this corner, donated by the Izard family. The original masonry building was blown up as a firebreak (unsuccessful) during the 1796 fire, and its simpler replacement, closed due to an inactive congregation in 1823, was torn down by the next generation of Huguenot descendants in order to erect the present church. Begun in 1844 and completed in 1845, the French Huguenot Church was designed by the Charleston architect Edward Brickell White. Built at the cost of $12,000, the Huguenot Church was Charleston's first Gothic Revival ecclesiastical building. The simple gable form of the exterior derives its ornamentation from the buttresses surmounted by cast-iron pinnacles, the lancet windows, and the crenellated parapet. On the interior the railed chancel and pulpit stand beneath the Gothic case of the original Henry Erben organ installed in 1847, and the

Postcard view of the Huguenot Church, 140 Church Street, early 1900s

liturgical tablets and marble memorial plaques dedicated to prominent Huguenot families line walls below a vaulted ceiling of plaster with rosette bosses.

The restoration of the building—damaged in the siege of 1864 and nearly destroyed in the earthquake—by the Lanier family of New York inaugurated a period of the church's primary use as a shrine to all Huguenot settlers of the New World, marked by the marble plaques dating from the late-nineteenth century to the early-twentieth century. Relegated for several decades to a single service a year in French, descendants of original members came back in the 1980s and restored the church's regular membership with weekly services and programs and rehabilitated the building. The paint scheme with scored plaster walls, the restoration of the chandelier and light fixtures, and the regilding and painting of the tablets are the most tangible results of the interior restoration. The churchyard retains several large family vaults including that of the Manigault family, used 1729–1870, and eighteenth-century New England gravestones marking the burials of members of the Bocquet, Neufville and other families.

141–145 CHURCH STREET, ALEXANDER PERONNEAU TENEMENTS

Constructed circa 1740; restored 1920s

Two of Charleston's earliest town houses, these buildings, two-and-a-half stories tall and two rooms deep, are largely constructed of Bermuda stone, a coquina stone imported from the Caribbean. Early research indicates that the merchant Alexander Peronneau built the buildings as investments, probably after the fire of 1740.

Unheated front rooms and full cellar with a large cooking fireplace and bake oven suggest that the tenement at 141

The Alexander Peronneau Tenements, 141–145 Church Street, as they appeared before restoration in the 1920s

Church was built as a combination commercial building and residence with the family quarters located behind the shop room opening onto the street. It was owned by the well-to-do craftsman and planter Paul Smiser in the late-eighteenth century and described in his will as "my Bermudian stone tenement in New Church Street." The structure at 143–145 Church Street is an example of a double tenement. It was heavily restored in the 1920s by Mrs. R. Goodwyn Rhett with the assistance of Thomas Pinckney, an African American builder trained in Charleston's masonry traditions. They added the Neoclassical Revival style door surrounds and the shutters.

142 CHURCH STREET, ST. PHILIP'S EPISCOPAL CHURCH HOME

East portion constructed 1780–97; remainder constructed 1842; remodeled 1887, 1972

Owned by St. Philip's since 1866 and remodeled in the Victorian style after the earthquake of 1886, the Church Home consists on its south end of a block of three former late-eighteenth-century row houses or tenements that faced Queen Street and were incorporated in 1842 into a new hotel called the Commercial House. In the late-nineteenth century the rubbed brick, arched window heads and other Victorian modifications were accomplished in the conversion to an Episcopal home with large piazzas on the south end topping a brick first story.

146 CHURCH STREET, ST. PHILIP'S CHURCH

L *Original church on this site completed 1722–1723; present building constructed 1835–1838; additions and chancel renovated 1920; restored 1993–94*

On February 16, 1835, the *Mercury* newspaper commented on the burning of St. Philip's Church: "such deep and general regret as prevails among our citizens.

Engraving of St. Philip's Church from London Magazine, *1735*

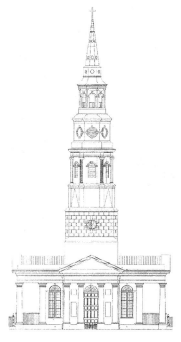

Measured drawing of the front (west) elevation of St. Philip's

. . . Unsurpassed in architectural beauty by any edifice in the union. . . ." The sentiment was made manifest in the timely reconstruction that re-created many aspects of the 1711–23 structure, most notably the triple Tuscan portico. The earlier design responded little to the provincial influences of southern colonial ecclesiastical construction and aggressively reflected the influences of English Baroque church design of the late-seventeenth and early-eighteenth centuries. Replacing a 1682 cypress structure at Meeting and Broad Streets, this building served the principal parish of the official church of the colony. In 1753 the *Gentleman's Magazine* in London published an elevation of the building's west facade. Surviving early-nineteenth-century interior views correspond to a description of the interior with its "lofty arches" and massive pillars adorned with elegant sepulchral monuments.

Although it is commonly asserted that the local architect Joseph Hyde was involved in the redesign and reconstruction of the building in 1835, the participation of additional architects is likely. Edward Brickell White, the architect of the French Huguenot Church, designed the later (1848–50) steeple of St. Philip's.

The 1835 building underwent significant changes to the east end in the 1920s under the direction of local architect Albert Simons. Changes included the extension of the east end one full bay to include a choir. The Boston architect Ralph Adams Cram was consulted for this project. His contributions included the Decalogue and the Lord's Prayer tablets and possibly the splendid "All Saints" window by Clement Heaton. The churchyard contains many early English carved markers and box tombs, as does the burial ground across the street. John C. Calhoun's splendid Roman sarcophagus style monument dominates this part of the graveyard.

CORDES STREET

Developed between 1790 and 1800

This is one of Charleston's more picturesque old wharf streets. It was originally taken from an area known as Prioleau's Wharves and is first mentioned in a deed of conveyance from 1800. Samuel Prioleau, a wealthy merchant of Huguenot descent and original owner of the wharves, developed nearby Prioleau Street and Gendron Street, as well as Cordes, which he named for his wife. 5 Cordes Street is typical of the older warehouse structures dispersed through the area. It was probably built by William Dewees in the 1790s. Like most of its neighbors, it was adapted in recent years for offices.

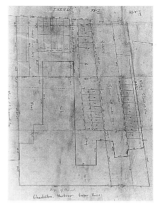

Plat showing Cordes Street's proximity to various wharves and docks

21 CUMBERLAND STREET, OLD POWDER MAGAZINE

🅛 *Constructed circa 1713; restored 1898–1902; conserved and restored 1995–96*

The Powder Magazine is the oldest secular public building surviving in South Carolina and the only one from the period of Proprietary rule. It is also the first building in the city deliberately restored for its historical associations.

The magazine was part of an early effort by the government of Carolina to build proper storage buildings for powder and arms. The 36-inch brick walls and the groin vaulting on the interior are somewhat characteristic of contemporary British magazines, but the exterior with central hip roof and gables covered with pantiles has a decidedly vernacular quality. Probably built under the direction of the Proprietary governor Nathaniel Johnson, the central column supporting groin vaults and in turn the massive roof system constituted an inherent structural problem discovered in the recent renovations.

View of the Old Powder Magazine, circa 1898

Interior view of the Old Powder Magazine after its opening to the public, early 1900s

Generally serving as a magazine until the end of the eighteenth century, despite the construction of another near the corner of Logan and Queen Streets, the building underwent repeated attempts at repair, particularly with the installation of cast-iron tie rods, forged in England and affixed by local masons in the 1740s. In the nineteenth century the structure went back to the descendants of the original owner of the site. It was used as a livery stable, as a printing shop, and for various other industrial purposes. At one point, it was a private wine cellar for the Manigault family. By 1860 the Powder Magazine was noted as a tourist destination for those visiting Charleston. The National Society of Colonial Dames in the State of South Carolina purchased the property in 1902. In 1993 Historic Charleston Foundation obtained a long-term lease from the Dames, undertook a full restoration, and reopened this public site.

39 EAST BAY STREET, GEORGE CHISOLM HOUSE

Constructed circa 1810; various twentieth-century renovations

Built by George Chisolm on the footage of two Grand Modell lots, this structure, including the former kitchen dependency, follows the bend in the peninsula and thus allows harbor views from every window. The Federal style wooden dwelling in an L-shape presents a two-story, five-bay front facade with a pediment and lunette window projecting from the hip roof. A street doorway formerly accessed the northeast room from East Bay Street. The double-tiered side piazzas follow the shape of the building and provide access to the principal entry architrave with its elliptical fanlight. The Frost family, who acquired the property in 1877, eventually purchased the lot to the south, demolishing an early-nineteenth-century single house to provide a site for formal and informal gardens, which were designed by landscape architect Loutrel Briggs in the 1930s.

40 EAST BAY STREET, GRANT-MISSROON HOUSE

Constructed 1789; altered with additions 1905, 1925

This brick edifice, owned by the English merchant Hary Grant in the late-eighteenth century, passed briefly through the Kinloch family and then the Fraser family before Capt. James Missroon purchased the property in 1808. Missroon, a native of Londonderry, and his descendants, involved in maritime trade, occupied the house for fifty years. During this time the family amalgamated adjacent properties and added a two-story dependency connected by a hyphen to the main house.

Detail of S. Barnard's View along the East Battery, Charleston, *1831, showing the Grant-Missroon House, circa 1792*

The original dwelling, the central portion of the present structure, includes a third-story lunette window surmounting a pedimented, tripartite window on the second story, an elliptical fanlighted doorway on the ground story, and stucco quoining. First converted to a boardinghouse known as the Shamrock Terrace, the building sustained extensive damage in the hurricane of 1911. Purchased by the Omar Shrine (a fraternal Masonic order) for its temple in 1925, Charleston restoration architects Simons and Lapham converted the house, adding a three-story section to the north and wrapping brick columned piazzas on the south and east, surmounted by an expanded third story; these new piazzas were later enclosed. During this work the remains of the Granville Bastion were uncovered; these were left intact. The house is now the headquarters of Historic Charleston Foundation and under long-term restoration.

41 EAST BAY STREET, WHALEY-HUIET HOUSE
Constructed 1901–02

Attorney W. Gibbes Whaley, who served for many years as master in equity, completed this stuccoed wood dwelling by 1902. The two-story, hipped-roof building with mixed Beaux Arts and Neoclassical detailing was sold within two years of its completion to William and Louisa Fait. William Fait had moved to Charleston only a few years earlier to manage the Charleston Canning Company but sold this house in 1906. The Huiet and Paul families owned 41 East Bay Street for most of the twentieth century. The bowed porch with a ground-story masonry arcade and upper balustrade was apparently added soon after construction.

43 EAST BAY STREET, GEORGE SOMMERS HOUSE
Constructed circa 1755; restored 1935

View of 43 East Bay Street before restoration in 1935

This house lies very close, if not immediately adjacent, to the site of the original city wall and was constructed on a portion of Grand Modell lot no. 1. Adam Daniel conveyed this lot, inherited from his father, to George Sommers with a "tenement" in 1755. Stylistically the house seems to date from the mid-eighteenth century, particularly due to the profiles of the moldings in its second-floor rooms and the paneling in its first-floor dining room. A surviving plat shows the layout of the single house and its extensive two-story outbuildings to the rear of the lot; these structures still survive.

Formerly this building, like many Charleston single houses, maintained an entrance on the street facade and a front ground-floor room for commercial purposes. In the early-nineteenth century the door was closed and the piazzas added, as was the late-Federal style piazza door screen. The bend in East Bay just beyond this lot led the area to be known in the 1700s as Sommers Corner. This very bend impelled the builder of the Sommers House to follow the diagonal of the street in the construction of the front facade.

Passing through several prominent merchant families, including those of John Teasdale, a British officer who became the first Charleston factor to ship cotton to Europe, and John Fraser, founder of the important mercantile firm Fraser and Trenholm, the dwelling suffered from deterioration in the early-twentieth century. Elizabeth Hanahan, a pioneering realtor in Charleston, restored the house in 1935 as her family's residence, with the assistance of preservation architects Albert Simons and Samuel S. Lapham.

45 EAST BAY STREET, SOMERSALL-DESAUSSURE HOUSE

Constructed circa 1790–1800; renovated 1850–60; altered as condominiums 1985

George Sommers sold this lot to the merchant James Hartley, who ordered his executors in his 1759 will to complete a house then under construction on this site. The present house, however, was apparently constructed by Hartley's son-in-law, merchant William Somersall. Due to a mid-nineteenth-century renovation by Wilmot G. deSaussure, later a Confederate general, the large-scale, three-story single house employs nineteenth-century Greek Revival and Italianate detailing, including a wide overhanging eave, heavy window hoods, and a bracketed piazza door hood, along with a triple-tiered piazza with fluted Doric columns. Although the exterior remains largely intact, some interior fabric was removed with the conversion of the house to condominiums in the mid-1980s.

47 EAST BAY STREET, ANNE BOONE HOUSE

Constructed after 1740; renovated 1840; restored twentieth century

Mrs. Boone's dwelling may have been built within the massive brick shell of an early-eighteenth-century house remaining on the site after the fire of 1740. The property offers a link with one of the lesser-known facets of early Charleston history. Anne Boone was the daughter of the landgrave Daniel Axtell, son of a Puritan leader who helped execute King Charles I and one of the refugees welcomed to Carolina by the Lords Proprietors. Her husband Joseph, also a Puritan or Dissenter, figured prominently in many of the colony's political struggles.

The north wall of the house with its original stucco finish and arched staircase windows survives almost intact from original construction. The other facades, however, have some alterations, including the replacement of the earlier porch with the present Tuscan piazza in 1840, the addition of an old balcony from another house in the early-twentieth century, and the rebuilding of the gable end in its nineteenth-century closed pediment profile after its collapse in Hurricane Hugo in 1989.

50 EAST BAY STREET, CAROLINA YACHT CLUB

Front portion constructed mid-nineteenth century; altered 1907, 1974

Housing the oldest continuous boating institution and one of the most exclusive private men's groups in Charleston, the Carolina Yacht Club incorporates both nineteenth- and twentieth-century architectural elements in its present clubhouse. Begun as a sculling group and successor to several such organizations founded by former Confederate soldiers who entered their first interstate competition in Savannah in 1874, the Carolina Yacht Club was chartered in 1888. Its original charter enumerated "yachting, bathing, social, literary, and aquatic purposes." Sailing became the organization's primary focus in the 1890s. In 1906, eighteen years after its establishment, the Carolina Yacht Club moved from Adger's Wharf to its present location, a range of cotton factors' offices with polygonal brick openings, built along a wharf. By 1907 the club leadership built a massive brick addition with a large square cupola. The clubhouse was commandeered as a naval officers' club during World War II. Returned to its membership in 1945, the Carolina Yacht Club has gone through additional renovations, including demolition of part of the original structure for a new wing in 1974 and the addition of a large concrete pier and waterfront sailing facility in recent years.

51 EAST BAY STREET, CASPAR CHRISTIAN SCHUTT HOUSE

Constructed 1800–02; restored 1994–95

The vast scale of this residence makes it one of the largest single houses ever built in Charleston. Standing three stories with corner quoining, a dentiled brick cornice, and hipped roof, the house was stuccoed on the east and south elevations but retains its brick finish on the north. The triple-tiered piazzas with graduating orders of Doric, Ionic, and Corinthian columns and the enormous windows with their original six-over-six sash hint at the scale and decoration of the interior: splendid Adamesque plaster friezes and cornices, mantels and door architraves with composition moldings, and a curved elliptical stair rising under a plaster ceiling medallion.

Caspar Christian Schutt, one of Charleston's first wealthy German mer-

Measured plan of the first floor, 51 East Bay Street

chants, completed the house within a few years after his 1799 purchase of the lot, locating his stores and countinghouse here. Passing successively to several other merchants, it became the residence of John Fraser following his tenure at *43 East Bay*. One of Charleston's most complete ranges of outbuildings stretch to the west and south, including the original kitchen, carriage house, servants' quarters, and stables. The enclosure of the property includes a paneled coping with banded piers and balustrade and wrought-iron gates with a curious star motif. Splendidly restored by new owners who rescued it from a planned condominium project, the Schutt House remains a single family residence.

55 EAST BAY STREET, JONATHAN SIMPSON HOUSE

Constructed circa 1782–85; partially restored 1960s, 1985

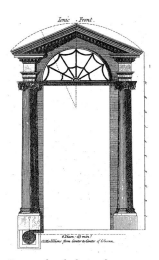

Pattern-book design by William Pain for an entry architrave that may have been the influence for the transom and pediment used for the entry of 55 East Bay Street

A British merchant with a fleet of ships engaged in Atlantic and Caribbean trade built a most up-to-date house on Charleston's East Bay waterfront after buying this lot from the Pinckney family property to the north in the early-1780s. The entry architrave with engaged Tuscan columns, pediment, and semicircular fanlight appears to be derived from the pattern book of the English builder William Pain. The front room originally served as a countinghouse, and the staircase in the large rear hall climbs to a drawing room with Adamesque detailing stretching across the front of the second floor. This room opens onto an exterior wrought-iron balcony with a motif of interlocking curves.

Owned by various merchants and an Episcopal minister, the dwelling declined in the twentieth century and holds the dubious distinction of serving as one of the final houses of prostitution in this part of Charleston, last raided by the police in 1958.

It was restored as a single family residence a few years later. An alley shared with the house next door accesses an original brick kitchen building renovated as a separate residence. A slightly smaller single house stands immediately to the south at *53 East Bay*. Constructed in the mid-1780s and ornamented by a dentiled brick cornice and wrought-iron balcony with a crossed star center panel, the building has served since 1957 as the sixth home of the Charleston Club, a venerable private men's organization established in 1852. In antebellum times considered one of the wealthiest men's clubs in America, the organization lost its three-story Meeting Street building after the Civil War but was sufficiently rejuvenated by 1881 to buy *7 Meeting Street*. Difficulties in the 1920s almost ended the club again, but a few members stayed on, it was revived, and this building was purchased.

57 EAST BAY STREET, GEN. THOMAS PINCKNEY HOUSE

Constructed circa 1783; altered and renovated mid- and late-twentieth century

Thomas Pinckney, the founder of Charleston's leading political family, bought this lot, with a house already built, shortly after his arrival in 1692. The original house on the site burned in 1778, and the present stuccoed brick dwelling has been dated to 1783. Stylistically similar to other post-Revolutionary houses in Charleston, particularly the Simpson house across the alley to the south, the three-story house with its low hipped roof also has a wrought-iron balcony on the second floor. Gen. Pinckney lived at *14 George Street* from the 1790s on, and this served as a rental property, although he attempted to sell it to a tenant at this juncture. The house subsequently became the home and grocery store of William Porter in 1826, thus explaining the large shop window opening on the first floor.

76–80 EAST BAY STREET, VANDERHORST ROW

Constructed 1798–1800; restored 1930s

Built in or before 1800 by Gov. Arnoldus Vanderhorst, this triple tenement served as the southernmost of two similar rental complexes, each divided into three three-story town house dwellings. Only the primary building of the southern grouping survives; the northern group was demolished by the end of the nineteenth century, and a parking lot occupies the site. Both rows originally included a complex series of service structures behind each unit and accessed various storehouses and wharves. All of this has disappeared, but several plats and early photographs portray the thriving maritime activity that once characterized this relatively quiet commercial area. The facade of Vanderhorst Row is an excellent example of Neoclassical design with its central pedimented pavilion constructed with splendid Flemish-bonded brickwork and marble detailing; it bears a strong resemblance to London's terrace architecture of the same period. Vanderhorst, a descendant of a Dutch family who immigrated to Carolina in the seventeenth century, lived in a house across the street that was demolished many years ago. He served successively as intendant (mayor), South Carolina governor, and a general in the War of 1812. The Vanderhorst Plantation comprised most of Kiawah Island, and his house there has recently been restored.

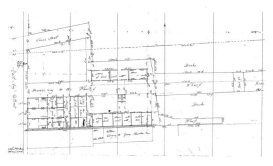

Plat showing Vanderhorst Row and its outbuildings and wharves, 1806

View of 79–97 East Bay Street, looking south, before 1930

RAINBOW ROW (79–107 EAST BAY STREET)

Excellent examples of early-eighteenth-century wharfside construction, the dwellings along East Bay Street provide insight into the colonial mercantile life of Charleston. Initially these buildings were all separately constructed (save 97–101 East Bay Street) and served as both residences and businesses for prosperous merchants: the ground floors were used by factors as counting rooms and stores, while families lived on the stories above. As the docks silted, the wharves were moved to more navigable locations, and the greatest part of the mercantile trade moved also. Consequently, this area stood relatively neglected for many years. In the 1930s Dorothy Porcher Legge, a decorator and preservationist, began the rehabilitation of the row with her own house at 99–101 East Bay Street and conceived the painting of the houses in different pastel colors reminiscent particularly of colors associated with Colonial Caribbean architecture. This block has retained the resultant appellation.

Rainbow Row from 83 to 101 East Bay Street, 1979

79–81 EAST BAY STREET, LINDSAY-BULWINKLE PROPERTY

Constructed 1845, 1778–85 respectively; renovated 1887, 1953, early 1980s

Lots no. 7 and no. 8 of the original Grand Modell served as the site for a succession of commercial and residential buildings. Earlier structures were destroyed in the fires of 1740 and 1778. The northernmost section at 81 East Bay Street was formerly occupied by a brick house and countinghouse built by Robert Lindsay that stood three and a half stories high. Much of this building collapsed in the earthquake of 1886. The first two floors of 79 East Bay Street were part of a corner two-story grocery store built by Henry Bulwinkle and later operated by John Henry Klenke. The Gaud School used the building from 1940 to 1953, but it was converted into residential units in 1953. The present building retains a late-nineteenth-century bracketed frieze and cornice at the parapet line over a range of seven two-over-two windows on the second floor. Crossed earthquake bolts run through the upper portion of the structure.

83 EAST BAY STREET, WILLIAM STONE HOUSE

Constructed circa 1784; restored circa 1941

Gutted in the fires of 1740 and 1778, this four-and-a-half-story house is named for William Stone, a Tory merchant who constructed the post-1740 building and retired to England during the Revolution. Apparently Stone's representatives rebuilt the damaged building almost immediately after the 1778 fire, for it was conveyed in 1784 for a price indicating its presence on the lot. The property passed through a succession of merchant owners who used the ground story as countinghouses and later as a grain and feed store, always maintaining a residence on the three stories above. Susan Pringle Frost restored the building in 1941 and added a Neoclassical wrought-iron balcony (brought from a State Street house) to the second story and a Colonial Revival style doorway to the front facade, replacing the nineteenth-century storefront. At the rear of the property an early brick warehouse was demolished except for its exterior walls. These ruins serve as part of a court-yard landscape designed by Loutrel Briggs.

85 EAST BAY STREET, SMITH, DESAUSSURE AND DARRELL BUILDING

Constructed circa 1785–87; restored 1930s, 1996–97

The house of an English merchant, James Osmond, was destroyed on this site in the fire of 1778. Passing to another English merchant, the site was conveyed to one of Charleston's leading mercantile firms, who built the present four-story dwelling with a low hipped roof prior to 1788. A series of merchants including British capitalists Thomas Hingham of England and Charles Hubert owned the property prior to the Civil War, after which it was sold to Luder Sahlmann, who used it as a storage warehouse for his feed-and-grain business next door. A small gauged railway ran through the present entry door, which was a covered passage through the building. In this condition, the house was acquired by Louise Graves, a founder of the Slave Mart Museum with her sister, and restored as a residence. The building retains its original fenestration including large shop style windows on the first story and belt courses between floors; the slightly longer windows on the second story indicate that this was the floor used for entertaining. The former shop entry was replaced by a window moved from the rear of the house at the time of restoration. The interior is largely intact and contains woodwork, particularly on the second story, with transitional Georgian/Neoclassical moldings. The house was restored by a restoration architect craftsman and his wife for use as their own residence in 1997.

87 EAST BAY STREET, JAMES GORDON HOUSE

Constructed circa 1792; rehabilitated circa 1930

A Scottish merchant and planter built this, the most massive of all the buildings in Rainbow Row, after acquiring the site in 1792. A previous tenement belonging to the English merchant George Seaman was destroyed in the fire of 1778. James Gordon mentioned the property in his 1816 will as "my house and store on East Bay," and it was sold by his executor, Charles Edmondston, in 1818 to Thomas Higham, who with his partner Charles Hubert owned *85 East Bay Street* next door. The stucco brick house has its original fenestration and low hipped roof with corner quoining. Purchased by Susan Pringle Frost in 1920, the second-floor balcony and other changes were made by her prior to her sale of the house in 1955. Unlike the rest of Rainbow Row, the house largely retains its aged stucco finish.

89 EAST BAY STREET, DEAS-TUNNO HOUSE

Constructed circa 1780–87

The Scottish merchant George Seaman owned this property. It passed from him to his friend David Deas and then to Deas's nephew John Deas Jr., married to Seaman's step-daughter. Seaman's tenement was destroyed in 1778, and Deas rebuilt the present house either during or just after the

Revolution. Adam Tunno, who rose to be one of Charleston's richest merchants, bought the property in 1787. Tunno, called the "King of the Scotch in Charleston," served as steward of the St. Andrew's Society until his death in 1834. One story retains its original fenestration and interior on its upper floors. A stone-lined cellar, possibly used for wine and spirits, survives under the structure. The lower story was remodeled with a garage and service addition to the south in 1936 with the assistance of the Charleston restoration firm of Simons and Lapham. Tunno's property stretched to Bedon's Alley, and his extensive outbuildings, including slave quarters and former warehouses, today comprise some of the most valued restored residences on the alley.

91 EAST BAY STREET, INGLIS ARCH HOUSE

Constructed circa 1778, circa 1782; restored 1938

This has been called the "Inglis Arch House" for many years because it is on the site of a pre-Revolutionary building leased by George Inglis and possessing an archway leading to an alley; the original dwelling burned in the fire of 1778. After the Revolution the mercantile firm of Leger and Greenwood rebuilt on the site. Leger and Greenwood are famous as importers of tea in the years immediately before the Revolution; it was their tea seized by Charleston citizens in the Charleston Tea Party of 1775. Briefly owned by Nathaniel Russell, the structure was sold to Frederick Kohne, who prospered at this site and willed the building to the Charleston Orphan House. Remodeled in the Greek Revival style, probably by Charles West, who operated a ship chandlery on the ground story, the building received extensive damage during the siege of the city in 1864. After several commercial uses the house was restored in 1938. The Greek Revival facade with its storefront and parapeted roofline was replaced with the current ground story and the upper pediment with a bull's-eye opening.

93 EAST BAY STREET, JAMES COOK HOUSE

Constructed circa 1782–87; altered 1836, restored and renovated 1941, early 1990s

This house was built to replace the house and shop with a Flemish gable that belonged to the Tory Fenwicke Bull, destroyed in the 1778 fire. James Cook purchased the property in 1778 and completed the present house within a decade. The ground story was rented for various mercantile uses while Cook's widow, who had subsequently remarried, lived upstairs until her death in 1826. Passing to Moses Hyams, a commission merchant, in 1836, the house was subsequently remodeled with a Greek Revival facade. Susan Pringle Frost purchased the building in 1920 and sold it to John McGowans, who, it seems, restored it in 1941 along with several other houses in this block. The three-story stucco dwelling rises to an original hipped roof with a single projecting dormer. Most of the interior detailing of the building has been lost, and a balcony was added to the central bay of the second story in a recent renovation. Loutrel Briggs designed the present garden in the 1940s.

95–101 EAST BAY STREET, OTHNIEL BEALE HOUSES

Constructed circa 1740; restored 1932, 1936

Although these houses were rebuilt after the fire of 1740, they seem to have survived the fire of 1778 unscathed. Col. Othniel Beale came to Charleston from Marblehead, Massachusetts, and became a wealthy wharf owner and eventually, after successfully re-

95 East Bay Street

building the city's harbor fortifications, a member of the Governor's Council. These dwellings, built on the site of a house inherited by Beale's wife Katherine "Hannah" Gale and on a lot Othniel Beale purchased across from his wharf, were originally envisioned for a single family dwelling attached to a tenement. The larger building at 99–101 East Bay Street was built by Beale for his family residence and contains an open central passage on the ground floor dividing two ground-story shop spaces and leading to the outbuildings at the rear. Beale died in 1772 and left to his wife the houses and buildings built on the land inherited from her parents and one half of the profits from the rental of the "house and Store adjoining to the South" at 97 East Bay Street. Both buildings share a common steep gable roof covered with early pantiles, an egg and dart molded cornice, and a continuous stuccoed brick facade.

99–101 East Bay

In the first rejuvenation of Rainbow Row, 99–101 was restored by Judge and Mrs. Lionel Legge in 1932 with early-eighteenth-century style nine-over-nine windows and cargo doors replacing the storefronts. The interior retains its early woodwork including cypress paneling in the front two-story rooms and mantels with central keystones. The second-floor wrought-iron balcony came from the now-demolished C. F. Prigge House at *7 Elizabeth Street*—hence the initials "CP" visible on the piece. The rear of the Beale House faces a courtyard once leading to warehouses but still bordered by an early kitchen dependency and numerous old walls. Loutrel Briggs assisted the Legges in the use of this courtyard and in designing a period garden.

The house at 97 East Bay Street, sold by Susan Pringle Frost to Mr. and Mrs. Thomas Dunham in 1936, retains its basic upper fenestration, but a nineteenth-century storefront was removed, the arch on the north of the front face was filled in with a Neoclassical Revival fanlighted doorway, and a balcony from another site was placed on the second-story front. The curvilinear gable-roofed house at 95 East Bay Street seems also to have survived the 1778 fire. It shares the egg and dart mold and pilaster treatment with its northern neighbors. Charles Cotesworth Pinckney owned 95 East Bay in the late-eighteenth century.

103 EAST BAY STREET, JOSEPH DULLES HOUSE
Constructed circa 1787; renovated 1930s

Joseph Dulles, the Scottish merchant ancestor of the cold war secretary of state John Foster Dulles and CIA founding director Allen Dulles, built this edifice as his countinghouse and family dwelling shortly after the Revolution. Although he moved to another residence on Church Street in 1800 and thence to Philadelphia, Joseph Dulles returned and died in Charleston. His family kept this building until 1836. The records of slaves on the Dulles family plantation, Good Hope, served as the evidence for much of the theory in the groundbreaking 1970s book, *The Black Family in Slavery and Freedom,* by Herbert Gutman. When the house was rehabilitated in the 1930s by the art historian Miss Anna Wells Rutledge, with the assistance of architects Simons and Lapham, the roof was raised to create the curious off-center gable, and door and garage door openings replaced the existing storefront.

105 EAST BAY STREET, DUTARQUE-GUIDA HOUSE
Constructed 1782–84; renovated circa 1890; rehabilitated circa 1970

The only house in Rainbow Row to retain its Victorian storefront, this dwelling was built by Lewis Dutarque, a planter of Huguenot descent, after he acquired the site in 1778. He sold it to John Robertson in

1784. The house again changed hands in 1797 and served successively as merchants' offices, a notary's office, and a paint store. In 1890 Giovanni Domenico Guida, an Italian immigrant, bought the house and added the pressed metal storefront, window heads, and entablature emblazoned with the name "Guida"; it was held by Guida's family as a grocery store until the 1960s. Anna Wells Rutledge, who also owned *103 East Bay Street*, purchased it in 1970, keeping the storefront in its evolved state.

107 EAST BAY STREET, JOHN BLAKE BUILDING

Constructed circa 1792, present facade circa 1887–90

In the pre-Revolutionary period this was the site of George Flagg's paint shop, which stocked pigment and oils for the painting of Charleston's houses. After the structure was destroyed in the fire of 1778, Flagg sold the empty lot in 1791 to John Blake. The present structure began as three stories with a hip roof. Sometime after the earthquake of 1886 a gable roof with a double window was added, the window openings were enlarged, and eight-over-eight sashes were installed. The structure retains evidence of a Victorian period cast-iron facade. A two-story brick kitchen building at *1 Elliott Street*, probably built by an early-nineteenth-century owner, serves as a separate residence.

109–115 EAST BAY STREET, PRINTER'S ROW (COGSWELL BUILDING)

Constructed circa 1909; rehabilitated as condominiums 1983

Henry Oliver, contractor

A series of buildings formerly occupying this site, including a double tenement of four stories, another four-story structure,

Detail of center section of 109–115 East Bay Street

and a corner two-story building, were damaged in the earthquake of 1886. By the late-nineteenth century these had been used as a hotel, a restaurant, a billiard parlor, and upper-floor residences. Walker, Evans, and Cogswell, engravers and stationers in the offices next door at *117 East Bay Street* and around the block at *3 Broad Street*, built this as their new printing plant by 1909.

114–120 EAST BAY STREET, COATES' ROW

Constructed circa 1788–1806; additions and alterations 1841

Thomas Coates apparently purchased or constructed this group of commercial buildings by 1806 to house, among other ventures, Harris' Tavern, later known as the French Coffee House, at 120 East Bay. This building served as the meeting place of Charleston's Jacobin Club in the 1790s, a group largely made up of French immigrants who wholeheartedly embraced the spirit of the French Revolution. Coates's wife Catherine also operated a noted tavern near the foot of Tradd Street, later called the Carolina Coffee House. Exemplary of early vernacular commercial structures in Charleston, the two-story, gable-roofed building at 120 East Bay contains extensive underground wine cellars. Its street doorway and northwest corner were removed to provide the standard Charleston corner store entry, with cast-iron column, in the late-nineteenth century. The three-story structure at 118 East Bay, constructed of stained red brick, features a projecting bracketed two-story bay and roof lantern, probably added in the early-1840s, nearly contemporary with the construction of the double tenement at 114–116 East Bay Street. After the death of Catherine Coates in 1829, the northern

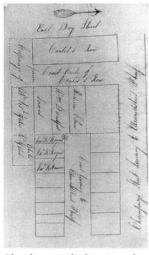

Plat showing the location of Coates' Row

section was sold in 1831 to John Michel, while the middle portion passed to Isaac Barrett. In these transactions the property was styled "Coates' Row." The unit at 114 East Bay was in use as a tobacconist's shop at the time of the war. Throughout their history these buildings have remained in use as commercial structures with some upstairs residences.

122 EAST BAY STREET, OLD EXCHANGE BUILDING

L *Constructed 1767–71; altered 1818, 1886; partially restored 1949, 1979–83*

William Rigby Naylor, architect-draftsman; Peter and John Adam Horlbeck, builders

In order to support Charleston's burgeoning transatlantic trade, the Commons House of Assembly voted a large sum of money for the building of an "Exchange and Custom House and a new Watch House" on the site of the original Half-Moon Battery at the foot of Broad Street. An Anglo-Irish draftsman, William Rigby Naylor, prepared drawings for one of the largest and grandest public buildings yet built in the colonies. Immigrant masons from Saxony, Peter and John Adam Horlbeck, contracted to undertake the construction, and the latter traveled to England to secure the specified materials. When completed, the building stood two stories above its massive basement with arcaded and rusticated openings on the first floor, pedimented pavilions with engaged Ionic columns on the west and Ionic pilasters on the east elevations of the second story, projecting stair towers with Venetian windows on the street elevation, and a surrounding portland stone parapet, ornamented by Neoclassical urns, partially disguising a hipped roof sheathed in Welsh Caernarvon slate. A columned, octagonal cupola with Venetian

William Rigby Naylor's elevation plan for the harbor side of the Exchange, 1767

Early-nineteenth-century engraving of the Broad Street elevation of the Old Exchange showing stair towers removed

Exchange Building, 1979, just before its most recent restoration

windows and a dome capped the center of the roof. The middle of the ground floor remained an open room, paved in Purbeck stone, for the exchange of commodities and specie, while a great hall on the second floor served as the center of the city's social life. The last royal governor, Lord William Campbell, was reluctantly greeted here while 257 chests of tea, detained in protest by the colonists, were stored in the building. The scene of an important meeting of the Patriots before the Revolution, the structure's basement became the Provost dungeon during the British occupation, providing a place for the detention of revolutionaries. After 1782 the building served as a city hall, site of the Ratification Convention of the Constitution (after the fire in the statehouse), and a point of welcome for President Washington when he landed at Prioleau's Wharf in 1791.

When the structure was conveyed to the federal government in 1818, the stair towers were demolished as a hindrance to East Bay Street, the Great Hall was divided for the installation of a staircase, and the original cupola was replaced by a large arcaded example, sited on a new base. Since it was damaged in the Civil War, the federal government considered its demolition during Reconstruction, a move protested by the preservationist Charlestonians. After earthquake damage in 1886, the original parapet and urns were lost, and the new cupola was removed and other Victorian alterations were made. Again threatened with destruction in 1912, the Exchange became the property of the Rebecca Motte Chapter of the Daughters of the American Revolution in 1921. An extensive bicentennial restoration project planned in 1976 resulted in much replacement of missing elements, including the cupola and windows. This renewal also included the cast stone replacement of the urns on a stuccoed parapet, the closing in of the central hall with large colonial style transomed doors, new fire stair towers on the east side, and a conjectural restoration of the upstairs great hall, a space which again serves the community for social events. The Old Exchange Building operates as a museum by the City of Charleston, and its basement provides an opportunity to view the city's original fortifications: the curving brick wall of the Half-Moon Battery.

132 EAST BAY STREET, GABRIEL MANIGAULT TENEMENT

Constructed circa 1797; renovated circa 1890–1900; rehabilitated 1983

Charleston's wealthy "gentleman architect" Gabriel Manigault probably designed and built this structure sometime after purchasing the property as an investment in 1797. Originally a hip roofed, brick double tenement of three stories, the structure's Flemish-bonded brick side walls and evidence of fenestration remain on the north and south elevations. A dramatic redesign of the front facade from the late-nineteenth century with roughcut sandstone masks Manigault's original scheme yet provides an example of a heavily rusticated Victorian facade of the period.

141 EAST BAY STREET, FARMERS' AND EXCHANGE BANK

L *Constructed 1853–54; rehabilitated 1970, 1990*

Francis D. Lee, architect; David Lopez and C. C. Trumbo, contractors

Designed in the Moorish Revival style by architect Francis D. Lee, who called it "Saracenic" in style, this building exemplifies eclecticism in the Victorian age. Muquarnas, commonly referred to as honeycomb vaulting, form the mass of the cornice, while horseshoe arches (compared to the Alcazar at Seville and the Mosque at Cordoba) and red sandstone work with striping balance the ornamented facade of this structure. Interior architectural elements in its original two-story counting room with its coffered ceiling also represent the eclecticism reflected on the exterior facade. The building's appealing features stood in contrast to the Roman Doric–columned bank next door, designed by Lee's former partner Edward Jones but demolished in the 1950s. The author William Gilmore Simms described Lee's building as a "toybox sitting under the eaves" of Jones's "Tower of Babel."

154–162 EAST BAY STREET, PRIOLEAU'S RANGE

Constructed before 1813; renovated circa 1836, 1867, 1977

Samuel Prioleau, owner of the nearby wharves, built this range before 1813. His son Dr. Philip Gendron Prioleau and Catherine Prioleau Ravenel remodeled the structures in about 1836, with pilasters and lintels of Quincy granite on the first floor, six-over-six windows with stone lintels and sills, and a surmounting parapet.

161 EAST BAY STREET, WAGENER-OHLANDT BUILDING

Constructed 1880; rehabilitated 1980, 1996

Richard P. Southard, builder

This structure was originally built by F. W. Wagener & Co., perhaps incorporating some earlier structures, such as a wholesale grocery store. The property also included a warehouse at Queen Street, supporting the firm's wide-ranging enterprises, including cotton, naval stores, fertilizers, as well as liquor and foodstuffs. Wagener's building epitomizes the transition between the Romanesque and the emerging commercial version of the Queen Anne style. Featuring elaborate glazed and pressed red brickwork walls and pilasters, with yellow brick forming a series of arches and belt courses, a pavilion dominates the central east facade, while the principal entry stands within a three-story turret at the northeast corner. The arcaded first story includes flanking cast-iron columns hinting at similar columns supporting the interior. By contrast, on the Queen Street side, the attached three-story warehouse of roughly pointed brownish brick was constructed in a Classical Revival style with pilasters on the first floor and a blind arch capped by an arched pediment on the second floor. This warehouse, which has been attributed to the hand of antebellum architect Francis Lee, once featured 80-by-260-foot open floor spaces on each level.

Early view of the many groceries on East Bay Street with the Wagener-Ohlandt Building on the right

Wagener was the consummate entrepreneur in late-Victorian Charleston. His family had emigrated from Hanover, and his brother served as mayor of Charleston, while he, as chairman, sank his fortune into the Interstate and West Indian Exposition of 1901–02. His country house property, Lowndes Grove, was subdivided as the Wagener Terrace Neighborhood. John F. Ohlandt, scion of another family of German-Charlestonian grocers, continued their business at this location from the mid-1930s. In 1980 the front building was rehabilitated as a restaurant. In 1987 developers adapted the warehouse as condominiums, placing a parking garage in the gabled one-story section at State Street.

167–169 EAST BAY STREET, ROPER-MELCHERS BUILDING

Constructed 1834–37; altered 1890s; rehabilitated 1985

Thomas Roper left this site to his son Robert William with the stipulation that if

Mid-nineteenth-century view of 167–169 East Bay Street with its original cornice

he died "without issue," then the property was to be devised to the Medical Society of South Carolina. Originally constructed by the younger Roper as a three-story double tenement, the building was reduced to two stories. Owned by the Medical Society for decades, the property was refaced with an Italianate style double shop front, pedimented window hoods, and a pressed metal entablature for Melchers & Company, wholesale grocers and dealers in Carolina rice.

After the building deteriorated with East Bay Street for most of the mid-twentieth century, the cornice was removed, but the remaining elements were restored when the building was rehabilitated as shops and offices in the mid-1980s.

178–180 EAST BAY STREET, STEPHEN LEFEVRE BUILDINGS

Constructed circa 1800; altered circa 1834–50; rehabilitated 1980s

This building stands on a lot formerly bordering a Cooper River wharf owned after the Revolution by Commodore Alexander Gillon, as was much of this side of the street. By 1794 a subsequent owner, Michael Lajonchere, leased the site to fellow French merchant Stephen Lefevre. By 1803 directories show Lefevre's place of business as Nichols Wharf (later Accommodation Wharf) lying nearly behind this building. In 1834 Lefevre or his son and heir, then living in Paris, sold the property to Nathaniel Fields. The new owner probably added the stucco window surrounds and possibly the wrought-iron window grilles. An early-twentieth-century owner removed a pantiled, hipped roof with three dormers, replacing it with the stepped parapet. From 1916 to 1951 this served as the wholesale grocery of E. F. A. Wieters and Sons, yet another of the German-owned businesses of this type along East Bay Street.

183–197 EAST BAY STREET, LODGE ALLEY PROJECT

Variously constructed 1797–1890; rehabilitated 1982–86

View of Lodge Alley from East Bay, circa 1905

This site is the East Bay Street end of what became the Lodge Alley Project. This project combined a collection of stores and warehouses bounded by Cumberland Street, State Street, East Bay Street, and Lodge Alley into restaurants, stores, and an inn (on the upper story of the northern row). In the nineteenth and early-twentieth centuries most of these buildings served wholesale grocers, commission merchants, and rice dealers. The youngest structure, 183–185 East Bay Street, is a three-story building built for the grocers W. C. Marjenhoff and O. T. Wieters. The Italianate style facade of 187–189 East Bay, with its cast-iron Corinthian pilasters on the first floor and Tuscan pilasters above supporting a massive entablature and shaped parapet, masks a building constructed in 1845 by Etienne Poincignon incorporating brick houses built circa 1800 by Samuel Cordes and Samuel Porcher. The Flemish bonded brickwork of these structures is visible along the adjacent Lodge Alley. The three-story building at 191 East Bay began as a single house constructed circa 1800 by the planter and merchant Theodore Gaillard. Its cast-iron storefront and window lintels date from its renovation after the earthquake by Bernard O'Neill and Sons, wholesale grocers and rice factors who owned several large plantations, supplying rice and cotton as well as truck farms by 1900, giving them "a trade all over the South Atlantic States." Isaac Barrett built 195 East Bay in the 1850s contemporary with the double building of James Walker at 197–199 East Bay Street; both retain their cast-iron storefronts. The three-story corner edifice at *201–203 East Bay Street* with its distinctive gable parapet was built in the 1850s by S. S. Farrar and Company grocers from the design of architect Francis D. Lee. Its successor firm, H. Bischoff and Company, boasted that their complex stretching the full block along Cumberland Street gave them 78,000 square feet of floored surface for their various specialty departments.

184 EAST BAY STREET, GAILLARD-BARKER BUILDING

Constructed circa 1810; rehabilitated mid-1980s

Built on a lot owned by the estate of Theodore Gaillard Sr., this three-and-a-half-story building exemplifies Federal style brick construction in Charleston with many later repairs and alterations. Flemish bond walls and a sawtooth brick cornice are examples of this masonry work. The building passed to the wholesale grocer O. F. Wieters in 1887.

4 ELLIOTT STREET, DAVID SAYLOR HOUSE

Constructed before 1779; restored 1986

This house survives as one of the only eighteenth-century Charleston single houses to which a later owner never added piazzas. The asymmetrical facade and narrow two-bay street elevation of the three-story brick building are reminiscent of Moxon's 1694 pattern book, *Mechanick Exercises,* showing the plan of a town house. The house retains its left doorway formerly leading to a shop, and the family entrance on the west opens to a stair hall rising to upper floors that still retain much of their original woodwork, including paneled chimney walls and cypress interior partitions. It is thought that this dwelling was rebuilt almost immediately after the fire of 1778 by the cooper David Saylor and his partner William McKimmy. Saylor owned a smaller structure on the lot to the east as well. With its off-center doorway and interior molding profiles, the Saylor House definitely precedes the full advent of the Neoclassical architecture of post-Revolutionary Charleston. Surviving in a dilapidated but almost original state, the house was purchased and restored in the mid-1980s.

16–18 ELLIOTT STREET, WILLIAM MILLS TENEMENTS

20 ELLIOTT STREET, GEORGE GIBBS TENEMENT

Constructed circa 1802; restored mid-twentieth century

These three tenements probably retain the shells of earlier eighteenth-century structures dating from the heyday of Elliott Street as Charleston's most important commercial thoroughfare and burned in the fires of 1740 and 1778. For most of their history these three-story, three-bay, stucco edifices housed commercial spaces on the ground floors and residences above. A tailor who immigrated to Charleston from Dundee, Scotland, and prospered in the city built the two attached structures at 16–18 Elliott Street by 1802, eventually bequeathing the easternmost tenement to his daughter, Mrs. George Lusher, who lived at 18 Legare Street, and the building at 18 Elliott to his famous architect son, Robert Mills. Neither sibling lived in these buildings, and they were sold in 1835 and 1807 respectively. The wealthy baker George Gibbs, who lived on State Street, built the tenement at 20 Elliott at about the same time as the adjacent structures. In the late-1930s the Chisolm family restored 16 Elliott, inspired by the example of Susan Pringle Frost, then rejuvenating Bedon's Alley. By 1949 they completed the work on 18–20 Elliott Street and also adaptively reused the ruins

18 and 20 Elliott Street

20 Elliott Street

of the old Evening Post printing plant across the street. By lowering the walls and putting on a colonial style brick cap, retaining the arched openings and the shutters on the windows, and completing extensive exterior and interior plantings, the Chisolms created a lot that became an innovative solution for neighborhood parking, and many current residents retain spaces here today.

22 ELLIOTT STREET, GIBBS-BLACKWOOD TENEMENT

Constructed circa 1793–1800; rehabilitated 1947, 1990

The baker George Gibbs, owner of the circa 1802 tenement to the east, rebuilt on this site a few years earlier, constructing a substantial stuccoed brick house of three stories. He bequeathed the building to his daughter Caroline Gibbs Blackwood, who lived here for some years before moving to Montagu Street, where she and her husband John Blackwood had extensive properties. The enclosure of the arched entry occurred in the first restoration of 1947; this open passage formerly led to a rear staircase to the residence above. The wrought-iron lunette in the arch is a particularly noted example of post-Revolutionary Charleston ironwork. The first floor, originally a commercial space, retains much of its old woodwork, including cypress sheathing. It was renovated as part of the residence and contains the dining room and kitchen with a new staircase accessing the original rooms above.

EXCHANGE STREET

Originally developed by 1788

It is possible that the walls of 17–19 Exchange Street survive from a building constructed on this site before 1788 on a thoroughfare that came to be known as Champney's Alley after that family's adjacent wharf. By 1829 Charles Edmondston acquired this and other properties in the immediate vicinity to support a growing import-export business, which eventually allowed him to erect the mansion at *21 East Battery*. A handsome brick building at the corner of Exchange Street and Prioleau Street known as the cotton exchange met its demise in 1956. The surviving two-story portion of 10 Exchange Street, an antebellum warehouse, retains a splendid cast-iron balcony probably dating from the 1850s.

Prioleau Street facade at 10 Exchange Street with mid-nineteenth-century cast-iron balcony

12 GILLON STREET

Constructed circa 1740

Gillon Street, one of Charleston's few cobblestone streets, contains several significant pre- and post-Revolutionary structures. 12 Gillon housed a tavern shortly after construction in 1740. It was occupied by the colorful merchant and politician Alexander Gillon in the 1780s. Gillon rose to great wealth within a decade of his arrival in Charleston in 1764. In the 1790s he championed anti-Federalist causes and also was largely responsible for the brief reintroduction of the African slave trade between 1803 and 1808. At the east end of the street an 1840s range of factors' offices, *9 Mid-Atlantic Wharf*, survives, although it was given a Colonial Revival style facade in a 1941 renovation.

LONGITUDE LANE

Developed before 1788

Developed by the mid-eighteenth century, Charleston's urban core included several narrow alleys. One of these alleys, Longitude Lane, bisected larger central blocks, thus creating new lots for future development. Fully improved by the end of the eighteenth century, some of these lots contained substantial structures, many owned by the

Early-twentieth-century view of Longitude Lane

Russell-Dehon families. At the southwest corner of East Bay Street and Longitude Lane stood the seventeenth-century house of the landgrave Thomas Smith, governor of Carolina from 1693 to 1694.

54 MEETING STREET, TIMOTHY FORD HOUSE

Constructed circa 1800–06; restored and renovated 1910, 1937, 1970s

By the early-nineteenth century a newly constructed single house of sizable scale invariably included a side piazza with a screen as an entrance, as can be seen in this original arrangement at the Timothy Ford House, although the piazza columns appear to be Greek Revival and the doorway itself is a Neoclassical style example of the twentieth century. Ford, who built the house, was an affluent attorney from Morristown, New Jersey, who came to Charleston after graduating from Princeton and went into practice with Chancellor Henry W. deSaussure. Ford lived in the now-vanished tenement adjacent to deSaussure's at *58 Meeting Street* until 1807 when he moved to this site purchased from Francis Mulligan. Raising their family here, the Fords entertained the Marquis de Lafayette in the house in 1824 during his triumphal revisit to the United States. Ford's daughter Louisa married Dr. Edmund Ravenel, a physician and pioneering American conchologist who built the small one-and-a-half-story building with weatherboarded siding at *52 Meeting Street* as his office. The Ford House is a simple three-and-a-half-story stuccoed brick dwelling with a hipped slate roof; it is ornamented only by simple belt coursing on the front facade and a dentiled masonry cornice. On the interior, however, it retains extravagant Neoclassical woodwork in its first- and second-floor rooms. A substantial line of kitchen and carriage house buildings have been incorporated into the present dwelling through a series of restorations beginning in 1915. These buildings and several other small structures line adjacent Ford's Court, where John Bartlam, a colonial potter of note, once lived and operated a kiln. With the assistance of the landscape architect Loutrel Briggs, the current owners established a noted new garden on the site including formal beds and an arbor.

58 MEETING STREET

Constructed before 1772, altered nineteenth century; renovated and restored 1982

Originally constructed as the western half of a double tenement with a single house plan by William Harvey, a merchant and planter (also owner of *61 Tradd Street*), 58 Meeting Street has surviving eighteenth-century fabric only on the upper two floors and original framing under the hipped roofline. This tenement and that across Tradd Street on the other corner were mirror images in their original form. From 1799 to 1809, after acquiring the property from the estate of Daniel deSaussure, Chancellor Henry William deSaussure lived in this house, while his law partner Timothy Ford lived in the vanished adjacent dwelling to the eastward. After the Civil War, the German grocer Gerard Logeman owned the property, selling by 1872 to John H. Doscher. Doscher's grocery, complete with storefront, occupied the ground floor, dramatically altering the building's appearance. Peter Christantou bought the building in 1917 and continued to run a store here until 1977. "Pete's," long a downtown tradition, was purchased by Historic Charleston Foundation and, after some civic controversy over a proposed rehabilitation for a Preservation Center on the site, was sold for single family use. A 1982 rehabilitation restored much of the upper-story fenestration and interior but created a new arched street-level entry and ground-story windows larger and lower than the raised originals.

64 MEETING STREET, ANDREW HASELL HOUSE

Constructed circa 1789; altered circa 1850; restored circa 1930

The classic Federal style Charleston single house at 64 Meeting Street stands with only small alterations from the dwelling built by Andrew Hasell, a planter in St. James, Santee, and St. Thomas parishes. Hasell acquired the site upon his marriage to Mary Milner, daughter of the Congregationalist merchant Job Milner. After his wife's death the property descended to their daughters and was sold in 1818 to Alexander England. Some alterations were made on the interior in 1850; the piazzas were probably added at that juncture, and a new hyphen addition connected the main house with the original kitchen house. Albert Simons, an architect prominent in Charleston's preservation history, restored the house by the 1930s for Thomas A. Huguenin and his wife Mary Vereen Huguenin, designing a Neoclassical style door screen on the piazza. Simons's firm also assisted the Huguenins in their restoration two decades later of the plantation house at Halidon Hill on the Cooper River. Ropemaker's Lane, formerly Rope Lane, probably named for an early ropewalk (a manufactory for cords used for sailing ships) runs to the north of this house.

68 MEETING STREET, JOHN CORDES PRIOLEAU HOUSE

Constructed circa 1810; altered circa 1900

The typical early-nineteenth-century single house at 68 Meeting Street is distinguished from others of its class by the dramatic turn-of-the-century alterations to the facade and piazzas. A projecting oriel window on the second floor and a single plate window on the first replace the traditional three-bay facade, and two semicircular bays and Victorian detailing embellish the simple two-story piazza. John Cordes Prioleau, a planter on the Back River, built the structure after he purchased the property from his father in 1808. William Bachman Chisolm, a prosperous fertilizer dealer, updated the building after his purchase of the house in 1894.

150 MEETING STREET, CIRCULAR CONGREGATIONAL CHURCH

🇱 *Constructed 1892 on the site of three previous structures*

Stevenson and Green, architects

Ruins of Robert Mills's Circular Congregational Church looking west, 1865

The Independent or Congregational Church has met at this location since its establishment in 1681. Founding members included most of the 45 percent of the early Charleston population who worshipped according to the dictates of John Calvin. Huguenots, Scottish and Irish Presbyterians, and Congregationalists from England and the New England colonies made up the first congregation; but at various points the first three founded their own meetinghouses or churches. Of the four buildings that have occupied the site, only the last two were of circular design. Before completing designs for the Octagon Church for the Unitarians in Philadelphia and the Monumental Church in Richmond, the Charleston architect Robert Mills, self-proclaimed as the first native-born professional American architect, designed a building in 1806 for the Congregational Church, this becoming the first circular American ecclesiastical structure.

Mills described the church as set off by "a rotunda of near 90 feet diameter surmounted by a dome, crowned by a horn

123

light. From that part of the rotunda which faces west, a square projection runs out, supporting a tower. Before this rises a portico of six columns, surmounted by a pediment which forms the facade of the building." In the original design a steeple was contemplated, but it was not completed for several decades.

Mills's church burned in the fire of 1861, and the ruins stood until shaken by the 1886 earthquake. The New York architectural firm of Stevenson and Green designed the fourth and surviving building in 1892. This building contains bricks from the original structure and reflects the Victorian Romanesque style popularized by Henry Hobson Richardson. Despite its much smaller scale, the structure exhibits design similarities to Richardson's Trinity Church in Boston.

The churchyard surrounding the building has been in use since 1681 and retains a large concentration of various gravestones, box tombs, and monuments. More than fifty slate stones imported from New England constitute the largest concentration of the work of Boston and Rhode Island carvers in the Southeast.

8 QUEEN STREET, JOSEPH OLMAN HOUSE

Constructed circa 1800; rehabilitated 1973, 1981

Situated on one of the streets of the Grand Modell of 1680, 8 Queen Street stands as an example of combined domestic and commercial spaces. Built after the fire of 1796, this three-story stuccoed brick building was constructed by Joseph Olman, a chandler, and completed before his death in 1813. More than likely, the principal rooms of the upper floors served as Olman's living spaces and the ground floor functioned as commercial space. The structure was used in this fashion in the twentieth century when it housed the workshop and residence of Edwin H. Smith, a well-known Charleston cabinetmaker operating in the city until his death in 1979.

18 QUEEN STREET, DANIEL CRUICKSHANK HOUSE

Constructed after 1796; restored and renovated 1958

Queen Street, looking west to Johnson's Row, circa 1905

An early settler in Charleston, Jonathan Amory, took up a grant on this and several adjacent lots in 1694. The original building on the site probably burned in the fire of 1796. Daniel Cruickshank, a tanner, built this and probably the adjacent side of a double tenement with hipped roofs between 1796 and 1800. The three-story single house retains segmental arched windows on the second and third stories surmounted by a simple stucco cornice and a pantile, hipped roof with a single dormer. The first floor of this typical single house was entered directly through a central door from the street and used as a tanner's shop. 18 Queen remained in the family of Daniel Cruickshank until around 1860, and 1958 restoration work on the home revealed traces of salt residue and a large hook on the ground level (items used in preserving and hanging hides).

20 QUEEN STREET, FOOTLIGHT PLAYERS' WORKSHOP

Constructed circa 1830; rehabilitated mid-1930s

This two-story building, built as a cotton warehouse in about 1830 by Arthur Kiddle, retains a high degree of its original exterior character with its arched ground-floor openings, gabled parapet with a central lunette, and weathered coat of lime and sand stucco. Running 140 feet to the rear along Philadelphia Alley, once called Cow Alley, the building served as a warehouse until 1932. The Footlight Players, founded as a community theater effort, acquired the building through the generosity of Eliza Dunkin Kammerer, a preservationist and philanthropic figure in Charleston's artistic renaissance. The theater seats nearly 300, and a wood carving from the Academy of Music hangs over the stage. The Footlight Players presented the last production at the Academy on King Street before its destruction. The group moved to the Dock Street Theatre in 1954 and retained this building for training and for productions by other groups.

22–28 QUEEN STREET, JOHNSON'S ROW

Constructed circa 1802; renovated and restored 1940–50

The row houses at 22–28 Queen Street are reminders of Charleston's post-Revolutionary successes. The city's economy and its middle class burgeoned after the war, creating opportunities for builders seeking to accommodate the large numbers of merchants and professionals wishing to reside near the commercial activities of the port. Attached row houses that could be massed on relatively small plots of land responded to this demand. This sequence of row houses on Queen Street is distinguished by its fine interior woodwork, perhaps the product of its notable builders and developers, William Johnson Sr. and William Johnson Jr. The elder Johnson came to Charleston from New York in 1741 and as a prosperous blacksmith became a member of the Sons of Liberty. After the Revolution he became a planter and served in the South Carolina House of Representatives. The younger Johnson graduated from Princeton and after various judgeships and a stint as Speaker in the South Carolina House was named by

Thomas Jefferson as a U.S. Supreme Court Justice, serving until his death in 1834. The three-story stuccoed brick dwellings retain their original second-story fenestration with three-bays each and a continuous belt course between the second and third stories. A continuous gable roof provides each tenement with two front dormers and two rear dormers and shelters two large chimneys. The arched openings on the ground story date to the first renovations of this row in the 1940s and 1950. The westernmost tenement at 28 Queen Street retains its corner quoining and a wrought-iron balcony.

23–25 QUEEN STREET, BENJAMIN CASEY TENEMENTS

Constructed circa 1806; no. 23 rebuilt after 1865; restored and renovated circa 1935

Like *83–85 Church Street*, 23 and 25 Queen Street form a double two-and-a-half-story stuccoed brick tenement structure. Built on Grand Modell lot no. 86, the first house may have been constructed by Francis Gracia, an olive oil merchant of Portuguese and possibly Sephardic Jewish extraction. The tenements passed through the Amory, Mayrant, and Moncrieff families. The latter was in control of the site when the fire of 1796 passed through the area. Creditors foreclosed on Moncrieff's mortgage, and Benjamin Casey, a coach maker, bought the property with money left to Mrs. Casey by her uncle, merchant John Eberly. The ground level of these double tenements functioned as a shop or office space, the upstairs rooms served domestic needs, and the double kitchen buildings behind provided for cooking, laundry, and servants' sleeping quarters. Heavily damaged during the Federal bombardment of the city during the Civil War, the front wall of no. 23 was rebuilt after 1865, and both structures were restored in the twentieth century by resident owners.

44–46 QUEEN STREET, ABRAHAM SASPORTAS TENEMENTS

Constructed circa 1800; altered mid-nineteenth century

A native of the Bordeaux region of France, Jewish merchant Abraham Sasportas immigrated to Charleston by 1778. After amassing numerous properties, including slaves and town lots, Sasportas returned to France in 1818, leaving his wife behind and providing her with a residence on Queen Street. The westernmost tenement boasts a double-tiered Tuscan columned piazza and red sandstone window heads probably dating from the mid-nineteenth century.

54 QUEEN STREET, THOMAS ELFE HOUSE

Constructed circa 1760–70; moved to back of lot and restored mid-twentieth century

Thomas Elfe, Charleston's most noted colonial cabinetmaker, built this two-and-a-half-story weatherboarded single house on this parcel some years before the Revolution. In its mid-twentieth-century restoration the house was shifted on the property for the construction of an adjacent retail space.

7 STATE STREET, UNION INSURANCE COMPANY BUILDING

Constructed circa 1811–19

This temple-form building of Classical Revival style survives as one of Charleston's earliest office buildings. The state of South Carolina chartered the Union Insurance Company to write marine and fire insurance locally and elsewhere and to make loans. The company's headquarters moved to this location during the second decade of the nineteenth century. Possessing its

The seal of Union Insurance in the pediment at 7 State Street

own fire engine and band of firefighters, the company was obligated to fight fires on the premises as certified by the cast-iron seals on the building. A large-scale version of the seal remains, centered in the tympanum of the front pediment. Fine Tuscan-order pilasters and belt coursing also ornament the front facade of 7 State Street.

11 STATE STREET
Constructed circa 1790–1800

This three-story single house was owned in the late-eighteenth century by the South Carolina Society. In the nineteenth century it, like an adjoining house, was owned by the New England–born slave trader Ziba B. Oakes, who possessed a nearby slave mart at 6 Chalmers Street. Slave traders also used the Greek Revival style three-story masonry building at *15–17 State Street*, constructed by William Caldwell or his predecessor before 1848.

12 STATE STREET,
ELEANOR COOK TENEMENT
Constructed circa 1820

The widow of Jonathan Cook, a shoemaker and vintner, built this three-story stucco building before her death in 1821. For much of its early history the ground story served as a coffeehouse, and the building's interior plan reflects this usage. Daniel Hart, a Sephardic merchant, owned the masonry single house to the south at *10 State Street*, which was apparently gutted and rebuilt after a fire swept through the block in 1810.

10–12 State Street

18 STATE STREET,
NATHAN HART HOUSE
Constructed before 1815; altered circa 1905

Owned for investment purposes by the same family from 1815 to 1905, this two-

story masonry building reflects the changing uses and status of the neighborhood. It was used at various times as a bake house, a junk shop, and the home of a river pilot. A subsequent owner probably altered the front window fenestration and added the turned-columned side piazza. The house received a major renovation in the 1980s, as did the unassuming dwelling to the north, *20 State Street*, which has a ground-story brick section dating from circa 1870 and a second-story frame portion built circa 1901. Between these two dwellings Unity Alley stretches toward East Bay Street.

19 STATE STREET, FREDERICK WOLFE HOUSE

Constructed circa 1796; restored circa 1968

Frederick Wolfe built this simple two-and-a-half-story, weatherboarded house after the fire of 1796. After Wolfe's death his widow and her second husband conveyed the building to Thomas N. Gadsden, the wealthy investor who lived at *116 Broad Street*. Gadsden held it as one of his many investment properties.

In 1968, instead of a threatened demolition, First Federal Savings and Loan gave the house to the Preservation Society of Charleston on the condition that it be moved a few feet to the south to provide access for a parking lot. Generally, most details of the house remained intact in the subsequent restoration, although the Victorian piazza columns were replaced with the current square stock. Most of the simple interior woodwork has survived as well.

22–24 STATE STREET, JOHNSON-POINSETT TENEMENTS

Constructed circa 1841

Some controversy remains over the date and builder of these double tenements. A leading Charleston statesman and importer of the plant that bears his name, Joel Poinsett amalgamated several lots formerly belonging to Dr. Joseph Johnson in order to construct a double tenement on the property. This building has a central archway surmounted by curious stucco scoring and three-story facade with gable roof and dormers.

23 STATE STREET, GEORGE LOCKE BUILDING

Constructed circa 1853; restored 1978

George Locke's two-story store building exemplifies the ongoing quality of Charleston's brick masonry through the late-antebellum period. The Flemish bond front elevation with seven bays, ornamented by brick jack arches, features an entablature with dogtoothed ornamentation. Locke operated a grocery on East Bay Street and built this structure as an investment. Two separate shops occupied the ground story while a family lived upstairs. In the late-1970s new owners restored 23 State Street as a double tenement, retaining many of its interior Greek Revival features and creating a garden at the rear beyond its double-tiered piazzas.

25 STATE STREET, ROBERT DORRILL HOUSE

Constructed circa 1815; rehabilitated 1957

Robert Dorrill built a three-story, stucco single house on this lot acquired in 1815 from French tinsmith P. A. Poincignon. Although it was constructed with a front central entry that most recently led to a grocery store, a new owner closed this doorway in a 1957 renovation of the house. The original second-floor drawing room retains its simple Neoclassical woodwork.

Early-twentieth-century view of 25 State Street

27 STATE STREET, WURDEMAN-FERAND HOUSE

Constructed circa 1814 with addition of outbuilding at 25 State circa 1816

John Wurdeman owned this corner site long enough to construct a mixed use commercial space and residence of three and a half stories, selling it to Thomas Ferand by 1816. Ferand added an outbuilding, and either he or a later owner fronted it with an elliptically arched piazza, louvered on the second story. This latter feature led the architectural historian Samuel G. Stoney to relate the appearance of the building to the houses of St. Thomas and St. Croix in the Virgin Islands.

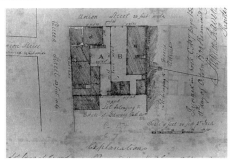

Plat showing 27 State Street, 1800

32–34 STATE STREET, HENRY SEEDORF TENEMENTS

Constructed 1858–60

A soda water manufacturer and grocer, whose principal store operated from his building at *49 Elizabeth Street*, constructed this double tenement after acquiring the site of two "burnt" wooden buildings in 1858. The asymmetrical first floors hint at the ground-story commercial uses. The stuccoed brick facade boasts decorative scoring, a belt course between floors, and a banded parapet with vertical openings. The present doors, added by the early-twentieth century, fill a first-floor opening at the center that extended from the sidewalk to the rear yard.

33 STATE STREET, VIGILANT FIRE COMPANY

Constructed 1849; rehabilitated 1959

Built by order of the City Council for one of the leading private fire companies operating in antebellum Charleston, this two-story stucco building with gabled parapet evolved through a series of uses until the 1950s, when it served as a maritime union hall and a grocery store. The second floor was adapted from a single room with fourteen-foot ceilings to an apartment before its initial rehabilitation as a residence in 1959.

35 STATE STREET, ARNOLDUS VENNING HOUSE

Constructed circa 1821; rehabilitated 1974

The widow of the colonial portraitist Jeremiah Theus owned a house on this site that may have been rebuilt after the fire of 1796. The present house dates to 1821, when it was acquired by the wealthy Christ Church Parish planter and factor Arnoldus Venning. The ground floor formerly housing a shop received the most alteration in its rehabilitation. The parapet with inset panels and dogtoothed cornicing continues to the dwelling next door at *37 State Street*, an exposed brick house with similar fenestration. The latter building appears to be of identical construction to its southern neighbor except for the larger size of its windows and its central door architrave with Greek Revival style fluted columns, central swag motif, and a four-paneled Italianate style door. This property was listed in the 1850s as being "new brick— 3 stories" and passed to Michael McMorty, a "lamplighter" by trade who lit the new gas streetlights each evening. McMorty lived next door at *39 State Street*.

38–40 STATE STREET, JAMES ROSS HOUSE

Constructed circa 1815; rehabilitated 1980s, 1993

In 1814 the heir of the wealthy merchant Christopher Fitzsimmons sold a large property to the rising merchant James Ross, a Philadelphia native. The lot extended to East Bay Street until the 1980s. Ross's three-story stuccoed single house includes three bays on the street facade, a flared hipped roof, and a double-tiered piazza. A curious iron rail with sharp points surmounts the entry gates to the south of the residence. Ross acquired the adjoining two-story shop at 40 State Street in 1839. This building was demolished by 1950. A large wing straddling the two lots attaches to the back of 38 State Street. The noted Charleston artists William Halsey and Corrie McCallum lived here for many years before a new owner transformed the property into condominiums in the 1980s.

39 STATE STREET, JOHN GEORGE MAYER HOUSE

Constructed circa 1795; renovated 1983

Built by the grocer John George Mayer around 1795, this dwelling may be the only building on the street to have escaped the fire of 1796. Mayer married the daughter of neighbors Jeremiah Theus and his wife Roseannah. After Mayer's death, his widow married the Reverend Israel Munds, minister of Trinity Methodist Church. The Mundses opened an academy in their dwelling and operated it for several years. By the late-nineteenth century the structure became a rental property. This three-story stuccoed building with a hipped roof sits back from the street and faces a garden extensively improved in a 1983 renovation.

41 STATE STREET, VIGILANT FIRE INSURANCE COMPANY
Constructed circa 1882; rehabilitated 1980–81

No. 41 State Street was built by Moses Goldsmith to house the offices of the Vigilant Fire Insurance Company. The building retains its original storefront windows and their surmounting cornice on the brick ground floor. Although the triple-tiered piazzas on the south side were removed many years ago, a cantilevered two-story enclosure, built to provide needed bathrooms, remains. New owners completed an extensive rehabilitation of the house in 1981, including a contemporary rear kitchen wing.

Vigilant Fire Insurance Company, 41 State Street, and its lost neighbors, circa 1905

42 STATE STREET, WILLIAM PRITCHARD DOVE HOUSE
Constructed 1816–18; restored 1957

William Pritchard Dove, grandson of an important eighteenth-century shipbuilder and wharf owner and himself a ship fitter by trade, built this stuccoed brick house after acquiring a lot at the corner of State Street and Lodge Alley and another on Lodge Alley from the merchant Joseph Flint. Dove's daughters sold the property in 1836 to the wealthy merchant James Ross, who held it as rental property. By the twentieth century the dwelling had declined with the rest of the block to warehouse usage. In the 1950s Robert N. S. Whitelaw, director of the Gibbes Museum of Art and chief founder of Historic Charleston Foundation, purchased the house with his wife, the preservationist and art historian Patti Foos Whitelaw. In their subsequent restoration they helped encourage the rejuvenation of the State Street area.

Federal details ornament the exterior of the Dove House, including stucco quoins,

keystones above the windows, belt courses, and surmounting hipped roof. The interior retains its important second-floor woodwork, including a notable wainscoting with guilloche (intersecting circles) molding probably derived from the late-eighteenth-century pattern books of William and James Pain. First-floor woodwork and a marble-paved entry were salvaged by the Whitelaws from demolished uptown buildings and reused here. The innovative garden effectively uses the brick wall of the old "Lodge" in the alley as a backdrop.

44–52 STATE STREET, LODGE ALLEY COMPLEX

Constructed variously between 1799 and 1888; rehabilitated 1982–86

Lodge Alley, a surviving lane named for a Masonic building still standing on the south side of the alley, became the catalyst in the 1970s for the rescue of a whole complex of structures that had evolved in warehouse uses in the twentieth century. The circa 1799 stuccoed brick dwelling at 44 State Street, built by Simon Elstob, had become a coffee roasting factory by the late-nineteenth century. The Vigilant Fire Insurance Company, whose later headquarters still stands at *41 State Street*, originally used 46 State Street. Although the former warehouse doorways had been retained on the early-nineteenth-century brick building at 48 State Street, the 1982 rehabilitation of the complex strongly altered the fenestration of 50–52 State Street, which had formerly served as a part of the wholesale grocery complex at *201–203 East Bay Street*.

7 STOLL'S ALLEY, JUSTINUS STOLL HOUSE

Constructed circa 1745

This early Charleston alley, originally named for the local blacksmith Justinus Stoll, contains several early brick dwellings. 7 Stoll's Alley, built and inhabited by Stoll,

initially had a two-room plan, which was later changed with the addition of a passage to accommodate nineteenth-century tenants.

1 TRADD STREET, THOMAS BARKSDALE HOUSE
Constructed circa 1800; restored 1927

This simple single house built of brick and covered with stucco represents the typical dual residential and commercial occupation of this area in post-Revolutionary Charleston. The building was restored in 1927 with the addition of an old balcony to its second-floor front facade. Reflecting the reclamation of this street at the beginning of Charleston's preservation fervor, the structure was restored by Mrs. T. W. Punnett, a cousin of President Franklin D. Roosevelt.

5–7 TRADD STREET, ALLEN-HEXT TENEMENTS
Construction partially dating from 1727 with rebuilding in 1743 and 1782–85; renovated 1937 and 1952

The New England merchant Andrew Allen built adjoining tenement structures on these sites prior to his marriage in 1727. His widow owned them at the time of the great fire of 1740 and conveyed them to her stepson, who in turn sold the properties to Daniel Hext. Hext probably rebuilt both buildings utilizing some surviving walls, and while keeping the west tenement, he conveyed the eastern section. After the fire of 1778, the merchant owner Robert Brown probably rebuilt 5 Tradd Street and another owner rebuilt 7 Tradd Street before 1785, when it was in use as a grocery store. 7 Tradd retains irregularly placed ground-story windows with side entries on opposite ends; the arched opening, apparently extensively used by eighteenth-century commercial traffic, draws particular attention. The iron balcony on the eastern tenement is older than the semicircular balcony at 7 Tradd, executed by Philip Simons for William Gilbert, a sculptor who renovated the house in the 1940s.

6 TRADD STREET, JOHN FABRE JR. HOUSE

Constructed circa 1788; restored before 1920

The merchant John Fabre Jr., son of Charleston's Lutheran minister, bought this tall stuccoed brick house in 1789 shortly after its construction by the mercantile partners Josiah Smith, Daniel deSaussure, and Edward Darrell. It was subsequently the property of various prominent Charlestonians, including Alexander Jones, owner of *102 Tradd Street*, and Philip Messervey. At the time of the War Between the States it served as the store of merchant William Gatewood, builder of *21 Legare Street*. During Reconstruction the edifice became a school and church for African American children. It served a variety of uses before its rescue by Susan Pringle Frost.

8–10 TRADD STREET, LAMBOLL'S TENEMENTS

Constructed by 1726; rehabilitated mid-1980s

With its unusual surviving gambrel roofline, double tenement form, chimneys, and other features, the building at 8–10 Tradd Street has generally been ascribed to construction in 1726 due to surviving grants of common-use alleys on the eastern and western edges of the building. Thomas Lamboll, a merchant and horticulturist, constructed the brick structure, and, surviving the fire of 1778 more or less intact, it remained in the hands of his descendants until 1846. The gambrel or "dutch" roof form, common in mid-eighteenth-century Charleston, largely disappeared, particularly through early-twentieth-century demolitions. Its presence on this building may point to circa 1750 replacement of an earlier roof form; the surviving roofline has been somewhat altered with twentieth-century tin covering and later shed dormers.

12 TRADD STREET, LIGHTWOOD-SOMMERS HOUSE
Constructed 1748–50; rebuilt 1789–96

A wealthy merchant partner of Gabriel Manigault and co-owner of the ship *Neptune* built a substantial brick house on this lot after acquiring it from the Baker family of Archdale Hall Plantation in 1748. Lightwood devised the property to his illegitimate sons, Edward and John Lightwood, at his death in 1769. The younger Edward Lightwood owned McLeod Plantation on James Island. The prosperous contractor Humphrey Sommers purchased 12 Tradd Street in 1784 and directed his executors at his death in 1788 to build "substantial brick buildings" on the property. The building's form and its presence on this site on a 1788 map may indicate a renewal by Sommers's executors of a structure surviving the fire of 1778. Sommers bequeathed to his daughters the adjoining structures: the stuccoed double tenements at *16–18 Tradd Street* and the unpainted scored stucco facade of *2 Bedon's Alley*.

13 TRADD STREET, WILLIAM HOPTON TENEMENT
Constructed circa 1778–82; altered circa 1860

A rich Charleston merchant with extensive English connections built this three-story brick house as an investment, probably after the fire of 1778 to replace a

previous dwelling owned by the Hopton family. William Hopton's daughter Sarah carried the property to her marriage with Nathaniel Russell. Combined with Russell family properties on Longitude Lane, the site did not pass out of the family until Sarah Russell Dehon's death in 1859, and various plats exhibit altered property lines. Although retaining its basic window fenestration and Flemish-bond brick over ground story English bond (visible on the west facade), the Hopton tenement was altered in the nineteenth century with a flat roof and in the twentieth with a double first-floor window, Colonial Revival style pedimented entry architrave, and Greek Revival style cornice. Nineteenth-century changes similarly characterize the two-story, Charles Warham House at *17 Tradd Street*, also missing its pre-Revolutionary roofline and boasting a finely articulated parapet, along with a twentieth-century doorway and second-floor semicircular balcony. Between the two dwellings and down a gated walkway, a brick building, formerly a kitchen, provides an interesting vista; Henry Saltus's two-story kitchen with pantile roof may have survived the fire of 1778. An early-twentieth-century owner renovated it, with substantial additions, as a residence.

19 TRADD STREET, JOHN MCCALL HOUSE

Constructed circa 1745; possibly rebuilt after 1778; renovated late 1800s, 1948

Mary Fisher Crosse, a Quaker minister whose travels took her to Turkey and New England before her settlement in Charleston, owned a house on this site by 1698. Five years after the fire of 1740, Crosse's great-grandson John McCall built a new house on the site; he continued to live on the property until his death in 1785. A new house may have been built within the shell

In the foreground, 19 Tradd Street

of the earlier dwelling after the fire of 1778. Today the facade of the building remains as in the eighteenth century, with five asymmetrically placed bays on the upper floor front, and capped by a gable roof with two dormers. Substantially renovated several times, the last in the 1980s, little interior fabric remains from the building's heyday.

23 TRADD STREET, WILLIAM BELL HOUSE

Constructed circa 1800; restored 1931

23 Tradd Street is on the right; 17 Tradd Street is in the foreground.

An earlier house on the site was presumably a casualty of the fire of 1778. William Bell, a merchant, purchased an additional three feet of land to the west, adjacent to his burned-out lot, just before the construction of the present building. Bell's house follows the general pattern along this portion of Tradd Street with large, asymmetrically placed shop windows on the ground story and four regular windows on both the second and third floors, evenly spaced and hung with nine-over-nine windows. A small entablature with a brick cornice provides a transition to the clay-tile hip roof. The Bell House apparently needed particular attention after the earthquake, as all four walls were noted as "cracked" and inspectors recommended that the north and south walls be taken down. The owner, then using it as a tenement, opted for repair and the installation of earthquake bolts, nine of which are visible on the street facade. In 1931 the Ernest Drapers of Washington, D.C., purchased the house and, with the New York architect John Churchill, altered the interior floor plan. The rear garden became a much photographed showpiece and is overlooked by a wrought-iron balcony taken from another building.

Although immediately abutting to the north, the adjacent three-story single house at *25 Tradd Street* has long been considered a survivor of the fire and original to 1748, when it was built by Maj. William Boone. The property, along with adjacent sites on Longitude Lane, became part of the holdings in this area of Nathaniel and Sarah Hopton Russell and was owned by their descendants until the Civil War.

26 TRADD STREET, ROBERT EWING HOUSE

Constructed after 1778; renovated 1990s

These two adjacent three-story buildings typify the dense construction of this part of Tradd Street after the fire of 1778, and with their unevenly placed ground-floor shop windows, they exhibit the mixed uses of these structures. Robert Ewing, a Scots merchant, erected 26 Tradd Street after his 1785 marriage to Jane Bonneau on land inherited by her. Kept as his primary residence, the three-story stucco dwelling boasts a semicircular wrought-iron balcony on the second floor. Dr. Peter Joseph Moore built *28 Tradd Street* as a rental investment in about 1790. Although most of the upper-story brickwork remains, the interior was completely removed earlier in the twentieth century and now follows a modern floor plan.

27 TRADD STREET, JOSEPH JOHNSON HOUSE

Constructed circa 1779–82; renovated early-twentieth century

Although fieldwork on this building has never been completed, research indicates that a shopkeeper, Joseph Johnson, built this two-and-a-half-story wood house after his purchase of the lot in 1779. Although it retains its original beaded weatherboarding and gable roof with two pedimented dormers on the east, the Venetian (Palladian) window in the gable end and the first-floor window heads apparently reflect a much later renovation.

35 TRADD STREET, BREWTON'S CORNER DEPENDENCIES

Constructed by 1747; restored 1920s

35 Tradd Street is often used to illustrate early-eighteenth-century construction in the densely populated walled city. Most of the structures built in this area during this time contained passages to the rear work yards; most were only two stories with one or two rooms per story. During this time porches were restricted to outside rear stairs or small balconies on the exteriors of grander buildings. Street frontage in the walled city was at such a premium that most construction spanned from property line to property line, unlike later Charleston landscapes, which provide for a side yard. 35 Tradd Street was originally two buildings built by Col. Miles Brewton as part of Brewton's Corner (now 77 *Church Street*); these have been combined into a single family residence.

38–40 TRADD STREET, BULLOCK BUILDINGS

Constructed circa 1718; restored early-twentieth century

Restoration work done on these properties in 1979 revealed that both structures, built by John Bullock or his widow between 1718 and 1722, escaped damage from the plague of fires that swept through early Charleston. No. 38, currently the museum of the life and work of Elizabeth O'Neill Verner, served as the artist's home and studio from 1938 until her death in 1979. This easternmost building retains much of its original character, including small imported red brick laid in a Flemish bond pattern and a steeply pitched gable roof. Evidence of alterations in fenestration are apparent in the front facade, but on the interior a large fireplace substantiates the dwelling's early character. In the twentieth century

Miss Verner's studio was joined to the three-story stuccoed brick building at 79 *Church Street*. Although this lot was also owned by the Bullocks, their daughter Millicent and her husband Col. Robert Brewton sold the property in 1722 to John Fraser.

41–43 TRADD STREET, JONATHAN BADGER TENEMENTS
Constructed circa 1746–72

Long thought to have been built by the cabinetmaker Jonathan Badger after his acquisition of the lot in 1746, this substantial brick double tenement may constitute one of the best-preserved exposed-brick buildings in the city from the first three quarters of the eighteenth century. Flemish bond brickwork with brick jack arches and a pantile roof accentuate this building's early character, but interior detailing indicates 1770s rebuilding or alterations. Following the early Charleston single house plan, a door (Greek Revival) stands within the center street opening at 41 Tradd Street. The entire property was sold to the tailor Alexander Cormack in 1770. Recently a brick incised with the date "1772" has been discovered on the exterior.

46 TRADD STREET, JAMES VANDERHORST HOUSE
Constructed circa 1770; renovated 1927

Built by William Vanderhorst for his son James around 1770, this three story stuccoed brick single house was purchased in 1927 by Alfred Hutty, the Woodstock, New York, artist, as the site for his Charleston home and studio. In order to accommodate Hutty's needs, the adjacent brick store to the west was demolished and a new entry and garden were created behind a substantial wall and corbeled brick gateposts. This has created the curious juxtaposition of a Neoclassical, fanlighted entry door beneath an original arched stair window. When Hutty first came to Charleston in the winter of 1919 he telegraphed his wife, "Come quickly, have found Heaven." His numerous engravings and woodcuts have increasingly come to symbolize the best work of the Charleston Renaissance of the 1920s, particularly his portrayals of rural African Americans and Charleston's now-vanished street vendors. The original kitchen dependency, uniquely remaining as a separate building served as Hutty's studio and was described in the *News and Courier* in 1935 as having a fireplace that was "one of the city's quaintest."

49 TRADD STREET, COL. GEORGE CHICKEN HOUSE
Constructed circa 1731; altered 1793

Situated on lot no. 41 of the Grand Modell, this Georgian town house is one of the earliest extant structures in the Old and Historic district and most likely replaced a wooden structure on the site when it was erected. The property was originally owned by Col. George Chicken, a noted public figure instrumental in colonial Indian policy. The present Adamesque woodwork was added after the Inglesby family purchased the house in 1793. The four-bay facade is ornamented by corner quoining, and the second-story balcony was added in the early-nineteenth century.

51–53 TRADD STREET, HEXT TENEMENTS
Constructed circa 1736; restored 1966, 1980s

This three-story stuccoed double tenement building stands on lot no. 60 of the Grand Modell, which was granted to Richard Tradd (father of the first male European child born in Charleston) in 1694.

Quoining, belt coursing, and a simple cornice ornament this hipped-roof paired dwelling. Alexander Hext built the present structure shortly after he acquired this lot in 1736 and at his death left the property to his sisters: the eastern tenement to Mary Harvey, and the western tenement to Elizabeth Seabrook. Harvey's son, Alexander, was a well-known Tory, and Seabrook's husband, George Saxby, was the receiver-general of His Majesty's Quit-rents in 1763 and stamp distributor in 1765. Both tenements were, therefore, confiscated in 1782 and granted to those of more patriotic sentiment. Another member of the family, the merchant William Harvey, built the notable stucco style house at 61 Tradd Street by 1770, nearly contemporaneously with his double tenements at 58 Meeting Street and 63 Tradd Street. This important Georgian house lost the woodwork of one of its rooms to the St. Louis Museum of Art in 1929.

54 TRADD STREET, WILLIAM VANDERHORST HOUSE

Constructed 1740; restored 1930s, 1996

This three-story masonry structure covered with stucco is a fine example of early single house construction and is important in understanding the development of the single house. The house retains its original floor plan, the prototype for single house construction. The William Vanderhorst House is notable in that it retains its public entrance on the street facade.

The dwelling at 54 Tradd Street is attributed to William "Vander Horst." The lot was inherited by Vanderhorst's wife, whose grandfather owned nearly two-thirds of this block of Tradd Street. Constructed circa 1740, the house is believed to be one of the earliest examples of single house construction in Charleston.

A study of the plat in 1796, at which time William Robertson owned the property, reveals that the house was covered with a tile roof. A modest assemblage of outbuildings filled the rear yard back to Rope's Alley (now Ropemaker's Lane), but, oddly, the property was only accessible through a passage to Tradd Street instead of having a second access through the alley. The early introduction of piazzas to the city is evidenced on the house of John McIver next door at *56 Tradd*. William Vanderhorst's house had a series of distinguished and notable tenants. Thomas W. Bacot, Charleston's fifth postmaster, rented the house, and tradition holds that the post office was located in the front room.

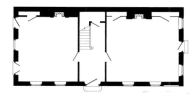

Measured plan of the first floor, 54 Tradd Street

56 TRADD STREET, GEORGE DUCAT HOUSE

Constructed circa 1740; renovated 1975

George Ducat, a shipbuilder, erected this two-and-a-half-story house of brick and Bermuda stone shortly after purchasing the property in 1739. Like many Charleston dwellings, the house was enlarged in the mid-nineteenth century by attaching the kitchen dependency to the main house; the double-tiered piazza was added in this period as well.

58 TRADD STREET, CLELAND-WELLS HOUSE

Constructed circa 1760; renovated 1935–36

Dr. William Cleland, who lived in the single house next door at *60 Tradd Street*, which was constructed as early as 1727, built this house in about 1760 for his son William. After William's death, the latter house passed in 1778 to Robert Wells. Wells with his son John operated a newspaper, supposedly in the cellar but probably on the first floor, known as the *South Carolina and American General Gazette*. As Tories, the Wellses were officially banished, and their house was sold at auction by the sheriff under the 1782 Act of Confiscation.

This is a three-story stuccoed single house with a clay-tile, hip roof with one dormer on the street elevation section. Sold in 1782 to a gunsmith, the building was conveyed in 1788 to Isaac Peace of *8 Courthouse Square*. The two Cleland dwellings passed through a succession of owners who made interior Victorian alterations. They are rare examples of eighteenth-century architecture that escaped the disastrous fires of that period. On the east side of *60 Tradd Street* one can see the original brick cornice at the roofline and corner quoins, as well as the original stucco on the eastern wall.

Plat of 1808 showing the long room and other buildings of McCrady's Tavern

2 UNITY ALLEY, LONG ROOM, MCCRADY'S TAVERN

N *Constructed 1779; rehabilitated and partially restored 1982*

Edward McCrady, a wealthy landowner and Revolutionary patriot, completed a tavern fronting on East Bay Street by 1779. The site included a separate kitchen across the rear courtyard topped by a space used as a long room, or ballroom. He constructed this two-story brick building as an assembly room for public entertainment; it subsequently became a venue for the Charleston Theatre. George Washington was entertained at a banquet in the long room during his visit in 1791. The brick arches and kitchen fireplaces still visible on the first floor constitute the most interesting original survivors of the tavern. By the late-nineteenth century the structure became a warehouse. In the 1970s it was restored and rehabilitated as a restaurant.

VENDUE RANGE

Developed after 1790

One of the centers of trade and commercial activity in the antebellum period,

Vendue Range has experienced great changes in the postwar and modern eras. Although 15–17 Vendue Range, built by the Scottish merchant Thomas Napier about 1830, stands as a monument to antebellum architecture, mid-nineteenth-century photographs depict numerous other landmarks, including an extensive Greek arcade, which have been lost. 18 Vendue Range is an early-nineteenth-century survivor of this row. Damage during the Civil War, extensive reconstruction in the late-nineteenth century at 23–25 Vendue Range, and the earthquake of 1886 have all taken their toll on this stage of antebellum architecture. The former brick warehouse at 22–24 Vendue Range, owned in the late-nineteenth century by the grocer Carsten Wulbern, has retained its original arched fenestration. An earlier structure to the southeast was demolished in 1989 following hurricane damage to make way for a planned waterfront hotel, which has not been built.

Vendue Range, looking west, after the 1886 earthquake

1–3 WATER STREET, JAMES CHAPMAN TENEMENTS

Constructed 1857

In 1847 the master in equity offered twenty-two lots, some with buildings, for auction on land formerly bounded by Vanderhorst Creek, now Water Street. James Chapman and three partners bought seventeen lots including this parcel. Chapman, a commission merchant in stocks and real estate and then resident owner of the dwelling across the street at 6 Water Street, added another small parcel and created two building lots here by 1857. The identical houses constructed by Chapman follow the Italianate or the urban version of the Italian Villa style, with central pavilions flanked by an entry bay on the east side and a screen for a masked piazza on the west. Stucco quoins on the

3 Water Street

first-floor corners become pilasters with bracketed capitals on the second story. The front gable with its dentiled cornice frames a Venetian window, and the roof behind boasts three dormers. Although rented to others by 1861, in the division of Chapman's estate his son Robert inherited 1 Water Street while James received 3 Water Street. Chapman descendants owned and occupied the former until 1927.

2 WATER STREET, NATHANIEL INGRAHAM HOUSE

Constructed before 1818; altered before 1885

Nathaniel Ingraham, a merchant who served on John Paul Jones's *Bon Homme Richard,* built this three-story brick and stucco dwelling between 1810 and 1818. Beginning as a hipped roof dwelling, the structure has always oriented to the harbor, even though its entry has continually faced Water Street. In the 1820s William Burgoyne owned the house and purchased the newly built Francis Saltus House next door at 6 *Water Street* as well. Otis Mills, developer of the Mills House, bought the combined properties in 1832. After it was shell damaged by the bombardment in 1864, its postwar owner, Anna Wells, and her husband, the Confederate hero and writer Dr. Edward Wells, made various changes, including a Second Empire mansard roof and cast-metal cornice and window heads. Wells's daughter Sabina Elliott Wells lived here prior to her career as a Newcomb potter.

5 WATER STREET, JOSEPH RIGHTON HOUSE

Constructed circa 1800–1880

A wealthy cooper, Joseph Righton, constructed several houses in the neighborhood, building this dwelling for his son. Originally built to face White Point and the river beyond, the house has a main entry that is accessed through an open arch in a brick wall and a staircase to the south elevation. In the nineteenth century a stucco pediment with dentiled masonry molding and a lunette window were added to the Water Street elevation.

10 WATER STREET, SWAIN-HUSSEY HOUSE

Constructed circa 1800

The entrance into 10 Water Street was originally on the garden side of the house, opposite its current location, as the lot that the mariner Luke Swain acquired stretched to Stoll's Alley on the north and to Church Street on the west. The house faced the alley currently behind the house and had piazzas overlooking Vanderhorst Creek, which soon thereafter became Water Street. Swain lived on the alley and sold the property, with or without a dwelling, to another mariner, George Hussey, in 1800. By the time of an 1826 plat, the building had assumed its present form, including its front piazza, hipped roof, and other features. Of particular note, two doors with twin Neoclassical architraves provide separate entries to the front rooms, a characteristic of some Cooper River plantation houses but unknown in the city. The vendue master, a public-market or auction official, lived next door at *8 Water Street*. This wood house was altered in the nineteenth century, notably with bowed front piazzas in the Eastlake style.

11 WATER STREET, MCCULLY RIGHTON HOUSE

Constructed circa 1778–80; altered circa 1858–1880

In 1778 McCully Righton, a brother of Joseph Righton and a wealthy cooper in his own right, purchased a portion of Grand Modell lot no. 298 on the south side of the canal that was filled to become Water Street. This traditional Charleston single house consists of a two-and-a-half-story main block on a high masonry foundation sheltered on the west by a double-tiered piazza screened by an Italianate style entry door that was probably added before the 1880s. Righton's family kept the property until 1858. David Briggs acquired it before the Civil War, but bankruptcy in 1868 required its forced sale. Henry Siegling of the Charleston family of music sellers purchased the house in 1874.

14 WATER STREET, YOUNG-KEENAN HOUSE

Constructed 1769

The placement of this single house on a corner lot has resulted in an address on Water Street. Thomas Young, the builder of *35 Church Street*, constructed this house in 1769. The date was confirmed with the discovery of a small piece of mahogany in the framing inscribed "T. Young, 1769." Young's widow, then living at *47 Church Street*, conveyed the house to Thomas Keenan in 1800 with a covenant not to open windows on the north side.

WATERFRONT PARK

Completed 1990

Sasaki Associates and Cooper-Robertson Partners, architects

Once a concentration of thriving wharves including Brown's Wharf and Accommodation Wharf, this area was in disuse by 1955 when fire destroyed the Clyde line steamship terminal here. In 1976 the philanthropists Charles and Elizabeth Woodward made a donation to the city for the restoration of Adger's Wharf and a small park to the south. This donation inspired Mayor Joseph P. Riley Jr. to formulate a concept for an expanded waterfront

park. By 1980 this overgrown area marred by charred pilings and gravel parking lots became the subject of a study supported by grants for the development of a waterfront park. Within a year twelve acres of highland and marsh were acquired. Planning and fund-raising for the park commenced along with work on the Adger's Wharf park. Construction of Waterfront Park itself began in 1988. Miraculously the nearly completed park endured relatively minor damages in Hurricane Hugo and opened just prior to the Spoleto Festival in 1990. The park's main entrance boasts a large paved plaza with a central fountain. The landscape includes a 400–foot wharf with a pergola and other structures, a lawn area with a large bronze pineapple fountain, and formal gardens with seating areas. The park contains 185 trees, mostly large-growth live oaks; 750 azaleas; 2,000 boxwoods; and more than 5,000 flowers.

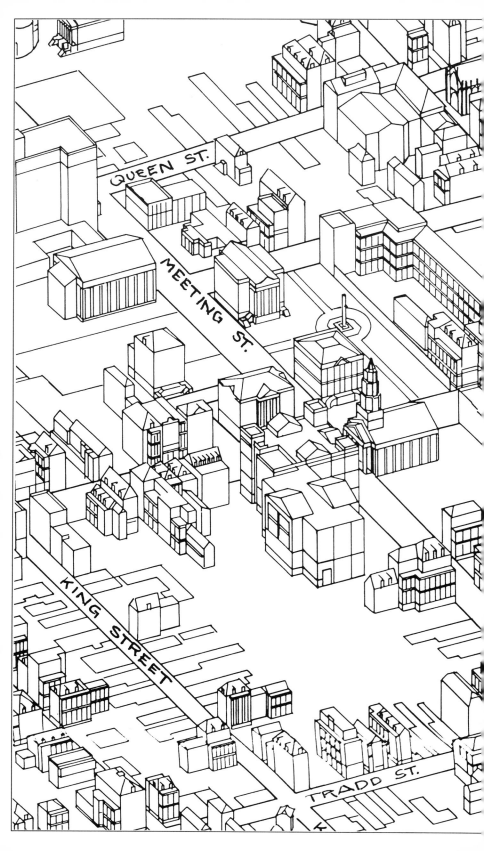

2

THE CIVIC SQUARE

The Heart of the Eighteenth-Century City

*T*he chief feature of the 1680s Grand Modell, according to Maurice Mathews, an original settler, was "a Square of two ackers of land upon which the four great streets of 60 foot wide doe center." This large Civic Square was intended to become the center of Charleston and the location of its most important public buildings. Implementation of the plan was slow, and Meeting Street, the north-south street that would form the square at its intersection with Broad Street, remained at the city's edge well into the eighteenth century. By 1739 the moat and gates of the walled city were gone and a brick market had been constructed on the site of the square's northeast corner. It had been decided by this point that the square would be an intersection of streets marked by four corner buildings. On the same day in 1751 the Commons House of Assembly authorized the establishment of the parish of St. Michael with the attendant construction of a new church, and the building of a statehouse on the opposite corner. Royal governor James Glen laid the cornerstone for the statehouse, which was sufficiently complete for use, if not finished, by 1756. The church was finished for services by 1761.

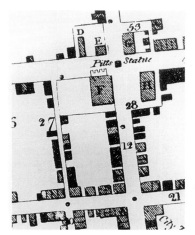

Detail of Ichonography of Charleston, South Carolina, *1788, showing the Civic Square*

View of Broad Street, *circa 1796, showing the intersection of Broad and Meeting Streets, watercolor sketch by Charles Fraser*

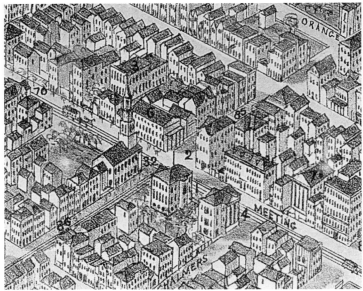

Detail of C. Drie's Birdseye View of the City of Charleston, South Carolina, 1872, *showing the Civic Square area after the Civil War*

On the fourth corner a public treasury and guardhouse were erected in 1768 from plans by William Rigby Naylor, son-in-law of St. Michael's contractor, Samuel Cardy. The area was described by a traveler as follows:

> Meeting Street lies nearly north and south, is open at the south end to another part of Coopers River and in running on from thence to the northward divides Broad street near the middle of it. At one of the four corners where the streets are divided stands the new English church, and at another is the State House where the members of the assembly meet to transact all the business of the province and the judges sit to hear and try causes etc. It is a large handsome substantial building and looks well. Opposite to it stands a plain good building much less than the other call'd the Town Watch House, over which are good apartments that are occupied as the Public Treasury Offices. These two buildings and the church are of brick inside and plaistered over so well on the outside to imitate stone that I really took them all for stone buildings at first. The fourth corner does not answer the other three, for it is only a low dirty looking brick market house for beef.

A marble statue of William Pitt, Earl of Chatham, executed on order of the colony by the London sculptor Joseph Wilton, arrived in 1767 and was placed on a base in the intersection. John and Peter Horlbeck constructed the pedestal and, along with a sculptor named William Adron sent from London, set the statue.

All of the structures save St. Michael's received heavy damage in the British siege of the city in 1779, but after the Revolution these edifices continued in their former uses. Nonetheless, after the vote in 1785 to move the capital of the new state to Columbia and the gutting of the building in a fire in 1788, the statehouse was refashioned with an additional story and altered fenestration as the Charleston District Courthouse. Due to traffic and the passions of the Revolution, Pitt's statue was removed to the grounds of the Orphan House above Boundary Street (now Calhoun Street). The Courthouse and the Treasury continued to house official departments of the eastern district of the state for several decades.

In 1796 a large fire burned much of the area between Broad and Meeting Streets, including the brick market described by Charles Fraser as "a neat building, supported by brick arches." The city conveyed the site in 1800 for replacement by a splendid Bank of the United States branch, possibly designed by Gabriel Manigault and constructed in the Neoclassical style. The city government took over the building as the city hall when the bank failed in 1819, moving its offices and council chamber here from the Exchange. In 1821 a public competition was held for the design of fireproof buildings to be built in a public square behind city hall. These were to include a district records building, possibly a new home for the Charleston Library Society, and an academy of arts. Despite stiff competition,

Detail from Officers of Volunteer Fire Department, *1844, by Christian Mayr, showing the brick City Hall, the Fireproof Building, and the steeple of the Circular Church*

Aerial view of the Civic Square area, 1969

Despite years of disuse, this 1887 city fire watchtower has recently been restored

including that from English architect William Jay, Charleston native Robert Mills won the competition. The following year construction began on the Charleston District Records Office, the only building of the original plan to be completed. City authorities cleared the old Beresford Alley, a venue of brothels and tipling houses, widening and reopening the thoroughfare adjacent to the records building as Chalmers Street. Thereafter the discovery of the plotted Denmark Vesey revolt and a slow economic decline ended plans for the completion of the square, and a small, temple form Academy of Fine Arts building was built instead on Broad Street.

The area around the Civic Square provided sites for the halls of a number of fraternal and benevolent organizations. In 1802 the South Carolina Society (1737), the former "Two Bit Club," commissioned Gabriel Manigault to design a new Meeting Street building to serve as its charity school and headquarters. Members of the St. Andrew's Society (1729) retained a "gentleman architect" named Hugh Smith to design a Neoclassical hall for their use. The St. Andrew's Society Hall became the city's most important setting for social functions, such as the Jockey Club and St. Cecilia Ball and the Secession convention, until its complete destruction in the fire of 1861. An office building next to the Courthouse was converted in 1833 by the Hebrew Orphan Society as their school and headquarters, and a site a block north became the location of the Hibernian Society building with a porticoed hall designed by Thomas U. Walter of Philadelphia.

The range of Charleston's eighteenth-century domestic architecture is represented by the Lining House at Broad and King Streets, believed to have been constructed before 1720; the Harvey House of 1728 and the Ramsay House, built before 1750, with their asymmetrical, chambered stair-

Flower sellers, antecedents of the vendors and basket makers who sell in this area today, standing across from the Hebrew Orphanage in the 1920s

case plans; the Blake double tenements on Courthouse Square; the single-house-plan shop and dwelling of Peter Bocquet at 95 Broad; and the single house of Daniel Ravenel to the east of the square on Broad Street. The Mills House hotel at 115 Meeting and the post–Civil War fire watchtower across the street mark the area's nineteenth-century architectural diversity, as does the Colonial Revival Standard Oil station designed by Albert Simons at Chalmers and Meeting Streets.

Late-nineteenth-century view
of 49 Broad Street

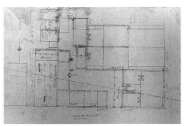

Plat showing the Benjamin
Smith House and its
outbuildings, 49 Broad Street,
in the late-eighteenth century

The Bank of South Carolina,
50 Broad Street, with the
pediment restored to its 1798
appearance

49 BROAD STREET, BENJAMIN SMITH HOUSE

Constructed circa 1740; altered nineteenth century; partially restored 1960s

This dwelling, built by the wealthy trader and assembly speaker Benjamin Smith, is an interesting contrast to the houses of other merchants such as Thomas Rose at *59 Church Street*, circa 1733, and George Eveleigh at *39 Church Street*, circa 1743, who built buildings in the first half of the eighteenth century. The first-floor fenestration and interior partitions were dramatically altered in the nineteenth century to accommodate a grocery store, but an eighteenth-century plat provides good evidence of the original first-floor room arrangement. Smith limited the commercial space in his house to a single large room on the first floor without smaller adjoining counting rooms. Smith's store, likely one of the largest private commercial spaces in pre-Revolutionary Charleston, was typical of the eighteenth-century houses that combined dwelling and store. It provided family access to second-floor living quarters through a rear entry off the piazza, which allowed entry to the stair passage without passing through the store.

50 BROAD STREET, BANK OF SOUTH CAROLINA

🅽 *Constructed 1798; earthquake damage and changes 1886; partially restored 1967–68*

The Bank of South Carolina constructed this T-shaped building in 1797–98. A pedimented central pavilion projects from the front facade on the street, with the principal entry delineated by a white marble arch. Window lintels, voussoirs, and a belt course are also of white marble. The Bank of South Carolina sold the building to the Charleston Library Society, the nation's third-oldest institution of its kind, in 1836. The Library Society housed its collections here until its move to King Street in 1914, selling the building to the Chamber of Commerce. The structure was partially restored by a bank in the 1960s and today serves as offices.

51–53 BROAD STREET, CLARK MILLS STUDIO

L *Constructed circa 1740; present facade added 1899*

This building, originally constructed by the merchant Benjamin Smith, has been heavily altered. Originally it was a simple three-story masonry double tenement with a high hipped roof. The present facade, added in 1899, obscures the original roof with its oversized gable accented by stylized Renaissance Revival details including pressed metal garlands and a dentiled cornice. Once the studio of sculptor Clark Mills (1815–53), who executed the famous statue of Andrew Jackson in Lafayette Park in Washington, D.C., in the twentieth century, it housed the law office of Mayor Thomas P. Stoney, who is remembered for establishing America's first historic district and zoning ordinance and for serving as an ardent ally of President Franklin D. Roosevelt's New Deal.

Stylized gable end of 51–53 Broad Street

54 BROAD STREET, GEIGER HOUSE

Constructed 1771–75; renovated circa 1800, late-nineteenth century

Thought by tradition to have been erected for the Geiger family shortly after completion of the Exchange in 1771, this structure features an early commercial floor plan on each level. At various times the room fronting Broad Street has been used as a drugstore and for retail sales. Its surviving circa 1800 woodwork is of great importance. It stands as one of the few Fed-

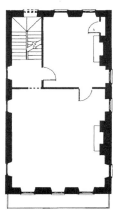

Measured plan of the first floor, 54 Broad Street

eral period shop interiors left in the Southeast. The German immigrant Geiger family held the building for nearly eighty years, selling it in 1854 to James McConkey.

55–57 BROAD STREET, MARSHALL BUILDINGS

Constructed 1907

T. K. and Alex Marshall, brokers, built these complementary two-story masonry buildings in 1907. The second floor of the eastern structure is fenestrated with a large bay window, while the matching floor of the western structure has a pair of bay windows.

56–58 BROAD STREET, NATIONAL FREEDMAN'S SAVINGS BANK

Constructed circa 1800 and circa 1798, respectively; altered 1890

Built by the attorney John Geddes, this double building originally served both residential and commercial functions. From 1869 to 1874, 58 Broad Street housed the National Freedman's Savings Bank, a national bank for African Americans. The Charleston branch, one of thirty in the nation, had 5,500 depositors and approximately $350,000 in deposits in 1873. In 1890, 56 and 58 Broad Street obtained the more unified facade that is visible today, although its pressed metal cornice was removed in the mid-twentieth century.

60–64 BROAD, CONFEDERATE HOME

Constructed circa 1800; additions circa 1835, circa 1900–10; earthquake repairs 1887

This large complex stretches through the block from Broad Street to Chalmers Street and is a nineteenth-century amalgamation of several different properties and buildings. On the site of a house formerly leased to a royal lieutenant governor the core of the front portion was built by Gilbert Chalmers, a well-to-do house carpenter, as a double tenement. Inherited by Chalmers's daughter and her husband, Gov. John Geddes of Ashley Hall Plantation, the building housed President James Monroe when he spent several weeks in Charleston in 1819. Forced by debt to sell, Geddes conveyed this building in 1825. By 1834 the Geddes House had passed to Angus Stewart, who converted it to the Carolina Hotel. Subsequent additions to the rear were later connected to an early-nineteenth-century tenement at *23–25 Chalmers Street*, the western side of which had served as the U.S. District Court from 1845 to 1860. It was here at the time of South Carolina's secession from the Union that District Judge Andrew G. Magrath took off his robes and suspended the Federal Court in South Carolina. An early-nineteenth-century doctor's office, adapted to modern office use and almost entirely reconstructed after Hurricane Hugo, stands on the southeastern edge of the site at *66 Broad Street*.

In 1867 the entire property was leased to Mrs. Amarinthea Yates Snowden and a group of nine women, who organized the Home for Mothers, Widows and Daughters of Confederate Soldiers of Charleston. By 1880 the home housed several hundred aged or infirm widows and a teacher's college for fifty-two women. After heavy damage in the earthquake of 1886, repairs were completed and the Broad Street facade was remodeled in the Second Empire style with a mansard slate roof and pressed metal dormers and cornices. Of particular interest from the street are the original wrought-iron balconies on the second floor and the mid-nineteenth-century storefronts below.

Detail of the door, 61 Broad Street

61–63 BROAD STREET, ROBERT DOWNIE BUILDINGS

Constructed circa 1815 and circa 1834, respectively; 61 Broad Street altered circa 1890s

Robert Downie, a prosperous tinsmith and metalworker, built 61 Broad Street as a shop/residence in about 1815. Much of its four-story facade has been altered. The building to the west was built by Downie as an investment after he purchased the site in 1834. It has a late-Victorian pressed metal facade in the Renaissance Revival style.

65 BROAD STREET, THOMAS FLEMING HOUSE

Constructed circa 1725–40; altered circa 1900

A late-nineteenth-century parapet masks the early-eighteenth-century roofline of a two-story house built by the planter Thomas Fleming after his acquisition of the lot in 1725. Fleming was a Quaker who belonged to the Charleston Meetinghouse and owned more than one thousand acres in St. Bartholomew's Parish in the south end of the county. The present metal facade details date from an early-twentieth-century renovation.

67–69 BROAD STREET, MANSION HOUSE HOTEL ANNEX

Constructed 1758–65; restored and rehabilitated 1973–74

Constructed by merchant John Hume, the son of a wealthy Goose Creek planter, this three-story brick building with a side passage originally housed a shop on the first floor and a residence above. A now-demolished outbuilding served as a winter studio for the American painter and later inventor Samuel F. B. Morse in 1820. In the nineteenth century the main building

Attorneys' signs on Broad Street, 1979

was the annex of the popular Jones or Mansion House Hotel, located next door to the west and since demolished. The ground story with rusticated detailing dates from a 1970s rehabilitation that returned the original side entrance.

68 BROAD STREET, DANIEL RAVENEL HOUSE

Constructed circa 1800; repaired after 1886 earthquake and after 1989 Hurricane Hugo

This typical Charleston single house, continuously occupied by descendants of the Ravenel/Mazyck families, is the oldest continuing legacy property in the city. Isaac Mazyck, a leading Charleston landowner and Huguenot immigrant, devised the lot to his daughter Charlotte in 1749. A wooden house shown on a mid-eighteenth-century plat burned in the fire of 1796, and Daniel Ravenel and his wife, of Wantoot Plantation, built the present single house.

The line of black-tiled outbuildings including kitchen, washhouse, stable, and slave quarters is visible from Washington Park (part of the original lot was condemned for the public square before 1820). The distinctive brick wall with arched, inset stucco panels follows a style traditional to Charleston.

Confederate Home (center) and the Daniel Ravenel House (left), 68 Broad, in the late-nineteenth century

71 BROAD STREET, SCHACHTE BUILDING (SITE OF THE MANSION HOUSE HOTEL)

Mansion House constructed 1772, dismantled 1928; Schachte building constructed 1930

Originally constructed in 1774 by William Burrows as his dwelling in town, a three-story wooden mansion on this site was only a fraction of the holdings of more than 10,000 acres owned by Burrows. Upon his death the property passed through the hands of several relatives before Jehu Jones, a free African American, purchased this site in 1815 and operated a hotel here until 1833. The name Jones Hotel stayed with the property until 1882 when Mrs. Jane Davis rented the property and renamed it the Mansion House. After the Civil War the structure became a boardinghouse, and by 1928 it was dismantled; a portion of its interior was bought by the New York collector Francis Garvan. The present office building of modified Beaux Arts design was constructed in 1930.

80 BROAD STREET, CHARLESTON CITY HALL

Constructed 1800–04; altered 1839, 1882; repaired 1866, 1898, 1938

Gabriel Manigault, attributed architect (1800–04); Charles Reichardt, architect (1839); Edward Magrath and Joseph Nicholson, carpenters; Andrew Gordon, mason; Colin McK. Grant, renovation contractor, 1882

Engraving, circa 1875, showing Charleston City Hall with its original exposed brick facade

Formerly the location of the 1739 beef market destroyed in the fire of 1796, this

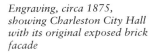

important site at the intersection of Broad and Meeting Streets was conveyed by the city to the president and directors of the Charleston branch of the first Bank of the United States in 1800. Gabriel Manigault (1758–1809) is often credited with its design, but the building itself was constructed under the guidance of the carpenters Edward Magrath and Joseph Nicholson and the mason Andrew Gordon. The building served as a state bank from 1811 to 1818, when it was designated as the city hall. The structure was denounced by the architect Robert Mills as "showy" and was dominated by a two-story hall across the front. The city engaged Prussian-born architect Charles Reichardt to perform the first renovations.

Aerial view of Charleston City Hall looking northward from St. Michael's steeple

The building was extensively altered again in 1882 when a new metal roof was added, the brick exterior was stuccoed, and the interior was completely gutted and reordered with a large second-story council chamber across the central front. After the earthquake of 1886 the Victorian council chamber was further ornamented with varnished wood sheathing and a decorative ceiling. The council chamber remains the heart of the city's government. This is the second-oldest city hall in continuous use in America and houses a notable collection of paintings, open free to the public, that includes portraits of presidents George Washington by John Trumbull, James Monroe by Samuel F. B. Morse, and Andrew Jackson by P. A. Healey. Virtually every dignitary to visit the city since the Marquis de Lafayette in 1824 has been welcomed in city hall.

The building today retains its extensive Adamesque marble detailing with arched window architraves and lintels, quoining, and engaged columns successively of the Doric, Ionic, and Corinthian orders. The city's seal, adopted in 1783, appears in a late-nineteenth-century low relief sculpture in the pediment and contains the following, in Latin, "The Body Politic, She Guards Her Buildings, Customs and Laws."

83 BROAD STREET,
FEDERAL COURTHOUSE AND POST OFFICE

Constructed 1896–97; restored with addition 1987

John Henry Devereux, architect

This southwest corner of the original Civic Square, today the "four corners," has successively contained a mid-eighteenth-century guardhouse and treasury building, a mid-nineteenth-century colonnaded city guardhouse, a building for the Charleston Club, and, since the earthquake of 1886, the present building. The current federal courthouse and post office was designed by the Irish-born architect John Henry Devereux, a former plasterer who became a noted architect in the city in the late-1860s.

Built in the Renaissance Revival style, the federal courthouse is constructed of Winnsboro, South Carolina, granite. Its rich interior exemplifies the opulence inherent in the construction of public buildings in this period. The post office on the ground floor is embellished with carved woodwork, marble staircase, and wrought-iron and brass railings. The federal district court still sits in the paneled Victorian courtroom on the second floor. In the early-1980s the General Services Administration commissioned an architectural firm to design a southern addition. Completed in 1987, the addition was dedicated as the Hollings Judicial Annex in honor of the U.S. senator from Charleston. The park contains an early-twentieth-century cast-iron fountain and bronze statue of James F. Byrnes, a Charlestonian who was an advisor to President Franklin D. Roosevelt and a United States Supreme Court justice.

84 BROAD STREET, OLD SOUTH CAROLINA STATEHOUSE/ CHARLESTON COUNTY COURTHOUSE

Constructed 1753; rehabilitated after fire 1788–92; additions and renovations 1883, 1921, 1940, 1968; restoration planned 1997–2000

First constructed in 1753 as the provincial capitol for the colony of South Carolina, the Charleston County Courthouse is one of the most important buildings in the state. Standing at its prominent position at the northwest corner of Broad and Meeting Streets, the old planned Civic Square, the Courthouse has withstood many vicissitudes in its nearly two and a half centuries of existence. Wars, fires, neglect, and numerous renovations and additions obscured its detailing until a recent architectural study and the advocacy of community organizations have led to a planned restoration of the building's 1792 appearance.

The structure originally served the ideal of symbolic display with its scale and plan indicative to citizens and travelers to Charleston of the power of English imperial rule. Originally two stories, the building contained a generous lobby and a grand staircase that opened from the pedimented engaged portico on Broad Street—all of which provided an appropriate setting for the affairs of state. The provincial court met in a large ground-floor courtroom, while the Commons House of Assembly and the Royal Governor's Council Chamber occupied separate quarters on the second floor. The latter was a lavishly finished room with paneling and gilded Ionic pilasters in which the governor sat in a ceremonial chair (which still survives) under a carved and gilded royal coat of arms. It was here that great affairs of state were announced to the public from a balcony overlooking Meeting Street. Here, too, after the end of royal government, the Declaration of Independence was first read in South Carolina.

The Charleston County Courthouse as it appeared from 1792 to 1883 (1875 engraving)

The building burned, suspiciously, during the Constitutional Ratification Convention of 1788. Debate during the convention divided Lowcountry merchants and planters eager for a strong national government and restoration of trade with Great Britain from farmers and upcountry planters desiring state autonomy. Determined to retain the state capitol, Charlestonians rebuilt within the shell of the statehouse in a Neoclassical style and added a third story. Some sources hint that James Hoban, the Irish-born architect of the White House then in residence in Charleston, may have assisted with the design and construction of the new statehouse. The restored building included state circuit courts and sheriff's offices on the ground floor off the lobby, federal district and circuit courts on the second floor, and rooms on the third floor that variously housed the Charleston Library Society, The Charleston Museum, and later the South Carolina Medical Society. Every visitor to Charleston from Lafayette to President James Monroe went to see the Museum. A renovation in 1883 destroyed the central lobby and, therefore, the old circulation patterns through the building. In 1926 and 1941 insensitive additions doubled the size of the building and a maze of corridors and partitions obscured the fabric of the original Courthouse. The building was heavily damaged during Hurricane Hugo in 1989.

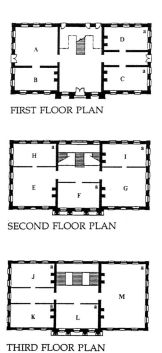

FIRST FLOOR PLAN

SECOND FLOOR PLAN

THIRD FLOOR PLAN

A. Court of Sessions &
    Common Pleas
B. Judges' Chambers
C. Prothonotary's Office
D. Sheriff's Office
E. Court of Equity
F. Register of Mesne
    Conveyance until 1826;
    S.C. Law Society
    Library, 1826
G. U.S. District Court
H. Register of the Court
    of Equity
I. Clerk of U.S. District
    Court & U.S. Marshal
J. Jury Rooms
K. State Treasurer until
    1826; Jury Room; &
    Medical Society until
    mid 1820s
L. State Comptroller
    & Grand Jury
M. Charleston Library
    Society & Museum
    until the 1820s

a. Subdivision of space
   unknown

*Conjectural plan of the Charleston
County Courthouse, 1788–1883*

85–87 BROAD STREET, JOSIAH SMITH TENEMENT

Constructed 1795; gutted in a fire and restored 1977

Originally constructed by Josiah Smith, a wealthy merchant, for two of his sons, this double tenement was constructed in the Neoclassical style then in vogue in Charleston. The arched entrance formerly opened as a passageway extending through the building to rear outbuildings, which have since been removed. Restored as a private dining club in the 1970s, damaged by a fire, and then restored as a restaurant, the building will become the entry to an addition to the Federal Courthouse Annex.

Josiah Smith Tenements, 85–87 Broad Street, in a photo taken circa 1898

88 BROAD STREET, HEBREW ORPHANAGE

Constructed before 1811

This site was sold to the Trescott family in 1804. At that time it was already occupied by "the Director of the Branch Bank of the United States of America." The bank moved to the new building at the northeast corner of Meeting and Broad Streets (City Hall) by 1804, and Trescott rented the structure on the site to the Bank of the State of South Carolina. 88 Broad Street was sold by 1833 to the Hebrew Orphan Society, an organization founded in 1801 to provide relief to widows and to educate, clothe, and maintain orphans of the Jewish faith. The building only briefly served residential purposes, primarily being used as meeting rooms and a school. After the loss of Beth Elohim Synagogue in the Ansonborough fire of 1838, the congregation used the building for services until completion of the new Beth Elohim in 1840.

The front facade is dominated by a central pavilion surmounted by a pediment with a lunette window. The principal door is flanked by engaged Corinthian columns. Much early woodwork survives despite mid-twentieth-century use of the building as offices.

Measured front (south) elevation, Hebrew Orphanage, 88 Broad Street

89–91 BROAD STREET

Constructed circa 1786–96; Victorian alterations 1880s; 89 Broad Street renovated 1978

These two buildings were once similar, simple Federal style, three-story, masonry, single houses. 89 Broad Street was probably erected after 1786 by Maj. Stephen Lee, a watchmaker and planter, on land inherited from his wife's father, Paul Smyser. The merchant James Piersen constructed 91 Broad Street, circa 1796, which retains the later Victorian alterations of metal window lintels, cornice, and parapet, masking earlier details. Its neighbor to the east had similar treatments removed in the renovations of the late-1970s.

92 BROAD STREET, DAVID RAMSAY HOUSE

Constructed before 1750; altered circa 1816

This mid-eighteenth-century double-pile house was originally built for the Congregational merchant Solomon Legare or his daughter Mary and her husband Thomas Ellis. Around 1784 the physician, patriot, and historian Dr. David Ramsay and his wife Martha Laurens purchased the house; they spent the rest of their lives at this address. Ramsay was a native of Lancaster, Pennsylvania, and graduate of the College of New Jersey (Princeton) and the College of Philadelphia, where he received his medical training under the noted Dr. Benjamin Rush. Ramsay moved to Charleston in 1773 and served in the South Carolina Assembly and later in the Continental Congress. Originally an opponent of slavery, he later came to accept the institution. He was most noted as the author of the first history of the American Revolution (1789) and an important history of South Carolina. His wife, daughter of the leading merchant Henry Laurens, was an important intellectual figure in Charleston in her own right. Martha died in 1811, while Dr. Ramsay was killed in 1815 by a patient whom he had determined to be insane.

As in the case of other remaining large houses built before 1750, the floor plan is slightly asymmetrical with a rear stair hall and a front room reserved for business. Upstairs a front drawing room adjoins a smaller withdrawing room. The house retains much of its original woodwork including several fully paneled rooms. Originally a two-story building with a front second-floor balcony, it was changed circa 1816–20 to three stories with a hip roof and a double-tiered front portico. A third story was added to the portico sometime after 1920.

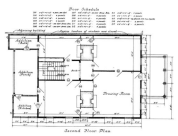

Measured plan of the first floor, 92 Broad Street

93–95 BROAD STREET, BOCQUET HOUSES

Constructed 1783 and 1770–71, respectively; additions and alterations circa 1820 and 1850; 95 Broad Street restored 1990–91

The earlier of these two houses was built by the son of the Huguenot baker who owned the property next door and several other lots in the area. After receiving the lot as a gift, Peter Bocquet Jr., a wealthy deerskin trader, militia officer, and assemblyman, built the house at 95 Broad in the years immediately prior to the Revolution. The first floor was altered in the mid-nineteenth century with two door surrounds: one to provide separate street access to the L-shaped stair hall and the other leading directly into a front room used for business. The floor plan is the same as that of the Phillips House at 55 Church Street. The eastern door surround with Federal style gougework is original, while the architrave of the west door is a modern reproduction.

The house is noted for the extraordinary quality of its woodwork. The overmantel

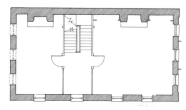

Measured plan of the second floor, 95 Broad Street

section of the drawing room chimneypiece, similar to the woodwork at *128 Tradd Street* and to the memorial to Lady Anne Murray in the First Scots Presbyterian Church, is attributable to one of several English carvers working in the city in the 1760s and 1770s.

Either Peter Bocquet Sr. or Peter Bocquet Jr. built the house at 93 Broad Street in 1783 in the restrained Neoclassical style with a ground-floor office space. In the 1850s the property was acquired by James Simons, an attorney, Speaker of the South Carolina House of Representatives, and commander of the militia forces in the initial attack on Fort Sumter in 1861. Simons added the large three-story wing and hyphens, connecting the main house with the rear kitchen building. At the same time the main dwelling was converted to a side-passage, double-parlor residence trimmed in the Greek Revival style.

97 BROAD STREET, MORDECAI COHEN TENEMENT

Constructed circa 1835

Sole survivor of three identical Greek Revival brick single houses whose sisters were demolished about 1940 for construction of a Piggly Wiggly grocery store, this two-and-a-half-story house on a raised basement was built as rental property by the prominent antebellum merchant Mordecai Cohen.

98 BROAD STREET, DR. HENRY FROST SURGERY

Constructed circa 1735 (front portion), circa 1800–10 (rear portion); renovated circa 1835

Dr. Frost's two-story, gable-ended office may incorporate a portion of a double tenement constructed about 1735 by the colonial physician Dr. John Martino and subsequently sold to Dr. Alexander Garden, the colonial horticulturist for whom the gardenia is named. Dr. Garden's principal plantation house, Otranto at Goose

Creek, is today surrounded by a modern subdivision. The front portion of the building was subsequently renovated after 1835 when Dr. Henry Frost took a mortgage on this site. The first-floor front room contains woodwork from Belvedere Plantation house, the circa 1800 Charleston Neck seat of Col. Thomas Shubrick. The plantation house was demolished in 1925 by the Standard Oil Company, and the interior detailing was subsequently installed. The front entry door with fluted pilasters and semicircular fanlight probably came from Belvedere.

102 BROAD STREET, DR. HENRY FROST HOUSE
Constructed circa 1844

This three-and-a-half-story, stucco, Greek Revival house was built by Dr. Henry Frost, whose physician's office still stands two doors away. Although unusual for this area of Broad Street, its design is typical of the side-passage, double-parlor plan that became common in Charleston's antebellum neighborhoods. A late-nineteenth-century rear piazza enclosure, with a bay window on the third story, is an exceptional feature of this building.

103 BROAD STREET, PETER BRASE HOUSE
Constructed circa 1837; rehabilitated mid-1980s

Constructed by the grocer Peter Brase, this frame building is a good example of the Greek Revival style in commercial architecture. For more than 140 years the structure housed a variety of groceries, including Brase's business, John Hurkamp & Company, the Automatic Grocery, and, finally, Piggly Wiggly supermarket, which closed this chain of occupation in 1983. The current Victorian style storefront was added in a 1984 rehabilitation.

104 BROAD STREET, ANN BOCQUET HOUSE

Constructed after 1758; altered early-twentieth century

Soon after their marriage Ann Bocquet and her husband John Wagner built this three-story stuccoed brick structure as their residence and as his place of business on a lot that was a dowry from Ann's father. Wagner was a merchant in the deerskin trade with his brother-in-law Peter Bocquet Jr. Today the original facade of the structure is masked by a later storefront, but the form of the projecting gable supported by stucco console brackets and the hipped roof survive from the eighteenth century.

29 CHALMERS STREET, GERMAN FRIENDLY SOCIETY

Constructed circa 1829

The German Friendly Society was founded in 1766, but this building has been its headquarters, and that of the later Arion Society, only since 1942 (the society was originally located at *27 Archdale Street*). The three-story brick structure was formerly capped by a hipped roof with a glass monitor or square cupola. This building originally housed a Bible depository, a response to prevailing evangelical currents in the early-nineteenth century, and retained that use until 1882 when the Carolina Art Association purchased the building as its headquarters. It housed the fledgling collection of the organization and served also as a studio until construction of the Gibbes Memorial Art Gallery began in 1905.

Late-nineteenth-century photo of the area around 29 Chalmers Street

34–38 CHALMERS STREET, WIGHTMAN AND McINNES HOUSES

Constructed 1835–51; restored 1930s

Formerly the location of late-eighteenth-century wooden tenements, this site was purchased by the adjacent property owner Dr. William Wightman in 1816. Wightman left these properties to his free black daughter Jane Prevost (Wightman). After a fire in 1835, Miss Wightman built the house at 36 Chalmers Street as her residence. A Greek Revival style building, it was "renovated" in the 1930s by the noted Charleston novelist Josephine Pinckney, author of *Three O'Clock Dinner*. Although the flat parapet and cast-iron grilles with anthemions are clues to the residence's Greek Revival past, Miss Pinckney, with the help of architect Albert Simons, added the Colonial Revival style piazza screen to the existing porch along with a wrought-iron balcony formerly used on a house that was demolished at *108 Meeting Street*. Jane Wightman, or her executor, built the house at 38 Chalmers Street as an investment before 1851, after which it was sold to Bernard O'Neill. His descendant, the noted Charleston artist Elizabeth O'Neill Verner, sold the residence to Miss Laura Bragg, a native of Massachusetts, who came to Charleston in 1927 as director of The Charleston Museum and later founded the Charleston Free Library. Miss Bragg was a central figure in the Charleston Renaissance, and her house was the salon for important southern literary figures of the era. The brick building at 34 Chalmers Street was constructed after1850 with the purchase of the lot by the blacksmith Benjamin McInnes. It remained a smith's shop and livery stable until the early years of the twentieth century and continues in the hands of his decendants.

34–36 Chalmers Street as seen through the fence around Washington Park

103 CHURCH STREET, GEORGE HOFFMAN HOUSE

Constructed circa 1816–20

This parcel owned by Joel Poinsett, the noted Charlestonian who was ambassador to Mexico and for whom the poinsettia is named, contained "two old brick buildings" at the time of its sale to George Hoffman in 1816. Hoffman apparently

razed the old structures and built the present edifice prior to an 1825 mortgage referring to a three-story brick building. This Flemish-bond brick single house retains evidence of a surviving shop on the ground story and residence above, and it boasts splendid original window lintels and sashes. Its north piazzas were later enclosed.

107 CHURCH STREET, ISAAC HOLMES TENEMENT

Constructed circa 1740

The wealthy planter and mariner Isaac Holmes, who lived a few doors to the south, built this three-story stuccoed dwelling to replace a structure burned in the fire of 1740. The house, which retains much of its important early woodwork, was altered in the late-eighteenth century with the addition of a wrought-iron balcony on the second floor. It was probably after the subdivision of the property in the 1780s that John and Elizabeth Geyer built the small stucco house at *105 Church Street*. Holmes also built another tenement at *2 St. Michael's Alley*, a two-story stucco dwelling with a Greek Revival piazza that was partially enclosed in the 1980s.

127 CHURCH STREET, CHARLES MOUZON HOUSE

Constructed circa 1815–25; renovated 1872; altered late-twentieth century

Charles Mouzon built this corner building shortly after acquiring the property in the early years of the nineteenth century. In 1872 E. H. Rickels renovated the building thoroughly, and twentieth-century owners have altered the structure even further. With its gable end to Church Street and three bays on each floor surmounted by a tripartite window, the building stretches eight bays along Chalmers Street. Mouzon apparently built the two-story single house with weatherboarded siding at *129 Church Street* at nearly the same time. Throughout much of the nineteenth century these two properties were held by the same owners.

131 CHURCH STREET, JAMES HUSTON HOUSE

Constructed circa 1809; restored 1929

Originally purchased by Alexander Calder, the former owner of nearby Planter's Hotel, this parcel was sold to Calder's son-in-law, a merchant tailor, who constructed this building with commercial space on the first floor and living quarters above. While the first floor is relatively re-strained, the second floor has exuberant Neoclassical woodwork. Calder lived and worked here until his death in 1824. The house was briefly owned by the Confeder-ate secretary of the Treasury George Trenholm (who owned many investment properties), but ater the war it declined into a slum. Restored in 1929, the three-bay brick house still retains the central front door that originally led into the shop space from the street, a relatively unusual survival.

135 CHURCH STREET, PLANTER'S HOTEL/DOCK STREET THEATRE

 *Constructed 1809; renovated 1935–37*

The present Dock Street Theatre includes the remnants of eighteenth-century buildings that were incorporated into a larger nine-teenth-century structure. Only fragmentary brick walls remain of the 1736 theater, probably the second edifice in America con-structed specifically for theatrical perfor-mances, which faced Dock Street (now Queen Street). This theater opened with a performance of the popular comedy *The Recruiting Officer*. Rebuilt in 1754 after a fire, the theater reopened with a production by a visiting London company of comedi-ans and subsequently played host to numer-

Door architraves from the Radcliffe-King House reused as balcony entries at Dock Street Theatre

ous productions of operas, farces, and Shakespearean plays in the ensuing decade. The principal portion of the Planter's Hotel dates from 1809, when Alexander Calder and his wife purchased the property and moved the hotel operation to this address (Calder was an ancestor of the famous twentieth-century sculptor Alexander Calder). The city's first major hotel was a "merry place" and provided lodging for notable visitors to the city as well as wealthy upcountry planters who brought their families and servants to Charleston for several weeks in February to take in the social season and attend the horse races. Noted for its service and cuisine, the hotel is reputed to be the birthplace of planter's punch.

The entry porch has unusual banded brownstone columns topped with heavily carved wooden brackets and balcony added in the mid-nineteenth century. In 1935 the city of Charleston restored the building as part of an innovative Works Progress Administration project. At this time an eighteenth-century style theater interior was created by the architect Albert Simons and the building was refit with exuberant Neoclassical woodwork from the demolished Radcliffe-King House. The Dock Street Theatre today serves as home to a local theatrical company and hosts numerous other performances, particularly during the Spoleto Festival.

4 COURTHOUSE SQUARE, BLAKE TENEMENTS

Plat showing the plan of the Blake Tenements, 1789

N *Constructed 1760–72; some renovation circa 1800, late-twentieth century*

Daniel Blake inherited this portion of the original Archdale Square, a site that had been reserved for an early Quaker governor on the old town plan. Blake sold much of the property for development of buildings that subsequently saw extensive use as lawyers' offices and lodgings for attorneys and judges. By 1772, as one deed noted, Blake had extensively improved the westernmost part of his property by building "two substantial brick tenements together with convenient outbuildings." The layout of the buildings, outbuildings, and formal garden with a privy for the western tenement are shown in a detailed plat of 1789. The outbuildings were demolished in the 1960s for county offices. Stone staircases lead to the original pedimented door architraves. Most of the windows were replaced about 1800, but a few eighteenth-century windows with heavy muntins remain on side and rear elevations. The brickwork of the front facade is laid in Flemish bond, while that of the less public facades is finished in English bond.

View of the Blake Tenements, 4 Courthouse Square, circa 1898

8 COURTHOUSE SQUARE, MEYER-PEACE HOUSE AND OFFICE

Constructed 1783–93; altered circa 1802, 1830, 1956

Philip Meyer, a leading sugar manufacturer, purchased this site, part of the old Archdale Square grant, from Henry Laurens prior to the Revolution. Meyer was a prominent Revolutionary patriot and was among those citizens interned on a prison ship in the harbor during the British occupation of the city in 1780–82. The three-story stuccoed brick house with pantile roof was constructed in the Federal style either by Meyer prior to his death in 1785 or by his wife Mary Meyer, who lived on the site until 1794. Mary Meyer continued to operate the sugar bakery here, and at her death the property devolved to her granddaughter, Mary Rudhall Peace. Mary Peace's husband Joseph lived and worked on this site through most of the first decade of the nineteenth century, practicing law with his partner, the future congressman Langdon Cheves, before moving his practice to Philadelphia in 1810.

Early-twentieth-century view of 8 Courthouse Square showing former gates, piazza, and landscape

Early-twentieth-century engraving by Elizabeth O'Neill Verner of the view from the porticoes of South Carolina Society Hall

72 MEETING STREET, SOUTH CAROLINA SOCIETY HALL

Constructed 1803–04; additions 1825, 1994

Gabriel Manigault, architect; renovations by Frederick Wesner, architect (1825)

This Neoclassical hall was constructed for a fraternal society of French Huguenot businessmen and artisans formed in 1737 as the "Two-Bit Club" in honor of the weekly dues each member raised for the assistance of indigent members and their families. The lots on Meeting Street were acquired in 1800, and responsibility for the design of a hall was given to one of its members, the gentleman architect Gabriel Manigault. Construction began in 1803 and was completed the next year. The T-shape plan provides two main stories over a service basement. The first level has three similarly sized rooms that served as billiards room, classroom (for a small school the Society once operated), and schoolmaster's apartment. The second floor contains a large meeting room separated by large doors from the ballroom, which has a colonnaded Neoclassical canopy at the east end. In the 1820s the current pedimented portico projecting over the sidewalk was added, as were the brownstone stairs and iron railings. Damage in the Civil War bombardment and the earthquake of 1886 led to interior Victorian changes, including the south staircase and the plaster ceilings. The seal of the Society with the motto "Posterati" appears in the pediment. The building is a popular setting for private receptions and other social events and contains extensive portrait collections of both the South Carolina Society and the St. Andrew's Society, the latter of which uses the front first-floor room. A documented parterre garden formerly located in the lot to the north side may someday be restored.

76 MEETING STREET, JUDGE ELIHU HALL BAY HOUSE

Constructed circa 1785

This three-story wooden single house with low-pitched hipped roof, built by Judge Elihu Hall Bay, presently serves as the rectory of St. Michael's Church. Judge Bay, a Maryland native, purchased the lot in 1785 and tore down the Indian trading store that originally stood here. He also owned the lot immediately south, where, according to a plat of 1792, he cultivated a formal parterre with shrubs and flower beds in front and a kitchen garden with fruit trees at the rear. The Neoclassical door screen of the piazza is of particular note, as is the line of original brick outbuildings, including kitchen, laundry, stables, and slave quarters, which stretches along St. Michael's Alley.

Plat showing the plan and adjacent garden of the house of Judge Elihu Hall Bay at 76 Meeting Street, 1792

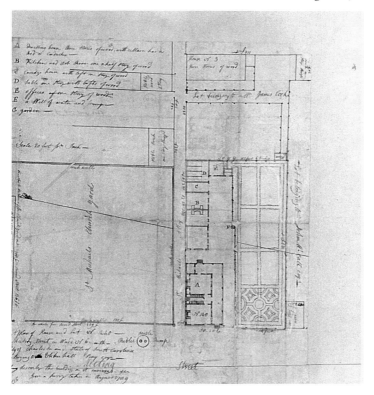

80 MEETING STREET, ST. MICHAEL'S CHURCH

L *Constructed 1752–61; interior completed 1772; renovated 1818, 1887, 1905; restored 1993–94*

Samuel Cardy, contractor; Humphrey Sommers, mason; Henry Burnet and Anthony Forehand, carvers

The steeple of St. Michael's Church seen from Washington Park

St. Michael's Church has long been considered one of America's most sophisticated colonial church buildings. It was begun in 1752 following an act of the Assembly for building a new parish church on the site of the first St. Philip's. Whatever the origin of the plan and the stylistic relationship between this building and the London city churches designed by Sir Christopher Wren and James Gibbs, St. Michael's cannot be tied to one source or definitively attributed to a single architect.

The exterior, except the Tuscan portico, was essentially complete by 1756. The steeple, which rises 186 feet, is today surmounted by a seven-and-a-half-foot weathervane with a gilt ball, an 1820s replacement of an earlier ball and dragon vane gilded by the artist Jeremiah Theus. Building commissioners' records reveal that Henry Burnet, a house and ship carver from London who died in 1761, carved the details for the steeple and interior details such as the capitals of the gallery columns, the narthex stair brackets, and the pulpit. The base and sounding board of the pulpit are late-nineteenth-century replacements. New research shows that Burnet also executed the flowers in the soffit that surrounds the crest of the cove ceiling and the central pendant from which a London brass chandelier of 1803 is suspended. Anthony Forehand carved the large column capitals of

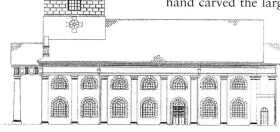

Measured drawing of the south elevation of St. Michael's

the chancel; English carver John Lord completed the altar. Most of this work was destroyed by Federal shelling in 1865, but the English wrought-iron altar rail, installed in 1772, survives and has been restored with Prussian blue paint and gilded components. The present chancel area was restored after the Civil War with plaster details and the insertion of a Tiffany stained glass window after Raphael's painting of St. Michael slaying the dragon. In 1906 Tiffany and Company was further engaged to enhance the chancel with the eight small plaster columns around the stained glass window and elaborate paintwork, especially the stenciled decoration in the apse. Further work was completed in this area by architect Albert Simons in the 1940s.

The box pews in the church are original and, like the columns, gallery facings, and soffits, are fashioned of red cedar. These have been restored with a vermilion wash, and the early-nineteenth-century pew numbers have been conserved. The noteworthy furnishings of the church include the 1770s font, ordered from London; the original case of the former 1768 Snetzler organ; and many marble memorial plaques, including one carved in London to Mary Blacklock located in the narthex under the steeple. In the surrounding burial ground, approached from Meeting Street through gates with funerary urns in wrought iron, is located one of the only in situ wooden grave boards in America, dated 1772. Also located here are gravestones for Edward Rutledge, signer of the Declaration of Independence; Charles Cotesworth Pinckney, signer of the U.S. Constitution; Gen. Mordecai Gist, Maryland Revolutionary War hero; and the Charleston jurist James Louis Petigru.

The church received shell damage to the chancel in the Civil War, but its steeple, painted black for the duration of the conflict, escaped damage. The bells, imported from England in 1764, were stolen by the British in 1782 and later returned. They were burned in Columbia in 1865 and returned to the Whitechapel Foundry of their origin to be recast. In 1993 they were again returned to Whitechapel and have been rehung as a full ring of bells. St. Michael's Church is one of Charleston's most enduring symbols. Often depicted by artists and described by writers, its bells are featured in the musical score of the opera *Porgy and Bess.*

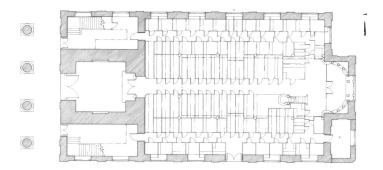

Measured plan of the first floor of St. Michael's

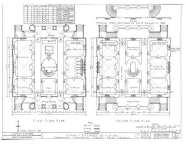

Measured plan of the first floor, Fireproof Building, 100 Meeting Street

100 MEETING STREET, FIREPROOF BUILDING (COUNTY RECORDS OFFICE)

L *Constructed 1822–27; earthquake damage and repair 1886–87; restored 1970*

Robert Mills, architect; John Spidle, construction architect; John Gordon, brickmason; James Rowe and John White, stonecutters

Originally constructed as a state office building with fireproof storage for records of the Charleston District, this structure was designed by Robert Mills at the city's behest in 1822 as part of the new city square plan. Mills's plans relied primarily on the removal of combustible materials from the fabric of the building. Brick, brownstone, and stucco for the exterior; stone groin and barrel vaults; stairways lit by a central skylight; and cast-iron windows were key components of the plans. The completed building differed from Mills's original plans. John Spidle, the on-site construction supervisor, may have directed the use of plain roughcast stucco columns instead of the fluted columns, the elimination of the belt course, the substitution of quoins for horizontal channeling, and changes to the cornice and the third-story window openings as designed by Mills. After serving generally as the county property record office and housing functions such as the coroner's and tax offices, the building was leased to the South Carolina Historical Society in 1955 and officially became the Society's headquarters in 1968.

105 MEETING STREET, HIBERNIAN HALL

L *Designed 1835; constructed 1839–41; earthquake repairs 1887*

Thomas U. Walter, architect; John White, stonecutter; Andrew Cunningham, carpenter; George Thompson, bricklayer

The hall of the Hibernian Society was built for an organization that was established in 1801 to provide aid to Irish immigrants and their families and that was the result of the amalgamation of two earlier Irish fraternal orders. The organization eventually attracted men of wealth and power, not necessarily of Irish origin, and welcomed both Protestant and Catholic members. The Hibernians hoped to follow the examples of the halls built for the South Carolina Society and the St. Andrew's Society and discussed the matter for fourteen years before buying a lot on Meeting Street. Architect Thomas U. Walter of Philadelphia, noted later for his design of the Capitol dome in Washington, D.C., was paid $100 in 1833 for plans for a building. Construction commenced on the hall in 1839 and was complete by January 1841 at a total cost of $40,000.

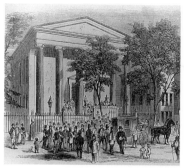

Engraving of Hibernian Hall, 105 Meeting Street, in the 1850s

The exterior, with its Ionic portico, reflects the simple and chaste design requested by the committee, save the gilded Irish harp in relief over the door. The interior, however, is an exciting space, dominated by a rotunda of three stories surrounded by stairs and circular columned balconies; the ceiling is finished with a coffered dome and oculus. Although the exterior portico was rebuilt after the earthquake of 1886 and changes included altering the proportions of the columns, as well as a more elaborate modillioned cornice and an Italianate window in the tympanum of the pediment, the building's interior is largely unchanged. The site of numerous Hibernian functions, including its annual St. Patrick's Day banquet, the building also hosts other large social events. Since the years following the Civil War it has been the annual site of the January Ball of the St. Cecilia Society, Charleston's oldest and most exclusive social function. On the portico stands a stone from the Giant's Causeway, brought to Charleston from County Antrim, Northern Ireland, in 1851. An elaborate wrought-iron fence and cast-iron gas lamps enclose the property from the street.

Batson's Exxon Station just before it closed in 1981

108 MEETING STREET, FRANCES R. EDMUNDS CENTER FOR HISTORIC PRESERVATION, HISTORIC CHARLESTON FOUNDATION

Constructed 1930–31; renovations and additions 1985–86

This building was originally constructed by Standard Oil of New Jersey as a gasoline filling station. Three houses dated between 1782 and 1805 had been built on this site, but they were torn down after Standard Oil acquired the property in 1929. Considerable public outrage ensued over this demolition. To assuage the local indignation, the company retained the Charleston preservation architect Albert Simons to design a suitable building for this corner lot that would be in keeping with the historic character of Charleston. Using brick, as well as elements such as columns, balusters, and window surrounds saved from the concurrent demolition of the Gabriel Manigault House at *279 Meeting Street*, Simons designed the service station in the Colonial Revival style. Some found the station charming, but most did not. The demolition of the original structures and the construction of this service station inspired the city council to enact America's first historic zoning ordinance in 1931 and also to create the nation's first historic district and Board of Architectural Review.

Acquired by partial gift from Standard Oil in 1985, Historic Charleston Foundation converted it to use as a preservation center, named for its longtime director Frances R. Edmunds.

Elevation by Albert Simons, 1929, of Standard Oil Station at 108 Meeting Street

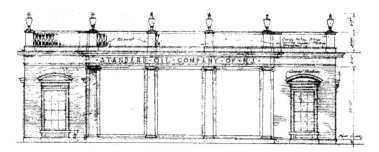

115 MEETING STREET, MILLS HOUSE HOTEL

Constructed 1853; reconstructed 1968

John E. Earle, architect

Reconstructed on the site of the original Mills House, this reproduction was completed in 1968. Otis Mills, a grain merchant and real estate developer, constructed the original in 1853. Mills, a native of Massachusetts, commissioned the architect John E. Earle, also an expatriate New Englander, to design the building, which contained the first large-scale running water and steam heat systems in the city. The five-story, 125-room hotel cost $200,000 to build and incorporated Philadelphia cast-iron balconies and New England terra cotta window cornices. The Mills House Hotel barely escaped the fire of 1861 and stood in its original configuration for over a century after the disaster. Remaining a splendid hostelry for most of the early-twentieth century, it was known as the St. John Hotel. By 1968 the original building was in a severe state of disrepair,

The Mills House, 115 Meeting Street, in 1853

and its new owners reluctantly demolished it. Although two stories were added in the reconstruction, architects carefully employed the original exterior design and used the nineteenth-century ironwork and some details from the first structure. Fiberglass copies replaced the original terra cotta window surrounds. The hotel opened for South Carolina's tricentennial in 1970.

116 MEETING STREET, OLD LOWER FIRE STATION

Constructed 1887–88; renovated 1970s

After earthquake damage to its old central fire station, the city embarked in 1887 on a campaign to build three new fire stations. This two-story, Flemish-bonded brick structure was the lower station, completed before the end of 1888 at a cost of about $7,000. A separate appropriation was made for an "Iron Bell Tower complete" of $2,344.50. The tower contained a 2,500 pound bell that was an essential part of the city's fire alarm system. The bell was also used to alert residents of hurricanes, severe temperature changes, important national events, and, until 1927 when the practice was discontinued, the time of day. Its use as a fire alarm was discontinued in 1953. In the 1970s the city rehabilitated the fire station as offices and a public hearing room. The bell tower was restored by the city in 1989.

45 QUEEN STREET, DANIEL CANNON TENEMENT OUTBUILDING

Constructed circa 1750; renovated circa 1955

This substantial brick outbuilding formerly served a wooden double tenement constructed in the mid-eighteenth century by Daniel Cannon, a wealthy pre-Revolutionary lumber mill owner and building contractor. The Cannon tenement was demolished (with some of its structure moved to the Crescent neighborhood) in the 1940s, but the brick kitchen/slave quarters remained and was renovated as a modern house. The building's primary interest arises from the gable-on-hip roof, an element rarely seen in surviving colonial Charleston buildings. A cypress paneled room from the interior of the Cannon House was preserved by The Charleston Museum.

57 QUEEN STREET, CITIZENS AND SOUTHERN NATIONAL BANK COUNTINGHOUSE
Constructed circa 1840; renovated circa 1958

Functioning in the nineteenth century as the office of the veterinary surgeon Dr. Benjamin McInnes and in the twentieth century as the offices of one of Charleston's pioneer urologists and heart surgeons, the younger Dr. Benjamin McInnes, this property remained in the hands of the McInnes family, who owned and operated the blacksmith's shop at *24 Chalmers Street* for nearly one hundred years. A two-story stuccoed brick structure with Italianate arches on the ground story and Craftsman period details on the second, the building was completely refashioned in the late-1950s to appear as a Colonial Revival style Charleston single house in its use as a branch bank; it adjoined a large bank parking lot that was constructed at that time surrounded by a splendid Charleston style brick wall.

QUEEN AND KING STREETS, QUAKER MEETINGHOUSE FENCE
Constructed circa 1858

This section of Gothic style, cast-iron fence and entry gates constitutes the sole remnant of the last of three Quaker meetinghouses that stood successively on this site from 1681 until the fire of 1861. The property was deeded to the Society of Friends by Gov. John Archdale, himself a Quaker and the holder of one of the largest individual sections of the Grand Modell, known as Archdale Square. Generations of Quakers met here, including several women ministers and missionaries, such as Mary Fisher Crosse, who tried to convert a Turkish sultan or vizier in 1660 and was persecuted in England and Puritan Boston before immigrating to South Carolina, and Fisher's granddaughter Sophia Hume, author of a tract exhorting her fellow Charlestonians to piety.

In 1970 Charleston County constructed a parking garage on the site and moved some remains to the yard of 2 *Courthouse Square*, including the gravestone of Daniel Latham, who carried the news of the 1775 victory at Fort Moultrie to the Continental Congress in Philadelphia.

5 ST. MICHAEL'S ALLEY, CLELIA MCGOWAN HOUSE

Constructed 1915

A rare example of the Craftsman Cottage style in lower Charleston, this house was built by Clelia Peronneau Mathewes McGowan, a poet, humanitarian, and politician. In 1919 Mrs. McGowan was elected the first alderwoman in Charleston and thus became the first major female officeholder in South Carolina history. McGowan constructed the two-story house with hipped roof and double, diamond-paned central windows on a raised basement on the former site of the Charleston Hydraulic Press, which had been pulled down a few years earlier. The building is set back from the street, in contrast to the tight placement of the houses on the other side of the alley.

7–9 St. Michael's Alley

6 ST. MICHAEL'S ALLEY, GEORGE DINGLE HOUSE

Constructed 1850; restored after 1918

Restoration of the buildings that line St. Michael's Alley began prior to World War I and were among the city's earliest rehabilitation efforts. Susan Pringle Frost, a preservation pioneer and cofounder of the Preservation Society of Charleston, purchased several houses along the alley then described by the *Post and Courier* as a "slum." George Dingle, a tradesman, built this small two-story, gabled roof dwelling as a tenement in the mid-nineteenth century almost contemporaneously with the similarly fenestrated house next door at *4 St. Michael's Alley*.

Early-twentieth-century view of 6 St. Michael's Alley

8 ST. MICHAEL'S ALLEY, JAMES L. PETIGRU LAW OFFICE

Constructed 1848; restored after 1918, 1983–84

Edward Brickell White, architect

Designed by the architect Edward B. White, this law office was built by the famed jurist James Louis Petigru on this site by 1849. Petigru, born in Abbeville, moved his practice to Charleston in 1819. He later served as attorney general of South

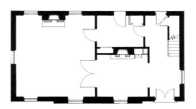

Measured plan of the first floor, James L. Petigru Law Office, 8 St. Michael's Alley

Carolina and as a member of the House. Defender of the liberties of the weak, particularly slaves and free blacks, Petigru opposed nullification and was Charleston's most outspoken unionist at the time of secession. After his residence on Legare and Broad Streets burned in the fire of 1861, Petigru and his wife moved into this building. According to an 1850s plat, Petigru's walled garden stood directly opposite.

The Petigru law office boasts some characteristics of Neoclassical design, out-of-fashion in the 1840s, with its brownstone window lintels and central pediment with a lunette window in the tympanum. The wrought-iron balcony with cast-iron panels was salvaged from a demolished building and installed by Susan Pringle Frost during her restoration of the area.

11 ST. MICHAEL'S ALLEY

Constructed 1780s

This house served as a carriage house for a now-vanished eighteenth-century dwelling to the east. Though rehabilitated in the 1920s, the building retained the arched entry, which is infilled by a window with Neoclassical moldings and the hipped roof and upper fenestration. The present house at *9 St. Michael's Alley* was built as a residence for DuBose Heyward in the late-1920s.

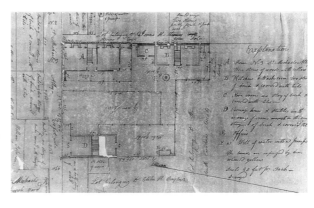

Plat of St. Michael's Alley showing number 11 as a carriage house, 1799

WASHINGTON PARK
Developed 1818; redesigned and renamed 1881

Originally laid out as part of the City Square following construction of the Bank of the United States building (city hall) but developed in its present form as part of a civic improvements program during the administration of Mayor William Ashmead Courtenay, this park was renamed in honor of George Washington to commemorate the centenary of the victory at Yorktown. In addition to the large granite obelisk in memory of Confederate soldiers, a bronze bust of the poet Henry Timrod and more modern commemorations of important figures such as Rachel Jackson, mother of President Andrew Jackson, and Francis Salvador, a member of the South Carolina Provincial Congress who was the first Jew elected to public office in America, ornament the park's double axial walks and east wall. The yellow brick statue base on the west end formerly supported the 1767 statue of William Pitt, moved here from the Orphan House grounds in the 1880s and relocated to The Charleston Museum one hundred years later.

Henry Timrod monument in Washington Park, circa 1903

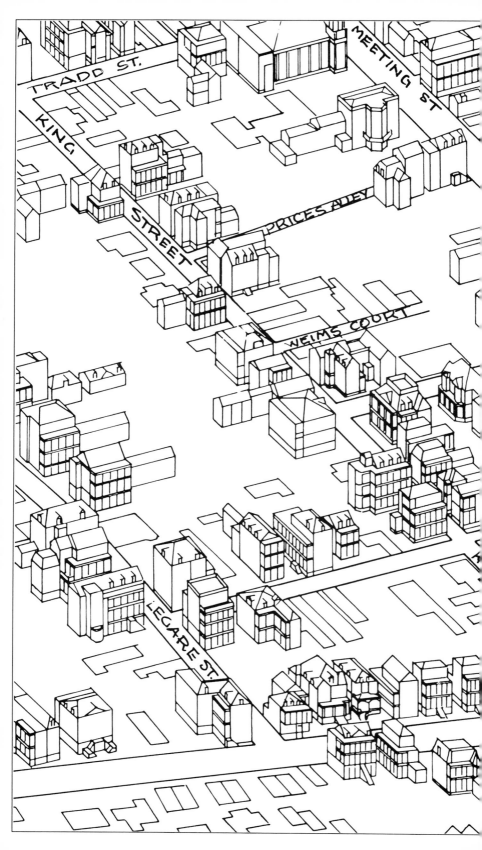

3

EIGHTEENTH-CENTURY EXPANSION

The Golden Age Continued

*A*n observer noted in the *South Caro-lina Gazette* in 1774 that White Point, until then almost a desolate spot, had recently been covered with houses, "many of them" very elegant, and estimated that more than three hundred houses had appeared in the city in the previous ten years. From 1750 onward, with ever greater rice crops and profits from indigo, Charleston prospered, and as it did, the construction of new houses and new commercial buildings caused the city to spill beyond the boundaries of the old walled area. Charleston's planters, merchants, and even prosperous mechanics looked to lower Meeting Street, East and South Bay Streets, and newly developing thoroughfares such as Legare Street as sites for personal residences or tenements for investment.

Individual single houses and double tenements of the same plan prevailed, with Georgian double houses filling larger lots. House carpenters and contractors such as Humphrey Sommers and John Fullerton, and carvers such as the recent English émigrés John Lord and Thomas Woodin were but a few of the house mechanics employed in this construction explosion. Orange Street, developed on the former pleasure ground of the Orange Garden af-

Detail of an ichnographic map by the Phoenix Fire Company of London showing the area south of Tradd Street, 1788

The Col. John Stuart House

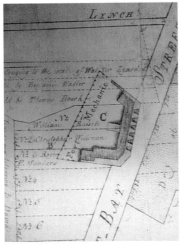

Plat *"Plan of the Public Lands Situated near East Bay Street"* showing Fort Mechanic, 1794

View of South Battery looking west, 1865

ter 1758, was one example; another was the development by entrepreneurs William Gibbes, Edward Blake, George Kincaid, and Robert MacKenzie of Legare, South Bay, and Gibbes Streets, accomplished by the filling of creek and marsh. The double house of William Gibbes, which commanded his 300-foot wharf stretching into the Ashley River channel; the double tenement finished by George Kincaid; and the house of Edward Blake's son John punctuated this early expansion. On Broad Street the substantial James Laurens House faced another double house; both were respectively acquired by the colony's Revolutionary leaders Edward and John Rutledge.

After the Revolution the vast, deep lots of Legare, western Tradd, and Logan Streets created opportunities for construction of large houses, much like contemporary suburban development north of the Boundary (Calhoun Street). Generally, owners such as Amarinthea Elliott and Francis Simmons opted for the single house form. In 1819 the completion of the city seawall allowed the development of lots south of Atlantic Street and the mansions of East Battery, beginning with the Holmes House and including the late-Neoclassical Edmondston-Alston House and the Greek Revival dwellings of William Ravenel and William Roper, all constructed during the antebellum period. The Battery did not remain architecturally stagnant, however, as the bombardment of 1861, the earthquake of 1886, and the hurricane of 1911 each removed major buildings and provided infill opportunities.

As the nineteenth century progressed, more large lots on the western edge of the city were subdivided, creating additional building opportunities. William Pinckney Shingler, a wealthy cotton factor, built one of the last great Greek Revival Charleston houses in 1857 and a year later built an-

East Battery, late-nineteenth-century view

other similar house across the street. The fire of 1861 burned most of the area of Broad Street west of Legare Street but generally spared the "eighteenth-century expansion" area. The shelling of the city beginning in August 1863 cleared this area first, and those who went uptown or upcountry, such as prominent Charlestonian Susan Middleton, learned much later of the "devastation" to the lower part of the city. Groups of soldiers stationed in Charleston were perhaps the only frequent visitors to the Battery, going down at night to watch burning shells come across the water.

After the war, many of Charleston's old aristocracy tried to hold on to their houses in lower Charleston: Middletons, Hugers, and Pringles. However, some, such as the executors of the late Governor R. F. W. Allston of 51 Meeting Street, were forced to sell. The new construction of the postbellum era included the imposing Victorian mansion of George Williams and later the magnificent house that the banker Andrew Simonds built for his New Orleans bride. Some of Charleston's "New South" men and their families eventually moved to this area and merged with the old elite, but most of Charleston's rising businessmen did not. The alleyways of the area were the homes of Irish immigrants and slaves before the war. By the late-1860s they were crowded with freedmen living in rental properties. The wedge formed by South and East Battery has remained Charleston's most fashionable address. Since 1950 even the alleys have been gentrified and are now upscale addresses.

1–3 ATLANTIC STREET, BENJAMIN SMITH HOUSES
Constructed 1830s

This portion of Atlantic Street from East Bay Street to Church Street was known from the late-eighteenth century until 1837 as Lynch's Lane. During that period Capt. Benjamin Smith, a shipbuilder, built these identical dwellings following the Charleston single house plan with two rooms on either side of a central hall. Unlike the typical single house placement, these structures lie directly on the street and have no piazzas. Simple weatherboarding, deep plain entablatures, and corner boards sheathe these simple five-bay dwellings capped with gable roofs, dormers, and end chimneys. Identical Neoclassical style doorways accent both buildings, which are fronted by modern staircases. Elizabeth O'Neill Verner, founder of the Charleston Etchers' Club and a leading exponent of the fledgling historic preservation movement, maintained a studio and residence at 3 Atlantic Street.

2 ATLANTIC STREET, MAY AND LEILA WARING HOUSE
Constructed circa 1890

This two-story Queen Anne style dwelling, which has a double-tiered front piazza that wraps around the building to the east and terminates with an octagonal tower topped by a conical roof, survives from a pair of identical dwellings built circa 1890 after the earthquake destroyed a large house on the site. Two unmarried sisters of the Waring family bought the house in 1923. Leila Waring painted miniatures of Charlestonians in the first half of the twentieth century, carrying on an art form generally associated with the prephotography era. She added a northeast room as her studio shortly after moving into the building. May Waring, her sister, was a well-known local writer.

5 ATLANTIC STREET, WILLIAM E. HOLMES TENEMENT

Constructed circa 1893

A pressed-metal hood supported by console brackets and matching window lintels and cornice ornament this three-bay, side-hall plan, bay windowed dwelling. William Holmes, proprietor of Holmes, Calder and Company, Charleston's leading paint and oil dealer and manufacturer, built this house as a rental unit in 1893, replacing an earlier house on the site. This property was held as an investment by his family for eighty-one years.

8 ATLANTIC STREET, THOMAS YOUNG HOUSE

Constructed circa 1805

Thomas Young, the keeper of a boardinghouse on State Street, built this two-and-a-half-story, two-bay, stuccoed single house in the early years of the nineteenth century. Although the structure retains its molded brick cornice, nine-over-nine windows, and scored stucco, numerous additions have been made in the twentieth century, including the front wrought-iron balcony, east side entry tower, and various rear modifications. Even more extensive additions obscure the original wooden single house to the west at *10 Atlantic Street*, constructed circa 1769 by William Hinckley.

14 ATLANTIC STREET, W. E. GAILLARD HOUSE

Constructed 1920; altered 1980s

An enterprising and civic-minded Charlestonian businessman completed this simple Colonial Revival style house in 1920. The five-bay structure is capped by a low hipped roof; a portion of the former west porches has been recently enclosed.

16 ATLANTIC STREET, STELLING-PELZER HOUSE

Constructed circa 1849–72; altered 1949

This two-story, hipped-roof brick building in the Colonial Revival style apparently incorporates an earlier wooden structure on the site. The property began as a frame, one-story grocery built by A. E. Stelling on land purchased in 1849 from the Lightwood estate; a second-story dwelling unit had been added by 1872 when it became the property of grocer John F. Meyer. After being occupied by a variety of groceries until 1927, it became a store for A&P. The building was bricked over by 1930 and converted some years later by Mary Branch Chisolm Pelzer as a residence.

105 BROAD STREET, WILLIAM L. BREDENBURG STORE AND RESIDENCE

Constructed 1879; renovated before 1930

A notice in the Charleston newspaper of October 23, 1879, reported that "W. L. Bredenburg who owns the lot at the southwest corner of Broad and King Streets, has commenced to rebuild." A few months before, a three-story wooden store and dwelling, owned for decades by Bredenburg's brother, had burned on the same site. The newspaper added that the planned brick building would be "an ornament to the vicinity." Bredenburg built his new structure in Philadelphia pressed brick and in a style still reminiscent of late–Greek Revival precedents. Cast-iron detailing with square pilasters ornaments the storefront on Broad Street, while masonry lintels and sills, quoins cornice, and parapet add distinction to the brick facade. Interior changes in the early-twentieth century primarily centered on the reconfiguration of the central staircase.

106 BROAD STREET, JOHN LINING HOUSE

Constructed before 1715; additions 1900s; restored 1972

This dwelling holds claim to distinction as the oldest frame structure in Charleston. The building's cypress structural members support architectural detailing that, in a modern context, appears rather plain but in the context of first period construction was rather advanced. The fully beaded siding, front door architrave, and dormers all reflect a well-developed architectural vocabulary. Most construction in this early period would not have boasted such details. The house stands on lot no. 160 of the Grand Modell, granted to Huguenot James De Bordeaux. A house is mentioned in a deed of 1715 conveying it to William Harvey, then the tenant in the property. John Lining, the first person to conduct scientific and systematic weather observations in America, may never have lived on the property. It belonged to his wife's family for more than twenty years before their brief tenure as owners.

106 Broad Street before restoration

106 Broad Street after restoration

Between 1783 and 1793, 106 Broad Street housed the *Gazette of the State of South Carolina,* which was published by Mrs. Ann Timothy. In the 1780s it became an apothecary for Dr. Andrew Turnbull, proprietor of a failed experimental colony in Florida called New Smyrna. In the 1960s the Preservation Society purchased and restored the building, which had long housed a storefront drugstore.

109 BROAD STREET, MARTIN CAMPBELL HOUSE

Constructed circa 1783; rehabilitated 1965

Although this lot was acquired by Martin Campbell in 1773, stylistic comparison indicates that the building was probably built after the Revolution and just before

its transfer by Campbell family members to the merchant William Price in 1784. The house has undergone significant renovation, but it retains the reverse graduation of its front windows, its hipped roof, and its triple-tiered piazzas with simple colonettes.

110 BROAD STREET, WILLIAM HARVEY HOUSE

Constructed circa 1728; altered circa 1800, 1837; renovated 1981, 1985

Escaping the great fires of the eighteenth and nineteenth centuries, 110 Broad Street stands as an example of a relatively intact pre-Revolutionary structure. The merchant's house plan follows that of *92 Broad Street* and other large dwellings of the pre-1740 period with a front office entry and a chambered rear stair hall ascending to a second story dominated by a large front drawing room and smaller withdrawing room. The house is composed of thick masonry walls accentuated by corner quoins and rises three stories to a bellcast hipped roof, pierced by large chimneys with corbeled caps. The Harveys, the builders, leased this substantial dwelling to royal governor James Glen from 1743 to 1756. Notable exterior changes were made about 1800, including the Neoclassical fanlighted front door with delicate gougework surround and the wrought-iron balcony. The yard includes a variety of former dependencies, with a Gothic style carriage house on a garden lot subdivided by the second owners, the Izards, from the Lining property in 1796, a privy and kitchen building with original cooking fireplace, bake oven, and warming oven. Ralph Stead Izard sold the house in 1837 to his aunt Mary and her husband, Ambassador Joel Poinsett, famous for bringing the poinsettia back from Mexico. The Poinsetts lived here for many years and added several Italian marble mantels to the interior before selling to Judge Mitchell King.

114 BROAD STREET, COL. THOMAS PINCKNEY HOUSE

Constructed circa 1829

Ralph Izard Jr. of Broad Street acquired this site before his death. Passing into his sister's estate, the property was sold to Col. Thomas Pinckney in 1829 with an "unfinished house." Pinckney, whose father owned *14 George Street*, completed the present T-shaped, two-and-a-half-story brick dwelling, with construction assistance from the Horlbeck Brothers, by 1829. Standing on a high basement, which is supported on the interior by groin vaulting, a stone columned front portico projects from the tinted red brick facade. Marble lintels surmount the triple sash front windows, and there is a gable roof with a lunette window in the transom. A plat of 1829 depicts the U-shaped line of dependencies, including stables, kitchen, and slave quarters, a portion of which survives. Pinckney spent the winter social season in this house, particularly in the upstairs parlor where satin damask curtains, rosewood sofas, Wilton carpets, and double chandeliers provided a grand space for the elaborate entertaining that characterized Charleston society. He served his guests from his extensive wine cellar in the basement. Pinckney kept most of his 190 slaves on his rice lands at Fairfield Plantation on the Santee River, where he spent the fall and early spring. He summered at Altamont, his farm in South Carolina's Pendleton district. The Pinckney family retained title to the site until 1866, when his daughter, Rosetta Ella Pinckney Izard, sold it to the Roman Catholic bishop of Charleston. It has since remained as the residence for Charleston's bishops. The house is one of the finest examples of the Classical Revival style in the city.

A marble staircase ascends to the cast-iron porticoes by Christopher Werner added to 116 Broad Street in 1853

116 BROAD STREET, JOHN RUTLEDGE HOUSE

🅛 *Constructed circa 1763; altered circa 1853, 1890; rehabilitated 1988–89*

When constructed, this building had a Georgian facade that lacked the ornate ironwork and Greek Revival details employed in the design today. John Rutledge, "Dictator" and governor of South Carolina during the Revolution, built this house before 1770 for his wife Elizabeth Grimké. Rutledge went on to serve as an associate justice of the U.S. Supreme Court and held a brief, unconfirmed term as chief justice before illness hastened his demise in 1800. The house passed through a number of different owners from 1790 until 1835, when it served briefly as the residence of Charleston's first Roman Catholic bishop, Rev. John England. Thomas Norman Gadsden, a wealthy slave trader and landowner, was responsible for the renovations of the Rutledge House in 1853 and added terra cotta window lintels to the exterior as well as the intricate cast-ironwork, utilizing P. H. Hammarskold as his architect. Hammarskold, a native of Sweden, was then working on the new statehouse in Columbia. The cast-ironwork, executed by German-born blacksmith Christopher Werner, includes palmetto and eagle designs in the end columns as well as acanthus and anthemion motifs popular in the late–Greek Revival period. In the late-nineteenth century, the house served as the residence of Mayor R. Goodwin Rhett. Supposedly Rhett entertained President William Howard Taft here during his visit in 1909, during which William Deas, the butler, introduced his now-famous she-crab soup.

117 BROAD STREET, LAURENS-RUTLEDGE HOUSE

Constructed circa 1760; altered circa 1885–90, 1935

Miller & Fullerton, architect-builders

Built in the Georgian style for James Laurens, brother of Henry Laurens, this house retains only a portion of its original eighteenth-century appearance. Nonetheless, it has long been celebrated due to its purchase in 1788 by Edward Rutledge, signer of the Declaration of Independence. The five-bay main block with a projecting pediment supported by console brackets and a steep pitched roof survives from the building's early construction as a Georgian double house. Greek Revival piazzas, added first to the east and later to the west end, survive, although the former was partially removed when a wing was added after 1885 by the Wagener family, who made other exterior and interior renovations. Frederick Wagener, who held one of Charleston's largest grocery companies (headquartered at *163 East Bay Street*), established the South Carolina West Indian Exposition and maintained this residence; he also used the eighteenth-century house at Lowndes Grove in the upper peninsula. When the house was remodeled again in 1935 it acquired its present Colonial Revival exterior.

Engraving of the Georgian style double house at 117 Broad Street as it appeared before 1880s alterations

119 BROAD STREET, MORTON WARING HOUSE

Constructed circa 1803; renovated circa 1890–1900

Built by the local factor Morton Waring in 1803, this structure originally stood as a large three-and-a-half-story, exposed brick Charleston single house. Waring sold the property, following severe financial reversals in 1811, to Mordecai Cohen. Cohen, who immigrated to Charleston from Poland as a peddler in the 1780s, rose to be a banker and merchant, and was considered to be the second-wealthiest man in South Carolina by 1830. However, Cohen, too, experienced financial losses, and he was forced to sell this property in 1844.

The house was owned in the late-nineteenth century by the Smith and Heyward families, who significantly altered the building with the addition of a marble veneer at the turn of the century. The principal three-bay facade now features marble quoining, marble console brackets over the first-floor windows, and a masked piazza, although the house retains its early-Neoclassical piazza door screen. In 1961 the Roman Catholic Diocese of Charleston purchased the house for office space.

122 BROAD STREET, CATHEDRAL OF ST. JOHN THE BAPTIST

Constructed circa 1890–1907; renovated 1980s; restored 1994–95

Patrick C. Keely and Decimus C. Barbot, architects

Although the cornerstone was laid for this stippled brownstone cathedral in 1890, it is actually the second such building to occupy the site. The Right Reverend John England was consecrated in St. Finbar's Cathedral in Cork, Ireland, and arrived to take up his duties over the diocese of the Carolinas and Georgia early in 1821. England purchased Charleston's favorite pleasure garden, the "New Vauxhall" gardens, shortly after his arrival and built a small wooden building during the planning of a larger cathedral. England did not live to see the completion by 1854 of the first large Gothic cathedral designed by the Brooklyn architect P. C. Keely, the leading architect of American Catholic churches of the mid-nineteenth century. Tradition holds that Keely studied under the great English Gothic Revivalist A. W. Pugin, architect of the Houses of Parliament. This influence appears in the decorated Gothic cathedral Keely completed in Charleston called St. John the Baptist and St. Finbar. With a nave of 54 feet in height, side aisles of 25 feet, and a tower and spire of 200 feet, this was the largest and most elaborate of Charleston's antebellum religious buildings.

With the loss of that structure in the fire of 1861 and a lack of funds due to the War Between the States, plans were developed for a nearly identical building by Keely during the episcopate of a former Confederate officer, the Right Reverend Henry B. Northrop. The cornerstone was laid in 1890 by Cardinal Gibbons of Baltimore. Due to funding problems and various delays, however, the present cathedral was not dedicated until April 1907. It stands slightly larger than the former building and is known only as St. John the Baptist; the planned spire for the 100-foot tower has never been built. On the interior, fourteen lancet arched Gothic windows depict the life of Christ, while the great rose window over the altar depicts the Last Supper (taken from Leonardo da Vinci) below the Baptism of Christ by John. The glazing was manufactured by the Franz Mayer Company of Munich and installed in 1907. The windows and interior plasterwork were splendidly restored in 1994–95. The front iron fence to the east, now a part of the cathedral property, is the sole remnant of the 1815 St. Andrew's Society Hall, burned in 1861.

The ruins of the original Cathedral of St. John the Baptist and St. Finbar, engraving, circa 1875

125 BROAD STREET, CHARLES ROBERT VALK HOUSE

Constructed 1886

Although the builder of this house was born in Connecticut in 1848, he spent much of his childhood in South Carolina and served in the Confederate army during the War Between the States. Starting in business as the superintendent of a fertilizer company, he organized a firm that grew to be known as Charleston Shipbuilding and

Dry Dock Company. Considered one of the chief exponents of Charleston's "New South" business elite, he completed this ambitious Tudor Revival style dwelling of Stoney Landing brick immediately after the earthquake of 1886. Tall stained glass windows and a second-story bay window ornament the front cross gable end topped by a closed gable with half-timbered decoration.

7 CHURCH STREET, CARRINGTON-CHENEY HOUSE

Constructed 1892; renovated with additions 1949

The Charleston preservationist Salley Carrington Cheney subdivided this lot from her parents' property at *2 Meeting Street* and renovated an existing servants' quarters and garage with the assistance of Charleston's preservation architect Albert Simons. The noted landscape architect Loutrel Briggs designed the garden, and the master ironworker Philip Simons completed the gates with the initials *S* and *C*, reflecting the owner of the address.

12 CHURCH STREET, DR. JOSEPH JOHNSON HOUSE

Constructed circa 1810; renovated circa 1920s, 1950s, 1992

This traditional single house has a large extension to the north and east. Dr. Joseph Johnson, intendant (mayor) of Charleston and president of the Medical Society of South Carolina, lived here shortly after the building's construction and later lived at *35 Church Street*. Even after numerous renovations, the house retains its original beaded cypress weatherboarding, several pairs of old paneled shutters, and an early-nineteenth-century fanlighted piazza door screen.

13 CHURCH STREET, THOMAS BALL HOUSE

Constructed before 1800; restored 1990–92

Standing on land owned in the early-eighteenth century by Landgrave Thomas Smith, one of the most powerful figures in colonial Charleston, most of the houses in this area of Church Street were built after the Revolution. The building at 13 Church shows a rare survival of a clipped gambrel or jerkin head roof, and its interior reflects late-Georgian, post-Revolutionary details with alterations made in the early-nineteenth century. Thomas Ball's executor's deed in 1820 describes the structure as a wooden house in need of repairs. The property was owned and rented out by Harriet Schutt, daughter of the builder of *51 East Bay Street*, and her husband, Robert T. Chisolm; they conveyed the property to the wealthy slave trader Thomas N. Gadsden in 1834. Gadsden lived here before moving to 116 Broad Street in the mid-1840s.

15 CHURCH STREET, SNOWDEN HOUSE

Constructed circa 1842; altered circa 1887–1888

This, the third dwelling to stand on the site, was occupied in the antebellum period by Dr. William Snowden and his wife Amarinthia Yates and was used as a Confederate hospital during the War Between the States. The Snowdens fled to Columbia when shells struck the house during the bombardment of Charleston in 1864. Mrs. Snowden, who had been chief fundraiser for the Calhoun monument before the war, returned here in 1865. It was in this house that the meetings leading to the formation of the Ladies' Memorial Association and The Confederate Home and College were held by Mrs. Snowden and her sister. The raised two-and-a-half-story, side-hall plan dwelling retains its original Flemish-bonded brickwork, entry door architrave, and double-tiered side piazzas. The present mansard roof was added during repairs following the earthquake of 1886.

19 CHURCH STREET, GEORGE WILLIAMS COACH HOUSE
Constructed 1875; rehabilitated 1940

Originally the coach house for George Williams's house on Meeting Street, now commonly known as the Calhoun Mansion, this structure was adapted to modern residential use in 1938 by Humphrey W. Chadbourne, a nationally known mining engineer, and his wife Margaret. The square, quoined building with hipped roof was modified with Georgian Revival style windows, an arched doorway, and a projecting pediment. The eastern section, along Church Street, of the enclosing brick wall is original, while the south and west walls are 1940s additions. The garden was designed by Loutrel Briggs in 1940.

20 CHURCH STREET, WILLIAM HOLMES HOUSE
Constructed circa 1809; restored mid-twentieth century

Prior to the building of the present house, this and the two parcels to the north were occupied by tenements built by Edward Fenwick, of Fenwick Hall Plantation. The adjacent tenements burned before 1785, leaving only the kitchen houses. This large single house was erected by 1809. The typical three-and-a-half-story Charleston single house, ornamented with stucco quoining and elaborate belt courses as well as a projecting pediment on the south side, still has an early-Neoclassical piazza door screen with a rectangular fanlight. As Holmes lived elsewhere, the 1809 directory lists James Ancrum as the resident on this property.

22 CHURCH STREET, DANIEL BROWN (SUNRISING) HOUSE

Constructed 1796; restored mid-twentieth century

A mariner, Daniel Brown, was the first to rebuild on the site of the Fenwick tenements, completing this three-story stuccoed house as his residence by 1796. Though largely original, it underwent certain renovations in the Greek Revival period. Its stucco belt coursing and fenestration nearly match the adjoining dwelling at *24 Church Street* completed by George Chisolm, a factor operating on Vanderhorst's Wharf, by 1800.

26 CHURCH STREET, JACKSON-WATT HOUSE

Constructed by 1794; altered circa 1840; partially restored 1961

James Watt, a grocer, completed the shell of a two-story house that Watt's predecessor, Charlotte Fenwick, daughter of Edward Fenwick, had inherited. After marrying continental officer Ebenezer Jackson and moving to Florida, she had sold the incomplete tenement to Watt. The three-story single house retains its basic form but includes significant alterations made in the Greek Revival period, including a parapeted gable framing a tripartite window. Its early natural stuccoed surface shows evidence of original scoring, early lime wash, and paint colors.

32 CHURCH STREET, LINDSAY-FOWLER HOUSE

Constructed 1804; various twentieth-century renovations

Robert Lindsay, builder

The dwelling at 32 Church Street, the oldest of three adjoining single houses, was built by Robert Lindsay, a joiner and lessee of the

property, in 1804. The simple two-bay, two-and-a-half-story dwelling retains its beaded weatherboarding and closed front gable. The taller single house at *34 Church*, to the north, was built before 1847 by James McBeth, a Civil War–period intendant (mayor), while the house at 30 Church Street was not built until the turn of the twentieth century.

33 CHURCH STREET, PETER TAMPLET HOUSE

Constructed before 1790; altered before 1920

This simple weatherboarded, two-story single house retains its original beaded siding on the piazza elevation. After a fire in the early-1900s a third story was removed, and several additional changes have been made to the structure. The form of this house bears an interesting relationship to the Richard Birnie House built a century later at *31 Church Street*.

35 CHURCH STREET, YOUNG-JOHNSON HOUSE

Constructed circa 1770; restored 1941

An early example of the Charleston single house, this three-story brick dwelling was built by Thomas Young shortly after he purchased the property in 1770 and represents a smaller, slightly more modest example of the dwelling he built at *30 Meeting Street* and sold to Col. Isaac Motte. Today the house is most noted as the former residence of Dr. Joseph Johnson, a prominent nineteenth-century Charlestonian who served as president of the city's branch of the second Bank of the United States, led South Carolina's Unionist Party during the nullification controversy, and wrote *Traditions of the American Revolution*. It was restored in the 1940s and owned by the sculptor Wilmer Hoffman.

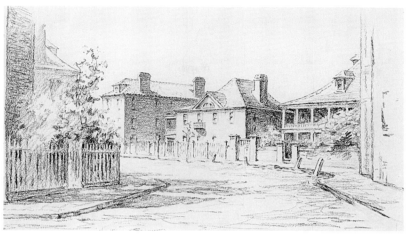

37 CHURCH STREET, GEORGE MATTHEWS HOUSE

Constructed circa 1743

The son of Anthony Matthews, one of Charleston's early prominent merchants, bought this property in 1743. Containing an asymmetrical interior plan, the house has later alterations, including the Federal period wrought-iron balcony and projecting pediment with lunette window.

38 CHURCH STREET, DR. VINCENT LE SEIGNEUR HOUSE

Constructed circa 1819; renovated circa 1900, 1980s

Dr. Vincent Le Seigneur, native of Normandy and refugee from Santo Domingo, purchased this lot in 1814 and completed this masonry single house circa 1819. The house remained untouched until the end of the nineteenth century, when the crenellated stair tower on the north wall was added by successive owners. Late-twentieth-century alterations include restoration of the kitchen house and extensive landscaping. The house and extensive dependencies were joined by 1900.

39 CHURCH STREET, GEORGE EVELEIGH HOUSE

Constructed 1743; renovated and restored early-twentieth century

Although this house is set back from the street and has an asymmetrically placed front door leading onto a front piazza, it originally had a center door leading to the larger of two front rooms. Front and rear piazzas appear on the 1795 plat of the property, indicating a feature usually added after the Revolution. Nonetheless, an account of the hurricane of 1752 refers to the destruction of brick columns on the front of the building, and closer bricks in the central aperture of the second-floor brickwork confirm the presence of an early piazza. The Eveleigh House is of the same floor plan as the Thomas Rose House at *59 Church Street*, built eight years earlier, if slightly smaller in scale. As in the Rose House, much of the original paneling remains, with similar arched cupboards or bowfats in the second-floor drawing room. Most of the original mantels were removed long ago. In the early-twentieth century mantels from the demolished Nathaniel Heyward House on East Bay Street were installed in the principal room and the two rear rooms on the first floor were combined to create a dining room. Of particular interest on the exterior are the brickwork and window openings with segmental arched heads.

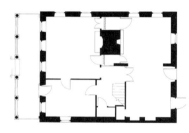

Measured plan of the first floor, George Eveleigh House, 39 Church Street

George Eveleigh was a prosperous deerskin trader in Charles Town when he purchased a lot lying across Vanderhorst Creek just outside the former city wall line. The creek was filled and is known today as Water Street, and with this filling Church Street was extended to White Point. Eveleigh sold the property about ten years later to John Bull, a wealthy planter in Prince William Parish. The Bull family later subdivided the rear of the lot facing Meeting Street, where they subsequently constructed *34 Meeting Street*. A later purchaser of 39 Church Street was the eighteenth-century chemist and naturalist Jean Louis Polony, a Santo Domingan refugee.

41 CHURCH STREET, ALBERT W. TODD HOUSE
Constructed 1909

This Colonial Revival style dwelling with Craftsman detailing and parged with a rough coating of stucco over wood lathe, known as spatterdash, was designed by its architect/owner to fit the attenuated lot. Todd's building (by tradition designed as the result of a wager) incorporates a uniquely linear floor plan.

43 CHURCH STREET JOHN ROSE HOUSE
Constructed circa 1769–75

The owner of Charleston's largest shipyard built this pre-Revolutionary Charleston single house. It retains its original weatherboarding as well as fine details such as paneled bases under its front windows, a compass-headed stair window on the north facade, and a unique egg and dart cornice mold below the roofline.

1 EAST BATTERY, LOUIS DESAUSSURE HOUSE
Constructed 1858–60; altered circa 1898; rehabilitated 1970s

The scion of a leading plantation family in Beaufort, Thomas Coffin, owned this lot, deeding it in 1858 to Louis deSaussure, who built this substantial three-story, late–Greek Revival style house with Italianate elements just before the War Between the States. Wartime photographs show the building with its current triple-tiered piazzas but with simpler window detailing. Before the war deSaussure and his neighbors seem to have joined in the construction of a lengthy coping wall with stuccoed piers and surmounting balustrade. The curved section in front of 1 East Battery and that before *5 East Battery* have survived. Bernard O'Neill, a wealthy wholesale grocer, bought the house in 1888 and added the cast-iron balconies and the window and door surrounds, as well as an elaborate pressed-metal entablature and balustrade (now removed). Owned briefly by Mrs. Robert E. Lee III (formerly Mary Middleton Pinckney, a native of Charleston), the house passed through several owners before becoming three condominiums, as it stands today.

5 EAST BATTERY, JOHN RAVENEL HOUSE
Constructed circa 1848

This house was built by the Ravenel family on one of the reclaimed marshland lots sold by the city in 1838. Though originally erected by John Ravenel, it passed a few years later to his son Dr. St. Julien Ravenel, the planter whose scientific efforts resulted in numerous contributions to his native region, including the design for the Confederate semisubmersible craft *Little David,* and as a pioneer in Charleston's postwar phosphate fertilizer industry. Ravenel was also considered the father of Charleston's artesian well system. His wife, Harriott Horry Rutledge Ravenel, wrote many books on Charleston history, including the classic *Charleston, The Place and the People* (1912). The Italianate style entablature and lintels were added when the house was rebuilt following the 1886 earthquake. The large dependency and garden to the south remain part of the property.

9 EAST BATTERY, ROBERT WILLIAM ROPER HOUSE
🛈 *Constructed 1838–39; addition late-nineteenth century; restored 1982–83*

The Robert William Roper House is one of Charleston's most monumental Greek Revival houses. With its prominent position on the southern edge of the Battery, its massive five-columned Ionic portico could be seen by approaching ships miles away. The city originally intended for this section of the Battery to be part of White Point Gardens, an L-shaped public park running from Atlantic to Church Streets, on East and South Battery. The financial panic of 1837 encouraged the city to sell the lands on the eastern side, predicting that they "will produce a beautiful row of ornamental buildings along the whole line of East Bay Battery." The income generated from the sale of these lots was used to finance the development of the southern section of the park, extending it westward to Meeting and later to King Street.

With the development of the park and the high retaining wall, the Battery became a social gathering place in Charleston. In April 1838 Robert William Roper purchased two lots along the Battery from the city for $8,200. For $1,439 he also acquired a triangular section of the lot which bounded his to the north and which Isaac Holmes had recently bought from the city. Roper's house on East Battery was grand in scale and execution, with possible design by Charles F. Reichardt. With narrow end facing the street, the colossal Ionic columns of the piazza stretch down the length of the lot. At the time of its construction, however, nothing stood between Roper's house and the harbor beyond. The house follows a side-hall, double-parlor plan but boasts a large west wing added by late-nineteenth-century owners. Original interior detailing includes classical imagery likely inspired by widely available pattern books.

Roper died of malaria in 1845. Post–Civil War purchasers, the Sieglings of the music emporium at *243 King Street*, lived here for a half century, selling to New Yorker Solomon Guggenheim in 1929. The current owner completed one of America's most notable restorations of a Greek Revival house in the early-1980s.

The Robert William Roper House, 9 East Battery, in the late-nineteenth century

Detail of the door at 13 East Battery

13 EAST BATTERY, WILLIAM RAVENEL HOUSE

Constructed circa 1845

A two-story portico with Tower of the Winds, Corinthian columns came down in the earthquake of 1886, leaving the front of this large house with an arcaded stucco base and a simple pedimented gable. The original builder, William Ravenel, owner of one of Charleston's major steamship lines and brother of John Ravenel of *5 East Battery*, completed this house by the mid-1840s. Held until the 1930s by the Ravenel family, who also owned Farmfield Plantation west of the Ashley River, the townhouse has been occupied by only two other families. An exceptionally large drawing room extends across the front of the building. The significant complex of rear dependencies survives.

Gate detail of 19 East Battery drawn by Simons and Lapham

19 EAST BATTERY, JULIUS M. VISANSKA HOUSE

Constructed 1920

Albert Simons, architect

This two-story, yellow brick house on a high foundation was designed for a prominent haberdasher by Charleston's leading restoration architect, Albert Simons. The house replaced the notable Federal style Holmes Mansion, which had been the first of the great Battery houses completed after the removal of Fort Mechanic following the War of 1812. The Holmes Mansion was wrecked in the hurricane of 1911 and was taken down shortly thereafter. Its lot had already been subdivided in the late-nineteenth century for the construction of *17 East Battery*. Simons's design reflects a curious mix of features, including corner brick quoining, Renaissance style loggia entry, and tripartite windows in the Greek Revival manner. Local tradition holds that Visanska asked Simons to design a house that resembled a mansion he admired in Atlanta. Charlestonians raised eyebrows at the expensive interior details including parquet floors and the costly yellow brick on the exterior. The residence was taken over by the navy in 1942, which used it for the duration of World War II. An 1896 weatherboarded residence to the east at *17 East Battery* was also dressed up in the early-twentieth century in the Colonial Revival style. This house has remained in the Mevers family since 1922.

21 EAST BATTERY, EDMONDSTON-ALSTON HOUSE
Constructed 1828; renovated 1838

This house was built in the Regency style by Charles Edmondston, a Scottish-born Charleston merchant, and remodeled by Charles Alston, a prominent rice planter, after he purchased the property in 1838. It reflects a modified Charleston single house plan with its front entry accessing a separate vestibule on East Battery. Alston added a third tier with Corinthian columns to the side piazzas, a cast-iron balcony, and a surmounting parapet with the Alston coat of arms. Although changes were made to the exterior to accommodate Greek Revival fashion, the use of the structure most likely remained the same. Business visitors were received on the first floor, renovated in the Greek Revival manner by the Alstons; the drawing rooms on the second floor, where piazza doors could be thrown open to catch sea breezes or provide a backdrop for formal events, functioned as the family's social spaces and retain late-Federal or Regency style decoration. The two small rooms behind the drawing rooms served as separate withdrawing spaces for men and women, and the family bedrooms oc-

Detail of S. Barnard's View along East Battery Charleston, *1831, showing 21 East Battery before Charles Alston's exterior alterations*

cupied the third floor. A substantial kitchen dependency is attached to the rear of the dwelling, while a separate stable and slave quarters remain at the back of the lot. Descending through Alston's daughter Susan Pringle Alston to her favorite cousin, the historian Henry Augustus Middleton Smith, the property and many of its furnishings have remained in the family. The house is currently shown as a museum administered by Middleton Place Foundation.

25 EAST BATTERY, CHARLES DRAYTON HOUSE

Constructed 1883–86; rehabilitated early 1970s

Measured elevation of the tack house, 25 East Battery

This house boasts possibly the finest Eastlake detailing in Charleston and has a collection of antebellum dependencies to the rear. Prior to the Civil War, a significant Greek Revival house, with outbuildings, stood on the property. It was shelled during the war, and its ruins stood abandoned for almost two decades. The current dwelling was built by Charles Drayton, of the family of Drayton Hall Plantation, between 1883 and 1886 with a fortune accumulated in the postwar phosphate industry. Although tradition claims that Charles built the house, the deed records his wife, Eliza Drayton, as the owner of the property.

The antebellum use of the rear structure along Atlantic Street is uncertain, though the arch at the western end suggests a carriage entrance to the yard from the side street. This access is quite unlike the primary street access employed by most of Charleston's nineteenth-century lots. The smaller building in the rear yard was likely a tack house that fronted the row of stables running behind the Atlantic Street lots. Some woodwork, such as the balcony on the kitchen house and the doors to the stables, date to the 1883–86 construction of the main house.

29 EAST BATTERY, PORCHER-SIMONDS HOUSE

Constructed circa 1856; altered 1890s, 1940s; rehabilitated 1983

Cotton broker Francis Porcher built this house a few years before the War Between the States in the same Greek Revival style as neighboring dwellings. John C. Simonds, son of the builder of the Villa Margharita at *4 South Battery*, renovated the house in a mix of Beaux Arts Classicism and Renaissance Revival detailing after 1894 with paired columns on the square portico and a double- tiered semicircular front piazza. All of the side piazzas were enclosed during the Second World War, when the house was used by the U.S. Office of Naval Intelligence; John F. Kennedy occupied one of the offices. Once a single family dwelling, this house was converted into three condominiums in 1983.

31 EAST BATTERY, HENRY PORTER WILLIAMS HOUSE

Constructed circa 1837; renovated 1903

When Henry Porter Williams was given the choice between this home and his father's, the Calhoun Mansion on Meeting Street, he chose this dwelling. Williams remodeled the house in 1903, raised the structure three feet above ground level, and stuccoed the exterior. Also during the renovation, part of the rear piazza was enclosed and the kitchen dependency was connected to the main house.

0 GIBBES STREET

Constructed circa 1890; rehabilitated with additions 1968

The roof and cupola retain the original form of this large stable and carriage house that formerly served a large Victorian dwelling to the east that faced Legare Street. It was pulled down in the 1960s. In 1968 this dependency was saved and adapted as a new residence with a contemporary front addition and garden.

2 GIBBES STREET, ROBERT FENWICK GILES HOUSE

Constructed circa 1850; altered 1885

This two-and-a-half-story, side-hall-plan house retains the customary closed front gable and the double-tiered piazzas with Tuscan columns usually associated with Charleston's Greek Revival period. A subsequent owner, William P. Holmes, applied Victorian detailing in 1885. Most of these changes have been removed, although a Neoclassical revival door surround has been added.

5 GIBBES STREET, MANIGAULT-SINKLER HOUSE

Constructed circa 1872; altered circa 1910–20

A member of the Manigault family, then owners of 6 *Gibbes Street*, completed this two-and-a-half-story, side-hall plan dwelling, which has a mix of Greek Revival and Italianate details. A bracketed overhang above the entry door and one-story bay window ornament the closed gabled front facade. The west piazzas were removed in the early-twentieth century when the Huger-Sinkler family, later owners, bought their first automobile and needed access to the rear of the lot.

6 GIBBES STREET, PARKER-DRAYTON HOUSE

Constructed circa 1806; altered 1820s

Isaac Parker, a planter and brickyard owner, built this substantial Neoclassical villa in 1806. When it was sold in 1820 to Col. William Drayton, the new owner extended the building to the east and west and probably added the large bowed front piazzas. Drayton moved his family to Philadelphia in 1837, and Charles Manigault, son of the architect Gabriel Manigault, purchased the house. Manigault filled the house with art collected in Europe as well as family heirlooms. His son Louis Manigault became a distinguished scientist and professor at the College of Charleston. Before the filling of the western edge of the peninsula, the windows of the house looked out over the marshes to the Ashley River.

1 KING STREET, FORT SUMTER HOUSE

Constructed 1923; rehabilitated mid-1970s

G. Lloyd Preacher, architect

Completed in 1923 as the city's first modern hotel, the Fort Sumter Hotel's Spanish Colonial design alarmed the city's fledgling preservation community. Rising six stories above a ground lobby floor, the hotel represented burgeoning winter tourism in the city and was viewed as representative of "progressive modern architecture" that could threaten the character of Charleston's streetscapes. The Fort Sumter Hotel closed in 1974, a few years before the tourist boat docks were removed from this section of the Battery. Known today as the Fort Sumter House, the building contains condominiums.

The Fort Sumter Hotel and the nearby boat dock in the 1920s

8 KING STREET, WILLIAM HOLMES HOUSE

Constructed circa 1791; renovated 1850s

William Holmes spent his youth in the house of his stepfather, John Edwards, at *15 Meeting Street*. In 1784 Holmes purchased this lot, apparently vacant, and built on it shortly after his marriage to his stepsister, Margaret Edwards. After brief ownership by Anne Peronneau, kinswoman of the "martyred" patriot Isaac Hayne and of the heroine Rebecca Motte, occupant of the Miles Brewton House at *27 King Street*, Nathaniel Ingraham acquired the property in 1799.

The Ingrahams may have added the double-tiered piazza and the Ionic-columned architrave of the piazza screen, as well as particularly exuberant composition work in the interior. After 1851 a new owner, the Reverend John Forrest, minister of First Scots Presbyterian Church, made minor changes. The relative purity of the Holmes House contrasts with the single house at *10 King Street*, with its later siding and early-twentieth-century side portico.

16–24 KING STREET

Constructed nineteenth century; variously altered twentieth century

This interesting collection of single houses reflects a typical nineteenth-century Charleston streetscape. While some of the structures date from the early-nineteenth century, the John Laurens North House (24 King Street) predates the 1820s. Some late-nineteenth-century alterations, such as the mansard roof on 22 King Street, reflect changes over time. Even the wrought-iron balconies that adorn the facade of 24 King Street provide insight to the evolutionary changes of a streetscape. Although their craftsmanship might date them to the construction of the house, this balcony and its likeness across the street on the mid-eighteenth-century dwelling at 23 King Street were moved here from the facade of *56–58 Broad Street.*

19 KING STREET, THOMAS LAMBOLL HOUSE
Constructed 1735–39; altered 1840–50

Tradition holds that this Charleston single house preceded the fire of 1740. Serving as the residence of merchant and colonial leader Thomas Lamboll and his botanist wife, Elizabeth, the original property stretched south to White Point gardens. After changes were made reflecting the Greek Revival period, with fluted Doric-columned piazzas and contemporary window surrounds, the house was shifted by the contractor Patrick O'Donnell in 1849 to make way for the widening of Lamboll Street. O'Donnell lived here while supervising the construction of his house to the north.

21 KING STREET, PATRICK O'DONNELL HOUSE
Constructed 1852–70; restored late-1980s

A contractor who moved to Charleston from his native Galway, Ireland, gained sufficient fortune by the 1850s to amalgamate several lots and begin construction of the city's largest Italianate style house. Recent evidence indicates that Patrick O'Donnell failed to complete the house until after 1865, thus giving some reality to the appellation "O'Donnell's Folly" for the building. During author Josephine Pinckney's ownership, 1907–1937, the Poetry Society and the Society for the Preservation of Spirituals were organized here.

The monumental three-story masonry building rises above a rusticated stucco ground floor. A Greek Revival architrave with arched doors leads to the stair hall, while a central pavilion rises to an open, modillioned gable with triple-tiered piazzas on the south. Arched window hoods, supported by console brackets and including shell motifs, decorate the second story. In its recent restoration the owner returned a period paint scheme to the building.

27 KING STREET, MILES BREWTON HOUSE AND OUTBUILDINGS

L *Constructed circa 1769; altered circa 1820s, 1840s; restored 1988–92*

Richard Moncrieff, contractor; Ezra Waite, John Lord, Thomas Woodin, and others, woodworkers

Chevaux-de-frise over the front iron fence, 27 King Street

East dependency of 27 King Street, engraving by Alice Ravenel Huger Smith, circa 1911

This house is considered the finest double-pile house in Charleston and with its outbuildings constitutes the most complete Georgian town house complex surviving in America. Miles Brewton, a wealthy slave trader and merchant, inherited the land on which the house was built from his prosperous grandfather and father. Although Ezra Waite claimed correctly to have performed much of the interior carving, recent research has indicated the hands of at least two others in the upstairs drawing (dining) room, including John Lord and Thomas Woodin, master carvers who had immigrated to Charleston from London. Much has been made in recent years of the use of pattern books in the design of the house and of the carving of the woodwork on the exterior and interior. In 1773 Josiah Quincy of Boston visited Miles Brewton and wrote enthusiastically in his diary:

> *Dined with considerable company at Miles Brewton, Esqr's, a gentleman of very large fortune: a most superb house said to have cost him 8,000 of sterling. The grandest hall I ever beheld, azure blue satin window curtains, rich blue paper with gilt, mashee borders, most elegant pictures, excessive grand and costly looking glasses, etc.*

The current owners have recently completed a major new restoration of the building. The original line of outbuildings on the northern edge of the property is relatively intact. The first portion consists of a kitchen, laundry, and carriage house built in 1769. The facade of the carriage house was remodeled at the time of other modifications by the Pringles (in Gothic Revival style) in the 1840s. Immediately behind the kitchen lies the cistern and an arcade with stables and storerooms leading to a substantial brick, two-story structure containing slave quarters and dating from about 1820. Another arcade stretches west from the quarters to an eighteenth-century building used originally as either a dairy, privy, or garden folly. These outbuildings relate exclusively to a paved courtyard and the cellar of the house and are separated from the garden by a brick coping and wooden fence.

30 KING STREET, ROBERT HAYNE HOUSE

Constructed before 1775; renovated with additions 1820, 1890

Gen. Robert Hayne built the northern portion of this two-and-a-half-story wood dwelling before the American Revolution. Hayne's son Robert Y. Hayne served as a governor of the state and as the mayor of Charleston. In keeping with Victorian construction on adjacent Ladson Street, the house evolved to its current form by 1890.

33 KING STREET, JOHN FICKEN TENEMENT

Constructed circa 1906

The John Ficken tenement at 33 King Street and the Buist residence at 37 King Street

A wealthy former mayor of Charleston built this house with its side-hall plan and Italianate detailing as an investment property. It took the place of a small brick store and a wooden dwelling, both of the antebellum period. The Buist family built the more substantial house next door at *37 King Street* in the Colonial Revival style.

41 KING STREET, JOHN PRUE HOUSE

Constructed circa 1746; partially restored with addition 1930s; restored 1995–97

This stuccoed brick dwelling is constructed on the northern portion of three lots acquired by Miles Brewton I in 1732. This portion of the property was inherited by the elder Brewton's daughter, Rebecca Roche, who in turn sold it to John Prue, a successful Charleston house carpenter. Prue probably built the present house with his own workmen in 1746. In his will, probated in 1773, Prue referred to himself as a "Cabinet Maker" and directed his executors to "sell and dispose of the Wooden and Brick Work of all that my Working Shop constructed and built in the yard of my massuage where I now live in Charles Town aforesaid as also all my Carpenters Joiners and Working Tools." Prue's holdings were apparently fairly extensive, as his will mentions other real estate in Charleston and a plantation on Charleston Neck. Upon the death of Prue's widow without surviving issue, the property was devised to the College of Charleston and sold for the benefit of the college. In the early-nineteenth century the southern portion of Prue's property was subdivided. The front room on the first floor contains an important carved mantel and overmantel dating from construction. The rear dependency, built as the kitchen and laundry, has most of its original asymmetrical fenestration. The dependency was joined to the main house with a hyphen addition in the 1930s.

The two-story, stucco single house to the south at *39 King Street* stands on property originally incorporated into this parcel. Richard Yeadon, an antebellum newspaper editor and philanthropist, probably built this house in 1847 incorporating a portion of a 1730s dwelling. It lost its third story as a result of the earthquake of 1886.

Measured plan of the first floor, John Prue House, 41 King Street

46 KING STREET, WALTER WEBB STORE

Constructed circa 1851

Walter Webb, a botanist, florist, and garden designer, purchased this lot "with a wooden building thereon" in 1851 and shortly thereafter began the construction of 46 King Street as his shop and residence. Unlike the earlier building at *44 King Street*, which stood on its site by 1794, Webb built his dwelling with the long facade parallel to the street, a less typical site arrangement in Charleston.

50–52 KING STREET, JOHN COWAN AND EDGAR WELLS HOUSES

Constructed 1729–30; restored mid-twentieth century

These two houses of similar fenestration are among the earliest datable dwellings outside the former walled city and are precursors of the standard Charleston single house. The original floor plan of the Wells House is uncertain, but John Cowan's dwelling is of a two-room "hall-parlor" plan with a staircase rising along the rear wall of the hall.

54 KING STREET, JAMES BROWN HOUSE

Constructed between 1768 and 1777; renovated with addition 1994

James Brown, a carpenter, erected this three-story single house sometime after he purchased the property in 1768 and sold the land for a significantly increased price nine years later. The detailing of the main house supports this eighteenth-century construction date, although the piazza appears to postdate the construction of the house by several decades. Recent renovations and repairs have included a new hyphen addition joining the main house and the rear dependency.

55 KING STREET, GRIMKÉ-FRASER TENEMENTS

Constructed circa 1762

Originally built as a double tenement by the jeweler Frederick Grimké, this property was inherited in the late-eighteenth century by his grandson, Charles Fraser. Fraser, Charleston's most noted early miniaturist, painted likenesses of more than 500 of Charleston's elite during his long career. The two-and-a-half-story Flemish bonded brick dwelling was converted to a single family residence in the mid-twentieth century, but a fire wall is still visible through the slate hipped roof.

71 KING STREET,
FORT SUMTER FILLING STATION

Constructed 1930s

This late-Craftsman style gasoline station until recently was one of only a few businesses remaining in the "South of Broad" neighborhood. Its stucco has a spatterdash finish characteristic of the few peninsular Charleston buildings built in variants of the Craftsman style after World War I.

71 King Street as the Fort Sumter Filling Station, 1994

75 KING STREET,
WILLIAM ELLIOTT HOUSE

Constructed before 1739; restored and renovated early-1950s, mid-1980s

William Elliott, whose distinguished family began here as a "brotherhood of builders," appears to have had this three-and-a-half-story house constructed sometime before 1740. The less regular design and floor plan of the structure are common attributes of earlier eighteenth-century construction. One of the oldest surviving Charleston single houses, the building retains much of its interior woodwork. A shop door in the center of the front elevation was converted to a window more than a century ago. Mentioned in Elliott's 1765 will, the house was then used as Mary Stokes's boarding school.

View of the William Elliott House, 75 King Street, looking north, 1950

79 KING STREET,
CAPT. FRANCIS BAKER HOUSE

Constructed circa 1747–49; altered 1875; restored 1935, late-1980s

The merchant Francis Baker built this small, two-and-a-half-story stuccoed brick single house after purchasing the lot from the vintner Elias Hancock before Baker's death in 1749. His will specified that his lot on King Street be "built upon." The house was converted to a dry goods store in the nineteenth century and first restored in 1935. The brick, gable-end structure next door at *77 King Street* may have served Baker as a shop, and the rear stucco dwelling may have been a kitchen and slave quarters. Both of these buildings had extensive alterations in the twentieth century.

80 KING STREET, MAURICE SIMONS HOUSE

Constructed circa 1782; variously restored and renovated twentieth century

A grandson of the French Huguenot immigrant who established Middleburg Plantation on the Cooper River completed this diminutive two-and-a-half-story Charleston single house just after the American Revolution. Though it retains its original weatherboarding, nine-over-nine windows, and even some of its shutters, the house has gone through numerous renovations. Simons lost much of his property in the Revolution. Shortly after building this house, he was killed in a duel.

82 KING STREET, ROBERT HAIG HOUSE

Constructed circa 1786; restored 1930s, 1990

Building contractors Robert Haig and Alexander Don completed this beaded weatherboard single house by the latter months of 1787 on land purchased from the larger lot to the north owned by George Ross, a Scottish tin merchant. A piazza was first added to the building in 1815 and replaced many years later by the two-story Neoclassical Revival style portico.

84 KING STREET, GEORGE ROSS HOUSE

Constructed circa 1785; renovated 1980

Strikingly different from the smaller eighteenth-century structures that line this section of King Street, the dwelling of tinsmith George Ross at 84 King represents the large-scale construction in Charleston of the post-Revolutionary economic boom. Stylistically this building results from the transition between the Georgian and Federal periods in the late-eighteenth century. The earthquake of 1886 destroyed all of the existing dependencies on the site and damaged the exterior masonry walls of the main house. In 1989 Hurricane Hugo damaged the roof as well as the stucco work.

85 KING STREET, MARX COHEN HOUSE

Constructed circa 1844; renovated 1992–93

The son of the first Mordecai Cohen, himself an Ashley River planter, built this two-and-a-half-story masonry single house on a Grand Modell lot formerly occupied by a small wooden house. Marx Cohen Jr., a distinguished Confederate officer, was killed by a Union artillery shell during the battle of Bentonville, North Carolina.

98 KING STREET, JOHN VAUN HOUSE

Constructed before 1840

John Vaun, a local carpenter, leased this lot from the Huguenot Church and built this two-and-a-half-story brick single house. It is typical of others along King Street that were built well into the nineteenth century without piazzas.

2 LADSON STREET, JOHN DRAYTON HOUSE

Constructed after 1746; altered circa 1813, 1900

Presumably constructed by planter John Drayton, builder of nearby Drayton Hall, this dwelling reaffirms Drayton's interest

Mid-nineteenth-century photo of 2 Ladson Street

in Palladian design and symmetrical architectural space. This dwelling maintains a floor plan that includes four-over-four rooms separated by a central hall and stair hall. The house has been remodeled twice: once prior to 1813 when the bowed expansion was added to the west end of the house; and again at the turn of this century when the shallow pediment and the rear wing were added in the spirit of the Colonial Revival movement. A brick dependency survives to the northeast.

9 LADSON STREET, W. M. WALLACE HOUSE

Constructed circa 1900–10; altered 1937

Rutledge Holmes, architect

This structure was originally built in the Queen Anne style and was designed by architect Rutledge Holmes in much the same manner as *7 Ladson Street*, built in the same decade by Mary Kinloch. A new owner removed the bay windows and tower and modified the house in the Colonial Revival style in 1937. The square front porch was removed, and the present semicircular portico framing a Neoclassical Revival style door was added. The house at *5 Ladson Street*, built in 1894 by James Hemphill, was the earliest of what originally constituted three Queen Anne/Colonial Revival style houses on the south side of Ladson Street.

6 LAMBOLL STREET, REBECCA ROSE HOUSE

Constructed circa 1788–90; altered midnineteenth century

Rebecca Rose, the widow of an Ashley River planter, inherited this land bordering Lamboll Street, then called Smith's Lane. The essential form of this wooden single house was altered in 1830 in the

Greek Revival style. The house also boasts piazzas on both the east and west sides and a parapeted flat roof reflecting the mid-nineteenth-century alterations.

8 LAMBOLL STREET, DRENNIS WHITNEY TENEMENT

Constructed circa 1840; rehabilitated late-1980s

This double tenement, built by a family of bakers prior to the Civil War, once contained an open passage on the first floor that clearly separated the two dwellings. On the second floor a party wall delineates the break between the units. Although the term *tenement* may have negative connotations in the twentieth century, in the nineteenth century it was common for the working class to rent space in such structures. Several dwellings like this were constructed in Ansonborough after the fire of 1838 and can still be seen today.

14 LAMBOLL STREET, PATRICK O'DONNELL TENEMENT

Constructed circa 1850–60

This eclectic two-story dwelling with square columned portico and Italianate/late–Greek Revival style window and door surrounds was probably completed before 1860 by the prolific builder Patrick O'Donnell. It contrasts sharply with the simplicity of the tall three-story single house at *18 Lamboll Street* built in 1807 for Josiah Taylor.

22 LAMBOLL STREET, BOHUN BAKER HOUSE

Constructed circa 1820; renovated circa 1850, 1983

Although begun as a Charleston single house, this tall Federal period dwelling was renovated in 1850 with front-facing, triple-tiered piazzas. The building served as the rectory for St. Michael's Church from 1895 to 1927.

23 LAMBOLL STREET, POYAS-EDWARDS HOUSE

Constructed circa 1837–45

A member of a family of wealthy ship-builders and merchants built this two-and-a-half-story single house as an investment before he sold it to Mrs. Edward H. Edwards in 1845. The Greek Revival detailing of its piazza and entry architrave confirm its date of construction.

25 LAMBOLL STREET, WARING HOUSE

Constructed circa 1912; partially restored 1992

Todd and Benson, architects

A splendid example of the Colonial Revival style in Charleston, this dwelling incorporates many of the elements of American colonial architecture in its twentieth-century design. Ionic-order detailing in the engaged portico on the front facade along with the Neoclassical fanlighted door and the surmounting lunette in the pediment reflect the mix of earlier styles characteristic of the best of this house style. Thomas R. Waring, editor of the *Evening Post*, built this house on a lot inherited by his wife Laura Witte Waring, the daughter of the real estate baron, German consul, and banker Charles O. Witte. An earlier house, probably dating to 1815, was pulled down, and the surviving specifications note that framing materials should be saved and reused.

27 LAMBOLL STREET, RICHARD REYNOLDS HOUSE

Constructed before 1851; renovated and partially restored 1995

Richard F. Reynolds purchased this residence in March 1851. Reynolds owned the firm of Reynolds and Company, which manufactured carriages in Charleston. He sold the property to Thomas Savage Heyward, an auctioneer, in 1857. Elizabeth Allston Pringle described coming here to the "first big dance" held in Charleston after the Civil War and noted, "I went to the party and had a grand time, no refreshments but water, but a beautifully waxed floor, a great big cool room, that is, two opening into each other with folding doors, and a great wide piazza all round outside to walk in after dancing." In November 1869 the house was sold at a sheriff's sale to Charles O. Witte. At the turn of the century Mrs. W. S. Coates operated a boardinghouse in the building. The structure became Melrose Apartments in the 1930s and during the 1940s continued as an apartment building, with tenants including the president of the Atlantic Lime Corporation, the vice president of the Standard Fertilizer Company, and a local architect with the firm of Halsey and Cummings.

1 LEGARE STREET, EDWARD BLAKE HOUSE

Constructed circa 1760–70; moved, altered 1870s

This two-and-a-half-story wood Charleston single house was moved, supposedly rolled on palmetto logs, to its present location in 1873 from a nearby lot. The original owner, Edward Blake, a Revolutionary patriot and commissioner of the South Carolina navy, was captured by the British after the fall of Charleston and imprisoned along with other southern patriots in the fortress at St. Augustine. Although retaining its original roofline, the house has undergone substantial alterations, including the addition of its present nineteenth-century piazza. An eighteenth-century Bermuda stone wall survives on the south boundary of the lot.

4 LEGARE STREET, KINCAID'S WESTERN TENEMENT

Constructed circa 1777; altered circa 1788–1800; restored 1970s

George Kincaid, one of the original developers of the Legare Street area in the 1770s, built a double tenement on filled marshland in 1777. Later acquired by the wealthy English merchant and landowner William Hopton as an investment, the house was devised to his daughter Sarah in 1785. Miss Hopton sold the property shortly before her marriage to Nathaniel Russell. The westernmost dwelling retains more of its early character and still has original full paneling in its principal rooms. Late-eighteenth-century alterations include gib doors and wrought-iron balconies on the second-floor Lamboll Street elevation. Piazzas added in the early-twentieth century were removed in the 1970s. The eastern tenement at *28 Lamboll Street* was heavily altered in the late-nineteenth and early-twentieth centuries with a piazza addition and the installation of decorative, pedimented window hoods. The dense character of this block, especially the use of the double tenement form, contrasts with the more spacious quality of lot layouts northward along Legare Street.

7 LEGARE STREET, HENRY LAURENS HOUSE

Constructed circa 1887

Built by a descendant of the Charlestonian of the same name, who served as the president of the Continental Congress, the house on this site replaced a substantial masonry building occupied in the antebellum period by Martha Laurens Roper, widow of the builder of *9 East Battery*. After the earthquake the building was considered too damaged to be repaired, and Laurens built a new house on the old masonry foundation, using high-grade heart pine lumber. When complete the building stood two and a half stories tall with an unusual closed gambrel or modified mansard roof, with mansard overhangs surmounting both its central dormer and its front door. In the mid-1930s Dr. and Mrs. Joseph I. Waring acquired the house and changed it to a mix of Georgian and Neoclassical styles. Raising the roof by one story to a pedimented gable, he added pedimented window heads over the first- and second-story windows and a Neoclassical style fanlight over the front door, in addition to many other changes. Dr. Waring was one of South Carolina's leading historians, particularly expert on its early medical history, writing the book *A History of Medicine in South Carolina*. The antebellum house to the south at *5 Legare Street*, owned in the late-nineteenth century by the Jervey family, received severe damage in the earthquake as well. An inspector noted about its condition, "Rebuild east wall from ground." A wooden Victorian front added in 1887 was removed nearly 100 years later in the rehabilitation of this structure as three condominiums.

8 LEGARE STREET, CLELAND KINLOCH HUGER HOUSE

Constructed circa 1857; restored late 1980s

Patrick O'Donnell, contractor

The contractor Patrick O'Donnell, owner-builder of the nearby house at *21 King Street*, supervised the construction of this imposing Italianate style dwelling. The house is enclosed by substantial stucco walls. Ironwork lyre gates open onto a marble-tiled walk that approaches a projecting tower entry with an arched door architrave. Retaining its unpainted stucco finish, the house boasts red sandstone sills and window lintels, corner quoining, and a deep entablature with a dentiled cornice.

A two-story piazza on the south stands on square stucco columns. In the early-twentieth century the property became the residence of Burnet Rhett Maybank, successively mayor of Charleston, governor of South Carolina, and a United States senator. Retaining many of its original features, the interior boasts much original gilt paint on its cornice moldings and many original gas lighting fixtures restored by the present owners. The Huger House and its similarly styled neighbor to the north, *10 Legare Street*, were both constructed on lots subdivided in the 1850s from the pre-Revolutionary Miles Brewton property to the east, the houses replacing the original garden temple. O'Donnell also constructed the latter building for Edward North Thurston. In 1953 the extensive kitchen house and quarters at 10 ½ Legare Street was subdivided and renovated as a substantial separate residence.

9 LEGARE STREET, HARTH-MACBETH HOUSE

Constructed circa 1817–25; renovated early-1900s

William Harth built 9 Legare Street as a tenement. It at different times became the home of Charles Macbeth, Charleston's Civil War mayor, and William H. Brawley, U.S. district judge. The building was originally constructed as a large single house of three and a half stories on a high English basement, and nineteenth-century maps show double tiers of piazzas extending along the south elevation. By the early-twentieth century the front portions of the piazzas were enclosed and double-tiered bay windows had been added on the south matching a polygonal bay addition near the southwest corner of the dwelling. Pedimented window heads and other details were added as well. A two-story kitchen dependency now accessed from Gibbes Street stretches along the north elevation.

14 LEGARE STREET, SIMMONS-EDWARDS HOUSE

🅛 *Constructed circa 1800; present garden 1950; variously altered twentieth century*

Francis Simmons, a Johns Island planter, constructed this dwelling as his town house in about 1800. It is one of a group of masonry, Neoclassical single houses of this decade (including *18 Meeting Street* and *51 East Bay*) that are related in scale, fenestration, exterior brickwork, marble detailing, wood trim profiles, and interior plasterwork. Simmons also owned an earlier wooden house on the site of the present garden. At his death in 1814, his appraisers completed a room-by-room inventory listing furniture in "the back room on the first or ground floor," "the first room on the first floor" (the dining room), the "Passage way of the lst floor," "the Drawing Room on the 2nd. Floor," the "Passage on the 2d. floor," "the chamber opposite the drawing on the 2nd Floor or drawing room chamber," "the small room on the 2nd floor of the Drawing room chamber," "the Back chamber on the 3rd. Floor," "the front room on the 3rd. floor," and "the back Garret."

The large brick gates with decorative wrought-iron panels were installed during the ownership of George Edwards, who acquired the house in 1816, and bear his initials. The brickwork is one of several examples in Charleston of true English tuckpointing with the mortar tinted red to straighten visual lines of the irregularly shaped bricks and a white lime mortar joint added within a recess in the tinted mortar. The stone pineapple finials dating from the Edwardses' occupancy were carved to resemble Italian pinecones. Although said to have been carved in Italy, they may be the work of an Italian mason working in Philadelphia, as it is known that Charlestonians

Pineapple gates, circa 1816–1820, Simmons-Edwards House, 14 Legare Street

were ordering marble work from Philadelphia in this period.

The original two-story kitchen building and one-and-a-half-story carriage house survive, the former joined to the main house by a series of late-nineteenth-century hyphens. The plan of the nineteenth-century garden is unknown, but the owners of the 1950s engaged Umberto Innocenti to design the current formalistic garden at the rear of the site, reusing the stone posts with spherical finials and the hexagonal summerhouse already in the garden.

15 LEGARE STREET, JOHN FULLERTON HOUSE

Constructed circa 1772; restored 1985, 1990–91

This structure stands as one of fewer than seventy-five dwellings that remain in Charleston from the pre-Revolutionary period. The Scottish carpenter and joiner John Fullerton, responsible for a number of noteworthy Charleston buildings, erected this dwelling shortly after he acquired the land from William Gibbes in 1772. Perhaps built as a speculative venture, the house was erected on what was then a sandy street with few buildings. Initially detached, the two-story dependency functioned as a kitchen on the first floor and servants' quarters on the second. British officers under Cornwallis were quartered on the property during the Revolutionary War. A two-story Neoclassical piazza was added to the west and south facades of the main house around 1800, and a Victorian addition was added around 1875. The grounds were landscaped to add a formal garden in 1985.

16 LEGARE STREET, AMARINTHEA ELLIOTT HOUSE

Constructed 1789–90; restored 1948; restored with addition 1987

John Morrison and Hume Greenhill, builders

This wooden residence constructed by Miss Amarinthea Elliott about 1790 owns the distinction of being the first to be specified in its contract as a "single house." A deed between Miss Elliott, first owner of the house, and John Morrison and Hume Greenhill, builders, dated 1789, offers explicit detail about the plans for construction of a single house and dependencies.

All of the elements that combine to create a single house (two rooms per floor; central stair hall; constructed at the front of the lot; one fireplace in each room; and rear dependencies constructed contiguously behind, along with the later additions of piazzas) are present. Thus, Charleston's pre-eminent architectural form, the single house, was clearly delineated as a building tradition by the end of the eighteenth century. The finely crafted building lost its dependencies many years ago and now boasts a modern rear wing which looks out onto an extensive early-twentieth-century garden.

Detail from the building contract of Amarinthea Elliott with Morrison and Greenhill, August 13, 1789

17 LEGARE STREET, ANTHONY TOOMER HOUSE

Constructed circa 1797; additions circa 1840

Anthony Toomer, a Revolutionary War veteran and master builder, erected this dwelling as a tenement investment soon after acquiring a 40-by-296-foot lot on Legare Street in 1796. First containing a simple two-bay house with beaded weatherboarding and a low pitched roof at a substantial distance from the street line, the property was described in an 1811 advertisement as having "a two story wooden dwelling house, brick kitchen, etc. thereon."

Apparently Thomas F. Purse added a two-story masonry addition to the front of the house, as well as a one-story piazza with a Greek Revival transomed screen. Most of the interior of the original house, including Neoclassical wainscoting, mantel, and staircase, remain.

18 LEGARE STREET, GEORGE LUSHER HOUSE
Constructed circa 1810; renovated 1928

Although often cited as indicative of West Indian architectural tradition, the Lusher House is simply a small Federal style Charleston single house with a bellcast hipped roof and wrapping piazzas, set back on the street, with a front garden space in the early tradition of this area. Hipped dormers project from the slate roof with tile ridge caps, and two interior chimneys rise above the north wall with stucco banding, corbeled caps, and Gothic arched hoods. Doorways with original semicircular fanlights ornament the front facade, but in single house fashion, the principal entry stands on the south elevation. In 1928 the eastern end of the piazza on the second-floor level was enclosed with a frame addition, while at the first-floor level the piazza was screened in. Lusher served as the attorney for the previous owner of the lot. His wife, Sarah, was the sister of the noted architect Robert Mills.

21 LEGARE STREET, WILLIAM GATEWOOD HOUSE
Constructed circa 1843

Virginia-born William Gatewood, an important factor or export agent of sea-island cotton and rice, built this imposing structure. Ornamented by brownstone details on the ground story and marble belt coursing and window architraves on the second, this brick facade with red-dyed mortar utilizes elements of Classical Revival and Greek Revival design. Piazzas, masked from the street by a fenestrated brick wall, present an imposing facade to the public way, thereby insuring privacy to the inhabitants as well as balancing the recessed stair tower on the other side. Large Tuscan columns support the piazzas, with paneled plinth bases on the second story matching the marble plinths under the window architraves. The drive to the north, formerly known as Sass's Alley, provided access to the brick kitchen as well as to the substantial house at *23 Legare Street*, owned in the 1840s by the well-to-do German craftsman Jacob Sass.

22 LEGARE STREET, CHARLES ELLIOTT HOUSE

Constructed circa 1764

An interesting architectural response to the threat of fire in the eighteenth century, the Elliott House, although mostly constructed of black cypress, employs thick masonry fire walls between the main rooms of the first floor extending into both the cellar and the attic. The house has further distinction as it follows the orientation of a single house but is actually two rooms deep, possibly because the north end may be an addition. The dwelling retains its eighteenth-century pedimented window hoods and dormers but boasts Greek Revival style piazzas and Neoclassical and Gothic woodwork, in addition to Georgian details on its interior. The upstairs mantelpieces and other carvings have been attributed by recent scholarship to the same carver who executed work on the Sommers House at *128 Tradd Street* and *95 Broad Street*. Charles Elliott, a wealthy planter, owned Sandy Hill Plantation in the south end of the county and built this house af-

ter purchasing the lot (formerly no. 240 of the Grand Modell) from James Skirving in 1764. He built *43 Legare Street* as well. The house eventually became the home of the naturalist and writer Herbert Ravenel Sass.

25 LEGARE STREET, WHITE-WILLIMAN HOUSE

Constructed circa 1840–50; altered late-nineteenth century

25 Legare Street after the earthquake of 1886

Originally completed with paired two-story, square-columned porticos on each end of its front facade, this long stucco dwelling was altered following damage from the earthquake of 1886. John B. White built the house following his 1838 purchase of the lot from Robert Chisolm. It was later owned by the Williman family and then by Mr. and Mrs. Edwin Frost, who made certain Italianate style alterations, including the central bay window and pediment.

29 LEGARE STREET, REV. PAUL TRAPIER GERVAIS HOUSE

Constructed circa 1835; restored with addition 1995–97

In 1835 the Reverend Gervais apparently reused the foundation and basement story of an eighteenth-century house built by the organist and composer Benjamin Yarnold. Standing three and a half stories above the basement, the simple frame, Greek Revival dwelling retains its original double-tiered Tuscan-columned piazza and simple Greek Revival entry architrave and piazza screen. The original lot measured 300 feet in depth, 280 feet today. Succeeding owners included the Robinson, Memminger, Rhett, and Gaud families. In the 1890s Capt. Thomas Pinckney and his wife Camilla Scott Pinckney rented the Gervais House. Here in 1895 their daughter, Josephine Pinckney, a nationally renowned writer and poet, was born.

31 LEGARE STREET, HANNAH HEYWARD HOUSE

Constructed circa 1789

The sister-in-law of the wealthy rice planter Thomas Heyward completed this simple Neoclassical villa within a few years after the Revolution. The curvilinear bay on the south facade boasts a Venetian (Palladian) window lighting a large upstairs drawing room. Rented by Mrs. Heyward's daughter to Julia Datty, the dwelling served as a girls' school run by this native of French Santo Domingo. The Augustine T. Smythe family acquired the house in 1868, and his descendants have resided here ever since. An extensive line of kitchens and stables survive along the south side of the dwelling. Smythe relations also owned the two houses to the north. The noted antebellum writer Louisa Cheves McCord bought the single house at 35 Legare Street in 1879. She was probably responsible for the Victorian alterations, including the mansard roof and the bay windows, added to the Federal-period dwelling. In the early-twentieth century Augustine T. Smythe bought the circa 1818 Glen House at 37 Legare Street for his daughter Susan, wife of the noted writer John Bennett.

The Hannah Heyward House, 31 Legare Street, showing bowed projection

32 LEGARE STREET, SWORD GATE HOUSE

Constructed before 1810; renovated twentieth century; additions 1840s

The wrought-iron gates leading to this property from Legare Street bear an elaborate sword and spear design and were made by the ironworker Christopher Werner "by mistake" when he was completing a similar pair for the Charleston Guardhouse in 1830. The gates were installed by 1850 by George Hopley, Charleston's British consul. The three-story wooden house with fanlighted piazzas had been completed be-

Detail of the Sword Gates, 32 Legare Street

fore 1810 by Solomon Legare and sold nearly a decade later to the Talvande family, refugees from Santo Domingo. Madame Talvande's girls' school was considered the best by Charleston's elite in the 1820s and 1830s. By tradition, the high brick walls were added to enclose the property during this period. Before Hopley's purchase of the site in 1849 a large stuccoed brick section was added to the building. After passing through a number of owners, including the daughter of Robert Todd Lincoln, the property was subdivided. Its brick wing became an inn. The setback of this edifice perhaps inspired that of the Colonial Revival house next door at *26 Legare Street*. Built in the 1920s by the Whaley family, it was entirely refaced several decades later by the next owners, the T. Wilbur Thornhills.

34 LEGARE STREET, WHALEY-LAPHAM HOUSE

Constructed circa 1905

Although completed just after 1900 by Richard S. Whaley, son of the owner of *26 Legare Street*, this stucco house was conveyed to the mother of Samuel S. Lapham, one of Charleston's leading restoration architects of the twentieth century. This eclectic residence has Jacobean syle and Craftsman detailing, with front curvilinear gable, large square dormers, and, in the Charleston tradition, a double-tiered side piazza.

43 LEGARE STREET, CHARLES ELLIOTT HOUSE

Constructed circa 1759; altered 1911

The builder of *22 Legare Street* constructed this three-and-a-half-story brick single house. Early plats show that it had a large fenced garden at the rear. The front elevation was renovated in 1911, with the addition of brownstone panels below the windows and a curvilinear parapet.

51 LEGARE STREET, W. W. WILKINSON HOUSE
Constructed 1876–77

W. W. Wilkinson built this large Queen Anne style wood house with a turret shortly after his purchase of the lot. An earlier one-and-a-half-story brick dependency survived the fire of 1861. The two-story, gable-end, stuccoed single house to the north at *53 Legare Street* also survived.

1 MEETING STREET, GEORGE ROBERTSON HOUSE
Constructed circa 1846

George Robertson built this house on the site of Sen. Ralph Izard's late-eighteenth-century town house destroyed in a fire some years earlier. Izard's mansion was designed by James Hoban, architect of the White House. Robertson's later side-hall plan house, among the largest in Charleston, included the most recent innovations. The primary entrance from Meeting Street boasts splendid double doors with glazed panels and flanking cast-iron lanterns. The piazza is masked on the east for the entire three floors. After the War Between the States, the Ross family acquired the house and Miss Mary Jane Ross filled the dwelling with exotic art objects and splendid decoration in the Victorian manner. At her death in 1922, her will attempted to leave the house in trust as a museum, but the legacy provisions were struck down by the South Carolina Supreme Court in 1944 and most of the collection sold at auction.

2 MEETING STREET, CARRINGTON-CARR HOUSE
Constructed 1890–92; restored early-1980s

This large Queen Anne style dwelling at the foot of Meeting Street occupies one of the city's best sites overlooking White Point Garden and the Charleston harbor. The

house replaced a structure destroyed in the earthquake of 1886 and is a good example of the adaptation of Queen Anne decorative elements to Charleston's vernacular traditions.

Waring P. Carrington acquired the site for this house in 1889. Carrington's wife, Martha Williams, was a daughter of George W. Williams, the wealthy banker who resided at *16 Meeting Street* (the Calhoun Mansion). Tradition holds that Williams gave his daughter and son-in-law a wedding gift of $75,000, which was then used to construct their residence. Carrington, a King Street jeweler, purchased two Tiffany windows, now in the first-floor parlor, to celebrate the couple's fifth wedding anniversary in 1895. The bandstand in White Point Garden was built and donated to the city by Martha W. Carrington in memory of Mr. and Mrs. George W. Williams.

7 MEETING STREET, JOSIAH SMITH HOUSE
Constructed circa 1783; various twentieth-century renovations

The structure at 7 Meeting Street stands as one of the few large double houses built in Charleston immediately following the Revolutionary War. With brick infill amid the major framing members, the house is clad with weatherboarding and rests on a brick foundation. Its Georgian facade, demi-lune portico, southern-facing piazzas, and rooftop lantern or cupola all proclaim the wealth of the builder. Although other examples of cupolas on eighteenth-century domestic structures can be found, this feature is typically reserved for public or institutional buildings. Josiah Smith, the descendant of one of Charleston's oldest Congregationalist families, was one of the city's wealthiest merchants and bankers. With his partners, he owned substantial properties, including 85 East Bay Street and *6 Tradd Street*, near the center of their mercantile activities on the Cooper River waterfront. Josiah Smith and his partners were not only important federalists but provided the leadership for the first Chamber of Commerce.

8 MEETING STREET, THOMAS TUCKER HOUSE

Constructed before 1806; renovated 1821, circa 1850

The earliest surviving construction on this lot is a weatherboarded single house located immediately behind the imposing masonry facade. The stuccoed front building section, retaining its early patina, boasts a mid-nineteenth-century cast-iron balcony overlooking the street. Located behind this 1821 addition and the original house are two brick dependencies that once functioned as the kitchen, laundry, and servants' quarters of the main house. Probably built by Capt. Thomas Tucker, it was purchased in 1806 by Abraham Crouch. Later the dwelling passed into the Ladson family, who retained it until 1960.

12 MEETING STREET, JOHN LEWIS HOUSE

Constructed circa 1822

Built by the factor John Lewis in 1822, this two-and-a-half-story residence stands on land once belonging to Charles Pinckney. The original wood-frame house appears to have had three rooms on each floor with a central stair and entrance and a large semicircular porch to the rear. The original house is capped by a hipped roof with dormer windows with a low projecting pediment in front.

15 MEETING STREET, JOHN EDWARDS HOUSE

Constructed circa 1770; additions late-nineteenth century

This structure, built by John Edwards, is typical of Charleston double houses of the 1760s and 1770s. It features four rooms on the first floor divided by a central entrance stair hall and four rooms on the second floor. The house is unusual, however, in its rusticated wood front: cypress siding cut and beveled to resemble stonework, a practice also employed by George Washington in his house at Mount Vernon. Records indicate that a number of other Charleston houses featured this detailing. Edwards was prominent in local politics during the American Revolution, serving with "Dictator" John Rutledge's privy council. He was later imprisoned by the British and exiled to St. Augustine for his role in the Revolution. The semicircular piazza on the south side of the house was added before the beginning of this century.

16 MEETING STREET, CALHOUN MANSION

Constructed circa 1876; restored 1970s, 1980s

William P. Russell, architect

The planned front elevation of the Calhoun Mansion, 16 Meeting Street, engraving, circa 1875

When this house was completed, an article in the *News and Courier* referred to it as probably "the handsomest and most complete private residence in the South." Encompassing nearly 24,000 square feet of living space, the residence was built by George Walton Williams, a local businessman who made a large fortune in the years before and during the Civil War. Williams, a native of Augusta, Georgia, began his Charleston business career in 1852, importing sugar and molasses from the West Indies and bagging from India. By the 1860s he had stores, warehouses, and industrial complexes in the peninsular city, as well as the Carolina Savings Bank at *1 Broad Street.*

With its twenty-five rooms, the Williams House is considered to be the largest single family residence in the city and includes elements of Italianate and Renaissance Revival styles. Its contrasting colors and textures of pressed brick, Corinthian-columned portico and side piazzas, as well as the period rope design around openings reflect the eclectic mix of national styles with homage to Charleston vernacular building traditions. The interior of this building boasts original walnut and oak woodwork, Minton encaustic tiles, and splendid gas chandeliers. For several generations the structure has been called the Calhoun Mansion in honor of one of its former owners, Patrick Calhoun, a grandson of John C. Calhoun, who married one of George Walton Williams's daughters. The house is privately owned but is open to the public as a museum.

18 MEETING STREET, THOMAS HEYWARD HOUSE

Constructed circa 1803

The deed transferring the "messuage and the buildings thereon" from Nathaniel Heyward and his wife Henrietta to his half brother Thomas Heyward, a signer of the Declaration of Independence, suggests that this large brick single house was complete by 1803. This dwelling is distinguished by oversized interior proportions. The facade exhibits remnants of nineteenth-century ironwork of exclusionary nature commonly called a chevaux-de-frise. The most prominent example of this type of ironwork is at the Miles Brewton House (*27 King Street*). This property retains original arcaded piazzas and early kitchen and slave quarters buildings. Neoclassicism was an aesthetic of classical detailing and attenuated proportions. 18 Meeting Street typifies these qualities in its brickwork with quoining and other fine detailing, its classical door architrave, and its exterior proportions.

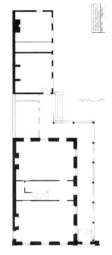

Measured plan of the first floor, 18 Meeting Street

23–27 MEETING STREET

Constructed 1760–1800; altered nineteenth century

These three single houses comprise an important streetscape of eighteenth-century masonry structures. All three have had Victorian changes, but 23 Meeting Street, originally built by provision merchant Albert Detmar, has retained its late-nineteenth-century alterations. The two southernmost of the three, 23 Meeting Street and 25 Meeting Street, date from 1770 and 1760 respectively, while 27 Meeting Street was erected after the Revolution.

Postearthquake photograph of 26 Meeting Street

26 MEETING STREET, WILLIAM MASON SMITH HOUSE

Constructed 1819–21

William Jay, architect

The Greek key fretwork in the window brownstone enlivens the subdued roughcast facade of 26 Meeting Street and foreshadows innovative Regency details inside. The facade presents an unusual adaptation of the traditional single house arrangement and indicates the side hall plan variation of the interior. This house has often been attributed to William Jay, and recent evidence found in William Mason Smith's papers—Jay's signature on a bill for the slate roof—assures this linkage. While many of his buildings in Savannah are known, knowledge of his activities in Charleston are unfortunately less clear. In 1820 he advertised in the *Courier:* "WILLIAM JAY offers his services to the inhabitants of Charleston, and the State generally, in his profession as an ARCHITECT. Any command left at this office in Jones Building, St. Michael's Alley, will meet with immediate attention." Later that month he was appointed architect to the Board of Public Works, a position he held for only a short time and which Robert Mills later occupied. It was in this capacity that Jay left a series of designs for public buildings in Charleston. Jay was last listed in the city directory in 1822, and it was soon thereafter that he returned to England.

30 MEETING STREET, YOUNG-MOTTE HOUSE
Constructed circa 1770

Thomas Young originally owned a lot which extended from Meeting through to Church Street. A masonry single house was begun on Meeting Street and was sold before completion to Col. Isaac Motte, an officer in the Royal Americans, 60th Regiment. The pedimented gable and tripartite window are nineteenth-century Greek Revival alterations.

31 MEETING STREET, JAMES LADSON HOUSE
Constructed circa 1792; altered after 1884

In 1792 Lt. Gov. James Ladson erected a two-story single house on a large lot facing a small court then called Ladson Court. The court was not cut through to King Street to become Ladson Street until 1895. The third floor was added in the middle of the nineteenth century, and the Poppenheim family, who purchased the property in 1877, installed bay windows on the first and second floors and erected the Victorian garden house.

Detail of the fountain at 31 Meeting Street

34 MEETING STREET, DANIEL ELLIOTT HUGER HOUSE
Constructed circa 1760; some alterations circa 1795–1800, circa 1850, circa 1900

The lots on which this substantial double-pile house was constructed were subdivided in 1759 from the Eveleigh House property at *39 Church Street*. The

34 Meeting Street in 1898

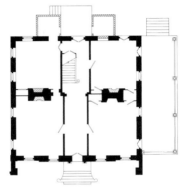

Measured plan of the first floor 34 Meeting Street

purchaser was Capt. John Bull (1693–1767) of Bull's (now Coosaw) Island. The Bull dwelling, rented by Lord William Campbell in 1775, is one of the few royal governors' houses to survive from the colonial period. A room-by-room inventory was taken in April 1777 by Campbell's wife's family and filed later with the British government as a claim. On the first floor was "The Passage, Parlour The Breakfast, Parlour The Dining, Library, and Steward's Room." The second floor included, on the front of the house, the "Dining Room" and "Drawing Room" and, behind these, bed chambers. The third floor included bed chambers for secretary, housekeeper, servants, and the nursery, with the loft above all. Outbuildings included the kitchen with its loft, coach house, and stables. The latter building does not survive, but the rest of the property and the rooms in the main house are essentially intact. Somewhat damaged in the shelling of the city in 1864 and sacked by Union troops in 1865, the dwelling was eventually repaired. It was sold in 1795 to the Morris family and in 1818 to Francis K. Huger. His descendants occupy it to the present day.

35 MEETING STREET, BULL HOUSE
Constructed circa 1720; altered 1800–10, 1895–1905

The first lieutenant governor of the Royal Colony of South Carolina apparently built a portion of this house around 1720. The house was owned and occupied by Governor Bull's son, William Bull II, who was also a lieutenant governor. The second Bull was the first native South Carolinian to receive a medical degree. This three-and-a-half-story stuccoed brick dwelling on a high brick basement sits on a large lot at the corner of Meeting and Ladson Streets. The principal facade features quoining, stucco lintels and keystones. Some alterations in the Colonial Revival style date from its ownership at the turn of the century by the family of Mayor John Ficken. According to tradition, this house was nearly identical to the Ashley Hall Plantation house, country seat of the Bull family, which was destroyed in 1865.

36 MEETING STREET, BRUNCH-HALL HOUSE
Constructed 1743; altered 1850s

This typical Charleston single house built by 1743 was altered in the nineteenth century to a double-parlor plan with parlor doors opening onto a central passageway. The three-story house with fine Georgian interior woodwork also has an addition of a mid-nineteenth-century Greek Revival parapet.

37 MEETING STREET, JAMES SIMMONS HOUSE
Constructed circa 1760; altered 1840s

Charlestonian James Simmons is believed to have built 37 Meeting Street in 1760. As originally constructed, the house follows a formal Georgian plan with a center hall dividing the four principal rooms on each floor. At Simmons's death in 1775 the house became the home of Gov. Robert Gibbes. He and his family were forced to abandon the house during the British occupation of the city in the Revolutionary War and returned to find it heavily damaged. In the next century it became the home of builder and financier Otis Mills. It was during Mills's occupancy in the 1840s that the facade of the house was greatly altered with the addition of the two projecting bays that are joined on the second floor of the house with an ornate cast-iron balcony. In 1862 the house became the headquarters of Gen. Pierre G. T. Beauregard, the commander of the Confederate forces at Charleston. Beauregard occupied the house until Federal shelling in the area forced him to shift his operations to a less vulnerable position at the northern end of the city.

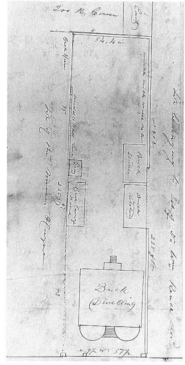

Plat of 1846 showing the double bays of 37 Meeting Street

Old St. Michael's Rectory showing 1886 earthquake damage

39 MEETING STREET, OLD ST. MICHAEL'S RECTORY

Constructed 1767; altered 1886–87
Miller & Fullerton, builders

One of the few known partnerships of housebuilders in colonial Charleston designed and executed this stuccoed brick single house for St. Michael's Church. It served as the parish's first minister's house but became a rental property after the Revolution and was eventually sold to rice planter William Read in 1825. Although retaining its notable compass-headed stair window on the north, the dwelling received considerable damage in the earthquake and now boasts a bracketed Victorian cornice.

43 MEETING STREET, JAMES MITCHELL HOUSE

Constructed circa 1798

A prosperous cooper built this narrow, masonry single house shortly before 1800. In the 1830s it served as the last residence of Henry William deSaussure, the former director of the U.S. Mint and appeals judge. The piazzas were removed and the current iron gates added in the early-twentieth century. A notable garden winding to Price's Alley and a distinctive contemporary addition to the rear dependency add interest to this property.

47 MEETING STREET, ROBERT M. ALLAN HOUSE

Constructed circa 1833

Originally constructed by Robert M. Allan, a factor-planter, this structure's piazzas were removed in the mid-twentieth century. Nonetheless, the glazed fan and rectangular transoms can clearly be seen from the street. Immediately to the north of the house stretches Price's Alley, established in the eighteenth century, the site of numerous tenements occupied in the antebellum period by Irish immigrants.

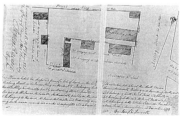

Plat of 1799 showing the location of 47 Meeting Street

51 MEETING STREET, NATHANIEL RUSSELL HOUSE

L *Constructed 1808; altered 1857, 1908, 1915; restored 1955, 1990s*

Completed in 1808 on an original lot of Charleston's Grand Modell, the Nathaniel Russell House is recognized as one of America's finest examples of Neoclassical domestic architecture. Its builder, Nathaniel Russell (1738–1820), was a prominent merchant from New England who came to Charleston as a young man of twenty-seven and quickly amassed a huge fortune.

In landscape setting Russell's house differs from most of Charleston's early urban dwellings; it sits back from the street approximately 30 feet, creating a front garden entrance through which the house is entered at ground level. Wrought-iron balconies on the second-floor exterior wrap around the house and overlook the garden. The main house was originally part of a large town house complex that included the two-story brick kitchen and laundry connected to a larger two-story, T-shaped brick carriage house with stables, storerooms,

Staircase in the Nathaniel Russell House, 51 Meeting Street

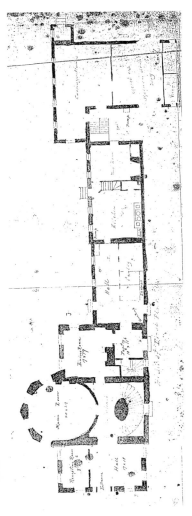

First-floor plan, 51 Meeting Street, at the time of the conveyance to the Sisters of Charity of Our Lady of Mercy in the 1870s

privies, and quarters for the Russells' approximately eighteen slaves on the second floor. Running along the south side of the property is Price's Alley, a thoroughfare since the eighteenth century that housed Irish immigrants and African American tradesmen in the antebellum period.

This house points to a reliance on architectural pattern books for detail, although the architect for the Russell House remains unknown. The three-story house contains only three rooms on each floor. Each floor utilizes the geometric patterns of a square room, an oval room, and a rectangular room. A free-flying, or cantilever, staircase connects the three floors and is perhaps the most stunning interior architectural feature in the city.

In 1809 one of Russell's daughters, Alicia, married Arthur Middleton, and the house served as their residence for the next ten years. Sarah Russell, another daughter, married the Reverend Theodore Dehon, whose death four years later of yellow fever sent Mrs. Dehon and her three children back to live at the Russell House. After Nathaniel Russell's death in 1820 and his wife's death in 1832, the house was inherited by Sarah Russell Dehon, who continued to live here with her daughter, her son-in-law, and their twelve children. In 1857 the house was purchased by Gov. R. F. W. Allston. He, his family, and their slaves were forced to evacuate the house during Charleston's 500-day bombardment by Federal troops. The house survived intact, although after Governor Allston's death one year later, Mrs. Allston had to open it as a female academy. In 1870 the Allston executors sold the property to the Sisters of Charity of Our Lady of Mercy, who owned the house for the next thirty-eight years, after which it was returned to single family residential use. Purchased by Historic Charleston Foundation in 1955 and designated as a National Historic Landmark in 1974, the Russell House is today open to the public as a house museum.

57 MEETING STREET, FIRST (SCOTS) PRESBYTERIAN CHURCH

Constructed circa 1814; renovated 1887, 1945, 1987

Perhaps inspired by the architect Benjamin Henry Latrobe's Baltimore Cathedral or designs by Robert Adam for the church at Mistley in Essex, the present structure replaced an earlier church dating to the 1760s. An even earlier building stood to the west of the current site. The pedimented portico supported by Tuscan columns is flanked by twin towers with gilded spheres and ironwork finials. First Scots is the fifth-oldest ecclesiastical building in the city, and the churchyard contains over fifty eighteenth-century gravestones. It was probably designed and constructed by the Scottish master builders John and James Gordon, who were members of the congregation. Much of the interior has been altered, due to severe earthquake damage and a fire in 1945. An important carved wooden memorial with rococo decoration survives from the earlier meetinghouse and memorializes Lady Anne Murray, a young Scottish noblewoman and member of the congregation who died in 1772. It hangs on the sanctuary wall along with marble memorials to the church's prominent nineteenth-century members, most of Scottish extraction. Ties to the Church of Scotland are exemplified by the stained glass window depicting the seal of the Church of Scotland, the burning bush, with the Latin motto around the seal: "Nec tamen consumbatur" (Nevertheless it was not consumed).

Central portico window, First (Scots) Presbyterian Church, depicting the great seal of the Church of Scotland

59 MEETING STREET, BRANFORD-HORRY HOUSE

Constructed 1750; portico added 1830; various twentieth-century restorations

The merchant Benjamin Savage acquired the lot at the corner of Tradd and Meeting

Streets from John Allen and his wife in 1747. Savage in 1750 then bequeathed to "Elizabeth Savage, the daughter of my Brother Thomas Savage (now living with me) my houses and Ground in Charleston . . . with all and singular buildings and appurtenances it being the ground and houses in Tradd Street." Elizabeth subsequently married William Branford, a wealthy planter, whose holdings included Old Towne Plantation, the original site of Charles Town. Elizabeth's daughter, Ann, and then her grandson Elias Horry, second president of the South Carolina Canal and Railroad Company, inherited the house after her death in 1801. It was Horry who apparently added the Greek piazzas that now cover the sidewalk on the Meeting Street side of the property.

The house has a double-pile plan, with one large room and one smaller room on the second-floor front. On the first floor both front-room doorways were widened during the Horry occupancy to create a double-parlor plan. The stable associated with the house is now *61 Meeting Street*. A kitchen building west of the stable was demolished in the early-twentieth century.

69 MEETING STREET, JOHN POYAS HOUSE
Constructed 1796–1800

Daniel Bourgett purchased this lot (a part of lot no. 89 of the Grand Modell) in 1730. At his death forty years later, the lot passed to his daughter and son-in-law, Rachel and Dr. John Poyas. Poyas constructed the three-and-a-half-story Charleston single house on a high basement in the last years of the eighteenth century. Built of stuccoed brick, this Federal style house is distinguished by its unusual height and by its many north-facing windows. These windows may have been added after the earthquake of 1886 since the adjacent property had been destroyed, thus eliminating the privacy motivation which traditionally precluded them. 69 Meeting Street remained in the Poyas family until 1837 when it was sold to Moses Mordecai. Although initially opposed to secession, Mordecai supported the Confederacy as a blockade runner.

3 ORANGE STREET, ELIZABETH PETRIE HOUSE

Constructed circa 1768; renovated and partially restored 1970s

The widow of the silversmith Alexander Petrie occupied this house, which was built by her husband's estate on one of the lots he subdivided from the former Orange Garden. The basic form of this pre-Revolutionary single house survives, and, like other dwellings on this street, it stands on a deep lot affording a substantial rear garden.

4 ORANGE STREET, SAMUEL CARNE HOUSE

Constructed circa 1776

The Tory Samuel Carne lived in this weatherboarded single house from 1777 to 1782. In plan it closely resembles neighboring contemporary houses, including the Walker House at *6 Orange Street*, the Miller House at *8 Orange Street* (a stuccoed single house with a side entry and a substantial 1920s addition), and the Tobias Cambridge House at *12 Orange Street* (which has a Victorian rear addition).

Floor plan of 4 Orange Street

7 ORANGE STREET, CHARLES PINCKNEY HOUSE

Constructed circa 1769; altered circa 1850; restored and renovated late-1980s

Charles Pinckney, a noted colonial jurist and father of a signer of the Constitution, built this two-and-a-half-story,

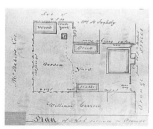

Mid-nineteenth-century plat showing 7 Orange Street and its work yard and garden

weatherboarded, double-pile dwelling on a high foundation. Although the house retains much of its original detailing, including an early front portico, its interior was altered in the mid-nineteenth century. Early plats show an extensive garden area at the rear, as well as a work yard adjacent to the surviving dependencies along the north side of the property.

9–11 ORANGE STREET, SIMONS TENEMENTS
Constructed circa 1770

Built as a three-and-a-half-story double tenement just before the Revolution, the northern house retains most of its original detailing. The exterior of the south residence, however, had some mid-nineteenth-century alterations. The Reverend Samuel Gilman and his wife, the author Caroline Gilman, lived most of their married life at 11 Orange Street. Gilman, the pastor of the Unitarian Church, wrote the poem "Fair Harvard" for his alma mater, while Caroline Gilman edited the first American magazine for children.

4 SOUTH BATTERY, VILLA MARGHERITA
Constructed circa 1895

Frederick P. Dinkelberg, architect

Although originally constructed as a residence, the Villa Margherita served for more than forty years as a leading hotel. Andrew Simonds, a bank president and financier, purchased the site with an existing eighteenth-century house and decided to build a new house for his New Orleans–born wife, Daisy. He retained Frederick P. Dinkelberg, a New York and Chicago architect who later became famous as a principal designer of the Flatiron Building in New York City, to plan a lavish residence to reflect his expanding fortune. Dinkelberg's building reflects the emerging Beaux Arts style while retaining some features of the Renaissance Revival style, in its grand Corinthian-columned portico, attenuated cornice, second-story cast-iron balcony, and impressive door architrave with engaged columns, fanlighted transom, and elaborate bracketed keystone. The decorative balustrade and cupola that formerly ornamented the stepped flat roof have been removed, along with the balustrade that surrounded the black and white marble front terrace. The interior, however, still includes an atrium surrounding a marble pool and a second-floor ballroom.

Villa Margherita, 4 South Battery, soon after its completion in the 1890s

Following Simonds's untimely death in 1905, his widow leased the property to Miss Ina Liese Dawson, who added an annex and converted the house to a fashionable small hotel called Villa Margherita. The hotel served wealthy northerners on their winter excursions to South Carolina hunting plantations, as well as other seasonal guests. Henry Ford and Alexander Graham Bell stayed at this select hostelry during its heyday. After its use by the United Seaman's Service in World War II, the house eventually returned to use as a single-family residence.

8 SOUTH BATTERY, COL. WILLIAM WASHINGTON HOUSE

Constructed circa 1768; additions and alterations circa 1800, 1840; restored with additions and alterations circa 1916

This building is the only pre-Revolutionary dwelling on the Battery. Thomas Savage built the house before 1770, and his widow, Mary Elliott Savage, sold it in 1785 to a young Virginia Revolutionary officer, William Washington, cousin of George Washington and hero of the battles of Cowpens and Eutaw Springs. Washington married Jane Elliott, daughter of Charles Elliott of Charleston, and they divided their married life between her Sandy Hill Plantation in the south end of Charleston County and this town house.

The original portion of the Washington House stands two and a half stories high on a raised brick basement. Its first-floor east windows are capped by the original pedimented hoods, exceptionally similar to those on the Charles Elliott House at 22 *Legare Street*. Similar hoods were added to the South Battery elevation in 1916. Pairs of dormers project on the south and north sides of its slate, hipped roof. During William and Jane Washington's occupancy, the house was referred to as "1 Church Street" and a brick staircase rose from Church Street to a center door that gave entry to the larger of the two first-floor rooms. With the staircase positioned in a rear chamber, 8 South Battery's original plan is reminiscent of *37* and *59 Church Street*. Alterations to the house in the early-nineteenth century included the pedimented portico on the east elevation and a similar portico serving as the central pavilion of a full double-tiered piazza on the west, along with interior Neoclassical changes such as marble insets in the fireplaces. Greek Revival pocket doors dividing the drawing rooms were added some years later. The formal garden with paisley-patterned brick beds probably dates from the antebellum period. The architectural firm of Todd, Simons, and Todd masterminded the restoration of the house in 1916 for Julian Mitchell; extensive alterations included the shuttered enclosures of the piazzas, the removal of a wall on the interior to enlarge the stair hall, and an addition to the north for a kitchen and other amenities.

20 SOUTH BATTERY, STEVENS-LATHERS HOUSE

Constructed circa 1843; altered 1870; partially restored 1970s, 1990s

Samuel N. Stevens, a factor in partnership with John and William Ravenel, purchased this property in 1843. Stevens's house stood three stories tall with a T-shaped floor plan and piazzas on the front elevation facing South Battery; the original front door stood in an ell toward the western rear of the first elevation of this porch. Colonel Lathers, a native of Georgetown, S.C., went to New York in 1847 and made a fortune in banking insurance, railroads, and other pursuits. By tradition, Colonel Lathers decided to assist in the reconstruction of his native state after the war, so he moved to Charleston. The *Charleston Courier* stated on March 31, 1870, that Colonel Lathers's residence on South Battery was "in [the] charge of Mr. J. H. Devereux." Architect John H. Devereux's enlargements for Lathers included a substantial addition with a large frieze and cornice with supporting brackets and a fish-scaled slate mansard roof with an arched tripartite dormer projection. The top floor of the dwelling housed an exceptional library described by a visitor as "filled with books and engravings." Receptions were held in the house for important Union leaders, including Gov. Horatio Seymour of New York and William Cullen Bryant. After attempting for nearly four years to restore goodwill between men of the North and the South, Lathers sold the house and returned to New York. Since the 1970s the main house and dependency have been utilized as a private residence and as an inn.

22 SOUTH BATTERY, NATHANIEL RUSSELL MIDDLETON HOUSE

Constructed 1857–58

Nathaniel Russell Middleton, who served as city treasurer and later as president of the College of Charleston, built the substantial three-and-a-half-story house at 22 South Battery in 1857–58 after demolishing a portion of an eighteenth-century double tenement on the site. Middleton, the grandson of wealthy merchant Nathaniel Russell, married Anne DeWolf of Bristol,

Rhode Island. This stuccoed brick house is fronted by a three-story piazza with fluted Doric columns on the first floor and fluted Corinthian columns on the upper stories. Each window on the second and third floors of the piazza opens through transomed French doors. The elegant second-floor double drawing rooms retain their original plasterwork and are reached via an impressive side staircase. There was extensive earthquake damage in 1886, and Middleton's detailed specifications for repair work to the South Battery house still survive. The house at 24 South Battery boasts Italianate and Gothic Revival detailing as well as some Victorian period decorative painting.

26 SOUTH BATTERY, COL. JOHN ALGERNON SYDNEY ASHE HOUSE

Constructed circa 1853

Edward C. Jones, architect

John A. S. Ashe, a wealthy planter, banker, and South Carolina politician, inherited this lot in 1828 as well as $10,000 for use in building a house. More than two decades later Ashe, a bachelor in his fifties, proceeded with construction of this sophisticated dwell-

ing that stands as one of the few major surviving Italianate buildings erected in Charleston before the Civil War. The front facade includes many of the best features of this architectural style, including an L-shaped asymmetrical plan with pedimented front gable, a double-tiered polygonal piazza with arched wooden loggias, and double bracketed cornices and surmounting roof balustrades. The scale of the house, its interior arrangement, and its ornamentation suggest social uses. The octagonal stair hall holds a semicircular staircase lit by an octagonal skylight. The mahogany stair incorporates two motifs, leaf and rice stems, and rises to a height of nine feet. An octagonal drawing room on the west features an ornamental cornice with a frieze of grapes and a marble mantel recessed in a square alcove in the north center. A portion of the extensive original outbuildings, which formerly provided living space for John Ashe's thirty domestic slaves, remains at the rear.

26–34 South Battery shown in a post–Civil War engraving

The noted photographer George Cook constructed a three-story structure next door at *28 South Battery* in 1860. The house has a similar arcaded piazza on the second story but, following more the style of the picturesque movement, features paired arched windows and a balcony projecting from the gable roof.

30 SOUTH BATTERY, JAMES E. SPEAR HOUSE

Constructed circa 1860

Although built at the same time as its eastern neighbor and bearing details of the Italianate style, particularly in its arched front doorway, Spear's house follows a more conservative Charleston Greek Revival pattern with its squared masonry columns, supporting a Tuscan-columned second-story portico and surmounting balustrade. French windows

on each floor of the front elevation give access to these outdoor spaces. Spear's property had formerly been a part of the adjoining Col. John Ashe House site and had been inherited by Ashe's daughter Harriett. Spear's house was apparently the first to be constructed on the lot.

32 SOUTH BATTERY, COL. JOHN ASHE HOUSE

Constructed circa 1782; renovated 1930s

A nineteenth-century writer credited the design of this post-Revolutionary house to a builder who worked in partnership with the great pre-Revolutionary Charleston housewright John Fullerton. This impressive three-story masonry house retains its original eighteenth-century cupola. The Tuscan-columned, double-tiered piazza with French doors and the Italianate style balustrades are probably mid-nineteenth-century additions. The first-floor nine-over-nine windows, the front doorway, and the dormer with an arched window may remain from the original construction of the house. Some Neoclassical woodwork survives on the interior. Certain alterations were made to the house in the 1930s.

34 South Battery, late-nineteenth-century view

34 SOUTH BATTERY, GADSDEN-BURCKMEYER HOUSE

Constructed 1820–30; altered early-1900s

Col. John Ashe of *32 South Battery* left this lot to his daughter Mary, the wife of Capt. Christopher Gadsden. The Gadsdens built this three-story masonry house with front pediment, probably in the 1820s. In the early-twentieth century the double-tiered, bow-front piazzas were removed and a Neoclassical Revival style doorway, ironwork balcony, and lunette window were added to the front facade.

39 SOUTH BATTERY, MAGWOOD-MORELAND HOUSE

Constructed circa 1825

Samuel Magwood, an Ashley River planter, built this two-and-a-half-story weatherboard single house for his daughter Susan at the time of her marriage. Constructed on a criss-cross foundation of palmetto logs sunk in mud, the house, despite its filled-marsh location, has remained relatively intact through most earthquakes and hurricanes. Two notable fanlights, one over the street door and the other over the entrance door, grace the exterior facade. The street door stands within a pedimented architrave with fluted pilasters and guilloche frieze. Its fanlight is semicircular with delicate double-looped wood tracery.

44 SOUTH BATTERY, JOHNSTON HOUSE

Constructed circa 1835

This three-story plantation style house was built about 1835 by spinster sisters Anne and Catherine Johnston on lots left by their grandfather, McKenzie. The residence was purchased by Gen. Benjamin Huger Rutledge after the Civil War, and the art historian Anna Wells Rutledge lived much of her life here. The house and its contemporary neighbor at *46 South Battery* retain their original substantial wood picket fences on masonry piers, along with carved lattice gates. Such fences tended to be more common devices for enclosure of early Charleston lots and have progressively deteriorated and disappeared from most neighborhoods in the city.

47 SOUTH BATTERY, HENRY CHEVES HOUSE

Constructed circa 1886–87

Before the earthquake of 1886 Henry Cheves purchased this lot, which was adjacent to numerous wharves and docking facilities, with a deed that prohibited him from putting up any commercial concerns except "a private wharf or bathhouse." This dwelling was probably built to face the Ashley River. It has Italianate style front cross gables and a later Colonial Revival style piazza on the South Battery elevation.

48 SOUTH BATTERY, JAMES MACBETH HOUSE
Constructed 1846

James MacBeth, who served as mayor of Charleston during the Civil War, constructed this three-story, gable-ended Greek Revival house in 1846. It has a substantial two-tiered piazza consisting of a masonry arcade on the ground story and a fluted Tuscan-columned porch on the second story. Sandstone pediments and lintels survive over the principal exterior door and windows. The MacBeth House, like its two neighbors to the east, retains its original wood fence and curved lattice gate. The dependency to the rear of the house dates from 1790; it was the first home of the Charleston Day School (1937–39).

49 SOUTH BATTERY, COL. JAMES ENGLISH HOUSE
Constructed circa 1795

Colonel English constructed his house on a lot formerly owned by Francis Salters and which abutted the former Charleston seawall along the shore of the Ashley River. The exterior stucco was apparently used to cover the brickwork and scored to resemble stone blocks with corner quoining. The house retains its original Neoclassical double-tiered side piazzas and most of its original nine-over-nine light window sashes.

50 SOUTH BATTERY, CHARLES DRAKE HOUSE

Constructed circa 1890

This house, with its rusticated stone foundation, painted stone columns supporting an attenuated arcade (infilled with glass), and second-story curvilinear projections under an extensive overhanging roof, was constructed by Charles Drake. An eclectic mix, the dwelling seems to incorporate elements from the Colonial Revival, Queen Anne, and Arts and Crafts styles. Real estate tycoon and attorney Benjamin Huger Rutledge, owner of *44 South Battery*, built a new large house at *52 South Battery* in the Colonial Revival style with French chateau-esque style turrets and front gable in 1899.

51 SOUTH BATTERY, WILKINSON HOUSE

Constructed circa 1795

Though built in the Federal period as a two-and-a-half-story single house on a raised masonry foundation with its piazzas facing the harbor, this house went through numerous nineteenth- and twentieth-century alterations. In the 1940s and 1950s Mrs. James Wilkinson operated an inn here, as well as a beloved local kindergarten.

56 SOUTH BATTERY, OSBORN-MCCRADY HOUSE

Constructed circa 1799–1801; altered 1850s

Thomas Osborn, from a prominent plantation family south of Charleston, built this two-and-a-half-story double house with beaded weatherboard siding and hipped roof late in the eighteenth century. A mid-nineteenth-century owner apparently added the second-floor cast-iron balcony, and a Car-

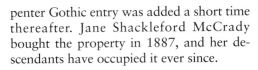

penter Gothic entry was added a short time thereafter. Jane Shackleford McCrady bought the property in 1887, and her descendants have occupied it ever since.

58 SOUTH BATTERY, JOHN BLAKE HOUSE
Constructed circa 1800; restored 1985

Built by John Blake, an early president of the Bank of South Carolina, this L-shaped structure exemplifies the endurance of early Charleston construction. Many surrounding buildings of the period succumbed to the natural disasters that plagued Charleston during the nineteenth century; yet this building, constructed on a masonry foundation with cypress and heart pine framing, survived. The structure possesses a wealth of late-Georgian and Federal details on both the exterior and interior, especially in its modillioned cornice. Its old parterre, visible through early-nineteenth-century wrought-iron gates, was restored by the present owner.

64 SOUTH BATTERY, WILLIAM GIBBES HOUSE
L *Constructed circa 1772; altered circa 1795–1810; restored and altered 1929; restored 1986*

Once the house of one of Charleston's wealthiest pre-Revolutionary merchant-planters, the dwelling presently known as 64 South Battery was intended to be viewed, not from the street, but from the Ashley River channel by boats approaching Gibbes's impressive 300-foot wharf. Adjacent to the wharf the owner had a host of stores, warehouse support structures, and a coffeehouse. Gibbes completed this wood double house with elaborate tabernacle-framed windows and console-bracketed central pediment in 1772; he enjoyed the property only briefly. In the occupation of

Charleston in 1780 Gibbes was interned in St. Augustine, his family was evicted from the house, and the building was used as a hospital by the British army. A room-by-room inventory taken after Gibbes's death in 1789 mentioned extensive furnishings in rooms such as those on the first floor described as the "Front Blue Parlour" and the "Front Wainscot Parlour." Gibbes kept twenty-two slaves on his town property.

The estate sold the property to Sarah Moore Smith, a widow, in 1794. Mrs. Smith or her son Peter made significant alterations to the house with Neoclassical mantels and door surrounds in the large upstairs drawing room and adjoining chamber, and a Federal style wrought-iron balustrade and columns in the large central hall. Mrs. Smith was the grandmother of the famous Sarah and Angelina Grimké, abolitionists and pioneers of women's rights who grew up at 321 East Bay Street. In 1928 Cornelia Roebling of New York, a native of South Carolina and daughter-in-law of the designer of the Brooklyn Bridge, bought the house and made a number of alterations, including the installation of an eighteenth-century chinoiserie style room on the first floor and an extensive garden designed by Loutrel Briggs. Briggs rediscovered the double-axial parterre of the late-eighteenth century in the eastern front yard and restored it as a rose garden for Mrs. Roebling. He augmented the rest of the site with additional features including an allée and a garden pool with a fountain in the best Colonial Revival manner, completing this project in 1933. The grounds of the William Gibbes site offer a unique perspective on an elite Charleston town property in evolution since the eighteenth century. The original kitchen and washhouse and the antebellum stable–carriage house block of brick and tabby con-

GIBBES's WHARF,
At SOUTH-BAY,

BEING now capable of admitting Vessels of any Burthen, to load or unload at it, the Subscriber will be obliged to all those Persons who will favour the said Wharf with their Business, as he has been at great Expence and Trouble in making it convenient, especially to Boats that pass down Ashley-River; which, by unloading there, will avoid the many Risks and Inconveniencies they are exposed to by going round White-Point, and which are very obvious to every difcerning Person, more particularly open Boats : And, as it is of Public Utility, by being a Security to the South-West Side of the Town, he hopes for the Public Patronage.

His Friends, the PLANTERS, need not be under any Apprehenfions of RICE not felling as well there as at any other Wharf, as has been experienced during the laft and prefent Year, as very little Rice has been ftored there from the quick Sale of what has been landed there : And having had Affurances from many refpectable Gentlemen, both in the Planting and Mercantile Intereft, of their friendly Intentions to land Veffels there to load, being convinced of the Safety of that River, and the Conveniency of the Wharf and Stores, with the Difpatch they meet with ; he likewife flatters himfelf, that the many Perfons that ufe it as a Ferry, and do not land their Crops there, will not have any Objections to contribute to the Support of it, by an annual Subfcription.

He has fixed a SCALE-HOUSE at the Head of the Wharf, for the more convenient weighing of Rice that may be fold on landing and to be immediately fhipped, and will, as foon as it is neceffary, add to the Number of Stores.

From the Quantity of LUMBER already fhipped from thence, it is evident no Place in Town is more proper for that Article, as well as for NAVAL STORES.

All Veffels fhall, for their BALLAST, be entitled to their Wharfage and Water, with Liberty to heave down and clean, as a proper Place is fixed for that Purpofe, and to which the Pilot-Boats are alfo welcome.
                    WILLIAM GIBBES.

Advertisement for Gibbes Wharf, South Carolina Gazette, September 1773

struction with tile roofing have survived largely intact, although the stable was converted to garages with servants' rooms above in 1929–30. Other early landscape features include the brick wall with arched, stuccoed recesses that surrounds the 140-by-268-foot lot (.83 acres), constructed in the 1830s; a brick privy (or "rabbit house" in Albert Simons's 1929 drawing); and a "tea house" with romantic curvilinear gables shading a marble relief, identical to that on the family tomb at Magnolia Plantation.

68 SOUTH BATTERY, HARTH-MIDDLETON HOUSE

Constructed circa 1800; renovated after earthquake 1886–87; restored 1920s

A lumber mill owner and planter, John Harth, purchased a lot subdivided from the holdings of William Gibbes, builder of the house next door and owner of the large wharf that stretched in front of this property in the eighteenth century. At that time Harth owned the westernmost lot on South Bay Street. He apparently built the core of the present house after 1797 and completed it just before 1802, when the city directory shows his residence as South Bay Street. Harth's lumber mill operated from the foot of this property and from nearby sites. At the time of John Harth's move to the Orangeburg district in 1816, he sold the property designated as "One South Battery" to Thomas Legare. Legare probably added the polygonal projection. Unlike most Charleston houses with side piazzas, the building is entered from the ground story through wrought-iron gates and a staircase leads to the principal floors. Much of Harth's original wood frame house was covered with stucco in the nineteenth century, an uncommon practice. With extensive damage in the earthquake of 1886, the older piazzas were rebuilt as enclosed additional living spaces and new side piazzas were added to the west, intersecting with the polygonal rear wing. In 1843 Legare's executor sold the property to Henry A. Middleton. The dwelling remained in the Middleton family for seventy years before being sold to William J. Pettus of Maryland, who completed the restoration of the house in the 1920s and added a garden by Loutrel Briggs in the extensive walled lot to the west.

70 TRADD STREET, ROBERT PRINGLE HOUSE

Constructed circa 1774

70 Tradd Street is an excellent example of the arrangement of an eighteenth-century single house site. This building was constructed for Judge Robert Pringle in 1774 (as denoted by an old plaque on the exterior wall). The existing piazza dates to the late-eighteenth century. A plat of 1787 portrays a "dwelling house three stories of brick with seller [sic] covered with shingles and a rod or conductor with a piazza"; "kitchen and wash room two stories of wood"; "carriage house and stables one story with lofts of wood"; and "garden." A significant change is the addition of a Victorian bay window on the first floor of the street facade. Unlike the brick single houses on Church Street, which mixed commercial and residential functions, this

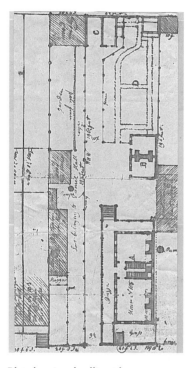

Plat showing dwelling plan, outbuildings, and garden, 70 Tradd Street, 1787

70–76 Tradd Street, early-twentieth-century photo looking east

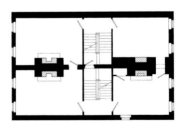

Measured plan of the first floor, Fotheringham-McNeil Tenements, 72–74 Tradd Street

property's only street access was by steps leading to the piazza. Most single houses do, however, allow for carriage access through the side yard. The 1787 plat shows a building on the second half of this double lot abutting the double tenement at 72–74 Tradd Street. 70 Tradd has occupied the second half of the double lot since 1839.

72–74 TRADD STREET, FOTHERINGHAM-MCNEIL TENEMENTS

Constructed before 1765; restored 1960s, 1990s

The gambrel roof on the double tenement at 72–74 Tradd Street is a rare surviving example of a relatively common eighteenth-century roof form found in Charleston. Although tenement housing was common in Charleston at that time, few examples are known in which the tenement was occupied by the owner, since most tenements were built strictly for use as rental properties. The street facade was altered when the building was converted into a single family dwelling in the mid-nineteenth century, eliminating the need for a second stair. The interior is largely unaltered.

75 TRADD STREET, DR. AARON WHITNEY LELAND HOUSE

Constructed circa 1815; renovated early-twentieth century

Dr. Aaron Leland, a native of Massachusetts who served as minister of the nearby First Scots Presbyterian Church, constructed this three-story weatherboarded house around 1815. Its engaged Ionic-columned entry leads directly into a stair which rises from the raised masonry basement to the first floor. A New England visitor, Ebenezer Kellog, recorded his 1817 impressions in a diary: "Dr. Leland's yard is accessible but small. He has one of the most comfortable though not one of the most elegant houses in the city. It is of his own building and accommodated to the climate, having a very large piazza on the south which looks into his garden." Leland sold the house in 1821 to Joel Stevens. Beginning in 1869 the house was owned by the Charleston physician and philanthropist John L. Dawson. Dawson's will specified that the building be sold to provide an infirmary at the William Enston Home complex, *900 King Street*. During the course of this century most of the rear piazzas have been enclosed to create additional living spaces.

84 TRADD STREET, CASEY HOUSE

Constructed circa 1916

This house and *90 Tradd Street*, its neighbor to the west, were constructed by Michael Casey by 1916 in a modified version of the single house form with Queen Anne style side piazzas. Renovations in recent years, including a contemporary wing at the rear, have altered these original late Victorian vernacular structures.

92 Tradd Street, late-nineteenth-century photograph

92 TRADD STREET, DEWAR-LEE-PRINGLE HOUSE

Constructed circa 1762; altered circa 1850

Charles Dewar built this house shortly after purchasing the lot in 1762. The Dewar family sold the property in 1835 to Eliza Seymour Lee, daughter of the famous Charleston cook Sally Seymour and wife of John Lee. The Lees were prominent members of Charleston's free African American elite. They first operated Lee's Boarding House and then in 1847 took over operation of the world-renowned Jones's Hotel. This hotel, located in the Mansion House on Broad Street, had been famous for its service since its founding in 1816 by the free black Jehu Jones. During the Lees' ownership the house was remodeled in a mix of Greek Revival and Egyptian Revival styles. The latter influence can particularly be seen in the decorative window surrounds on the facade. The house began with a single-house plan, but this has been somewhat altered by enclosed piazza sections and a penthouse addition. The Lees remained in the house until after the Civil War. In 1873 it was sold to Ernest Pringle, a president of the Bank of South Carolina. His descendants have occupied the dwelling ever since.

94 TRADD STREET, SAMUEL WAINWRIGHT HOUSE

Constructed circa 1760; altered nineteenth century; renovated late-1970s

Described with its outbuildings and called "a capital and well-known house" in a 1784 newspaper advertisement, this three-and-a-half-story Charleston single house was probably completed by 1760. Its ground story served as a bakery through most of the nineteenth and early-twentieth centuries and as Schwettman's Drug Store from 1949 to the 1970s before the building was returned to residential use.

101 TRADD STREET, JANE THOMSON HOUSE

Constructed circa 1778; altered and renovated mid- and late-twentieth century

Standing on a Grand Modell lot granted in 1689 to Direck Hugland, a New York mariner, this three-story Charleston single house was built for Jane Thomson in the late-1770s. According to newspaper advertisements, Thomson's millinery business was sufficiently thriving by the early-1770s to compel her to advertise in the *South Carolina Gazette* for young women to join her shop as apprentices. In the twentieth century the new owners raised the roofline of the house to create a full third story, and in more recent years a double-tiered side piazza was removed.

102 TRADD STREET, GRIMKÉ-FRASER HOUSE

Constructed mid-eighteenth century; renovated with additions mid-nineteenth century

This site was acquired in 1743 by the merchant and planter Frederick Grimké. Following his death in 1778, the property descended to his daughter Mary Grimké Fraser. The house and land remained in the possession of Fraser women until the mid-1800s, when it passed out of the family. Today the Grimké-Fraser house reflects two major periods of architectural activity. Built as a two-story, hipped-roof structure in the mid-1700s, the house originally stood at right angles to its present position and occupied the corner of the lot at Tradd and Orange Streets. The actual plan of the house in this early period appears to have been close to its present arrangement. A piazza (most likely of single-story height) wrapped around the east and north sides of the building. Access into the house from the piazza led di-

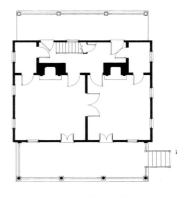

First-floor plan, 102 Tradd Street

rectly into the principal first-floor living spaces (a front parlor and back dining room). Associated with the house were a brick kitchen building and a large rear yard surrounded by a wooden fence. Dr. Hopson Pinckney, an assistant teller at the State Bank on Broad Street, purchased the house in 1847 from the Fraser descendants. Pinckney purchased a property that required significant work, as indicated in an 1846 description: "the old yellow house," wrote Charles Fraser, "is very old, as you know and ruinous." Pinckney began his renovations by moving the house back from Tradd Street, turning it ninety degrees, inserting new underpinnings, making extensive sill repairs, adding new front and rear piazzas, and inserting Greek Revival detailing, including pocket doors between the principal rooms and double doors onto the piazzas.

103 TRADD STREET, JACOB ECKHARD HOUSE

Constructed circa 1797; restored circa 1960

A German organist, often called the "Father of Music in Charleston," constructed this two-and-a-half-story Charleston single house of stuccoed brick. The structure formerly had three bays on the Tradd Street elevation on the first and second floors, but the central street door was later closed in. Piazzas added in the nineteenth century were removed by 1960. The dwelling retains an old clay tile roof and some of its interior woodwork. Eckhard, born at Eschwege in Hesse, began his career as a church organist at the age of twelve. Traveling to America as a Hessian soldier in 1776, he settled, after the Revolution, in Richmond, Virginia. Eckhard came to Charleston in 1786 as organist at St. John's Lutheran Church and in 1809 became organist and choirmaster at St. Michael's Episcopal Church, where he began the first boys' choir in America and published a collection of tunes, chants, and anthems. Eckhard taught music to private pupils throughout his career and used a portion of the ground floor of the house for their instruction.

106 TRADD STREET, COL. JOHN STUART HOUSE

L *Constructed circa 1767–72; wing and piazzas added before 1850; restored with additions 1934*

A rare example of a side-passage plan from the Colonial period, this lavishly fitted house was built by John Stuart, a Scotsman who became superintendent of Indian affairs for the southern colonies and thereby held seats on the governors' councils of Virginia, North Carolina, South Carolina, and Georgia. Stuart acquired the large lots at the southernmost end of the Orange Garden tract by mortgage to the owner Alexander Petrie. He fled the house in 1775, and it was sold in 1782 as confiscated property to the merchant Alexander Gillon. The exterior of the building has flush weatherboarding, pedimented window surrounds, and one of Charleston's most elaborately carved wooden door surrounds: a pediment supported by engaged, fluted Corinthian columns, possibly derived from a plate in Edward Oakley's *Magazine of Architecture, Perspective, and Sculpture* (1730). The first floor of the side wing and the piazzas were added in the nineteenth century. In the 1920s the woodwork from the first-floor sitting room and the large drawing room on the second floor was sold to the Minneapolis Institute of Arts for display in a period room. In 1934 the architectural historian John Mead Howells of New York and Portsmouth, New Hampshire, bought the property as a winter home and reproduced the original woodwork in these rooms. He added a second floor to the polygonal wing and developed a formal French garden west of the house. Howells became a pivotal figure in the Charleston preservation movement in the 1930s and 1940s.

108 TRADD STREET, JAMES MCCALL WARD HOUSE
Constructed 1810–23

A Charleston attorney built this small, vernacular wooden house at a substantial setback on Tradd Street. A double-tiered, Tuscan-columned piazza provides the only ornamentation to the asymmetrical four-bay front facade. After Ward's death, his widow repurchased the property when the mortgage was foreclosed by the Fellowship Society. In the 1850s John B. P. Alley, owner of a substantial undertaking establishment, purchased the property. Alley added a one-story building to the north for making coffins and lived on the site as well. Although the undertaking business ceased by 1900, his descendants, the Poulnot family, owned 108 Tradd Street until 1977.

110 TRADD STREET, SNELSON-MULLER HOUSE
Constructed circa 1900; renovated with addition circa 1980

A contractor of the Mormon faith replaced an earlier single house on this site at the turn of the century. Built in the Shingle style, the dwelling with hipped roof and cross gables features a one-story front piazza with shingled square columns, a curvilinear bay on the second story, and overhanging eaves with long rectangular brackets. Mrs. Margaretta Agnes Muller bought the completed residence in 1904. Her son, John D. Muller Jr., later a leading Charleston preservationist, spent his childhood in this house.

122 TRADD STREET, WILLIAM C. BEE HOUSE

Constructed circa 1850

William C. Bee, owner of the leading blockade running business in Charleston during the War Between the States, served as a commissioner from South Carolina negotiating a withdrawal of Federal troops and the end of Reconstruction. Bee built this three-and-a-half-story brick single house as his family's residence in the second quarter of the nineteenth century. The two-bay, three-story brick facade consists of Flemish bond brickwork, brick jack arches above each window, and a gabled parapet with a tripartite window. The two-story, Tuscan-columned piazza features an Italianate style architrave screen with a console bracketed hood. Bee also helped establish the phosphate industry in the Charleston area after the war.

125 TRADD STREET, CAPT. JOHN MORRISON HOUSE

Constructed circa 1807; restored 1930s

One of the most distinctive of Charleston's single houses, the Morrison dwelling's wide street frontage points to the exceptional depth of its stair hall and flanking rooms on each floor. John Morrison, a mariner, purchased the property from the estate of Isaac Mazyck in 1800 and built within five years. Following the Federal style, the house retains its nine-over-nine white sash windows on the first two floors and smaller six-over-six third-floor windows. A modillioned cornice and boxed soffit or fascia encircles the building, including its triple-tiered, columned piazzas. With the death of Captain Morrison, the property was sold in 1826 to the Peronneau family. In the 1930s Mr. and Mrs. Frederick Allen, a wealthy northern couple, restored the house as their winter residence, replacing the piazza screen with a period fanlighted doorway brought from the North. Apparently this site and the lots to the west were part of the garden of Robert Squibb. Squibb, a scientific horticulturist, authored *The Gardener's Calendar,* first published in 1787. He introduced a number of rare species of plants into the Charleston area.

126 TRADD STREET, DR. PETER FAYSSOUX HOUSE

Constructed circa 1732; restored 1965

Beginning as a two-story house with an asymmetrical floor plan like those at *59 Church* and *94 Broad*, this early dwelling evolved through several periods of alteration. Surviving interior corner posts still visible in the front rooms have often been noted as the building's most unusual architectural feature and as an indication of its construction by a carpenter accustomed to seventeenth-century English building techniques. In the antebellum period a double-tiered piazza was appended to the west elevation. Other alterations in the nineteenth and early-twentieth centuries included the construction of a brick ell on the rear of the house and the removal of the front street door.

Probably built by the tailor Alexander Smith between 1732 and 1740, the house became the property of Anne Fayssoux and her husband Dr. Peter Fayssoux, surgeon general of the Continental army in the Revolution. One of their descendants who grew up in the house, Gen. Bernard Elliott Bee, supposedly gave Gen. Thomas J. Jackson his famous nickname, saying "there stands Jackson like a stone wall." In 1863 Charles O. Witte acquired the Fayssoux House and used it as one of his many rental properties. Beatrice Witte Ravenel inherited the house, and her daughter Beatrice St. Julien Ravenel restored it as her residence in 1965, adding the long subdivided back lot to the parcel. Miss Ravenel is best remembered for her scholarly book, *The Architects of Charleston.*

128 TRADD STREET, HUMPHREY SOMMERS HOUSE

Constructed circa 1765; additions 1790– 1800, 1840s

Charleston's most noted eighteenth-century builder-contractor constructed the original section of this L-shaped wooden dwelling on a raised masonry foundation on a point overlooking "Councellair's Creek" (now long filled) and the marshes of the Ashley River in 1765. Immigrating to Charleston from the west of England as a "slater," Humphrey Sommers prospered with commissions, one of which was as chief subcontractor of St. Michael's Church. Sommers fully utilized some of the best work of independent craftsman carvers on the interior of the house, which he built on a lot that may have been acquired through the dowry of his wife, Susanna. The interior woodwork, particularly the parlor chimney piece with extensive rococo style carving,

has become famous in recent years and was reproduced in the Museum of Early Southern Decorative Arts in Winston Salem, North Carolina, as a hallmark of a Charleston room. The exterior of the house retains its original pedimented window surrounds with console supported sills, weatherboard siding, wide entablature with a modillioned cornice, and a bellcast slate roof. A central projection from the east elevation provides a stair hall on the interior and contains an elaborate Venetian (Palladian) window. A portico may have graced the south elevation, but a Tuscan-columned piazza was added in the nineteenth century. Sommers rose to be a member of the Commons House of Assembly by 1762 and achieved sufficient wealth to leave a substantial estate of town and country property at his death in 1789. Judge Edward Frost purchased 128 Tradd Street in 1841, and the house has remained in the hands of his descendants ever since.

129 TRADD STREET, JOSEPH WINTHROP HOUSE
Constructed circa 1797; restored 1940s

Joseph Winthrop, a member of one of Boston's oldest families, came to Charleston from Connecticut as a young merchant in 1788. After wedding Mary, the elder sister of the miniaturist Charles Fraser, he built this three-story single house on a large lot set back from Tradd Street. The structure is austerely simple on the exterior with beaded weatherboarding, large six-over-six windows, and a deep modillioned cornice. The interior retains much of its original Federal woodwork. Architectural historian Samuel G. Stoney lived in the rear dependency for much of his later career as a Charleston historian.

WHITE POINT GARDEN
Developed 1848–60 with subsequent improvements

This "public pleasure ground" (also known as the Battery) was developed in the years after the city began to buy up land in this area for a park. Known as "White Point" or "Oyster Point" from the initial settlement of Charles Town due to the oyster shells found along the south shore of the peninsula, it served as the site of a series of forts and batteries. A mid-nineteenth-century bird's-eye view shows the present park with immature plantings and double axial paths. A bathing house served as a popular attraction on the water side of the park through much of the nineteenth century. Although the cannons and mortars are commemorative rather than relics of the wars they represent, the park, with its mature live oaks, serves as the setting for a number of statues, memorials, and monuments. These include E. T. Viett's statuary monument to the Palmetto Guard and the magnificent bronze memorial to the Confederate defenders of Charleston. The latter sculpture, a bronze figure standing before a representation of the goddess Minerva, carved by H. A. MacNeil and cast in Paris in 1932, allegorically depicts the soldiers' defense of the city. The cast-iron bandstand was given in 1905 in memory of Mr. and Mrs. George W. Williams.

Detail of John William Hill's Charleston, S.C., *1851, showing White Point Garden*

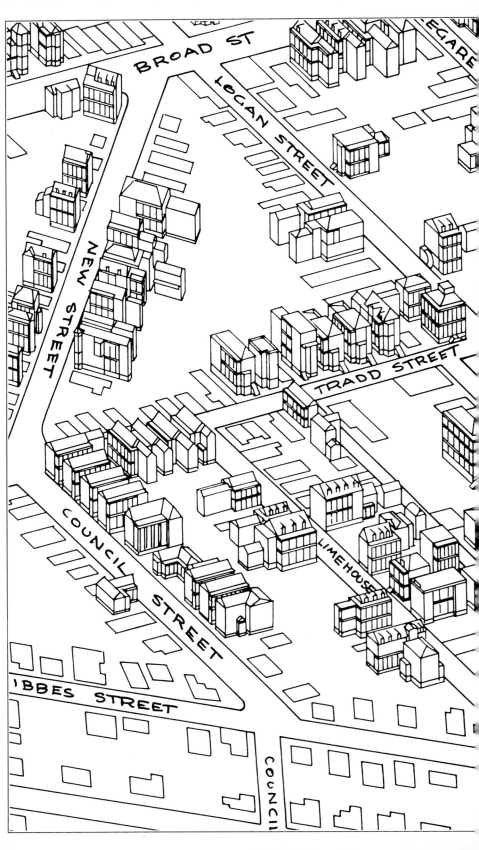

4

THE LOWER WESTERN PENINSULA

Nineteenth-Century Rebuilding and Twentieth-Century Infill

Charleston's earliest buildings generally occupied the higher dry ground encompassed by the Grand Modell, and for nearly a century that was land enough to fill the demand for construction sites. Planners and mapmakers drew pen-and-ink boundaries that imagined the city extending into some of the vast marshland that bordered the western edges of the city along the Ashley River, but there was little need for these wet sites until the city spilled beyond its early boundaries. As the nineteenth century progressed, more large lots on the western edge of the city were subdivided and marshes were filled to create additional building sites. A small parcel called Savages' Green was developed in 1792 with the construction of a new theater on a wedge of land between creeks. Its dividing streets, Savage and New, were laid

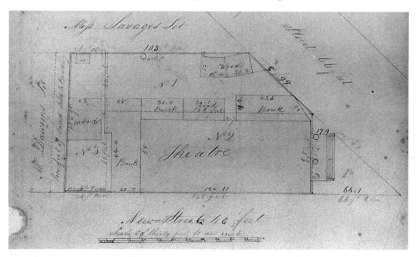

Plat showing Charleston Theatre at Broad between Savage and New Streets, 1833

Simons Houses, 168 and 170 Broad Street, in the early-twentieth century

The extension of the city seawall to create Murray Boulevard, circa 1911

out from the subdivision of lands formerly owned by individual families. New Street, originally called Middleton Street after the wealthy plantation family who owned town property there, underwent the name change in 1832. The fire of 1861 traveled in a near perfect diagonal from the edge of Hasell Street on the waterfront southwest to the Ashley River at the foot of Tradd Street and destroyed most of the area of Broad Street west of Legare Street and to the southwest much of Logan, New, Savage, and Council Streets. However, the very west end of Tradd Street where the Chisolm family's imposing Greek Revival mansion and their adjacent complex of rice mills stood was spared.

Much of this area of Charleston was rebuilt between 1870 and 1890, often in the Queen Anne style and in many cases by German merchants. The use of the side-hall, double-parlor plan with front bay windows and double-tiered side piazzas prevailed. Other Victorian styles such as Stick, Italianate, Gothic Revival, and Second

South Battery and Gibbes Street during the development of Murray Boulevard

Empire are be found in this section as well.

In 1909 the Charleston businessman Andrew Buist Murray, an orphan who became the ward of the wealthy Jefferson Bennett, promoted a plan originated by C. Bissell Jenkins and under the leadership of Mayor R. Godwyn Rhett to fill about fifty acres of mudflats and marshes south of Tradd Street to South Battery. The extension of the seawall from Whitepoint along the Ashley River shore permitted the development of this "Boulevard" section by 1911. Extensions of old streets such as South Battery and Gibbes tying into the prolongations of existing north-south thoroughfares such as Rutledge and Ashley created new building lots. These lots gave rise to the construction of an eclectic mix of new houses in the prevailing early-twentieth-century styles of Beaux Arts, Colonial Revival, and Tudor Revival. Some developers built up whole blocks of investment houses, or in the case of Colonial Street, an entire street. The larger, grander Georgian Revival buildings went up along Battery (renamed Murray) Boulevard on the Ashley facing the harbor, as their East Battery counterparts did a century before. The intrinsic architectural significance of these houses is only now becoming apparent.

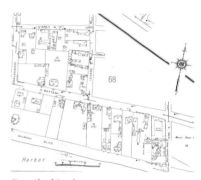

Detail of Sanborn map showing Murray Boulevard and its environs, 1930s

J. C. Tiedeman House showing original polychrome paint scheme, circa 1893

130 BROAD STREET, J. C. TIEDEMAN HOUSE
Constructed 1881–82; renovated and restored 1996

John C. Tiedeman built this side-hall, double-parlor-plan house with low pitched, hip roof on an important corner lot. The facade exhibits rich Italianate detail, including the bracketed hood over its entry, approached by marble steps with a cast-iron balustrade; a bay window with balustraded base and parapet; bracketed window heads; bracketed cornice within the wide entablature; and a two-story piazza with square columns. Another family member, Otto Tiedeman Jr., erected a similar dwelling immediately to the north at *63 Legare Street* at the same time. The latter building includes more conservative detailing, however, with its Tuscan columns and omission of the bay window. Both houses joined a smaller-scaled version of the same plan at *65 Legare Street*, finished in 1879 by C. J. Harvey.

131–137 BROAD STREET
Constructed 1877–83

Different owners constructed the side-hall, double-parlor-plan houses of varying sizes and detailing on lots burned out in the fire of 1861. The earliest of these, 135 Broad Street, was constructed by John P. Merkhardt by 1877. Merkhardt also built an almost identical house next door at 137 Broad by 1879, a property still held by his family into the third decade of the twentieth century. With three and a half stories, 133 Broad Street is the tallest of the ensemble. This dwelling was constructed by Arthur Mazyck in 1884–85 and was soon thereafter acquired by the Waring family. John Voight, a shoe dealer on Market Street, constructed 131 Broad Street with its prominent bay window and door over-

Measured first-floor plan, 131 Broad Street

hang before 1887. In recent years, the owners discovered original stenciled ceiling decoration consisting of the Greek Revival anthemion motif.

134 BROAD STREET, JOHN KLINCK HOUSE

Constructed 1872; restored 1996

John Henry Devereux, architect

The owner of the grocery at the northeast corner of Broad and Church Streets constructed this house in 1872 with the assistance of the architect John Henry Devereux. As Klinck's business expanded, he obviously desired to move out of his old-fashioned residence at *116 Church Street* and retire to this area where other German families were rebuilding on lots burned out in the fire of 1861. Klinck's two-story house reflects a mixture of period romantic styles including a two-story Gothic piazza with quatrefoil shaped columns, Italianate style bracketed cornice, and first-floor bay with semicircular headed windows.

136–138 BROAD STREET, WILLIAM B. SMITH HOUSE AND A. E. CARADUC HOUSE

Constructed circa 1875–79; 136 altered circa 1905; 138 rehabilitated mid-1980s

A large antebellum house on this double lot burned in the fire of 1861. In the mid-1870s William B. Smith subdivided the property into two lots, apparently building an elaborate side-hall, double-parlor-plan dwelling on the eastern half, while a purchaser of 138 Broad Street constructed a two-and-a-half-story side-hall, double-parlor-plan house with a Second Empire mansard roof and double-tiered front piazzas. Henry and Sarah I'On Lowndes purchased 136 Broad Street in 1881 and eventually sold it to A. T. Litschgi, who added various Georgian Revival details

The Colonial Revival style doorway of 136 Broad Street

with the help of the architect-contractor Henry T. Zacharias. These include the door architrave with engaged Corinthian columns and semicircular transom and the pedimented screen on the piazza.

140 BROAD STREET, ALFRED HUGER HOUSE
Constructed circa 1870

Alfred Huger, planter and postmaster of Charleston, owned a fine antebellum house on this site that burned in the fire of 1861. Legend has it that he stoically watched the fire consume his house from an armchair that he pulled into the middle of the street. One of the few property owners on the western end of Broad Street who chose to rebuild on the sites of their former houses, Huger completed a substantial two-story house with closed cross gable and projecting bay window, and giant order, Italianate style door architrave. A two-story piazza with Tuscan columns faces Logan Street on the western side of the dwelling. Huger left the property to his son, Dr. William Huger, and it was occupied until the early-twentieth century by William's widow, Sabina Huger. Long noted for its massive date palm in the yard, the house today is still owned by the late Mrs. Huger's estate.

Early-twentieth-century photograph of 152 Broad Street

152 BROAD STREET, BIRD-TIEDEMAN HOUSE
Constructed 1885

John Henry Devereux, architect

William M. Bird, a dealer in paint, glass, and hardware, lived on lower Meeting Street but built this house in 1885. The house reflects the transition between the Italianate and Queen Anne styles, apparent in its double-tiered front bay window, curved piazzas with saw-cut-patterned balustrades, and intermediary cross gable. Early photographs depict the original polychrome paint treatment of this building, as well as the lost detailing of its rear carriage house, formerly surmounted by a cupola. Bird sold the house to the German grocer Otto Tiedeman, relative of other German families on Broad Street, in 1889.

157 BROAD STREET, LUTJEN'S (BURBAGE'S) GROCERY
Constructed 1874

This is the only active corner grocery store in the South of Broad neighborhood. This type of corner store remains a viable part of some neighborhoods to the north, but it is one of Charleston's most threatened vernacular building types. Burbage's was built in 1874 by the Lutjen family, who immigrated to Charleston from Hanover, Germany, to house their store and saloon. A former house on the site was destroyed in the fire of 1861, and much of this part of Broad Street was rebuilt in the 1870s and 1880s by persons of German extraction. Berend Lutjen built the single houses at *159–163 Broad Street* in 1878–80. Burbage's grocery store moved to this address from another downtown location in 1961. Although the interior has been modernized, the piazza still leads to a stairway accessing family living quarters above.

159–163 BROAD STREET, BEREND LUTJEN TENEMENTS
Constructed 1874–80; restored and renovated 1980s

Berend Lutjen, a German grocer and saloon keeper whose family emigrated from Hanover, acquired several Broad Street lots burned over in the fire of 1861, including the property of the Horlbeck family. A few years later Lutjen built *157 Broad Street* to house his store and saloon. He built the wooden side-hall-plan house at 159 Broad Street and the traditional Charleston single houses with closed gable ends and double-

161 Broad Street

tiered piazzas at 161 Broad Street and 163 Broad Street. Although the upper story of the piazza on the latter dwelling was enclosed, both buildings retain their Italianate style door architraves and six-over-six sash windows. The surviving interiors of these houses retain mantel and staircase trim typical of Greek Revival dwellings in the antebellum period and reflect the adoption by Charleston's nineteenth-century immigrants of the most typical vernacular house types.

160 BROAD STREET, WILLIAM WRAGG HOUSE

Originally constructed by 1855; renovated or rebuilt 1866–70, 1940

This building was originally a three-story dwelling owned by one of South Carolina's leading physicians, William Wragg, who lived primarily on this site from 1855 until his death thirty years later. Passing to the McLeod family, the house was lowered or refenestrated and renovated in the Colonial Revival style with a portico. Wragg built the adjacent dwelling at *162 Broad Street* for his daughters.

164–172 BROAD STREET, SIMONS HOUSES

Constructed 1888–91

A scion of one of Charleston's ancient Huguenot families, Samuel Wragg Simons, built three of the houses in this block between 1886 and 1891, a group presenting the most eclectic mix of Victorian styles in the city of Charleston. The house that now occupies the lot at 164 Broad Street originally stood at 3 Franklin Street and was moved to its present location on rollers. Caroline Simons's house at 170 Broad Street features a mix of Queen Anne with some Italianate and Eastlake (Stick) details, including its front bracketed gable with projecting arcaded balcony and mixed diagonal/vertical stickwork, second-story shingle sheathing, and pedimented, metal window heads.

170 Broad Street, shown circa 1893, a decade after its completion

167 BROAD STREET, HEILBRON-GIBBON HOUSE
Constructed circa 1836–40

This two-and-a-half-story raised brick single house may be the only dwelling on the south side of Broad Street, west of Legare Street, to survive the 1861 fire. Apparently built by James Heilbron, it was owned at the time of the Civil War by George Gibbon, a merchant of Massachusetts origin who lived nearby on New Street.

173 BROAD STREET, PRIOLEAU-MILES HOUSE
Constructed circa 1873

Although built by a member of the Prioleau family, this large house was acquired in the 1880s by C. Richardson Miles, a South Carolina attorney general and president of the College of Charleston Trustees. Considered a pillar of Charleston's "old guard," Miles was eulogized at his death as "bending his best efforts towards preserving the essentials of good breeding and polite intercourse in the midst of change." Incorporating a mix of Queen Anne and Colonial Revival style detailing, the house has an entry that is capped by a large bracketed pediment while an adjacent cross gable with square and bowed bay windows projects from the front facade. A front balustraded balcony curves to the west and joins a double-tiered Ionic-columned piazza. The side-hall-plan building contains twenty-three rooms.

177 BROAD STREET, JONES-SMITH HOUSE
Constructed before 1870

Lucius M. Jones built this two-and-a-half-story Charleston double house on a large lot near the western end of Broad Street by 1870. His house reflects many of Charleston's antebellum architectural traditions yet pays homage to the prevailing

Italianate style. A small pedimented portico shades the front doorway, which has a semicircular transom. A large-scale pediment projects from the roof with a central Venetian window. A double-tiered piazza faces out on the adjacent garden lot that remains with the property. Jones sold the house to his partner, William B. Smith, in 1874.

180 BROAD STREET, COOPER-O'CONNOR HOUSE
Constructed circa 1855

180 Broad Street, Mathew Brady photograph taken during Union occupation, 1865

A two-story portico with Temple of the Winds capitals ornaments the front tower of this three-story wooden house constructed in the Greek Revival style at the former western end of Broad Street (before later filling) near Colonial Lake, then popularly known as "the pond." George Washington Cooper acquired the property from a trustee of the estate of Louis Trapman, who had received the site through his marriage to Mary Bowen Moore. A lengthy lawsuit resulted in the sale of this and other properties for distribution to the four heirs, including the Baroness de Lengenuil of Canada. After Cooper's financial reversals, Michael P. O'Connor bought the lot with its "mansion house and outbuildings" from the Bank of South Carolina in 1859. This block survived the fire of 1861, and the house was used by the Confederacy as a prison for Union officers. Five generals were imprisoned here prior to the fall of the city in February 1865. After the war George Cunningham, a butcher who rose to be mayor of Charleston, purchased this property.

191 BROAD STREET, CLARENCE WARING HOUSE
Constructed 1913

Clarence Waring, a native Charleston businessman, constructed this two-and-a-half-story Colonial Revival style house in

1913 on one of several newly reclaimed lots. A projecting closed gable emanates asymmetrically from the hipped roof facade. A full-width porch with paired Doric columns and balustrade wraps partially around the western elevation. Waring's house bears a striking similarity to its two western neighbors, the George Carroll House (1912) at *193 Broad Street* and the Taft-Simons House (1911) at *195 Broad Street.*

CHISOLM STREET

This street, named for the family that built the adjoining rice mill, borders a filled mill pond commonly referred to as the "Horse Lot." This former grazing space provides a popular venue for soccer matches and other local sports. On the west side of the street 3 Chisolm Street opened in 1923 as the Murray Vocational School, one of the first schools of its kind in the state. David B. Hyer, whose career began in civil engineering and construction at the Charleston Navy Yard, designed the $180,000 vocational school that was named in honor of the philanthropist Andrew Buist Murray. Murray School features significant characteristics of the Neoclassical Revival style with its stone, engaged column portico and handsome fanlighted doorway in the Adamesque mode.

Neoclassical doorway, 3 Chisolm Street

1–20 COLONIAL STREET, CALHOUN SECURITIES HOUSES
Constructed beginning 1914–15

Nearly all the dwellings on the street were completed within a few years; Calhoun Securities Company constructed most of the buildings as an investment, but a few individual owners built their own houses. Colonial Street constitutes one of the most diverse collections of early-twentieth-century houses in the city; they show the wide mix of architectural styles used throughout the nation in this period.

Although the Queen Anne style character-izes the dwelling at 3 Colonial Street with its cross gable front bay and conical tower, most of the residences represent the Colonial Revival and Craftsman styles with wide, hipped dormers, full-width porches or front porticos, and closed gabled roofs. The front facing gambrel roof at 19 Colonial Street nearly duplicates the roofline of the more sophisticated Shingle style dwelling at 5 Colonial Street with paired and triple windows, classical portico with Colonial Revival architrave, and shed dormers projecting from the sides of the metal gambrel roof.

2–6 COUNCIL STREET, RICHARD MORRIS HOUSES
Constructed 1881

Three nearly identical single houses anchor the corner of Council and Tradd Streets. Richard J. Morris, a house furnishings dealer, constructed these buildings as an investment in 1881. Each of the dwellings retains its closed gable ends and two-story side piazzas. The house at 2 Council Street retains an original late–Greek Revival architrave in the piazza screen, matching that at 6 Council Street, although the latter now features an overhanging pediment. 4 Council Street lost its piazza screen in the conversion of the house to a duplex some years ago. By contrast with these regularly proportioned structures, the investor Henry Klaven built the diminutive two-bay single house at *8 Council Street* with Queen Anne style detailing.

10 COUNCIL STREET, H. L. GRADDICK HOUSE
Constructed 1885–86; altered twentieth century

H. L. Graddick, an African American mariner, and/or his son, H. T. Graddick, captain of the schooner *Robert E. Lee*, constructed this Greek Revival style single house as a residence more than a decade after this type of construction passed out of fashion. The building retains its six-over-six sash windows, plain Greek Revival style door architraves, and tripartite window set in the front closed gable. Several years ago a subsequent owner removed the original piazzas and added a discordant Colonial Revival style portico and L-shaped addition. Graddick also constructed two small freedman's cottages on the lots immediately to the south. John Ahrens built another freedman's cottage at *13 Council Street* before 1890, and he was also the owner of *14 Council Street*. The large L-shaped cottage at 14 Council Street retains its original wrap-around piazzas and Gothic hooded chimneys, while the more diminutive *16 Council Street* retains its simple two-bay front facade with closed gable, despite numerous additions to the rear.

13 Council Street

18–20 COUNCIL STREET, CASEY TENEMENTS
Constructed before 1886

Mrs. T. Arthur Casey, wife of an appraiser, erected these two identical Charleston single houses with Italianate style attic windows in their closed gable ends and Italianate style piazza door architraves. The piazza screen at 20 Council Street features a rectangular transom with clipped corners. The Caseys, according to the directory of 1893, lived at *22 Council Street*, which was also built before 1886. 22 Council Street is an identical single house altered in the twentieth century as a duplex with extensive additions.

20 Council Street

9 FRANKLIN STREET, B. C. PRESSLEY HOUSE
Constructed 1855

B. C. Pressley, a partner in the law firm of Pressley, Lord, and Inglesby, built this

two-story, gable-ended house with a side-hall entry a few years before the Civil War. Pressley's house reflects the transition between the Greek Revival style, evident in its double-tiered piazza with fluted Doric columns, and the Italianate style, as demonstrated through the bracketed cornice and bracketed door hood, which shelters a fanlighted transom. The eclectic mix of elements on Pressley's house contrasts with the smaller-scaled detailing of the residence at *11 Franklin Street*.

13 FRANKLIN STREET, GEORGE WASHINGTON COOPER HOUSE

Constructed circa 1850

Adding to the mix of romantic styles utilized in the building of this part of Franklin Street in the antebellum period, George Washington Cooper, owner of *180 Broad Street*, selected a Carpenter Gothic style for this 1850s house. Sheathed in narrow-width siding, the side-hall-plan house boasts an entry portico and two-story side piazza with lattice columns, decorative verge board on its gable, and a cantilevered third-story window with harmonious gable trim.

15 FRANKLIN STREET, ETIENNE POINCIGNON HOUSE

Constructed circa 1850; rebuilt 1886–87

The wealthy tinsmith and real estate baron Etienne Poincignon built this simple three-story masonry house in the side-hall plan in 1850 and shortly thereafter conveyed it to Caroline McNulty. Only the arched windows, the upper cast-iron grilles with anthemion motifs, and the decorative brick parapet interrupt the general austerity of the design, probably owing to the severe damage inflicted on the house by the earthquake of 1886, requiring that "all walls be rebuilt above the first story."

17 FRANKLIN STREET, THEODORE WHITNEY HOUSE

Constructed circa 1850; renovated 1983

Exhibiting features of the late–Greek Revival and early-Italianate styles with its columned front portico, double-tiered side piazzas, and oversized closed gable, masking a lower pitched roof, Whitney's house incorporates other eclectic trends of mid-nineteenth-century America. Although obscured by the shutters, the first- and second-story windows are framed by Egyptian Revival style architraves. In the conversion of the structure as a designer show house in 1983, extensive decorative paint schemes were discovered on the interior. The building housed Charleston's French consul, Paul Dejardin, in the 1870s and 1880s.

GREENHILL STREET

Primarily developed in the early-nineteenth century, much of the eastern side of the street down to the marshline running just south of 4 Greenhill Street was acquired in the 1790s by the noted Charleston cabinetmaker William Axson Jr. Axson, generally associated with the carving of the pulpit at Pompion Hill Chapel on the Cooper River, as well as other eighteenth-century Charleston woodwork and furniture, devised this property to his son, Samuel Edward Axson, a house carpenter, along with a sum of money "sufficient to built a house thereon 35 feet by 18." Noted by the late architectural historian Albert Simons for its meticulous craftsmanship and its representation of the "continuity of pre-Revolutionary skill," this two-and-a-half-story Charleston single house with a slightly asymmetrical plan retains its original beaded weatherboarding. A double-axial-plan garden designed in the 1940s by Loutrel Briggs survives despite a subdivision of the parcel to the south. The remainder of the west side of the street has a number of wooden dwellings of mid- and late-nineteenth-century construction, such

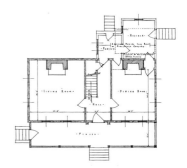

Measured front (west) facade and measured plan of the first floor of the Axson House, 4 Greenhill Street

as 3 and 7 Greenhill Street, adapted as larger residences in recent years, as well as Colonial Revival style houses such as 13 Greenhill Street.

7 LIMEHOUSE STREET, ROBERT LIMEHOUSE HOUSE
Constructed circa 1830

A member of the family that owned the land from which this street was created in the antebellum period built this two-and-a-half-story brick single house with pedimented gable and double-tiered Tuscan piazza. A simple Greek Revival architrave survives in the piazza screen. In scale and simplicity the Limehouse dwelling closely resembles its contemporary in stucco at *14 Limehouse Street.*

9 & 10 LIMEHOUSE STREET, WILLIAM PINCKNEY SHINGLER HOUSES
Constructed 1857, 1859

The wealthy cotton factor William Pinckney Shingler bought several lots on the west side of the street in 1856 from the Limehouse family. Within the year Shingler, with the assistance of a master builder, completed the late–Greek Revival style dwelling with a double-tiered, Doric-columned piazza on the south facing the large garden area and a closed gable front with a central tripartite window. A marble staircase with a wrought- and cast-iron railing and brass trim approaches the Rococo Revival style doorway, an indication of the architectural treatment of the lavish interior. The brickwork of the building was originally pointed with a tinted mortar and scored and lined with a white lime mortar, an extraordinary technique used to cause the uneven bricks to appear straight and evenly molded. The extensive brick coping along Limehouse Street is similarly treated

10 Limehouse Street

and topped by a wooden balustrade. With the death of his wife and a temporary decline in cotton prices in the Panic of 1857, Shingler sold the house a few months after its completion. Tradition holds that within a year he married his late wife's sister and began construction of a similarly styled but larger-scaled brick dwelling at 10 Limehouse Street. This house has a street-level pedimented doorway with a guilloche molding and a "masked piazza," a brick wall with false windows shielding a double-tiered piazza from the street. Its former dependency, now a separate dwelling, remains at *12 Limehouse Street.*

View of 9 Limehouse Street with former piazza stair, 1880s

15 LIMEHOUSE STREET, ANDREW CUNNINGHAM HOUSE
Constructed circa 1854

An artisan named Andrew Cunningham bought this parcel in 1853 from Thomas Limehouse following a subdivision of the family property. Although the Tuscan-columned, double-tiered piazza and most interior features link this house to the antebellum Greek Revival style, the window lintels with segmental arches and keystones on the second story, the stucco belt courses, and stucco quoining reflect the out-of-date Federal style. The house was purchased in 1914 by Wade Humphreys, antecedent of the contemporary Charleston writer Josephine Humphreys, and remained in this family until 1984.

18 LIMEHOUSE STREET, OPTIMUS E. HUGHES HOUSE
Constructed circa 1853

An unusual paired bracket cornice supporting a deep fascia, and an Italianate style parapet with a central panel flanked by pedestaled urns cap this house built by Optimus E. Hughes around 1853. Hughes took out a mortgage on his house in 1853

and by 1856 sold it to John Eddings. The southernmost antebellum house on the street, the dwelling lost a third story and gabled roof years after its construction.

21 LIMEHOUSE STREET, JOSEPH E. JENKINS HOUSE

Constructed 1917

Walter H. Smith, architect

Architect Walter H. Smith designed this austere two-story frame dwelling in the Colonial Revival style for the Charleston businessman Joseph Jenkins. A pediment with a Neoclassical lunette extends from the hipped roof, while the one-story front portico shades the transomed entry.

3 LOGAN STREET, FANNIE WERNER HOUSE

Constructed 1902

The English architect Richard Norman Shaw popularized the Queen Anne movement that borrowed heavily from late-medieval models. Many characteristics of this style are evident in the house built for Fannie Werner, including the triple-columned front portico with spindle-work balustrade, the double-tiered bay windows with diamond-work upper sashes, the closed front gable with ornamental trim, and the double-tiered side piazza with unusual bowed front. The wrought-iron front fence features the lyre pattern popular in Charleston during the latter years of the nineteenth century.

4 LOGAN STREET, FROST HOUSE

Constructed circa 1852

When the fire of 1861 swept the neighborhood, the Frost House survived the conflagration and thus remains the only antebellum dwelling on Logan Street between Tradd and Broad Streets. Edward Frost of *128 Tradd Street* built this house for his son, Thomas. A marble staircase with cast-iron balustrade rises to the main entry, sheltered by a pedimented architrave. Brownstone lintels and sills ornament the window fenestration of the principal two floors. Susan Pringle Frost, Charleston suffragist, realtor, and founder of the Preservation Society, lived here in the early years of the twentieth century. Miss Frost hosted a meeting of the National Women's Party at 4 Logan Street in 1915.

6–10 LOGAN STREET, ST. PETER'S EPISCOPAL CHURCH SITE AND GRAVEYARD

Established 1834–36

Charleston Episcopalians established a fourth congregation on this site in the 1830s. The fire of 1861 destroyed a substantial colonnaded church building here. Only the wrought-iron fence with single and double gates, which feature elaborate scrollwork cresting, and a churchyard with numerous marble monuments remain. This area was used until the early-twentieth century as a cemetery by another parish. Part of the church parcel was sold for construction of condominiums in the early-1970s.

9 LOGAN STREET, JOHN LEGE HOUSE

Constructed 1874; renovated late-1950s

John Lege, a cotton broker and partner in the firm of Mottet, Huchet and Company, built this plain, late–Greek Revival style house after the Civil War in an area of Logan Street burned out in the fire of 1861. After using a fire loan from the city for the "rebuilding of the burnt district" Lege sold the building to William Leidler. The current door architrave with fluted Doric columns and semicircular transom was added by Mr. and Mrs. S. Henry Edmunds, the owners of the house in the 1950s and 1960s.

9 and 11 Logan Street

11 LOGAN STREET, MARIA WILSON HOUSE

Constructed 1882

Mrs. Wilson conservatively chose the Charleston single house style for her new residence in 1882. Distinguishable from antebellum examples by its one-over-one sashes, Italianate style piazza door architrave, and flat hooded window heads, the Wilson House, like its other postbellum neighbors, employs a setback to create a front yard. A Victorian cast-iron fence separates this space from the sidewalk.

14 LOGAN STREET, N. S. NIPSON HOUSE

Constructed 1874

N. S. Nipson, a shoe dealer on King Street, built this two-story, side-hall-plan house in 1874. Nipson's house was probably the first to be rebuilt on the east side of Logan Street after the fire of 1861.

8 MURRAY BOULEVARD, HENRY CHEVES HOUSE

Constructed 1930; altered 1987

Henry Cheves, descendant of a noted nineteenth-century politician and himself a banker and resident at *47 South Battery*, constructed this two-story brick house with a double-tiered Colonial Revival porch in 1930 east of houses he built fifteen years earlier for his son and daughter. A subsequent owner added a third story with proportionately smaller windows in the late-1980s.

10–12 MURRAY BOULEVARD, CHEVES HOUSES

Constructed 1916

McCrady Brothers, architects

In 1916 Henry Cheves built these matching two-story, curvilinear-gable-ended houses for his son, Henry Cheves Jr., and daughter, Charlotte Cheves Hardison, on two newly reclaimed lots on Battery (now Murray) Boulevard. These stucco-on-wire frame houses reflect an eclectic late–Queen Anne style reminiscent of seventeenth-century Jacobean architecture.

36 MURRAY BOULEVARD, ARCHIBALD BAKER JR. HOUSE
Constructed 1938

Dr. Archibald Baker Jr., son of the founder of Baker Memorial Hospital and himself a prominent Charleston physician, built this Colonial Revival house with Neoclassical overtones in 1938. A pedimented portico with Temple of the Winds columns and an oval window in the tympanum dominate the five-bay facade. A doorway surmounted by an elliptical transom serves as the main entry for this central-hall-plan dwelling.

46 MURRAY BOULEVARD, DR. ROBERT BARNWELL RHETT HOUSE
Constructed 1926–28
Simons and Lapham, architects

The newly formed partnership of Albert Simons and Samuel Lapham utilized their exceptional knowledge of Charleston Neoclassical detailing in the planning of this Revival style dwelling for Dr. and Mrs. Robert Barnwell Rhett. Standing on a large lot enclosed by a handsome brick coping with wrought-iron fence and gates topped with cast stone Neoclassical caps and spheres, the building is constructed of hand-molded brick laid in a variant of the Flemish bond pattern. A double curvilinear stair approaches a Neoclassical portico with fluted Tuscan columns, detailing that is repeated in a piazza on the east side of the building. A pediment supported by console brackets projects from the slate roof, echoing the other Federal houses in the city.

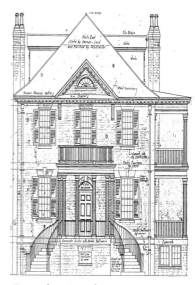

Front elevation of 46 Murray Boulevard by Simons and Lapham, 1925

48 MURRAY BOULEVARD, G. ABBOTT MIDDLETON HOUSE

Constructed circa 1929

A large Neoclassical Revival portico with attenuated columns fronts a brick house constructed for a leading Charleston cotton exporting family about 1929. A Georgian Revival style door architrave provides entry into this building, reflecting the mix of precedents used in large traditional houses in the early-twentieth century. In 1942, while stationed in Charleston, Lt. John F. Kennedy lived in the garage apartment at the rear of the lot.

52 MURRAY BOULEVARD, C. BISSELL JENKINS HOUSE

Constructed 1913; renovated and restored 1992

Walker and Burden, architects

C. Bissell Jenkins, the originator of the reclamation project that led to the completion of Murray Boulevard and other streets in this area, became the first to build a residence on the new, grand thoroughfare. Designed by the architectural firm of Walker and Burden, the house remains the most imposing of the Colonial Revival style dwellings built on the peninsula in the early-twentieth century. The monumental dwelling is fronted by a giant-order Tuscan portico and is constructed of Summerville brick and trimmed in limestone. The four faces of the red tiled roof terminate in a deck surrounded by a balustrade. Jenkins also developed the first residential subdivision on James Island, creating Riverland Terrace in 1925. Sold in 1927 to John B. Farrow, president of the Charleston Country Club, the house served as a veritable center for early-twentieth-century Charleston society.

62 MURRAY BOULEVARD, ALFRED HUGER HOUSE

Constructed 1915

Alfred Huger, a Broad Street attorney, constructed this house in the early-twentieth century. One of the first houses completed along the new boulevard, the Huger House is constructed in a modified Colonial Revival style. It is a two-and-a-half-story rectangular structure sheathed in weatherboard siding and seated on a low masonry foundation. The principal south facade is five bays wide with a two-tier piazza extending across the three central bays. Of particular note is the front door architrave set within an elliptical arched opening with multipane fanlight and sidelights.

70 MURRAY BOULEVARD, ARCHIBALD BAKER SR. HOUSE

Constructed 1914

Dr. Archibald E. Baker Sr., founder of Baker Sanitorium (later Baker Hospital) and father of the builder of *36 Murray Boulevard*, erected another of the early houses on the newly filled Battery (now Murray) Boulevard. Dr. Baker's brick dwelling features a two-story, double-tiered piazza on its front facade. The square columns on the side of the building are original, while the front Tuscan style columns reflect recent alterations. The building has a notable interior with mantels and other woodwork reminiscent of the Neoclassical style.

74 MURRAY BOULEVARD, TRISTRAM HYDE HOUSE

Constructed 1914

Albert W. Todd, architect

Albert Todd, a native South Carolinian, moved his architectural practice from Augusta, Georgia, to Charleston in 1899 and designed a number of projects in and around the city, including several structures at the Citadel, the main building for the Medical University of South Carolina, and the town hall for Sullivan's Island. Himself an elected official, as a member of the state legislature from 1910 to 1924, Todd designed this Neoclassical Revival style residence for Mayor Tristram T. Hyde in 1914. Hyde, initially defeated in his run for mayor in 1911, was elected in 1915 and served two four-year terms. Considered a representative of the old aristocracy, Hyde was noted for his ability to lead a "Sunday school delegation in a parade [while] countenancing an alliance with bootleggers." The two-story, Ionic-columned portico fronts a large pressed-brick house with Neoclassical door and window trim. In keeping with Charleston tradition, a side piazza extends from the west elevation of the building.

104 MURRAY BOULEVARD, LOUIS FISCHER HOUSE

Constructed 1930

This well-detailed wooden house stands apart from its brick-veneered neighbors near the western edge of Murray Boulevard. Louis Fischer, president of his family's lumber company, built this two-and-a-half-story dwelling in 1930. The architect must have been thoroughly versed in Federal style southern houses, evident through the detail of its double-tiered, pedimented portico with a lunette window in the tympanum. The house contrasts stylistically with its neighbors, particularly the white Southern Colonial style dwelling with two-story portico at *96 Murray Boulevard* and the pressed brick, white pilastered house with a pedimented gable, built in 1943, at *98 Murray Boulevard*.

8 NEW STREET, WILLIAM OSTENDORFF TENEMENT
Constructed 1894

William Ostendorff, member of a large family of German craftsmen, was a saddler and carriage maker. He built this Queen Anne style Victorian house as an investment in 1894 while living next door at *10 New Street.* Ostendorff's dwelling follows the traditional Charleston style found in other New Street houses; it has a front double-tiered piazza and a door in the left front bay leading to a side hall. The tower on the southwest corner of the front facade marks a unique departure from the traditional conservatism of Charleston construction in buildings of this scale and adds a more typical Queen Anne characteristic.

9 NEW STREET, JAMES J. IGOE HOUSE
Constructed 1887

James J. Igoe, a harbor pilot, constructed this two-story, side-hall, double-parlor-plan house for his family shortly after the earthquake of 1886. Reflecting Charleston's general postwar conservatism, the house is distinguishable from Greek Revival examples of this type by its low hipped roof, Queen Anne style columns on its double-tiered piazza, and its Italianate style door hood. Like several Victorian houses in the area, its entry is approached by a flight of stone steps with a wrought-iron balustrade. Also in 1887 Joseph Thompson, who lived at 134 Tradd Street, built similarly styled dwellings at *13* and *15 New Street.* Although both are somewhat disfigured by side piazza enclosures, these structures retain Italianate style bay windows with engaged balustrades and double bracketed cornices.

14 New Street

14 NEW STREET, LOUIS BARBOT HOUSE
Constructed before 1873

Louis Barbot, descendant of a French immigrant family from Santo Domingo, studied with Edward C. Jones and entered the architectural field in 1853. He later served as city engineer from 1837 to 1884. Although most of Barbot's family lived at *59 Meeting Street*, by 1873 he apparently constructed this house for his own residence, at that point the southernmost dwelling to be rebuilt on this side of New Street. Larger scaled than most of the neighboring dwellings, Barbot's building features a pedimented, Italianate style hood surmounting a transom doorway, a two-story front bay window, and a large square-columned, double-tiered piazza accessed by numerous French doors. The piazza side of the house overlooks a fine garden on the adjacent lot, always part of this property and surrounded by an early-nineteenth-century brick wall with arcaded stucco panels. On the interior the entry hall includes a tall Victorian stairway and opens into double parlors separated by full-height sliding doors. The present owners found a framing board during 1970s renovations signed by a craftsman and dated "1868," but documentary evidence indicates that the building was not finished until 1872. In the same year of Barbot's construction, merchant James Salvo, a member of a family of cabinetmakers living and working on King Street, built a small single house with inset double-tiered side piazzas and closed gable roof at *16 New Street*. Salvo never occupied the house, which was apparently altered in the early-twentieth century with an addition to the eastern section of the south facade that changed the traditional single house plan of the building.

20 NEW STREET, ROUSE-AICHEL HOUSE
Constructed 1875

George Rouse, a partner in a Chalmers Street printing firm, and his wife, Cordelia, built this substantial two-story wood dwelling, similar in scale to *14 New Street*, with brick gates and wrought-iron fencing in 1875. The house is of the usual side-hall, double-parlor plan with Italianate style front door and two-story front bay, and its side piazzas are masked by an extension which afforded additional bays to the front rooms. The Rouses retained the property only briefly, selling it to the Aichel family, who lived here for almost a century.

21 NEW STREET, SIMONS-JAGER HOUSE
Constructed circa 1880

Brothers James and Manning Simons built this frame house for $3,500. James Simons resided on the property for only three years, but the family retained ownership and rented the house until 1920. Dr. Eugene L. Jagar, a professor of neurology at the Medical College, purchased the property in 1925 and lived here for fifty years. A closed gable roof and front bay window with surmounting balustrade and a paneled base ornament a facade that is otherwise typical of the side-hall, double-parlor houses on New Street.

24 NEW STREET, E. A. MACKEY HOUSE
Constructed 1875

E. A. Mackey constructed the most architecturally distinguished of the Italianate style houses on New Street. A double-tiered staircase rises to the front doorway, which includes a semicircular architrave supported by engaged Corinthian columns. The house features an elaborate front bay window with engaged and surmounting balustrades. Hearkening to an older Charleston tradition, quoins accent the corners of the buildings. Three years after the construction of the Mackey House, the machinist Isaac Hayne constructed a similarly styled but smaller-scaled dwelling at *26 New Street*. Its paired bracketed door hood and arched windows distinguish it from its taller neighbor.

27 NEW STREET, ESTILL HOUSE

Constructed 1873

Iphegenia Estill built this Greek Revival style Charleston house with double-tiered, Tuscan-columned piazzas in 1873. The building's late use of elements commonly found in Charleston in the antebellum period, particularly its closed gable roof with tripartite and dormer windows, delineates it from the Italianate and Queen Anne style houses on the street. In the late-nineteenth century the house became the home of Gustave M. Pollitzer, a leading businessman whose noted suffragette daughters later lived at *5 Beaufain Street*.

31 NEW STREET, MARTIN HOUSE

Constructed 1900–02

One of the later residences on the street, Sarah Martin's house exemplifies the fully developed Queen Anne style in a Charleston context. A gable-ended porch sheathed in overlapping wood shingles surmounts the front entry. Similar shingles cover the gabled roof and the cross gable of its projecting front bay. A double-tiered piazza with Queen Anne style columns and balusters shades its south facade.

37 NEW STREET, HAMMER-SAMS HOUSE

Constructed circa 1860–66

The Hammer-Sams House occupies a distinctive triangular lot at New and Broad Streets formerly called Savage's Green. Here

in 1792 Charlestonians constructed a new theater, designed by James Hoban, the Irish-born Charleston architect who later designed the White House. Although the theater was simple and barnlike on the exterior, a hand-some Tuscan portico was added in the late-1820s shortly before it became a medical college, a short-lived rival to the present Medical University of South Carolina. The building was demolished before the construc-tion of the present house, and with the fill-ing of the adjacent parcels, a number of houses arose along New Street in the ante-bellum period.

According to real property records, in 1863 William C. Hammer purchased the lot on which 37 New Street now stands. The house may have been under contstruction just before or during the Civil War, a time when building of new houses was at a mini-mum. Donald D. Sams bought the property with a completed dwelling in 1868, and his family occupied it for almost a century. Sams owned Dataw Plantation near Beaufort prior to the war, and Union troops destroyed his house there in 1862. The Hammer-Sams House, with its corbeled brick gable end, Gothic hooded chimneys, brick belt course between floors, and double-tiered side piazza with a Greek Revival entry screen, exhibits features common to antebellum Charleston single houses.

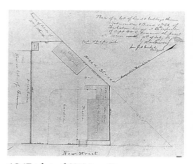

1867 plat of 37 New Street with its garden and two-story brick kitchen

22 RUTLEDGE AVENUE, MANNING SIMONS HOUSE

Constructed circa 1902

Bradford Lee Gilbert, architect

This two-story, stuccoed brick residence was built in the early-twentieth century for Dr. Manning Simons. Simons's house was designed by architect Bradford Lee Gilbert, who designed many of the buildings for the South Carolina Interstate and West Indian Exposition. The house shows influences of the Renaissance Revival style, which was showcased at the Exposition.

The corner of Rutledge Avenue and Broad Street in the early-twentieth century

28 RUTLEDGE AVENUE, SEABROOK-FITZSIMMONS HOUSE
Constructed circa 1885

Edward Seabrook, scion of an Edisto Island family, built this wood dwelling with a projecting entry and a wrapping porch by the mid-1880s. The house faced the newly redeveloped pond designated as a "commons" by the Assembly in 1768 but by the 1880s called "Colonial Lake." Christopher Fitzsimmons, a descendant of a family of wharf owners, purchased the property shortly after construction.

9–15 SAVAGE STREET, LAURA MARTELLE HOUSES
Constructed circa 1894–98

Well-detailed wood parapets with curvilinear features surmount these two-story dwellings constructed by Miss Laura Martelle, who lived at 19 Limehouse Street in the late-1890s. While only 9, 11, and 13 Savage Street still have their curvilinear window hoods, all of the houses retain their bracketed cornices and other features in the Italianate style. The original piazza at 15

15 Savage Street

Savage Street has been replaced with a ponderous contemporary variant, but the Queen Anne style turned columns with jigsaw-cut brackets and spindle-work balustrades remain in the three southernmost examples.

20 SAVAGE STREET, MARGARET ALDERT HOUSE
Constructed circa 1873

The Aldert House, with its front closed gable end framing a tripartite window, its double-tiered Tuscan piazza, and its Greek Revival door architrave, closely resembles the typical Charleston single houses of the antebellum period. The front picket fence standing on a diminutive brick coping constitutes a rare survival of the wooden fences seen throughout this and other neighborhoods in nineteenth-century Charleston. The centered addition on the second story of the piazza, sheltering an upstairs bathroom, exhibits one of the most common methods for adding modern conveniences to Charleston single houses in the early-twentieth century.

31 SAVAGE STREET, GEORGE N. BARNARD TENEMENT
Constructed circa 1872

A folk variant of a one-story front piazza, supported by jigsaw-cut columns and Italianate style balustrades, fronts a plain two-story Greek Revival style house built in 1872 by George N. Barnard, the Civil War photographer who operated a studio on King Street. The first-floor facade retains its simple Greek Revival central architrave with narrow lines of transom and side lights and full-height sash windows that open directly onto the front piazza. A plain parapet screens the low hipped roof. Barnard built other houses along the street for speculation: for example, the flat roofed, side-hall-plan dwellings at *36 Savage Street* and *38 Savage Street*.

35 SAVAGE STREET,
BEREND LUTJEN HOUSE

Constructed circa 1880

The builder of three houses and a corner grocery store at Broad and Savage Streets completed this substantial L-shaped dwelling a few years before the earthquake. The dwelling retains its original two-over-two windows and Italianate door hood framing an oval glass transom.

46–48 SAVAGE STREET,
JOSEPH THOMPSON HOUSES

Constructed circa 1880

Joseph Thompson constructed these nearly identical two-story single houses by 1880. Both buildings retain their wide faces, surmounted by closed gables with small louvered attic openings. The piazza at 46 Savage is screened from the street by a bracketed door architrave with a pedimented hood and a rectangular glass transom with clipped corners. From an alteration common to Charleston houses during the early-twentieth century, the piazza door screen at 48 Savage Street is missing, as is the raised wooden decking of the first floor of the piazza. The columns of this porch have been altered with the addition of nine-course brick pedestals, and they now rest on a brick paved terrace.

74 SOUTH BATTERY,
LOUIS DEB. MCCRADY HOUSE

Constructed 1935–36

Albert Simons and Samuel S. Lapham, architects

Charleston's premier restoration firm designed this new Colonial Revival house for Mr. and Mrs. Louis deB. McCrady just prior to World War II. McCrady, a Charleston-born engineer and part of a long family tradition in the surveying and engineering field, had spent several years practicing his profession in Canada. Perhaps the most correct among the Colonial Revival houses on the

Charleston peninsula in its derivations, the McCrady House, with its red brick facade, more closely resembles James River plantation houses in Virginia than Lowcountry precedents. Wrought-iron gates flanked by red brick piers and coping mark the approach to the front door of the house, which is set in a Georgian style architrave with engaged Tuscan columns and a semicircular transom. The facade rises two floors to a slate hipped roof ornamented by dormers and large chimneys with stucco banding.

84 SOUTH BATTERY, HARRIETT PORCHER SIMONS HOUSE

Constructed 1924

Albert Simons designed this house for his wife and family about a decade after his graduation from the University of Pennsylvania School of Architecture. His wife, Harriett Simons, founded the League of Women Voters in South Carolina. Although the front facade of the house appears to follow a traditional Charleston single house plan, a side-facing T provides an entry porch and alters the essential single house form. The brickwork, shutters with cut-out upper squares, and window details demonstrate a subtle Arts and Crafts influence on Simons's design.

95 SOUTH BATTERY, MATTHEW BARKLEY HOUSE

Constructed 1914

The Barkley House remains the most imposing of the Neoclassical Revival style houses built in early-twentieth-century Charleston. Its wooden facade, semicircular entry portico, large sash windows and shutters, and hipped roof with four massive chimneys seem more reminiscent of New England Federal houses. This impression was more pronounced when the building retained its front wooden fence, recently replaced with a modern iron fence set on a mottled brick coping.

120 SOUTH BATTERY, A. MARION STONE HOUSE

Constructed 1922

David Heyer, architect

This two-and-a-half-story masonry Colonial Revival style building with a semicircular front portico was designed in the 1920s by David Heyer for a leading Charleston businessman, A. Marion Stone. It was one of the first new dwellings in the filled area of South Battery.

130 TRADD STREET, PORTER-GUERARD HOUSE

Constructed 1882–85

Mrs. Emma A. Porter built this two-story wood dwelling with front and west piazzas in the early-1880s after acquiring the site from Mrs. A. A. Ravenel. This and the buildings to the west and north were placed on the site of an eighteenth-century mansion, which burned in the fire of 1861. A large roof monitor or cupola rises from the center of the hipped roof. Edward P. Guerard purchased the house by 1910.

132–136 TRADD STREET, LEE, THOMPSON, AND KENNY HOUSES

Constructed 1882–85

These three side-hall-plan dwellings were built in the mid-1880s with rich Queen Anne detailing, including two-story bay windows and Italianate style entries approached by balustraded staircases springing from marble tiled walkways. John Kenny, a leading builder and contractor who owned 136 Tradd Street as an investment, was probably responsible for the construction of all three. A. Markley Lee, who lived at 132 Tradd, was a prominent attorney in practice with Augustine T. Smythe on Broad Street. Joseph Thompson resided at 134 Tradd Street. Kenny also built *138 Tradd Street*, a three-story wood dwelling now missing its double-tiered front portico, and *144 Tradd Street*, also in the side-hall-plan style, built before 1870. He lived at *142 Tradd Street,* a three-story masonry dwelling that may have survived the fire of 1861 but received heavy damage in the earthquake of 1886.

143 TRADD STREET, BOWLES-LEGARE-PARKER HOUSE

Constructed 1797–1801; altered circa 1855

The merchant Tobias Bowles constructed this house in suburban fashion with an extensive setback from Tradd Street and a prospect over the Ashley River. Though several periods of subsequent filling interrupted the river prospect, the front garden remains, despite the density of later construction in the immediate neighborhood. The wrought- and cast-iron entry gates, with crossed arrow pickets and surmounting scrollwork, sit atop a molded stucco coping and create a striking entry to the property. Although the front fenestration hints at the dwelling's early-nineteenth-century origin, piazza details, second- and third-story doorways, and interior trim indicate the structure's substantial remodeling by Solomon Legare Jr. in the mid-nineteenth century.

149 TRADD STREET, DANIEL Z. DUNCAN HOUSE

Constructed circa 1880; renovated 1997

The Duncan House is a typical example of a working-class single house of the post–Civil War period. The structure has a unique gable roof with closed pediment and a simple side piazza. The building originally included a separate one-story kitchen ell to the rear. Only a few alterations have been made to the dwelling in the twentieth century. This simple 1880s frame single house was built by a freedman as his residence fifteen years after the end of the Civil War. African Americans lived throughout the "South of Broad" neighborhood in the late-nineteenth and early-twentieth centuries, often on alleys and smaller streets. The elder Daniel Duncan acquired a substantial lot on Greenhill Street in 1872, probably a site burned over in the fire of 1861. Within a few years the property was subdivided, and Daniel Z. Duncan, apparently the elder Daniel's son, built a small house facing Tradd Street. The senior Duncan was a laborer, and his son followed the opportunities for blacks in the navy positions and became, consecutively, a buoy tender, a fireman for the steamer *Wisteria*, and eventually assistant inspection officer at the Navy Yard.

151–159 TRADD STREET, S. J. L. MATTHEWS HOUSE
Constructed 1883–86

S. J. L. Matthews, who lived at *3 Limehouse Street*, built these four speculative houses in the mid-1880s. Three of the four dwellings follow the style of the two-and-a-half-story wood Charleston single house, while 153 Tradd Street has had extensive modifications.

172 TRADD STREET, CHISOLM-ALSTON HOUSE
Constructed 1834–36

Alexander Hext Chisolm acquired this site near his thriving rice mill in 1829 and built a notable Greek Revival structure here in the mid-1830s. Several experts attribute the design to Charles F. Reichardt, Prussian trained architect of the Charleston Hotel, the Washington Racecourse Grandstand, and the facade of the guardhouse at Meeting and Broad Streets. Corinthian columns, similar to those Reichardt designed for the Charleston Hotel and Gov. John Manning's plantation house at Milford on the upper Santee River, modeled on the Choragic Monument of Lysicrates, support the Chisolm House portico. Similar columns appear in the front door architrave and in various doorways in the front hall. William Algernon Alston Jr., owner of five plantations in lower All Saints

Parish in Georgetown County, bought the house for his town residence in 1855. Alston probably added the massive stucco wall and gates to the front of the property, which faced directly over the former seawall that separated Tradd Street from the marshes of the Ashley River. This house once commanded the waterfront western edge of the city much the way the houses on Murray Boulevard dominate the Ashley River side today. The Chisolm-Alston House was purchased by a member of the DuPont family in the early-twentieth century and was known locally as the DuPont House for many years.

Civil War torpedo boat Little David *beached in front of the Chisolm-Alston House at 172 Tradd Street, 1865*

174 TRADD STREET, THOMAS YOUNG HOUSE

Constructed circa 1883–84

Late-Italianate style door and cornice trim and double-tiered Queen Anne style piazzas distinguish this large two-and-a-half-story frame house constructed by Thomas Young, a stevedore, on land subdivided by the Chisolm family. The exceptionally high basement of this house indicates its precarious position on lands adjacent to the marshes and the Ashley River. The rear piazzas end midway along the west elevation with a gabled ell addition, a modification of the traditional Charleston plan generally seen in the 1870s and 1880s. In 1896 it became the home of Francis Rodgers Jr.

182 TRADD STREET, DINGLE HOUSE
Constructed 1912

The large-scale Dingle House provides a strong corner at the wide intersection of Tradd Street and Ashley Avenue. John and Olive O. Dingle purchased this lot in 1910, and by virtue of the west-end filling program of 1911, they were able to develop the site by 1913. Dingle, then Charleston's city engineer, constructed a two-and-a-half-story Colonial Revival style house with a front Doric-columned porch, paired second-story central windows, and a slate gable roof with deep, overhanging soffit and three pedimented dormers. Grace Goodhue Coolidge, wife of President Calvin Coolidge, stayed in this house during her visit to Charleston in the 1920s. Shortly after completion of the Dingle House, John Reeves built a smaller-scaled Colonial Revival house at *180 Tradd Street*, similar to its neighbor but with Craftsman overtones including a central diamond-paned window flanked by unusual oval windows on the second floor.

190 TRADD STREET, CHISOLM'S MILL SUPERINTENDENT'S HOUSE
Constructed circa 1840; renovated early-twentieth century

A Civil War view of a damaged Confederate semisubmersible gunboat, sitting adjacent to the Tradd Street seawall, shows the Chisolm's Mill superintendent's house in nearly its original condition. This dwelling, built to house the keeper of the mill, retains its original closed-pediment gable end, double chimneys on the east elevation, and nine-over-nine sash windows. Early-twentieth-century alterations include the addition of a second-story piazza, subsequently partially enclosed; an L-shaped addition; and replacement of the wood shingle roof with a

tin roof. The author and playwright DuBose Heyward lived here briefly as a child in the 1880s, and in the twentieth century the noted South Carolina historian Dr. George C. Rogers Jr. grew up in the house, then owned by his father, Charleston school superintendent George C. Rogers Sr.

Another 1865 view (see above, p. 329) of the abandoned semi-submersible Little David, *with 190 Tradd Street in the background*

200 TRADD STREET, CHISOLM'S MILL

Constructed circa 1830

After an 1826 fire destroyed a sawmill on this site, the Chisolm family completed a large masonry rice and lumber mill complex. Located at the western edge of Tradd Street, it looked out over the marshes of the Ashley River. Although damaged in a fire in 1859, the mill was subsequently rebuilt and continued to operate until it was virtually destroyed in the hurricane of 1911, an event which also dealt a final blow to the rice industry in the Lowcountry. Acquired first by the U.S. Lighthouse Department for its headquarters and later by the U.S. Coast Guard, this property continues in the hands of the latter service.

Late-nineteenth-century photo of the Old Chisolm's Rice Mill

The mill's main block, a four-story building with a central pedimented pavilion, arched windows, and decorative quoins, surmounted by a cupola, no longer survives. Nonetheless the Coast Guard uses the remaining west wing, a three-story brick building, as a storage area, machine shops, and a post exchange. A two-story building constructed circa 1915 serves as headquarters for the base.

1 TRAPMAN STREET, FOGARTY HOUSE

Constructed 1850s

Dr. Simon Fogarty built the first house on Trapman Street, a two-and-a-half-story closed-gable single house, in the 1850s. Much of the early detailing of the house survives, including the front pediment, the two-tiered Tuscan piazza, and the slate roof with three projecting dormers. The principal doors on each floor of the south elevation feature rectilinear Greek Revival architraves with surmounting transoms and side lights.

Trapman Street in the early-twentieth century; this house is now gone

6–12 TRAPMAN STREET, KELLERS TENEMENTS

Constructed 1870–80

Dr. H. H. Kellers constructed this interesting group of two-story single houses as tenements between 1870 and 1880. 8 and 12 Trapman are single houses with gable-ended front facades, while 6 and 10 Trapman are nearly identical flat-roofed single houses. 6, 10, and 12 Trapman were enlarged in the early-twentieth century with L-shaped additions. 8 and 10 Trapman retained their square-columned piazzas. The building at 12 Trapman has a more sophisticated closed-gable front and Tuscan-columned piazza.

TRUMBO STREET

The prosperous contractor C. C. Trumbo built 20 Trumbo Street, the first of two houses constructed on the street that bears his name. These dwellings follow the side-hall house plan, have west-facing piazzas, and boast late–Greek Revival style detailing. Records referring to this thoroughfare as "Trumbo's Court" start with the late 1860s.

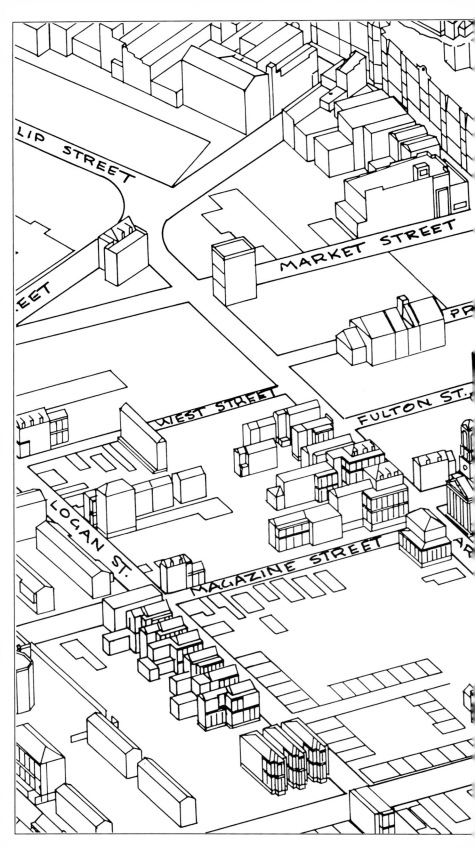

5

COMMERCIAL AND PUBLIC LIFE
Dynamic Nineteenth-Century City

Charleston's earliest commercial activities centered on Church and East Bay Streets, but as the city grew in the eighteenth century and continued to expand in the early-nineteenth century, the focus of commercial and public life took root in other locations, notably King Street and its neighborhoods and, slightly later, Market Street. Even though it was the principal highway to the early settlement, King Street, running along the spine of high ground in the center of the peninsula, lay outside the original fortified Charles Town. It was often known as the "Broad Path" or the "Broad Way," not to be mistaken for Broad Street, and wagons from the interior of South Carolina found their way into the city via its path. Although primarily residential before 1800, it was a bustling retail corridor by the 1830s and remains the heart of

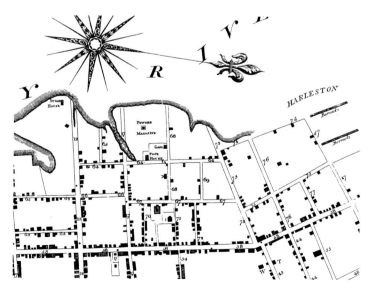

Detail of ichnography of Charleston showing King Street and the city's western edge

Antebellum photograph of Siegling's Music House, 243 King Street, before 1853

King Street above Hasell Street, circa 1905

Charleston's downtown commercial district to the present day.

The houses and shops that lined King Street and which spilled along the side streets leading to it provide some of the clearest glimpses of Charleston's commercial expansion during the early-nineteenth century. Charles Fraser in his memoirs in the 1850s said of its earlier years: "King Street, now so attractive, with its gorgeous windows and dazzling display of goods emulating a Turkish Bazaar, and inviting them to a daily fashionable promenade, was then chiefly, occupied by hucksters, peddlers, and tavern keepers." Here merchants, from Sephardic Jews and Germans to later eastern and southern European immigrants, lived above their shops. The upper floors often followed the single-house plan. There were usually no full piazzas but rather truncated versions accessing the residential entry on the second floor. Upper King Street, stretching toward the railroad complex and the upper boroughs, was developed for commercial activity in the late-nineteenth and early-twentieth centuries. Retail shops of all types thrived on King Street, as did theaters, beginning with the Academy of Music at Market and King Streets and continuing with vaudeville houses such as the Beaux Arts style Garden Theatre. More than six movie theaters operated on the street by the early-twentieth century, including the Riviera, constructed in Art Deco style on the Academy of Music site in the late 1930s.

Before commercial activity burgeoned along King Street, lots to the west had been long developed for public purposes. Lands lying just west of King Street and south to Beaufain Street were conveyed to the proprietary governor James Moore and subsequently acquired by the wealthy merchant Isaac Mazyck. These Mazyck lands were partitioned for sale in the 1740s.

*Engraving, circa 1875, of Old
Roper Hospital, Queen and
Franklin Streets*

Substantial dwellings such as that of Philip
Porcher with its large garden lot contrasted
with small single houses in the alleys and
along Mazyck (now Logan) Street. Still
further toward the Ashley River, between
the Mazyck lands and the original public
burying ground (now vanished without a
trace), the Colonial Assembly partitioned
off a public square divided in 1740 and
bounded by present-day Logan, Queen,
Franklin, and Magazine Streets. On this site
the colony constructed a neighborhood of
civic buildings that included an almshouse,
a public hospital (asylum), a jail and pillory, and a new powder magazine.

By the latter part of the eighteenth century, the old Mazyck lands became known
for two things: the German Lutheran
Church and some of its congregation, giving rise to the term "Dutch Town"; and
strings of taverns and, eventually, brothels
along Beresford (now Fulton) and West
Streets. A new jail and a workhouse of sto-
ried horror were constructed in the public
block in the early-nineteenth century. These
edifices were eventually joined by much
more progressive institutions: a seamen's
hospital designed by Robert Mills, a Neoclassical home for the Medical College of
South Carolina (demolished by 1940) on
the site of the old jail and pillory, and a

*Central portion of Old Roper
Hospital after Hurricane
Hugo, September 1989*

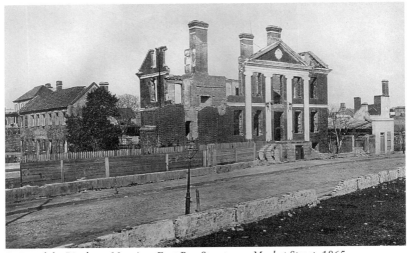

Ruins of the Pinckney Mansion, East Bay Street near Market Street, 1865

John McAlister Livery Stable and Horlbeck Alley, circa 1905

Vulcan Iron Works on Cumberland Street, looking east, 1865

magnificent hospital constructed by the Roper Foundation in the Italianate style in the 1850s (the final remnant was virtually destroyed in Hurricane Hugo in 1989).

The city's market area of the nineteenth century lay east of King Street in what became the epicenter of the antebellum city. As the city's walls were removed in the second quarter of the eighteenth century, new Church Street reached beyond St. Philip's Church by crossing over a creek via "Governor's Bridge" to lot no. 80 of the Grand Modell, granted to the original proprietor's son Sir Peter Colleton, and adjacent lots that were granted to other members of his family. These parcels came to be known as Colleton Square. The third generation of Colletons sold the property in 1738 to three prominent citizens including Charles Pinckney, who built his Mansion House on the best site in 1746. The Pinckney family later gave the whole of present-day Market Street, which was built on filled marsh, to the city with a reversion clause (i.e., the Pinckneys could reclaim the property if the city ceased using the site for a public market) that continues to the present day. The Market Hall, designed by Edward Brickell White, was built in 1841. The city market sheds stretch 1,240 feet in length today but originally reached on the other side of East Bay Street to the harbor. Several sections have been rebuilt following earthquake, hurricane, and tornado damage. The street still prolongs itself to a dock and passenger terminal adjacent to the imposing Custom House, designed by Ammi B. Young.

From the late-nineteenth century to the mid-twentieth, the market area contained a varied mix of commercial uses. As the city's "Tenderloin" district, it was lined with tattoo parlors and speakeasies, or "blind tigers," during Prohibition. These contrasted sharply with a sailors' chapel on the northwest corner of North Market and East Bay Streets that was given to the city by the Pinckney family. The area also had an industrial impulse as home to ships' chandlers, seafood packing warehouses, wholesale grocers, and a carriage factory. The tumbledown character of the area, accentuated by damage in a tornado in 1938, made it a thorn in the city's side by the 1960s. Eventually "gentrification" in the form of renovations for bars, restaurants, inns, and shops, primarily geared for Charleston's tourist economy, took over, and while old buildings were rehabilitated, new infill structures were added to the once localized landscape. New developments from Charleston Place to Majestic Square as well as ongoing plans for a new marina near the waterfront end of Market Street promise even further activity.

Charles Hamilton's Charleston Square, *showing the market area in 1865*

*Unitarian Church, interior
view looking west*

6 ARCHDALE STREET, UNITARIAN CHURCH

🅛 *Constructed 1772–87; remodeled 1852*

Francis D. Lee, architect

Construction of the Unitarian Church was halted for the duration of British occupation of Charleston during the American Revolution. Begun in 1772, it was finally dedicated in 1787 and was called the Second Independent Church. The congregation was born out of the Independent Congregational Church at the White Meeting House, now the Circular Congregational Church, on Meeting Street and continued as one body with that group for thirty years. A Unitarian minister, the Reverend Anthony Forster, was the first pastor of the newly chartered Second Independent church in 1817, and his successor, Dr. Samuel Gilman, served from 1819 to 1858. Gilman wrote Harvard's anthem "Fair Harvard." His wife, Caroline Gilman, is remembered for publishing the first children's newspaper in the country, the *Rosebud,* and for laying out the gardens on the south side of the church. Today the gardens, with many old varieties of plants, are intermixed with later gravestones in a portion of the cemetery and dominated by a Gothic monument to the Gilmans. The graveyard connects to King Street and then Meeting Street via the Gateway garden walk, which crosses from brick gates on King Street through the Charleston Library Society yard, through the courtyard of the Gibbes Museum of Art, and across Meeting Street through the graveyards of the Circular Church and St. Philip's Church.

The church was rechartered as the first Unitarian church in the South in 1839 and was remodeled into its present perpendicular Gothic style in 1852. The architect Francis D. Lee designed a new tower on the west end and a chancel at the east end. A prevailing respect for the old structure encouraged the retention of elements from the original building, while Lee added loftier details to the edifice. Inspired by the Chapel of Henry VII at Westminster, Lee added the decorative fan vaulting of plaster which adorns the interior and also added buttresses to the building and changed the fenestration to reflect the Gothic style. The church suffered extensive damage during the earthquake of 1886; while the interior was repaired, surviving ornamentation on the tower was stripped away.

10 ARCHDALE STREET, ST. JOHN'S LUTHERAN CHURCH

Constructed 1816–18; additions 1859, 1896; restored 1990–91

Frederick Wesner, architect; Abraham Reeves, ironwork designer

St. John's Lutheran Church
and Unitarian Church steeples

St. John's Lutheran Church is a rectangular, stuccoed brick edifice which combines Federal and Baroque elements. Erected in 1816–18 to replace a gambrel-roofed wooden building, the church is thought to have been designed by Frederick Wesner, an architect of German descent who also designed the Old Citadel Building and the portico of the South Carolina Society Hall at *72 Meeting Street*. Wesner guided construction of the wooden portions of the church, while John Horlbeck Jr. and Henry Horlbeck were responsible for the brickwork. St. John's pastor during this period, the Reverend John Bachman, was a noted Lutheran theologian and a naturalist. He served the church for almost sixty years.

It is not known who designed the tower that rises from the west gable to a height of eighty feet, although the artist Charles Fraser submitted a more traditional design that the committee rejected. This tower has four sections: the first has louvered bull's-eyes; the second has shallow scrolls with heavy strap-work; the third is the cupola with Italianate pilasters flanking open

Elizabeth O'Neill Verner's Magazine Street, *showing St. John's Lutheran Church in the vista of the street*

arches; and the fourth is the four-sided dome with a bulbous finial. The portico, with its four Tuscan columns, wide entablature, and lunette in the pediment, is approached through iron gates designed by Wesner's brother-in-law, Abraham P. Reeves, and executed by Jacob S. Roh in 1822.

On the interior St. John's Lutheran Church has galleries on three sides supported by slender cast-iron Corinthian columns and a recessed chancel with a window flanked by arched tablets. The pulpit was donated by the late-nineteenth-century cabinetmaker Jacob Sass and was added in 1896. In the churchyard numerous gravestones in German combine with several slates imported from New England and large monuments to the great Lutheran merchant families of mid-nineteenth-century Charleston.

19 ARCHDALE STREET, PHILIP PORCHER HOUSE

Constructed circa 1773; renovated with additions circa 1835; restored 1980–81, 1986–87

The facade of this two-story frame dwelling with a hipped roof has had only slight changes since its construction in the 1770s. The piazza is an early addition. Access to the front chamber was originally, and is now, through a door in the center of the facade. However, this door was blocked when a piazza entrance was added in the early 1800s, an entryway that assumed a secondary role when the original entrance was reopened during a 1980s restoration. This house occupies a lot that stood outside the original walled city. Philip Porcher of St. Stephen's Parish on the Santee River and his wife Mary received the lot from Mary's father, the entrepreneur Isaac Mazyck, in 1765. Porcher bequeathed the house to his daughter Mary, who resided here until her death in 1835. The next owner, Augustus Theodore Gaillard, was probably responsible for some alterations to the interior's splendid eighteenth-century paneling.

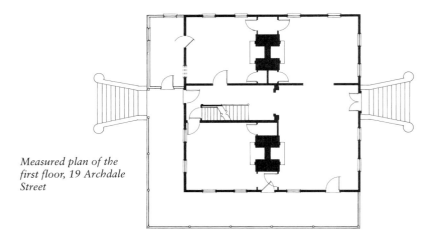

Measured plan of the first floor, 19 Archdale Street

21–23 ARCHDALE STREET, SAMUEL WILSON HOUSES

Constructed 1808–15; restored and rehabilitated mid-twentieth century

The piazza door screen with its elaborate scrollwork, at 21 Archdale Street

Dr. Samuel Wilson constructed these similar three-story brick single houses on a portion of the Mazyck lands inherited by his wife, Catherine Mazyck, granddaughter of the Huguenot immigrant Isaac Mazyck. Wilson built 23 Archdale Street first, but by 1808 the Wilson family was living in 21 Archdale Street at the corner of Magazine and Archdale Streets. Wilson's will devised this house to his son William Handy Wilson. The elder Wilson left his son Dr. Isaac Mazyck Wilson the slightly larger and later house at 21 Archdale Street. The houses were among a number of properties purchased in 1840 by Etienne Poincignon, a wealthy landowner whose family had emigrated from the French West Indies to Charleston in the 1790s. Family tradition holds that this area was saved from a large fire in 1864 by Poincignon's efficient organization of his family with wet blankets and water buckets to stop flames from erupting on the roofs.

Although both houses have exceptional brickwork laid in Flemish bond, 23 Archdale Street retains its original piazza door screen, designed after a plate in the late-eighteenth-century pattern book of William Pain, as well as much of its original exterior and interior Federal details. By contrast, significant Greek Revival style alterations, probably added by Poincignon, mark 21 Archdale Street, including the pedimented dormers, the piazza columns and balustrade, and particularly the piazza door screen with its carved anthemion motifs ornamenting the overhang and the scrolled pilasters. These houses were saved and restored by John Muller, a leading Charleston preservationist.

27 ARCHDALE STREET, GERMAN FRIENDLY SOCIETY KITCHEN
Constructed circa 1802

John Horlbeck Jr. and Henry Horlbeck, builders

Charleston's German fraternal society, founded in 1766, built a grand hall at this address, completed before Christmas in 1801, and undertook soon thereafter to construct a 36-by-16-foot stuccoed brick kitchen on the site. The upper story with three rooms eventually became a residence for the schoolmaster of the society's school. The main hall burned in the 1864 fire that engulfed this portion of the street, but the kitchen survived. In its rehabilitation as apartments some years ago, certain features were lost, and its tile roof has long since been replaced. On another portion of the property, a colorful Austrian mariner who repeatedly ran the blockade during the Civil War built a two-story wood single house on a site where he also operated a woodyard. Capt. Jacob Francis purchased the lot at *25 Archdale Street* in 1884 and constructed a typical mid-nineteenth-century style Charleston single house with a double-tiered side piazza and featuring square posts supporting an arcade on the first story and square, chamfered posts on the second. John Muller restored both houses in recent years as rental properties. The Muller Trust more recently renovated the small stucco single house at *29 Archdale Street*, built as a tenement investment by Mrs. Ann Ross of *1 Meeting Street* in the mid-1870s on the site of an earlier dwelling. Like the Francis House, the Ross Tenement contains features more common in antebellum Charleston dwellings, including Gothic Revival interior woodwork, out of fashion by the time this house was constructed. A single brick gate pier, now cut off, remains at the southeast corner of the Ross property.

40 ARCHDALE STREET, BULWINKLE-OHLANDT BUILDING
Constructed circa 1880; renovated circa 1995–96

John Henry Bulwinkle constructed a grocery store around 1880 on the site of a house that burned in 1864. The simple three-story building with red pressed brick, tightly laid and surmounted by a simple arcaded brick cornice, housed Bulwinkle's grocery and a saloon with a rented residence above. During Prohibition the grocery housed a blind tiger in its back room; it appropriately became a liquor store before its renovation as part of the Majestic Square complex to the east.

49 ARCHDALE STREET, DARBY BUILDING
Constructed circa 1802; altered 1886; renovated 1994

The brick building at Archdale and Beaufain Streets with a curious stepped brick gable end, probably added after the earthquake of 1886, stands as a lone survivor of a continuous block on both sides of early-nineteenth-century masonry and wood dwellings and shops. Possibly constructed before 1802 by the goldsmith John Darby, the building contains interior woodwork dating from the mid-nineteenth century and retains a storefront with a corner iron column, a feature associated with corner store buildings throughout Charleston in the mid-nineteenth century. The city created the triangular spit of land on which the building stands by lengthening Market Street and demolishing several houses along these portions of Archdale and Beaufain Streets.

BEAUFAIN STREET, ROBERT MILLS MANOR PROJECT

Constructed 1939–41

Douglas Ellington, Simons and Lapham, architects; Loutrel Briggs, landscape architect

The antebellum houses at 63 and 65 Beaufain Street reflect nineteenth-century design in the tradition of the Charleston single house. Both structures of stuccoed brick have west-facing piazzas on the first and second floors. Tuscan columns support the piazzas, and vermiculated quoins decorate the structure at 63 Beaufain Street. Side lights and a glazed transom accentuate the main entry off the piazza. Flanked by mid-twentieth-century multiunit brick dwellings, these earlier two structures have been incorporated into the Robert Mills Manor Project, designed by local architects in the late 1930s. The thirty-four-unit Manor Project was one of the first in the Charleston area and is reflective of the creativity of Charlestonians in adapting the New Deal programs for low-income housing. The two-story, gable-roofed brick structures were built in the form of those in other areas, but in their materials and detailing as well as scale they seem like dependencies behind old Charleston houses, arranged in a courtyard fashion. This grouping, which replaced older, dilapidated structures along Beaufain, Magazine, Franklin, and Smith Streets and Cromwell Alley, remains a residential complex for persons of fixed income today.

Aerial view of 63–65 Beaufain Street, Robert Mills Manor and Old Charleston District Jail

CLIFFORD STREET
Established before 1788

This short thoroughfare running between Archdale and King Streets was formerly known as Dutch Church Alley due to the adjacent St. John's Lutheran Church. Casimir Patrick, a German tradesman who lived in Harleston Village, built the two-and-a-half-story weatherboarded single house at 24 Clifford Street by 1827 with late-Federal woodwork on its interior. Several lots to the east, the dwelling at 16 Clifford Street was built in 1859–60 by the master house builder Albert Elfe as a tenement. This small-scale rubbed brick single house was restored in recent years with a second-story balcony instead of a piazza.

171 CHURCH STREET, C. D. FRANKE WAREHOUSE
Constructed circa 1909; rehabilitated 1984

John D. Newcomer, architect

The Franke Warehouse, at the northwest corner of Market and Church Streets, is an important example of early-twentieth-century industrial architecture. It was constructed as a manufacturing and storage building for a carriage company founded in 1859 by C. D. Franke, a Prussian immigrant. His carriages and wagons were marketed throughout the Southeast. By the 1870s the company had also become a supplier for carriage parts, iron products, and hardware. By the early-1900s Franke

Detail from C. D. Franke letterhead showing Franke (later Jahnz) Carriage Works

(Jahnz) Company was manufacturing auto parts in this building. It closed in 1981, was rehabilitated, and now serves as an office complex. It is one of only a few surviving examples of the industrial nature of the Market Street area prior to World War II.

6–8 CUMBERLAND STREET, THEODORE GAILLARD RANGE

Constructed circa 1789–1804; renovated 1960s

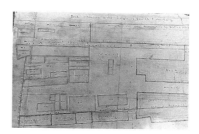

Plat showing the eastern end of Cumberland Street and the Market area

The lower arched openings of this stuccoed masonry building survive as the only indication of its former use as a range of four three-story stores and factors' offices. Theodore Gaillard, the son of a prominent merchant and planter who bought the site in 1777 with the confiscation of the Loyalist Wragg family's wharf, in turn had his property confiscated by South Carolina authorities due to his own Tory leanings during the British occupation of Charleston. Sold to John Vanderhorst, it was repurchased by Theodore Gaillard Jr. at auction in 1789. The younger Gaillard then lived at *198 East Bay Street* and later joined the rest of his family in Harleston Village. Gaillard sold the completed warehouses to John Christopher Faber in 1804, and they were later known as Faber's North Range. The third floor was removed due to damage during the earthquake of 1886, and late-twentieth-century renovations as office buildings have obscured many of the early characteristics of this site.

26 CUMBERLAND STREET, MARTSCHINK BUILDING

Constructed 1941–42; rehabilitated 1986

This building was constructed by the Martschinks, a family with extensive real estate interests in this section of Charleston, and originally housed a wholesale magazine distributorship and warehouse.

One of Charleston's few urban examples of the Art Deco style, the structure has a front brick facade with a central pavilion that is flanked by stylized pilasters terminating in decorative panels. The windows on either side are surmounted by decorative spandrels with a Greek key motif. Later serving as an electric supply company, the building has since become a restaurant and bar.

200 EAST BAY STREET, UNITED STATES CUSTOM HOUSE

Constructed 1849–79; restored 1968

Ammi B. Young, architect; Edward Brickell White, supervising architect

The Custom House is Charleston's only major building in the national Classical Revival style, an imposing edifice on a level with comparable buildings constructed in Washington, D.C., during the same period. At least nine architects entered a competition for this project after the site was purchased by an act of Congress in 1847. Portions of four designs were included in the final plan developed by Boston architect Ammi Burnham Young. Young, the first supervising architect of the U.S. Treasury, apparently had the edge on the design of such structures at this period, designing the customhouses in Boston, Galveston, and Norfolk (in similar style), as well as other new federal buildings. Construction, which began in 1849, was interrupted just before the Civil War by lack of appropriations, revived by Congressional authorization in 1867, and com-

Custom House, 200 East Bay Street, about 1900

pleted twelve years later. Despite the cost estimate of $370,000 at the outset, the total outlay for the building reached $3 million accomplished through nineteen separate acts of Congress.

The original design included a large dome and four porticoes, but the final building included only a front and rear portico without the dome and with a somewhat diminished interior plan. The Custom House as completed is 149 feet by 71 feet, constructed with New York and New Jersey granite. On the exterior a rusticated base supports the principal floors of the structure, with porticoes approached by triple-tiered steps, and side bays divided by engaged Corinthian columns, surmounted by a roof balustrade. The interior is one of Charleston's most impressive, with a heavy cast-iron stair to a great central, marble-floored hall with second-floor gallery, oak grained doors (recently restored), and a cove ceiling decoratively painted with shields and flags of the United States surrounding a skylight. After avoiding a proposed demolition in the 1950s, the Custom House still houses federal offices. The structure also provides Charlestonians with a venue for outdoor concerts, and Spoleto performances and other events take place within its great hall.

Elevation of the planned Custom House, circa 1857, showing the dome that was never built

Engraving, circa 1880, of the completed Custom House

205–211 EAST BAY STREET, WILLIAM BIRD BUILDINGS

Constructed before 1831; altered circa 1850, 1870, 1886–87; rehabilitated 1980s

These structures may retain some brick walls dating from the 1770s tenements owned by the Manigault family. The present Greek Revival character of 205 East Bay and particularly the range to the north probably date after 1831, when Dr. Philip Moser acquired the corner. One of the many owners, Charles H. Bass, sold 205

Detail from an 1890 bill from William Bird Company, showing the company building before and after the earthquake of 1886

East Bay to William Bird in 1870. The William Bird Company, a hardware and paint firm, occupied the corner building and eventually spread its operations to the adjacent range owned by James Marsh. The cast-iron colonnade on the first floor and the Italianate window heads above date from the postbellum period. The pilastered granite storefront unites the three buildings to the north.

234 EAST BAY STREET, CARROLL BUILDING

Constructed 1906–10; rehabilitated 1984

Thomas W. Carroll, the son of an English immigrant stevedore, established an icehouse and fish business on this site in 1895. When his ice concern was purchased by Southern Ice Company, he continued to sell fish at the same location. The present brick structure just north of the corner, with arched windows and simple brick banding, was built by Carroll between 1906 and 1910. Wooden buildings on the corner were torn down for parking in the 1970s, and after the Carroll family closed the seafood company in 1984, this street-front site was developed with a modern office building connected to the earlier structure.

241 EAST BAY STREET, SYLVESTER JANCOVITCH BUILDING

Constructed 1871; rehabilitated with addition 1985–86

A ship's chandler completed the stuccoed masonry dwelling on this site shortly after acquiring the property from the merchant Moses Hyams, who had lost his buildings here in the fire of 1861. Sylvester Jancovitch had immigrated to Charleston from Austria in the early-1850s and died shortly after completing his handsome late–Greek Revival store and residence. The three-bay facade features a belt course between floors, decorative window heads, and a corbeled brick cornice surmounted by a parapeted gable. The building was the subject of a historic rehabilitation in 1985–86, at which point the contemporary addition to the north was constructed and joined to the original edifice by a stucco and glass hyphen.

20 FRANKLIN STREET, MARINE HOSPITAL

L *Constructed 1831–34*

Robert Mills, architect

Robert Mills, a Charleston native, had moved to Baltimore and was working for the federal government when funds were appropriated for construction and operation of a marine hospital in his hometown. Mills served as the architect for the Marine Hospital, the city's first Gothic Revival structure. Initially built for sick and disabled merchant seamen, it has since been used as a teaching hospital by the Medical University of South Carolina, a Confederate military hospital, a free school for black children, an orphanage, and a library and office space for the Housing Authority of the City of Charleston. Rectangular in plan, the Mills building boasts Gothic ornamen-

Measured front (west) facade of the old Marine Hospital

tation such as lancet arches and cluster or quatrefoil-shaped columns supporting the piazzas. It served as a hospital until after the Civil War. Later it was run by the Reverend Daniel Jenkins as an orphanage for African American children, many of whom donned band uniforms and performed on the streets of Charleston. The Jenkins Orphanage band later earned an international reputation, visiting England, and was given credit for helping develop the dance called "The Charleston." The Reverend Jenkins's son Edmund studied music in Europe and was a fellow of the Royal Academy of Music in England. He became a figure in the Harlem Renaissance but died before attaining recognition of his significant body of work.

11 FULTON STREET, GRACE PEIXOTTO HOUSE

Constructed circa 1852; renovated mid-1980s, 1991

In 1851 the entrepreneur Grace Peixotto purchased a lot on what was then called Beresford Street and built a brothel. After her death in 1879 or 1880, the property passed to Jacob S. Myers. Although Myers, a mariner and dealer in cigars and tobacco, is listed as the owner, various madams are noted as residents until the end of World War II. At this time the property contained, in addition to the main building, a two-story brick building and a three-story brick building arranged around a courtyard and linked by piazzas. After the building was vacated in the postwar era, it was rented to navy petty officers and their families. These tenants petitioned the changing of the street name to Fulton to put an end to any ties to the former address. Subsequently, the building served as a furniture warehouse, a storage facility, a bar, and offices.

16 HAYNE STREET, YOUNG AMERICA STEAM FIRE ENGINE HOUSE

Constructed circa 1847; rebuilt circa 1872

Louis Barbot, architect

This fire engine house stands as one of two survivors of the volunteer fire company buildings that dotted the peninsula before the organization of the Charleston Fire Department in 1882. These individual companies built small engine houses throughout the peninsula. Young America Company, founded in 1866, grew to sixty members. The current structure, a stuccoed brick two-story building, has architectural details relating to the Greek Revival and Italianate styles, including pilasters surmounted by classical console brackets topped by a parapet with a modillioned cornice.

125 KING STREET, PETER GUILLEMINE BUILDING

Constructed circa 1885; rehabilitated 1983–84

This building survives as one of the few remaining Queen Anne style wooden commercial structures in Charleston. After it was built, the property became the shop for Guillemine and Riley, a firm dealing in tinware and stoves. The Guillemine family lived upstairs and enjoyed the projecting front bay with its paired windows overlooking King Street. Adapted as a pharmacy by the early-twentieth century, this site, purchased by the Tellis family in the 1940s, may be the oldest continuous location for a drugstore in the city. In its recent rehabilitation preservationists and the Board of Architectural Review supported the reinstallation of the pharmacy's old neon sign because of its historic importance to early-twentieth-century King Street.

147–149 KING STREET, HESSE GROCERY

Constructed 1878–80; renovated with additions 1890

The three-story brick double building at 147–149 King Street was constructed between 1878 and 1880 as the grocery of Ernst J. Hesse, a prosperous merchant of German descent who lived in Harleston Village. By 1890 the property was divided and featured two storefronts of equal proportion. Occupants have included a series of grocers, furniture and tinware merchants, booksellers, antiquarians, and florists. The Preservation Society of Charleston purchased 147 King Street in 1978 as its headquarters. The design of this structure is typical of late-nineteenth-century commercial buildings on King Street. Distinguishing features of the storefronts include oversized glazed windows, paneled bulkhead, cornice molding, and central entries with double doors and transoms. Rear piazzas with an entry to the upper stories of 147 King Street mark the west side of the building.

150–154 KING STREET, PATRICK KUGEN'S STORES

Constructed circa 1868

Patrick Kugen, who later served as treasurer of the city, constructed this triple storefronted building in 1868 on a lot burned over in the fire of 1861. The architectural details of cornice and window lintels survive on the southernmost building at 150 King Street. At Kugen's death his son inherited the southernmost building while his daughter inherited the double structure at 152–154 King Street. Recently a later coat of stucco fell, revealing original scored stucco on the facade. The cornice was removed from 152–154 King Street and the storefronts altered, excepting the pilasters, in the mid-twentieth century. These storefronts have since been restored.

159 KING STREET,
GEORGE W. FLACH BUILDING

Constructed circa 1865–66

A Gothic style crenellated parapet caps an otherwise unremarkable two-bay, Greek Revival brick structure at the corner of Clifford's Alley and King Street. The builder, George W. Flach, a German immigrant, dealt in watches and silver on this site occupied in the eighteenth century by the Charleston silversmith Thomas You. Several years after Flach's death the property was sold to Patrick Conroy, operator of a furniture shop, and was utilized for several different commercial purposes.

164 KING STREET,
CHARLESTON LIBRARY SOCIETY

Constructed circa 1914; additions 1970s, 1995–96

McGoodwin and Hawley, architects

Considered the third-oldest private library organization in the U.S., the Charleston Library Society was organized in 1748 by seventeen citizens of varying professions for the purpose of saving "their descendants from sinking into savagery." Its first collection was destroyed in the fire of 1778, and it was located on the third floor of the Charleston County Courthouse until 1836, when it bought the vacated building of the Bank of South Carolina at *50 Broad Street*. The Philadelphia architects McGoodwin and Hawley designed a new structure in 1914 at this address.

The Beaux Arts classical style building stands above a rusticated ground story with double pilasters topped by Ionic capitals separating five bays with arched openings. The stuccoed brick structure has marble detailing and a dentiled cornice capped by a paneled parapet. In recent years the Society has expanded by connecting to adjacent historic structures. In 1995 the organization restored the surviving pressed-metal facade of *158–160 King Street*, the former Carolina Rifles Building, circa 1870, constructing new spaces behind it.

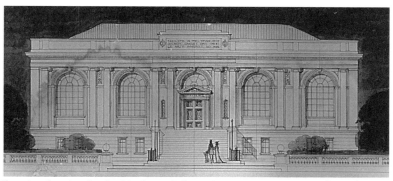

Elevation drawing for the Charleston Library Society, 164 King Street, by architects McGoodwin and Hawley, 1912

165 KING STREET, WILLIAM BYRNE HOUSE
Constructed 1875

William Byrne, a grocer operating nearby on King Street, constructed this building and occupied it as a residence. Though the early storefront was removed many years ago, the first-floor cornice with end cast-iron brackets survives, as do the pedimented window heads of the second floor and simple lintels on the third. The building retains its six-over-six windows on the upper stories of the side elevation as well as its molded cornice.

169–171 KING STREET, BALLARD-MCKENZIE BUILDING
Constructed circa 1870

Elizabeth Ballard, a widow, inherited a lot bequeathed to her by her husband. The site had contained a building before the fire of 1861. Mrs. Emma McKenzie bought the property in 1866 and completed construction on this three-story brick store and residence. Mrs. McKenzie's building appears deliberately simple in detailing and lacks a cornice on its large exposed parapet. Whether a cornice existed and was removed is a matter of some debate. Beneath the parapet three recesses hold iron grilles depicting eagles. Mrs. McKenzie's property was rented for a number of years to the Rugheimer family, drapers and tailors from Germany. Several modern condominiums have been constructed at the rear of the property adjacent to the three-story kitchen building. This construction interrupted a walk which formerly led to the Unitarian churchyard.

186 KING STREET, HAHNBAUM-MOFFETT BUILDING
Constructed before 1788; restored 1978

The restoration of this decorative wooden corner structure was hailed by preservationists in the 1970s as a triumph of commercial restoration. The pre-1800 structure was built by a German physician, Dr. George Hahnbaum, one of the founders of the Medical Society of South Carolina. Hahnbaum's building with beaded wood siding on the north wall and a stuccoed south wall was refronted in the early-nineteenth century, probably by John Rudolph Switzer, a saddler who used the building until his death in 1811. Switzer may have lived here, but he also constructed a residence at 6 *Montagu Street* in 1803. Andrew Moffett, a dry goods dealer, bought the site in 1835. Moffett built the fine brick house at 328 East Bay Street as his residence.

The outstanding feature of the building is its front facade with a ground-story, classical entablature with a triglyph frieze supported by four engaged, fluted columns, surmounted by two levels ornamented with Ionic pilasters and topped by a modillioned cornice and parapet. Frances Edmunds, then executive director of Historic Charleston Foundation, saved the first-floor columns when the ground story was demolished in an insensitive 1940s conversion of the building to a tavern. In the 1978 rehabilitation these columns were returned and the building was fully restored.

191 KING STREET, WILLIAM ENSTON BUILDING

Constructed 1850

This three-story gray brick building with a granite Gothic Revival storefront, consisting of an arched entablature supported by trefoil-shaped columns, was built by the furniture merchant William Enston in 1850 as the flagship for his stores. This English merchant who came to Charleston also built a major real estate and steamship empire. At his death in 1860, he left a remainder interest in his $1 million estate for

Silcox Furniture (formerly William Enston Furniture Company), 191 King Street, 1875 engraving

the founding of the William Enston Home, built at *900 King Street*. In 1887 the structure became the home of Phoenix Furniture, a company eventually managed by A. W. Litschgi of *136 Broad Street*. Although the facade has been well preserved, the original cornice was removed in recent years.

192–198 KING STREET, COL. BLUM RANGE

Constructed circa 1853; altered circa 1870; rehabilitated 1983

Francis D. Lee, architect

This range was actually designed as two double buildings, but in a manner to appear as a single facade. Lee utilized the Greek Revival style for the upper stories with their six-over-six windows with brownstone lintels and sills and an overhanging dentiled cornice and entablature. Sometime after the War Between the States, Italianate detailing and cast-iron columns with Egyptian Revival style capitals replaced simpler brick columns and the lower facade designed by Lee. This ground story served many uses in the nineteenth century, from a confectioner's, a dressmaker's, and a furniture dealer's to Singer Manufacturing Company and a fraternal hall; the upper floors were utilized as an inn. Heavily deteriorated by the 1950s, the range was thoroughly rehabilitated by 1984 and again used as shops and an inn.

193 KING STREET, WILLIAM BELL BUILDING

Constructed before 1840; ground story altered circa 1890

Surviving as an excellent example of a mixed commercial and residential building of the early-nineteenth century, the tile-roofed Bell Building retains its splendid three-bay facade with red sandstone win-

dow lintels and sills on both upper stories, topped by a belt course, cast-iron grilles, and a pedimented parapet. The ground story was altered in the mid-nineteenth century with cast-iron columns. In the emerging King Street tradition, a side staircase leads up to the residence's entry and the single house plan is preserved on the upper floors. A well-preserved kitchen dependency survives at the rear of the property.

200 KING STREET, FLAGG BUILDING

Constructed circa 1800–06; renovated 1870–1900

George Flagg, a prominent paint dealer and craftsman who in his younger years achieved notoriety as one of the pre-Revolutionary Sons of Liberty, may have built this three-story brick structure in the early years of the nineteenth century. Flagg had already leased the property for four years when he purchased it from Lawrence Benson. Flagg sold it in 1810 to Dr. Michael Fronty, a French surgeon and doctor formerly engaged at the University of Montpellier—in France. Fronty practiced medicine and lived in the building, providing care for the poor as well as paying patients. Although the structure retains its basic upper-floor fenestration, Renaissance Revival style pedimented window heads were added to the second story. A heavy cast-iron entablature and parapet were added by the Blum and Ficken families, who owned most of the property in this block in the late-nineteenth century.

202 KING STREET, RUGHEIMER BUILDING

Constructed circa 1912; rehabilitated 1980, 1992

Walker and Burden, architects

John Rugheimer, a German immigrant, settled in antebellum Charleston and, after a stint as a blockade runner, opened a tailor shop later at *169–171 King Street*. After his death, his sons purchased this site in 1911, demolishing a nineteenth-century structure except for the north common wall and building the three-story brick edifice. The arched ground story with banded pilasters and bracketed granite capitals supports a yellow brick upper facade divided by brick pilasters topped by a granite entablature and a parapet with a panel designating the family name. The simpler south wall of red Philadelphia pressed brick has typical arched window openings of the early-twentieth-century commercial type. When it was rehabilitated as an inn in 1992, the developers purchased the site next door, where a two-story double building with a pressed-tin facade lost its entire front to Hurricane Hugo. It was replaced with a three-story masonry structure with reminiscent stucco detailing.

208 KING STREET, OLD YMCA-WOMEN'S EXCHANGE

Constructed 1889; altered 1950s, 1980; exterior partially restored and interior rehabilitated 1993

S. W. Foulk, architect; Henry Oliver, contractor

Victorian America's leading designer of YMCAs, S. W. Foulk of Newcastle, Pennsylvania, designed this pressed-brick, three-story building in the Richardsonian Romanesque style to house the Charleston YMCA, which had been organized in 1854. With the Charleston business magnate George Walton Williams as chairman of the building committee, Foulk was selected as the architect and funds were raised locally for the construction. The building retains much of its fenestration despite severe mid-twentieth-century alterations. The shop spaces on the ground story are divided by banded, rough-cut stone that also appears in the detailing of the base of the north tower and the arches above the bands of windows. In the twentieth century the roof of the tower and the peak of the central gable were removed and the extensive glass of the large arch was infilled. These exterior features have not been restored.

216 KING STREET, MCBRIDE-CHICCO BUILDING

Constructed 1839–40; renovated and rehabilitated 1980s

Patrick McBride, a merchant who immigrated to Charleston from Ireland, constructed this three-story masonry building after the fire of 1838. Sold in 1846 with a "three story brick dwelling house thereon and outbuildings," the property passed briefly through the hands of a dry goods merchant and became the property of Patrick Coogan. Vincent Chicco, a colorful figure in early-twentieth-century Charleston, acquired the property in 1906. Known as the "king of the blind tigers," he was famous for his opposition to Prohibition laws. Chicco apparently added the pressed-metal decoration to the building, including the semicircular window hoods and bracketed entablature and arched parapet. After this work was complete, the building was occupied by the Academy Inn. In more recent years it was renovated and the facade was entirely removed and rebuilt, although the decorative elements were retained and replaced. The adjacent properties to the south, including the red pressed-brick structure with pressed-metal window architraves at *214 King Street* and the site of *212 King Street*, were owned by Henry Brown, a men's clothier, from 1888 until after the turn of the century. In 1909 the Hampton Lee family, owners of Southern Furniture Company, constructed the three-story gray brick building at 212 King Street, with its large windows and cast-metal entablature over its first-floor storefront.

212–216 King Street

217 KING STREET, MAJESTIC SQUARE

Constructed 1995–96

Samuel S. Logan III, LS3P Architects

A newly constructed commercial and office building named by its owners, descendants of Albert Sottile, for the grandest of his King Street theaters (now demolished), Majestic Square stands four stories above the street on the site of the Victoria Hotel, demolished in 1970 for a bank, now removed. The corner entry is reminiscent of earlier King Street buildings, while the cast stone detailing, albeit contemporary, relates the structure to the Riviera theater across Market Street.

218–220 King Street

220 KING STREET, NATHAN HART BUILDING

Constructed 1838–40; rehabilitated 1988

The Charleston hardware merchant Nathan Hart lost his business in the fire of 1838 when the conflagration consumed a three-story house on this site that he leased from the trustee for the owners, the Schmidt family. Purchasing this site, Hart constructed his own building shortly thereafter, and it remained in his family until the late-nineteenth century. Reflecting the high quality of Charleston construction in the antebellum period, the red brick facade is beak jointed with a fine white mortar, and the King Street facade second-story windows have granite lintels. A late-nineteenth-century style storefront has been added spanning the corner of the first floor. Beyond the main block of the building, along Market Street, late-nineteenth-century pressed-metal window and door hoods survive. An arched brick two-story hyphen, typical of King Street, separates this from the adjacent structure at *218 King Street*. The latter building with similar brick detailing and a surviving modillioned cornice and parapet was also built in the years immediately after the fire.

227 KING STREET, RIVIERA THEATER

Constructed 1937–39; rehabilitated and renovated, 1996–97

Charles C. Benton and Sons, architects

One of Charleston's most beloved buildings, the Riviera theatre, was built at the end of the 1930s as the city's first motion picture theater and is a significant example of the Art Deco style. The Riviera supplanted the earlier Academy of Music, a structure erected in 1838 and converted to use as a theater in 1869. The Pastime Amusement Company, operators of motion picture theaters in the early-twentieth century, acquired the Academy in 1920 but did not announce plans to demolish it and replace it with a new structure until 1936. Charles C. Benton, a Fayetteville, North Carolina, architect who designed theaters and churches throughout the South, planned the present structure with its Aztec temple shape, stylized geometric motifs, and vertical projections from the roofline. A terrazzo entry leads to an interior with a seating capacity for nearly 2,000 people. A sign of the times, balcony seating was originally divided for whites and blacks.

The Riviera theater opened to Charleston audiences on January 28, 1939, with the feature *Secrets of a Nurse*, starring Edmund Lowe. Some of the wall murals, polychrome plaster details, and other Art Deco features remain intact. Recently acquired by the Charleston Place Hotel, the old theater is under conversion into a convention hall above and galleria shops along the Market Street facade.

229–233 KING STREET, RACHEL LAZARUS BUILDING

Constructed circa 1839; variously rehabilitated late-1980s

Rachel Florence Lazarus, one of a number of "sole traders" (women permitted by South Carolina equity courts to operate businesses separate from their husbands), first acquired this status in 1804 and entered the dry goods business in 1817. A woman of great strength and talent, she was the only female subscriber to the Hebrew Harmonic Society, a group that provided the funds for the installation of an organ in the rebuilt Beth Elohim Synagogue in 1841, and she bore seventeen children. After the fire of 1838, Mrs. Lazarus received one of the loans under the Act for the Rebuilding of the City of Charleston and used the funds to construct these three buildings as tenements. Although the storefronts have been altered over the years, the three-story stuccoed brick facades retain their original fenestration with stone lintels and sills, as well as masonry belt courses, and molded cornices. On the upper stories each structure follows the Charleston single house plan and most retain their Greek Revival mantels and staircases. Between the buildings, hyphen infills feature cast-iron panels boasting circular devices also with anthemion motifs. Cabinetmakers Martin Vogel and Francis Salvo completed a contemporary building of four bays next door at *235 King Street* with thistle motifs in its parapet grilles.

237 KING STREET, AHRENS GROCERY BUILDING

Constructed 1870; restored 1986

Abrahams and Seyle, architects; John H. Lopez, contractor

Charles D. Ahrens and George Kriette bought this burned-out site with the shell of a building in 1870, immediately thereafter beginning construction of the present edifice. When completed, Ahrens Grocery wholesale and retail operation was moved here, and Ahrens lived upstairs for about seven years before the rooms were rented to a succession of men's clubs. The *Charleston Daily Courier* wrote about the building upon its completion, describing its exterior with cast-iron Corinthian columns and cornice and its "handsome iron lintels" over each window, and further stating, "the whole iron work is colored in vermillion after the prevailing style of the New York coffee and tea houses." The interior in its original form was extensively described as having Carolina pine shelving ornamented with "gilt moldings" and varnished counters of yellow pine and walnut. The building's exterior was thoroughly restored, even with its original color, in 1986.

239 KING STREET, CAROLINA SAVINGS BANK BUILDING

Constructed 1926–27; rehabilitated 1997

This small building, exhibiting some characteristics of Beaux Arts classicism, was built at the same time as several other similarly styled banks throughout the city, in keeping with the financial boom of the 1920s. Retaining its terra cotta detailed facade boasting Neoclassical Revival pilasters and console bracketed door architrave, the building has been occupied until recently by a succession of banks and offices.

243 KING STREET, SIEGLING MUSIC HOUSE

Constructed circa 1838; exterior rehabilitated and interior altered 1984–85

John Siegling, a native of Erfurt, Germany, established a music store in 1819, selling harps, pianos, and wind instruments. Moving his business from Meeting Street to King Street, he rebuilt on the site

Siegling Music House, 243 King Street, in an etching from an 1880s advertisement

of a building destroyed in the fire in 1838 at the corner of King and Beaufain Streets. Remaining in business until the early 1970s, the company was advertised as "America's oldest music house." The three-story masonry building was remodeled in the mid-nineteenth century and again circa 1900 with the application of Italianate style window hoods and a modillioned cornice with bracketed corners. Acquired in the early-1980s by the present owners, members of a religious order, the structure was renovated and the storefront, with its cast-iron pilasters, was partially renewed.

245–247 KING STREET, NATHAN HART BUILDINGS
Constructed circa 1838; rehabilitated 1986

Nathan Hart, who also constructed *220 King Street*, built these two brick edifices, probably just before his death in 1840. When auctioned by his estate, Hart's widow purchased 245 King Street and his daughter, Mrs. Mordecai Levy, bought 247 King Street. The building's original third story was removed in the late-nineteenth century. The first floor of the corner building retains its cast-iron pilasters, supporting an arcade infilled with banded-glazed brick and featuring windows with pressed-metal, semicircular lintels. The bracketed cornice, with modillions, is different from that at *249 King Street*; the latter structure contains a plain stuccoed facade and arched two-over-two windows. By 1918 these buildings were used as an S. H. Kress and Co. store. The "five and dime" later became a Silver's store until 1978. Silver's also used the three-story building immediately to the north. This edifice, 249 King Street, was designed by the architect John Henry Devereux and built by Susan Wood in 1876. Mrs. Wood's new Italianate style building, with its flattened arched windows and banded corner pilasters, stood ready for occupancy by April of that year. With the ground floor of 249 King Street rented to J. R. Read Co., the upper floors served as the dwelling and studio for the noted Civil War photographer George N. Barnard.

253 KING STREET, CARRINGTON-THOMAS BUILDING

Constructed circa 1890; renovated 1918

Originally built as a men's clothing store, this structure was later renovated for use by the Citizens Bank. Exhibiting a form of Beaux Arts classicism, an engaged, pedimented portico with Ionic columns frames an arched doorway with a central console bracket. Although the building is now a jewelry store, its original bank interior, used from 1918 to 1958, still survives.

254 KING STREET, MOSES LEVY BUILDING

Constructed 1838

Moses Levy, who also built *311 East Bay Street* and lost numerous buildings in the fire of 1838, began construction of this three-story building shortly before his death in 1839. From the start the structure was rented to Charleston's most famous antebellum silversmithing firm, Hayden, Gregg and Company. Generally used as a hardware store since the late-nineteenth century, the building has lost most of its original storefront in the process of numerous renovations, although it retained its scored stucco facade with stone lintels and cast-iron grilles with palmetto designs in the parapet. The building experienced major deterioration until recent renovations. The Levy family also owned the property next door at *256 King Street* at the time of the fire, then sold it to the jeweler William H. Jones a few months later. After the structure passed through numerous owners, the cornice was replaced by a tile parapet. 256 King Street was built simultaneously with *258 King Street*, with a common passage through the middle. The latter structure, built by Jacob Hersman, served for most of the nineteenth century as a jewelry store.

260 KING STREET, KERRISON DRY GOODS BUILDING

Constructed circa 1920; storefront rehabilitated 1996–97

Front elevation of the new Kerrison's store, 1920s illustration

Kerrison's Dry Goods spent its early years, after its founding in 1830, at the site of the Riviera theater (*227 King Street*). It took over new quarters in the 1860s on Hasell Street. The latter building was enlarged in 1920 with the four-story yellow brick section facing King Street. The first-floor storefront, infilled with architectural glasswork, provided the chief ornamentation for the otherwise simple facade, now with three bays of triple windows on each floor but missing its modillioned cornice. Billed in recent years as the South's oldest department store, this headquarters facility closed after Hurricane Hugo in 1989, and remaining suburban operations ceased in 1996. The building has undergone a recent renovation for a new clothing store.

265–267 KING STREET, GEORGE COOK STUDIO BUILDING

Constructed circa 1840; rehabilitated 1995

This front-facing Classical Revival style building, with arched windows at the ends of the front facade and in the center, served as the studio for Charleston's most prominent mid-nineteenth-century photographer, George Cook. His photographs of Charleston following the earthquake of 1886 remain the best documentation of that natural disaster. Cook later moved to Richmond, Virginia, and expanded his photography business. Once covered over with curtain wall facades, the building has recently been rehabilitated.

Cook's photographic studios shown in an 1880s engraving

King Street, decorated for a Confederate veterans' reunion, 1899

268 KING STREET, JOHN THOMPSON BUILDING

Constructed circa 1850; first floor rehabilitated mid-1980s

John Thompson's seed store occupied this building in 1850. Its successor company, William McIntosh Co., continued on the site until 1968. During the McIntosh occupancy a rusticated sandstone facade with flat headed windows and corbeled parapet were added to the front of the structure.

270 KING STREET, MASONIC TEMPLE BUILDING

Constructed 1871–72; partially rehabilitated 1984

John Henry Devereux, architect

The Grand Lodge of Ancient Free Masons of South Carolina laid the cornerstone for this building in 1871. When completed, the three-story Gothic Revival style structure had three stories facing King Street and a stair hall entry on Wentworth Street that rose to a grand lodge room with a forty-foot coved ceiling studded with five gas chandeliers. Alterations through various renovations in 1877, 1885, 1886, and 1895 and extensive remodeling in 1920 and again in the late-1940s led to the loss of much of the original character of this monumental edifice. In 1984 the ground-story, Gothic-arched storefronts were restored, but the infill in the upper stories and the modern awning windows remain.

273 KING STREET, PARISH-POINCIGNON BUILDING

Constructed circa 1840; rehabilitated 1987–88

Long considered to be one of Charleston's most commanding corner commercial structures, this building was begun as early as the 1830s when it was owned by Daniel Parish and stood as a three-story, square-ended store and dwelling. Owned in the 1850s by the Charleston real estate magnate Etienne Poincignon, the building passed through his descendants, the McNulty and the Storen families, until the 1980s. For much of the late-nineteenth century the property was rented to the Hirsch Israel Company, a clothing store. This company renovated the building with a multistory central arch and a domed corner tower. The tower was later removed and the arch was infilled, but evidence of the pressed-metal Italianate cornice and the elaborate window lintels supported by console brackets partially survives. The lintels and certain other features were restored in the late-1980s.

274–276 KING STREET, COMMER-CIAL SAVINGS BANK BUILDING

Constructed 1908–09; altered 1953; renovated 1990s

John D. Newcomer, architect

An early-nineteenth-century building was demolished at this site in 1908 to permit the construction of a new three-story stuccoed brick bank building in a simplified version of the Italian Renaissance style. The architect, John D. Newcomer, a native of Pennsylvania, designed numerous buildings throughout Charleston, including *172 Meeting Street* and *302 King Street*. He also remodeled several of the city's historic buildings. This bank, presided over by future mayor Tristram T. Hyde, opened its doors with a capital stock of $50,000, a respectable sum at the turn of the century. In the 1950s the deep modillioned cornice and stucco ornamentation were stripped off the building, leaving only the remnants of two pilasters flanking the storefront opening and interlocking arches supported by Corinthian pilasters on the third-story level. Recent renovations have stabilized the building, but its lost features have not been restored.

275 KING STREET, HIRSCH ISRAEL BUILDING

Constructed 1897–99; renovated 1996

The Hirsch Israel Company, which rented *273 King Street* across Wentworth street, completed a monumental structure on this site by 1899. In 1919 the building with a domed corner tower was sold for the Dime Savings Bank. The tower and much of the facade were later stripped away, and the Hirsch Israel building became a discount clothing store with a yellow brick facade. The building has recently been renovated with a contemporary interior, revealing the surviving framing of the upper stories.

281 KING STREET, KRESS BUILDING

Constructed 1931

Despite the distinction of enclosed hyphens or piazzas and adaptations of the single house, King Street has elements that are common to most Main Streets in the United States. One of these elements is the dime store. Samuel H. Kress was a schoolteacher and entrepreneur who began his company in 1887 by purchasing a stationery shop in Pennsylvania. By 1896 Kress had developed his first chain, with a second store in Pennsylvania and a third in Memphis, Tennessee. A national headquarters was established in New York City in 1900 to oversee his twelve stores. S. H. Kress set his chain apart by building his stores with unusual designs and never leasing. He was so interested in architectural design that he developed his own architectural division in his New York office. Kress's personal touch to every store was the incorporation of his German family coat of arms on the interiors and, by the 1930s, on all storefronts. 281 King Street is typical of Kress's Art Deco buildings with its yellow brick facade, its polychrome terra cotta detailing, vertical orientation, and abstract and geometric designs.

View of 285–299 King Street with a crowd before the 5 and 10 cent store, circa 1905

285 KING STREET, ALLAN-KERRISON COMPANY BUILDING

Constructed before 1860; renovated 1890s

This mid-nineteenth-century Greek Revival style building was substantially refaced in the 1890s with a Beaux Arts Neoclassical facade. A stuccoed frieze with a floral motif tops the original surviving storefront, while decorative panels with delicate reliefs and vertical Corinthian pilasters terminate above the arched third-story windows. A bracketed parapet with a garland frieze, dentiled cornice, and surmounting balustrade provides an elegant cap to this building used for many generations as a jewelry store. Neoclassical urns that once decorated the balustrade have been lost.

Perhaps the oldest building in continual use as a jewelry store in the city, it housed the antebellum firm of James Allan and Company from 1865 until the 1920s. Allan's company survived the Civil War and enjoyed a wide reputation for its "reliability."

Allan's jewelry store, 1875 engraving

286–288 KING STREET, GEORGE MILLER BUILDING

Constructed 1839–40; altered 1883

Rebuilt after the fire of 1838 by the merchant George N. Miller, the building was described in an 1853 conveyance to Thomas N. Gadsden as "a Three story Double Tenement Brick Store." The stuccoed brick Greek Revival building with six bays on each floor and an upper facade decorated by cast-iron grilles with anthemion motif was renovated after its purchase by John Henry Steinmeyer in 1883. The Steinmeyer family, owners of extensive properties in Harleston Village and a large lumber mill on the Ashley River near Gadsden and Beaufain Streets, added Italianate style pressed-metal window hoods and a bracketed cornice. Used as a dry goods store and drugstore, the building retains its interior paneling, shelving, and drawers.

290–292 KING STREET, MILLER, RIPLEY AND COMPANY BUILDINGS

Constructed 1838–39; altered 1890, 1950

Miller, Ripley and Company signed a contract with the builder/architect John Gordon to construct two three-story brick stores on these sites before the fire of 1838. Rebuilt immediately after the fire as double tenements in the Greek Revival style, 290 King Street was purchased by Samuel Johnston. Johnston added an Italianate storefront to the building as well as the pressed-metal window surrounds and a cornice placed over the surviving Greek Revival parapet grilles. The Bernard family purchased the corner building at 292 King Street, and it remained in their hands until 1912, when it was passed to a company owned by the Sottile family. Remodeled in 1950 in the Art Moderne style, the structure has wide horizontal bands between floors and fluted pilasters.

297 KING STREET, MORDECAI COHEN BUILDING

Constructed circa 1839; altered late-1880s, 1950

Mordecai Cohen, who owned property throughout Charleston, including the tenements at *97–101 Broad Street*, built a three-and-a-half-story brick structure with a front gabled parapet on his property after the 1838 fire. Miles Drake, a dry goods merchant, purchased the building in 1851, and his family held it until 1912. In the late-nineteenth century Italianate detailing was added, but much of this was removed in 1950 during the ownership of Pastime Amusement Company, a Sottile family real estate firm. Cohen built *293* and *295 King Street* as well, but these buildings have experienced even more twentieth-century alteration than their neighbor to the north.

302 *King Street*

Present-day King Street,
300 block, looking
north

302 KING STREET, TITLE GUARANTEE BUILDING
Constructed 1915–16

John Newcomer, architect

The architect John D. Newcomer designed this edifice for a building and loan company, and its construction was completed by 1916 at a cost of $13,000. Built of brick with a veneer of limestone, the upper floor with a semicircular window topped by a console bracket and a surmounting cornice supporting a roof balustrade derives from the Beaux Arts style. The Title Guarantee Building contrasts with the late-Italianate style storefront added to a 1790s building at *300 King Street*. The Onslow Candy Company added the surviving pressed-metal window hoods and the bracketed cornice. The arch with the bracketed keystone at the Title Guarantee Building, however, harmonizes with the surviving arched entry at *304 King Street*. The console bracketed arch on this latter structure and the now-restored front interior remain from the Princess Theater, built on this site in 1911 by Albert Sottile and first leased to Eddie Riddock. The latter building served Charleston as a soda shop. When this business failed, Sottile announced plans to convert the facility to a movie theater. Surviving as a movie house exclusively, the Princess boasted a mirror screen and a five-piece orchestra for film accompaniment and intermittent entertainment.

308 KING STREET, SAMUEL SCOTTOW BUILDING

Constructed before 1793

This edifice is one of several survivors in this part of King Street of late-eighteenth-century dwellings that were later converted to commercial uses. Scottow's widow died here in 1812, and the property was purchased by Christian Henry Faber. The parcel was subdivided with the creation of two lots to the south, including the surviving Greek Revival building at *306 King Street*, built by Faber. The Georgian character of both buildings survives in the diminishment of the window sizes from the second to the third floors in the Classical architectural tradition, and in the scored stucco facade and stucco cornice. The building retains few features of its Victorian period storefront with cast-iron components. The remnant of the piazza to the south was infilled, in the King Street tradition, many years ago and serves as a separate shop on the ground story.

313 KING STREET, JOHN ANTHONY BUILDING

Constructed circa 1812–15; rehabilitated before 1940

Saddler John Anthony built one of King Street's finer commercial buildings on this site shortly after 1812. Although the structure experienced alterations in the 1840s, it retains its Flemish-bonded brickwork, marble belt course, stone lintels, tile roof, and a projecting dormer. While it was the site of the Jack Krawcheck Men's Clothing Store for many decades, the owners completed significant restoration, a rear courtyard designed by Loutrel Briggs, and renovation of an adjoining store at *311 King Street*, designed in the Neoclassical Revival style.

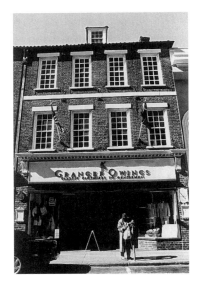

314 KING STREET, FELDMAN-TESKEY BUILDING

Constructed circa 1878; rehabilitated 1993–94

This three-story stuccoed building was built in 1878 as a grocery by the wholesale grocer and liquor dealer Benjamin Feldman and his partner Robert Teskey; it replaced a wooden structure on the site which they had leased before purchasing the property in 1871. The structure served a mixed use for many years, with various businesses occupying the ground floor and the upstairs serving as a residence and later as a boarding-house. By 1890 it served as J. N. Peeckson Choice Family Groceries. A bracketed cornice surmounts a front para-peted shed roof. The facade features quoining at the corners of the upper floors and segmentally arched windows with decorative surrounds. A piazza original to the building was enclosed in the 1920s and today houses the separate business desig-nated as 312½ King Street.

Advertisement for 314 King Street as a grocery and "importers of Teas, Coffees and Spices"

319–325 KING STREET, AMERICAN HOTEL BUILDING

Constructed before 1850; renovated circa 1890–1900; restored 1975 after a fire

The owner of extensive real estate in Charleston and Philadelphia, Robert F. Henry held these properties prior to death in 1846. Henry's estate probably amalgam-ated several other buildings on the site to create one of Charleston's most elegant antebellum facades and one of its finest small nineteenth-century hotels. Although the ground story has seen much alteration, pilasters with stylized Corinthian capitals remain. The upper-story fenestration is di-vided by Tuscan pilasters, topped by deco-rative panels with American eagle and floral motifs, and fronted by engaged cast-iron panels. A roof balustrade caps the building. Descending from Henry to his nieces and nephews, the hotel became the property of Miss Mary Jane Ross of *1 Meeting Street* and was included in legal battles over the settlement of her estate. One of Charleston's most virulent political battles, the 1915 primary race for mayor between incumbent Tristram T. Hyde and John P. Grace, resulted in a tense democratic committee meeting on the second story. With a disturbance at the door, a volley of gunfire caused the death of Sidney Cohen, a young reporter assigned to cover the meeting.

320 KING STREET, SAMUEL PENDERGRASS BUILDING

Constructed early-nineteenth century

This three-story brick building, which retains its Greek Revival fenestration and chimneys, has undergone extensive remodeling since its construction in the first decade of the 1800s by Samuel Pendergrass. The first of these changes was undertaken by Thomas Fleming, a merchant who purchased the property in 1820 at public auction. Fleming raised the height of the structure, extending the top half-story into a full story, and added the hipped roof. The property eventually passed to Mordecai David, who enclosed the piazza on the south side of the building, creating the separate two-story structure now known as *318 King*. This section shares walls with both of its neighboring buildings and features Italianate windows and a bracketed cornice.

327–329 KING STREET, GLORIA THEATER BUILDING

Constructed circa 1855–56; facade remodeled 1923–27; rehabilitated 1992–93

Barbot and Seyle, original architects

The real estate and movie theater tycoon Albert Sottile purchased this property containing a mid-1850s double tenement built for John D. Meyers's grocery. The architects Barbot and Seyle had originally designed the front facade, but later it was altered with the addition of Italianate style windows. In 1922 Sottile began construction of a pressed-brick theater section at the rear and completed the renovation of the front section with ground-story commercial spaces. When opened in 1927 the facility housed movies as well as traveling vaudeville companies. Although some of its original decorative features were stripped away after the movie house closed in 1975, the remaining details were restored by the College of Charleston in its conversion of this site in 1993 as the Sottile Theater. The main auditorium still features side archways covered with ornamental ironwork and the original domed ceiling, which is surrounded by a plaster oculus; a shimmering blue, skylike expanse with "twinkling stars" is created through the effect of lighting within. South Carolina's premiere of *Gone with the Wind,* a festive celebration for the filming of a story that highlighted Charleston's "charm and grace" (and included Charlestonian Alicia Rhett in the cast), was held at the Gloria Theater in 1939. Some of Charleston's most socially prominent young women dressed in authentic antebellum clothing for the premiere and its accompanying events.

336–338 KING STREET, JOHN CUNNINGHAM BUILDING
Constructed after 1794

The merchant John Cunningham purchased this site in 1794 and probably built the present three-story double building within the first decade of his ownership. This stuccoed brick Federal style building has a common facade on the upper floors, and its rear yards were formerly accessed through the central archway, although the buildings are now two separate parcels as a

result of a court order in 1879 in the settlement of debts of Mrs. Sarah Ottolengui, a later owner. Jacob Capel purchased 336 King Street and Dorothea Blohme bought 338 King Street, both renting to a myriad of tenants, including David and Epstein, jewelers and watchmakers; Charles Holle, barber; Cable Piano; and None Such Lunch. The 1940s brought such lessees as the Arcade Shooting Gallery, the Barn Tavern, and Bert's Locker Club, reflecting changing uses. Throughout the pre–World War II history of the site, most of the commercial tenants lived upstairs. The Italianate style cornices with side brackets and the pedimented window hoods probably date from the years immediately before 1879. The former feature obscures the hipped roof dating from the late-nineteenth century. These later details and the double form reflect the same pattern as the smaller two-story double building across the street, *337–339 King Street*, built by the baker Henry Dorre in 1859 and subsequently divided into separate properties.

341 KING STREET, JAMES WHITE BUILDING

Constructed circa 1819

James White, a merchant, mortgaged a new building on this site in 1819. Retaining many of its late-Federal features including corner quoining, window heads, and belt course, the house has a pilastered pediment that once included a tripartite window, since reduced to the current small opening. White never lived here, but Henry Loomis, a hardware merchant, had his business and residence here by 1819. Like many of the early-nineteenth-century buildings surviving in this part of King Street, the upstairs follows the single house plan and retains its original woodwork. The property formerly included a bakery and extensive outbuildings at the rear; part of the stuccoed kitchen dependency survives.

342 KING STREET, MILLER BUILDING

Constructed after 1821; renovated 1970, 1991

This building retains its Federal character with its hipped roof and finely pointed Flemish bond facade, divided by belt coursing and three bays with nine-over-nine windows surmounted by rubbed brick jack arches. Miller, a jeweler, replaced two earlier wooden buildings on the site after buying it at auction in 1821; he retained it until his death in 1840. Although the upper floors of 342 King have remained as built, the small, adjacent two-story structure at *340 King Street* was refaced in the 1940s in a late-Moderne fashion with molded bands of vertical concrete and a merlon in the stepped parapet. The brick form and fenestration of 340 King Street are similar to that of the early–Greek Revival store and dwelling at *348 King Street*, built by the Santo Domingan refugee Margaret Gidiere for her dry goods store and residence by 1830. This latter structure was held by numerous owners, including the German tavern keeper John Schachte. It later served as the Lyric Theater, the place where burlesque was introduced to Charleston, and eventually provided the venue for a series of discotheques and bars.

363 KING STREET, POPPENHEIM HARDWARE STORE

Constructed 1891–92; facade rehabilitated 1982

W. B. W. Howe, architect; J. D. Murphy, builder-contractor; Thomas H. Reynolds, mason

The son of an Episcopal bishop who designed the Drayton House at *25 East Battery* and the William Enston Home complex at *900 King Street* executed the plans for a new hardware store for the merchant Christopher P. Poppenheim. Called "an ornament to the street" in a

headline for a story in the March 23, 1892, edition of the *News and Courier*, the Richardsonian Romanesque building rises two stories with a facade of Philadelphia pressed brick and terra cotta detailing terminating in a tile roof with a central pediment sheltering a plaque marked 1891.

The front arcaded portico was supported by cast-iron pillars set on bases of Winnsboro (S.C.) granite. The newspaper account enthusiastically described the floor of the vestibule as being formed by "the largest single block of granite ever brought to Charleston." Poppenheim's business had been housed since 1883 in a smaller store at *345 King Street*, a more simply detailed building in the Romanesque style. Since losing its storefront in the mid-twentieth century and with the painting of its masonry, the relationship to the later structure has been obscured. The building at 363 King was rehabilitated with additions in 1982.

370 KING STREET, FELLOWSHIP SOCIETY
Constructed early-nineteenth century; renovated circa 1880–1900

This stuccoed, three-bay building with pressed-metal window heads and cornice houses one of Charleston's historically significant eighteenth-century organizations. The Fellowship Society has been headquartered here since the early-twentieth century. The Society was founded in 1762 by a group of "mechanics," or craftsmen, who were active in the promotion of American liberties in the period before the Revolution. The Society remains in existence. Its original stated purpose was to assist widows and orphans of former members.

371 KING STREET, GARDEN THEATER
Constructed 1917–18; restored 1980s, 1990

C. K. Howell and David B. Heyer, architects

This vaudeville theater, more than four years in construction, marked an architectural high point for the city with its use of Beaux Arts Neoclassical style. Albert Sottile's building also became a popular venue for photo plays, as movies were called, and vitaphone talking pictures. A central pavilion and arch is flanked by Corinthian pilasters and decorated with classical allegory figures representing music; end bays provide spaces for small shops. Those visiting the theater passed beneath the coffered barrel vault into a vestibule decorated as a garden with trellis, flower baskets, and caged singing canaries. The lobby retains its Neoclassical plaques and other decoration. The present theater was extensively rehabilitated in the early-1980s to provide a venue for community performances and Spoleto concerts.

The Garden theater in its pre–World War II heyday, Christmas, 1938

375 KING STREET, MARTHA GIVEN BUILDING

Constructed circa 1868

A two-story stuccoed brick building was built on this site just after 1868 to provide income for a widow of a Charleston shoe dealer. It retains later pressed-metal detailing in its pedimented window surrounds and bracketed cornice.

379–381 KING STREET, ENSTON BUILDINGS

Constructed circa 1860s, 1870s; altered 1940s; rehabilitated 1980s

William Enston, the furniture magnate whose principal store remains at *187–191 King Street*, apparently replaced an eighteenth-century building in the late 1850s with the present structure at 381 King Street completed in the Italianate style. Enston's estate retained the building for the use of his widow after his death. Hannah Enston also built the two-story structure to the south in the 1870s. These became part of the legacy used to build the Enston Home at *900 King Street*. Passing through numerous remodelings, 381

King Street lost its cast-iron storefront in the late-1940s but retains the arched window hoods on the second story and pedimented window hoods set in blind arches on the front facade of the third story. Although the piazza has been infilled on the first two stories, a remnant on the third tier retains its Tuscan columns. The two-story building at 379 King was built after William Enston's death and is a small wood structure that retains its second-story Italianate style windows and end brackets flanking a simple entablature.

387 KING STREET, FRANCIS MARION HOTEL

Constructed 1922–24; renovated 1980s; rehabilitated and restored 1994–96

William Lee Stoddard, architect

The New York architect who designed some of the South's finest hotels, including the Tutwiler in Birmingham and the Georgian Terrace in Atlanta, designed a large new hotel for Charleston in 1920. Part of a movement to give Charleston an up-to-date modern hotel, the Francis Marion Hotel Company included some of Charleston's leading businessmen and two former mayors. Although the newspaper referred to the style of the structure as "Italian Renaissance," the building reflects elements of the Georgian Revival and Neoclassical Revival styles. The first-floor lobby and mezzanine are fronted on the exterior by arched window openings framed in the central pavilion by double Corinthian pilasters surmounted by an "attic story" with Neoclassical urns and cartouches. A balcony surrounded the twelfth floor, and above it an entablature with fanlight and cartouche decoration terminated in a Greek style parapet with acroteria. The penthouse floor rose above this decorated level. Serving as an important part of the city's tourism and business life, the Francis Marion also became a social center after its completion, particularly with the use of its elegant ballroom for debutante dances and other events. After declining in the 1960s and 1970s, the hotel was renovated in the 1980s and completely rehabilitated in 1994–96.

404 KING STREET, CHARLESTON COUNTY LIBRARY

Constructed 1960

Cummings and McCrady, architects

In May 1958 Charleston County ordered the demolition of the west wing of the Old Citadel, designed by Edward B. White in 1850, due to the proposal to build a new library on the site. The demolition drew less protest than the firestorm of citizen and preservationist ire invoked over what was described by planners as a "modernistic curtain wall library." The structure was called a "birdcage" by some opponents and "violative of every principle of historic Charleston architecture" by a trustee of Historic Charleston Foundation; the sculptor Willard Hirsch, on the other hand, pronounced it "very beautiful." When completed, the two-story building with pink marble veneering, metal plaques by sculpter Hirsch, and aluminum trim cost more than $750,000. It has served as the main branch of the county public library until the present. A new Calhoun Street structure is set for completion in 1997.

405 KING STREET, ST. MATTHEW'S GERMAN LUTHERAN CHURCH

Constructed 1867–72; restored and steeple rebuilt after fire damage 1965–66

John Henry Devereux, architect

With the tremendous expansion of Charleston's German community, the congregation of St. Matthew's Lutheran Church on Hasell Street bought a new site on King Street near Vanderhorst Street for its congregation. The cornerstone was laid in 1869, and the church was complete for Holy Thursday, March 28, 1872, and dedicated with a crowd of 3,000 inside and outside. The 297-foot spire of the structure commands this section of the city and was once the tallest structure in South Carolina. The Gothicism employed by the architect was said to be related to the German versions of Gothic architecture. The building was once decoratively painted to appear as though it were of stone construction. A disastrous fire in January 1965 gutted the sanctuary and toppled the steeple. The spire projected upside down to the ground just southwest of the doorway and penetrated the soil to a depth of eighteen feet. A section of the spire has been left in place as a reminder. On the interior the marble altar and the German stained-glass windows in the apse remained intact. The Charleston firm of Simons, Lapham, Mitchell and Small oversaw the restoration of St. Matthew's Church.

409 KING STREET, RADCLIFFE-AIMAR BUILDING

Constructed circa 1808; rehabilitated 1983–84

Lucretia Radcliffe, developer of her husband's estate as the new suburb of Radcliffeborough, built this large four-and-a-half-story stuccoed brick building by 1808, conveying it eight years later to Samuel Maverick. Serving for a time as the Reverend Ferdinand Jacobs's Seminary for

View showing the south elevation of 409 King Street, 1865

Girls, the site became an apothecary hall for George Washington Aimar in 1852. Securing title in 1871, Aimar built his thriving drugstore business in this structure; its doors were closed in 1978. The building stretches six bays along King Street and the same distance along Vanderhorst Street. Stucco belt courses divide the upper floor, and two dormers project from the front and side of the roof. In a 1983–84 renovation the rear piazzas were enclosed in glass and the ground floor and part of the additional stories were altered. A stair tower was added on the north.

416 KING STREET, BROWNLEE FURNITURE BUILDING

Constructed 1803–27; renovated with new facade 1947

In 1947 the architect Augustus Constantine altered a three-story, stuccoed brick single house with a hipped roof, dating from the early-nineteenth century and built by the merchant John Brownlee, adjacent to his 1945 store for Chase Furniture Company. The latter building is respected for the quality of its modernistic style facade with white marble sheathing, gray marble banding, circular windows, and glass block banding flanking the 1940s neon sign. The shell of the house at *418 King Street*, an early-nineteenth-century version of the original single house form of the Brownlee Building, retains its English bond brickwork and a remnant of its dentiled cornice and slate hip roof. This building was built for Mrs. Elizabeth Wragg before 1803.

426 KING STREET, FRANCIS MARKS HOUSE

Constructed 1806–10; altered 1942; rehabilitated 1990–91

Francis Marks, a member of a family of King Street shopkeepers, built this three-

THE BUILDINGS OF CHARLESTON

story stuccoed brick single house with a low hipped roof after acquiring the site in 1806 from Joseph Manigault. Although the building was rehabilitated in recent years, the fenestration of the upper floors remains intact in the late Federal manner with larger windows on the second floor and smaller openings on the third story.

442 KING STREET, FERGERSON-AMME HOUSE
Constructed before 1840

James Fergerson, a planter in St. John's Parish, Berkeley, bought this parcel from Ann Wragg Fergerson, the widow of a Revolutionary War hero, and built a two-story brick dwelling in the 1830s. The gabled-roof house retains the remnants of its double-tiered Greek Revival style piazzas on the south and the shell of extensive outbuildings to the rear. This structure became a bakery with the sale of the site to the Amme family in 1856. They owned the property until 1931. An Italianate style facade with pressed-metal ornament was added in the late- nineteenth century, but most of this has been removed. In the 1980s the Board of Architectural Review repeatedly denied petitions for its demolition.

446 KING STREET, AMERICAN THEATRE
Constructed 1942; remodeled 1947

Augustus Constantine, architect

Constructed in the Modern style for the Pastime Amusement Company, this uptown theater was named in honor of American servicemen and others working for "victory over the axis powers." Seating 900, this simple building was outfitted with the latest technology, and a large American eagle topped its proscenium arch. Rehabilitation of the building, which retains its exterior marquee and curtain wall facade with stepped parapet, began in 1996 for its use as a virtual reality theater.

456 KING STREET, WILLIAM AIKEN HOUSE

L *Constructed 1811; addition circa 1830s*

This structure was purchased by William Aiken Sr. in 1811 from the trustees of the minor James Mackie for $14,000. It was originally built as a brick single house with associated outbuildings located on the Ann Street side of the property. A ballroom addition was constructed sometime after Aiken's death in 1831, as was the Gothic Revival style carriage house at the rear. The property was extensively damaged in the 1886 earthquake. It remains a strong presence on King Street. Its fence was removed in the early-twentieth century and given to the Gibbes Museum of Art.

View of the north elevation, 456 King Street, circa 1925

Aiken, the father of South Carolina governor William Aiken Jr., born in County Antrim, Ireland, is perhaps best remembered as the president of the South Carolina Canal and Railroad Company, which was begun in 1827 in an attempt to regain a portion of the shipping trade lost to the port of Savannah. The railroad was completed to Hamburgh (now Aiken), South Carolina, by 1833. The company later became part of Norfolk Southern, which still operates its district sales office in part of the house, thus maintaining the long railroad history of the property. In 1977 the property was donated to the National Trust for Historic Preservation and now houses its Southern Regional Office.

67 LEGARE STREET, CRAFTS SCHOOL

Constructed 1881; renovated with addition 1915; rehabilitated mid-1980s

Abrahams and Seyle, architects

This building was constructed as the Crafts School in 1881. Built to replace the Friend Street School, which was founded in 1859 and destroyed in the fire of 1861,

389

it rises three stories on a high basement. Architects Abrahams and Seyle designed the Gothic Revival style school, which features buttresses and lancet arches. The school was named for William Crafts, the noted Charleston antebellum poet and intellectual, who is buried in the graveyard of King's Chapel in Boston. David Hyer designed the three-story wing in 1915. The building has recently been converted to condominiums.

87–101 LOGAN STREET, HEINSOHN TENEMENTS
Constructed 1885

A member of a large family of German tradesmen purchased seven of nine lots subdivided from the city-owned "Hospital Land" in the mid-1880s. In the eighteenth century this area was the site of a public hospital largely for the insane. All of the dwellings on these lots were built contemporaneously and were similarly designed with Queen Anne detailing and single house plans. One property was purchased separately by Fredericka Martin. Herman Rosebrock built a substantial corner store on the seventh lot at Logan and Magazine Streets.

122 LOGAN STREET, MATTHIAS WOLFE HOUSE
Constructed 1790–1800; rehabilitated 1980s

A well-to-do butcher built this three-story, stuccoed brick single house with a hipped, pantile roof in the late-eighteenth century. The structure retains its original form with some intact window sash and shutters, and the interior still features its late-Georgian style staircase and several mantels. For several decades this building has provided a site for Fielding's Home for Funerals, formerly located at the corner of Logan and Short Streets, and it has been restored by that company.

126 LOGAN STREET, HENRY GEFKEN HOUSE

Constructed circa 1805

An unrestored, two-story wooden house with beaded weatherboarding, hipped roof, and corbeled brick chimneys with a stucco band stands on this small lot. Built by the carpenter Henry Gefken around 1805, the building retains its large nine-over-nine first-floor windows above and smaller six-over-six windows, a detail recognizable in most Georgian and Federal period houses. The small late-nineteenth-century wooden house to the south fronts a circa 1816 masonry dwelling constructed by the bank clerk John Pickenpack that was used in the early-twentieth century as a school.

138 LOGAN STREET, HUGUENOT SOCIETY

Constructed circa 1850–60; rehabilitated 1990

The first recorded ownership of this property is in 1851, when it was purchased by Henry F. Strohecker, executor for the deceased John Strohecker. 138 Logan Street is an example of nineteenth-century commercial construction and has Greek Revival detailing. The Huguenot Society moved to this building from a former site (the Confederate Home). The Society's library contains volumes pertaining to Huguenot history and extensive genealogical records and papers of Huguenot émigrés and their families.

12 MAGAZINE STREET, BENJAMIN MAZYCK TENEMENT

Constructed 1783–1800

This small gable-roof dwelling with beaded weatherboarding was built by a member of the Mazyck family, original owners of this area, after the Revolution. On the exterior of the first floor it retains its original trim and nine-over-nine windows, and some Federal style mantels and a staircase remain on the interior.

21 MAGAZINE STREET, OLD CITY JAIL

Constructed 1802; altered 1820s; wings constructed 1855

Improvements by Robert Mills, architect; wing designed by Barbot and Seyle

The four blocks surrounding the city jail were designated in 1680 as public lands and were the location of institutions serving the poor, the sick, and the dispossessed. In addition to housing a series of powder magazines that were erected on Magazine Street beginning in 1737, this land was used for a public burying ground, the poorhouse, the marine and other hospitals, the workhouse, and the jail. In his *Statistics of South Carolina*, published in 1826, Robert Mills describes the institutions of this block:

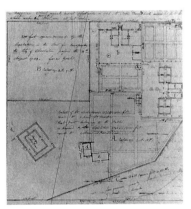

Plat showing Charleston jail site with magazine, gaol, almshouse, and hospital

Lunatic Asylum—This benevolent institution was founded in 1822; the building is now ready for the reception of patients; it will contain 150, nearly all in separate rooms; the plan of the building is such as to admit of any extension, without departure from the original design. . . . The original act of Legislature making appropriations for a Lunatic Asylum including also an Asylum for the Deaf and Dumb. . . . The public prison is situated on Magazine Street. . . . It is a large three-story brick building with very roomy and comfortable accommodations. . . . There has been lately added to it a four-story wing building, devoted exclusively to the confinement of criminals. It is divided into solitary cells, one for each criminal, and the whole made general fire proof. A spacious court is attached. . . . Very good health is enjoyed by the prisoners. The work house, adjoining the jail is appropriated entirely to the confinement and punishment of slaves. These were formerly compelled only occasionally to work; no means then existing of employing them regularly and effectually. The last year the City Council ordered the erection of a tread-mill; this has proved a valuable appendage to the prison, and will supercede every other species of punishment there.

The building was renovated by the architects Barbot and Seyle in the 1850s. Until the earthquake of 1886, the design also included a substantial tower. The wing described by Mills was his own design, but it was replaced by the 1850s wing, which remains. Union troops, including the remnant of the 54th Massachusetts Regiment, were quartered here during the Civil War. The facility served as the county jail until the 1930s. Today the building is the property of the Housing Authority of the City of Charleston.

MARION SQUARE
(CITADEL SQUARE)

🅽 *Developed by 1830; attained present conformity by 1883*

During the Revolutionary War tabby fortifications stretched across this site for the defense of Charleston from British attack. Developed after the war, with Lowndes Street running east-west through this space and Tobacco Street at its northern end, it soon became a muster ground for the State Arsenal, designed by Frederick Wesner and erected in the wake of the discovery of the Denmark Vesey insurrection plot in 1822. Finished some years later, the arsenal stood two stories with a central arch

Tourist souvenir photo of Marion Square looking toward the Calhoun monument and the Francis Marion Hotel, 1920s

and interior courtyard. The site became
home to the South Carolina Military College in 1843. The Old Citadel, as it is now
called, was renovated on several occasions
before the college relocated to Hampton Park
in 1822. The structure was raised in the late-
nineteenth century, and two wings were
added on the east and west in 1950. Although the central arch is original, the upper stories are additions and some of the
fenestration has been altered. Extensively
gutted in 1995–96 for reuse as an inn, the
building is now entered from a new porte
cochere on Meeting Street.

A row of houses standing along the western edge of the square was removed by 1883.
Various monuments are scattered throughout the space. A memorial to John C.
Calhoun was finally erected in 1887 by the
Ladies Calhoun Monument Association, after decades of debate and fundraising. The
initial statue on a pedestal was removed by
1896 for the present fluted stone pillar with
cast-iron palmettos flanking its base and a
raised statue of Calhoun, his back to the
north, seemingly brooding over the street
bearing his name. The square also includes
a section of the Revolutionary War tabby
fort, surrounded by a cast-iron fence; an
obelisk monument to Gen. Wade Hampton;
a memorial to Gen. Francis Marion; a cast-
iron fountain capping an artesian well; and
a memorial to Charleston's great twentieth-
century statesman and Supreme Court justice, James F. Byrnes. The latter accompanies
the red brick bandstand, designed in the
Moderne style by Augustus Constantine in
1944 and dedicated to Charlestonians in the
armed forces of World War II.

The city covenanted long ago that the
square should be kept open as a parade
ground for the Washington Light Infantry
and the Sumter Guards, antebellum organizations. A 1961 proposal to put a parking lot on this square was shelved after
public outcry.

MARKET AREA
188 MEETING STREET, MARKET
HALL AND MARKET SHEDS

L *Constructed 1840–41*

Edward Brickell White, architect; Andrew Cunningham and John White, contractors

Market Hall and the public market sheds that stretch for several blocks behind the hall are located in the heart of Charleston's nineteenth-century commercial district. The land was conveyed to the city in 1788 by the Revolutionary War general Charles Cotesworth Pinckney and other citizens "to lay out a street from the channel of the Cooper River to Meeting Street 100 feet broad, and in said street to establish a public market or markets for the purpose of vending all sorts of butcher meats, poultry, game, fish, vegetables and provisions."

From 1790 to 1806 markets were erected, and in 1837 the cornerstone was laid for a combination masons' hall and market on the site of the present Market Hall. The following year a fire destroyed several blocks of the city including the newly constructed masons' hall. The fire prompted the city to enact legislation that

Photo of west (front) elevation of Market Hall, 188 Meeting Street

Detail of measured drawing of the portico, Market Hall

City market with turkey buzzards at work cleaning up trash, circa 1900

discouraged the erection of wooden buildings, and it also inspired the city to contemplate a more permanent market complex. The local architect Edward Brickell White was chosen as the architect for the project.

Set on the narrow lot between North and South Market Streets, facing onto busy Meeting Street, Market Hall is located on one of the most conspicuous sites in Charleston. Its temple form rise is two stories in height with a double flight of brownstone steps ascending to a pedimented portico supported by four Roman Doric columns. The intended appearance is that of a stone structure, when, in fact, the building is constructed primarily of brick covered with a brownstone stucco. The ground level is heavily rusticated, and the upper story is scored in an ashlar pattern. The cornice, portico, and Doric capitals are red sandstone, while the triglyphs and moldings are cast cement. The bucrania and ram's heads, signifying the presence of a meat market, are made of cast-iron.

According to local tradition, the upper meeting room served as a recruitment center as well as a ballroom for benefits of "the cause" during the War Between the States. The Palmetto Guard, a distinguished military unit of volunteers, was honored with a farewell reception here before leaving for battle, and its members returned annually to toast their fallen comrades. The last two survivors met in 1917.

Since 1899 the United Daughters of the Confederacy have held their functions in the meeting room. Their Confederate Museum has occupied the upper floor for most of the twentieth century; however, the upper story was closed after Hurricane Hugo in 1989, and the entire building is awaiting extensive interior and exterior restoration.

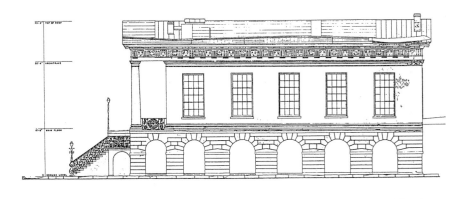

SOUTH ELEVATION

Measured drawing of south elevation, Market Hall

34 NORTH MARKET STREET, OLD CHURCH OF THE REDEEMER

Constructed circa 1916; rehabilitated late-1960s–80s

This rough brick Gothic church was built in 1916 as a chapel for mariners and sailors, replacing Mariner's Church at *50 Church Street*, which was damaged in the earthquake. This church adjoined the seamen's home located to the west on North Market Street. The Pinckney family held this site longer than most of its other area property, giving these parcels to the Charleston Port Society. Miss Harriott Pinckney donated the property because she "almost daily watched the sailors loitering around the waterfront apparently with no home and no place to

Interior, 34 North Market Street before its conversion to a restaurant in the 1960s

go." The chapel was constructed in the traditional Gothic manner but, like its predecessor on Church Street, contains a pulpit made from the prow of a small boat and other nautical features. The seamen's home is a two-story building with matching brick detailing and Gothic trim, including a lancet-arched loggia on the southeast corner of the building. These structures ceased their charitable functions in the 1960s and have been converted as restaurants.

36–38 NORTH MARKET STREET, J. C. H. CLAUSSEN RANGE

Constructed circa 1850; renovated 1970s

J. C. H. Claussen operated various wholesale businesses in the antebellum period including a candy factory, a grist and meal mill, and a cracker manufactory. Of these buildings, the one at 36–38 North Market, including a central section and two side portions, retains its original cast-iron storefront. While bowed metal window heads survive on the second story, the third story was lost in the tornado of 1938. The Bay Fruit Company and other produce wholesalers operated in the range until the 1960s. The spaces were renovated in the 1970s and 1980s to house various shops and restaurants.

Engraving, J.C. H. Claussen & Co., candy factory, 1880s

50-54 NORTH MARKET STREET, HENRY'S BUILDING

Constructed before 1850; renovated 1932, 1984

This three-part range of two-story brick buildings was built before 1850 and has served a succession of uses. The 52 North Market Street portion was occupied by a barber, A. S. Clark, and 54 North Market was a grocery for A. J. W. Gorse. In 1932 Henry Otto Hasselmeyer and Walter L. Shaffer converted the buildings into one of Charleston's longest running restaurants, which operated under their family ownership until 1984. The structures have altered fenestration but are unified through a series of segmental first-floor openings. The easternmost buildings have similar arches on the second story framing paired windows. In recent years a former dependency, running along Anson Street to the north, was altered with the addition of a storefront.

90–98 NORTH MARKET STREET, J. S. WEEKS AND COMPANY RANGE

Constructed circa 1845; altered 1935, 1940, 1950; rehabilitated 1988–89

The City Land Company conveyed these lots in the early-1840s, and a series of wholesale grocers occupied the 90–98 North Market Street section. These buildings, constructed as a range, were divided into five sections separated by interior fire walls. All five of these sections have served multiple uses, with either individual or overlapping common tenants, and several have been linked on one or more floors. The granite lintels and window sills on the upper stories are original and support a built-up roof, sloping from front to rear, which is concealed by a flat parapet. 86–88 North Market Street to the east has been the most altered, with the loss of its upper story and the addition of a stepped parapet. Overall, however, the range remains a good example of the type of commercial architecture that once predominated in the market area.

102 NORTH MARKET STREET, TOWNSEND, ARNOLD-HORNIK BUILDING

Constructed 1850–52; rehabilitated 1982–83, 1995

This substantial four-story building with a granite columnar storefront and matching lintels, sills, and projecting cornice was built soon after the acquisition of this key site in the beginning of the 1850s. Serving a succession of clothing and dry goods stores, it continued this use with the Hornik family, who leased the property in 1892 from the owners, the Claussens, and eventually purchased the parcel after 1917. The small building to the east lost much of its facade in the mid-twentieth century but regained some of its earlier detailing in a massive historic rehabilitation of the structures in 1982–83.

View of 102 North Market Street, before its 1982 rehabilitation

43 SOUTH MARKET STREET, AIKEN-WYATT BUILDING

Constructed circa 1830s; renovated 1972, 1980, 1990

This two-story building with Flemish bond brick was probably built in the 1830s and was held in the antebellum period as investment by South Carolina governor William Aiken Jr. Aiken owned a continuous line of fourteen separate brick buildings on South Market Street at the time of the Civil War. This structure remained in the Wyatt-Aiken-Rhett-Maybank line for more than a century. It has been heavily altered, particularly in recent years for use by various restaurants.

49 SOUTH MARKET STREET, WILLIAM AIKEN TENEMENT

Constructed 1820–30; rehabilitated 1970s

This three-and-a-half-story Flemish bond brick building constitutes the lone intact survivor of a range of similar dwellings constructed by William Aiken Sr. after his 1819 purchase of the block bounded by State, Church, Market, and Linguard Streets from Peter and Violetta Wyatt. It was one of the first buildings to be thoroughly rehabilitated in the rejuvenation of Market Street.

139 SOUTH MARKET STREET, MCKINLAY BUILDING

Constructed 1846; renovated 1875–90; rehabilitated 1988

Archibald and William McKinlay, prosperous free African American brothers, purchased this as well as other Market Street properties in the 1840s. Possibly of three stories originally, the surviving structure served its owners as a tenement until the McKinlay estate sold it in 1875 to Robert Martin, a purveyor of diverse goods, from shoes to washing machines. Martin probably renovated the facade with Italianate style window hoods, deep cornice, and new glazed face brick in white and brown. A concrete block infill was removed in recent years for restoration of the storefront.

The area became the center of a rough nightlife for sailors and gamblers. In 1927 one of Charleston's leading bootleggers, Frank "Rumpty Rattles" Hogan, was shot while picking up his waitress girlfriend from her job across the street. The killers, who shot from the upper windows of 139 Market Street, were acquitted in a sensational trial.

135 MEETING STREET, GIBBES MEMORIAL ART GALLERY (MUSEUM OF ART)

Constructed circa 1905; addition 1978

Frank P. Milburn, architect

Frank P. Milburn, an architect whose practice was centered in Charlotte, North Carolina, and Columbia, South Carolina, and who was influential from Washington southward, designed the Gibbes Memorial Art Gallery, Charleston's best example of the Beaux Arts style. In addition to participating in the design of the Gibbes, Milburn, as an architect for the Southern Railway, designed train stations and public buildings throughout the South. H. T. Zacharias served as contractor for the gallery, which opened on April 11, 1905. The engaged front portico stands on a ground-story entry with stylized rustication, while a dome topped by pantile shaped copper shingles, surrounded by a bronze anthemion border, rises from the parapeted flat roof. A contemporary rear addition of gray stucco with large tinted glass openings was completed in 1978.

Interior, Gibbes Memorial Art Gallery

The Carolina Art Association—founded in 1857, disbanded during the Civil War, and reorganized in 1878— operated out of an art school in the Bible Depository Building at *22 Chalmers Street*. A bequest of more than $10,000 from the estate of the Charleston businessman James Shoolbred Gibbes to the city, under the direction of the progressive mayor J. Adger Smyth and the Association, provided the necessary funding for construction of the new James S. Gibbes Memorial Art Gallery. The museum houses not only a definitive collection of early portraits, paintings, and miniatures related to Charleston and the Lowcountry but contemporary works as well.

141 MEETING STREET, CHARLESTON GAS LIGHT COMPANY

Constructed 1876–78

Edward Brickell White, architect

Built and designed for the Charleston Gas Light Company, this building uses Palladian style architectural elements manufactured in cast-iron. The three-bay, stuccoed, masonry facade boasts an engaged front portico with Tuscan columns supporting a balustraded second tier with Corinthian columns and a surmounting modillioned pediment; the upper windows feature two flanking pediment hoods and a semicircular one, also in iron. The Charleston Gas Light Company, incorporated in 1846, began illuminating the city streets by gas two years after its establishment. Charleston plats show that the original gas plant stood on the west side of Church Street, between Cumberland and Market Streets. The iron gates in front of the present structure initially stood at the former site. The Gas Light Company's successor, South Carolina Electric and Gas Company, maintains local offices in the building.

172 MEETING STREET, C. D. FRANKE BUILDING

Constructed 1908; rehabilitated 1974

John D. Newcomer, architect

The C. D. Franke Company, carriage makers and formerly suppliers of gun carriages, bought this block extending to Church Street in 1905. Then controlled by Emil Jahnz, the company built its large factory at *171 Church Street* and this three-story, pressed brick building as its showroom and office by 1908. The window surrounds, flat on the second story and segmentally arched on the third, harmonize with the pressed-metal pedimented entablature giving the Franke name and dates. The entablature and parapet were heavily damaged in Hurricane Hugo in 1989 but fully restored by the present owner afterward.

173 MEETING STREET, ALBERT TIEFENTHAL BUILDING

Constructed 1874; rehabilitated 1982

D. A. J. Sullivan, contractor and builder

The front portion of this three-story structure was constructed a decade after the War Between the States by an immigrant German businessman as his restaurant and saloon, with a residence on the upper floors. After construction commenced, the *News and Courier* stated that it would be "handsome" with "water works" throughout and the front finished with "decorated metal." The arcaded first-floor portico with two central engaged Corinthian columns survives, as do the Italianate style window surrounds. The cornice has long since been removed, but pressed-metal quoining at the corners survives. Originally the interior plan of this structure departed from the Charleston single house model with suites of rooms and a rear staircase. After Tiefenthal's death in 1889, his widow married the son of the owner of the nearby Pavilion Hotel, Francois Opdebeeck Jr., and sold this site to William J. O'Hagan. After declining through the 1970s, the structure was rehabilitated in 1982 as one of the first bed-and-breakfast inns in Charleston's tourism boom of the 1980s.

MEETING AND MARKET STREETS, CHARLESTON PLACE

Constructed 1984–86

John Carl Warnecke and Partners, architects

Beginning in Mayor Palmer Gaillard's administration in the early-1970s, plans were formulated to rejuvenate King Street. This effort accelerated by 1975 and led Mayor Joseph P. Riley Jr. and city planners to lure a major hotel or convention center to a block bounded by Meeting, Hasell, King, and Market Streets. Although the

*Meeting Street shops
(Charleston Place storefronts)*

city's intent was the renewal of the street, the issue sharply divided preservationists and the general citizenry. An early plan with a ten-story hotel tower of starkly contemporary design was shelved, and a compromise plan with a new developer and the Washington, D.C., architect John Carl Warnecke was finally accepted in the early-1980s. The resulting complex features a hotel with restaurants and retail spaces along King, Market, and Meeting Streets. The complex itself is a mix of contemporary Neo-Georgian and Second Empire styles with synthetic green slate mansard roofs, varying textures and colors of brick, and rusticated cladding. A large gateway from Market Street with a forecourt provides an approach to the main hotel block, while the King Street side is dominated by interspersed curvilinear gables and square parapets with a clock tower, designed to hearken back to similar towers now lost from 273 and 275 King Street.

Although preservationists considered retention of the facades of the buildings at 209–235 Meeting Street to be a major victory, the extensive rear sections of all of these, primarily antebellum commercial structures, were removed to construct the hotel parking garage. These edifices include the Samuel Seyle building at 209 Meeting, built right after the fire of 1838 and sold by the fancy-goods merchant Gustav Sussdorf in 1859 to George S. Cameron. Cameron owned the three buildings to the north at 211, 213, and 215 Meeting Street, which have unified cast-iron grand-story facades consisting of Corinthian columns, modillions, and side brackets with human mask motifs, probably added just before or after the Civil War. These stuctures were gutted and several refaced after a fire in 1910, and the facade of 213 Meeting Street was saved again after a 1979 fire. The five buildings to the north were owned before the Civil War by the Strohecker family and rented to a variety of brokerage houses. The Ansonborough entrepreneur Charles W. Seignious apparently owned the double-fronted edifice at 229 Meeting Street and fitted it out with Italianate style detailing.

Postcard view showing the Charleston Hotel and streetscape across Meeting Street, circa 1900

200 MEETING STREET, NATIONS BANK PLACE

Constructed 1989–90

Aubry Architects; SBF Design

Designed by a Florida architectural firm in the modern classical style, this large bank building with a raised multistory portico hearkens back to its predecessor on this site. This was the location from 1838 to 1960 of the great Charleston Hotel, a magnificent Greek Revival structure with giant order Corinthian columns probably designed by the Prussian-born architect Charles F. Reichardt. The demolition of the hotel in 1960 for a motor inn (now removed) remains a dark memory for many Charleston preservationists.

375 MEETING STREET, SOUTH CAROLINA RAILROAD COMPLEX (BLOCK BOUNDED BY MEETING, JOHN, KING, AND MARY STREETS)

Constructed between 1849 and 1853

Charleston Freight Station photographed in 1917

Most of these structures were built by the Camden line of the South Carolina Railroad in the mid-nineteenth century. The complex stretches from the depot (the shell of which survives at *37 John Street*), along the rail line, through various warehouse complexes, to the carpentry shops several blocks northward at the city line. Other surviving associated structures include the William Aiken House at *456 King Street*; the Gas Engine Building, constructed in 1858 (now *81 Mary Street*, used as offices for the Chamber of Commerce); the Dean's Warehouse, 375 Meeting Street (now in use as the Charleston Visitor Center); and the Martschink— Warehouse, surviving as a structural frame and covering the present visitor transportation mall. Charleston was at the center of an ambitious scheme developed in the 1820s to link the port with

Eastern piers of the railroad gates in 1925

Detail of C. Drie's Bird's Eye View of the City of Charleston, South Carolina, 1872, *showing the railroad complex*

the cotton transport of the Savannah River and perhaps farther west. With 133 miles of track between Charleston and Hamburgh (now Aiken), South Carolina, the city had the distinction of being the longest railroad operation in the world at that time. Later a second line was developed in Camden, South Carolina. Various problems in the antebellum years, such as rising operating costs and its inefficiency as a passenger station, spelled change in just a few short years, and the complex shifted to warehouses for freight.

76 QUEEN STREET, GRAHAM HOUSE
Constructed 1893–94; rehabilitated 1970s

The Gibbes Memorial Art Gallery now uses this front-facing, plantation style Charleston house built in the Queen Anne style. With its form essentially the same as Greek Revival examples, the Graham House with turned columns and two-over-two windows shows the way Victorian details were often imposed on this earlier Charleston building pattern.

78 QUEEN STREET, JOHN O'MARA BUILDING
Constructed 1865; rehabilitated 1981

A bookseller completed this three-story masonry single house right after the War Between the States on the site of a building lost in the fire of 1861. Most burned-over lots were not built on until long after the war, but O'Mara was perhaps one of the first to rebuild. He obtained a city loan to erect the two-story structure at *82 Queen Street* in 1869 as an investment. Restored some years ago as a restaurant, it has a unique inner wrought-iron gate with an egret motif. The restaurant has incorporated the neighboring stuccoed brick building at *84 Queen Street*, built as an investment by William Ufferhardt, a German merchant, in 1876.

92 QUEEN STREET, EDWARD LEWITH HOUSE

Constructed 1876–78

Lewith, a King Street merchant, built this structure and two other houses at 96–98 Queen Street on lots left vacant by the fire of 1861. The house at 98 Queen Street was demolished some years ago. Generally repeating the patterns of houses built in antebellum Charleston and exhibiting the holdover of such styles for smaller dwellings until the end of the nineteenth century, 92 Queen Street and *96 Queen Street*, a house which Lewith's family retained for more than sixty years, are reversed, mirror images of each other. The former dwelling was slightly updated with a bay window and Italianate style door overhang, but both have the side-hall plan, six-over-six windows, and closed gable end that would be expected in late antebellum dwellings. *90 Queen Street* was built circa 1885 as an investment and bought the next year by Ernest Hesse of *147–149 King Street*.

94 QUEEN STREET, UNITED STATES ELECTRIC ILLUMINATING COMPANY

Constructed 1882; rehabilitated 1983

This functional wooden building with a brick front facade served a fledgling electrical company, organized in 1881, that failed to secure a contract with the city for electrical street illumination. The group went out of business, and Charleston did not begin the electrification process until five years later. The structure's history was rediscovered during its rehabilitation in the early-1980s.

112 QUEEN STREET, ALEX MATTSON HOUSE

Constructed by 1880

This two-story Greek Revival style stuccoed brick single house was built fifteen years after the Civil War by a draymaster.

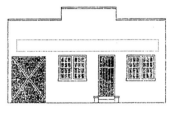

94 Queen Street, drawing of front elevation

Mattson acquired the adjoining lots and within three years built wooden dwellings to the west at *114* and *114½ Queen Street*, using a mix of the Queen Anne and Carpenter Gothic styles. The construction of yet another such building by A. Stanhope Johnson at *116 Queen Street*, with its distinctive bargeboard, created one of Charleston's most eclectic groupings of variants on the vernacular single house form.

118 QUEEN STREET, BOLLMANN HOUSE
Constructed 1867–68

H. Bollmann, a German grocer, built this three-story stuccoed brick single house right after buying the lot from the Dazier trust. The Italianate window heads and cornice add distinction to an otherwise severe facade. On its west line, the Bollmann House formerly bordered the orphanage of the Sisters of Our Lady of Mercy, a substantial brick building demolished in the 1960s. Modern townhouses now occupy the site.

132–136 QUEEN STREET & 140 QUEEN STREET, MARLBOROUGH REALTY HOUSES
Constructed 1913

Although it had faded in fashion, the Queen Anne style was employed in the design and construction of these four two-story wooden dwellings with double-tiered front piazzas. Marlborough Realty acquired these and the surviving main block of Roper Hospital some years after the hospital wings that occupied the house sites went down in the earthquake of 1886. The main section of the hospital was divided into apartments and the residence of the realty company's owner. His descendants lived in the building until Hurricane Hugo demolished it entirely.

133 QUEEN STREET, JOHN HENRY BULWINKLE GROCERY

Constructed circa 1869;
twentieth-century renovation

Rebuilding on the site of his prefire grocery, Bulwinkle, a German merchant, constructed a flat-roofed, stuccoed brick building of two stories. He later built the more substantial grocery at *40 Archdale Street* and eventually retired in prosperity to upper Harleston Village. Retaining part of its storefront fenestration, the building has continued in neighborhood grocery use with various owners since construction.

153–155 QUEEN STREET, DAVID LOPEZ TENEMENTS

Constructed circa 1837–38

David Lopez, the owner of other real estate in this area of the city and the builder of houses as well as the Civil War semisubmersible *Little David,* apparently built these tenements shortly after acquiring the site in 1837. These paired rental houses follow the classic eighteenth-century Charleston double tenement form, but the interior chimneys, wide weatherboarding, and nine-over-nine window sashes present the impression of earlier construction. After passing through a series of transactions with the settlement of Lopez's estate, the buildings became the property of Eliza Hopkins after the Civil War. In the 1870s the houses were sold separately to different owners.

WEST STREET

This small thoroughfare, like the rest of the area, became a prime site for brothels by the mid-nineteenth century, and most of its original buildings have been demolished. A fine two-story dwelling at 9 West Street, however, was built before 1830 as an investment by Dr. William Kirkland, the owner of *116 Church Street.*

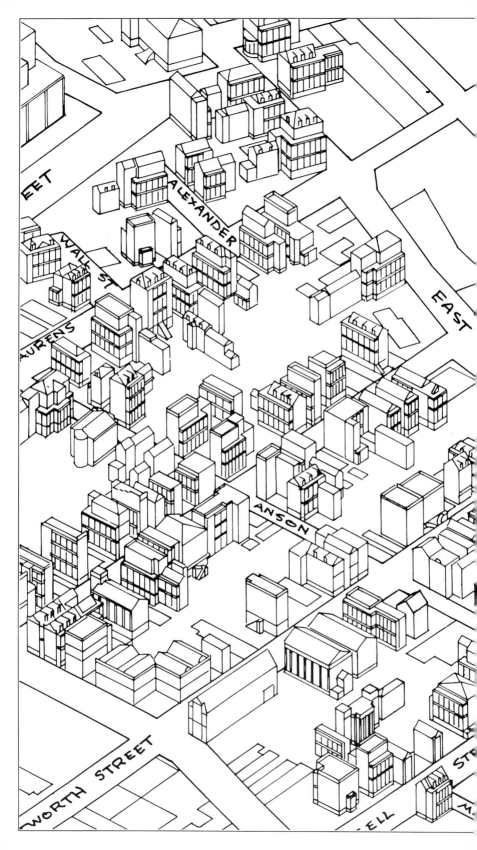

6

ANSONBOROUGH
The Original "Borough"

The original Ansonborough district incorporated an area formerly known as the "Bowling Green." This, the city's first borough or suburb, was bounded by King Street, Anson Street, present-day Calhoun Street, and the Rhettsbury area. Captain (later Admiral and Baron) George Anson acquired this tract of about sixty-four acres from Thomas Gadsden in 1726. An old story repeated by Carolina historians avers that Anson won the parcel in a card game. Anson's holdings were gradually sold for building. When the tract was platted in 1746, Anson initially named some streets for his ships: *Centurion, Scarborough,* and *Squirrel;* two streets, George and Anson, he named for himself. The former three eventually became portions of Meeting, Anson, and Society Streets, respectively. Anson had circumnavigated the globe by the early 1740s. He eventually gained peerage and after that never returned to South Carolina.

By the eighteenth century this borough was home to various merchants, relatively prosperous tradesmen, and even a few planters. A number of lots were bought as an investment on Society Street by the South Carolina Society, but these, developed with interspersed single houses and double tene-

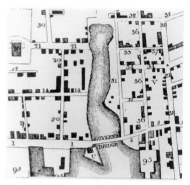

Detail of Ichnography of Charleston, South Carolina, *1788, showing creek (future Market area) and Rhettsbury and Ansonborough*

Photo of the Gabriel Manigault House, Ansonborough, Meeting and George Streets, 1929, shortly before its demolition

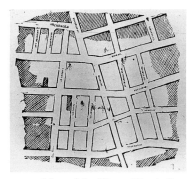

Map of the "Burnt District" from the Charleston Courier, *showing the extent of the 1838 fire*

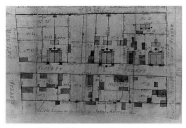

Plat of Society Street in Ansonborough before the fire of 1838

ments, were gradually sold. The architectural masterpieces of the area, however, lay northwest of its heart, at Meeting and George Streets, where corner mansions built by Thomas Radcliffe and Gabriel Manigault vied for superlatives with adjacent villas. The lone survivor of the group, the Middleton-Pinckney House of 1797, represents the apogee of Charleston's Neoclassical style.

By 1838 the commercial boundaries of the neighborhood were dominated by dry goods merchants, confectioners, saddlers, cabinetmakers, cobblers, grocers, fruiterers, and milliners; the interior of the area was filled with dwellings housing white and free or enslaved black occupants. On April 24, 1838, a fire broke out at King and Beresford (Fulton) Streets, spreading to the northeast and proving to be "the largest and most distressing fire" in the city to that date. One diarist described the worst casualties as resulting from the practice of blowing up houses at the edge of the fire in the attempt to create a break, adding, "there are about 1,000 houses burnt, distress is beyond description." The state of South Carolina was able to offer loans for rebuilding, with the stipulation of brick as the primary material. Building contractors and investors built entire rows of single houses as well as a few attached dwellings. The presence of two Lutheran churches and a German Catholic church in the center of the neighborhood attested to a strong German population in the area in the 1840s and 1850s, while the eastern edge along the Cooper River became an area of small wooden structures, occupied by recently arrived Irish laborers as well as hired-out slaves living in tenements.

An extended area, which had experienced significant decline before World War II, was targeted by Historic Charleston Foundation in 1958 as its first revolving fund enterprise, the Ansonborough Rehabilitation Project. This effort centered on a twelve-block area of 135 antebellum houses, comprising not only the majority of the original Ansonborough but also the suburbs of Rhettsbury, Laurens Square, and Gadsden's Middlesex. All of this area today, plus the blocks between Meeting and King Streets, is considered to be the Ansonborough neighborhood.

Rhettsbury, comprising most of Hasell and Wentworth Streets and bordering on Pinckney Street, was divided by Col. William Rhett's great-granddaughters from his former plantation in 1767. At least two Methodist meetinghouses sprang up along Hasell Street; the one at the western end became Charleston's first Roman Catholic church, St. Mary's, by 1788. That area of buildings was occupied by various prominent members of Charleston's Sephardic congregation, including the Moise, Cohen, Lopez, and Solomon families, and became the site of their synagogue.

The Gadsden and Laurens families were the most prominent residents living north of Ansonborough. A plot of land containing twenty acres of high ground and twenty acres of marsh that adjoined Charleston's largest pre-Revolutionary dock complex, Gadsden's Wharf, was subdivided by the patriot leader Christopher Gadsden (creator of the motto "Don't Tread on Me" and the flag that bore it) into six wharf lots and 197 single lots. The lots lay along streets named after John Wilkes, a favorite English patriot, and Pasquale di Paoli, a parliamentary representative for Middlesex and a Corsican patriot. The plan also included a brick market. Gadsden's own asymmetrical wood dwelling lay along the extension of East Bay Street. After the Revolution much of the area was designated as "Federal Green." The development of Middlesex was much like the middle-class evolution of Ansonborough, with a few larger houses built along East Bay Street, including the now-destroyed Nathaniel Heyward House. Most of the Middlesex neighborhood was demolished in 1966 by "urban renewal" for the municipal auditorium project. Some houses were moved out of harm's way into Ansonborough by Historic Charleston Foundation.

Lithograph of Meeting Street, Charleston, S.C., *by T. Addison Richards, 1844*

Nathaniel Heyward House, East Bay Street at Society Street, circa 1915, prior to its demolition

Early-twentieth-century photograph of the house of Henry Laurens, built circa 1740, now demolished

Aerial view of Ansonborough and Middlesex neighborhoods at the beginning of the Ansonborough Project

Between Ansonborough and Middlesex stood the house and four-acre square of Henry Laurens, wealthy merchant and a president of the Continental Congress. Laurens's wife had, as he described it, an "ardor" for gardening. He brought the English gardener John Watson to Charleston in 1767 to assist her in this avocation, including the growing of olives, capers, limes, ginger, guinea grass, Alpine strawberries, raspberries, grapes, apples, pears, and plums, in addition to many flowering shrubs and herbs. The mid-eighteenth-century house with its jerkin-head roof survived until 1916, when it was pulled down due to the adjacent railway and port activities that still characterize the area today. The former Laurens Square was subdivided into building lots in 1804, and the houses in this zone essentially formed the backbone of the Ansonborough Rehabilitation Project.

ALEXANDER STREET (MIDDLE STREET)

Established by 1772; developed 1790–1820

Christopher Gadsden established this street originally as Middle Street in the center of his Village of Middlesex. Renamed in 1903 to correspond to the street that continues northward from Calhoun Street, this small remaining section was blocked off by the construction of the Gaillard Municipal Auditorium in the late-1960s. With its many smaller houses of Charleston's working class, it offers the opportunity to see the scale of Middlesex as it developed in the post-Revolutionary period. Francis Nelson, a ship's carpenter, built the oldest of the three remaining houses, 6 Alexander Street, after acquiring the lot from Mary Middleton in 1799. It is somewhat smaller than its neighbor at 8 Alexander Street but noteworthy in that it is a two-room house lacking a central hall, a floor plan common in the city before 1740. The brickwork of the house also reflects a pre-Revolutionary practice with the front and south end in Flemish bond and the other sides in the simpler English bond. Simon Jude Chancognie constructed the comparatively large three-story single house across the street at 5 Alexander Street in about 1813. Chancognie's dwelling retains excellent Federal woodwork on its interior.

6 Alexander Street

13–25 ANSON STREET, GOLDSMITH'S ROW

Constructed 1894; rehabilitated 1980s

These wooden houses constitute a rare example of a late-nineteenth-century housing development built by a single investor in downtown Charleston. Isaac A. Goldsmith, a dentist and holder of extensive real estate, built this row of single houses as tenements in 1894 on property formerly occupied by a cotton press and a small flour mill. The brick

Goldsmith's Row as shown in a Sanborn Map, early- to mid-twentieth century

dwelling south of this row, *11 Anson Street*, was constructed before the Civil War by a German immigrant. The houses were originally rented to immigrant laborers. The 1896 directory lists three of the seven on Anson Street as vacant. Inhabitants of the other four were Giovanni B. Singuinate; Margaret Pozaro, a laborer; Michael Gorman, a stevedore; and John W. Bouson, the manager of the Bay Fish Company.

27 ANSON STREET, PALMETTO FIRE COMPANY HALL

Constructed circa 1850; converted to apartments circa 1940; rehabilitated in 1986 as a single family residence

Edward C. Jones, architect

This masonry, Italianate structure was completed about 1850 and designed by one of Charleston's leading architects for a volunteer company of firemen. The property had been acquired by the new city fire department by the 1880s and remained in this use until the end of the decade. The building retains its pediment supported by console brackets and its arched side doorways, but its open central bay was filled in the 1940s during the conversion of the building to apartments. It has since become a single family residence.

28 ANSON STREET, OLD WEILS MATTRESS FACTORY

Constructed before 1872; rehabilitated as condominiums 1990

The rear, two-story brick section of this building began as a cotton warehouse owned by George W. Williams and later served as the center of a complex belonging to Robertson, Taylor and Company, who processed cotton brought into Charleston from the plantations. The Weils family added the front section of the building in the twentieth century when the structure became a mattress factory; it retained this use until the

1970s. After the Board of Architectural Review had denied applications for demolition for years, a group of investors renovated the entire building as condominiums. The rear of the property borders a tiny thoroughfare called Motley Lane, formerly called Mott's Lane. It traverses in an L-shaped path from Pinckney Street to Anson Street, accessing small houses and outbuildings of some of the large dwellings facing onto Hasell Street.

30 ANSON STREET, EDWARD MCCRADY HOUSE

Constructed circa 1848

One of Charleston's most prominent nineteenth-century citizens, Edward McCrady, a Yale graduate and descendant of an eighteenth-century tavern owner, erected this flat-roofed brick house as his residence. Although McCrady originally opposed the Nullification Doctrine, by 1850 he became a follower of states' rights views, and he eventually signed the Ordinance of Secession in 1860. He is best known for defending black soldiers captured in the war and as a prominent Episcopal layman. One of his sons became chairman of the zoology department at Harvard University, while the other became president of the College of Charleston and a leading historian of South Carolina. Set back from the street, the house lost its nineteenth-century parterre in the 1960s.

34 ANSON STREET, MARY LANNEAU HOUSE

Constructed circa 1848; rehabilitated 1969

The widow of a member of a family of French Acadians with large real estate holdings constructed this two-story single house a decade after the 1838 fire, using fashionable pressed brick rather than the locally made, handmolded variety. The house was passed through numerous owners until it was rehabilitated in the Ansonborough Project in 1969.

45 ANSON STREET, ANN HUNT TENEMENTS

Constructed circa 1829–38; rehabilitated 1970s

This interesting masonry house with American bond brick partly covered by a mellowed coat of lime stucco was probably built as a paired kitchen house and slave quarters for a double tenement that has since disappeared from the front of the lot. Mrs. Hunt owned several wooden houses on this part of the street that were destroyed in the fire of 1838, and she rebuilt these structures before selling the lots in 1847.

46–52 ANSON STREET, THOMAS WALLACE HOUSE AND MARTIN DOWD TENEMENTS

Constructed circa 1845–50; rehabilitated 1969

Although the Wallace House at 46 Anson Street was constructed separately from the others, by the mid-1850s most of these structures seem to have become part of a complex of rental properties owned by Martin Dowd, a bottle dealer. Wallace's house was built as a rental property by a substantial dry goods merchant and is un- usual in its setback from the street and L shape. A one-story shop formerly stood in front and served through much of the late- 1800s as a barbershop. The brick double tenement at 48–50 Anson Street, with a cigar store in one end and a bakery in the other; the brick building at 52 Anson Street, housing a grocery store on the first floor; and the brick house with arched gate around the corner at *27 Wentworth Street* formed a connected complex when in Dowd's ownership.

53 ANSON STREET, WILLIAM THOMPSON TENEMENT

Constructed circa 1843; rehabilitated 1966

A bricklayer and mason who lived nearby on George Street built this house and its adjacent neighbor at *30 Wentworth Street* as double tenements (with different rooflines) and also constructed the single house at *32 Wentworth Street* after the fire of 1838. In its rehabilitation of these structures in the 1960s, Historic Charleston Foundation eliminated the metal Victorian window heads and permitted the removal of the piazza at 30 Wentworth Street.

58–60 ANSON STREET, VENNING HOUSES

Constructed circa 1851; rehabilitated mid-1960s

These two brick single houses were constructed by the Charleston factor Robert M. Venning, whose family owned extensive plantations, as well as a brickyard, in Christ Church Parish, near present-day Mount Pleasant. They are part of a complex of four Venning Houses near this corner of Anson and Society Streets. These dwellings are characteristic of Ansonborough single houses but unusual in their tall, narrow window openings, with nine-over- nine light window sashes (out-of-date by 1840), and their kitchen buildings, placed perpendicular to the rear of the main structures.

58 Anson Street

The house at 60 Anson Street has a flat parapeted roofline and is a near duplicate of the building at *43 Society Street*, built by Venning circa 1840, possibly for one of his sons. While Robert Venning had this house under construction, his father, Jonah Venning, replaced a dwelling he had lost in the fire of 1838 with the present edifice at *46 Society Street*. This latter building appears slightly more substantial than its neighbors and retains its original kitchen house and stable. All of these houses are constructed from similar brick, possibly produced at the Vennings' own brickyard.

63–65 ANSON STREET, SUSAN ROBINSON DEPENDENCIES
Constructed circa 1839; rehabilitated mid-1960s

These small gable-ended, masonry buildings were constructed as dependencies for *48 Society Street*. Mrs. Robinson rented these properties separately before the Civil War, and 63 Anson Street was listed as being occupied by slaves in the 1861 census.

66 ANSON STREET, CHAZAL HOUSE
Constructed circa 1839; rehabilitated 1963

The widow of a well-to-do privateer built this house the year after the Ansonborough fire. The Chazal family had immigrated to Charleston with other Santo Domingan refugees in 1794. Jean Pierre Chazal, whose privateer *The Saucy Jack* captured some forty British vessels in the War of 1812, eventually owned numerous lots in Ansonborough and nearby Middlesex prior to his death in 1823. His widow and her sons leased this lot in the same year from the free black A. M. E. minister (and later bishop) Morris Brown, who was forced to leave Charleston in 1823 in the hysteria following the discovery of the Denmark Vesey insurrection plot. Mrs. Chazal's son, Dr. J. P. Chazal Jr., served as professor of anatomy and later dean of the Medical College. He leased a building immediately to the south as his office (now demolished) and the Venning House at *46 Society Street* as his residence.

The austerity of the Chazal House, with its Philadelphia brick in simple running bond and flat parapet, is somewhat relieved by the Tuscan-columned piazza raised on brick piers, the Greek Revival piazza door screen, and the segmental arched windows on the south elevation. The current brick cornice is probably the result of post-1886 earthquake repair.

67 ANSON STREET, ST. STEPHEN'S EPISCOPAL CHURCH
Constructed 1835–37

John and Henry Horlbeck, builders

In 1819 the Ladies' Benevolent Society of Charleston recognized the need for a place of worship for those unable to afford pew rent in other churches. Forming a new group, the Charleston Female Domestic Missionary Society, these women rented a room and arranged services there until Mrs. Nathaniel Russell (Sarah Hopton) donated a lot on Guignard Street. The building on the Guignard site, built by James or John Gordon, burned in the fire that swept the area near the market in June 1835.

The current St. Stephen's Church was built by the Horlbeck brothers, and possibly designed by them as well, at a total cost of $11,285. The firm's surviving records indicate that the bricks from the former building were cleaned and reused in a project that lasted from December 1835 to November 1836, after which the building was dedicated. The church's restrained classicism is evident in its arched center doorway, surmounted by a tablet and flanking stucco recesses with interspersed Tuscan pilasters on three sides of the building. On the interior the simplicity of the room is relieved only by the Doric columns supporting the gallery, the barrel-vaulted ceiling, and the arched chancel window. Also of interest are marble memorials to Sarah Hopton Russell and Sarah Russell Dehon.

Due to the changing ethnic and economic character of Ansonborough, the church building has passed through several congregational changes. A black Methodist congregation, Mount Moriah Methodist Church, received the St. Stephen's Church building in 1923 when the group joined the Episcopal Church as a body. The church's membership was solely African American for more than sixty years. Since 1987 its racially mixed congregation has been considered exemplary of a diocesan goal toward more integrated Episcopal worship.

Measured floor plan of St. Stephen's Episcopal Church, 67 Anson Street

71 ANSON STREET, THOMAS DOUGHTY HOUSE

Constructed circa 1806; restored 1960

At the death of Daniel Legare, whose residence stands to the north at *79 Anson Street*, his daughter Mary Legare, wife of Thomas Doughty, inherited the lot. The Doughtys had apparently constructed a previous house on the site, replacing it by 1806 with the present structure. The dwelling has an unusual T-shaped plan that allows for windows on three sides of the principal rooms. A chambered staircase stands at the north end of the center hall. On the exterior the simple brick face is ornamented by a curvilinear, Anglo-Dutch style brick screen. On the interior the building contains finely detailed Adamesque woodwork.

72 ANSON STREET, KOHNE-LESLIE HOUSE

Constructed 1846–47; restored and rehabilitated 1962, 1994

One of the larger houses in Ansonborough, 72 Anson Street was constructed by Eliza Neufville Kohne of Charleston and Philadelphia shortly after she acquired this lot in 1846. An earlier two-story wooden single house of circa 1805 had burned in the fire of 1838 and Mrs. Kohne replaced it with a three-and-a-half-story brick house of the side-hall, double-parlor plan. She willed the building to her nephew, the merchant Benjamin Neufville, in 1852 as "my house and lot on Anson Street," although she seems to have resided on Broad Street. Mrs. Kohne also attempted to leave an annuity to her freed slave, Emma Harbeaux, but the Neufville family challenged the bequest. Harbeaux's case was argued before the U.S. Supreme Court by the noted Charleston attorney James Louis Petigru. The Neufville heirs sold the house in 1904 to Charles C. Leslie, one of Charleston's most prominent black businessmen and a member of the family that stood among the free black elite before the Civil War. The Leslies lived in the house for more than half a century. The original kitchen dependency remains at the rear as a freestanding structure and may have survived the fire of 1838. When the house was restored during the Ansonborough Project, a later wooden building on the lot to the south was removed and the garden was enlarged to its present size.

74 ANSON STREET, MICHAEL FOUCAUT HOUSE

Constructed circa 1812; moved to its present location from 15 Wall Street in 1966

The Michael Foucaut House was originally built by a carpenter as his residence on Wall Street in the developing neighborhood of Middlesex. The building is a two-and-a-half-story Charleston single house with beaded weatherboard siding and a simple one-story piazza. When the city decided to clear the former Middlesex neighborhood for construction of the Gaillard Auditorium, Historic Charleston Foundation bought the house for one dollar and moved it to this location in 1966. The Michael Foucaut House is similar in form to its larger neighbor at *61 Laurens Street*, the James Mackie House, built in 1800 at *114 Anson Street* and similarly moved to its present site in 1966.

Photo showing 15 Wall Street being moved to 74 Anson Street, 1966

75 ANSON STREET, JOSEPH LEGARE HOUSE

Constructed circa 1800; rehabilitated 1969

This two-and-a-half-story wooden house raised on a brick basement was built by the wealthy planter and factor Joseph Legare, whose family had owned the property next door since 1760. The exceptional front staircase with marble steps and iron balustrade was added by Benjamin Howland in 1844 along with the Greek

Revival style piazza. The house had a third story added at about the same time; this story was removed and the roof restored in 1969. A late-Victorian house to the south was also removed and the lot restored, while the extensive line of outbuildings became individual residences.

79 ANSON STREET, DANIEL LEGARE HOUSE

Constructed circa 1760

Extensive changes make it difficult to ascertain the exact date of construction of this wood house on a raised stucco foundation. Nonetheless, it has long been considered one of the earliest surviving structures within the original Ansonborough suburb. Certain details, such as the heavy heart-pine framing sheathed in beaded black cypress weatherboarding and the low pitched hip roof, indicate an eighteenth-century date. Construction of the building began before or after the lot (part of lot no. 5 of the original George Anson tract) was sold by Daniel Crawford to the Christ Church planter Daniel Legare in 1760. The Legare family sold the house in 1806 to the Mortimers, who renovated some rooms with new woodwork in the fashionable Neoclassical style.

82 ANSON STREET, MARY SMITH HOUSE

Constructed circa 1799; moved to its present location from 88 Anson Street in 1967; restored 1973

One of Charleston's wealthiest eighteenth-century merchants, Josiah Smith, of *8 Meeting Street*, leased and subsequently conveyed this house and its former lot to his spinster daughter, Mary Smith, in 1799. The building is a tall brick Charleston single house, formerly situated on a lot 100 feet north of its present site. It was moved in 1967, out of the path of the city's extension of George Street east from Anson Street to connect with East Bay Street, in conjunction with the Gaillard Auditorium construction. The dwelling is now arranged to face a large garden that fronts on Laurens Street. Although the house had suffered since passing out of the Smith family in 1869, its Federal interior remained largely intact and was partially restored by Historic Charleston Foundation, with the remainder of the work completed by a new owner in 1973.

89–93 ANSON STREET, ST. JOHN'S REFORMED EPISCOPAL CHURCH, ST. JOSEPH'S RECTORY, AND PHILIP SIMMONS GARDEN

Church constructed 1850 with alterations in 1887; rectory and school constructed circa 1850, 1887; garden established 1991

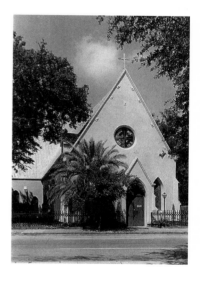

Possessing a most diverse history, the Gothic Revival church on this site has served slave and free black Presbyterians, Irish Catholics, and, more recently, African American Reformed Episcopalians. The Presbyterians constructed the building as the Anson Street Chapel for black members who later moved to Calhoun Street and established Zion Presbyterian Church. The bishop of Charleston acquired the property in 1861 and organized the fourth Roman Catholic parish in the city, primarily to serve a laboring Irish population recruited from northeastern cities and living in small houses next to the Cooper River waterfront just east of East Bay Street and above Calhoun Street. A rectory was established in the older single house next door, and Bishop Patrick Lynch took residence here after the cathedral and bishop's residence on Broad Street were destroyed in the fire of 1861. The church building was heavily damaged by shells in the siege of Charleston. Initially repaired in 1866, the chancel, roof, and interior were rebuilt in

1883 with the addition of transepts, a Gothic ceiling, and fourteen stained-glass windows.

The simple board and batten school building next door at *87 Anson Street* was completed by 1887 and continued as St. Joseph's School until the 1950s. The Diocese closed the church in 1965 due to a declining congregation and reestablished it in the suburbs west of the Ashley River. Six years later the St. John's Reformed congregation acquired the property and has occupied the entire site up to the present. Organized in 1906, St. John's was first located on nearby Calhoun Street in a building that was moved by the city in 1942 to the corner of East Bay and Calhoun Streets in the expansion of East Bay Street. The St. John's congregation has retained most of the structure's interior features, including stenciled decoration and gilded Gothic elements.

The grounds of the church were dedicated in 1991 as a commemorative landscaped garden in honor of member Philip Simmons, renowned African American ironworker. The garden development is ongoing; a "Heart Gate" designed by Simmons and executed by his apprentices marks the entry to the space.

BURNS LANE (FORMERLY BLACKBIRD ALLEY)
Established by 1801

Small tradesmen and laborers lived in Blackbird Alley, later named Burns Lane, through the nineteenth century. Most of the small dwellings have been removed, but the scale and finish of 20 Burns Lane are indicative of some of those buildings that were demolished. The Horlbeck family built this house before 1852, as well as the building at 22 Burns Lane, possibly an outbuilding to a Horlbeck house that faced Calhoun Street. The structure at 21 Burns Lane was built as an inexpensive tavern or brothel by 1820 and formerly contained more than ten fireplaces. As a tenement occupied by black families until the mid-twentieth century, the structure was renovated with additions by a developer in 1987.

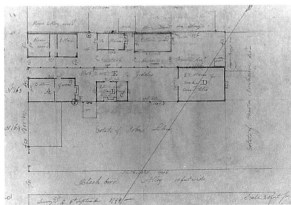

Plat showing Blackbird Alley, 1799

77 CALHOUN STREET, GAILLARD MUNICIPAL AUDITORIUM
Constructed 1966–68

Lucas and Stubbs, architects

Gaillard Auditorium has served for thirty years as Charleston's leading venue for large musical performances, trade shows, conventions, and public assemblies. The Civic Auditorium, as it was originally called, was the consummate 1960s urban renewal project, built under the administration of Charleston's progressive mayor J. Palmer Gaillard. The removal of the Middlesex neighborhood as well as the realignment of George Street, the elimination of Minority Street, and the cutting off of Wall and Alexander Streets were the first steps to its construction. At the time of its planning, it was hailed as a major architectural step for a city that was "lagging behind in architectural design." After months of heated debate local voters later rejected an extension of the urban renewal concept to the rest of the city. Lucas and Stubbs designed a building in the prevailing interpretation of the International style, with certain walls completed in tan brick with precast concrete detailing, accented by large cast-metal city seals over the principal entrances, all at a cost of more than $3,796,000. The auditorium seats 2,701 persons and has provided a venue for numerous Spoleto events, operas, ballets, and visiting orchestras, as well as the Charleston Symphony Orchestra. The first portrait of an African American in a Charleston city building, a representation of the insurrection plot leader Denmark Vesey with his back to the viewer, was hung in the hall after some controversy in 1970. The lines of the building have been softened by formal gardens to the northwest and the recent construction of a new parking garage and a massive four-story stucco headquarters for the Charleston School Board and city departments facing Calhoun Street. LS3P, the successor firm to Lucas and Stubbs, designed these latter buildings in a modern Neoclassical style.

Gaillard Auditorium soon after its completion, 1968

85 CALHOUN STREET, ARCH BUILDING

Constructed circa 1800; renovated circa 1850, 1967

Owned through most of the nineteenth century by the James English family and descendants, the building has an unusually wide first-floor center archway that has been thought to denote a use of the property as a way station for freight wagons in the years prior to the development of railroads. Although the upper floors were generally occupied as residences, the first floor of the building housed grocers, dry goods stores, taverns, and a restaurant at various dates prior to its disuse after World War II. It was the only building saved in this block from the auditorium project.

103 CALHOUN STREET, BUIST SCHOOL

Constructed 1920

David B. Hyer, architect; James O. Betelle, consulting architect

Buist School was built during the days of segregated education. The Charleston school board retained James O. Betelle, America's leading designer of school buildings, to work with the architect David Hyer on the structure for African American pupils. Construction costs totaled $100,000. A wrought-iron gateway executed by the noted artisan Philip Simmons, an alumnus of the school, leads to the three-story brick building. Although its windows have been altered, some Colonial Revival features remain, including belt coursing, keystones over the windows, a central pavilion, and a decorative parapet. Buist School has been transformed in recent years as a magnet school for elementary age students.

121 CALHOUN STREET, HARLESTON-BOAGS FUNERAL HOME

Constructed 1915

Edwin G. Harleston, a prominent African American who planted rice along the Cooper River and spent twenty years as a sea captain, entered the undertaking business in 1901 with his brother. Reorganizing the firm in 1913, Captain Harleston constructed a new three-story wood building in the traditional Charleston vernacular style to house his extensive business, including office, showroom, morgue, embalming room, and chapel seating 150 persons. Captain Harleston's son Edwin A. Harleston, following studies at Atlanta University, Harvard, and the Museum of Fine Arts School in Boston, returned to Charleston to become a portrait and genre painter and to assist in the family undertaking business. The younger Harleston was the lead organizer of the Charleston NAACP chapter in 1917. Harleston and his wife, the photographer Elise Forrest Harleston, set up the Harleston Studio in the building and resided here as well after 1920. From the outset, meetings of the NAACP were often held at 121 Calhoun Street, and various prominent black leaders visited here, including W. E. B. Du Bois, Mary White Ovington, James Weldon Johnson, and Mary McLeod Bethune.

143 CALHOUN STREET, KNIGHTS OF COLUMBUS HALL

Constructed 1907; repaired after fire 1947

Decimus C. Barbot, architect; J. T. Snelson, contractor

This brick, Gothic style building on a high basement continues to house the Charleston Chapter of the Knights of Columbus, a Catholic men's fraternal order

dedicated to charitable causes. In 1923 the building served as the venue for a speech by the Irish leader Eamonn DeValera, later the first president of the Irish Republic. DeValera was invited by then mayor John P. Grace to speak at a public auditorium. Grace, Charleston's first Irish Catholic mayor, was forced by local opinion to move the speech from the original public site to this building. In 1947 a fire gutted the upper story; repairs were accomplished through a loan of $12,000 from Charleston's churches.

290 EAST BAY STREET, SEABOARD RAILWAY FREIGHT STATION (NOW HARRIS TEETER GROCERY)
Constructed 1914; rehabilitated 1979–80

This yellow-brick freight warehouse built by the Seaboard Coastline Railway was part of a line of structures to the northeast that served as the railway terminus for the Charleston port. A spur rail line formerly ran in front of this building. The station was ingeniously adapted in recent years as a downtown supermarket, just as the former Leland Moore Paint and Oil Company at *272 East Bay Street* was adapted as an inn and corporate offices and *279 East Bay Street*, a former cotton warehouse, was rehabilitated as a shop. Although the surrounding area remains an active part of the State Ports Authority operation, most of the older structures in the vicinity have disappeared. Some sixty acres to the east comprise the Union Pier, one of four SPA terminals and an area slated for long-term redevelopment.

EAST BAY STREET (BEHIND 290 EAST BAY STREET), BENNETT RICE MILL
Constructed 1844; three walls demolished 1960

Thomas Bennett, architect

One facade remains of a large brick mill designed in the Classical Revival style, possibly by its owner, Gov. Thomas Bennett. The structure contained steam-powered mill apparatus that separated rice grains from husks. The Bennett and Lucas families owned most of the six mills operating in the city by 1860, producing more than 470 barrels of rice daily, each containing 600 pounds. Operating from the time of construction until 1911, when a hurricane in that year virtually ended the Lowcountry production of the crop, the building was part of a complex that included other buildings, water and rail access, and a mill pond. Bennett acquired the site by 1829, but the construction of this mill did not commence until 1844, and operation began in January 1845. Beginning as a 90-by-60-foot building, the Bennett Mill was slightly smaller than Chisolm's Mill at 200 Tradd Street and substantially smaller than the West Point Mill, a Bennett-owned facility at *14 Lockwood Drive.*

A large wing was added in the mid-nineteenth century. The mill continued under Bennett family ownership and was capably managed by Washington Bennett's foster son, Andrew Buist Murray. After closure the mill progressively deteriorated while national recognition of its architectural character increased. In 1952 the building was condemned, but both Historic Charleston Foundation and the Preservation Society worked toward its preservation, leasing the building for five years in 1958. Hurricane Donna in 1960 substantially weakened the deteriorated Bennett Mill. The city ordered the building demolished except for sixty feet of the west wall, which was saved by local preservationists as a reminder of the mill's industrial grandeur.

Bennett Rice Mill before its near destruction in the hurricane of 1960

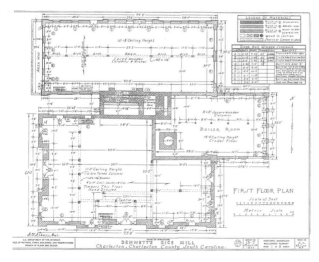

Measured plan of the first floor, Bennett Rice Mill

301 EAST BAY STREET, MOSES LEVY HOUSE

Constructed circa 1816; rehabilitated 1980s

The leader, or hazan, of Temple Beth Elohim constructed this three-story brick house. Moses Levy is best known for having saved the sacred scrolls from the burning synagogue during the fire of 1838, while five of his own properties burned in the conflagration. Moses Levy's son Jacob and daughter-in-law Fanny Yates Levy took up residence in the house by 1819. Jacob Levy was educated in Europe and met his bride in her native city of Liverpool. Her noted portrait by Thomas Sully now hangs in the Corcoran Gallery. The house was sold to the steamship entrepreneur James Adger in 1849, and it briefly served as the home of the South's famous proslavery novelist William Grayson. The structure is particularly noted for the elaborate Federal style architrave with oval paterae and gougework that serves as its piazza entrance. Similarly exuberant Neoclassical woodwork ornaments the interior.

311 EAST BAY STREET, STEPHEN SHREWSBURY HOUSE

Constructed circa 1809; rehabilitated 1971; restored late-1980s

An important Federal doorway surmounted by an elliptical fanlight provides the main entrance for this tall masonry dwelling at the corner of East Bay and Laurens Streets. Stephen Shrewsbury, member of a family of shipwrights and himself a carpenter, rose to be clerk of the South Carolina Bank by 1796 and acquired this lot in 1800 from a grocer. By 1809 he had completed this house and moved to the site. After many years of use as an office, it is again a single family dwelling, although the former kitchen dependency, now *42 Laurens Street*, was subdivided and renovated as a separate residence.

317 EAST BAY STREET, BENJAMIN DUPRÉ HOUSE

Constructed circa 1803–05; rehabilitated 1985

A prosperous tailor constructed this weatherboarded single house before 1805. Like the Shrewsbury House, it is raised on a high foundation and its principal rooms are on the upper floors. The staircase is lit by an original Venetian (Palladian) window, and much of the interior woodwork has survived. The present owners restored this house in 1985 as an inn and moved two other houses to the lot, one to the back of this site facing George Street and another to the adjoining lot at *315 East Bay Street*, where only a rear brick kitchen dependency had survived. These two wooden single houses, brought from the north side of Calhoun Street ahead of demolition, were built in the 1830s and have been rehabilitated as part of the inn complex.

321 EAST BAY STREET, BLAKE-GRIMKÉ HOUSE

Constructed circa 1789; north wing added circa 1850; renovated 1960s

The only eighteenth-century double house surviving in the Ansonborough area, this large weatherboarded dwelling was probably built before 1789 by William Blake, descendant of a proprietary governor and a wealthy planter and slave owner in his own right. A late-eighteenth-century plat of the site shows the front and rear staircases much as they are today, as well as a missing front forecourt (like that of the Miles Brewton House) and the now-vanished rear outbuildings. Several important residents have occupied this house. Rented for a time by the widow of Declaration of Independence signer Arthur Middleton, it was sold to Judge John Faucheraud Grimké and utilized by his

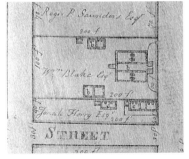

Detail of a plat of Gadsden's Middlesex showing 321 East Bay Street, 1795

large family, including his daughters Sarah and Anglina Grimké, later famous as abolitionists and pioneers of women's rights. Purchased by Charles O. Witte in 1862, it served as his residence until his wealth and prominence as a leading entrepreneur and German consul permitted his acquisition of the grander Patrick Duncan Villa at *172 Rutledge Avenue*. Witte, or his predecessor in title, William Martin, added the Victorian style north wing with bay windows. The house's other Victorian additions, except the cast-iron stair, were removed in 1965.

328 EAST BAY STREET, ANDREW MOFFETT HOUSE

Constructed circa 1839; rehabilitated 1962, 1986

A dry goods merchant with a shop at 188 King Street apparently built this two-and-a-half-story brick single house on the site of an earlier, similar dwelling that had been constructed in the 1790s by Philip Gadsden; Philip was the son of Gen. Christopher Gadsden, who lived next door and developed the surrounding village of Middlesex. The house has notable brickwork with quoining, belt coursing, dogtooth cornice, and pedimented gable, and the finish gives indication of the application of a late-nineteenth-century red paint to the surface. After her husband's death in 1853, Anna Moffett lived here until after the Civil War when she sold it to the Seignious family for rental property; it retained this use until its recent rehabilitation as an inn.

329 EAST BAY STREET, GADSDEN-MORRIS HOUSE

Constructed circa 1800; partially restored 1960

One of the tallest and most finely detailed of Charleston's Federal single houses, this dwelling was built after 1798 on land formerly owned by Christopher Gadsden.

Although traditionally called the Gadsden House, the building was probably built by Thomas Morris, a Gadsden son-in-law whose name appears on the lot on the 1790s map of this portion of Middlesex; Philip Gadsden is shown on the same map as living at *328 East Bay Street*. The property had subsequent owners of prominence, including Col. Elnathan Haskell, a Revolutionary War hero; Dr. Benjamin Bonneau Simons, an outstanding medical practitioner; and, after the Civil War, the Right Reverend W. B. W. Howe, Episcopal bishop of South Carolina. The building has fine brickwork as well as important carved marble keystones, window sills, and door architrave, along with surviving Neoclassical wooden elements. The present iron gates were designed in a collaboration between Samuel G. Stoney, architectural historian, and Philip Simmons, noted Charleston ironworker. The gates remain some of Simmons's most important works. This house was given to Historic Charleston Foundation by a Gadsden descendant in 1959.

329 East Bay Street and lost buildings to the north, circa 1930

332 EAST BAY STREET, ROBERT PRIMEROSE HOUSE

Constructed circa 1817; altered circa 1840–50

In 1817 Robert Primerose constructed a new brick house on a high basement on this lot, the former site of Christopher Gadsden's own residence. Primerose was an auctioneer and resident on the site, according to the directory of 1822. Although the house largely retains its Federal style elements, including the pediment projecting from the roof and the fine entry doorway with fanlight, the piazza and elliptical front portico are Greek Revival additions as are the French doors on all levels of the piazza side. A mid-nineteenth-century owner added the brick gates with brownstone caps, the marble steps, and the unusual cast-iron gas torchères topping the stair newels.

342 EAST BAY STREET, SCOTT-CASTENS HOUSE

Constructed 1817–19; rehabilitated circa 1990

This dwelling and a house at *35 Calhoun Street* are the sole survivors of an impressive group of early-nineteenth-century houses of variant scales and materials. The losses of most of these buildings, particularly those at the corner, were a watershed in the movement to strengthen Charleston's preservation laws in the 1960s. This weatherboarded single house on a stuccoed brick foundation was built in 1817–19 by James Scott, a vendue master, and his wife Mary. The house next passed to the Haud family and thence to Carston Castens, whose relatives owned the property for nearly one hundred years.

4 GEORGE STREET, JAMES W. BROWN HOUSE

Constructed circa 1852; renovated with addition late-1980s

This substantial two-story brick house stands on a lot that was conveyed to James W. Brown, a ship's grocer and commission

merchant. Through the heaviness of its columns and its simple window and door moldings, it is reflective of the solid simplicity of Greek Revival style. The brickwork is of importance because of its tuck-pointed surface: red mortar has been used between the irregularly shaped bricks; the mortar has then been scored or grooved; and a white mortar then has been "ruled in" to provide a straight, regular appearance.

8 GEORGE STREET, SARAH DANIELL LAWRENCE HOUSE

Constructed circa 1787–91; altered circa 1895; alterations removed 1973

Sarah Daniell Lawrence received this house and land by purchase from the estate of her father, Robert Daniell, in 1791. He specified that a house be built on this lot for benefit of his wife or daughters when he made his will in 1787. The building was apparently complete before his death. The house, with a central hall and one room on either side, directly faces the street. Its period can be deduced from the wide, beaded weatherboard siding and the unusual Palladian (Venetian) windows on each gable end of the attic story.

9 GEORGE STREET, ROBERT ROULAIN HOUSE

Constructed circa 1816; Victorian alterations circa 1870

This lot was bequeathed by Daniel Legare, out of his property at *79 Anson Street*, to his daughter Ann. It eventually was acquired by the brickmason Robert Roulain, who built the present dwelling by 1816. Roulain conveyed the house in 1834 to the Reverend Daniel Cobia, the young minister of the new St. Peter's Episcopal Church on Logan Street. Cobia died tragically only two years later, and the house was conveyed to Maj. William Laval, then the state treasurer for the eastern half of South Carolina. Laval lived around the corner on Anson Street and sold the building in the 1860s to the O'Neill family. They probably made the Italianate alterations to the house, such as the pressed metal window lintels and single light window sashes.

11 GEORGE STREET, MARY SCOTT HOUSE

Constructed circa 1813; altered circa 1850; renovated 1971

Daniel Legare bequeathed this parcel out of the *79 Anson Street* property to his granddaughter Mary Scott by a codicil in his will, which specified that she receive the lot "where the Taby [tabby] house now stands" when she reached twenty-one years of age (probably between 1793 and 1795). This two-and-a-half-story single house built in the early-nineteenth century has some surviving Federal detailing but was changed extensively by a subsequent owner in the 1850s. The early scored stucco, obscured on the front by later renovations, is still visible on the east wall of the building.

14 GEORGE STREET, MIDDLETON-PINCKNEY HOUSE

Constructed circa 1796–99; partially renovated and rehabilitated 1880s, 1980s

This three-story stuccoed-brick house on a raised basement was begun about 1796 by Mrs. Frances Motte Middleton and completed by her and her second husband, Maj. Gen. Thomas Pinckney, whom she married in 1797. Edward Hooker, a Connecticut visitor, described the house in 1805: "Maj. Thomas Pinckney's house is of brick, three stories high with an elegant rotund, of the same height, in front, which serves for a porch. It has an air of magnificence; but appears less advantageously from its having been left, for two or three years, in an unfinished state." General and Mrs. Pinckney sold the house to John Middleton, Mrs. Pinckney's eldest son, in 1822 for "natural love and affection" and $10,000. The polygonal front projection provides oval rooms on each floor, and a more truncated rear projection contains a winding staircase. The exterior is severe save its marble belt courses, window lintels, columned entrance, and other trim. Its interior is largely original but simple with Neoclassical doors and wainscoting and some later Regency style mantelpieces and cornices. The building has had little alteration despite its occupancy for more than one hundred years by the Charleston Commissioners of Public Works, who constructed a reservoir, water tower, and pumping station at the rear of the site, using the main house as offices. The reservoir later became a public swimming pool until closure in the 1960s. In the 1980s 14 George Street became the headquarters for the Spoleto Festival, and it is also the main office for the Charleston Symphony Orchestra. The rear lot and additional parcels have been subdivided and developed as a new street in Ansonborough called Menotti Street.

24 GEORGE STREET, COLLEGE OF CHARLESTON GYMNASIUM

Constructed 1938–39

Albert Simons, architect

This Georgian Revival style facility was constructed after the demolition of the Radcliffe-King Mansion, one of Charleston's most important Federal houses. The three-story house had been built in 1806 by the wealthy merchant Thomas Radcliffe, whose land was developed after his death as the suburb of Radcliffeborough. His widow, Lucretia, gave important receptions and social gatherings in the house, as did

The intersection of Meeting and George Streets, looking west past the Radcliffe-King Mansion, 1875 engraving

the later owner Judge Mitchell King. In 1880 the dwelling became the High School of Charleston and remained in this use until 1924. The school caretaker's cottage with a mansard roof remains at the corner of Meeting Street and Burns Lane. On October 27, 1938, the College of Charleston pulled the house down to make way for the new gymnasium, designed by Albert Simons. Nonetheless, the woodwork was saved and much of it reused in the renovated Dock Street Theatre. The brick coping, iron fence, and gates remained intact until 1982, when all but a section along Meeting Street were removed. The contemporary addition to the gymnasium on the west sits on the former site of the Thomas Walker House, a three-story masonry dwelling with front piazzas and a balustraded parapet that was demolished in 1911 for a YMCA. This site was also formerly occupied by the William Gilliland House, destroyed by the college during an attempt to move the house off the property in 1978.

27 GEORGE STREET, THOMAS BARKSDALE HOUSE
Constructed circa 1817; altered late-nineteenth century; rehabilitated 1985

Although the house was completed by 1817, the paired bay windows and mansard roof of this building create the impression that it was built in the Victorian era. These features were added in the late-1880s by a subsequent owner. The fenestration and beaded weatherboarding of 27 George Street, though, hearken back to an earlier date. After several decades as a fraternity house, the building was restored in the 1980s for an inn.

32 GEORGE STREET, ROBINSON-FRENEAU HOUSE

Constructed circa 1796

Although built by Elizabeth Robinson, this three-story wood single house was occupied from its completion until 1813 by Peter Freneau, an editor of the *City Gazette* and secretary of state for South Carolina. Freneau's more famous brother was Philip Freneau, an anti-Federalist editor. The house retains early-twentieth-century shingle sheathing that obscures its origins, but it also retains an early scored masonry ground story.

36 GEORGE STREET, LEQUEUX-WILLIAMS HOUSE

Constructed circa 1834

This house was on the site by 1834, when it was sold by the devisees of the wealthy merchant Edward Darrell, the Lequeux sisters, to Lawrence Benson, who held it as rental property. In 1890 it was purchased by Pauline Williams, who raised her nine children in the house, a family in whose ownership it remains. The dwelling once had piazzas to the west, now removed, but otherwise the building differs strongly from most Charleston antebellum domestic structures. Resembling New York town houses of the 1830s, particularly those following the designs of Minard Lefever and William Thompson, the Greek Revival features of 36 George Street include a rusticated ground floor with an off-center front doorway set in an Ionic-columned architrave, full-height brick pilasters, wrought-iron window grilles, and a large stucco entablature.

Pattern-book elevation for a town house from Asher Benjamin's American Builder's Companion, *1827*

28–36 HASELL STREET
Constructed variously 1840–44

These buildings constitute an unbroken line of brick Charleston single houses constructed after the fire of 1838. By 1861 all were owned by John McNellage and occupied by single-family tenants. The dwelling at 36 Hasell Street was constructed by the wealthy planter-factor Samuel N. Stevens after he acquired the lot in 1843. In the same year Stevens acquired the lot at *20 South Battery* and there constructed a large three-story brick residence that still survives. The building at 28 Hasell Street was converted to a ground-floor commercial space many years ago and stuccoed, but the houses at 30, 32, and 34 Hasell Street have identical parapeted gables, dormers, brick detailing with dogtooth cornices and belt courses, and Greek Revival style piazza door screens.

33 HASELL STREET, JOHN HAMILTON HOUSE
Constructed circa 1838; restored 1980s

Although the main house was built as the prototype for seven others after the fire of 1838, the English-bond brick kitchen was a survivor from the late-eighteenth or early-nineteenth century, when there was a cooperage on the site. The property was described in an advertisement in 1863 as having six finished rooms, a stable for three horses, and a carriage house for two vehicles. The main house stands apart from its later neighbors because of its simpler late-Federal (rather than Greek Revival) detailing. Its main entry door studded with sidelights featuring cast-lead ornaments of dogwood blossoms and wheat sprays hints at an interior that boasts some of the rare surviving stenciled ceiling decoration in the city.

Measured first-floor plan, 33 Hasell Street

35 HASELL STREET, JOHN MCNELLAGE HOUSE

Constructed circa 1843; rehabilitated mid-1980s

John McNellage acquired a vacant lot at this address from Robert Wilson at the beginning of 1843. Wilson and his family owned numerous city properties, particularly in Ansonborough. The three-story dwelling stands on a high brick foundation with two bays on each floor and a surmounting brick parapet, ornamented by cast-iron anthemion grilles. On the south facade the parapet steps down toward the south and a double-tiered piazza shades this elevation. The late-Italianate style arched door hood dates from a postbellum renovation.

37 HASELL STREET, JONES-HOWELL HOUSE

Constructed 1841

Fletcher and Sessions, builders

A recorded specification and contract dated July 17, 1841, evinces that Eliza Jones, through her agent S. S. Howell, and the carpentry firm of Robert Fletcher and T. V. Sessions contracted for work associated with a three-story brick house on a high basement with attached "back room or tea room" and pantry on this site. The document specifies that the piazza should be "10 feet wide as shown on the plan with fluted columns turned fancy balusters 3 inches in thickness with neat cornices." By tradition, Jones passed the house to her daughter, who married into the Sidney S. Howell family; it remained in the Howells' possession for a century. The large side yard of the property once had a Victorian style parterre.

42 HASELL STREET, GEORGE CANNON HOUSE

Constructed circa 1845

Like its near neighbor at *38 Hasell Street* and the Jones-Howell House across the

street at *37 Hasell Street*, this substantial dwelling follows the side-hall, double-parlor plan, but instead of a raised entrance, the front door is at street level. Although the scored stucco facade is largely original, the main door surround has been altered and the fluted Doric-columned piazzas encumbered by some enclosures.

The interior stair rises to a second level that is probably the most elaborate in Ansonborough. Despite the severity of the exterior, Cannon's house has double drawing rooms with black marble mantels, Greek Revival style pilasters flanking windows and doors, and extravagant plaster ceiling medallions and other decoration.

44 HASELL STREET, JAMES STOCKER HOUSE
Constructed 1840–42; restored late-1960s

This two-story, flat-roofed dwelling appears from the street to follow the same single house plan as its neighbors. Despite the regularity of its piazza screen entry, French doors from the porch lead into three different rooms. The stair hall is tucked into a rear projection. Although painted for most of this century, the building is constructed of red Philadelphia pressed brick, and its principal decoration can be found in its parapet with cast-iron grilles and a surmounting dogtoothed cornice. Stocker built the house as an investment, and it quickly passed through a succession of similar absentee owners, including the steamship magnate James Adger. The restoration of the building in the late-1960s by the Charleston police chief John Conroy was a strategic advance in the revitalization of Ansonborough.

45 HASELL STREET, CHARLES W. SEIGNIOUS BUILDING
Constructed circa 1851; rehabilitated 1965, 1994

Charles W. Seignious acquired the lot with or without this three-story brick store and dwelling in 1851 from Samuel Wagner. The structure is notable for the retention of its early storefront pattern, especially the stone lintel and the cast-iron pilasters. The first-floor shop windows are a conjectural restoration by Historic Charleston Foundation carried out when it acquired the property in 1965. A walled-up entry door at the northeast corner of the structure formerly gave access to the floors above. Similar access survives through the remaining doors on the rear of the west elevation.

47–53 HASELL STREET

Constructed circa 1840

These three Charleston single houses seem appropriately scaled in ascending order from the corner of Anson Street toward the west. Each shows characteristics of having been built immediately after the fire of 1838. The most historically important of the group is probably 51 Hasell Street. This house was apparently built by Charles Glover, a contractor of New England extraction who came to the city to rebuild some houses in the neighborhood after the fire of 1838. His young wife, Mary Baker of New Hampshire, quickly became part of a small group of intellectuals of New England extraction in the city. A few years after their arrival Charles Glover died and his young widow left Charleston. In 1866 after her remarriage, Mary Baker Glover Eddy became the founder of the Christian Science religion.

48 HASELL STREET, ST. JOHANNES LUTHERAN CHURCH

Constructed 1842; renovated 1913

Edward Brickell White, architect

This Greek Revival church was originally built for a congregation of German immigrants who broke away from the more

Americanized St. John's Lutheran Church when it dropped its monthly services in German. The building was originally of exposed brick and lacked the Tuscan-columned front portico. It had an interior with a centered pulpit and communion table below. When St. Matthew's completed its grand new edifice in 1872 on Marion Square, the building was first sold to Salem Baptist Church but was conveyed within a decade to another evangelical Lutheran congregation, St. Johannes. A number of improvements, including the installation of the art glass windows, were completed in 1913.

50 HASELL STREET,
ST. JOHANNES CHURCH RECTORY
Constructed circa 1846

Although serving as the church rectory since 1920, this substantial stuccoed brick house was built in 1846 as a town residence for Joel Smith, an Abbeville District planter. The rectory's scale, like that of its neighbors to the west, exhibits a marked difference in size from the houses east of Anson Street. Its most unusual feature is its Italianate style window in the front gable. A Victorian entrance door with etched glass panels also ornaments the front facade.

52 HASELL STREET,
GIBBONS-GILLILAND HOUSE
Constructed circa 1843; altered circa 1886

A New England merchant and prominent member of the Charleston Unitarian Church built this house on a lot purchased in 1843 for about $1,500. By 1861 it was occupied by William H. Gilliland, a successful wholesale druggist-merchant on nearby Hayne Street. A significant feature of the house is the pressed sheet-metal ornament, probably added after the earth-

quake. Prior to the Ansonborough Rehabilitation Project of the 1960s, many neighboring houses had such added decoration.

54 HASELL STREET,
COL. WILLIAM RHETT HOUSE

Constructed 1712–1728; altered 1800;
restored and renovated 1950

Long tradition has set the date of construction of this substantial stuccoed brick
house on a half basement at 1712, thus
making it one of the oldest houses in the
city. It is actually constructed well outside
the original walled city limits and was part
of Point Plantation, a tract first acquired
by the New England émigré Jonathan
Amory. Amory died in 1699, and his brick
house burned in 1707. The vacant tract of
twenty acres, eleven adjacent lots, and eight
acres of marsh was then acquired and renamed "Rhettsbury" by Col. William
Rhett, a leading merchant often remembered for his capture and prosecution of
the loathed pirate Stede Bonnet. Rhett had
completed the house by at least the time of
his death in 1728, when his estate inventory described the furnishings in a house
of similar description. The house is of a
slightly asymmetrical floor plan with two
adjoining larger rooms on the west and two
smaller rooms separated by a central hall
on the eastern end. The Rococo ornament
in the dining room of the house was probably added in the third quarter of the eighteenth century, while other substantial
changes were made in about 1800, including a northwest addition and other alterations to interior woodwork.

In 1730 Col. William Rhett's widow
married the colony's chief justice Nicholas
Trott and the property was briefly called
"Trott's Point." After Trott's death the
"Rhettsbury" appellation returned and the
plantation was subdivided for his grand-

daughters Susannah Hasell Quince and Mary Hasell Ancrum. In 1807 the house and remaining grounds were sold to Christopher Fitzsimmons, a wealthy wharf owner. It was here that Fitzsimmons's grandson, Wade Hampton, later a noted Confederate lieutenant general and governor of South Carolina, was born in 1818. The piazzas on both the east and west ends were added in the early-nineteenth century, following the development of the streets of Rhettsbury around the house. The steps and entry on the west end are older than those on the east, which were added in the 1940s. The garden was designed by New York landscape architect Umberto Innocenti in the 1940s.

Several owners used or rented the structure as a boardinghouse in the 1920s and 1930s. It is generally rumored that it was used as a "house of assignation" during this period, following the decline of the neighborhood around it. In 1941 Mr. and Mrs. Benjamin A. Kittredge Jr. of New York, owners of Dean Hall Plantation and creators of its famous Cypress Gardens on the Cooper River, purchased the property. The Kittredges thoroughly restored the house, and it became the first significant restoration in the neighborhood.

60 HASELL STREET, GEORGE REYNOLDS HOUSE

Constructed 1847

Perhaps one of Charleston's most eclectic antebellum houses, this dwelling was built by the merchant George Reynolds in 1847. It combines the Italianate-villa style, exemplified by twin Tuscan towers and the Egyptian Revival style, embodied in the detailing of the front square-columned portico. The house is the only one in Ansonborough set back from the street in this manner. Its flanking brick outbuildings provide a forecourt at the street line.

Portico detail, 60 Hasell Street

64 HASELL STREET, BENJAMIN SMITH HOUSE

Constructed circa 1843; rehabilitated 1982–83

A well-to-do building-supply merchant constructed this handsome Greek Revival style dwelling with a front double-tiered portico. The building has an unusual U-shaped plan with two large front rooms separated by a central hall and two smaller rooms at the rear. The interior is lavishly decorated with plaster friezes and extravagantly carved window and door frames in the Corinthian order. The double steps and wrought-iron rail add great distinction to the entry of the building. Held by a succession of noted Charleston families, the house passed to the Mazycks in 1852 and thence in 1853 to Mary Mazyck Gadsden, whose descendants held the property until 1937.

66 HASELL STREET, LAZARUS-GADSDEN BUILDING

Constructed circa 1839; rehabilitated 1984–85

Originally built as a lecture hall for the third Presbyterian Church, this building was sold in the 1870s to the Lazarus family. Formerly a tall single-story structure fronted with a fluted Doric-columned portico, it was converted, following substantial earthquake damage, by Floride Gadsden, who lived next door, as a residence for her daughter Phoebe Gadsden Smythe. The Gadsdens added a one-story columned piazza surmounted by a central pedimented portico. The latter feature was removed in the 1960s. Following a period of neglect, the house was completely rehabilitated as a law office in 1984.

66 Hasell Street before rehabilitation

449

90 HASELL STREET,
SYNAGOGUE OF KAHAL KADOSH BETH ELOHIM

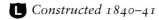 *Constructed 1840–41*

Cyrus Warner, draftsman-architect; David Lopez, contractor

A newspaper account in 1792 described the first synagogue on this site as a steepled, meetinghouse style building. This structure became the first permanent house of worship for a largely Sephardic community that had established its congregation by 1749. The fire of 1838 consumed this building with the rest of Ansonborough, and the congregation began planning for a new building on the same site, behind the surviving wrought-iron fence. Various architects and builders, including Charles Reichardt, James Curtis, David Lopez, and Frederick Wesner, submitted plans, and it is unclear which design was selected and sent to Cyrus Warner in New York to be formally drawn. Surviving specifications indicate the high quality of materials, including the use of marble portico tiles, various details of blue granite, and the brick and stuccoed columns. The building as finished has a Greek Doric portico with fluted columns and, on the interior, a coffered dome set into a vaulted ceiling. The mahogany ark sits within a Corinthian-columned canopy, surmounted by scrollwork and a central anthemion framing a pair of gilded tablets.

The Reformed Society of Israelites was founded by some members in 1824 and later merged again with the old congregation, causing a change in Sephardic ritual to a shorter English service. The rebuilding after the fire and the installation of an organ in the back gallery caused the departure of conservative and Orthodox members of the congregation, most of whom were immigrants from central and eastern Europe. Next door to the synagogue is the circa 1797 Anthony Toomer House at *86 Hasell Street.* This three-story brick dwelling with belt courses and banded and corbeled chimneys has been used by the congregation as the home of its archives.

Hasell Street Beth Elohim Synagogue, engraving of 1875

95 HASELL STREET,
ST. MARY'S ROMAN CATHOLIC CHURCH

 *Constructed 1838–39*

Christopher Kane, contractor

The present St. Mary's is the third church on the site of the first establishment of Roman Catholicism in the Carolinas and Georgia. Catholics in colonial Charleston worshipped quietly, as they were the only group not permitted toleration in the province from proprietary times. The first priest, the Reverend Ryan, found the local Catholics, numbering about two hundred, "few, poor and timid." After renting a Methodist meetinghouse on Hasell Street, the group purchased the site about the time that the congregation was incorporated by the South Carolina legislature in 1791. With the first boats of refugees from the slave insurrection in French Santo Domingo, the number of congregants swelled. A handsome brick church was built under the direction of the Reverend Simon Felix O'Gallagher in 1801, but this building burned in 1838.

A cornerstone was quickly laid for rebuilding on the site, and the new church was completed in 1839. The present building follows a Robert Mills–inspired tradition of the Classical Revival style already out of fashion in the 1830s. On the interior a fine 1814 altar painting by the local artist John Cogdell, rescued in the 1838 fire and restored by the artist for the new church, is surmounted by a ceiling executed by the decorative painter Chizzola. These images are in company with twenty-three ceiling and wall paintings, copies of European masterpieces, by the Italian artist Caesare Portia that were installed in 1896. The spectacular stained glass windows were completed in two campaigns by the Franz Mayer Firm of Munich. One of the most significant facets of St. Mary's is its graveyard, which holds the burials of eighteenth- and early-nineteenth-century immigrants of French, Irish, Italian, and Spanish extraction. Two daughters of the Comte De Grasse, the French admiral who helped George Washington secure victory at Yorktown, are buried here among other French refugees of the West Indies.

45 LAURENS STREET, THOMAS WALLACE HOUSE

Constructed circa 1804; rehabilitated 1968–69

The cabinetmaker Thomas Wallace, whose shop on Queen Street produced furniture in the prevailing Federal style for the Charleston elite, constructed this three-story wooden single house on a raised basement in about 1804. The closed gable end of the roof and the open Greek Revival piazzas, which do not have a street entry, are perhaps the only features that set this dwelling apart from its similarly styled neighbor at *43 Laurens Street*. Wallace sold the house in 1815 to Capt. Nathaniel Greene Hilliard, a Connecticut émigré.

48 LAURENS STREET, SIMON JUDE CHANCOGNIE HOUSE

Constructed circa 1814–16; rehabilitated 1961; addition 1988

A French merchant and consul built this three-story, hipped-roof dwelling on lands obtained from the estate of Christopher Gadsden in 1807. The house retains its simple Neoclassical detailing with the exception of the Greek Revival doorway in the piazza screen. Most of its simple woodwork survives in its interior. The expansive corner lot provides a notable walled garden. Visible from the Alexander Street elevation is a contemporary classical addition.

49 Laurens Street just prior to its 1970 restoration

49 LAURENS STREET, WILLIAM MONIES HOUSE

Constructed circa 1804; restored 1970

This simple Neoclassical dwelling was actually begun as an investment by the painter and glazier John Haslett and his partner Youngs Hasmer on one of two lots purchased from the Laurens Square property inherited by Henry Laurens II. It may have been completed by William Monies, a Scottish merchant, who was the first owner to occupy the building. The dwelling was purchased by the Paterson family when Monies returned to Scotland, and it was bought in 1867 by the Charleston attorney George Lamb Buist. By 1971 the house was one of the most deteriorated in the neighborhood, and its reclamation was one of the last in Historic Charleston Foundation's Ansonborough Rehabilitation Project. The small iron balconies on the second floor are apparently original.

50 LAURENS STREET, ADAMS-INGRAHAM HOUSE

Constructed 1807–08; restored after fire damage 1974

This dwelling was built after the purchase of a lot from the Gadsden estate, in this case by John Strong Adams, a merchant of Irish extraction. More grandly conceived than the Chancognie residence, the house boasts a period-style fanlighted doorway and marble steps, as well as a notable brick kitchen/carriage house. The third story and the iron fence were added in the antebellum period, probably by the Ingraham family, who owned the property from 1828 until the mid-nineteenth century.

53 LAURENS STREET, JAMES MARSH HOUSE

Constructed circa 1815

The only original brick house left on Laurens Street, this well-preserved Federal dwelling has tuckpointed Flemish-bond-pattern brickwork with belt courses between floors and brick quoining. The house has the further distinction of having been in the possession of only two families in its history. Descendants of James Marsh, the builder, owned the property until 1904, when it was conveyed to Mary Connor, the first of a succession of Connor-Renken family members who still live in the building.

55 LAURENS STREET, JAMES JERVEY HOUSE

Constructed circa 1818; rehabilitated 1980s

With its placement on a high brick basement and its double-house form, this dwelling presents a larger-scaled, more urban plan than other houses in the Ansonborough district. Although its windows were changed to two-over-two sashes in the mid-nineteenth century and the property changed to condominiums in the 1980s, the Flemish-bond building retains much of its exterior integrity, including belt courses, quoins, and cornice. The stair windows in the center bay on the front indicate that, unlike other houses in the city, the stair runs toward the street front instead of toward the rear.

57 LAURENS STREET, AUGUSTUS TAFT HOUSE

Constructed circa 1836; restored 1970s

This three-story town house is a good example of early–Greek Revival style in the emerging Charleston interpretation. The dwelling is built of black cypress and exhibits little ornamentation on its exterior save the simple Greek key motif in the pilasters of its door architrave and the fine marble staircase approaching it. The house retains much of its original interior, including black marble mantels, plaster cornices, and ceiling medallions in its downstairs double parlors. The site includes a three-story brick kitchen and quarters at the rear, built after the fire of 1838 (which narrowly missed this house) and a notable garden on the west side, occupying an additional lot that has always been part of the property. Although the black cypress siding is very durable, it has been painted in the past and is currently coated with a stain.

The house was built around 1836 by Augustus R. Taft, a member of a prominent New England family that also produced a president and a senator. The builder's daughter married Pierre Gaillard Stoney, and the house remained in their family for over a century, except for a six-month period in 1865 when it was confiscated by the Freedman's Bureau to provide housing for freed slaves.

MAIDEN LANE

Established by 1788

This short thoroughfare is one of the few Charleston streets to retain its original cobblestoned paving. Nonetheless, most of its historic structures had disappeared by the mid-twentieth century. The small brick single house at 5 Maiden Lane is the sole survivor of three nearly identical dwellings; the other two were demolished in the early-1960s. This remaining house was built by Robert F. Henry following his acquisition of the lot in 1838. Across the street the brick wall surrounds the original site of Trinity Methodist Church, established in 1792. Trinity was an offshoot of Charleston's original Methodist congregation, Cumberland Church, and followed the doctrines of the Reverend William Hammet, a "Primitive Methodist" who opposed the policies of Francis Asbury and other leaders of the Methodist Episcopal Church in America. Its first building, the Blue Meeting House, burned in the fire of 1838 and was replaced by a simple Greek Revival structure that was in turn replaced by a large Beaux Arts style church in 1902. Hundreds of church members were buried in the cemetery, which, now legally deactivated, remains underneath the parking lot now covering the site.

256 MEETING STREET, WILLIAM GAYER CARRIAGE FACTORY

Constructed circa 1838; rehabilitated with reconstructed facade 1985

The rehabilitation of this building is a testament to Charleston's preservationist

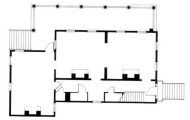

Measured plan of the first floor, 57 Laurens Street

5 Maiden Lane, south elevation (looking north)

perseverance, to the community spirit of local business leaders, and to the advantages of historic preservation in the 1980s. Built by a coach and carriage maker with loan funds following the disastrous Ansonborough fire of 1838, the structure had one of the most distinctive facades in the city, incorporating Classical and Greek Revival elements with hints of the later Italianate style. The site remained in the hands of successor carriage makers until 1898, later becoming a bottling plant and a wholesale shoe company. The Gayer building's most ignominious period came after the property's sale to the Tire Company: the elegant facade was removed and a driveway added to the front. After being abandoned by the 1950s and acquired by the neighboring church for parking, the Board of Architectural Review denied demolition requests on three occasions. In 1985 the front facade was reconstructed based on an early photograph and the structure became the headquarters of the bank that occupies the site.

262–264 MEETING STREET, CENTRAL FIRE STATION AND COURTENAY SQUARE

Pavilion constructed 1885; station constructed 1887–88

Daniel G. Wayne, architect-builder; Colin McK. Grant, contractor

On this site a cast-iron pavilion, erected in 1885, covers an artesian well, 1,800 feet deep, that served Charleston residents with pure water, especially during times of yellow fever epidemics. Designs for a small park on this site, named for Charleston's mayor William Ashmead Courtenay, were altered after the earthquake of 1886, when plans were developed to construct modern fire stations at convenient points in the city

rather than repairing the old damaged buildings. The L-shaped Central Fire Station, built in a restrained Italianate Renaissance Revival style with splendid brick detailing, was completed by 1888 at a cost of $14,000. Today the structure houses firemen and equipment as well as a well-maintained late-nineteenth-century engine, usually visible from Wentworth Street.

266–270 MEETING STREET, WILLIAM GAYER HOUSE AND DANIEL HART HOUSES
Constructed 1840–50; renovated 1970s

William Gayer, owner of the nearby carriage works, built the large three-story parapeted house with a later enclosed piazza at 266 Meeting Street in 1840. Used as a boardinghouse by the 1880s, the building continued as a hostelry until the 1960s, when it was known as the Southern Air Hotel and apartments. A new owner renovated it as an office and apartment building in the 1970s. The similarly styled Hart Houses were built more than a decade apart and received Italianate style detailing after the earthquake of 1886.

272 MEETING STREET, CAULTIER APOTHECARY-STOKES BUSINESS COLLEGE BUILDING
Constructed 1872; rehabilitated 1984

Although the adjoining house at 66½ *Society* was built in about 1853, the principal Meeting Street building at this site was erected after the Civil War by Dr. George Caultier, who kept his apothecary shop on the first floor. By 1898 the property had been acquired by Albert L. Stokes, who founded one of the first business colleges in the United States. Stokes's institution trained hundreds of women during the next four decades as they entered the business world in the World War II years. Caultier's building reflects an interesting variant on the Italianate style with its arched and rusticated first floor and its semicircular-headed windows on the upper floor.

275 MEETING STREET, TRINITY METHODIST CHURCH

Constructed 1848–50

Edward C. Jones, architect

Perhaps the least altered of Charleston's late–Greek Revival church buildings, Trinity was actually constructed for the Third (later Westminster) Presbyterian Church. Often compared to the Church of the Madeleine in Paris and its predecessor the Maison Carrée at Nîmes, primarily due to its monumental Corinthian-columned portico and massive dual flight of stone steps, the building nonetheless reflects its region with its large windows and contemporary technology with its cast column capitals. Inside the church louvered shutters over the tall windows, open galleries, and a central apse, decorated with molded plaster anthemions and other embellishments and flanked by four Corinthian columns, portend the end of the simplicity of the Greek and the emergence of the Roman Revival and the more elaborate styles of the late antebellum period.

275 Meeting Street, then the Central Presbyterian Church, 1875 engraving

In 1926 the Trinity Methodist congregation, sited at Hasell Street and Maiden Lane since 1792, purchased the building when Westminster Presbyterian Church moved to an uptown location. The Trinity congregation brought with them a large Tiffany window donated in memory of George Walton Williams, builder of the Calhoun Mansion, installing it in an existing chapel at the southwest end of the church.

278 MEETING STREET, JOSEPH BEUNBAULT HOUSE

Constructed 1845–52

With a rare setback from Meeting Street, this three-story stucco dwelling now stands behind a modern building, but it formerly faced a landscaped garden. In plan and detailing, with its side piazzas, the house exhibits characteristics of Charleston single houses. The front bay window, however, dates from a postbellum renovation, probably by the Buist family, owners of the property from 1876 until 1886.

286 MEETING STREET, NOYER-WILDHAGEN HOUSE

Constructed 1807; restored and rehabilitated 1984

The lone survivor of a splendid group of Federal style houses in the area of Meeting and George Streets, this residence was constructed for the spinster Abigail Noyer in 1807. Passed to Dr. A. C. Wildhagen, who kept an office on the ground floor, the house stayed in the hands of his descendants until the early-twentieth century, when it became a drugstore and seven apartments. Subsequent changes led to enclosures of the piazzas and a ground-floor storefront for Central Sundries Drug Store. Restoration in recent years included full replication of the piazzas and a truncated version of the old piazza screen.

287–289 MEETING STREET, DER DEUTSCHE FREUNDSCHAFTS-BUND HALL

Constructed 1870; rehabilitated early-1980s

Abrahams and Seyle, architects

This two-story Gothic Revival building stands on a raised basement at the intersection of Meeting and George Streets. Formerly serving a German fraternal or-

An 1890s photo of 289 Meeting Street, today the Washington Light Infantry headquarters

ganization, it had a number of uses before being taken over in 1984 as the headquarters of the Washington Light Infantry, a local military unit founded in 1807. Lancet arched windows and parapet provide the major decoration for this large stucco building, which is partially enclosed by fencing from the old Radcliffe-King House and is accessed from the street through gates designed by Albert Simons for the Infantry in 1955, reflecting the unit's service in most wars since the War of 1812.

296 MEETING STREET, STROBEL HOUSE

Constructed circa 1800

One of numerous small wooden houses that formerly lined upper Meeting Street, the Strobel House was built by one of Charleston's prominent mechanic families in 1800. Though threatened with demolition, it was retained on its original site and later restored as an office.

298–300 MEETING STREET, GIBSON-FRONENBERGER HOUSE AND ABIGAIL LEVY HOUSE

298 constructed circa 1824; renovated 1859, 1941; rehabilitated 1985;

300 constructed 1853; rehabilitated 1985

James Gibson built 298 Meeting Street in about 1824 on a large lot that also included 300 Meeting Street. The building took its present form in 1859 after its sale to Caleb Fronenberger, who remodeled it in the Italianate style with an addition that gave its roofline curious perpendicular gables and an arched Italianate-style center doorway. The site was subdivided in 1847. Abigail Levy purchased the new lot at 300 Meeting Street and constructed a simple wood single house in 1853 as a tenement. The tall Italianate gable end masks the roofline behind what is probably a later addition.

309–313 MEETING STREET, CONNELLEY'S FUNERAL HOME AND RESIDENCE

House constructed circa 1796, renovated 1890s; funeral home constructed 1894; complex rehabilitated as residential condominiums 1984

The Charleston single house at 313 Meeting Street was built about 1796 by John Horlbeck on that portion of the original Ansonborough suburb formerly owned by Peter Porcher. Though the house is said to retain much of its original interior woodwork, its exterior was heavily altered with Eastlake/Victorian style alterations after its purchase by Jesse M. Connelley in 1892. Connelley, an Edgefield businessman and salesman, purchased an undertaking business from Frederick Ansel and retained the builder J. D. Murphy to design and construct a new Romanesque Revival style mortuary in 1894 at 309 Meeting Street. This structure's facade, including sandstone detailing and stained glass windows, is essentially original to construction. Connelley also established Charleston Greenhouses on the site, selling tropical fish from a small outdoor aquarium, which partially survives in front of the greenhouses. Connelley also completed a large brick coffin warehouse at the rear of the site, a structure now facing Burns Lane.

309–313 Meeting Street, the J. M. Connelley establishment, shown in a late-1800s engraving

Connelley became South Carolina's first licensed mortician, when such laws were enacted early in the twentieth century, and operated the leading funeral home serving Charleston's elite families for several generations. In 1984 a group of Atlanta-based investors rehabilitated the house and mortuary as condominiums, retaining their exterior appearances and much of their interiors as well. The former coffin warehouse at Burns Lane/133 *Calhoun Street* now serves as a maintenance facility for the College of Charleston.

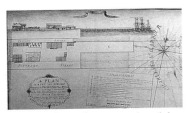

Eighteenth-century plat of the eastern end of Pinckney Street

PINCKNEY STREET

The southern edge of the Ansonborough neighborhood burned in the fire of 1861, and when rebuilt it was characterized by a mix of small wooden single houses and freedmen's cottages. The north side of the western end contained mostly brick single houses with businesses interspersed, while the south side contained several livery stables, including those associated with the Charleston Hotel. The finest surviving house on the street is 46 Pinckney Street, built in 1852 by Jacob Rabb after he purchased the lot from the neighboring Methodist Episcopal Church.

After removing an old engine house from the site, he seems to have constructed the present building, a typical brick single house with a pilastered brick gable end and slate roof. As one of the only two antebellum brick buildings surviving on the street, the Rabb House stands out from the neighboring industrial structures and simple wooden dwellings constructed after the Civil War, such as the freedmen's cottages at 14 and 17 Pinckney Street and the small wooden single houses at 18 and 19 Pinckney Street.

29–33 SOCIETY STREET, JOHN W. ROBINSON TENEMENTS

Constructed 1915; 33 Society rehabilitated early-1980s

These three wooden buildings, constructed originally as duplexes, stand on the site of the rear yard of the Thomas Heyward House. Heyward had constructed his substantial house in 1788 with a large two-story Tuscan portico. After the house was demolished prior to World War I, the property was subdivided and the three tenement houses were built on the site. The surviving door surrounds, bay windows, and wood detailing are characteristic of the late–Queen Anne/Victorian style, already out of date when the dwellings were completed and indicative of the Ansonborough neighborhood's changing demographics in the early-twentieth century.

32 SOCIETY STREET, GABRIEL B. BROWNE HOUSE

Constructed 1846; rehabilitated 1968; facade restored 1990

Gabriel Browne, a commercial merchant at Gibbes Wharf, built this well-detailed brick house on a raised basement in 1846. According to the city census, Browne was still the owner-occupant of the site in 1860. In exterior form the house matches those in the eastern block of Hasell Street, but it is a wider building with a more expansive interior than other Ansonborough single houses.

35–37 SOCIETY STREET, JULIANA DUPRÉ TENEMENTS

Constructed circa 1840; altered circa 1886, 1930s

The severe Greek Revival pressed-brick facades of 35–37 Society Street appear to stretch across one single building. This impression is dispelled when it is observed that the central entry door is placed within a filled brick archway. Although an analysis of this structure would indicate a double tenement such as those found in lower Charleston, the buildings are actually separate houses, the easternmost having an open archway that led to the rear of the property, an architectural feature seen in a few other Ansonborough locations. The two houses were joined in this century and changed into apartments by 1941, a use which continues on the site.

36 SOCIETY STREET, HENRY STREET HOUSE
Constructed 1840

A prosperous commission merchant built this exceptional two-story Greek Revival house in 1840 utilizing the high basement of the previous dwelling on a site that had been destroyed in the 1838 fire. Henry Street doubled the size of the house in 1845 by adding rooms and changing the plan from a single house to a double house. Double parlors open off each other on the east side of the first-floor hall, while a dining room and rear room mark the other side. While such a front-facing Greek Revival house is rare in the strict urban confines of Ansonborough, the Henry Street House has some similarities in its placement and scope of decoration to *64 Hasell Street.*

40–42 SOCIETY STREET, JULIANA DUPRÉ HOUSES
Constructed 1850, 1854; restored and rehabilitated 1961, 1980s

Juliana Dupré built these two stucco brick single houses in 1850 and 1854 respectively. The house at 40 Society Street lacks the expansive side lot of the westernmost house. The two differ because of the flat roof of 40 Society Street and the gable roof end of 42 Society Street. In a recent restoration, it was discovered that the house at 40 Society Street is actually built within the first-floor walls of the original house destroyed in the fire of 1838. The house, when rebuilt, was lengthened by nine feet, necessitating the recentering of all fireplaces and chimneys and the main stairwell. Mr. and Mrs. J. Blake Middleton bought the dwelling at 42 Society Street in 1961. It was one of the first houses to be rehabilitated in the Ansonborough Project.

44 SOCIETY STREET, ISAAC REEVES HOUSE

Constructed circa 1840; rehabilitated 1962, late-1980s

Isaac Reeves sited this small brick house on the lot in a manner that provides the most unique yard in Ansonborough. Set in a large garden, the simple two-story building with French windows and wide piazzas is constructed of Philadelphia brick. The dwelling was one of the first to be restored in the Ansonborough Rehabilitation Project. Reeves's widow, Ann, still owned the residence in 1860 but had turned the site into rental property.

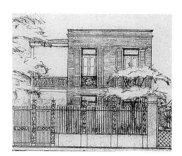

Drawing of 44 Society Street

48 SOCIETY STREET, SUSAN ROBINSON TENEMENTS

Constructed 1839–40; rehabilitated mid-1960s

An earlier house on this site owned by Joseph Sanford Barker of Mulberry Plantation burned in the fire of 1838 long after the site had been conveyed to a trust for the use of Susan Robinson, wife of the builder of numerous houses on Judith Street in Wraggborough. The easternmost portion of the tenements was occupied by a confectioner or baker, George R. Olson, after his purchase of the property in 1875. Prior to the historic Ansonborough Project the entire first floor of the structure served as a grocery store. In 1964 the present owners purchased the building for the offices that now occupy the first floor of the site.

52 SOCIETY STREET, JAMES M. STOCKER HOUSE

Constructed 1840–41

The James M. Stocker House is characterized by a flat roof and scored stucco facade and retains much of its original detailing, including its simple Greek Revival door surround. Stocker, a merchant, bought the lot in 1840 and probably began construction of the single house immediately, as his mortgage to the Bank of the State of South Carolina required that funds for construction be expended within a year. In 1847 the property was conveyed in trust for Louisa Lord, the wife of Stocker's business partner, Samuel Lord. The Lords lived in this residence for the next several decades.

54 SOCIETY STREET, GEORGE BLACK HOUSE

Constructed circa 1853

George Black built this finely crafted two-and-a-half-story, side-hall-plan house after his purchase of the lot in 1852. Italianate in style with stucco quoins, window lintels, and a gable end with a central arched window, the Black House offers variety in a block dominated by single houses.

55 SOCIETY STREET, OLD HIGH SCHOOL

Constructed 1840–42; portico constructed 1850; rehabilitated 1984

Edward Brickell White, architect

Capitals for 55 Society Street restorations, Robert Pringle, sculptor

The High School of Charleston was founded in 1839, replacing an early preparatory academy associated with the College of Charleston. Its construction was a response to the call for major improvements in the city's public education in the second quarter of the nineteenth century, led by Christopher G. Memminger. The school board approved the current plan by Edward Brickell White in 1840 after rejecting a more expensive scheme. White also designed a two-story portico, added to the high school in 1850, as well as one for the College of Charleston's main building. After correspondence with the Worcester, Massachusetts, architect Elbridge Boyden, White ordered from Worcester fabricated terra-cotta column capitals, probably manufactured by Tolman, Luther and Company. In 1881 the high school moved to the old Radcliffe-King Mansion at George and Meeting Streets and the building was leased through the 1930s to a series of African American fraternal orders. The column capitals were heavily damaged in the earthquake of 1886 and were later removed. In a rehabilitation in 1984 fragments of the capitals were located and the sculptor Robert Pringle was able to reconstruct them based on the Tolman catalog, newspaper accounts, City Council minutes, and the fragments. The current capitals are made from a fiberglass reinforced cement material. The wrought-iron gates were probably installed in 1840 and correspond to similar work in the city from the same decade. The buildings immediately to the east at *49–51 Society Street* constitute the former St. Peter's School, a separate African American school founded by Roman Catholics. The St. Peter's buildings grew from the westernmost portion of the structure, originally constructed by Edward Roach.

55 Society Street after restoration of its column capitals

56 SOCIETY STREET, DR. JOSEPH JOHNSON HOUSE

Constructed 1835–40; rehabilitated 1962, 1991

Dr. Joseph Johnson, one of South Carolina's leading medical scientists and an intendant (mayor) of Charleston, built this residence for his wife, Katherine Bonneau Johnson, a Charlestonian of French Huguenot descent. A versatile scholar, Johnson, who had lived on lower Church Street, carried on extensive research into the causes of yellow fever and also authored

the history book titled *Traditions of the American Revolution*. Saved in 1960 by the Ansonborough Rehabilitation Project, the house was sold to the British author Gordon Langley Hall, who initially restored the residence, and later became the home of Josephine Humphreys, one of Charleston's premier late-twentieth-century novelists. The Dr. Joseph Johnson House is similar to its westernmost neighbor, the J. C. Burckmeyer Building at *58 Society Street*, which was rebuilt by its owner after the fire of 1838 and served as the primary residence until 1871 of a family that owned numerous properties in Ansonborough.

57 SOCIETY STREET, WILLIAM MCELHERAN HOUSE

Constructed circa 1851

William McElheran rebuilt on this site after the fire and sold the dwelling with its appurtenances to James McClary, a blacksmith. McClary then lived at *24 Wentworth Street* and apparently used this house as an investment. 57 Society Street is a three-story Charleston single house similar to *59 Society Street*, another of the several dwellings in this area constructed by Jonah M. Venning as tenements after the fire of 1838.

62 SOCIETY STREET, HIERONYMUS-TIEDEMAN HOUSE

Constructed 1838–40; rehabilitated late-1980s

William T. Hieronymus, the co-owner of a nearby livery stable who also built *66 Society Street*, built this large three-story, stucco-coated brick dwelling. The house is particularly unusual because it has a masked piazza, a side porch which is shaded from the street by the extension of the front wall of the building, complete with windows and other facade features. After earthquake damage in 1886, Victorian window hoods were installed and a new cornice was added to the top of the facade.

63–65 SOCIETY STREET, ST. PAUL'S CATHOLIC CHURCH (GERMAN CHURCH)

Constructed circa 1840; renovated as a Catholic Church 1861; altered late-1940s

First constructed as a rectangular building to house a lecture room for the Second Presbyterian Church (replacing an earlier lecture room destroyed in the fire), the current edifice was subsequently acquired by the Philharmonic Society and then by the Diocese of Charleston, serving the Sisters of Charity of Our Lady of Mercy as the locus for a free school. With the desire for a new parish to serve German Catholics in the area, Bishop Lynch appointed the Reverend William Beerschneider as priest. After the raising of funds, the architect Louis Barbot was chosen to convert the lecture room into a church, and his additions of Romanesque style details and steeple were complete by 1861. After the war, dissension over the use of the German language and the shrinking of the congregation resulted in closure of St. Paul's in 1869. In the 1880s some of the congregation moved to a new church on Wentworth Street (now the site of St. Katherine's convent, a modern building at *36 Wentworth Street*) and the old St. Paul's was again used as St. Mary's School. Acquired by the Palmetto Post of the American Legion in 1947, the building was altered extensively on the ground floor, the windows of the sanctuary were filled in, and the openings of the remaining portion of the steeple were blocked.

66 SOCIETY STREET, HIERONYMOUS-ROPER HOUSE

Constructed 1839; renovated circa 1850– 52, 1966–68

The widow Martha Laurens Roper, former mistress of the splendid house at *9 East Battery* and a plantation owner in her own right, purchased a masonry single

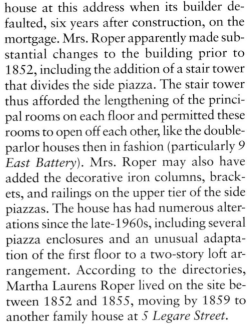

house at this address when its builder defaulted, six years after construction, on the mortgage. Mrs. Roper apparently made substantial changes to the building prior to 1852, including the addition of a stair tower that divides the side piazza. The stair tower thus afforded the lengthening of the principal rooms on each floor and permitted these rooms to open off each other, like the double-parlor houses then in fashion (particularly 9 *East Battery*). Mrs. Roper may also have added the decorative iron columns, brackets, and railings on the upper tier of the side piazzas. The house has had numerous alterations since the late-1960s, including several piazza enclosures and an unusual adaptation of the first floor to a two-story loft arrangement. According to the directories, Martha Laurens Roper lived on the site between 1852 and 1855, moving by 1859 to another family house at *5 Legare Street*.

75 SOCIETY STREET, ECKHARDT-PATRICK HOUSE
Constructed circa 1839

Mary Elizabeth Burckmeyer Elsworth Eckhardt rebuilt almost immediately after the fire on this site. Her three-story stuccoed-brick single house rises to a flat roof disguised by a banded parapet. A later Italianate style doorway stands in the screen of the double-tiered piazza. The dwelling was purchased in the 1850s by Dr. John Burckmeyer Patrick, a dentist who perfected several new dental techniques. Patrick also built the two-story Italianate style structure with pedimented second-story window and balcony at *82 Society Street* as his office.

WALL STREET
Established by 1788; mostly removed in 1966

A brick wall dividing Ansonborough from Middlesex supposedly served as the source for the name of this street. Only a single block survives of this thoroughfare that stretched to Calhoun Street prior to the clearing of Middlesex for the city auditorium. Three original houses survive in the west block, including 1 Wall Street (*54 Laurens Street*), a wooden side-passage-plan house built in the mid-nineteenth century, with a later barrel-vaulted entry. Another is 3 Wall Street, a late-eighteenth-century Charleston single house reminiscent of *39 Laurens Street* (another house moved by Historic Charleston Foundation from the Middlesex area) and built by the house carpenter George Nelson. Free persons of color, Paris and Susan Cooper, constructed the simple two-story brick building at 5 Wall Street in 1856. Eight free African American families lived on the street at the time of the Civil War, three of whom were owner-occupants.

3 Wall Street

3–13 WENTWORTH STREET, EDWARD WINSLOW BRICK TENEMENTS

Constructed circa 1841–42; rehabilitated 1970s–80s

After the fire of 1838 Edward Winslow borrowed $3,120 from the Bank of the State of South Carolina to purchase these lots, a site measuring 156 feet wide and 87 feet in depth, and began construction of seven row-house tenements (six survive). Such a row is rare in Charleston, as is the six-foot alley laid out by Winslow at the rear of the site. The easternmost tenements have two-story, front bay windows, probably added in the late-1800s, while the westernmost unit has a typical Charleston piazza. On the interior each dwelling has a typical side hall opening onto a parlor and dining room separated from each other by sliding pocket doors. Although four of the buildings were sold to James Chapman in 1849, by 1861 all of the tenements were held by different individuals and were owner occupied.

8–10 WENTWORTH STREET, JOHN T. HENERY AND CHARLES W. SEIGNIOUS HOUSES

Constructed 1850–56; renovated and restored 1964

These two contrasting 1850s Charleston single houses illustrate the variations within this set house plan. In 1850 John Henery built his stuccoed house at 8 Wentworth Street away from the street, affording a front garden. The simple gable and oversized second-story windows on this dwelling contrast with Seignious's brick house at 10 Wentworth Street, completed six years later, which is set at the street line and has elaborate brick detailing in its belt course and a closed, pilastered gable with a tripartite window.

12 WENTWORTH STREET, WILLIAM C. ARMSTRONG HOUSE

Constructed circa 1853–55; extensively renovated with alterations circa 1969

William C. Armstrong, then manager of the nearby Bennett's Rice Mill, constructed this unusual dwelling by the mid-1850s. Armstrong died in 1857, and his heirs sold the house to the Burckmeyer family, owners of many properties on Society Street. During renovation, new owners removed the front piazza, demolished later rear additions, added a new iron balcony to the second story, and filled the central arch leading to the rear.

15 WENTWORTH STREET, CHRISTOPHER MYERS HOUSE

Constructed circa 1847; renovated and restored 1966–67

Christopher Myers's house features a substantial basement story with triple-tiered side piazzas, in contrast to its contemporary neighbor at *17 Wentworth*

Street with truncated basement and a double piazza. Myers, a merchant, sold the building in 1853 to W. L. Chapin, a wholesale druggist who also kept a harness-making business on nearby Hayne Street.

18–20 WENTWORTH STREET, LOPEZ-MOISE TENEMENTS

Constructed circa 1839; restored 1970 and late-1970s, respectively

David Lopez, a merchant and builder whose Rhode Island–born father owned a store on King Street selling architectural ornamentation, built these dual tenements with his brother-in-law, Isaac Moise, between 1839 and 1841. At nearly the same time Lopez was active in some capacity in the construction of the new Beth Elohim Synagogue on nearby Hasell Street. Lopez sold out his interest, during or just after construction, to Moise, a founder of the Reformed Society of Israel and brother of Penina Moise, a noted antebellum poet and originator of the second Jewish Sunday school in America. Typical of Greek Revival row houses, both units stand two stories on raised basements and follow the side-hall, double-parlor plan.

18 Wentworth Street after restoration and 20 Wentworth Street before restoration, 1970

19 WENTWORTH STREET, WILLIAM LEBBY HOUSE

Constructed 1847–48

William Lebby, an engineer and machinist, acquired this burned-over lot in 1847 and was living on the site by 1849. Perhaps the most unusual dwelling in Ansonborough, the house follows the typical side-hall plan, but its double L-shape permitted the insertion of a piazza behind the front sitting room, which opened up communication to rear service areas of the house. The surmounting modillioned brick pediment and the front door architrave are typical Greek Revival features. Lebby probably had the cast-iron front fence with Rococo Revival elements installed in the 1850s.

20–24 WENTWORTH STREET, FRANCIS Q. MCHUGH TENEMENTS

Constructed circa 1840; renovated 1970

The enterprising attorney Francis Q. McHugh, who built six substantial brick buildings in this area in the 1840s and 1850s, constructed a double tenement on this site in about 1840. The house has brick details common to the area, but particularly noteworthy are the cast-iron grilles set into the dogtoothed brick parapet, featuring a palmetto motif rather than the formal Greek anthemion design. Saved in the Ansonborough Project, the building in the 1960s had no plumbing and only the barest wiring. The purchasers from the Foundation removed partitions between the two dwellings and converted the former double tenement into one substantial house. On the interior Greek Revival plaster cornices, ceiling medallions, and black marble mantels add distinction. Still the occupant in 1861, McHugh was also the builder of numerous rental properties in Harleston Village.

23 WENTWORTH STREET, JAMES J. JEFFORDS HOUSE

Constructed circa 1843; restored 1966

James Jeffords, a planter, built the house at 23 Wentworth Street as his personal town residence in the mid-nineteenth century. Jeffords's detailed stucco single house with corner quoins and stone window heads and sills stands apart from its eastern neighbor. Archibald Speers acquired his property next door at *21 Wentworth Street* as a vacant lot in 1845 and sold the site by 1848 with "a new brick dwelling and outbuilding." The houses are similarly scaled yet achieve a degree of individuality from their differing facades.

33 WENTWORTH STREET, WILLIAM PROCTOR HOUSE

Constructed circa 1840

Peter Desmerinese Jr. bought this lot after the fire of 1838 but sold it, with only the foundations of a building remaining, to William Proctor, an accountant with various mercantile firms. From 1849 to 1867 Proctor resided in the two-story, brick single house he completed on the site.

38 WENTWORTH STREET, WILLIAM C. MCELHERAN HOUSE

Constructed circa 1847

McElheran's property was purchased in 1860 by C. D. Franke and Ferdinand Benedict. Their company constructed gun carriages for the Confederacy on this site and adjacent properties. The Franke warehouse complex south of this property between Church and Meeting Streets was acquired several decades later, and the principal carriage-making operation was moved to that location. This property has returned to residential use in recent years.

43 WENTWORTH STREET, ST. ANDREW'S LUTHERAN CHURCH

Constructed circa 1840; interior altered 1903, 1936, 1977, 1989

St. Andrew's Lutheran Church

The Wentworth Street Methodist Protestant Church, originally completed on this site in 1834, was rebuilt after the fire of 1838 in the Greek Revival style. The congregation that presently meets here is the result of a post–Civil War merger of the original church with the Zion Evangelical Lutheran Church, then on Morris Street. The congregation of St. Andrew's Lutheran Church repaired the building's shell damage and continued its expansion with the completion in 1894 of a new Romanesque Revival Sunday school building with

Early-twentieth-century view of the old Sunday school building, St. Andrew's Lutheran Church

crenellated steeple. The main church building features a fairly typical Greek Revival portico, divided from the street by tall wrought-iron gates. The body of the building is decorated with pilasters dividing the bays of its side walls. The church's interior was extensively redecorated in 1908 with a refurbished, apsidal chancel (which contains a painting of Christ's Ascension, a copy of Gottlieb Peter Berman's painting of a century before), an arch with extensive plaster decoration, stenciled and frescoed walls, and stained glass windows. Much of the plasterwork in the arch and the painted decorations were removed in the late-1930s and the church's interior was simplified. The old Sunday school building had been removed a few years earlier and replaced by the present brick Colonial Revival style building. St. Andrew's also holds title to the two-story brick 1840s single house next door at *35 Wentworth Street*, used as an archive building.

46 WENTWORTH STREET, GEORGE PRATT TENEMENT

Constructed circa 1850

This narrow one-bay building originally made up a small part of a larger structure with similarly engaged pilasters and tripartite windows. Built as a triple tenement by George Pratt some years after the 1838 fire, a brick archway ran through the tenements just east of the surviving structure to a rear courtyard with several outbuildings. A subsequent owner sold the property in 1863 to Charleston real estate baron A. J. Salinas, who owned it until his death. It was held in Salinas's estate until the years after the earthquake of 1886. The larger portion of the building was demolished in the 1950s.

60 WENTWORTH STREET, CENTENARY METHODIST CHURCH

Constructed 1841–42; renovated 1911, 1953

Edward Brickell White, architect

Edward B. White designed one of Charleston's most chaste Greek Revival buildings for the congregation of Second Baptist Church in 1841–42. Some believe that the giant-order portico exemplifies the challenge to White to compete with the K. K. Beth Elohim Synagogue one block to the south. Lamenting the placement of the doors insisted upon by the building committee, an anonymous critic wrote an essay in the newspaper pointing out its "flawed" design, and a response by the architect indicated his own lament as well. At war's end the Wentworth Street congregation merged with Citadel Square Baptist and endeavored to sell their church buildings.

Contemporaneously, black members of Trinity Methodist Church left that congregation when offered membership after the war on the condition that they continue to worship in the gallery. After starting a church under the leadership of a New England minister and beginning services at Avery Normal Institute, the leaders negotiated to purchase the Wentworth Street building for $20,000. The requirement that the funds be paid in gold by a specified date nearly ended the transaction, but the congregation was aided in securing the gold by a Trinity member and the wealthy Charleston banker George W. Williams. The church was extensively repaired after the hurricane of 1911 and renovated in 1953. Its congregation has included some of Charleston's most important African Americans, including the late civil rights leader Septima Poinsett Clark.

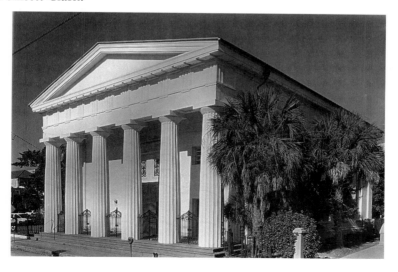

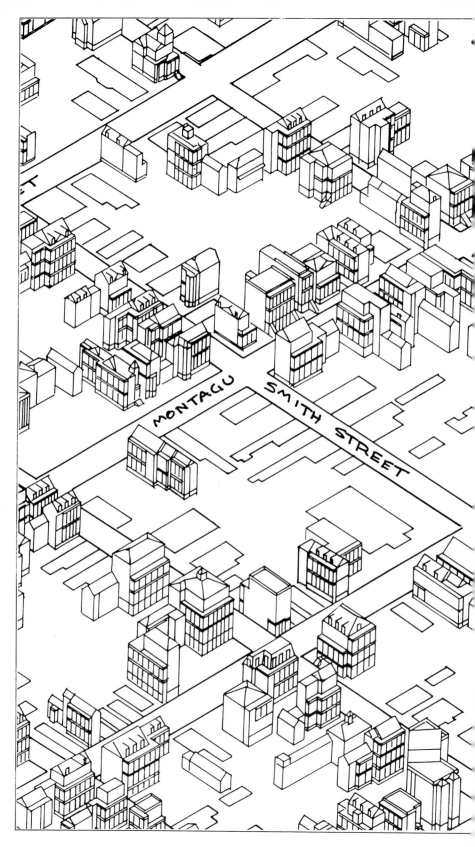

7

THE VILLAGE OF HARLESTON

Intellectuals and Entrepreneurs

*A*fter Ansonborough, this is Charleston's earliest suburb. Harleston Village was created from land originally granted to Henry Hughes and John Coming, first mate on the ship *Carolina*. Affra Harleston Coming, John Coming's powerful widow, deeded seventeen acres in the southeastern portion of this tract to the parish of St. Philip as a glebe, while the northeastern portion became known as the Free School Lands (eventually the site of the College of Charleston). The neighborhood today includes these two components, as well as a portion of the Mazyck lands south of Beaufain Street (included in this book in chapter 5, the "Commercial and Public Life" section) and Wragg's Pasture, bound by St. Philip, King, Calhoun, and Beaufain Streets.

In 1770 Mrs. Coming's nephew John Harleston, who also owned Bluff Plantation on the Cooper River and who had inherited much of the remaining Coming tract, subdivided it into lots along streets named for

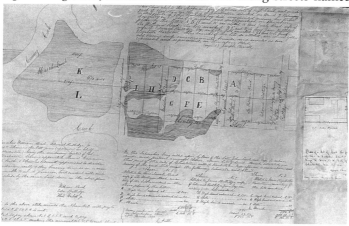

Plat showing subdivision of the remaining lands of John Harleston, 1795

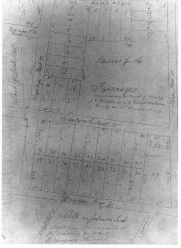

Plat of glebe lands and parsonage, early 1800s

important contemporary men, several of whom were associated with the cause of American liberty: William Pitt, the defender of American rights in the Stamp Act crisis; leaders of the South Carolina assembly, including John Rutledge, Thomas Lynch, and Christopher Gadsden; Hector Beringer de Beaufain, customs collector and member of the Governor's Council; Lt. William Bull; and royal governor Sir Charles Greville Montagu. Lots were slowly purchased and developed in Harleston, as in the glebe lands. The latter was broken down into lots in 1770 and further divided with the opening of Glebe Street in 1797. Most of the lots remained in the hands of the parish and were initially developed under long-term leases, due to the will of Affra Harleston. The will required that the church keep the land forever. Initially, the leases ran for twenty-one or thirty-one years and required that a lessee build a house of a certain size and within a specified period of time. Retained by the parishes of St. Philip's and St. Michael's after the Revolution, some ground leases in the area continue, although most of the lots were long ago sold.

The glebe lands contain several pre-Revolutionary dwellings, including the Minister's (later Bishop's) House on Glebe Street and 89 Wentworth, part of a mid-eighteenth-century double tenement with its original jerkin head roof. But only a few other structures built before 1775 remain in the Harleston Village area. The irregularity of tidal creeks and marshes provided a hindrance to quick residential development of Harleston. In the late-eighteenth century, however, the western edge of the lands was obtained by Thomas Bennett Sr., who joined with the wealthy mechanic Daniel Cannon and used the power of tides in large ponds to establish lumber mills and eventually rice mills. Several decades later the Bennett family, through business connection and marriage, became allied with Jonathan Lucas Jr., whose father had first introduced steam-powered rice mills to South Carolina. By the 1840s, with their West Point Mill on the edge of Harleston Village and the Bennett Mill on the Ansonborough side, as well as various plantation mills, the Bennett-Lucas clan controlled the milling of more than 40 percent of the rough rice from the plantation districts around Charleston.

The Bennetts were responsible for the construction of numerous large houses in the neighborhood and were associated with 113 Ashley Avenue, 104 Bull Street, and especially the Governor Thomas Bennett House at 69 Barre Street. Originally constructed in the manner of the Bennett residences, the former Theodore Gaillard House at 60 Montagu Street was embellished by successive owners, including Jefferson Bennett in the 1850s.

Throughout the early-nineteenth century lots were divided from larger tracts, and dwellings, mostly of a single-house plan, were constructed. In the 1840s and 1850s the neighborhood experienced a boom with the construction of many residences in Greek Revival, Gothic, and Italianate styles, often based on the side-hall, double-parlor plan. One of the few rows of town houses in Charleston, Bee's Row, was constructed on Bull Street. Churches such as Grace Episcopal, built on the St. Michael's portion of the former glebe lands, and Bethel Methodist, constructed with a slightly flawed Doric portico, marked the north and south boundaries of the neighborhood.

The neighborhood's character, while industrial on its western edge, owed much to its diverse population. While the college attracted a small professorial group, Charleston's antebellum intelligentsia lived here as well, including the essayist and poet Hugh Swinton Legare, the author William Rivers, and the progressive leader Christopher Gustavus Memminger. Meanwhile, Coming Street became the most popular residential address for Charleston's free black or "mulatto elite" population in the years before 1861. The Johnson family, daughter and son-in-law of the wealthiest African American planter in the state and themselves pros-

View of Cannon's windmill by Charles Fraser, 1796

perous free persons, lived at 7 Coming Street. Richard Holloway, a prominent carpenter, built several houses, including 96 Smith Street and 221 Calhoun Street, while he resided on Beaufain Street. Morris Brown, a free black minister and later bishop of the A. M. E. Church, built a house at 94 Smith Street before fleeing to Philadelphia during the closing of the city's black churches after discovery of the Denmark Vesey plot. Vesey is believed to have lived at 56 Bull Street, but the present house appears to be largely of later construction. After the war numerous black churches were founded in the area, as was the Avery Normal Institute. With the subdivision of large lots, small houses and tenements in courts crowded the once spacious quality of Harleston lots. The great Bennett Mill pond was gradually filled, allowing the extension of Rutledge and Ashley (Lynch) Avenues and the creation of Bennett Street, which even now is prone to flooding at high tide.

The filling of the mill pond provided the city with an opportunity to develop Cannon Park. New lots were made available along this park, and redevelopment occurred around the new public space created around a tidal pond to the south, renamed Colonial Lake. Postbellum industrialists, following the lead of the progressive mayor William Ashmead Courtenay, often lived in Harleston Village, either retrofitting old houses with new Victorian detailing or building new residences.

The largest mansion built in Charleston after the War Between the States was that of the cotton and phosphate merchant Francis Rodgers. Rodgers, a native of North Carolina, built the tallest house on the highest point of land in the city. The evolution of the area has continued in the twentieth century with the filling of additional areas after World War II along the Ashley River and the expansion of the College of Charleston throughout the old glebe lands and into much of the rest of the eastern end of the Village of Harleston. The college has restored many buildings, closed streets such as Green Street within the campus, and demolished some houses along St. Philip and George Streets.

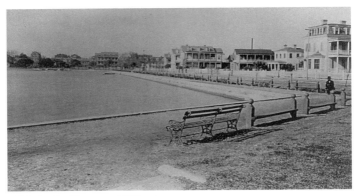

Colonial Lake, looking east, 1890s view

55 ASHLEY AVENUE, BAKER HOSPITAL BUILDING
Constructed 1912; rehabilitated 1983–84

The noted Charleston physician Dr. Archibald Baker Sr. and Dr. Lawrence Craig founded Baker Hospital in 1912, the same year in which this building was completed. The four-story brick structure combines elements of Italian Renaissance and Mission styles in its design. This was Charleston's first modern private hospital, specializing in surgical and obstetrical patients. With the move of Baker Hospital to North Charleston, this edifice was rehabilitated as residential condominiums.

Baker Hospital, 55 Ashley Avenue, soon after construction

61 ASHLEY AVENUE, RICHARD PEYTON HOUSE
Constructed 1803–07

Richard Peyton, a merchant who kept an office at the Custom House, built this dwelling on a site purchased in 1803 from Thomas Corbett, a Harleston relative. Tradition holds that the house, set far from the street behind a paneled stucco wall and front wooden fence, was intended to be the dependency building for a larger residence which was never completed. Nonetheless, the quality of the existing structure, particularly the surviving Neoclassical woodwork, indicates the building was constructed as a principal residence. A stable and carriage house probably dating from 1830–50 stands on the Beaufain Street side. Passing through a series of owners, the house belonged in the 1840s to Robert Martin, owner of *16 Charlotte Street*. After being sold in 1879 to the Bruns family, the building underwent substantial renovation with the addition of a double-tiered octagonal front bay and two-over-two windows. A Victorian style parterre probably dates from the mid-nineteenth century and incorporates beds in the shapes of hearts, periwinkles, and ovals.

69 ASHLEY AVENUE, ELI GEDDINGS HOUSE

Constructed after 1852; renovated 1992

A Charleston physician acquired this lot before 1852 and built a three-story wooden single house with a flat roof and parapet, probably just prior to the War Between the States. After passing to Anna Marscher by 1879, Victorian changes, including two-over-two windows, were carried out on the site. The building was extensively renovated in 1992, and additional units were added to the rear of the lot.

75 AND 79 ASHLEY AVENUE, DANIEL FAIRCHILD HOUSES

Constructed circa 1842

The present dwelling at 79 Ashley Avenue is the second house built by Daniel Fairchild to stand on this lot. A previous dwelling, a three-story weatherboarded single house, was constructed shortly after acquisition of the lot in 1830. This house was shifted in the 1840s to make way for the present three-story stuccoed brick residence. The original house now at 75 Ashley Avenue retains its exterior features including a unique door architrave, which consists of Ionic pilasters supporting a carved wooden frieze featuring Grecian style acanthus leaves. This structure has a near match in the flat-roofed single house at *73 Ashley Avenue*. The latter dwelling, however, has shorter piazzas, and its Greek Revival door screen lacks the decorative lintel of its neighbor.

79 Ashley Avenue was also built in the single-house style, with red sandstone window lintels and sills, and fine stucco detailing including banded trim surrounding the arched staircase windows, quoins, and belt courses. Tradition holds that the body of the house remained as exposed brick until the turn of the century. The house ap-

75 Ashley Avenue

pears to have been built and jointly used by the Fairchilds and the James Hamlin family until 1908. An earlier brick dependency remains. It formerly housed the kitchen and is visible along Wentworth Street.

76 ASHLEY AVENUE, JOHN HUME SIMONS HOUSE
Constructed circa 1855

The children of wealthy Santee River rice planters, John Hume Simons and his wife (and cousin) Mary Hume Lucas, built this enormous three-and-a-half-story brick town house at the corner of Wentworth Street and Ashley Avenue by 1855. The house follows a double-house plan and retains Greek Revival plaster marble mantels, fourteen-foot ceilings, and many of its original features. Its Flemish bond exterior has fine white lime pointing. Pressed-metal pedimented window heads were added to the street elevations in the late-nineteenth century. The closed gable roof has a lunette window surmounting two smaller windows, while wide pedimented dormers ornament each side of the roof on the north and south. The house was used during the siege of the city of 1864 for the congregation of Saint Mary's Roman Catholic Church. Remaining a single-family residence throughout its history, the building was purchased in 1961 by Mr. and Mrs. Emmet Robinson, founders of the Footlight Players, Charleston's local theater group.

81 ASHLEY AVENUE, HERIOT-GRIMBALL HOUSE
Constructed 1852–60

Catherine Heriot's trust estate acquired this large corner lot from Albert Elfe in the late-1850s. Shortly afterward construction began on a large two-and-a-half-story side-hall-plan house on a raised basement with a fenced garden on the south. The structure stands on a masonry foundation, and the two-story wood portion is surmounted by a closed gable with a tripartite window and shaded by a double-tiered Tuscan-columned piazza. In the late-nineteenth century Italianate brackets were apparently added to the cornice of all elevations. The house became the property of Mrs. M. A. Grimball by 1872 and eventually was owned by her son and her daughters, who held onto the site until 1902. Twentieth-century alterations include the enclosure of the piazza's ground story and the addition of rear bays on its other tiers. Elfe apparently kept the lot to the north at *83 Ashley Avenue* for himself. Before the War Between the States, he constructed a two-and-a-half-story Charleston single house, which also has a double-tiered side piazza. In the 1880s or 1890s the gable roof was changed to a full mansard roof with decoratively bracketed dormers and slate shingles.

90 ASHLEY AVENUE, JOSEPH GLOVER HOUSE

Constructed before 1838; renovated circa 1881–90

Originally completed as a fairly typical masonry single house, the dwelling at 90 Ashley Avenue set back from the street was altered with significant Victorian changes in the nineteenth century. Dr. Joseph Glover built this house on a lot purchased by his trustee in 1825 from the Harleston family, apparently using the building as a rental. At the time of Glover's death in 1838, Edward Simons resided in this house, although it was left to Glover's son. After ownership by the Chisolm family in the 1840s, the property passed to the Keith family, who lived at *96 Ashley Avenue* and rented this building to Amelia Parker, a free person of color. In the 1880s the house became the property of the Toale family, owners of a building-and-supply company on Hayne Street and a sash-and-blind factory on Ashley Avenue and Beaufain Street. Although the original house and the dependency were joined before the war with a hyphen addition (a practice normally followed after 1865), Queen Anne style changes were made to the front facade, including the semicircular bay window and the patterned triangular panel in the top of the gable in the surmounting finial.

91 ASHLEY AVENUE, FRANCES CARRERE ROBERTSON HOUSE
Constructed circa 1898

A finely crafted example of the Queen Anne style of Victorian architecture, this two-and-a-half-story dwelling was built by the wife of the president of an insurance company in the 1890s. A cross gable with a flat one-story bay surmounting an engaged portico attaches to the principal roof of this side-hall-plan house. A double-tiered piazza with square columns adjoins the south end of the dwelling and is accessed by shuttered French doors from the principal rooms.

95 ASHLEY AVENUE, MAYOR WILLIAM A. COURTENAY HOUSE
Constructed before 1852

Mayor William Ashmead Courtenay purchased this three-and-a-half-story Charleston single house from a trustee acting for Henry Sterling Lebby and his wife, Susan Ann, in 1870. Theodore Jervey probably built the original Greek Revival style house in the 1840s, conveying it to Lebby in the mid-1850s. Courtenay, who came to office in 1879, served as mayor of Charleston at a crucial time in its history. While modernizing city government, he greatly improved the area with new parks, fire and police stations, and a renovated city hall. He envisioned a quality expansion of the city

487

into the northern portion of the peninsula and worked for its recovery after the hurricane of 1885 and the earthquake of 1886. Basically a Greek Revival single house in form, the structure has triple-tiered piazzas that once overlooked a large garden, which was subdivided in the twentieth century. Although the piazzas and the pilastered door screen survive, the front facade of the dwelling was renovated after the earthquake of 1886 with a two-story projecting bay and triple front windows on both levels. The parapeted brick gable was reduced to create a bracketed roof overhang in the Italianate manner. Although rehabilitated many years ago as an apartment, the original separate kitchen dependency survives at *51½-A Montagu Street.*

96 ASHLEY AVENUE, THEODORE GAILLARD HOUSE

Constructed circa 1816

The well-to-do merchant and planter who built *60 Montagu Street* constructed this as his new residence by 1816. The Gaillard House presents an unusually wide elevation and large closed-ended gable to the street. The two-and-a-half-story wood dwelling with beaded weatherboards and a double-tiered south piazza stands on a high stuccoed basement. A lunette window caps the tympanum of the modillioned west gable. A modified double house on the interior, the dwelling retains its late-Federal and Regency style woodwork. After Gaillard's death the property was sold to Dr. Willis Wilkinson, whose daughter married Dr. Christopher G. Memminger, secretary of the treasury of the Confederacy and Charleston advocate of public education. In 1849, however, Dr. Paul Trapier Keith, a priest of St. Michael's Episcopal Church, purchased the property.

110 ASHLEY AVENUE, THAYER-LYNAH HOUSE

Constructed circa 1881

Francis J. Pelzer, a rising capitalist in postbellum Charleston, owned this site sometime before transferring it to William Thayer by 1881. Thayer subsequently built this house. After Thayer's death the property transferred to Arthur Lynah, who owned it until after World War I. An original late-nineteenth-century wooden fence, consisting of simple pickets between columnar posts, surrounds the property. This type of fence, formerly the most common in Charleston's uptown neighborhoods, has generally disappeared.

129–135 ASHLEY AVENUE, HALSEY LUMBER COMPANY HOUSES

Constructed 1910–18

These Queen Anne style dwellings were built by the Halsey family, who acquired the Bennett Mill property in the late-nineteenth century. With the filling of the mill pond in the 1880s and 1890s, new lots were created for the construction of dwellings. 133 Ashley Avenue was sold to David B. Hyer, one of Charleston's leading early-twentieth-century architects, who probably designed his own house at the time he opened his practice in 1912.

69 BARRE STREET, GOV. THOMAS BENNETT HOUSE

 *Constructed circa 1822; restored 1988*

This is the ambitious house of one of Charleston's wealthiest and most progressive antebellum residents. Thomas Bennett Jr. followed his father and namesake in the operation of the family's lumber and rice milling industries that surrounded this house. Although the vast mill pond with its floodgates and causeways, the lumber mill buildings, and the manager's house have disappeared, the Bennett residence survives as a testament to the family's prominence. Bennett served as governor of South Carolina from 1820 to 1822 as well as various terms in the General Assembly, and he continued to urge industrial and social progress for his native state. A curving marble stair approaches the raised door architrave leading to the south-facing piazza entry of the Bennett House. This architrave and the main door architrave within the piazza feature semicircular fanlights and elaborate surrounds with pilasters and modillioned cornices. Pediments with lunette windows project from the roof on the north and south elevations, while the closed front end gable features a Venetian (Palladian) window. The splendid exterior woodwork, created from wood produced in the Bennett mills and probably by their own carpenters, hints at the exceptional interior, which boasts a two-story free-flying staircase, marble mantelpieces, and elaborate plaster cornices and ceiling medallions.

In the late-nineteenth century E. L. Halsey became the owner of the remaining lumber mills as well as the house. After serving various uses after its sale by the Halseys following World War I, the building was restored by the Roper Foundation in 1988. Subsequently, the garden was renewed with a new plan and the kitchen and slave-quarters dependencies to the west were rehabilitated as guest accommodations. The remarkable wooden fence, with its columnar post topped by spherical finials, has remained, as have the wooden gates with a guilloche decoration. Formerly Lucas Street, the street name was changed to Barre Street when the thoroughfare was extended to Broad Street in the 1950s.

22 BEAUFAIN STREET, MEMMINGER AUDITORIUM

Constructed circa 1938

Albert Simons, architect

Scholars of Robert Mills have recognized the debt of the design of this school and civic auditorium to the work of Charleston's most famous native-born architect, particularly because of the inset Doric columns of the portico. Plans for restoration of this important classic theater, long a venue for Charleston musical and civic events, remain uncertain.

64–66 BEAUFAIN STREET, FRANCIS QUINLAN MCHUGH TENEMENTS

Constructed circa 1850–53; rehabilitated mid-1980s

The attorney Francis Q. McHugh purchased a parcel on the north side of Beaufain Street extending from Coming Street to Kirkland Lane. He intended to build speculative dwellings such as those he had constructed at *22–24 Wentworth Street* in Ansonborough. Apparently McHugh sold 68 Beaufain to the mason Thomas Divine with the provision that he complete a dwelling on the lot as well as buildings for McHugh that were already under construction. The two McHugh Houses were completed as three-story stuccoed single houses with flat roofs and simple parapets. Double-tiered piazzas with Tuscan columns shade the south facades of each structure. McHugh sold 64 Beaufain to Thomas N. Gadsden, a slave broker who owned numerous investment properties. Divine completed a two-story single house with similar detailing by 1853. It was later conveyed to Theodore Huchet, a merchant of Santo Domingan descent. Huchet or perhaps a subsequent purchaser added pressed tin window hoods and a surmounting entablature, as well as a wooden overhang in similar style.

70 BEAUFAIN STREET, CATHERINE MASHBURN HOUSE

Constructed circa 1868–71

The Divine-Huchet property was apparently subdivided by the 1860s when a small dwelling was constructed at 70 Beaufain Street, at the corner of Kirkland Lane, which is an alley running north toward Wentworth Street. Catherine Mashburn apparently built this small, gabled, two-story house with a front piazza between 1868 and 1871. By the 1880s Thomas Finlay was using the ground story as a grocery store.

88 Beaufain Street

86–88 BEAUFAIN STREET, KATE MCCLOY HOUSES

Constructed circa 1890

Following the earthquake of 1886, Kate McCloy purchased these properties, including the site of a brick house owned by the attorney B. Pressley Smith that was listed as "badly wrecked" by the disaster. McCloy built a large two-and-a-half-story, side-hall-plan house with a front closed gable, double-tiered bay window, and two-story piazza at 88 Beaufain Street. Her family built a smaller house of similar plan with an Italianate doorway at 86 Beaufain Street and retained it until 1910.

89 BEAUFAIN STREET, WILLIAM G. STEELE HOUSE

Constructed 1815–19

William Steele, a lumber merchant, built this late-Neoclassical, three-story stuccoed brick single house with a cross-gabled roof in the early-nineteenth century on parcels that were originally part of the Mazyck lands. The house is notable for its elegant detailing, especially the finely carved marble piazza door surround with delicate brackets and the lunette window positioned in the cross gable of the house. Duncan Nathaniel Ingraham was a later owner of the house. He achieved an international reputation for diplomacy, and after resigning from the U.S. Navy at the beginning of the Civil War, he supervised construction of two ironclads for the Confederacy.

91 BEAUFAIN STREET, STEELE-MOOD HOUSE

Constructed circa 1820–30

This two-and-a-half-story single house that sits at some distance from the street on a large lot—which once stretched more than 200 feet in depth—was probably built by William Steele, owner of *89 Beaufain*

Street. Steele conveyed this lot in trust to his wife in 1819. When her trustee initially sold it in 1838, the present late-Federal style house was already constructed. Standing two full stories on a raised basement, the building has two bays of nine-over-nine windows on each level of the front elevation and is surmounted by a closed gable roof with a flush boarded tympanum. The delicate columns of the double-tiered piazza are also a key to the date of construction. The merchant and silversmith William Mood purchased the property in two different conveyances in 1840 and 1851, selling the whole to Robert Alexander in 1856.

106 BEAUFAIN STREET, CARRIE STEINMEYER HOUSE
Constructed circa 1880

A female member of the Steinmeyer family, owners of extensive real estate in this area, built this simple two-story side-hall-plan house just before 1880. A banded parapet shelters the house as well as the double-tiered, Tuscan-columned piazza. A simple Italianate style doorway adds the only decorative element to the three-bay facade. Mary Marshall apparently built a similar dwelling to the east at *104 Beaufain Street* at approximately the same time. A gable roof and two-over-two windows are the major differences in this contemporary dwelling, sold in 1881 to Johanna Matthiessen.

108 BEAUFAIN STREET, JOHN STEINMEYER HOUSE
Constructed 1840–42

This imposing dwelling, originally of single-house style, was built in 1840–42 by John Steinmeyer, a successful lumber merchant, on land that was originally part of Harleston Green. Gov. Thomas Bennett acquired the property in 1842 for his grand-

daughters, Mary and Celia Campbell. The property had come full circle because the Bennett family sold it to Steinmeyer originally. The Campbell sisters were responsible for enlarging the dwelling, transforming it from a single house to a double house by adding an extension on the east side. The sisters also had the cypress exterior cut to resemble stone, a process called rustication. In 1904 Mary Campbell willed the house to the Presbyterian Church, creating a home for "Presbyterian and Huguenot women of gentle birth and small means." The house was returned to a single-family residence by a descendant of Governor Bennett in 1971.

110 BEAUFAIN STREET, ROBERT SHANDS SMITH HOUSE

Constructed circa 1840

During the 1830s land on the north side of what is now Colonial Lake was sold in parcels by the planter Robert Hume. The parcel on which 110 Beaufain Street and its neighbor to the west stand was purchased by Whiteford Smith. 110 Beaufain Street was transferred to Robert Shands Smith, a commission merchant, who built a three-and-a-half-story, scored stucco single house. The dwelling is a classic Charleston single house with restrained Greek Revival lines, a tripartite window in the front gable end, and double-tiered piazza with a flat roof. A modern addition off the third floor allows for another bathroom. Stuccoed belt coursing separates the second and third floors.

112 BEAUFAIN STREET, WHITEFORD SMITH HOUSE

Constructed 1837–40

This Greek Revival style double house with a double-tiered piazza, floor-to-ceiling windows, and unfluted Doric columns was built by Whiteford Smith around 1840 as the popularity of classicism began to sweep the Lowcountry. The house, faced with long-leaf pine weatherboarding, is topped by a hipped roof and rests on a partial basement. The double house plan is slightly unusual in that the two front rooms are nearly twice the size of the two rear rooms. The lumber merchant Joseph Ward Mott acquired the property before selling it to James Gray, master in equity, in 1849. The 1886 earthquake damage survey lists the property in good condition with the exception of the chimneys. Recent owners discovered the remains of an original painted ceiling.

118 BEAUFAIN STREET, JOHN HENRY STEINMEYER HOUSE

Constructed circa 1840s

Nathan Nathans, a dry-goods merchant, conveyed this lot at the west end of Beaufain Street to the lumber mill operator John Steinmeyer, who soon afterward built a two-story weatherboarded and stuccoed brick dwelling on it. A two-story rear extension, faced with wide clapboards, was added shortly after construction. Although small enough to be a dependency, the house may have served as a temporary home to the family while a larger house at *4 Gadsden Street* and three other Steinmeyer houses were under construction. The 1852 city ward book assessed Steinmeyer's mill at the end of the street and the three brick buildings together, describing 118 Beaufain Street as "kitchen only on lot."

2–8 BULL STREET, E. M. HACKER TENEMENTS

Constructed 1907

These identical two-and-a-half-story wood houses with front porches and pedimented entries were built by E. M.

Hacker as an investment in the early-twentieth century. These very simple late–Queen Anne houses boast little decoration save their porches and secondary gables projecting from the principal roof gables and incorporating polygonal bays on the first floor.

12 BULL STREET, HUGH P. CAMERON HOUSE
Constructed circa 1851; altered 1890s

Separated from the Blacklock House property in 1849 and purchased by the architect Edward B. White, the lot subsequently became the property of Hugh P. Cameron, a King Street crockery merchant. The two-story house is constructed of Charleston-made brick laid in a Flemish bond with stone lintels above its principal front windows and is faced by a double-tiered piazza. Late-Victorian and Colonial Revival changes made to the house after its acquisition in 1892 by David Benchner include the masonry piers and coping as well as the front gate, with his cast-iron initials. Other changes include the Colonial Revival French doors on the front windows, probably replacing Greek Revival triple sash, and substantial interior changes such as a Minton-style floor in the entry hall. Used at various times for several different programs at the College of Charleston, it currently houses the college's program in historic preservation.

15 BULL STREET, TRENHOLM-SMALL HOUSE
Constructed circa 1863–71

George A. Trenholm, wealthy Charleston blockade runner and secretary of the treasury of the Confederacy, probably built this two-and-a-half-story wood dwelling in the late-1860s. The house displays a mix of Italianate and Greek Revival style elements. A columned piazza with an arcade formed by jigsaw-cut trim stands on the front elevation of the three-bay facade, which features a closed gable roof with Italianate brackets and a central Venetian (Palladian) window. Trenholm sold this house in the early-1870s to Jacob Small, who also purchased *11 Bull Street*. Helena Kessler Eggers constructed the two-and-a-half-story dwelling at 11 Bull Street by 1876. The building has a deep entablature, with Italianate style brackets, that serves as the base for a Second Empire style mansard roof. A double-tiered bay further ornaments the front facade. The west-facing piazzas were enclosed in the early-twentieth century, when the upper sashes of the windows were replaced and other alterations were made.

18 BULL STREET, WILLIAM BLACKLOCK HOUSE

L *Constructed 1800; restored 1973*

Completed in 1800 for one of Charleston's wealthy British merchants, the William Blacklock House represents a suburban retreat from the bustle of Charleston's mercantile district. Previously Blacklock had been in partnership with the Scots merchant Adam Tunno in one of the largest import-export businesses on East Bay Street. In plan the house resembles Charleston's Georgian period double-pile houses, such as the Miles Brewton House (1769) and the William Gibbes House (1772), but the exterior and interior details are strictly Neoclassical. Blacklock's back buildings were designed in the Gothic taste. Blacklock's estate inventory of its room usage and early contents, taken on May 14, 1816, provides one of the most thorough descriptions of a Neoclassical period town house. The first floor consisted of the dining room, the parlor, a back bed chamber, and a servants' room in the northeast corner, located closest to the back buildings. The second floor contained the drawing room, two additional bed chambers, and a nursery.

Vaulted stair hall ceiling, William Blacklock House

24 BULL STREET, BENJAMIN LUCAS HOUSE
Constructed circa 1858; rehabilitated 1969

Benjamin Lucas, a builder or contractor who also served as city building inspector in the 1860s, bought this lot in 1858 five years after it was carved out of the Blacklock property. Constructed in the plantation style version of the Charleston single-house plan with double-tiered piazzas facing the street, this three-and-a-half-story stuccoed house has fine mid-nineteenth-century decoration with stone window lintels and sills and corner quoining. The house passed to female members of the Lucas family in the 1880s and served for more than forty years as the Lucas Academy, a school for young ladies. The sisters probably added the substantial rear addition at this time. For much of the twentieth century the house deteriorated in its use as eleven apartments. A 1969 rehabilitation by Richard Jenrette, of New York and Charleston, converted it into five units.

43 BULL STREET, JOHN C. SIMONS HOUSE
Constructed circa 1850

A deep lot allows this three-story dwelling to have a substantial setback from Bull Street, providing a degree of privacy. Built by the King Street merchant John Simons, the three-bay house is ornamented by extensive ironwork and a bracketed cornice. A false extension of the facade masks a triple-tiered piazza placed on the side of the building and fosters a sense of privacy.

Late-nineteenth-century photo of 43 Bull Street

48 BULL STREET, EMANUEL ANTONIO HOUSE
Constructed circa 1786–1808; additions 1813, after 1852

This masonry dwelling with a one-story front piazza; a two-story, six-bay facade; and a hipped roof with a projecting pedi-

ment has long interested neighborhood residents and Charleston historians seeking its origins. Recent research has shown that it began as a two- or three-room dwelling of the post-Revolutionary period constructed before 1808 by Isaac Holmes, a Johns Island planter, for Emanuel Antonio, a Charleston merchant. Conveyed by Antonio in 1808 to Peter Suau, the house and parcel of Antonio's original lot passed through six different owners before its acquisition in 1816 by the Hamilton family, who retained it until 1837. It was then sold to Samuel Seyle, who lived here until 1856. The house became numerous apartments at the beginning of World War II, and an additional building for more apartments was constructed. Since 1989 the house has undergone significant restoration.

51 BULL STREET, HOLY TRINITY REFORMED EPISCOPAL CHURCH
Constructed circa 1880

This congregation was formed as small groups of African Americans left the Protestant Episcopal Church to form the Reformed Episcopal Church. In 1875 this congregation was organized under its present name, and in 1876 the site at 51 Bull Street was acquired. Construction was begun by 1880, and the church was built in three weeks for the cost of $1,000.

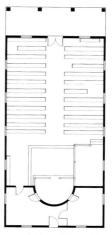

Measured plan, 51 Bull Street

52 BULL STREET, SAMUEL SEYLE HOUSE
Constructed circa 1838

In the late-1830s the owner of the plantation style house at *48 Bull Street* built this two-story single house for his son. Altered in the late-nineteenth century, the house now boasts a deep entablature with Queen Anne style brackets and Victorian turned columns on the side piazza.

54 BULL STREET
Constructed circa 1870–90

This is a typical frame single house of the late-nineteenth century built for working-class whites and, particularly, the freedmen who crowded into this area of Harleston Village after the Civil War. Large lots such as the one at *50 Bull Street* were increasingly subdivided. Even at this late date the pattern for kitchen dependencies remained fixed with middling single houses. This example retains a two-story outbuilding with only one room per floor.

56 BULL STREET, DENMARK VESEY HOUSE
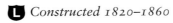 *Constructed 1820–1860*

Tradition holds that this is the residence of Denmark Vesey, leader of an aborted slave insurrection in 1822. The single-story frame building with vernacular characteristics follows the scheme of "freedmen's cottages" built in postbellum Charleston but may contain an earlier structure. Vesey, a native of the West Indies brought to Charleston as a slave, purchased his freedom in 1800 with money from a lottery prize. Vesey went on to become a carpenter, which left him in good financial standing. Accused of corresponding with Santo Domingan revolutionaries and planning to burn Charleston, Vesey and thirty-four other African Americans were hanged. Continuing documentation on this site may affirm the relationship of the front portion of the present building to Denmark Vesey.

Measured plan, 56 Bull Street

66 BULL STREET, JOHN CART HOUSE
Constructed circa 1819

John Cart, a prosperous fuel merchant dealing in lumber and coal, built this three-bay, two-and-a-half-story Charleston single

house nearly two decades after acquiring the lot through the will of his sister-in-law Ann Tighe. Although a number of Neoclassical decorations survive on the interior, only the beaded weatherboarding and the nine-over-nine windows on the piazza side evidence the construction date of the house. Greek Revival changes including the piazza and piazza door screen were probably added by Cart before his death in the 1840s. The house descended to Cart's daughter, and it then went through several owners and tenants. These included William Tarrant, who operated a school for boys in the house for almost twenty years; Mrs. E. A. St. Amand, a dancing teacher; Professor F. W. Ortmann, a music teacher; and, in the twentieth century, Walton Locke, a classical pianist.

76 BULL STREET, MATTHEWES-LEGARE HOUSE

Constructed circa 1813

This two-and-a-half-story plantation style dwelling wrapped by double-tiered piazzas was built by the vendue master and planter George Matthewes. Matthewes previously built *110 Rutledge Avenue* and lived on Wentworth Street until he moved to his new house at this address in 1813. After his death in 1815, the house was sold by his daughter to Mrs. Mary Swinton Legare. Her famous son, Hugh Swinton Legare, who was crippled, used this as his residence until his death in 1843. Educated in Paris and Edinburgh, Legare began the *Southern Review* while serving concurrently as a state legislator. He later served as ambassador to Brussels, congressman, U.S. attorney general, and U.S. secretary of state. At the time of his death he was being considered as a Whig presidential candidate for the election of 1884. The house passed in 1855 to Alexander Calder, ancestor of the artist with the same name, and it served as a Calder family residence until 1919. Much of the interior retains its Adamesque decoration, with the exception of a Regency style gray marble mantel in the front drawing room. Tradition holds that Legare kept quarters on the ground floor, where Charleston's literary figures of the antebellum period gathered.

96 BULL STREET, ISAAC BENNETT HOUSE

Constructed circa 1815; rehabilitated and restored mid-twentieth century

Detail of frieze, 96 Bull Street

This Federal style single house raised on a high foundation, with its one-story piazza accessed from a piazza screen and an ascending wooden staircase, retains some of the most unusual Neoclassical decoration in this area of Charleston. The main body of the house, with its black cypress weatherboarding with a beveled edge, terminates in a frieze and cornice with an Adamesque swag decoration. This same pattern can be found on the interior as well. The relationship of the builder, Isaac Bennett, to the family that owned the nearby mill remains a mystery. The house passed to the Shand family by the 1820s for income purposes and then to the Dawsons. In the mid-nineteenth century an additional bay was added to the rear of the building, copying the detailing of the original building. The piazza staircase and screen were altered a few decades later in the Italianate style. A two-story ell addition was put on the house in the mid-twentieth century.

99 BULL STREET, FRANCIS WARRINGTON DAWSON HOUSE

Constructed circa 1854; altered circa 1887; rehabilitated 1984

Frederick Richards, a prosperous merchant-tailor, owned and occupied the nucleus of this substantial masonry dwelling before the War Between the States. The British-born Francis Warrington Dawson purchased the dwelling in the 1870s at the same time he was forming part of the present-day *Post and Courier*. Dawson championed numerous liberal causes as a newspaper editor, including a ban on dueling, and diversification of the South Carolina economy. Dawson was influenced by Sarah Morgan, a Louisiana journalist, to champion woman's rights. In the late-1880s a Swiss governess in the Dawson household had an affair with a neighbor, Dr. Thomas McDow. In an altercation between Dawson and McDow, the editor was shot and killed. In one of Charleston's most sensational trials, McDow was acquitted and carried out of the courthouse on the shoulders of exuberant Charlestonians. Dawson probably added the Renaissance Revival style detailing to the house, including the double Corinthian columned front portico and the detailing on the polygonal bays on the east and west ends. The house was converted to apartments in the mid-twentieth century, and the double-tiered piazza at the rear has been enclosed with glass.

100 BULL STREET, MONPOEY-WILKES HOUSE

Constructed circa 1820

Honore Monpoey, a wealthy grocer, built a section of this two-and-a-half-story stuccoed brick house on a large lot that formerly stretched to the Bennett mill pond. Placed at a considerable distance from the street, the western part of the house was a typical Charleston single house in plan. He lived here until the 1850s, but after the Civil War the house passed through several merchant families. Monpoey purchased two plantations on the Ashley River in the 1830s and rose from shopkeeper to a member of Charleston's planter gentry. In 1894

Herman Wilkes bought the Bull Street property and probably was responsible for the Colonial Revival style addition with a hipped roof and wide front dormer to the eastern end, placing front piazzas across the entire structure.

101–109 BULL STREET, BEE'S ROW

Constructed circa 1853–54; partially restored and rehabilitated 1980s

Although built in 1853 by Sara Smith, probably with a contractor from the North, the row was taken over during the Civil War by William C. Bee, who owned a blockade-running firm. During the war the row was known as Bee's Block and was used partially as warehouses and stores. A small court running behind the buildings is today humorously called "Wasbee Range." These tall row houses resemble similar structures built in Savannah, Philadelphia, and Baltimore in the mid-nineteenth century. Terra-cotta decorations in the Italianate style with pedimented window heads and console-bracketed arch door surrounds were probably ordered from New England and resemble those on the original St. Johns (Mills House) Hotel at the corner of Queen and Meeting Streets. Although each house has been altered over the years, most retain their original plasterwork and Italianate style stone mantels. Each unit opens from the street onto an antefoyer and a foyer of an octagonal shape with niches intended for statuary. Sara Smith was the first to live on the row and seems to have built 101 Bull Street for her own residence.

104 BULL STREET, BENNETT-PRIOLEAU HOUSE

Constructed circa 1802

The noted builder-architect Thomas Bennett Sr. constructed this raised two-and-a-half-story Neoclassical style dwelling before March 1, 1802, when he sold it to

Henry Izard, who conveyed it to Nicholas Harleston. Similar in its weatherboarding to *96 Bull Street*, it also resembles *128 Bull Street* and the now-demolished *112 Bull Street* in its front-facing form. The house passed to the attorney Samuel Prioleau in 1818 and remained that family's residence until 1850. A double-tiered front piazza was probably added in the mid-nineteenth century. The Schirmer family owned the house through much of the twentieth century and reduced the front piazzas to the present double-tiered portico while retaining much of the interior Neoclassical decoration.

125 BULL STREET, AVERY RESEARCH CENTER FOR AFRICAN-AMERICAN HISTORY AND CULTURE

Constructed circa 1867

The Avery Normal Institute was established during the period of Reconstruction as the first free secondary school for African Americans in the area. Born out of the Saxton School, founded in 1865 by the Reverend Francis L. Cardozo, it was organized with the assistance of the American Missionary Association of New York, which also staffed the school. Ten thousand dollars was obtained from the estate of the northern philanthropist Charles Avery, and further financial aid was given by the Freedmen's Bureau and local merchants. The school was constructed by 1868 and by 1880 had an enrollment of nearly five hundred students. Although the institute was originally private and served Charleston's most prominent free African American families, by 1947 it became public and developed a reputation as one of the best schools in the region. This Italianate structure with its arched entry and cupola is now under the aegis of the College of Charleston and functions as a research library and museum for the nineteenth- and early-twentieth-century Charleston black experience.

Avery Normal Institute, engraving from Harper's Weekly, *November 1, 1879*

128 BULL STREET, JOSEPH BENNETT HOUSE (THOMAS GRANGE SIMONS HOUSE)

Constructed circa 1814

Joseph Bennett, a lesser-known son of Thomas Bennett, lived not far from the family sawmills in this house constructed by his father by 1814. The two-and-a-half-story weatherboarded dwelling with a central pedimented pavilion stands on a high masonry foundation, reflecting the short distance from the house to the marsh at the time of construction. The Bennetts conveyed the property in 1818 to the Simons family, wealthy factors who later owned the Crescent Plantation (now the West Ashley subdivision The Crescent) on Wappoo Creek. Thomas Grange Simons II was born in the house in 1819 and lived here until his death in 1904. For most of the twentieth century the house has been owned by a succession of Rivers and Porcher families.

129 BULL STREET, DRAYTON-GIRARDEAU HOUSE

Constructed circa 1822; altered circa 1846

Rebecca Drayton, who married the builder of Drayton Hall when she was sixteen years old, lived until the 1820s and apparently had her final residence on this site, which was sold by her executor in 1842. It is believed that the front Greek Revival portion and later Italianate style bays were built onto the Drayton residence. The house was sold in 1846 to the contractor-builder Louis Rebb, who probably made the first improvements. In the antebellum period the house was owned by the Reverend John Lafayette Girardeau, a Presbyterian minister who served as a chaplain in the Civil War as well as pastor of white and black Presbyterian congregations.

207 CALHOUN STREET, RICHARD BRENAN HOUSE

Constructed circa 1817; renovated as offices mid-1970s

Built on lot no. 156, the northeast corner of the original Harleston Village, the three-and-a-half-story single house constructed by Richard Brenan survives despite demolitions of numerous dwellings in the rest of the block. Brenan, a merchant, had moved to this site by 1822. The building features well-detailed quoins and a west-facing pediment as well as a double-tiered piazza supported by Neoclassical style Tuscan columns and a screen with a pedimented architrave on the first floor. The house was purchased in 1835 by Nathaniel Russell Middleton, grandson of Nathaniel Russell, who was the city treasurer and later president of the faculty of the College of Charleston. Middleton and his wife lived here briefly, eventually transferring ownership to his widowed sister-in-law Alice Izard Heyward in 1844. Used as a parsonage by Bethel Methodist Church from 1881 until 1965, the building deteriorated for several years before being rehabilitated in the mid-1970s by a land-surveying firm. In this period the old dependency was rebuilt as an office addition.

221 CALHOUN STREET, RICHARD HOLLOWAY TENEMENT

Constructed circa 1814

Holloway, a free African American builder who owned more than twenty houses at the time of his death in 1823, constructed this two-and-a-half-story Charleston single house sometime after 1814, along with a nearly identical house at *96 Smith Street*. Holloway's houses show impressive planning and detailing. The gable roof at 221 Calhoun covers the piazzas as well as the principal structure, and its tympanum is ornamented by a Venetian window with splayed Gothic muntins. A double-tiered piazza topped by a pediment projecting from the roof faces the west end of the property. Shuttered for many years, the building remains in a state of severe deterioration. Although the Holloways lived on Beaufain Street, this house was left to John Holloway, who in turn sold it in 1847 with a property description including "a Two Story Wooden Dwelling House, thereon together with a kitchen and a building formerly used as a schoolhouse and stable."

239 CALHOUN STREET, ALEXANDER LINDSTROM HOUSE

Constructed circa 1885

With the gradual filling of the Bennett rice pond, Charlestonians began to buy lots for the construction of modest houses. A bookkeeper built this straightforward two-story Charleston single house with two-story side piazzas and an open front gable just before the earthquake of 1886. With the exception of the front Italianate style window surrounds, the building uses the detailing of the late–Greek Revival period.

267–273 CALHOUN STREET, CALHOUN SECURITIES ROW HOUSES

Constructed 1910–12

Halsey Lumber Company, which built the houses at *129–135 Ashley Avenue*, subdivided these lots and conveyed them to Calhoun securities in 1910. Originally eight houses were constructed, but only five survive. The salesman Levi Boland built his own house at 267 Calhoun Street, which reflects the new Colonial Revival style with some hold-over Queen Anne features. A semicircular arch in the projecting front

gable end gives access to the principal entry, while a front porch with double columns wraps from Calhoun Street to the
Ashley Avenue side of the building.
Calhoun Securities completed the other
houses more simply with small front
porches, projecting bays, hipped roofs, and
hipped dormers.

281 CALHOUN STREET, BANKERS TRUST BUILDING (NATIONS BANK CENTER)

Constructed 1974

Jeffrey M. Rosenblum, architect

Because this site had long lost its historical context, an opportunity for the construction of a modern building presented
itself in the mid-1970s. This large bank
building with its reinforced concrete pedestal, exposed steel framing, and large ex-
panses of glass is unusual in the city's new
downtown architecture in that it is
unapologetically modern.

COLLEGE OF CHARLESTON (COLLEGE, GEORGE, AND GREEN STREETS)

CISTERN AND MAIN CAMPUS OF THE COLLEGE OF CHARLESTON (66 GEORGE STREET)

🇱 *Constructed circa 1820–56; additions 1930, 1975*
William Strickland, Edward B. White, George E. Walker, principal architects

The colony set aside free school lands by 1712, but this area was unused for this purpose until the chartering of the College of Charleston, when ten acres of school-designated land and the barracks were given to the college. During the Revolution the site had been the location of barracks for William Moultrie's 2nd South Carolina Regiment. When Robert Smith's family petitioned for repayment of loans he had made to the college in its early years, three-fourths of the college's original lands were sold. After the Reverend Jasper Adams, a graduate of Brown University, became principal of the college in 1824, he described the place as a "mass of ill looking and inconvenient buildings." Through efforts of the trustees, a new center building was begun in 1828. The central portion of the present main structure was designed by William Strickland of Philadelphia, a student of Benjamin Latrobe, one of the architects of the U.S. Capitol. Strickland probably learned of the College of Charleston from one of its former trustees, Langdon Cheves, who served as president of the Second Bank of the United States. Strickland was the architect for the bank building as well as for Cheves's Philadelphia residence.

In 1850 Edward Brickell White, Charleston's leading Greek Revival architect, designed wings and a third portico for the main building. Ionic capitals, ordered for the structure from Elbridge Boyden of Worcester, Massachusetts, in 1850, corresponded to those ordered by White for the Corinthian portico on the High School of Charleston at *55 Society Street*. Much of the building was used to house the paleontology and natural history museum collection now in The Charleston Museum, and scien-

Harrison Randolph Hall, College of Charleston

tific interest led to the construction of a small observatory on the roof, which is still visible. The wrought-iron fence erected around the college by Christopher Werner incorporates spears and axes.

Porter's Lodge at the college

The college building today, with its weathered stucco barely tinted due to numerous washings and paintings, has a six-columned fluted Ionic portico with a central clock in the temple of the pediment. It stands on an arcaded base approached by sweeping wrought-iron staircases. The wings designed by White feature curvilinear gables supported by Ionic pilasters. In 1854 George E. Walker, a Charleston architect-builder, drew the plans for the library building of the College of Charleston. The library was undertaken by William F. Patterson and completed by 1856. This building, which represents the transition between the Greek Revival and the Italianate styles, includes an engaged portico supported by Tuscan pilasters and two-story arched Italianate style windows with corner quoining. The structure includes a main room surrounded by a gallery, and a great central plaster ceiling medallion. The main college building was expanded first in 1930, using a design by Albert Simons and Samuel Lapham, and again in 1975 by the successor firm to Simons and Lapham, when a new portico was added on the north side facing the newly created college mall.

Aerial view of the College of Charleston area

5, 7, AND 9 COLLEGE STREET, BOLLES FEMALE ACADEMY

Constructed circa 1826–35; rehabilitated 1971–72

A teacher from Connecticut, Abiel Bolles, opened his own school a few years after his arrival in Charleston in 1807. After constructing 5 College Street with a pedimented gable roof and inset piazza, Bolles expanded his school by 1830 with the flat-roofed single house at 7 College Street. In the mid-1830s Bolles built an even larger two-and-a-half-story Charleston single house on a high

5 College Street

foundation with side piazzas in the emerging Greek Revival style. Bolles sold 9 College Street almost immediately to Dr. John Bellinger, surgery professor at the medical college and originator of certain operations of the abdomen. The College of Charleston rehabilitated these buildings in 1971–72 for use as offices for faculty and staff.

11 COLLEGE STREET, WILSON-SOTTILE HOUSE
Constructed circa 1891

S. W. Foulk, architect; Henry Oliver, builder

Samuel Wilson, one of Charleston's most progressive merchants of the postwar era, built this house in the emergent Queen Anne style in about 1891. It has been cited as probably the most extraordinary example of this architectural vocabulary in Charleston. S. W. Foulk, who also designed the YMCA building, undertook the planning for this building. Possessing numerous shapes and textures, the Wilson-Sottile House boasts a central hipped roof from which emanate several gable roofs as well as an additional hip to the west. The building features turrets on the southwest corner and on the front elevation, as well as double-tiered bowed porches with Queen Anne style turned columns and elaborate jigsaw-cut and spindlework trim. Fish-scale shingling on the turret and other locations provides some relief from the thin clapboarding of the principal walls of the structure. Stained-glass windows in the stair tower add ornament to the exterior and interior, while the latter features elaborate woodwork and an entry paved with minted tiles. A central hall with staircase provides entry on each side to downstairs rooms of varying shapes. The house was sold in 1912 to Albert Sottile, developer of most of the theaters in Charleston. The Sottile family gave the house to the college in 1964.

58 GEORGE STREET, BARNARD ELLIOTT HOUSE

Constructed circa 1802; restored 1971

Barnard Elliott, a wealthy planter whose family laid out Elliottborough in the northwest corner of the city after his death, built this house shortly after the end of the eighteenth century. The structure stands on a high masonry foundation, and the timber-framed walls were built with a double wall of studs to provide structural stability as well as the customary depth of a masonry building. Altered in the Victorian manner in 1870, the house contains woodwork from the Walker House at *26 George Street* that was installed in the early-twentieth century. The house became apartments in 1952 before being acquired by the college in 1971 and restored. The building retains its eighteenth-century double-house shape with hipped roof, now covered by a standing seam tin roof, hipped gables, and chimneys.

*Doorway detail,
58 George Street*

66 GEORGE STREET, PORTER'S LODGE

*Constructed circa 1850s
Edward B. White, architect*

66 George Street is part of the original main campus of the College of Charleston. This small Classical-Revival building was designed by Edward Brickell White, also responsible for the porticoes and wings of Harrison Randolph Hall. The location of the building adds a sense of definition and axis to the campus. The college never hired a porter, but the building once served as the residence for a succession of college janitors.

72 GEORGE STREET, JOHN KING HOUSE

Constructed circa 1837; moved and rehabilitated 1972

John King built this impressive three-and-a-half-story Greek Revival style Charleston single house at the time of the

War Between the States. The property was held in trust for Virgil A. Berry, a free person of color. The college was responsible for shifting the house a full ninety degrees to make room for the Physicians Memorial Auditorium in 1972. The move was made after the building was braced with steel crossbeams and adjusted every few feet to prevent cracking. *74 George Street*, a three-and-a-half-story masonry Charleston single house, was shifted some years later to make way for a second phase of the science building.

2 GREEN STREET, JOHNSON HOUSE

Constructed circa 1817–22; rehabilitated 1972

In 1971 the College of Charleston acquired this house from the descendants of a free person of color who had owned the property since buying it at auction in 1844. Apparently the dwelling was built on a lot sold as a result of a suit by Bishop Robert Smith's heirs in 1817. James C. Martindale, a planter, probably constructed the house within a few years after purchasing the lot at auction. It went through various owners until being purchased by Joseph Johnson. Beginning as a small two-and-a-half-story weatherboarded house, the structure retains a two-story rear addition with a flat roof, but another side addition was removed in the twentieth century.

4 GREEN STREET

Constructed circa 1817

This three-and-a-half-story Charleston single house with a hipped roof retains its Flemish bonded brickwork on its east side, while stucco and Italianate style window heads and a two-story Tuscan piazza remain on the front and west sides. The house was held in the estate of James Martin in

1860 and served as rental property for a number of years. Its use as a dormitory for men from the early-twentieth century to the present has earned the structure its colorful title "The Shack."

6 GREEN STREET, WAGONER HOUSE

Constructed circa 1817; rehabilitated 1970s

Although owned at the time of the Civil War by Samuel S. Mills, this two-story stucco single house with a full-tiered Tuscan piazza has been moved twice by the college to make way for construction of the small library and college mall. The Wagoner House is named for a teacher of French and German who apparently lived on the site in the late-1800s. Three College of Charleston alumnae in 1971 stood in front of the building to stop an approaching bulldozer from destroying it. This event led to the college's creation of a preservation committee.

10 GREEN STREET, GOV. WILLIAM AIKEN HOUSE

Constructed circa 1841; rehabilitated 1970s

This two-story house with raised parapet was built around 1841 by William Aiken as one of a pair of identical rental houses. The twin house at *8 Green Street* was demolished in 1971–72 to make way for the Robert Scott Small Library. The surviving house was built with the same solid construction methods and extraordinary details as those seen in Aiken's rental properties at Wragg Mall. Original Greek Revival woodwork, as well as evidence of graining, has survived. The two-story piazza has French doors on the elevations similar to the houses at Wragg Mall.

14 GREEN STREET, KNOX-LESESNE HOUSE

Constructed circa 1846; rehabilitated 1972–73

Walter Knox, a carpenter, bought this lot following the dismemberment of the college property in 1817. After his death, Katherine Knox built this dwelling with Greek Revival and Tuscan or Italianate style detailing. Mrs. Knox lived here at the time of the war. The house is three stories tall with a surmounting hipped roof and cupola. Several tiers of cast-iron front piazzas as well as triple-tiered Tuscan piazzas ornament the house. Owned by Albert Osceola Jones, an African American who served as a South Carolina state representative between 1870 and 1881, the house was sold to Charlestonian Willie James Lesesne in the early-twentieth century. The college restored the house in 1972–73, and it serves as a women's dormitory.

1 COMING STREET, PETER CHRISTOPHER SCHRODER STORE

Constructed circa 1850

At the time of the Civil War this three-story late–Greek Revival store building was owned by a German grocer named Peter Christopher Schroder, who lived on the floors above. Italianate style alterations from the late-nineteenth century included the removal of the southeast corner for a typical Charleston store entry with a cast-iron column. Later occupied by the Doscher family as a grocery store, it served as the forerunner for a family business that expanded to a supermarket chain still in existence.

7–9 COMING STREET, JAMES DRAYTON JOHNSON HOUSES

Constructed circa 1850

James Drayton Johnson, a free African American tailor whose son married the daughter of William Ellison, a wealthy African American plantation owner in the up-per Santee region, probably built these two small vernacular single houses with gable roofs in the mid-1800s. Johnson lived in the smaller of the two houses at 9 Coming Street while renting the larger at 7 Coming Street to Julius Kaufman. Although the house at 7 Coming Street has been fully rehabilitated in recent years, the smaller dwelling is sheathed in synthetic shingles. The Ellison-Johnson family letters survived, and the ed-ited manuscript version, *No Chariot Let Down*, was published by the historians Michael T. Johnson and James L. Roark in 1984. The letters provide a unique glimpse of the lives of Charleston's free black community in the de-cade before the War Between the States.

10 COMING STREET, ST. MICHAEL'S GLEBE TENEMENT

Constructed circa 1820–30; altered mid-twentieth century

Preservationists have long recognized the graceful character of this late-Neoclassical style house, built on St. Michael's portion of the glebe lands. The projecting pediment from the front-facing gable roof boasts a Neoclassical style fanlight.

10 Coming Street, late-nineteenth-century photograph

17 COMING STREET, SARAH A. COHRS HOUSE

Constructed circa 1839; rehabilitated 1991

This two-and-a-half-story wood Charleston single house, constructed as an investment for Mrs. Sarah Cohrs, stands on a high stuccoed brick foundation and has side Tuscan piazzas, gable roof with a tripartite window, and paired chimneys with later Gothic style arched hoods. It bears all the characteristics of typical Charleston single houses of the Greek Re-vival period. By contrast, the brick house to the south at *15 Coming Street* follows the side-hall plan with pilaster caps sup-porting the base of the gable roof. Both of these houses experienced severe deterioration since the 1960s, although 17 Coming Street has undergone historical rehabilitation. 15 Coming Street remains divided into apartments, with a facade that was poorly rebuilt in the 1980s.

23 COMING STREET, MARY GRAY HOUSE

Constructed circa 1830

A widow, Mary Gray, acquired this house in 1841 from James Stevens, the trustee for the "marriage settlement" of Ann Hunt and her husband, Nathaniel Hunt. The dwelling passed through various owners, but it was W. K. Brown who held it until the end of the nineteenth century. The early-nineteenth-century single house form—with nine-over-nine windows on the first story, surmounted by an open gable roof with three projecting dormers—was altered in the late-nineteenth century by construction of a north addition with a new Italianate style entry. These alterations transformed the structure into a duplex. The property to the south at *21 Coming Street* passed as a vacant lot to Mrs. Gray when she acquired 23 Coming Street. Either John Zanoga or W. K. Brown built the two-story Italianate style dwelling here in the 1870s.

26 COMING STREET, JAMES DENTON HOUSE

Constructed circa 1798; moved from 25 St. Philip Street in 1977

James Denton, tavern keeper, wharf master, and carpenter, built this small two-and-a-half-story, open-gabled single house on the glebe lands at *25 St. Philip Street*. Significant Victorian changes to the building include the Italianate style piazza screen and two-over-two windows. After the house was moved to Coming Street in 1977, the middle dormer was rebuilt to create a third-story bathroom.

28–38 COMING STREET,
COLLEGE OF CHARLESTON
SORORITY HOUSES

Variously constructed between 1771 and 1908

Five houses on the east side of Coming Street, as well as one dwelling across the street, became home in the 1970s to various sororities at the College of Charleston. The large two-and-a-half-story Charleston single house at 28 Coming Street sits on a fully raised brick basement and has a double-tiered piazza on the south side. Its closed gable front features a modified Venetian (Palladian) window. It bears striking similarity to the Scott House at 38 Coming Street, which was first built on a glebe land leased by John Scott in 1771. Remodeled in the Greek Revival manner in the 1830s, its interior, nonetheless, retains some Georgian woodwork, and it still possesses its eighteenth-century hipped dormers and beaded weatherboarding.

The smaller single house at 34 Coming Street may also date from the Revolutionary period, but its Queen Anne closed gable and remodeled piazza entry belie an early date. Constructed by the vintner Thomas Harvey, the property originally contained a separate brick distillery building.

The only masonry example of the group, the Graves House at 36 Coming Street was built in the 1840s by a wealthy planter who leased the site from the glebe. Standing three and a half stories tall on a raised basement, the house retains its Greek Revival piazza door screen and an unusually wide dormer with a tripartite window projecting from its hipped roof.

The more eclectic styles of the late-nineteenth and early-twentieth centuries are exhibited in the Queen Anne style dwelling at 35 Coming Street with its square tower, first-floor bay window, closed gable with patterned wood decoration, and two-story, square-columned piazza.

In contrast to all of these buildings sited close to the street, the Colonial Revival style house at 32 Coming Street, with front and side porches, second-story bay, and hipped roof, is situated at the back of a deep lot.

28 Coming Street

35 Coming Street

40 COMING STREET, W. J. RIVERS HOUSE

Constructed 1851

William J. Rivers, founder of the South Carolina Historical Society and author of the most important history of the state published in the nineteenth century, built this fine two-and-a-half-story brick dwelling in 1851 while running a private school nearby. Rivers became a professor of classical languages in 1857 at the University of South Carolina and moved to Columbia, leaving behind an elite Charleston circle, including neighbors Hugh Swinton Legare, Christopher G. Memminger, and Dr. John Bachman. The house retains its finely pointed Flemish bond front facade with brick jack arches, red sandstone window sills, belt courses, and a closed front gable with a central tripartite window. The architrave in the side piazza screen, probably original, has unusually large Rococo style console brackets supporting the overhanging lintel.

57 COMING STREET, KORNAHRENS-GUENVEUR HOUSE

Constructed circa 1884

This two-story Charleston single house, which retains many elements associated with the Greek Revival expression of this style, was constructed by John H. Kornahrens, a manufacturer of soda water, who had a bottling facility in the basement. Edward Leon Guenveur, an African American plumbing contractor, bought the house in 1925, and it has been retained by his descendants ever since. Five years earlier Francis Ran built the two-story corner grocery next door as his shop and residence. The structure retains a masonry ground story. The weatherboarded second story is topped by a wide cornice and a deep parapet that screens the flat roof.

69 COMING STREET, FARR HOUSE

Constructed circa 1817

This two-and-a-half story weather-boarded Charleston single house, with its principal piazza standing on a stuccoed and arcaded brick basement, was built on land given by William Blacklock, of *18 Bull Street*, to his daughter Katherine and her husband Nathaniel Farr. With its perpendicular stone staircase rising to a Greek Revival door screen, the house seems reminiscent of the Legare House at *75 Anson Street*.

70–72 COMING STREET, HENRY HORLBECK HOUSES

Constructed before 1852; renovated 1971–72

Henry Horlbeck, scion of the brickmaking family that owned Boone Hall Plantation, built these two stuccoed brick dwellings as investments on lots that had been subdivided from the college lands in 1817. Horlbeck sold the larger three-story single house with parapeted and corbeled gable roof to J. C. Johnson while retaining the smaller house to the north as a rental property. The latter is a two-and-a-half-story single house with a similar parapeted gable. It was conveyed by Horlbeck's estate by 1894 to the businessman and real estate baron Samuel Wilson. The College of Charleston rehabilitated both structures for use as student residences in the early-1970s.

4 GADSDEN STREET, JOHN H. STEINMEYER HOUSE

Constructed circa 1852

John H. Steinmeyer, a member of a Charleston family with extensive real estate holdings, owned a steam sawmill nearby and probably built this house on land leased by Nathan Nathans, a King Street dry goods merchant. The Steinmeyers were living here by 1852 on land that had only recently been

Ashley River marshes. As the family lumber business expanded in the 1850s, J. H. Steinmeyer continued to live at this site. The three-story Greek Revival dwelling is of the side-hall, double-parlor plan. A Temple of the Winds portico shelters the front entry on the north end of the Gadsden Street elevation. The flat roof is capped by a stucco parapet with dentiled cornice, while triple-tiered piazzas on the south overlook Beaufain Street. Heavily damaged in the hurricane of 1885 and the earthquake of 1886, the property was sold by the Nathans to George W. Egan, builder of the Charleston jetties.

19 GADSDEN STREET, THOMAS HAMLIN HOUSE
Constructed 1828–30; restored 1957

Thomas Hamlin, a planter whose family was prominent in Christ Church Parish and who later owned Snee Farm Plantation (built circa 1820), built this one-and-a-half-story single house on a raised brick basement in the Greek Revival style in the late-1820s. Hamlin's house was the first to be built on Gadsden Street above Wentworth and originally had a spectacular view of the Ashley River, thus accounting for the influences of plantation style architecture on the structure. Resembling the more typical planters' houses found east of the Cooper River, the dwelling has a front piazza, a gable roof with three dormers, and two chimney stacks projecting from the ridge of the roof. On the interior this compact version of the Charleston double house had four heated rooms on each floor divided by a central hall. This may have been built as a summer residence for the Hamlins, as it was placed on the notably healthy western edge of the city.

22–24 GADSDEN STREET, C. HENRY HESSE HOUSES
Constructed 1885–86

C. H. Hesse purchased these lots from J. H. Renneker Jr. prior to 1883. Within three years he constructed two two-story

Charleston single houses at 22 and 24 Gadsden Street with nearly identical weatherboarding, corner posts, fenestration, and open front gables. A double-tiered, square-columned piazza shades the south side of 22 Gadsden, while the matching piazza at 24 Gadsden now has Tuscan columns. The ground level of 24 Gadsden has been altered with a brick floor and brick tiers supporting the column bases. Renneker retained the original portion of the lot at *26 Gadsden Street* only briefly, selling it by 1883 with buildings already on it.

23–25 GADSDEN STREET, SAMUEL WILSON TENEMENTS
Constructed circa 1880

At the death of Louis Sherfesee, who owned a parcel measuring 218 by 118 feet on Gadsden Street, a section of this lot was sold to Samuel Wilson. Wilson built two houses for investment purposes on the site. These two nearly identical single houses, with flat roofs extending over their south-facing double-tiered piazzas, retain their original Italianate door architraves and turned columns. The windows on 23 Gadsden have Italianate surrounds, while the lintels on 25 Gadsden are flat. Originally the houses had four-over-four light windows on the front elevation. The second story and windows on 23 Gadsden have been altered.

47 GADSDEN STREET, HERMAN ESDORN HOUSE
Constructed before 1872

A former Confederate soldier built this one-and-a-half-story Charleston single house, which is set back from the street. Of a style often called "freedman's cottage," Herman Esdorn's dwelling evidences the universal appeal of its form. At some point its kitchen building was attached to the house, creating an L-shape. Esdorn operated a store and saloon in a building that once stood at the front of the lot.

6 GLEBE STREET, ST. PHILIP'S PARSONAGE HOUSE (BISHOP ROBERT SMITH HOUSE)

Constructed circa 1770; restored 1965

Built by Affra Harleston Coming around 1770 as the parsonage house for the rector of St. Philip's Church in the center of a four-acre tract carved from glebe lands left to the parish, this brick dwelling has served as the home of the state's first Episcopal bishop and is now the residence for the president of the College of Charleston.

The rectory follows the Georgian double-house plan, although its side end now faces the street. It has a simple six-bay facade with central pedimented pavilion on its south principal elevation. Central door architraves approached by brick staircases with stuccoed rails, rubbed brick jack arches surmounting the principal windows, and bull's-eye windows in the tympanum of the pediments add ornamentation to the Flemish bonded-brick facade. Although its stairway was replaced in the Federal period, the building retains much of its original Georgian paneling as well as some mantels and doors. Outbuildings, orchards, and pastures originally surrounded the building, then set in an undeveloped block. The Reverend Robert Smith, a graduate of Cambridge University who served after ordination under the bishop of London, arrived in Charleston in the late-1750s and became the rector of St. Philip's Church by 1759. Unlike most Anglican clergy, he fought as a patriot during the Revolution. Afterward he was a key figure in the organization of the Episcopal Church. After beginning an academy in the basement of this house, he was named the first president of the College of Charleston in 1785. He resigned the post after he became bishop of South Carolina.

Known as Mrs. Eason's Boarding House at the time of the Civil War but still owned by the glebe, the house suffered substantial deterioration until 1965, when the college bought it from St. Philip's Church.

7 GLEBE STREET, MT. ZION A.M.E. CHURCH

Constructed circa 1847–48; repaired after fire damage 1938–39

Edward C. Jones, architect

Originally built as the Glebe Street Presbyterian Church, this building served a new congregation spawned from the Second Presbyterian Church. Unique among Charleston ecclesiastical buildings, Jones's design exhibits the influence of the late, simplified classicism of Sir John Soane, who died a decade before. Albert Simons, an F. A. I. A. Charleston architectural historian, likened the rusticated base and square piers on the central bay of the Glebe Street church to the tower of St. Johns Church in Bethnel Green, London. He also noted the influence of Soane's Dulwich Picture Gallery in explaining the sarcophagus terminus of the central tower, as well as Soane's design for the windows of the waiting-room court loggia of the Bank of England as the inspiration for the central window beneath. In 1888 the building was sold to the Mt. Zion A.M.E. Church. A new congregation formed from the Emanuel A.M.E. Church on Calhoun Street. Despite a 1938 fire, the original exterior and most of the simple interior have been preserved in their original form.

9 GLEBE STREET, GLEBE HOUSE

Constructed circa 1854

The glebe of St. Philip's Church built a two-story Charleston single house on this site in about 1854. Probably formerly resembling its immediate neighbor at 11 Glebe Street, with a parapeted front gable and Palladian style central window, the dwelling was altered by the 1880s with a full mansard roof and Italianate style pressed metal window heads. It retains its basic Greek Revival fenestration and double-tiered piazzas.

12 GLEBE STREET, WILLIAM HARRAL HOUSE

Constructed circa 1855; rehabilitated 1970s

William Harral acquired this lot from the glebe and built a simple but finely crafted side-hall-plan house by 1855. Retaining most of its original fabric, the house features a pedimented Greek Revival style entry with matching lintels above the first floor windows. A roof with a front-facing gable and tripartite window surmounts the dwelling, while a two-story piazza with square masonry columns on the first level supports the lighter Tuscan colonnade of the second tier. Transomed French doors on this elevation provide easy access to the side piazza.

The glebe apparently retained the lots at *14* and *16 Glebe Street*. These two-and-a-half-story brick single houses have finely detailed entablatures and gables, and Venetian style windows, features usually not found in Charleston architecture after 1830. Both dwellings retain original Tuscan-columned piazzas with simple Greek Revival door screens.

20 GLEBE STREET, THOMPSON-MULLER HOUSE

Constructed circa 1846; restored circa 1970

George Thompson was apparently one of the first to break the glebe, purchasing this lot and building a wide Charleston single house with three bays on the site in the mid-1840s. Thompson's dwelling includes brick quoining on the corners of the front facade, a banded entablature, and a corbeled pediment with a Neoclassical style

Palladian window in the tympanum. Stone window lintels accent the heads of each opening, while marble steps lead from the street to the first tier of the two-story Greek Revival style piazza. Thompson also built the side-hall-plan house at *26 Glebe* by the 1850s. It was later altered with Italianate style pressed window and door hoods and a Queen Anne style double-tiered piazza.

6 MONTAGU STREET, JOHN RUDOLPH SWITZER HOUSE
Constructed circa 1803; rehabilitated 1964

John Switzer, a saddler with a shop on King Street, built this plantation style dwelling in the emerging suburb of Harleston Village sometime after acquiring the property in 1803. A two-story piazza supported on an arcaded brick foundation fronts the two-and-a-half-story wooden dwelling, which has a pediment in the roof. The principal tier of the piazza, with a columned arcade, is original, while the second story constitutes a slightly later addition. A fanlighted Neoclassical style doorway with attenuated fluted pilasters provides entry into the house, which retains much of its delicate Federal style woodwork. Although a later owner changed the windows to two-over-two lights in the postbellum period, the house otherwise retains a high degree of integrity.

The house passed through several owners, including Keating Simons Laurens, grandson of Henry Laurens. Mr. and Mrs. George A. Z. Johnson, natives of Harleston Village, restored the house in the mid-1960s.

8 MONTAGU STREET, SARAH CAMPBELL HOUSE
Constructed circa 1883

Sarah Campbell, whose family also owned the property immediately to the west, built this unique Charleston single house in the Second Empire style in around

1883. Mrs. Campbell's dwelling follows the normal single-house pattern with a double-tiered piazza and a pedimented door screen supported by Victorian style brackets. However, the entire building is surmounted by a Second Empire style mansard roof over a deep cornice with alternating brackets and raised ovolo panels. A square turret projects from the second story through the roof, which has pedimented dormers.

11 MONTAGU STREET, SCHMIDT-CONNER HOUSE
Constructed 1819–29

This three-story residence, combining Neoclassical and Classical Revival detailing of the 1820s, survives as one of the most exuberant of Charleston's early-nineteenth-century single houses. Mrs. Elizabeth Schmidt, a widow, began construction of a brick dwelling shortly after her family acquired the lot in 1818. Living across the street without the means to complete the house, she sold the lot, with "an unfinished Brick Dwelling House and kitchen," in November 1828 to the grain merchant Robert Eason Conner. Conner, who completed the building by 1829, died in 1840 and left the property in trust for his minor son. John Y. Stock, an exchange broker, bought the house and lived here for more than forty years.

The Schmidt-Conner House, with its three-story stuccoed mass, follows the typical single house pattern with a two-bay front, north-side interior end chimneys with stucco banding, and double-tiered side piazzas. The piazza, however, distinctly relates the house to the Classical Revival style practiced by the Charlestonian Robert Mills, particularly evident in its banded Tuscan columns and its exceptional piazza door screen with an engaged columned architrave and a semicircular transom with muntins ornamented with a guilloche motif. A modern owner added the polygonal second- and third-story bays to accommodate bathrooms for the interior. Unlike many Charleston houses, this dwelling has been owner occupied through nearly all of its history.

12 MONTAGU STREET, MCNEILL-EGAN HOUSE

Constructed circa 1812; renovated 1900

This house was constructed for a mariner in 1812 on land bought by Capt. Daniel McNeill from the subdivision of the properties of the plantation owner Benjamin Smith. Much of the Neoclassical detailing of the house was obscured in the early-twentieth century. Although the structure retains its original fenestration on the first two floors, George W. Egan, a contractor who built the Charleston jetties, added a third story and an extension with a polygonal bay connecting to the rear dependencies shortly after acquiring the property in 1900. Before Egan's purchase, the house passed through the Chisolm family to George Gibbs, the builder of *20 Elliot Street*, who purchased it for the use of his daughter, Mrs. Caroline Blackwood. Mrs. Blackwood eventually married George W. Brown, a commission merchant. Although she died in 1882, her estate held onto her considerable properties in the area until 1894.

A family member began construction of the house at *14 Montagu Street* in 1885. The newer dwelling provides a late-nineteenth-century note amidst this concentration of antebellum architecture. Following the Queen Anne style, the two-story, hipped-roof dwelling includes a wrapping piazza with turned columns and spindle work surmounted by an arched entry hood, a shingled second story, and gable styled dormers with Venetian windows.

13 MONTAGU STREET, WILLIMAN HOUSE

Constructed before 1789

Jacob Williman, a successful butcher and tanner, bought a lot in the original Harleston Green section in the early-1780s. He lived on the site by 1790 and stayed until his death in 1813, when the property passed through his son, Dr. Jacob Williman, to the Schmidt family next door, which retained it until 1871. This eighteenth-century style single house standing on a high masonry foundation boasts a one-story piazza protected from the street by a tall screen with beaded flush boarding, and a late-Neoclassical style architrave and fanlighted, square transom. The low hipped roof, beaded weatherboard siding, and T-shaped central chimney stack indicate the building's eighteenth-century origins. Its hall-parlor interior plan and woodwork actually hearken back to earlier Georgian precedents.

Even though it was transferred in 1871 with the proviso in the will that it was "in exceeding bad condition and falling into ruin," the Williman House retains enough historic fabric to represent the earliest dwellings in the village.

16 MONTAGU STREET, CAROLINE BLACKWOOD BROWN HOUSE

Constructed circa 1830; rehabilitated 1971

The daughter of George Gibbs, who also owned *12 Montagu Street*, built this three-story Charleston single house shortly after 1830. Although the house contains some holdovers from the Federal period, such as the nine-over-nine windows and the attenuated Tuscan columns of the piazza, the remnant of the original piazza door screen and the parapeted termination and flat roof relate the building to the emerging Greek Revival style. The latter two features may reflect alterations to the house completed after sale of the property in 1848 by Caroline Blackwood and her new husband, George W. Brown, to Thomas E. Baker, or changes made after Baker's sale to the stockbroker Isaac Moise in 1851. This house, like many others in the neighborhood, was rehabilitated in the 1970s by George A. Z. Johnson.

18 MONTAGU STREET, BENJAMIN SMITH HOUSE

Constructed before 1788

Goose Creek planter Benjamin Smith, a delegate to the Constitutional Ratification Convention, built this suburban retreat soon after the Revolution. This structure has housed some of the most distinguished residents of the village. Smith lived here and sold it in 1811 to Chancellor William Henry deSaussure, the first director of the U.S. Mint and supervisor of the coining of the first American silver dollars. Although considerably altered on the exterior with double-tiered Greek Revival piazzas and double windows, the house retains much interior Georgian woodwork from the Smith period, particularly in the second-story drawing room.

The hurricane of 1811 wreaked considerable havoc on the house. A local newspaper account described the damage to the mansion, reporting that "one of the chimneys was thrown down and a part of the family who were in an upper room at the time were precipitated with the falling bricks, through two floors into the kitchen." The carriage house at 28½ Pitt Street, a two-story brick structure, was converted in 1949 into two apartments.

20 MONTAGU STREET, COBIA-MOULTRIE HOUSE

Constructed circa 1808

This three-and-a-half-story brick house on a high foundation with a molded brick

water table represents the apogee of the Neoclassical Charleston single house in Harleston Village. Built at the same time as the Nathaniel Russell House at *51 Meeting Street*, the dwelling at 20 Montagu Street features the same finely crafted brickwork laid in Flemish bond with rubbed brick jack arches over the windows, semicircular stair-hall windows on the east elevation, marble window sills, and a dentiled brick cornice. The double-tiered piazzas, with arcades supported by slender Tuscan columns and screened by a notable door architrave with Ionic pilasters and a rectangular fanlight, survive as the most distinctive Neoclassical version of this tradition in the boroughs of Charleston.

Daniel Cobia built this house by 1809 and lived here with his mother, Christiana Cobia, a planter in her own right. After Cobia's death in the 1820s, the house passed to Dr. James Moultrie Jr., cousin of Gen. William Moultrie, leader of the movement to found a medical college in South Carolina and eventually professor of physiology. Moultrie's executors sold the property in 1879 to Mary Frazier Davie McCrady, daughter of a North Carolina governor and wife of Confederate general Edward McCrady. The McCradys lived here for nearly twelve years. Here the general, an attorney and historian, completed much of his four-volume history of South Carolina.

23 MONTAGU STREET, RIVERS-BULWINKLE HOUSE
Constructed 1843–44; restored 1980s

In 1843 Dr. Thomas Eveleigh arranged for the holding in trust of this lot and the subsequent construction of the house for his widowed daughter, Mrs. Eliza Rivers. Built as a typical Charleston single house of stuccoed brick on the front elevation and with double-tiered side piazzas, the residence went through major changes about forty years later when it was conveyed to the grocer and saloon keeper J. H. Bulwinkle with stores at *133 Queen Street* and *40 Archdale Street*. Family members who lived here until the mid-1930s added the metal cornice with end brackets as well as a matching wood overhang above the piazza door screen.

Eveleigh also built a small two-story brick single house with a dogtoothed cornice and two-story piazza for another daughter, Mrs. D. T. Heriot. Altered in the 1890s with Victorian additions and in the late-1930s converted into apartments, *27 Montagu Street* retains splendid Flemish bond brickwork on its front elevation. It has recently been restored as a single family residence.

24 MONTAGU STREET, BRUCKNER-COBIA HOUSE
Constructed 1802–06

In one of Harleston Village's most picturesque settings, this two-and-a-half-story single house with a simple wrapping piazza provides a distinct impression of the early rural character of the neighborhood. The merchant Daniel Bruckner purchased this lot from a fellow German tradesman in 1801 and probably completed the house by 1806. Christiana Elizabeth Cobia, mother of Daniel Cobia, purchased the property shortly before completion of the family's house nearby at *20 Montagu Street*. The Cobia family held the property through several generations, selling it in 1938. The house displays exterior details such as wide-beaded weatherboarding and a hipped roof, as well as interior features such as Federal style woodwork and early hardware.

25 MONTAGU STREET, JOHN ROBINSON JR. HOUSE
Constructed circa 1848

The son of merchant John Robinson, builder of numerous houses in Wraggborough, built this typical three-and-a-half-story Greek

Revival single house on a lot purchased in 1847. Brick banding just below the front gable end and rubbed brick jack arches provide the only ornamentation for the front facade, while a double-tiered, Tuscan-columned piazza rests on a masonry ground story, which has an arcaded entry. Jane Gaillard Thomas, daughter of Judge Theodore Gaillard of Charleston, acquired the property in 1859, eventually conveying it to her son, Dr. Theodore Gaillard Thomas, and his wife Mary Theodosia Willard of Troy, New York. Thomas, gained international fame practicing obstetrics at the Rotunda Hospital in Dublin and later in New York State. His wife was a granddaughter of the noted educator Emma Willard.

The Thomases probably never lived in the house. But while it was owned by the Siegling family from 1881 to 1921, it was primarily the residence of William Lanneau, owner of the arts store at *238 King Street*.

28 MONTAGU STREET, HANNAH GRONING HOUSE

Constructed circa 1809

Defaced by later changes, including the addition of a late–Greek Revival style piazza and two-over-two windows, the loss of the console brackets supporting its central pediment, and the alteration of its lunette window, this Federal house nonetheless retains its basic form as well as its hipped roof with corbeled chimneys. Mrs. Hannah Groning, the wife of a merchant, built the house around 1809 and retained it until 1833. Converted into apartments in the 1940s, the house still features splendid Neoclassical mantels and wainscoting.

29 MONTAGU STREET, ETTSEL ADAMS HOUSE

Constructed circa 1850; rehabilitated 1975

The merchant Ettsel Adams built this three-story brick side-hall, double-parlor house after his purchase in 1839 of the westernmost of the four lots belonging to Dr. Thomas Eveleigh. The dwelling retains its austere antebellum brickwork, its six-over-six windows, and its double-tiered Tuscan piazzas. A Victorian style door hood was added, and other changes have been made to the entry from the sidewalk.

Adams sold the house soon after construction, and it eventually became the property of the Hart family, who used it as a tenement while renting a residence for themselves on Wragg Mall.

Door and iron rail detail, 29 Montagu Street

30, 32–34 MONTAGU STREET, CHRISTOPHER WHITE AND TOBIAS-LOPEZ TENEMENTS

Constructed 1854

Attributed to Edward C. Jones, architect

Apparently planned as a portion of a four-to-six-unit row of dwellings, these Italianate villa style houses may have been designed by Charleston architect Edward C. Jones, noted for using similar detailing in his design for Roper Hospital. Dr. Christopher G. White built the easternmost single dwelling, but upon default on his payments, it was acquired by a member of the Tobias family, which owned all three dwellings at the time of the War Between the States. The house at 30 Montagu Street probably lost its interior during its conversion to three apartments in the early-twentieth century, but the houses at 32 and 34 Montagu Street have generally remained single family residences and have retained their original interior features. A cast-iron fence and a double gate with allegorical figures adorn the entrance into 34 Montagu Street.

Detail of gate, 34 Montagu Street

38 MONTAGU STREET, CHARLES PATRICK HOUSE

Constructed circa 1886–90

This two-story, side-hall-plan house retains its bracketed cornice and low-pitched hipped roof along with a one-story front bay, a double-tiered side piazza with Queen Anne columns, and a rear polygonal projection. Charles Patrick acquired the lot on this site in the late-1880s and probably built the dwelling soon thereafter.

39 MONTAGU STREET, HARRIET R. SIMONS HOUSE

Constructed circa 1881

Harriet R. Simons built a Queen Anne version of the traditional side-hall, double-parlor-plan Charleston single house more than a decade after the War Between the States. Retaining the typical closed-gable end and tripartite window characteristic of Greek Revival houses, Mrs. Simons's dwelling—with its bracketed entry hood, front bay window, two-over-two windows, and deep entablature—relates to buildings built on Broad and New Streets in the same period. Larger suburban properties in the neighborhood were frequently divided into smaller lots after 1865. This house was built on a lot subdivided from one of the Rutledge Avenue properties. The Deveaux family, leaders in the local Democratic Party, rented the house from 1914 to 1922 before building a new house at *7 Gadsden Street*.

40 MONTAGU STREET, BERNARD WOHLERS HOUSE

Constructed 1891–94; restored and rehabilitated 1963

In the 1890s a wholesale grocery manager built a Queen Anne style dwelling with certain Eastlake overtones on a newly created lot at 40 Montagu Street. Constructed in the same time period as houses at *36* and *38 Montagu Street*, the exuberant Wohlers House follows a multi-cross-gable plan with varying spindle-work detailing in its first-floor entry porch and its second-story front balcony. The front gable, with triple windows and shell-work patterning in its upper part, flanks a west double-tiered piazza with spindle-work detailing similar to that in the front entry. Passing through numerous owners, the Wohlers House was restored as apartments in 1963 by Mr. and Mrs. Charles Woodward, who also restored the I. Jenkins Mikell House at *94 Rutledge Avenue.*

43–45 MONTAGU STREET, GERTRUDE MORDECAI TENEMENTS

Constructed 1897–1902

Gertrude A. Mordecai, who lived at *93 Rutledge Avenue*, built these identical side-hall-plan houses in the Queen Anne style around the turn of the century. Used as rental property through much of their early history, the two-story dwellings retain double-level front bay windows and Queen Anne style double-tiered piazzas with spindle-work detailing. Original L-shaped wings intersect with the rear ends of the piazzas on both houses. The Deveaux family rented 45 Montagu Street prior to their move to *39 Montagu Street* a few years later.

44 MONTAGU STREET, JOHN HARLESTON READ HOUSE

Constructed circa 1847; restored 1946

John Harleston Read, a grandson of the developer of Harleston Village, built this two-and-a-half-story dwelling with a front-facing double-tiered piazza set back at some distance from Montagu Street. The dominance of the second story of the house, with its front porches, long windows, and three gabled dormers, is reminiscent of Creole style houses in New Orleans. Read died at the beginning of the Civil War, and the house passed through many owners and tenants before restoration in 1946. A recessed piazza on the north side overlooks a brick courtyard leading to stable and kitchen buildings, now restored as separate residences.

47 MONTAGU STREET, STEEDMAN-GNANN HOUSE

Constructed 1896–98

F. L. Steedman, who purchased this property in a master's sale in 1896, probably built the two-story wooden house on this site. Held by a bank for many years, it was eventually conveyed to Walter Gnann, a partner in the Jet White Stream laundry on King Street. Even though the building looks like a Charleston single house, its stair hall fits within an original western appendage recessed behind a one-bay entry porch.

49 MONTAGU STREET, HYDE TENEMENT

Constructed between 1919 and 1922

Charleston mayor Tristram T. Hyde, through his Equitable Real Estate Company, acquired this lot by 1902, conveying the property to his son a few years later. Another family member, Mabel Hyde, built the dwelling between 1919 and 1922. Equitable Real Estate Company built *51 Montagu Street* by 1902 and conveyed it within a few years to Frank M. Smith.

54 MONTAGU STREET, ISAAC MOTTE DART HOUSE

Constructed circa 1806; porches added 1820s; back porch enclosed and second story added 1840s–50s; restored with new addition 1994–95

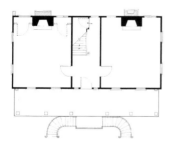

Measured plan of the first floor of 54 Montagu Street before restoration

In 1795 eleven lots on the estate of the late John Harleston were divided among his three surviving daughters. On July 21, 1801, Isaac Motte Dart, a Charleston attorney and factor, purchased the two halves of one lot, although he is listed as residing on Hasell Street until 1806. Dart built the typical Charleston single house now known as 54 Montagu Street between 1806 and 1809.

This two-and-a-half-story wooden building on a raised basement has a front staircase or portico and is reminiscent of plantation construction. Nineteenth-century changes included the large rear (northern) addition, removed after Hurricane Hugo. Also of note is the early–Gothic Revival carriage house on the property. The main building was purchased by the American Missionary Association in 1930 and retained until 1950. The property was then used by a local nursing school as a dormitory.

60 MONTAGU STREET, THEODORE GAILLARD (GAILLARD-BENNETT) HOUSE

Constructed 1800; restored 1992

Rice planter and merchant Theodore Gaillard began to assemble the three lots on which he would build his residence in the spring of 1800. When the *New Charleston Directory and Stranger's Guide* appeared in 1802, it noted that Gaillard had completed his house. He owned it for fifteen years, then sold it for $11,000 to Gen. Jacob Read during the depression that followed the War of 1812. Read died four years later. His estate sold the house in 1819 to James Shoolbred, a Santee River rice planter who was Charleston's first British consul. It is likely that early in Shoolbred's tenure (1819 until his death in 1851) he added the Regency style portico, the rusticated double entrance steps, and the robust quoining to the basement level. During his postwar visit to Charleston, Gen. Robert E. Lee addressed well-wishers from the second level of the portico as a guest of the owner, Washington Jefferson Bennett.

The interior of this double house is one of Charleston's best of the Federal period. Restored recently with great care, the structure contains elaborate plaster cornices and ceiling decorations and well-preserved examples of composition mantel decorations.

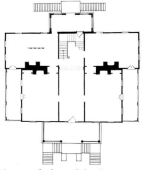

Measured plan of the first floor, 60 Montagu Street

62 MONTAGU STREET, JONATHAN STEINMEYER HOUSE

Constructed circa 1854–60

A member of a wealthy lumber mill family, Jonathan Steinmeyer, acquired this significant corner lot in Harleston Village in 1854, purchasing it from Keating L. Simons. Although briefly conveyed after the war to Elias Horlbeck, the house became the property of Samuel Prioleau Ravenel in 1872. Ravenel, scion of an old Huguenot plantation family, joined the ranks of Charleston's rising industrialists in the postbellum period with his interest in the Coosaw Mining Company, a phosphate extracting firm.

Long cited by the city and by preservationists as one of Charleston's most visibly dilapidated antebellum dwellings, the Steinmeyer House still retains much of its original historic fabric. A staircase on Gadsden Street approaches a raised entry to the principal levels. On these floors wooden piazzas with fluted Doric columns face southward. These at one time afforded a view across the marshes to the Ashley River. Masonry pillars line the ground floor on the southern side of the house. A large wooden dependency building survives to the north and remains with the property as a separate residence.

64 MONTAGU STREET, BENNETT-SIMONS HOUSE

Constructed 1800–12

The wealthy lumberman Thomas Bennett Sr., a contractor and amateur architect, built this house as a family residence sometime before his death in 1814. Bennett's grandson later owned the property but sold it in 1830. Passing though the Guerard and Moultrie families, the house was acquired in 1857 by Thomas Grange Simons. A plat prepared at the same time described the lot as containing "one large three story building being the mansion house, and the outbuildings and offices to wit, one two-story brick building and another brick building in one story, another one-story building of wood, together with two other small buildings."

The principal two-and-a-half-story wood house retains its essential form, although two-over-two windows replaced the original sashes in the late-nineteenth century. Probably at the same time, the portico was changed to create a wide overhanging piazza. The Ionic columns at the end of the first floor stand on individual masonry piers, while a stone staircase rises to the original portico in the same arrangement as *54 Montagu Street*. The brick carriage house, visible from Gadsden Street and now known as *40 Barre Street*, retains its original arched openings and other fenestration despite its conversion in the 1980s to a separate residence.

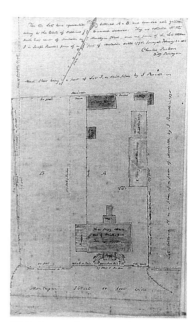

Mid-nineteenth-century plat showing 64 Montagu Street and its outbuildings

1 PITT STREET,
CHARLES HENRY LANNEAU HOUSE
Constructed circa 1848

Basile Lanneau, a tanner and currier, acquired these lots in the easternmost section of Harleston Village in 1788. The Lanneaus, French Catholic settlers from Acadia, arrived in South Carolina with other exiles in 1755. Basile was befriended by the wealthy merchant Henry Laurens, converted to Protestantism, and thrived as a craftsman and businessman. A number of houses in this area of Pitt Street were constructed by members of the Lanneau family.

1 and 3 Pitt Street

Charles Henry Lanneau built this house by 1848, after which he conveyed it to William D. Porter, who supposedly allowed the house to be used as a prison for Federal soldiers during the Civil War. Acquired by William Baynard Simons in 1889, the house was held by his family until the end of the 1930s.

Built of local brick, the Charles Henry Lanneau House follows the side-hall, double-parlor plan, with a rear addition for a dining room. Rubbed brick jack arches, a brick belt course between floors, and a dogtoothed cornice ornament the front facade. The flat-roofed dwelling has a two-tiered piazza facing Beaufain Street, accessed by triple sashed windows from the double parlors and rear dining room.

The Lanneau family also built a similar stuccoed side-hall-plan house at *5 Pitt Street* around 1830. A small Greek Revival portico fronts the entry door to this flat-roofed dwelling. In the early-twentieth century this house became the home of Carrie and Mabel Pollitzer, sisters active in suffrage, art, and music circles. Their other sister, Anita Pollitzer, was a friend and biographer of Georgia O'Keeffe.

3 PITT STREET, BASILE LANNEAU HOUSE
Constructed 1790–1820; restored 1970s

Basile Lanneau bought this property before the Revolution but apparently did not build on it until the late-eighteenth century. The original two-story, wood single house received a third-story addition and a double-tiered Greek Revival piazza in the mid-1800s. An Italianate door hood was added to the piazza door screen in the late-nineteenth century, and the building was eventually converted into apartments. Badly deteriorated from neglect by the 1970s, the house was subsequently restored. A small two-and-a-half-story single house standing directly across the street at *2 Pitt Street* was moved to the site in 1974 from 34 St. Philip Street. The Preservation Society relocated the building to prevent its destruction for a city parking garage. This house was also built by Basile Lanneau, probably between 1782 and 1787.

7–9 PITT STREET, LANNEAU HOUSES

Constructed 1830–40

The younger Basile Lanneau built the two-story, pressed-brick house at 7 Pitt Street between 1837 and 1840 on a lot purchased by his father. This flat-roofed Greek Revival dwelling retains its side piazza and interior detailing. Its stone window lintels and sills, masonry detailing, and cast-iron grilles with anthemion motifs match those on the Lanneau dwelling at 9 Pitt Street, a three-story, side-hall-plan house built by the family sometime between 1830 and 1840. The latter building has its principal rooms on the second floor and an upper piazza resting on masonry piers. Several original outbuildings survive at the rear of 7 Pitt Street.

9 Pitt Street

13 PITT STREET, HENRY GERDTS HOUSE

Constructed 1859–60

A brownstone pediment supported by carved console brackets marks the front doorway of this two-and-a-half-story house built by a wholesale grocer and commission merchant a few years before the War Between the States. Built on a corner lot, the house is ornamented on the front, facing Pitt Street, with brick corbeling and brownstone lintels and sills. A double-tiered piazza with Ionic columns on the first floor and Corinthian columns on the second shades the Wentworth Street side of the house and overlooks a garden space enclosed by a nineteenth-century wall with brick piers, paneled brick coping, and a wooden balustrade.

13 Pitt Street, with its piazzas and dependencies along Wentworth Street, 1930s

Gerdts left the house to those of his daughters who were unmarried or widowed, and the house remained in the family until 1955. Extensive dependencies, visible from Wentworth Street, were long ago converted to apartments.

543

18–20 PITT STREET, SAMUEL H. WILSON TENEMENTS
Constructed 1880

A King Street merchant built both of these two-story frame dwellings as rental properties in 1880.

21 PITT STREET, EMILY GAILLARD HOUSE
Constructed circa 1838; restored 1971

In keeping with the system of marriage settlements, this property was conveyed in trust in 1837 for Emily Rutledge Parker, daughter of John Parker, upon her marriage to the merchant Theodore Gaillard. Mrs. Gaillard apparently lived here by 1840 and stayed until 1852, when the house was leased to the merchant Augustus Jones. Mrs. Gaillard's trustee sold the house in 1887 to Mrs. Julia Boag, a widow. Typical of two-and-a-half-story masonry single houses built in uptown Charleston, the front gable end is separated from the main body of the house by a corbeled brick band. A double-tiered piazza shades the western elevation of the building, and a late-nineteenth-century ell addition joins the house to a dependency. In 1940 the structure was turned into apartments. The restoration of the house in 1971 marked one of the first revitalization projects in this part of Harleston Village.

31 PITT STREET, JOHN M. SCHNIERLE HOUSE
Constructed circa 1830–40

John Schnierle, a German carpenter, bought this lot from a Virginia physician in 1817. Although he and his family continued to live on Friend (now Legare) Street, Schnierle apparently built this house in the 1830s. It stands two and a half stories tall on a raised brick basement and has weatherboard sheathing. A closed gable end faces the street, while a double-tiered piazza faces a sizable side lot. Schnierle died in 1846, and his property was partitioned among his sons, John and William, and his daughters, who had married other prominent German families, the Sieglings and the Horlbecks.

33 PITT STREET, JOHN SCHNIERLE JR. HOUSE
Constructed circa 1849

John Schnierle Jr. built this house around 1849. Typical of the single house form found in Harleston Village, the two-and-a-half-story dwelling with a closed gable roof stands on a high masonry foundation. The double-tiered, Tuscan-columned piazza also stands on masonry piers. Elected as the city's second German mayor, Schnierle followed the first, Mayor Jacob Mintzing, upon his death in 1843. Both Mintzing and Schnierle were lumber merchants and marked the rise of Charleston's German Lutheran community to virtual dominance in city politics and certain economic spheres in the nineteenth century. Schnierle, still residing here after the Civil War, died in 1869.

41–43 PITT STREET, OLD PLYMOUTH CONGREGATIONAL CHURCH
Constructed 1871–72

A group of black Congregationalists left the Circular Congregational Church and worshipped in various locations, including the chapel at the Avery Institute, forming, by 1867, the Plymouth Congregational Church. Backed by the American Missionary Association, the congregation grew slowly. Under the leadership of the Reverend James T. Ford, pastor and teacher at Avery, the congregation purchased a lot at the corner of Pitt and Bull Streets and built a church and a parsonage. The church, dedicated on March 10, 1872, was a Greek Revival style New England meetinghouse with a steeply pitched gable roof and six tall sash windows on the north and south facades. Only the Pitt Street entry and its roof overhang show the influence of Ecclesiastical Gothic architecture.

The contemporary parsonage dwelling at *32 Bull Street* exhibits the Queen Anne style with a cross gable and a square tower at the corner of the front facade, topped by a bellcast roof. The church moved to Spring Street in 1958. The Charleston Association for the Blind purchased the former church building and used it until 1995.

57 PITT STREET, BETHEL METHODIST CHURCH

 Constructed 1852–53

Ephraim Curtis, architect; Reb and Busby, contractors

The congregation of the Blue Meeting House on Cumberland Street bought this site for a church and cemetery in 1793. A wooden meetinghouse constructed in 1797 was moved to the western side of the lot to make way for the present Greek Revival building and was eventually moved across Calhoun Street to become Old Bethel Methodist Church. The (new) Bethel Methodist Church is a simple temple-form building with six large fluted Doric columns supporting a pedimented portico. On the interior, a late-nineteenth-century stenciled paint scheme has been restored and the pressed metal ceiling panels in the cove ceiling have been preserved. An antebellum cast- and wrought-iron fence encloses the front of the property, while masonry piers and wooden fencing surround the grave-

Bethel Methodist Church, Pitt and Calhoun Streets, 1875 engraving

yard. A large, columned Sunday school building once serving as host to one of Charleston's most thriving congregations was removed several decades ago, and an earlier Italianate structure built for the same purpose was demolished in 1994. A large monument in the graveyard marks the burial site of the phosphate tycoon Francis J. Pelzer.

157 QUEEN STREET, DR. WILLIAM MICHEL BUILDING

Constructed circa 1855–60

Dr. William Michell purchased this property and two lots to the west a few years after the subdivision of a number of parcels in this block in 1849. The structure retains its stuccoed brick ground story, which by the 1880s served as a store. The one and a half stories above retain weatherboarded siding as well as a closed gable roof with three dormers along Queen Street and a tripartite window facing Franklin Street. A double-tiered piazza on the south side has been enclosed, as has a rear piazza at the western edge of the building. Michel left the property to Middleton Michel at his death in 1871. The younger Michel experienced financial reversals, and 157 Queen Street became the property of Berend Puckhaber, owner of a large wholesale grocery complex on upper King Street. In 1879 Puckhaber built two houses on the parcels to the west at *159* and *161 Queen Street*. These identical wooden houses still possess two-bay front facades with six-over-six windows and closed gable ends. They have single, centered chimney stacks rising from the ridges of the roofs. Asymmetrical in plan, the four-bay facades on the west side are shaded by double-tiered piazzas.

162 QUEEN STREET, FOX-MAGEE HOUSE
Constructed circa 1852

On its original sale in 1852 to George Mansfield, this site was described as a "low water lot." Maria Fox, who bought the property in 1852, apparently began construction of the present house, which she was forced to convey a year later to Capt. Arthur Magee, holder of a mortgage on the house. Magee died within a year, but his widow lived here until 1893. Dogtoothed brickwork, a wrought-iron balcony, and a pair of banded chimneys characterize this dwelling as well as the slightly taller exposed brick single house to the east at *160 Queen Street*, owned and occupied in 1860 by Henry Campsen.

163 QUEEN STREET, SAMUEL COURTENAY TENEMENT
Constructed circa 1856–57

Broad Street's leading bookseller, Samuel Courtenay, bought this property as a vacant lot in 1856 and constructed a house as an investment. A mariner named Deforrest purchased the building in 1863 and conveyed it a decade later to Mary E. Miller, who lived here for the rest of the century. The two-and-a-half-story dwelling, topped by an open gable roof with wide overhanging eaves, follows the side-hall plan. Although most of the front windows have been replaced with two-over-two sashes and the front door is capped by a late-Victorian window hood, the structure nonetheless retains an unusual second-story cast-iron balcony overlooking a small thoroughfare formerly known as Cooper's Court (named after its antebellum owner, George Washington Cooper). Today the lane is called Michel Place. In 1860 twenty-five people, including nine slaves, lived in the four houses of nineteenth-century vintage that are still on the alley.

192 QUEEN STREET, LOPEZ HOUSE

Constructed circa 1852

A member of one of Charleston's leading Sephardic Jewish families built this unusual dwelling as a rental property by 1852. Rented in 1861 to the Frenchman Napoleon L. Coste, the house was owned by the Lopez family for several decades. The dwelling is constructed in the side-hall plan, and the front facade is constructed with board and batten cladding, fronted by a double-tiered piazza with open-work wood columns. All of these characteristics are hallmarks of the Carpenter Gothic style.

40 RUTLEDGE AVENUE, ALBERT W. TODD HOUSE

Constructed circa 1900; rehabilitated 1986

Charleston's first leading Colonial Revival architect, Albert W. Todd, who also served as a state senator, designed this house as his own residence at the turn of the century. The building's exterior, previously stuccoed, now has beaded cypress weatherboard siding. A semicircular Neoclassical portico with smaller side porches, all with Ionic columns, ornaments the front facade facing Colonial Lake. A massive rectilinear doorway with a square fanlight, flanked by oval windows, marks the primary entry, while on the second-story balcony a semicircular fanlight ornaments the surmounting doorway. On the south elevation a two-story piazza, also with Ionic columns, overlooks the western end of Queen Street, while a massive entablature with a deep frieze, dentils, and modillions supports the deep soffit of the roof.

Todd sold the house five years after construction to Dr. William Frampton and his wife Pauline. Frampton, a woodworking

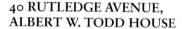

enthusiast, installed a significant amount of wood taken from the demolished Cooper River plantation house Belvedere. In addition to the cornices, mantels, and wainscoting from Belvedere, he added parquet floors to a number of rooms. After purchasing the house in 1938, Mr. and Mrs. G. Simms McDowell made further changes, including the cypress siding and the present cast-iron fence. The house was renovated as a bed-and-breakfast inn in 1986 and is now referred to as The Belvedere.

42 RUTLEDGE AVENUE, THOMAS O'BRIEN HOUSE

Constructed circa 1859

Thomas O'Brien, a grocer and liquor dealer, constructed this large-scale Charleston single house a few years after purchasing the lot in 1856. A deep entablature with large modillions frames the front end pediment. The first-floor windows, as well as the third-story Palladian window, follow the Italianate style of architecture. Although the present piazza door screen is a Colonial Revival replacement, the piazza appears to be original, with large fluted Doric columns on the first floor and slightly smaller columns of the same order on the second tier. O'Brien also built the house next door at *44 Rutledge Avenue*. Somewhat simpler in detail, the piazza retains its nineteenth-century door screen with acanthus leaf console brackets supporting a dentiled entablature.

52 RUTLEDGE AVENUE, HARRIET F. CREIGHTON HOUSE

Constructed circa 1913

One of Charleston's most eclectically decorated wooden houses, the Creighton House was built in the name of the wife of the owner of Charleston's largest lumber firm, the Whipple Lumber Company. Constructed at the end of the period of Queen

Anne fashion, the house displays numerous elements of that architectural style. An Ionic-columned porch wraps the front and south elevations. A pediment marks the entry to the house and is flanked to the north by an octagonal tower sheathed in fish-scale shingles, topped by a conical roof and ornamented by a bull's-eye window. On the south end of the front elevation, a pedimented gable supported by brackets tops a curvilinear bay. The Creightons kept the house until 1918, when it was sold to the Poulnot family, owners of Kerrison's Department Store, who lived here for forty-four years.

The somewhat earlier Queen Anne style house at *50 Rutledge Avenue* had been transferred by 1912 as the headquarters of the Society for the Welfare of the Aged of Charleston. This house, with its two-story side piazza and front porch supported by turned Queen Anne columns, sports the same pattern of turret and projecting front gable but offers an earlier example of the same architectural style.

63 RUTLEDGE AVENUE, BERKELEY COURT

Constructed 1922

This apartment building is set back at a diagonal on a corner lot at Beaufain Street and Rutledge Avenue. It has Italian villa detailing with a bracketed cornice and low-pitched roof. The front entry is Italian Renaissance in style with overtones of Spanish Colonial and Craftsman features. It was constructed by Edward J. Murphy, who also built the Fort Sumter Hotel at the Battery. The apartments are fireproof, made entirely of concrete, brick, and tile.

65 RUTLEDGE AVENUE, JAMES HENRY TAYLOR HOUSE (I)

Constructed circa 1840

The builder of this three-and-a-half-story, side-hall-plan house came to Charles-

65–67 Rutledge

ton from New England and rose to be one of the leading merchants in the city. Active in promoting industrialism and becoming one of the earliest manufacturers of cotton goods in the state, James Taylor also helped found the Carolina Art Association. The simple Greek Revival dwelling, still retaining its early stucco coating, was embellished with pressed metal detailing in the late-nineteenth century, including the semicircular window heads and the pedimented door overhang supported by metal brackets. A triple-tiered piazza with three levels of Tuscan columns shades the south elevation of the house, which at the time of construction overlooked Colonial Lake. This house, like the residence Taylor constructed next door at *67 Rutledge Avenue* in 1850, remained in the hands of Taylor descendants until 1968.

67 RUTLEDGE AVENUE, COL. JAMES HENRY TAYLOR HOUSE (II)

Constructed circa 1852

James Taylor's later residence, this brick-stucco, two-story, side-hall-plan dwelling exhibits Italianate and Gothic features, including double bracketed eaves supporting a pyramidal, hipped roof and central cupola, as well as a Carpenter Gothic front piazza with trefoil shaped columns flanking three latticework Moorish arches. The same arch appears in the masonry drive gate on the south. The house is notable not only because it retained, until recently, many of its original lighting fixtures, fireplace equipment, and bell system, but because its full complement of yard buildings also survives. Constructed about 1852, the house contains one of the earliest examples of interior plumbing in Charleston. An original copper bathtub survives, as do a rooftop rainwater cachement and a basement cistern.

71 RUTLEDGE AVENUE, CORBETT-JERVEY HOUSE

Constructed circa 1831

Elizabeth Corbett, a niece of Elizabeth Harleston, whose family still owned much of this area in the early-nineteenth century, built this three-story weatherboarded house in the early-1830s. Modified, possibly in the Greek Revival period, with a front entry and later with changes including French doors on the piazza side and two-over-two windows, the house retains its spacious lot. Owned for many years by the family of Judge Theodore Jervey, the building was occupied by the Braid family in the twentieth century.

71 Rutledge Avenue and environs in the 1960s

73 RUTLEDGE AVENUE, WHILDEN-HIRSCH HOUSE

Constructed circa 1856

Elizabeth Corbett, builder of the house next door, inherited this lot from the estate of her aunt Elizabeth Harleston in 1831. Eventually the estate passed to William Whilden, who built the nucleus of the present residence by 1856. Owned by the Manson family during the Civil War, the property was purchased in 1893 by the clothier Isaac W. Hirsch. It has been theorized that Hirsch used T. H. Abrahams from the firm of Abrahams and Seyle to remodel or largely rebuild the house. The resulting Second Empire style structure, with a mansard roof sheathed in fish-scale slate shingles supported by a deep metal cornice, stands nearly intact as completed in the 1890s. A large bay window with a bracketed cornice and a hooded entry architrave with a cut-glass transom ornament the front facade. A diagonal wall faces the corner of Wentworth Street and Rutledge Avenue, and several stained-glass windows are visible from this elevation. One of these depicts a stag, a reference to the German word *Hirsch*. The house retains an unusual survival in its natural-colored stucco scored with a red joint.

74 RUTLEDGE AVENUE, HARLESTON-BOCQUET HOUSE
Constructed circa 1782–83

One of the most distinguished eighteenth-century houses in uptown Charleston, this two-and-a-half-story weatherboarded double house stands on a high Flemish bonded-brick foundation. Resembling a country villa or suburban seat, the house is on land once owned by the Harleston family. Isaac Child Harleston, a Revolutionary War soldier and provincial congressman, may have built the present residence. The property was conveyed to Peter Bocquet, owner of *95 Broad Street*, in 1783. Advertised for sale after his death in 1793, a house and other buildings were specified for this site. Gov. John Matthews, a former member of the Continental Congress and second chief executive of South Carolina, lived here until his death in 1802.

The house passed through numerous owners until it was acquired by the Aimar family in 1912. They or their immediate predecessors probably changed the dormers in the hipped roof to the Colonial Revival style examples seen today. The garden is perhaps the most important element of this property to survive. It retains its late-eighteenth-century plan, including quatrefoil, circular, and other shaped beds edged with brick and box. Larkspurs, old *camellia japonicas,* and periwinkles survive as plantings of one of Charleston's oldest town gardens.

81 RUTLEDGE AVENUE, GLOVER-SOTTILE HOUSE
Constructed circa 1826; altered late-nineteenth century

Joseph Glover, a physician, built the present dwelling as a three-story Charleston single house on a raised foundation. In the late-nineteenth century Italianate details were added to the building, including the cast-iron pedimented window heads and rusticated piazza door architrave, matching the stucco rustication of the ground floor and the corner quoining of the facade. Semicircular iron balconies and ironwork railings were probably added to the piazza at the same time. Charleston businessman Cavaliere Giovanni Sottile, later the Italian consul, purchased the house in 1906. Appended to the northwest corner of the building, a pedimented three-and-a-half-story dependency structure apparently stood on the site in the eighteenth century when this section of Harleston Village was still largely undeveloped.

89 RUTLEDGE AVENUE, JAMES WHITE HOUSE

Constructed circa 1852

Elizabeth Smith White inherited a portion of this property from her father's estate in 1840, and through partition and subsequent purchase she and her husband created two building lots at Rutledge Avenue and Wentworth Street. By 1852 White built 89 Rutledge Avenue on the corner as a two-and-a-half-story stuccoed brick Charleston single house with stone lintels and sills on the principal windows of the front elevation topped by a pilaster gable with a tripartite window. The present loggia entry and piazza are later additions. An early-twentieth-century addition to the rear dependency created a substantial additional unit accessed from Montagu Street. Shortly after constructing this residence for himself, White built a similar masonry Charleston single house with a corbeled brick gable end at *87 Rutledge Avenue.*

93 RUTLEDGE AVENUE, EDWARD L. TRENHOLM HOUSE

Constructed circa 1850

A giant order Tower of the Winds columned portico commands the Montagu Street elevation of one of Charleston's most

elaborate antebellum houses. Serving as an interesting foil to the similarly oriented Mikell House across the street, this dwelling was built by Edward L. Trenholm. Trenholm spent some years in England as the managing partner of Fraser, Trenholm and Company. Reflecting the transition between Greek Revival and Italianate influences in Charleston, a pedimented doorway on the Rutledge Avenue side leads to a stair hall rising to the principal entertaining floor, which has large double drawing rooms. The window heads on the east side become more exuberant on the south portico side with broken pediments and central shell motifs supported by brackets. 93 Rutledge Avenue has been made into apartments, with a ground-floor office.

94 RUTLEDGE AVENUE, ISAAC JENKINS MIKELL HOUSE

Constructed 1853–54; restored 1960s, 1980s

One of the most visually imposing houses in Charleston constructed before the Civil War, the Isaac Jenkins Mikell House more closely resembles an Italian villa than a Charleston house. In July 1853 Mikell purchased lots 97 and 98 in Harleston Village for $13,300. Nearly a year later he sold half of that land to Edward H. Lane for a bond of $12,000. It is assumed that Mikell began construction on his house located on lot 98 shortly after its purchase in 1853. The house appears much as it did then, with a Minton-tiled portico supported by Corinthian column capitals carved from cypress and ornamented by rams' heads. Mikell was one of several millionaire Sea Island cotton planters from Edisto Island. This town house is believed to have been built for Mary Martha Pope, his third wife.

The house passed through a series of owners until 1934, when it was listed as vacant. In 1935 the house was sold to the

Detail of one of the columns at 94 Rutledge Avenue

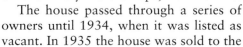

Charleston Free Library, and it began twenty-five years of public service. It was saved and restored as a residence in the 1960s by Mr. and Mrs. Charles Woodward.

95 RUTLEDGE AVENUE, GRIMKÉ-SEABROOK HOUSE
Constructed circa 1815–26

Judge John Faucheraud Grimké began construction of this house in 1815. Father of the abolitionist Grimké sisters, he lived with his family at *321 East Bay Street* and probably never resided on this site. Thomas Banister Seabrook, a cotton planter from Edisto Island, completed the house and probably installed the Adamesque mantels and other decorations. The dwelling was conveyed by Seabrook's daughter, Caroline Geddes, to Edward Trenholm in 1850. Trenholm lived here briefly while finishing his own house on the south side of the lot.

This house retains its original stuccoed quoining and dogtooth cornicing in its closed gable front. It has a double-tiered south piazza with an arched soffit on the principal story. Late-nineteenth-century changes to the house include the Victorian pressed-metal window heads and the two-over-two windows.

97 RUTLEDGE AVENUE, GIBBON HOUSE
Constructed circa 1885

Constructed in the late-Italianate style variant of the Charleston side-hall plan, this dwelling built by George Gibbon just before the earthquake of 1886 is noted for its fine balustraded front stair, a bracketed front gable with a semicircular headed window, and double-tiered piazza with similar brackets. Held by the Gibbon family for nearly a century, it descended to Maude Gibbon, who founded the Charleston Symphony in 1919. She reorganized the symphony in 1936 and personally collected needed musical scores and instruments, as well as housing guest artists such as Pablo Casals. Miss Gibbon left the house to the Charleston Symphony in the 1960s, and it served as that organization's headquarters for several years before returning to a single-family residence.

101 RUTLEDGE AVENUE, WILLIAM STEVENS SMITH HOUSE
Constructed circa 1796–1804

This substantial three-and-a-half-story, stuccoed-brick single house retains its original street-level door, which accesses an office space as it has for many decades. The rusticated arched piazza screen provides access to an inner wooden staircase, rising to the principal level of the piazza. A plantation-owning politician and attorney, William Stevens Smith, a grandson of Josiah Smith, the builder of *7 Meeting Street*, constructed this house on land he believed belonged to his wife but actually was held by her uncle Benjamin Waring. He received title after lamenting to a court of equity that it was "inconvenient" to allow a large proportion of his property to remain vested in a house he had "declined using as a family residence." He sold the property in 1804 without ever having lived here.

Passing through a variety of planters and merchants, the dwelling eventually was owned by William Laughton, a rice and cotton merchant, from 1846 to 1877. Laughton probably made most of the Greek Revival changes to the house. Late-Italianate changes include window heads and two-over-two windows, which were probably made by Dr. Thomas McDow. McDow was acquited for the murder of Francis Warrington Dawson of *99 Bull Street*, who was shot while in the basement of this house. The interior includes a mix of Neoclassical wainscoting, doors, and staircase, with some mantels in the late-Victorian style. Several Greek Revival ceiling medallions can be seen in the drawing room and dining room.

104 RUTLEDGE AVENUE, THOMAS BANNISTER SEABROOK HOUSE
Constructed circa 1816

Edisto Island planter Thomas B. Seabrook, who completed the house at 95 Rutledge Avenue, built this three-and-a-half-story dwelling on a high foundation for himself in about 1816. The house retains arched piazzas of its Neoclassical period as well as a pediment with a lunette roof window. Queen Anne style window heads, a bracketed Queen Anne cornice, and a three-story tower with triple bracketing, shingling, and a conical bell-shaped roof were probably added by Arthur A. Lynah in the late-1880s.

105 RUTLEDGE AVENUE, SMITH-MIKELL HOUSE
Constructed circa 1820–35

William Stevens Smith, who built the house at *101 Rutledge Avenue*, constructed this single house sometime before 1837. He conveyed it first to his daughter Henrietta, who married into the Mikell family, and later to another daughter, Juliette. The dwelling, with its nine-over-nine windows and modillioned front gable, reflects the transitional period between the late-Federal style and the advent of the Greek Revival style.

112 RUTLEDGE AVENUE, HUGHES-MOLONY HOUSE
Constructed circa 1830; altered 1940s

This finely detailed two-and-a-half-story building follows many of the design elements found on other large-scale Harleston Village buildings, particularly those built

by the Bennett family. The house retains its closed gable roof and modillioned cornice. A pedimented second-story pavilion projects above the principal tier of the side piazza. When completed, this house stood on the southern edge of the Bennett mill pond and faced a spacious lot of its own to the east, as well as that of the Huchet House on the corner. Owned by the Hughes family at the time of the War Between the States, the house was retrimmed with Queen Anne detailing in the late-nineteenth century. It passed out of the family by 1904, when it became the residence of H. A. Molony, a grain and fertilizer dealer. The dwelling was converted to apartments in the 1940s and to condominiums in the 1980s.

114 RUTLEDGE AVENUE, BRODIE HOUSE

Constructed circa 1893–94

The Bennett mill pond was filled by 1893, and the newly created lots there were gradually sold for construction. Through a trust estate, Dr. Robert L. Brodie purchased this lot and built the existing house before 1894. Raised a full story off the ground, the dwelling has a piazza that is approached by a wide stair. Queen Anne style columns wrap the building, which also boasts an elaborate spindle-work balustrade.

121 RUTLEDGE AVENUE, CANNON PARK AND RUINS OF THE CHARLESTON MUSEUM

Established by 1880; some redevelopment circa 1985

After the Bennett mill pond was filled, Mayor William Ashmead Courtenay was wise to retain Frederick Law Olmstead to design a park for this site. But before the park was completed, the city decided in May 1899 to build an auditorium here to serve as convention space, particularly for the United Confederate Veterans. A bequest from John Thompson to the city was used to finance the auditorium construction. Although designed by the architect Frank Milburn, who was selected early in his career for this commission, the structure was built in a temporary manner with a cast-iron frame and exterior stucco with applied ornament in the Beaux Arts style. By 1907 the auditorium became the home of The Charleston Museum, which remained here until the collection was moved into a new building on Meeting Street in 1980. Within a month, the old building burned. The original semicircular colonnade has been preserved as an architectural folly. The city partially restored the plan of the original Cannon Park, and much of the site remains as open green space.

The old Charleston Museum building in the 1960s, before fire destroyed all but the portico

122 RUTLEDGE AVENUE, JAMES S. SIMONS HOUSE
Constructed 1893

Businessman James S. Simons built the first of a series of Queen Anne style houses on the newly filled mill pond lots facing Cannon Park. An extending gable surmounting a double-tiered bay and a corner turret ornament the upper stories of this wood dwelling. It has encircling fluted-columned piazzas and a pedimented entry. Favorite period features, such as fish-scale shingling within the gables and on the tower, as well as paired windows and console brackets, add further distinction to the facade.

126 RUTLEDGE AVENUE, ADELE G. BAKER HOUSE
Constructed 1898–1902

Cross gables with Tudor style wood decoration and diamond pane windows, as well as an ornamental turret with a conical roof, identify this late–Queen Anne style house built by Adele G. Baker on a lot purchased by Benjamin McCabe in 1893.

126 Rutledge Avenue as viewed from Cannon Park, circa 1905

McCabe, owner of a row of Queen Anne style houses on Chapel Street and developer of numerous sites on the peninsula, acquired several of these lots, obviously intending to build a row of investment houses. The McCabe lots, however, went to individual owners, who built an assortment of Queen Anne and Colonial Revival style houses in the ensuing decade.

34 SMITH STREET, ROBERTSON-PICKENS HOUSE

Constructed circa 1855; restored 1990s

George Robertson, a prosperous Scottish merchant, built this large Italianate style "villa" on the northeast corner of Beaufain and Smith Streets in about 1855. The house descended to Anna Ingraham Pickens, wife of a Citadel cadet who fired one of the first shots of the Civil War. By 1902 the Pickens family, through their trustee, sold the house to Julius Janhz, a partner in the C. D. Franke Company as well as a bank director. Serving as chairman of the Commission for Public Works, Janhz was responsible for a diversion of the Edisto River that still provides much of Charleston's present-day water supply.

The house's central pedimented pavilion, with arched windows and a balustrade bay, dominates the Smith Street side. The principal entry is on the north, approached by a flight of red sandstone steps. A masked piazza is on the south side. Used as apartments for several decades, the house was recently restored as a single-family residence.

39 SMITH STREET, HENRIETTA KELLY HOUSE

Constructed circa 1898; restored 1990s

Henrietta Kelly, owner and operator of Miss Kelly's School next door at 151 Wentworth Street, built the present Queen Anne style house with cross gables, corner turret, and encircling front piazza. For years this was one of the few Charleston Victorian houses to be painted in a palette reminiscent of its era of construction. It was rented for many years to the Hornik family, dry goods merchants.

52 SMITH STREET, ETTSEL ADAMS HOUSE

Constructed circa 1850; restored 1979

Ettsel Adams, a partner in Adams and Frost Commissions, built this town house around 1850 for rental or resale while living next door at *29 Montagu Street*. Italianate detailing, including the window and door heads as well as the double arched windows in the front arched gable end, cover earlier late–Greek Revival features. Original survivals include curious dentiled belt courses and cornice, and the double-tiered, Tuscan-columned piazzas. Arcaded, Italianate style chimneys emerge from the roof on the south elevation.

54 SMITH STREET, JOHN HUNTER HOUSE

Constructed circa 1830

Beaded-edge weatherboarding and a central lunette window in a pediment at the gable roof distinguish this late-Federal style dwelling built by John Hunter after he acquired the lot in 1830. The interesting console brackets supporting the hood over the front door probably date from the 1850s, as do French windows accessing the encircling side and rear piazza.

58 SMITH STREET, RAYMOND-DALY HOUSE

Constructed circa 1840–50

Mary and Henry Raymond completed this three-and-a-half-story stuccoed brick Charleston single house a few years before

selling it to John Daly, a boot and shoe dealer at *306 King Street.* Although the lower story of the side piazza remains open, enclosures of the second-story piazza and the remnant of the third-story piazza were probably done at the turn of the twentieth century. At that time the house was owned by Thomas Reynolds, a granite and marble worker, who raised eight children and several grandchildren in the house. Reynolds added marble tiles to the piazza, the interior foyer, and other spots within the building.

59 SMITH STREET, CAPT. JOSEPH JENKINS HOUSE
Constructed circa 1818; restored 1964

Capt. Joseph Jenkins, owner of Brick House Plantation on Edisto Island, built this single house as a town residence shortly after purchasing these two lots in 1818. The building stands on a high masonry foundation and retains the features that are hallmarks of Harleston Village single houses. The weatherboarded facade, with two bays on the street side and nine-over-nine windows, terminates in a closed gable roof. It has side dormers and a central pediment with a lunette window. A one-story piazza supported by an arcaded stucco ground story is accessed from the street by a ground-level piazza door screen with a pilastered architrave and rectangular fanlighted transom. Jenkins sold the house to his nephew, and it remained in the family until 1838, when it passed to William Birnie. After the War Between the States the original lot was subdivided and new houses in the Queen Anne style were constructed at *55* and *57 Smith Street.* Mr. and Mrs. Charles Woodward of Philadelphia, who restored *94 Rutledge Avenue* a few years earlier, rehabilitated this dwelling, removing asbestos siding and the remnants of numerous rental units.

67 SMITH STREET, COL. SIMON MAGWOOD HOUSE

Constructed 1818–24

The original dependency of 67 Smith Street, visible from Bull Street

Col. Simon Magwood was an Anglo-Irish immigrant who came to Charleston after the Revolution, constructed wharves along the Cooper River waterfront, and also served as a state senator. He built this two-and-a-half-story Charleston single house on a raised, stuccoed basement. An original pedimented door architrave accesses an arcaded ground story and stairway leading to the principal tier of the south piazza. A fanlighted doorway provides access from the piazza to an elaborate interior, with late-Neoclassical and early–Greek Revival plaster and wood decoration (sometimes referred to as Regency style). A paneled parapet with a modillioned cornice shields the roof of the piazza from the house. The gabled roof, with its closed tympanum on the street side, has a projecting pediment on the south side. The central lunette window was lost many years ago. Its original dependency, now a separate residence on Bull Street, retains its mid-nineteenth-century stucco and arched window heads.

Magwood built a similar dwelling for his son at *63 Smith Street*. This house has nearly identical pedimented window heads but a simpler arcaded double-tiered piazza on its south side. Although Magwood's daughter and son-in-law sold 67 Smith Street in 1863, his descendants retained 63 Smith until 1905.

84 SMITH STREET, ANNIE ACKERMAN HOUSE

Constructed 1896–97

Annie Ackerman, wife of a King Street paint dealer and resident of *45 Pitt Street*, built this finely detailed Queen Anne style house. A two-story bay sheathed in shaped shingles projects from the front elevation, while turned-columned piazzas with elaborate spindle work and cornice bracketing attach to the south elevation. A matching portico covers the front entry of this side-hall-plan house.

89 SMITH STREET, BENNETT-JONES HOUSE

Constructed circa 1840; renovated circa 1850; rehabilitated 1989

By 1840 either Gov. Thomas Bennett Jr. or his son, W. Jefferson Bennett, built this two-story Greek Revival house overlooking the marshes and family mill pond. Occupied in the 1850s by the noted architect Edward C. Jones, the house was renovated to relate to Smith Street with a Doric-columned front portico decorated with interesting reverse console brackets that flank the front doorway. Polygonal bay windows on the north and south ends feature a mix of Gothic, Roman, and Egyptian detailing. These last features create curious alcoves with Gothic plaster decoration in the principal first-floor rooms.

91 SMITH STREET, NATHANIEL MAXWELL HOUSE

Constructed circa 1808; renovated 1905; rehabilitated 1980s

Christian Henry Faber, a merchant of German extraction on King Street, leased a lot on Calhoun Street in 1808 to Nathaniel G. Maxwell. Maxwell built the present dwelling in the Federal style with weatherboarding, a low pitched hipped roof, and five bays on each elevation with nine-over-nine sash windows. Hewn and sash-sawn framing evidences the early character of the building. Moved from Calhoun Street to the present site, the house became a rental duplex in 1905 and continues to house tenants. The front piazza was later rebuilt, while the rear porch retains its Tuscan columns.

94 SMITH STREET, MORRIS BROWN HOUSE
Constructed circa 1818

The Reverend Morris Brown built this house as an investment property after acquiring the lot from master carpenter Richard Holloway, a fellow member of the free African American community. Holloway himself may have built this structure, as he did his own investment property next door at *96 Smith Street*. Brown, whose church was implicated in the Denmark Vesey slave insurrection plot, had to leave the state in 1822. He moved to Philadelphia and eventually became a founding bishop of the A.M.E. Church. Wide weatherboarding, six-over-six windows, and an open gable roof characterize this simple Charleston single house. It retains its original double-tiered piazza and an early–Greek Revival piazza door screen. An ell addition at the rear was added in the late-nineteenth century. Brown, while residing in Philadelphia, sold the house to William Gibson in 1829.

15, 17, & 19 ST. PHILIP STREET, JOHN S. RIGGS TENEMENTS
Constructed 1859–60; rehabilitated 1977

John S. Riggs, organizer of Charleston's horse-drawn streetcar system and president of the company when it merged with the Electric Railway Company, built these three identical houses and two others at *88–90 Wentworth Street* shortly after acquiring four lots from the glebe of St. Philip's Parish. The houses were finished by 1860 and rented to Octavius Willke, the Reverend Thomas O'Rice, and Elizabeth M. Archer. They followed the traditional Charleston single house pattern with a mix of Greek Revival and Italianate elements. The arched windows and quoining reflect the former style, while the peaked ground-stone window heads and certain other features represent the latter. The interior is a similar mix of details, from Italianate mantels in the parlors to Greek Revival moldings and ceiling medallions in other rooms. The tenements were rehabilitated by the College of Charleston in 1977.

25 ST. PHILIP STREET, THADDEUS STREET EDUCATION CENTER

Constructed 1980

Cummings and McCrady, architects

The firm of Cummings and McCrady designed this 52,000-square-foot building for the college's Center of Continuing Education graduate studies and learning resources, which was dedicated to Thaddeus Street, a business leader in twentieth-century Charleston. This building is the first of several that were attempts to imitate the Charleston streetscape through the streetline massing and indentation of most of the structure.

50 ST. PHILIP STREET, ALBERT SIMONS CENTER FOR THE ARTS

Constructed 1977

Simons, Lapham, Mitchell, and Small, architects

This structure is named for Charleston's most noted twentieth-century architect, college trustee, and professor of fine arts. The architectural firm that Albert Simons founded designed this contemporary brick building in 1977. Although set back from the street in a plaza, a pylon consisting of columns supporting a lintel stands on the street level and responds to the vocabulary of Charleston buildings. The 88,800-square-foot building not only houses the college's fine arts program but also serves as a venue for community theater, concerts, and Spoleto Festival USA performances.

87–89 WENTWORTH STREET, ST. PHILIP'S PARISH GLEBE TENEMENTS

Constructed circa 1750–75; 87 Wentworth altered nineteenth and twentieth centuries

These brick and bermuda stone tenements with massive central brick chimneys may be the oldest houses remaining on the former glebe lands. Although the eastern tenement was altered in the nineteenth century, 89 Wentworth retains its original jerkin-head roof and an early one-story piazza accessed through a rusticated, arched doorway from the street. The interior has some paneling and woodwork indicating construction from the third quarter of the eighteenth century.

89 Wentworth Street

88–90 WENTWORTH STREET, RIGGS TENEMENTS

Constructed circa 1859

These identical single houses were built by John Riggs in the late-1850s along with *15, 17,* and *19 St. Philip Street.* Riggs acquired these lots in 1859 and built the five Italianate houses as rental units. 90 Wentworth Street remains largely unchanged with its brick quoins, arched window in the gable end, and double-tiered piazza with a recessed piazza door screen containing carved decoration. However, a noticeable change in 88 Wentworth Street is the addition of a bay window in the second tier of its enclosed piazza. Riggs owned many properties around the city but is perhaps best remembered as the founder of Charleston's first street car system, established in 1866.

90 Wentworth Street, late-nineteenth-century view

92 WENTWORTH STREET, ST. PHILIP'S CHURCH TENEMENT

Constructed circa 1850; altered 1880s

Like many houses in this part of Harleston Village, 92 Wentworth Street was built on what was part of the glebe

lands left to the Church of England by the settler Affra Coming. In 1770 the church subdivided seventeen acres into building lots, which were leased to provide income. Two of the first lessees were John Commins and John Daly, who resided here in the last half of the 1850s. Jacob S. Schirmer, apparently the first secular owner of this house, bought the property from St. Philip's Church in 1859.

92 Wentworth Street appears to be on land that was once part of the garden of the Bishop Robert Smith House at 6 *Glebe Street*. This two-and-a-half-story wooden single house has been modified to reflect changing times. Notable changes include the mansard roof in the Second Empire style and the replacement of the smaller original windows with large paned glass. Most of these changes took place in the 1880s when Jacob Knobeloch owned the dwelling. Knobeloch was responsible for changing the orientation of the dwelling to Wentworth Street by moving it a full ninety degrees.

99–101 WENTWORTH STREET, QUEEN INVESTMENT COMPANY HOUSES

Constructed 1898–1902; rehabilitated 1970s

99 and 101 Wentworth Street are part of the College of Charleston's Fraternity Row. These Queen Anne style dwellings were constructed by Queen Investment Company in the late-nineteenth century. Identical in floor plan, both houses appear quite different at first glance. 101 Wentworth Street has a prominent second-story tower at the east of a truncated pediment with lunette window, while 99 Wentworth Street has notable corner brackets and spindle work on the front-facing porch.

100 WENTWORTH STREET, GRACE EPISCOPAL CHURCH

Constructed 1847–48; various twentieth-century additions; restored 1991

Edward Brickell White, architect; E. W. Brown, contractor

Charleston's restoration architect Albert Simons once remarked that the silhouette of the steeple of Grace Episcopal Church, with its successive pinnacles, recalled the steeple of St. Mary the Virgin on High Street in Oxford. Edward B. White's approach to the Gothic Revival style apparently emanated from Oxford, and after completion of his initial essay in this form, the Huguenot Church, he embarked on two other commissions in the late-1840s: Grace Church for a new Episcopal congregation on the old glebe lands adjacent to Harleston Village, and a larger structure for the congregation of Trinity Church (now Trinity Cathedral) in Columbia. His contractor, E. W. Brown, supervised construction of both buildings. When completed, the multitiered steeple with corner pinnacles surmounted by tall spire had, as intended, a significant effect upon the suburban landscape.

The arched Gothic window over the principal doorway and similar windows down both sides of the structure, as well as Gothic friezes in stucco and other details, hinted at the elaboration of the interior, with its vaulted nave, side aisles, and apsidal chancel. Although its chancel tablets and interior plaster are original, the altar window, rear window, twelve clerestory windows, and several other windows were planned by Ralph Sadler Meadowcroft, an Anglican rector who served the congregation for several decades. In the restoration after Hurricane Hugo, the original paint scheme, intended to create the impression of stone blocks, was restored, as was the gilded decoration in the chancel. Grace Church closed on January 20, 1864, because of shelling of the city by Union forces on Morris Island. Although damaged by a shell, it was the first Episcopal church to reopen in the city after the war.

Local tradition holds that when a Union commander ordered the rector, the Reverend Charles Cotesworth Pinckney, to pray for the president of the United States, with Union soldiers standing at attention in the aisle, Pinckney replied, "I will gladly obey your order, sir. I know of no one who needs praying for more than the president of the United States."

103–105 WENTWORTH STREET, MUTUAL REAL ESTATE COMPANY HOUSES

Constructed 1910; rehabilitated 1970s

The Mutual Real Estate Company built these two Queen Anne style dwellings several years after their neighbors to the east were constructed. Similar in style and identical in layout to *99* and *101 Wentworth Street*, these two buildings, also now used as College of Charleston fraternity houses, have subtle differences. The recessed gable ends of the buildings lend prominence to the flat-roofed, double-tiered, front-facing porches with turned columns and latticework balustrades.

107 WENTWORTH STREET, WILLIAM JOHNSON HOUSE

Constructed circa 1858

This dwelling was built around 1858 on land that had remained in the same family since 1771, when the first leases were granted for this area by St. Philip's Episcopal Church. This three-story house still retains its original Greek Revival style influences; however, some changes were made after the earthquake of 1886, including the large Italianate windows with pedimented crowns on the first floor and the pressed metal decoration on the facade. Perhaps the most notable occupant was Dr. William Henry Johnson, a leading orthopedist who introduced X-ray technology to Charleston. Dr. Johnson made his own splints and braces in a blacksmith shop that he had built behind the house. This interest in blacksmithing led him to experiment with an unusual exercise regimen: throwing his anvil around the yard. At least one of Johnson's inventions, a pressure cooker attached to the radiator of his car, earned him a certain degree of notoriety in Charleston. Today the dwelling is a College of Charleston fraternity house.

114 WENTWORTH STREET, JONAS BEARD HOUSE

Constructed circa 1805; altered 1980s

114 Wentworth Street

Jonas Beard purchased a thirty-one-year lease on this glebe lot from St. Philip's Church and, according to lease stipulations, was required to build upon the property within a specified number of years. 114 Wentworth Street, a two-and-a-half-story frame structure, was probably built by Beard as a residence but in the 1850s became a grocery run by John C. Mehrtens. This building and its two-story masonry neighbor at 112 Wentworth Street have been converted into faculty offices by the College of Charleston. The antebellum storefronts were removed, and the corner entry to 114 Wentworth Street was moved to the center of the principal facade at this time.

120 WENTWORTH STREET, JOHN BURCKMEYER HOUSE

Constructed circa 1791–1800

This two-and-a-half-story dwelling on a raised masonry basement was built by a German butcher and may be one of the earliest houses in the immediate area. John

Burckmeyer acquired the property in 1791 and completed construction before the end of the decade. The house retains much of its original fabric on the interior, including wainscoting and Adamesque detailing. However, much of the exterior was changed after the earthquake of 1886 by the Thomas family. The extensive renovations included adding rooms to the rear of the house, adding a second tier to the piazza, and changing the windows and siding to adopt a more up-to-date Victorian look.

121 WENTWORTH STREET, HENRY MUCKENFUSS TENEMENT
Constructed before 1871

Although the Muckenfuss family, who lived across the street, acquired this lot at auction in 1829, the present house on this site, constructed in the Italianate version of the Charleston side-hall-plan house, probably dates from the beginning of the 1870s. Although the side piazza has been altered with a ground-level extension on the first floor and a full twentieth-century addition on the second floor, the building retains its front fenestration and bracketed cornice, as well as its hooded door architrave.

122 WENTWORTH STREET, HOPTON-MUCKENFUSS HOUSE
Constructed circa 1830

Robert Hopton acquired this lot in 1821, a site formerly owned by John Burckmeyer, who built the house next door at *124 Wentworth Street*. The three-story, plantation style version of the Charleston single house faces the street with a double-tiered piazza and two central doorways on the first two floors with rectilinear transoms and sidelights. The wooden picket fence standing on a masonry coping is a rare form of this type of enclosure, once common in the neighborhood. After passing through several owners, the house became the property of H. W. Muckenfuss. W. Murragh Muckenfuss, an attorney on Broad Street, lived here for much of the late-nineteenth century.

124 WENTWORTH STREET, BURCKMEYER-MUCKENFUSS HOUSE

Constructed before 1812; altered circa 1845, circa 1880

When the prosperous butcher John Burckmeyer died in 1812, he left this house and lot to his daughter, Elizabeth. She sold the property in 1845 to H. W. Muckenfuss, and it became a family residence for the rest of the century. William G. Muckenfuss, who lived here beginning in 1876, was an executive in the phosphate firm of Pelzer, Rodgers and Company. H. W. Muckenfuss probably made the first changes to the house, including the 1840s style parapeted gable, and a later generation added the pedimented pressed window heads and made other alterations as well.

128 WENTWORTH STREET, HENRY COBIA HOUSE

Constructed circa 1840s

This Charleston double house was built by the auctioneer and commission merchant Henry Cobia. The dwelling, with its prominent double-tiered piazza, shows the influence of the late–Classical Revival style with its Tuscan columns and dentiled molding around the cornice. However, the Italianate double doors and pedimented first-floor windows illustrate the emergence of Victorian architecture. The house has an ell addition as well as a dependency in the rear. The dependency may have been built prior to the main house.

134 Wentworth Street, 1920s photograph showing the old storefront

134 WENTWORTH STREET, ELSWORTH-LOCKWOOD HOUSE

Constructed circa 1803; partially restored and rehabilitated 1990s

This two-and-a-half-story corner residence built on a raised basement has a hipped roof with dormers in the Federal style. Theophilus Elsworth, a gauger at the Custom House, built this as his residence. The building once was used as a private academy run by the Stuart family. Another owner, Dr. Joshua Lockwood, a druggist, bought the property in 1889 and converted the ground floor into a pharmacy. It was during this time that the storefront and cast-iron columns were added. The building has since been subdivided into apartments, and the storefront is gone.

137 WENTWORTH STREET, ALEXANDER BLACK HOUSE

Constructed 1837–38

Alexander Black, a merchant, bought this property from Basile Lanneau, who owned numerous parcels on Montagu Street. Black built what appears to be a typical Charleston single house with beaded siding, simple windows, and an enclosed piazza. Nevertheless, the piazzas are shorter than usual and terminate at the main stairwell, which, unlike those in most single houses, is not centrally located. The entrance, which once was the piazza door, is off center and Victorian in style. The original occupant was Mrs. Catherine Lopez, listed in the city ward book as a "free person of color."

138 WENTWORTH STREET, EDWIN L. KERRISON HOUSE

Constructed circa 1838; restored 1970s

Russell Warren, architect

Unlike most of the houses in the Village of Harleston this monumental dwelling sits back from the street and features a front-facing portico supported by columns with Temple of the Winds capitals. The house was designed by the Rhode Island architect Russell Warren, kinsman of Charleston merchant Nathaniel Russell. Built by a dry goods merchant, the house was advertised for rent with a description that mentioned its "handsomely laid out garden," its bathing house, and running-water conveniences.

144 WENTWORTH STREET, FLEMING-ROSS HOUSE
Constructed circa 1800; restored late-1980s

This large plantation style double house dates from the post-Revolutionary period, although its exact date of construction is unclear. For many years the home of the Fleming family, it was later used by Dr. Augustus Fitch, who had a medical office here. The property was used as two residential units into the early-twentieth century. During World War I, 144 Wentworth Street was turned over to the Red Cross for use as offices by Miss Mary Jane Ross of *1 Meeting Street*. Upon her death in 1922, the house was placed in a trust to be used for public charities. This two-and-a-half-story dwelling on a raised brick basement is located at the edge of the east lot line and faces a large garden. A double staircase of brownstone rises to the first floor of the piazza. Today it is a single-family residence again.

149 Wentworth Street when it was occupied by Atlantic Coast Life Insurance Co.

149 WENTWORTH STREET, FRANCIS SILAS RODGERS MANSION

Constructed 1885–87

Daniel G. Wayne, architect

Francis Rodgers, a wealthy cotton factor and councilman, built this stunning example of the Second Empire style of architecture. The four-story, 13,883-square-foot house dominates this neighborhood. Especially notable is the mansard roof with cast-iron railing and cupola. Finished with Philadelphia red brick, the dwelling is highlighted by stone lintels and quoins. A detail in the shape of a cotton plant positioned under a bay window clearly reflects Rodgers's business interests. The property had several outbuildings, including a small gas plant that provided lighting. The house was being planned by Rodgers as early as 1881 but was not completed until after the earthquake of 1886. Rodgers used the house as his residence until his death in 1911. His obituary stated that "the house in which Mr. Rodgers spent the last years of his life is considered one of the handsomest in the city." It stayed in the family until 1920, when it was sold to the Scottish Rite Cathedral Association. Atlantic Coast Life Insurance Co. held the building from 1940 until 1996.

The mansard roof at 149 Wentworth Street

151 WENTWORTH STREET, BENJAMIN LAZARUS HOUSE

Constructed 1849

Built by the wealthy merchant Benjamin Lazarus, a Sephardic Jew, this three-story frame dwelling on a masonry basement later was used as the Charleston Female Seminary, also known as Miss Kelly's School. Kelly's philosophy was that the school "is designed for the education and training of Christian women." It was during its tenure as a school in the late-nineteenth century that a large three-story wing was added to the south. However, many of the original elements survive, including beaded weatherboard siding and window surrounds.

The teachers and pupils of the Charleston Female Seminary on the piazzas of 151 Wentworth Street, 1890s

154 WENTWORTH STREET, HENRY MUCKENFUSS HOUSE

Constructed circa 1836

Elegant in its simplicity of detail, 154 Wentworth Street shows the influence of the Greek Revival style on Charleston architecture. The two-story house, originally only one-room deep, presents a double-tiered piazza supported by Tuscan columns to the street. Henry Muckenfuss, a mason, lived here until 1845, when he purchased a larger house at *122 Wentworth Street.* The dwelling subsequently passed through many different owners until 1950, when it was converted into a medical office and a two-story addition was added to the rear.

155 WENTWORTH STREET, JAMES SEIGNIOUS HOUSE

Constructed circa 1879

A cotton factor and member of a family with extensive real estate holdings throughout nineteenth-century Charleston built this dwelling as his own residence at the end of the 1870s. Retaining the scale and basic

579

conformity of a large antebellum Charleston side-hall-plan house, James Seignious's Victorian dwelling exhibits the effects of the Italianate style on Charleston's traditional house forms. The elaborate door architrave with a bracketed hood, approached by a granite staircase; the front bay window; and the front end gable, with an Italianate style version of a Venetian window, ornament the building. Despite a twentieth-century conversion to apartments, alterations to the house have been minimal.

156 WENTWORTH STREET, JAMES SANDERS HOUSE
Constructed 1851

James Sanders, a mason, built this two-and-a-half-story stuccoed brick Charleston single house on a raised basement in 1851 after acquiring a portion of a larger lot from the attorney Francis McHugh. An arched opening on the street level leads to a stairway and a raised piazza entry with a pedimented frontispiece. Many of the embellishments on the front facade, such as the segmental arches on the second story and the bracketed cornice, are Italianate in style; they are capped by a parapeted gable with a tripartite window.

157 WENTWORTH STREET, ELEANORA WILKINSON HOUSE
Constructed circa 1853

This two-and-a-half-story, side-hall, double-parlor-plan dwelling was built around 1853 by Mrs. Eleanora Wilkinson, following her husband's death. A Greek Revival architrave ornaments the front facade, and a double piazza attached to the west facade is supported by Tuscan columns. After Mrs. Wilkinson's death in 1874, the property passed to her son-in-law Christopher Gustavus Memminger, a secretary of the treasury for the Confederacy and the founder of Charleston's public school system. Memminger did not choose to reside at 157 Wentworth Street. He remained at his own dwelling nearby (now demolished) and sold the Wilkinson property in 1874 to Mrs. Miriam Valentine for $6,000. The second tier of the piazza was enclosed by a later owner.

162 WENTWORTH STREET, JOHN P. KEIP HOUSE
Constructed 1876–79

John Keip built one of Wentworth Street's most imposing commercial buildings in the late-1870s but kept it only briefly. It was sold for the store and residence of C. S. Hesse between 1881 and 1883. Retaining its second-story pedimented window heads, deep cornice, and north piazzas, the building continues in the mixed use for which it was originally constructed.

164 WENTWORTH STREET, DETREVILLE-LAFITTE HOUSE
Constructed circa 1853

Likely buried within the north portion of this three-and-a-half-story stuccoed brick structure with hip roof and two-story Doric-order piazzas is the remains of an early-nineteenth-century structure. When Richard DeTreville purchased the site in 1853, the deed indicated that the property contained a "mansion." It is not likely that DeTreville demolished the structure. Instead, it is probable that his large early-Victorian house incorporated the earlier building. Ten years after purchasing the property, DeTreville sold the dwelling to John B. L. Lafitte, a commission merchant from New York City. Not long afterward Lafitte purchased a mortgage by a firm that included George Alfred Trenholm, Christopher Memminger's successor as secretary of the treasury for the Confederacy. During the Civil War, Trenholm outfitted a flotilla of twelve boats to defend Charleston. More than sixty of his ships ran the blockade to England, exchanging cotton for war materials. Because of Lafitte's mortgage with Trenholm's firm, 164 Wentworth became part of the suit filed by the U.S. government following the war to seek payment for large wartime profits. The result was a referee's sale in 1873 at which Savage Deas Trenholm purchased the house for $27,000. The building was converted into eleven condominiums in 1984.

166 WENTWORTH STREET, JOB PALMER HOUSE
Constructed circa 1809; restored 1960s

Job Palmer, a carpenter, probably built his own residence at 166 Wentworth Street in the early-nineteenth century. This brick three-story Charleston single house on a raised basement has a double-tiered piazza with an elegant door architrave and simple rectangular transom. The piazza entrance was found in the basement of the house during a 1960s restoration. A portion of the second tier of the piazza was enclosed in recent years to accommodate twentieth-century needs.

169 WENTWORTH STREET, CORBETT-IRVING HOUSE
Constructed circa 1837

This two-story Greek Revival style dwelling was constructed sometime before 1837, although it is uncertain who built it. Elizabeth Corbett purchased the empty lot in 1831 from a relative, but when it was sold to Dr. John Beaufain Irving in 1840, a dwelling was listed on the property. This may point to Elizabeth Corbett as the builder since she owned the property at the time of its construction. However, she was never listed in the city directories as residing on Wentworth Street. Dr. Irving was listed as living in this house as early as 1837, yet he sold it a few days after purchase. The house is set back from Wentworth Street on a high brick basement. The projecting front entry, which originally may have been double tiered, is capped by a balustrade and supported by Tuscan columns. A modillioned cornice is just beneath the flat roofline.

174 WENTWORTH STREET, WILLIAM MATHIESSEN TENEMENT

Constructed 1860

This small two-story wooden single house with a front closed gable was built by William Mathiessen just after he acquired the lot from Albert Elfe. Although standing in a row of nineteenth-century single houses, Mathiessen's house retains its fine vernacular detailing and early character.

188 WENTWORTH STREET, STEINMEYER-SWEEGAN TENEMENT

Constructed 1851–60

John H. Steinmeyer, in partnership with L. T. Potter, bought a large parcel on the north side of Wentworth in 1851 at public auction. The lot on which the house now sits, fronting thirty-one feet on Wentworth Street, was created during a later subdivision. Steinmeyer sold the house in 1860 to Edward F. Sweegan, who probably added the first-floor polygonal bay in the late-nineteenth century. This simple single house has a double-tiered piazza and a flat, parapeted roof with a closed gable end.

CHAPEL STREET

ELIZABETH ST

'LOTTE STREET

HENRIETTA

TINCı STREET

8

MAZYCKBOROUGH AND WRAGGBOROUGH

Villas of the Antebellum Elite

Mazyckborough and Wraggborough have similar development patterns, and both originally were popular with wealthy families seeking suburban residences. Mazyck's Pasture, site of the "Liberty Oak" where the "Sons of Liberty" met before the Revolution, was surveyed in lots for Alexander Mazyck in 1786. Toward the north ten years later the heirs of John Wragg planned the development of his estate as the suburb of Wraggborough, naming streets for various members of the family, including John, Henrietta, Ann, Elizabeth, Mary, and Judith. In a progressive move, the family dedicated Wragg Mall and Wragg Square to the public, and these remain today as open greens. At the beginning of the development of both neighborhoods, large houses such as the Gibbes family "villa" on John Street and the Manigault House a block away served as the nucleus for an area that eventually included a Neoclassical church, Second Presbyterian Church, and a line of large houses along Charlotte and Chapel Streets. These houses were built for the rice-planting Toomer and Vanderhorst clans and eventually for newly risen merchants such as

Detail from Heyward family diary, 1835, recording a seasonal family move from the plantation to the house in Wraggborough

View toward Second Presbyterian Church, late-nineteenth-century photograph

Detail of C. Drie's Bird's Eye View of the City of Charleston, South Carolina, 1872, showing Mazyckborough and Wraggborough

Robert Martin and former mechanics such as William Henry Houston.

Scottish Presbyterian merchant John Robinson built several dwellings along Judith Street, including one acquired by Irish-born railroad baron William Aiken, whose son, Gov. William Aiken, extensively remodeled the house and added the row of Greek Revival tenements along the north side of Wragg Mall.

Early brick stores such as that at 19 Elizabeth Street and the two Victorian corner stores at the intersection of Elizabeth and Chapel Streets mark the diversity of these boroughs in the mid- and late-nineteenth centuries. The explosion in 1865 of the Northeastern Railroad Depot on the eastern edge of Wraggborough caused significant fire losses along Alexander Street. This coupled with some subdivision allowed the construction of numerous wooden Victorian dwellings in the third quarter of the nineteenth century. The row at 51–59 Chapel Street, built by Benjamin F. McCabe about 1890, constitutes one such unified development.

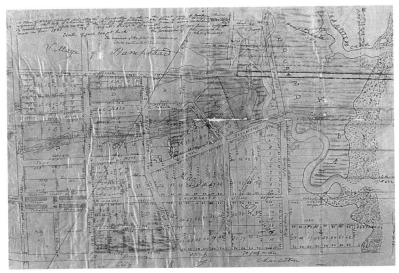

Plat of Mazyckborough and Wraggborough area, 1801

79 ALEXANDER STREET
Constructed 1951–52

This pavilioned one-story structure with Georgian Revival elements reflects a renovation of a 1950s cinderblock building, originally constructed for the Charleston Speech and Hearing Clinic by the Junior League of Charleston. A two-story wooden building of 1872 formerly stood on the site.

80 ALEXANDER STREET, GADSDEN-DEWEES HOUSE
Constructed 1800–1810; altered circa 1886

This is the site of that portion of Mazyck's Pasture where a "noble live oak tree" was formally dedicated to "liberty" by Charleston's John Wilkes Club in 1766. Christopher Gadsden, leader of this group, later called the Palmetto Society, first advocated independence from Britain beside this "liberty tree." The tree was cut down by the British during their occupation of the city in 1780–82. Owned by the Gadsden estate, this and adjoining parcels were acquired by William Dewees, a planter and wharf owner, in 1807. A subsequent owner added the piazzas, the Greek Revival door surrounds, and the Victorian window heads. A third story and roof were damaged and removed after the earthquake of 1886.

83–85 ALEXANDER STREET, PHILLIP SCHNEPF HOUSE
Constructed 1881–82

An earlier house on this site owned by Benjamin Lee burned in the evacuation fire of 1865. A German tradesman built a traditional two-and-a-half-story Charleston single house on this site shortly after 1880. An Italianate style hood caps the piazza screen on the front of Tuscan-columned piazzas. With the exception of the screen

83 Alexander Street

and the two-over-two windows, the dwelling, with its closed gable end and three dormers, continues in the Greek Revival style of single house construction. A nearly identical single house with six-over-six windows and Greek Revival piazza door surround survives next door at *85 Alexander Street*. John R. Pinckney, a freedman, erected this house between 1882 and 1885.

110 ALEXANDER STREET, MARION LAROCHE HOUSE

Constructed circa 1894

This frame Victorian house stands on a lot burned over in the evacuation fire. Marion LaRoche bought this lot after the subdivision of this parcel from *112 Alexander Street* and built the dwelling with its double-tiered front piazzas ornamented by Queen Anne style column brackets and spindle-work balustrade.

114 ALEXANDER STREET, FRANCIS B. HACKER HOUSE

Constructed circa 1880

Italianate details ornament this two-and-a-half-story dwelling built by Francis Hacker after he acquired the lot in 1876. The understated bowed piazza follows the lines of the first-floor bay window. The bracketed cornice, tripartite window, and second-story French doors reflect the solid craftsmanship of Charleston's postbellum carpenters.

126 ALEXANDER STREET, CORDT DIECKHOFF HOUSE

Constructed circa 1867

A grocer built this three-story masonry structure with flat roof on the site of a building destroyed in the evacuation fire of 1865. Prior to the war Dieckhoff owned five lots on this side of Alexander Street with tenements primarily rented to Afri-

can Americans and Irish immigrant laborers. Dieckhoff's building retains evidence of its early first-floor storefront and an enclosed piazza screen that still provides access to the residence above. The pressed metal window hoods and cornice add architectural distinction to this mixed-use building.

153 ALEXANDER STREET, MEMORIAL BAPTIST CHURCH

Constructed circa 1886; renovated mid-1970s

From 1818 onward this site served as a Baptist burial ground. In the years after the Civil War several different Baptist congregations occupied the property, including the Second Baptist Church and the First Colored Baptist Church, both with burial grounds. By the late-1880s Memorial Baptist purchased the property north of Second Baptist Church for its new congregation. Soon thereafter, the group built the wooden core of the present building in a vernacular meetinghouse style. Covered with brick veneer in 1976 and embellished with Colonial Revival details, Memorial Baptist Church continues at this site, long occupied by black and white Baptists.

1 ANN STREET, BOYCE-STOREN HOUSE

Constructed circa 1847–50

This two-story, late–Greek Revival wooden house with a flat parapeted roof and two-story tiered piazza features unusual Rococo Revival style brackets framing each bay. It, like its neighbors, was purchased by Michael Storen, a native of County Clare in Ireland, who prospered in Charleston just before the War Between the States. Storen owned a tannery and a farm in the upper peninsula, later the site of the William Enston Home at *900 King Street.*

3 ANN STREET, MICHAEL STOREN HOUSE

Constructed circa 1870

As a two-and-a-half-story wooden dwelling in the Queen Anne style with a front porch and second-story corner porch, the house bears little indication of using the traditional Charleston domestic style. Michael Storen lived in this house near the investment dwellings he built, including the single house next door at *5 Ann Street*.

110 CALHOUN STREET, EMANUEL A.M.E. CHURCH

Constructed 1891; restored 1990–91

The oldest African American congregation south of Baltimore and the oldest A.M.E. church in the South, Emanuel A.M.E. Church was organized in 1818 as the Hampstead Free African Church by Morris Brown. After the discovery of the Denmark Vesey plot in 1822, blacks were forbidden to worship in their own churches. A mob destroyed the original church, and its minister left for Philadelphia where he became the first bishop of the A.M.E. Church in America. Many of the congregants, however, continued to worship together underground. After 1865 Emanuel reorganized, acquired this site on Boundary (now Calhoun) Street, and constructed a wooden church under the direction of its minister, Richard Harvey Cain, who also served during Reconstruction as a congressman. After the destruction of the earlier church in the earthquake of 1886, the Reverend L. Ruffin Nichols presided over the completion of a brick Gothic building with a tall steeple on the west end of its front facade. Retaining its original altar, communion rail, pews, and light fixtures, Emanuel presents one of the few relatively unaltered religious interiors, particularly of the Victorian period, left in the city.

28 CHAPEL STREET, ELIAS VANDERHORST HOUSE

Constructed circa 1832; rehabilitated 1983; partially restored 1990s

Built as a suburban villa by a member of the wealthy Vanderhorst family, owners of much of Kiawah Island, the stuccoed brick house stands two stories above a raised basement and has a piazza approached on the main floor by a double, semicircular, brownstone staircase with a wrought-iron balustrade. A dogtooth corniced pediment projects from the center of the gable roof. After its conversion to apartments before World War II, the Vanderhorst House became a neighborhood eyesore. Rehabilitated as apartments with tax incentives in 1983, the house was partially restored as a private residence in the 1990s. Although the fluted Doric columns of the front piazza remain, the original front windows, semicircular door transoms, and a lunette window in the pediment did not survive the early-twentieth-century changes.

Elias Vanderhorst House, 28 Chapel Street, late-nineteenth-century view

34 CHAPEL STREET, DR. ANTHONY VANDERHORST TOOMER HOUSE (II)

Constructed circa 1840; restored 1980s

Dr. Anthony V. Toomer, a wealthy physician and planter, or his son built this two-story frame dwelling on a brick basement as one of three large suburban villas on antebellum Chapel Street. The distinctive double bows of the front piazza and other features once led some historians to attribute the house, wrongly, to the architect Robert Mills. The pedimented cross gables, interior doors, stair niches, and other details exhibit sophisticated Gothic Revival influences. The original stair hall floor coverings were linoleum, apparently ordered by the builder from England, reflecting the first documented use of this material in Charleston.

34 Chapel Street (right) in 1978, before restoration

36 CHAPEL STREET, DR. ANTHONY VANDERHORST TOOMER HOUSE (I)

Constructed circa 1809; restoration 1975–78

Prior to building *34 Chapel Street*, Dr. Anthony V. Toomer erected this simple, late-Federal style house on a large lot which he acquired shortly after the subdivision of the neighborhood by the Wragg family. The frame house, with a double-tiered front piazza approached by a stuccoed masonry stair, is surmounted by a hipped, slate roof with three front dormers. The restoration of this building in the 1970s served as a demonstration project for the rejuvenation of other uptown houses damaged by fire and subject to condemnation.

41–43 CHAPEL STREET, WILLIAM HENRY HOUSTON TENEMENTS

Constructed 1840–50

The prosperous contractor William Henry Houston built these nearly identical Greek Revival style single houses in the 1840s. On both buildings a wide frieze separates the two-bay body of the front facade from the closed gable roof with central tripartite window. One-story piazzas with various alterations mark the west facades of each house. By the time of the Civil War, Houston had rented 41 Chapel to the merchant Solomon Solomons and 43 Chapel to William Fraser.

45–47 CHAPEL STREET, JONAH M. VENNING TENEMENTS

Constructed 1840–50

Wealthy wharf owner Jonah M. Venning built these houses on lots subdivided from his principal residence at *40 Charlotte*

Street. Although some nine-over-nine window sashes, Tuscan columns on the second-floor piazza, and gable dormers survive on 45 Chapel Street from the original construction, Victorian style window hoods and mid-twentieth-century brick infill on the piazza mar the integrity of this original dwelling, which stands several feet taller than its contemporary neighbors. Venning built a more truncated version of the Charleston single house at 47 Chapel Street, later altered with two-over-two windows on the front facade and turned, Queen Anne style columns on the piazza.

49 CHAPEL STREET, WINSTANLEY-PARKER HOUSE

Constructed circa 1790–1810; altered 1960s

Thomas Winstanley, Middlesex businessman and intendant (mayor) of the city in 1804, built this asymmetrical, two-story weatherboarded and hipped-roof house. The building has a stair hall and three rooms on each floor and was one of the earliest structures in the new neighborhood of Mazyckborough. Originally intended to face Charlotte Street with an extensive front garden, the former parcel was subdivided to create the lot for *44 Charlotte Street*. By 1832 the house had been sold to Miss Rachel Parker, heiress of other properties in the area formerly owned by her uncle Benjamin Parker. Miss Parker lived in the house until her death in 1861, devising it in her will to her niece Sarah Drayton with bequests to Mrs. Drayton's sons, Robert Parker and Charles Drayton. Part of the Drayton Hall line, Sarah Drayton spent her last years in this small house. The chimneys were removed in the 1960s after the building had been cut into apartments.

View of train passing 49 Chapel Street in the 1950s

51–59 CHAPEL STREET, BENJAMIN MCCABE TENEMENTS

Constructed circa 1890

In 1890 Benjamin McCabe, a leading investor and captain in a local militia company, the Irish Volunteers, constructed these five dwellings in the Queen Anne style with pedimented gable roofs. Four of the houses have double-tiered front piazzas. The houses generally retain the stylized woodwork of their front porches, including lattice or turned balusters and chamfered columns and windows with triangular louvered heads. McCabe lived at 59 Chapel Street, which retains its original one-story front piazza. McCabe's investment company constructed three houses in similar style around the corner at *24, 26,* and *28 Elizabeth Street* in 1896, replacing an early-nineteenth-century tenement that had belonged to his parents.

1 CHARLOTTE STREET, CHARLESTON GAS WORKS

Constructed circa 1855

This one-story, gable-roofed brick building and a two-story, similarly styled structure, both surrounded by a brick wall, are the remains of South Carolina's earliest surviving public utility complex. This plant supplied Charleston houses with gas in the antebellum period; the structures are still owned by the power company and house electric generating facilities. Flemish bond brickwork and blind arches add architectural distinction to this otherwise plain industrial complex.

5 CHARLOTTE STREET, ELIZABETH SELL HOUSE

Constructed circa 1872; rehabilitated 1978

Elizabeth Sell, a member of the William Henry Houston family, built this small, two-and-a-half-story, wood Charleston single house in a block of similar style dwellings, including *3 Charlotte Street*, a wood single house owned by Mrs. J. P. Morrison, and another at *7 Charlotte Street*, owned by Charles Seignious and maintained as rental property. Within a few years after its construction, a Queen Anne style projecting bay window and bracketed cornice were added. The house was rehabilitated in 1978.

16 CHARLOTTE STREET, ROBERT MARTIN HOUSE

Constructed 1834–35; renovated 1996

Robert Martin, a wealthy trader in upland cotton, purchased this lot from the planter Thomas Milliken in 1834 for $2,500. The lot, now 100 feet wide along Charlotte Street and 200 feet deep, differs from the 1801 plat of Wraggborough. The 1835–36 city directory lists Robert Martin, a factor, living on Charlotte Street, suggesting that construction had begun after his purchase of the property. Martin's house has a traditional central hall plan with two symmetrical rooms on each side of the entry and staircase hall. Set on a high brick basement, this house resembles many of the earlier plantation houses of the Carolina Lowcountry with its piazza supported by massive Doric columns on the ground story and fluted Doric columns above. Paired dependencies at the rear form a domestic courtyard protected by a high brick wall from East Bay Street. The whole complex has been renovated as a law office.

20 CHARLOTTE STREET, JOSEPH AIKEN HOUSE

Constructed 1848

Joseph Aiken House, 20 Charlotte Street, late-nineteenth-century photograph

Constructed in 1848 by Robert Martin, this house was intended as a wedding gift to Martin's daughter, Ellen, who married her cousin Joseph Aiken, son of Gov. Wil-

595

liam Aiken. Like Martin's house next door at *16 Charlotte Street*, this house presents an unusual combination of stylistic elements. The facade is dominated by columns with large Tower of the Winds capitals. On the west side there is a recessed loggia with an arcade that contains Italianate elements. The floor plan features a central hall, and the interior is ornamented with both Egyptian Revival and Greek Revival details. The formal garden with patterned beds survives from the antebellum period along with the rear brick dependencies.

21 CHARLOTTE STREET, SARAH WESTCOAT HOUSE

Constructed 1873; addition 1890–1900

Sarah Westcoat acquired the lot and became one of a group of women builders of houses in Mazyckborough-Wraggborough during the Victorian period. Just before the turn of the century, Emily Alice Honour added an octagonally shaped three-story tower with shingle banding after purchasing this 1870s Italianate Charleston single house with simple double-tiered piazzas. The slight indentation of the tower from the body of the main building provides a curious set-back entry door and one-bay front porch.

22 CHARLOTTE STREET, MARIA SMITH HOUSE

Constructed 1879–80

This unusual T-shaped house with closed gable end and double-tiered front piazzas anchors the northwest corner of Charlotte and Alexander Streets. Gothic Revival influences in the window and door surrounds, with hold-over Greek Revival piazza columns and up-to-date two-over-two windows, accentuate the eclectic form of the house completed by Maria Smith in 1880.

29 CHARLOTTE STREET, CUNNINGHAM-GORDON HOUSE

Constructed circa 1815–28; restored 1970s, late-1980s

Among the oldest surviving houses in Mazyckborough, 29 Charlotte Street adheres more closely than any other house in the neighborhood to the Federal style. Richard Cunningham, a planter, purchased the lot in 1815 and apparently began construction soon thereafter. He sold the lot with a "large unfinished three story brick house thereon" to John Gordon in 1828. The deep brown brick, produced in the Charleston area, is laid in Flemish bond with sharp joints in a beaded lime mortar. In the best Neoclassical manner, the windows are set in the narrowest jambs, and the most significant exterior decoration can be found in the rubbed brick, jack arches heading the windows, the dogtoothed brick cornice, and the simple two-tiered, Tuscan-columned piazza. A two-story dependency remains at the rear of the property.

32 CHARLOTTE STREET, WEGMAN-HOLMES HOUSE

Constructed circa 1820; renovated and restored late-1980s

John Casken, carpenter

Several splendid craftsmen collaborated on the construction of the late-Neoclassical, three-story single house at 32 Charlotte Street. John Casken built the house in trust for Catherine Wegman. It has a three-story, Flemish-bond brick facade and a two-story wood piazza with a galleried second-story and pedimented door architrave. In 1849 William C. Holmes, partner in the paint manufactory firm of Holmes, Calder and Co., bought the property. His descendants owned it until 1931. The Holmes family made Victorian style changes to the building, including a large rear addition and piazza enclosure with a substantial bay window. This later addition created a family sitting and dining area, a typical add-on for some Charleston single houses following the Civil War. Considering the residence's tie to a leading color manufacturer, paint research was conducted on the building in recent years and revealed the survival of interior doors grain-painted to imitate mahogany and exterior wooden elements painted a cream tan with yellow green finishes applied to the shutters and blinds.

33 CHARLOTTE STREET, J. THOMAS HAMLIN WHITE HOUSE
Constructed circa 1854–55

J. T. H. White, a planter in Christ Church Parish, near Mt. Pleasant, purchased this parcel with an existing wooden building and two brick outbuildings in 1854. White pulled down these structures and began construction of a late–Greek Revival style dwelling, probably from brick produced at an East Cooper brick kiln partially owned by White. White's house sits majestically on a raised basement and has Flemish bond brick walls capped by a slate gable roof. A stone double staircase with elaborate cast-iron balustrade rises from the sidewalk to a landing before the projecting central bay, which boasts a pedimented door architrave, a second-story tripartite window, and a surmounting pediment with a circular, or bull's-eye, window.

White enjoyed his house until the Civil War, when it was used as a hospital and seized, in 1866, as headquarters for the commanding general of the occupying forces, Gen. Daniel Sickles. He was a controversial figure who claimed to have won the Battle of Gettysburg by disobeying General Meade's orders. Sickles held absolute power over North and South Carolina beginning in 1866. When President Andrew Johnson removed Sickles from his post, the Charleston newspaper observed, "There was a universal feeling of relief at his departure." The general went on to make several fortunes, and while U.S. minister to Spain he became the rumored lover of Queen Isabella.

35 CHARLOTTE STREET, SCHACHTE HOUSE

Constructed circa 1870

A Charlestonian of German extraction constructed this two-story wood Italianate house with Queen Anne details shortly after the Civil War. Delicate cast-iron detailing surmounts the finely crafted entry hood and first-floor bay window. Turned columns and spindle-work balustrades support the double-tiered west piazzas.

36 CHARLOTTE STREET, REBECCA CORDES HOUSE

Constructed circa 1830; rehabilitated mid-1980s

A family of French Huguenot descent, the Cordes owned extensive plantations in the Cooper River region and acquired several properties in Mazyckborough in the early-nineteenth century. Mrs. Rebecca Cordes, a widow, built a substantial two-and-a-half-story single house with closed front gable on a high brick basement. A triple-tiered, Greek Revival style piazza graces the west elevation, while on the east a Venetian (Palladian) window illuminates the staircase. Small wooden quoins decorate the corners of the building. Mrs. Cordes's house passed to Thomas Cordes Harleston in trust for Elizabeth Cordes Waring prior to the Civil War.

40 CHARLOTTE STREET, JONAH M. VENNING HOUSE

Constructed circa 1831

The Venning House stands on a lot sold in the eighteenth century to the carpenter Samuel Harn of nearby Middlesex and subsequently acquired by a Hampstead (East Side) butcher, John Eberley Halsall. Venning, a lumber merchant and factor with extensive interests in the Mt. Pleasant area, bought the lot and three years later built this three-story wood single house, which faces the street in the plantation style. It has been suggested by architectural historians that this is one of the oldest Greek Revival houses in Charleston, and heavy Tuscan columns, simple cornice, and rectilinear transom door architraves indicate this influence.

43 CHARLOTTE STREET, WILLIAM A. HUSSEY HOUSE

Constructed circa 1849; restored 1990s

Similar in scale to its eastern neighbor, *33 Charlotte Street*, William Hussey's Greek Revival style dwelling reflects Federal and Italianate influences as well. A double brownstone staircase with a wrought-iron balustrade rises from the street level to a Greek Revival door architrave set in a two-and-a-half-story central pavilion. Stucco quoins accent the pavilion as well as the corners of the dwelling. Black marble mantels with inset, gilded cast-iron decoration, cove plaster cornices, and exuberant plaster ceiling medallions add distinction to the interior of this late-antebellum, suburban villa. After being rented to various tenants and later acquired by the Colburn family, the property deteriorated in the early-twentieth century before a recent restoration.

44 CHARLOTTE STREET, WILLIAM HENRY HOUSTON HOUSE

Constructed 1834; rehabilitated 1966–74

With its piazzas facing the street in the plantation style, like its neighbor at *40 Charlotte Street*, William Henry Houston's raised, two-and-a-half-story house over-looks the western edge of Mazyckborough. Substantial Greek Revival door architraves and oversized dormers with tripartite windows differentiate the Houston House from its more traditional neighbors. In the ante-bellum period Houston added a stucco coping with Gothic Revival style piers and a wrought-iron fence to protect his front property line. Beginning his career as a carpenter in the neighborhood of Middlesex to the south, Houston became a wealthy building contractor and by the 1830s owned properties throughout Charleston, including seven houses on Charlotte Street alone. The Houston family lived at this address until the 1880s when it was sold at auction to the secretary of the Northeastern Railroad. After decades of twentieth-century neglect and two fires, it was rehabilitated.

44 Charlotte Street (in the foreground) in 1966, after fire damage and before rehabilitation

527 EAST BAY STREET, NORTHEASTERN RAILWAY DEPOT

Constructed 1866–67; rehabilitated late-1980s

A masonry building on this site, the original Northeastern Railway Depot, burned in the evacuation fire in 1865. The railroad company had begun construction of a new depot on this lot by 1866 and completed it by 1867. The present building, the eastern core of the former depot complex, retains its closed gable roof, brick walls, and arched openings along East Bay Street. Through various renovations, however, the latticework in the gable, the doors, and other features were lost.

4 ELIZABETH STREET, DEREEF HOUSE

Constructed circa 1870

The Dereefs, a wealthy free African American family with substantial holdings before the Civil War, built this two-story wood Charleston single house on a corner adjacent to an early lane now called Harlem Court. This alley, largely peopled with African American laborers, experienced a significant decline in the twentieth century. This and the construction of the new Charleston County Library resulted in the demolition of most of the houses in this area.

10 and 12 Elizabeth Street

12 ELIZABETH STREET, JOHN CARBURRY HOUSE

Constructed circa 1851

Originally constructed as a typical Charleston single house by John Carburry, a clerk-bookkeeper on Atlantic Wharf, the house was subsequently altered with an Italianate bay, bracketed cornice, and piazza door screen, probably in the late-1890s. The slightly larger scale of Carburry's house can be compared to the adjacent single house at *10 Elizabeth Street*, which has similar window trim and was constructed nearly contemporaneously by Aberdeen Gregorie, a free person of color.

14 ELIZABETH STREET, SARAH RUTLEDGE HORT HOUSE

Constructed circa 1860

The spinster Sarah Rutledge Hort's house, with its high-quality Greek Revival design, exceptional brickwork, and large scale, stands significantly apart from its simpler wooden neighbors. Miss Hort acquired the vacant lot at 14 Elizabeth Street, a property formerly held for investment by the planter William Matthews, from one of several short-term owners. With Hort's death at the end of the Civil War the house passed to her executor before its purchase in 1882 by the grocer Henry Bulwinkle, whose descendants owned the property for nearly a century. The gable-ended building with corner quoining and brownstone window sills and lintels follows the side-hall, double-parlor plan popular for the city's larger houses in the antebellum period. The interior of the house features original marble mantels on both floors and several large plaster ceiling medallions.

19 ELIZABETH STREET, HENRY BULWINKLE GROCERY

Constructed circa 1831

Bulwinkle's grocery store follows the traditional pattern of the Charleston single house with first-story concessions to commercial use. Original entry doors on both the Elizabeth Street and Charlotte Street elevations provided access to the shop, while a masked piazza included an early staircase which gave access to the second-floor porch and the accompanying dwelling unit. The Flemish bond brickwork and the dogtooth cornice at the gable end are modest architectural flourishes.

22 ELIZABETH STREET, NEW TABERNACLE FOURTH BAPTIST CHURCH

Constructed 1859

Francis D. Lee, architect

Charleston's premier Gothic Revival architect, Francis D. Lee, designed a soaring Gothic church for the St. Luke's Episcopal congregation in the Mazyckborough-Wraggborough neighborhood. The *Charleston Courier* noted at the time of the laying of the cornerstone in May 1859 that the style was to be "Perpendicular Gothic . . . peculiarly adapted to our Southern cli-

Early-twentieth-century view of the interior of St. Luke's Episcopal Church, 22 Elizabeth Street, before it was purchased by New Tabernacle Baptist Church

mate." The church was constructed in a Greek cross layout, but the planned 210-foot steeple was never completed. Intended to be stuccoed, the building remained exposed brick with indifferent pointing techniques. Giant lancet Gothic windows with elaborate tracery decorate the gable ends of each point of the cross. On the interior, soaring Gothic vaults resting on quatrefoil columns support the central 55-foot ceiling. The galleries are decorated with Gothic style spindle work and quatrefoil center panels. Damaged by shelling and stripped by Union troops during the Civil War, the barely completed building continued in use by the St. Luke's congregation until 1949. At that time the church merged with St. Paul's in Radcliffeborough and became the Cathedral of St. Luke and St. Paul at 126 Coming Street. New Tabernacle Fourth Baptist Church, founded in 1875 and rebuilt in 1904 under the leadership of the Reverend D. J. Jenkins, founder of Jenkins's Orphanage, purchased St. Luke's in 1950. Most of the detailed elements of St. Luke's Church have been preserved with the change in congregation, and the building often serves as a popular venue for Spoleto performances.

31 ELIZABETH STREET, KOENNECKE-COSTA GROCERY STORE
Constructed circa 1830

Although originally constructed in the Greek Revival style with a tripartite window in its gable end, this structure was altered by a subsequent owner, probably about 1890. The first floor was changed to create a typical corner grocery, even though the building was used as a bakery before it was converted to its present grocery store use. The side piazzas were enclosed at the same time.

48 ELIZABETH STREET, AIKEN-RHETT HOUSE

Constructed circa 1818; renovated with additions circa 1833, 1858

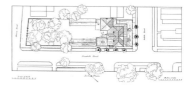

Aiken-Rhett House, 48 Elizabeth Street, in 1898

The Aiken-Rhett House is the best-preserved complex of antebellum domestic structures left in the city. John Robinson, a well-to-do merchant, began construction shortly after acquiring the site, which was at the head of the Public Mall reserved in the development of Wraggborough, in December 1817. Following financial reversals, Robinson advertised his residence for sale, stating that it included four rooms on each floor "all well finished, cypress and cedar piazzas and fences, and large cellars and store rooms under the dwelling." William Aiken Sr. then acquired the site as rental property. By deed of partition William Aiken Jr. and his wife Harriet Lowndes Aiken obtained the lot and began the first series of alterations. At this point the floor plan of the house was dramatically altered. The central hallway was closed, the entry was moved from Judith Street to Elizabeth Street, an entrance foyer was created, and a double-parlor plan was arranged. A new eastern wing with a service staircase, a large dining room on the first floor, and a ballroom above enlarged the house for large-scale entertaining. In the 1830s Aiken added significantly to the outbuildings with additions to the kitchen and slave quarters on the east and the carriage house stable on the west. Entries to these buildings from the street were blocked, and Aiken altered their fenestration with some Gothic Revival detailing, also using this style for an ornamental cow shed, chicken coop, and matching corner privies. By the end of the 1850s Aiken was one of the largest slaveholders in South Carolina, keeping

Site plan of 48 Elizabeth Street showing the locations of outbuildings

Measured plan of the first floor, Aiken-Rhett House

Measured front (south) elevation of the Aiken-Rhett House

more than seven hundred slaves at his Jehosee Island cotton and rice plantation and nineteen slaves at his town property. In this period Aiken further remodeled his house, redecorating with fashionable gas lighting fixtures, wallpapers, and carpets and adding on the northwest an art gallery wing with Rococo Revival plaster decoration to house items acquired in Europe.

Aiken supported the Confederacy, although he opposed secession. He died during the war, and after the death of Harriet Aiken the house descended to their daughter and her descendants, the Rhett family. With most of the house closed off, the Aiken family descendants lived in only six rooms by the 1970s, when the property was transferred to The Charleston Museum with some of its original furnishings. Historic Charleston Foundation acquired the property from the Museum in 1995 and has begun further conservation while operating it as a house museum.

51–55 ELIZABETH STREET, JOHN P. DALY HOUSES
Constructed 1845–50

51–53 Elizabeth Street

John P. Daly purchased these properties as vacant lots from Frances Moore in 1845. Shortly thereafter he built three houses, two nearly identical stuccoed brick Charleston single houses and the northernmost dwelling, a smaller frame single house. The buildings at 51–53 Elizabeth Street stand out as particularly fine examples of masonry single houses with rusticated ground stories, pilasters, and dogtooth cornices in the gable ends, central tripartite windows, and double-tiered Tuscan columns in the piazza; only 53 Elizabeth Street retains its original door screen.

HENRIETTA STREET

This short street, only one block in length, has lost all but three of its antebellum houses. Many free blacks lived along

this street before the Civil War, and it continued as home to a large African American population in the late-nineteenth century. Septima Poinsett Clark, a civil rights leader, spent her early adulthood in the two-and-a-half-story wood single house at 16 Henrietta Street, now gone.

2–4 JOHN STREET, GIBBES HOUSE

Constructed circa 1805–10

Robert Gibbes Jr., a Johns Island planter, lived in the suburban villa on this lot by 1819. The lot had been devised by his mother, Mary, from the estate of her brother, John Wragg. Gabriel Manigault in 1805 acquired a partial interest in this property from John Gibbes, father of Robert Gibbes Jr., but the disposition of his interest and any role he may have had in the construction of this house are unknown. Either Robert Gibbes Jr. or his father built the present plantation style dwelling. Robert sold the property to his brother Benjamin in 1825 and the property remained in the family until 1863. Apparently the late-nineteenth-century owner, William Moran, constructed the small one-story corner store in the front yard of the house. The kitchen building served a commercial use after the Civil War as a German bakery.

17–25 JOHN STREET, WILLIAM HENRY HOUSTON TENEMENTS

Constructed 1852–56

The wealthy builder William Henry Houston constructed these four nearly identical two-and-a-half-story, frame Charleston single houses. A resident at this time on nearby Charlotte Street, Houston rented the dwellings to a succession of clerks, clothiers, and craftsmen. Although all of the buildings retain double-tiered piazzas and closed gable ends with tripartite windows, each property reflects differing approaches to renovation. Unlike 21 and 23 John Street, which retain their Italianate door hoods and shutters, 25 John Street has had alterations to its piazza which include Queen Anne style columns and a brick door screen.

3 JUDITH STREET, ANNA TIEDEMAN TENEMENT
Constructed 1870–80

The widow of a German merchant, then residing at *9 Judith Street*, built this small single house and the slightly larger versions at *5 Judith Street* and *7 Judith Street* in the late-nineteenth century as rental properties. Mrs. Tiedeman and her husband apparently filled in a creek bed to create these lots. The piazza at 3 Judith Street features an unusual arcaded opening and recessed door screen. The real estate investor Morris Jervey built the small two-story cottage with front piazzas at *1 Judith Street* in the 1930s, utilizing similar vernacular detailing. Both houses reflect the changing economic character in the neighborhood.

6–8 JUDITH STREET, JOHN ROBINSON TENEMENTS
Constructed 1817–20

John Robinson, the builder of the Aiken-Rhett House, erected these nearly identical weatherboarded Charleston single houses on raised brick basements in the second decade of the nineteenth century. Exemplifying the contemporary Neoclassical style, both houses retain their nine-over-nine windows, paired east chimneys, pilasters, and architraves on the piazza screens. Robinson constructed these houses with one-story piazzas, but a later owner constructed a second-story piazza at 6 Judith Street some years later.

9 JUDITH STREET, JOHN TIEDEMAN HOUSE

Constructed 1870; rehabilitated 1977–88

A German immigrant who prospered as a hay and grain merchant built a traditional Charleston single house on this lot shortly after the Civil War. Although most of the Tiedemans lived on Broad Street and in other neighborhoods in the late-nineteenth century, John Tiedeman's widow continued to live in this house until 1934. Only an Italianate style hooded door screen strays from the Greek Revival character of the building, seen particularly in its closed gable end and the Tuscan columns of its piazza.

10 JUDITH STREET, JOHN ROBINSON HOUSE

Constructed 1814

After the Aiken-Rhett House, this was John Robinson's most finely crafted Wraggborough building. Retained by his widow after Robinson's other properties were lost due to debt, the house has since generally remained as a single family residence. The two-and-a-half-story stuccoed brick dwelling with a front-facing Neoclassical piazza features corner quoining and a cross pediment with a well-detailed lunette window.

15–17 JUDITH STREET, JOHN ROBINSON HOUSES

Constructed 1835–38

Robinson, the Wraggborough real estate developer, built these Greek Revival, side-hall, double-parlor houses as investments for his children. He obviously employed the same builder or craftsman used by Augustus Taft in the construction of the house at *57 Laurens Street*. All three frame houses retain the same pattern-book door surrounds approached by marble staircases with iron balustrades and identical fenes-

17 Judith Street

609

tration. The Laurens Street example, like 17 Judith Street, possesses a flat roof with masking parapet, while 15 Judith Street rises to a closed gable roof with a tripartite window and projecting dormers. Extensive enclosures added by modern owners mar the piazzas of both Judith Street houses.

338 MEETING STREET, CITADEL SQUARE BAPTIST CHURCH

Constructed 1855–56; steeple restored 1990–91

Formed in 1854 by twelve members from First Baptist Church who were eventually joined by members of the Wentworth Street Baptist Church in Ansonborough and the Morris Street Baptist Church in Radcliffeborough, this amalgamated congregation began construction of a new church building within a few months. Edward C. Jones and Francis D. Lee apparently designed the new Baptist church with a style referred to in the *Charleston Courier* as "pure Norman," following the Romanesque structures found particularly in France. Jones and Lee's design predates the more famous work in this style by Henry Hobson Richardson. On the exterior a massive gable roof fronts Meeting Street with arched entries surmounted by elaborate Romanesque windows, the central one supporting a rose window. The 224-foot spire was toppled by the hurricane of 1885. Its replacement, a shorter, late-Victorian version of the earlier steeple, was in turn replaced following damage in Hurricane Hugo. In 1990 the congregation raised funds to restore the steeple to its original height, with some concessions on the design to incorporate the post-1885 work. In the interior, ribbed vaulting and plaster bosses decorate the ceilings and the pulpit area where an alcove was originally wainscoted in oak. The interior was formerly painted in an imitation of stone.

Citadel Square Baptist Church with its original steeple, 1875 engraving

342 MEETING STREET, SECOND PRESBYTERIAN CHURCH

Constructed circa 1811; restored 1990–91

James and John Gordon, architect-builders

Organized as an outgrowth of the First (Scots) Presbyterian Church and officially known as the Second Presbyterian Church of the City and Suburbs of Charleston, the congregation attracted a new generation of Scottish merchants who planned an ambitious building outside the boundaries of the city. This church faces the public space known initially as Wragg Square and later dubbed Ashmead Place. It was designed and built by James and John Gordon, Scottish masons and builders who subsequently built St. Paul's Church at *126 Coming Street* in Radcliffeborough. A portico in the Tuscan order with a deep entablature and ribbed frieze supports a pediment in which there is a large lunette window. Similar fanlights appear over the doors. Lacking side doorways, the south facade of the church features a fully developed pediment supported by a wide entablature and engaged Tuscan columns. The spire, intended by an early minister of the church to be a "finger pointing upward," was never completed. Its rusticated base, decorated with bull's-eye windows, supports a single octagonal cupola supported by Corinthian pilasters. The first minister of the church, the Reverend Andrew Flynn, was replaced after about twenty years by the Reverend Dr. Thomas Smyth, an Irish Presbyterian minister who kept close ties with Calvinists in the British Isles. Severe acoustical problems inspired church leaders to alter the interior in 1833 by raising the floor three feet and lowering the ceiling by sixteen feet. After severe damage by Hurricane Hugo in 1989 the original ceiling height was restored, and remnants of a plaster decoration incorporating the seal of South Carolina and other devices served to permit the restoration of this ornament in the area above the Venetian stained-glass window on the east wall.

350 MEETING STREET, JOSEPH MANIGAULT HOUSE

L *Constructed circa 1803; restored late-1980s, early-1990s*

Gabriel Manigault, architect

The Manigault House is a paradigm for the advance of the preservation movement in early-twentieth-century Charleston. The wealthy planter Joseph Manigault inherited the southern portion of the property from his uncle Joseph Wragg and, after purchasing the northern lot from his sister, commissioned his brother Gabriel Manigault to design a house in the manner of a Neoclassical suburban villa. The building as completed stands three stories high over a high basement. It boasts a curvilinear bay on the north side providing an entry door and Palladian window, another curvilinear bay on the east side, a semicircular double-tiered piazza on the west, and a rectangular piazza on the south facing the garden. Constructed of distinctive locally made reddish brown brick and trimmed with various sandstones, the house is covered by a slate, hipped roof. On the interior a broad curved stair rises on the north side of a large entry hall to a second-floor drawing room and a withdrawing room. There are large bedchambers on both the second and third floors. Extensive Neoclassical composition work decorates the various mantels and doorways of the principal rooms, and a large plaster medallion ornaments the ceiling of the stairway. A garden temple with a bellcast roof fronts the south end of the property where a parterre adjoins the south facade of the house. To the east and northeast a kitchen, stable, and other dependencies, all now gone, made up a work yard. Architecturally, Joseph Manigault's town residence, without its third story, resembled the now-lost Manigault Plantation house at White Oak on the North Santee River.

A carriage maker, George N. Reynolds, bought the property in 1852 from the Manigault heirs and, after reorienting the house to the south,

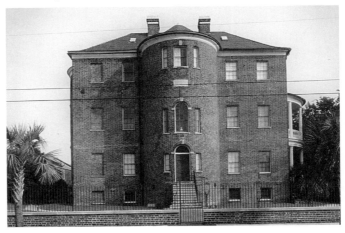

sold the southeast portion of the lot. Later the kitchen building and the entire north yard were sold and replaced by a dry cleaning establishment. Eventually the house declined to a tenement, and by 1920 it was threatened with demolition. Susan Pringle Frost founded the Society for the Preservation of Old Dwellings largely to save the Manigault House, and the fledgling group purchased it on May 19, 1920. By 1922 the financially distressed Society sold the property to Mrs. Ernest Pringle, who attempted valiantly to secure its future, reluctantly selling the garden to Standard Oil Company for a filling station. During this tenure the gatehouse became a comfort station, and purchasers of full tanks of gasoline could receive free tours of the house. When the property was auctioned for default on the mortgage, The Charleston Museum purchased it in 1933 with funds donated by Harriet Pollitzer, Princess Pignatelli, the South Carolina–born socialite who wintered at Wando Plantation near Mt. Pleasant.

Through the negotiations of museum director Milby Burton and Mayor Burnet Maybank, Standard Oil deeded back the garden, but the restoration of the property was delayed for more than fifteen years due to the lack of funding. The house was used as a USO facility in World War II, after which sufficient funds were raised for its restoration. The Garden Club of Charleston restored the garden according to a surviving 1820 watercolor by Charlotte Manigault, and the museum furnished the house with a splendid collection of Charleston-made Federal furnishings. By 1986 the museum had demolished the modern building. Following years of study by architectural historians, conservators, and archaeologists, a restoration program reconstructed a conjectural fence and stair to the surviving door entry on John Street, divided the former work yard with outlines of the lost outbuildings, and restored some of the original colors and paint finishes.

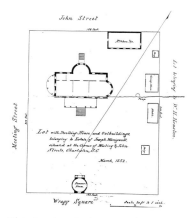

Plat showing site layout and floor plan of 350 Meeting Street

The southern facade and garden temple of the Joseph Manigault House during World War II

360 MEETING STREET, THE CHARLESTON MUSEUM

Constructed 1979–80

Chrissman and Solomon, architects

A Boston architectural firm won the design competition to produce the plans for the new Charleston Museum in 1976. The monumental contemporary structure was intended to appear contextual but deliberately planned to lack historical references to the surrounding area. A planned mall, a series of four rectangles connected by glass corridors linking the new museum to its Joseph Manigault House, was never undertaken. The construction of this building, particularly in a neighborhood then lacking revitalization, was considered by the City Council and planners as a major first step toward rejuvenation of the area and greater access to the nation's oldest museum.

2–4 WRAGG SQUARE, AIKEN'S ROW
Constructed 1845

Two of the seven identical rental houses built by William Aiken still survive at these addresses. Earlier generations referred to these dwellings as the "Seven Wages" because of the often-told story that the rent from each of these houses supported the main Aiken residence on a given day of the week. These two-story houses have double-tiered front piazzas with Tuscan columns. All the interior and exterior woodwork derives from simple Greek Revival prototypes found in pattern books. The interior floor plan follows the double house tradition, but pocket doors separate the two rooms on each side of the hall. In the antebellum period each property had its own kitchen with piazza and a separate stable, forming a forecourt at the rear of the houses. Two houses were demolished in the first expansion of Courtenay School, circa 1940, while three more were removed for the new school building in 1957.

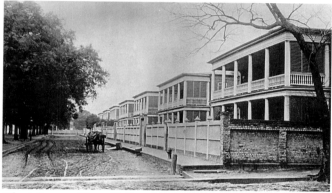

Aiken's Row on Wragg Mall, or Square, in the 1890s

Aiken's Row before the first demolitions in 1940

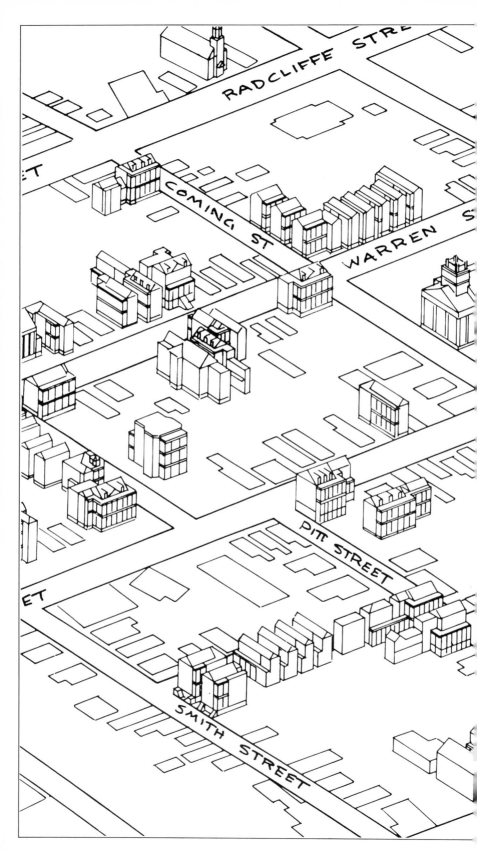

9

RADCLIFFEBOROUGH AND CANNONBOROUGH

Planters and Craftsmen

*R*adcliffeborough (originally Radcliffeboro) is an eight-block neigh borhood that was sectioned off into lots from farm property purchased by Thomas Radcliffe. Radcliffe's widow, Lucretia, and his estate continued the development of this borough after 1806. Mrs. Radcliffe donated a prominent square of land for the site of the Church of St. Paul's, Radcliffeborough, begun as the Third Episcopal Church in 1811. Designed by the Scottish builders James and John Gordon and executed by the carpenters Robert Jackson and Robert Galbraith, this undertaking was a conscious attempt to build a larger edifice than those downtown. St. Paul's served as the base of worship for a number of rice planters living in the uptown area, but it was generally surrounded by houses built by prosperous merchants and mechanics. The plantation style house at 57 Radcliffe Street, often referred to as "West Indian" in style, is an early remnant, as is 64 Warren Street, built in 1816. At Warren and Thomas Streets three prominent émigrés—Justice Benjamin Faneuil Dunkin, Lawrence Edmondston, and Samuel Mills—built substantial houses in

Henry Jackson's 1846 View of Charleston *showing the neighborhood of Radcliffeborough and Cannonborough across the mill pond (present-day Calhoun Street)*

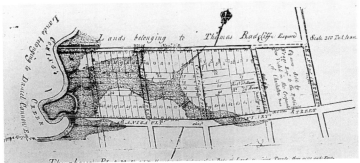

Plat of the Wragg lands, below Thomas Radcliffe's parcel, Radcliffeborough, 1786

the 1820s and 1830s. The latter two dwellings feature characteristics more applicable to New England houses of the period: recessed entries, Ionic pilasters and cornices, flush siding, and boxed interior plans.

Coming Street in Radcliffeborough, like Harleston Village, was home to several free black families before the War Between the States, and a "free woman of color" owned many of the lots on Radcliffe Street in the 1850s. Duncan Street in the same period, with a mix of single houses, cottages, and more substantial two-story dwellings, was nearly dominated by free African Americans and slaves living apart from their masters. After the war the free black elite of the antebellum period established St. Mark's Episcopal Church and retained the architect-engineer Louis Barbot to design a building with Roman Corinthian columns. Larger lots, such as those at Warren and Coming Streets, were sometimes subdivided for the construction of small single houses for newly freed slaves. Duncan Street and Desportes Court remained residential enclaves for working African Americans. Today Radcliffeborough is an economically and racially mixed neighborhood, and its stated boundaries also include former Wragg lands to the south and Elliott lands to the north.

West of Radcliffeborough the other early suburb of Cannonborough stretched west to the Ashley River and northward into the neck of the peninsula. This area encompassed a low marshy tract owned by the wealthy "mechanick" David Cannon and connecting to his western lumber mills. This area, even more than Radcliffeborough, was a setting for substantial villas for wealthy planters and merchants. On the east Cannonborough bordered lands formerly owned by the Wragg family. A potter's field in the western part of the Cannonborough section became the locus for a large federal arsenal in the 1820s, a complex that became a school for boys in the postbellum period. After the Civil War intense filling of marshland, providing links southward to streets such as Ashley, Rutledge, and Smith Streets, provided opportunities for construction of houses by middle- and working-class individuals, Irish and German immigrants, and freedmen. A substantial part of the original Cannonborough neighborhood has been encompassed by Charleston's hospital complex and the Medical University of South Carolina.

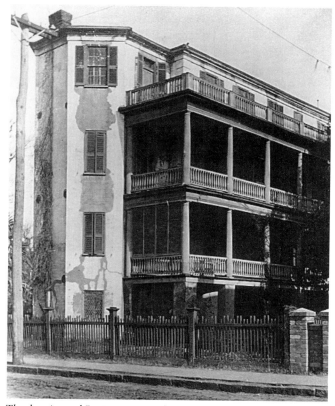

The deteriorated Benjamin Faneuil Dunkin House, Smith and Warren Streets, early-twentieth century

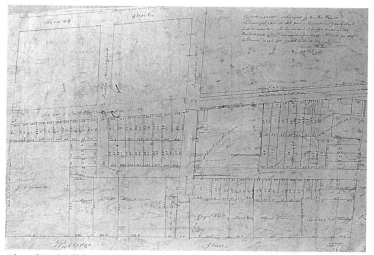

Plat of Radcliffeborough, early-nineteenth century

141 ASHLEY AVENUE, ALSTON HOUSE

Constructed circa 1817–19

This dwelling is an extraordinary survivor of small suburban villas built by wealthy rice planters in Cannonborough and Radcliffeborough in the early-nineteenth century. An advertisement from the *Charleston Courier* in 1818 described a building that may be the house or a dwelling similar to that at 141 Ashley Avenue:

> *For Sale/ A healthy Summer Residence. THE LOT and BUILDINGS at Cannonsborough, formerly occupied by the subscriber, and lately by Judge Cheves and Mr. Alston. The Lot is 100 feet in front by about 320 deep on two streets: The Dwelling House has ten rooms, one of them 31 feet by 16, with a cove ceiling, a kitchen and pantry, paved with Flag Stones; large room for servants, and every convenience for a genteel family; handsome Garden and Pigeon House on a large scale, & c. The situation for health is unexceptionable, and for a Southern Planter a most desirable one.*

The house originally sat back from Calhoun Street one block to the east with its piazza garden side looking out over the Bennetts' rice mill pond. Its entry faced Mill Street. The house has been moved three times in the twentieth century by St. Francis Xavier Hospital, occupants of a portion of the original lot by 1881, and the Medical University of South Carolina. The most important feature of the building is its surviving ornate ceiling plasterwork, including medallions and cornices. One of the second-floor rooms also has a barrel vaulted ceiling.

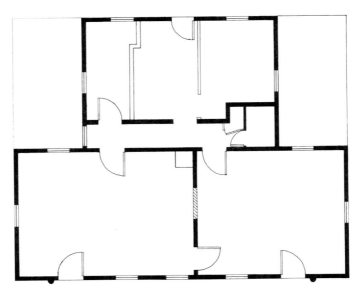

Measured plan of the second floor, 141 Ashley Avenue

167 ASHLEY AVENUE, U.S. ARSENAL/OLD PORTER MILITARY COMPLEX

Porter Military Academy's Hoffman Library, which is today the Waring Library of the Medical University of South Carolina

Established by 1825; various nineteenth-century construction dates; altered 1960s; restored 1980s–90s

The United States government established an arsenal on this uptown site in 1825 on the location of a paupers' cemetery. The arsenal continued in operation until the beginning of the Civil War, when it was taken over by the Confederacy. The only remnant of the first complex was extensively renovated in 1884 as a chapel for Porter Military Academy, a boys' school formed in 1867 by an Episcopal clergyman, the noted Confederate chaplain Dr. Toomer Porter. Dr. Porter had obtained the arsenal site from the federal government with the particular assistance of Gen. William T. Sherman. A leading African American builder helped Dr. Porter convert the former brick arsenal shed by adding a peaked Gothic roof and new windows.

Daily chapel service at St. Timothy's Chapel, Porter Military Academy, 1950s

An octagonal, Gothic Revival library donated by a New York Episcopal minister in 1887 and designed by New York architect J. B. Snooks also survives from the formative period of the school. Today this structure houses the extensive library and archive of the Medical Society of South Carolina. Colcock Hall, a two-story brick artillery building, remains from the 1862–64 use of the site by the Confederacy. Porter Military Academy, upon its merger with another school (today it is a coed private school known as Porter-Gaud), sold the campus to the Medical University of South Carolina. The Medical University in recent years has restored these buildings, especially St. Timothy's (now St. Luke's) Chapel, which has been brought back from near total destruction by Hurricane Hugo.

Colcock Hall

178 ASHLEY AVENUE, WICKLIFFE (JOHN HUME LUCAS) HOUSE

Constructed 1850–52; restored 1977

This two-story, hipped-roof house follows a typical side-hall, double-parlor floor plan seen in all of Charleston's nineteenth-century suburban neighborhoods. The dwelling, however, includes elements of mid-nineteenth-century grandeur that individualize the property from most of its neighbors. John Hume Lucas, a rice planter and an engineer, built the house between 1850, when he bought the land, and 1852, when he is listed as residing at the Ashley Avenue address. The most distinctive element of the house is the giant order portico with Tower of the Winds capitals as a side porch element instead of traditional double-tiered piazzas. Another detail distinctive of the mid-nineteenth century is the sunken double staircase in the entrance hall, an example of which can also be seen at the Aiken-Rhett House at *48 Elizabeth Street*. The Aiken-Rhett example, however, is an alteration to an earlier building, not planned in the original design, as in the case of the Wickliffe House. Restored by the Medical University of South Carolina as an alumni and faculty house, the dwelling is now named for its donor.

192 ASHLEY AVENUE, WICKENBERG HOUSE

Constructed 1859–61; rehabilitated 1980s

A family of prosperous grocers built this elaborate stuccoed brick dwelling with a mix of Greek Revival and Italianate details on the eve of the War Between the States. The elaborate terra-cotta door and window surrounds incorporating anthemion motifs accent a large, modified side-hall-plan dwelling with a closed front gable and double-tiered piazzas. Tradition holds that Gen. Pierre G. T. Beauregard used this house as a headquarters during the siege of Charleston. The original builders held onto the house for eight generations, although as the neighborhood developed surrounding garden and orchard lots were subdivided to create new building opportunities.

214 CALHOUN STREET, FREDERICK SHAFFER HOUSE
Constructed circa 1834

The Shaffer House survives as one of the great suburban villas that lined Boundary Street, later called Calhoun Street. This section of the former Wragg lands, today considered part of Radcliffeborough, devolved to the wealthy planter Joseph Manigault in the early-nineteenth century. Frederick Shaffer, a rising house carpenter or building contractor, purchased this lot as well as several others in this area from Manigault over a nine-year period. Shaffer apparently constructed this Greek Revival style house with his own craftsmen. The building holds many similarities with some of the other suburban houses built with their faces to front the street in the plantation style, such as the Robert Martin House at *16 Charlotte Street*. A balustraded wood staircase serves as an approach to the raised double-tiered piazza and a five-bay facade with a rectilinear, Gothic Style central architrave. Brick side wings and a rear addition add exceptional size to this dwelling. The rear dependency surviving at *63 Pitt Street* once housed eighteen slaves who served the Shaffer household. The front coping surmounted by a wood fence and the hatched front gates comprise unique survivals of the typical nineteenth-century enclosure of such a suburban property.

Shaffer's estate sold the residence in 1885 to Isaac J. Barden. During this occupancy the house became infamous due to the 1899 murder of Thomas Pinckney Jr., a prominent young Charleston attorney, who was found shot twice in the back following a call at the house. The younger members of the Barden family were associated with the crime, but after closed hearings no charges were ever brought in the case.

220 CALHOUN STREET, BURNHAM HUGER HOUSE

Constructed circa 1840; rehabilitated 1983–84

Although Thomas Burnham probably built this two-and-a-half-story wood dwelling on a raised basement story in 1840, he sold the property shortly after completion to the merchant David Levy. The building exhibits details more common to Federal style buildings, particularly with its nine-over-nine sash windows and gabled dormers, but its Doric-columned piazza elevated on a ground-story brick arcade represents the Greek Revival period of construction. Rear projections flank a centered two-story piazza that once looked out upon the work yard and garden.

In 1847 Levy sold the property to Dr. Benjamin Huger, the wealthy owner of Richmond Plantation on the Cooper River. Huger's daughter, Eliza, married Alfred Huger Dunkin, whose family lived at *87 Warren Street*. In more recent years the building was converted into apartments and then reconverted with more units in a Tax Act Rehabilitation in 1984.

222 CALHOUN STREET, OLD BETHEL METHODIST CHURCH

🅽 *Constructed 1797–98; moved from Pitt and Calhoun Streets 1880*

Bethel Methodist Church was organized in 1797, and the original church building was completed by 1798. The third-oldest church structure in Charleston, the building originally stood on the corner of Pitt and Calhoun Streets where the present brick church of Bethel Methodist now stands. The simple frame structure was moved to the rear corner of the property in 1852 after Bethel Methodist's brick church was completed. The old church became the meeting place of the African American members of Bethel's congregation. In 1880 the building was rolled across Calhoun Street to its present location, where it became known as Old Bethel Methodist. The present congregation includes descendants of the 1880 congregation. The church was designed with a simple rectangular floor plan measuring 40 by 60 feet. Originally its only ornamentation included the simple classical cornice and front and rear gables. The columned portico was added in 1880 after the church was moved to its present location. The galleried interior is plainly finished in keeping with the meetinghouse tradition. With the exception of the pressed ceiling, the pews, and the organ, the church retains much of its 1798 appearance.

Measured front (south) elevation of Old Bethel Methodist Church

268 CALHOUN STREET, SEBRING-AIMAR HOUSE

Constructed 1838–46; rehabilitated mid-1980s

The president of the State Bank at *1 Broad Street* and owners of *3 Broad Street* built this two-story, flat-roofed wooden dwelling on a high foundation overlooking the mill pond in the second quarter of the nineteenth century. Sebring's house fits the plantation style profile of Cannonborough dwellings with front-facing piazzas. A rear brick dependency formerly served as a kitchen and slave quarters.

Charles Pons Aimar, whose family business was sited at *409 King Street*, bought the house in 1882, and his family lived here for nearly a hundred years. The Medical University has adaptively rehabilitated both buildings for an alumni house and offices.

274 CALHOUN STREET, DANIEL CANNON HOUSE

Constructed circa 1802–15; altered nineteenth century

The wealthy lumberman Daniel Cannon apparently commenced construction of this large two-and-a-half-story wood house on a high brick basement in 1802, and after his death the structure was completed by his estate some years later for his daughter. The house retains some of its original exterior elements, including hipped roof and fenestration, and there are splendid Adamesque features on its interior. William Gregg, jeweler and founder of Graniteville Manufacturing Company, the South's most innovative antebellum industrial facility, lived here from 1838 to 1855. The property has notable Greek Revival additions, including the piazza columns and a Victorian cast-iron fence. A double brick dependency survives northwest of the main house.

274 Calhoun Street in the 1880s

126 COMING STREET,
CATHEDRAL OF ST. LUKE AND ST. PAUL (EPISCOPAL)
Constructed 1811–16; restored 1990–91

John and James Gordon, builders

The first discussion concerning the construction of a third Episcopal church in the city appears in the records of St. Michael's in 1806. This impetus, however, seems to have been thwarted by President Thomas Jefferson's embargo. The reasons for building a third church are, unfortunately, not clear. Both Robert Mills and church historian Frederick Dalcho allude to the increase in Episcopalian membership in the early-nineteenth century, but the *History of St. Paul's Church* argues that there were other reasons as well. It states that three factors encouraged the construction of a third church: the need for more room; the convenience of those living in the northern suburbs; and a group with personal preferences for a particular minister, Dr. Percy, who had recently been relieved of duties at St. Philip's.

In 1810 a building committee was formed, and the new congregation met in the Huguenot Church while their building was being constructed. Four lots were donated by Mrs. Lucretia Radcliffe on Coming Street, and the cornerstone was laid on November 19, 1811. James and John Gordon, builders of Second Presbyterian Church on Meeting Street, were chosen as builders and their plan for the church accepted. Robert Jackson and Robert Galbraith were responsible for the carpentry work. As with the other church, cost overruns and engineering difficulties plagued the structure, which was finally completed in 1816. Rev. J. Stewart Hanckel (assistant rector, 1838–51) recalled, "Its cost far exceeded the original estimates, having been greatly increased by errors in judgment, etc., on the part of the architects and contractors.

The Cathedral of St. Luke and St. Paul in 1989, damaged by Hurricane Hugo

Drawing of the Cathedral made by Jean Claude deMontfort, 1975

The construction of the steeple had to be abandoned and the present tower substituted; even this had to be lightened, by the removal of vast masses of brickwork, to arrest the settling of the steeple and the cracking of the main walls." He also reported that the building was in frequent need of repairs amounting to nearly $120,000 (as much as the original cost of the building).

Further information concerning the interior is provided by Reverend Hanckel, who reports that despite another description of a "richly painted" chancel, the interior was not as grandly fitted out as had been originally intended. Recent paint research confirms the use of gilding for capitals of pilasters and other details and also reveals extensive use of graining on doors, the balcony fronts, and the wainscot. Other evidence indicates a light yellow on the columns that may have been the base for a decorative treatment such as marbleizing, although clear evidence for such a treatment was not discovered. The plaster walls were painted a lime white, and much of the wood trim was painted a light gray. This general scheme was restored after Hurricane Hugo.

James Gordon died in 1814 before the church was completed. John Gordon continued his work as a bricklayer and builder after his brother's death, working on private commissions as well. In 1819 he purchased his first plantation, and as his fortunes rose so did his social aspirations, for in the 1831 directory he listed himself as a planter. John Gordon died in 1835 at the age of forty-eight.

135 COMING STREET, WILLIAM WHITEMAN TENEMENT

Constructed circa 1830; renovated with certain alterations 1990

A Charleston jeweler and silversmith built this two-and-a-half-story Charleston single house on a raised foundation with a front closed gable end and double-tiered piazzas in the 1830s. The pedimented window hoods and the Italianate style piazza door probably reflect alterations of the last quarter of the nineteenth century. The house has undergone a number of alterations, including, most recently, the rebuilding of the chimneys and other changes after Hurricane Hugo.

140–142 COMING STREET, JAMES REDDING TENEMENTS

Constructed circa 1889; rehabilitated 1979–80

140 Coming Street in 1979, before rehabilitation

Although Alexander Wilson owned this and the properties to the north in this block from the 1870s until the 1880s, only a few small one-story houses occupied the site. In 1884 James Redding bought these two properties from Wilson's heir, as well as acquiring the sites of *42,44,46,48,* and *50 Warren Street.* 140 and 142 Coming Street mirror the general single house plan for Wilson's tenements, including double-tiered piazzas screened by Italianate style doorways and simple wood sheathing, six-over-six sash windows, and double, Gothic hooded chimneys. Most of the Warren Street dwellings, constructed between 1890 and 1898, follow the same plan, although Redding or a subsequent owner added a roof overhang with brackets and square-cut decoration in the Queen Anne manner to 50 Warren Street. Another investor, J. H. Mindermann, built an L-shaped modified single house at *138 Coming Street.*

151 COMING STREET, HENRY OETJEN HOUSE

Constructed circa 1851–52; rehabilitated mid-1980s

A German merchant built this two-and-a-half-story brick single house on a lot acquired at public auction in December 1850. Stylistically the building, with its pilastered gable framing a tripartite window, brick belt coursing, and two-story side piazza, relates to the mid-nineteenth-century single houses found in Ansonborough. Altered as apartments some years ago, the Oetjen House became the subject of a tax act rehabilitation by investors in the mid-1980s. The ground-story doorway leading to a lower unit is one of several twentieth-century alterations.

71 PITT STREET, DESEL HOUSE
Constructed circa 1836

C. L. Desel constructed a well-detailed wood single house on a high stuccoed brick foundation on a lot acquired from Joseph Manigault. Similar in form to the house at *135 Coming Street*, the dwelling embraces the Greek Revival style with its one-story raised piazza, square door architrave, and closed front gable with tripartite window. Desel died during the Civil War, and the property passed to the Johnson and then the Shepard families.

72 PITT STREET, RICHARD HOLLOWAY HOUSE
Constructed circa 1827; rehabilitated 1980s

This building survives as one of several investment properties constructed or owned by the free black carpenter Richard Holloway. Holloway's extended family lived on Beaufain Street but had interests across the city. As an exhorter in the Methodist Church and a member in the elite Brown Fellowship Society, Holloway held a position of unique authority in Charleston's pre–Civil War free African American community. The high quality of wood craftsmanship exhibited in the Pitt Street house includes the double-tiered piazza with paneled parapet and a closed gable roof with a modified version of a Venetian (Palladian) window. 72 Pitt Street is closely related to

Holloway's contemporary property at *221 Calhoun Street* and received a thorough rehabilitation in the 1980s.

73 PITT STREET, WILLIAM WALLER HOUSE
Constructed circa 1832

The saddler William Waller built this two-and-a-half-story single house after acquiring the site in 1832 from Daniel Johnston, a butcher and member of Charleston's free black community. Richard Holloway probably acted as the contractor for this building since the modified Palladian window in the front gable and other features show similarities to Holloway's other work. In the late-nineteenth century another prominent African American family, the DeCostas, owned the property and probably made the minor Italianate style changes, including the bracketed cornice and piazza door screen.

82 PITT STREET, SANDERS HOUSE
Constructed circa 1843

This two-and-a-half-story brick single house is a good example of the suburban development that blossomed as Charleston's expanding antebellum population pushed development north up the peninsula. The builders of this house appear to have been two entrepreneurs: Septimus Sanders, a barber whose business was located at *43 Broad Street*; and Joseph A. Sanders, a bricklayer. The Sanders's acquired the property in 1843 and built a residence there, which was owned briefly by William Bell, a planter, and then by Mrs. Sarah O'Hear. Joseph Sanders then purchased the house in 1846, and the trustees of his estate acquired it the following year for his widow, Laura Sanders. Like several suburban Charleston houses, 82 Pitt Street is set back so that a small lawn separates the

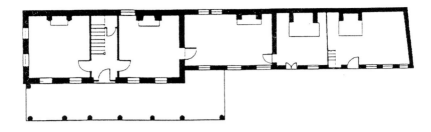

Measured plan of the first floor, 82 Pitt Street

house from activity on the street. The interior of this residence contains decorative elements in the Federal style, one indication of the cautious tastes of its builders and their clients. Its remarkably intact rear dependency was apparently joined to the main house in the 1870s by a hyphen addition.

84 PITT STREET, ELIAS WHILDEN HOUSE
Constructed circa 1827; altered 1840s

A successful rice planter from the Mount Pleasant area built this massive double house with its side to the street, in the single house manner, in about 1827. The structure stands on a brick foundation and has a weatherboarded facade with four bays, a closed gable on the street side, and a double-tiered, Tuscan-columned piazza that faces a large garden lot. Past the piazza door screen a staircase rises to the main elevation and the front entry, which is surmounted by a fanlight with a decorative eagle carving. The original lot underwent subdivision on several occasions, including the 1841 severance of the property known as *82 Pitt Street*. Whilden, who owned substantial town property in the developing Village of Mount Pleasant, retained this as a town house for several years. The house was owned by the T. A. Wilbur family at the time of the earthquake of 1886. After the earthquake the dwelling was rated in good condition except for collapsed chimneys.

26 RADCLIFFE STREET, CENTRAL BAPTIST CHURCH

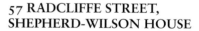 *Constructed 1891; restored 1990*

John P. Hutchinson, architect

The Central Baptist Church was designed by John P. Hutchinson, an African American architect, and built in 1891 by members of the congregation. The church has the distinction of being the first in the city to be designed, built, and financed by African Americans. With its tall Gothic windows and doors and Italianate detailing, the structure is a strong presence on Radcliffe Street. Perhaps its most distinguishing feature is its square central tower, which was replaced with a reproduction of the original after damage by Hurricane Hugo in 1989. Striking elements on the interior of this structure are the murals painted between 1912 and 1915 by the artist Amohamed Milai of Calcutta, India, which depict the life and death of Christ.

57 RADCLIFFE STREET, SHEPHERD-WILSON HOUSE

Constructed before 1817

Historians have proposed various theories to explain the history and architecture of this corner building. Generally called the "West Indian House" because of its original T-shaped form with a steep hipped roof overhanging an inset piazza, the building stands on a raised brick basement with several openings to the sidewalk. The dwelling faced open country and may have been part of an uptown farm or plantation. The great-niece of Thomas Radcliffe, Sophia Frances Perry Shepherd, received 57 Radcliffe upon her marriage to Alexander Barron Wilson in 1816. Documentary evidence remains unclear as to whether the Shepherd-Wilson House stood on this site prior to the marriage.

156 RUTLEDGE AVENUE, JOHNSON-WILBUR HOUSE

Constructed circa 1808; renovated circa 1900, 1990s

Formerly the residence of U.S. Supreme Court Justice William Johnson, this two-and-a-half-story Charleston single house passed to the A. N. Wilbur family in the late-nineteenth century. The Wilburs altered the windows and added a substantial rear addition. Threatened with demolition in 1968, the house has been adapted for new uses but retains its splendid interior decoration in the Neoclassical style.

172 RUTLEDGE AVENUE, ASHLEY HALL

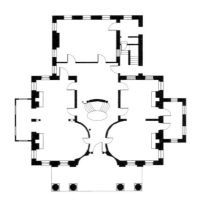

Measured plan, 172 Rutledge Avenue, Patrick Duncan House (Ashley Hall school)

N *Constructed circa 1802–16; various nineteenth-century additions*

Although this building's exact construction date remains in question, it is known that Patrick Duncan, a wealthy tallow chandler, purchased a lot in 1798 from Daniel Cannon and yet another lot in 1807 to the south from Elizabeth Combe. The purchases were made at the time when the neighborhood was becoming the fashionable suburb of Cannonborough. After his return to England in 1828, Duncan sold the house to James Nicholson for $11,800 in 1829.

In 1836 the property and building passed into the hands of James Reid Pringle, leader of the Unionist Party during the Nullification controversy. In 1845 George A. Trenholm, a noted Charleston merchant and onetime secretary of the treasury of the Confederacy, acquired the property. After the Trenholm tenure, the property was in the hands of Charles Otto White. Since 1909 the house has served as the home of Ashley Hall, a private school for girls.

The architecture of the building is believed to show the influence of William Jay. The house is entered through the basement portico, which has been glass enclosed to form a conservatory. The exterior of Ashley Hall is stuccoed and is probably original, as most homes such as this one from the Regency era were finished in this manner. The elaborate architectural detail in the Regency style, soaring elliptical stairway, curved walls and doors, round-headed openings, grandiose portico, and rounded balconies are similar to designs in Savannah by William Jay.

The three pointed arch windows in the pediment of the building's portico, defined by four Ionic columns, and the vaulted ceilings of the interior add Gothic motifs also used by Jay's contemporary, Robert Mills. An 1819 account describes the richness of Patrick Duncan's garden, but Charles Otto Witte is responsible for the present botanical diversity of the garden as well as the garden building clad with shells.

174 RUTLEDGE AVENUE, TRENHOLM-DARBY HOUSE

Constructed before 1861; renovated circa 1880s

Begun as a Charleston single house in the late-1850s by a wealthy railroad magnate, George Trenholm, this wooden structure was substantially renovated about twenty years later in the Queen Anne style by the Darby family.

179 RUTLEDGE AVENUE, BROWN-RANDOLPH HOUSE

Constructed 1876

Abrahams and Seyle, architects

The well-to-do merchant Edmonds Brown began construction of this massive, antebellum style brick house a decade after the end of the War Between the States.

Following the side-hall plan, with double-tiered piazzas supporting Tuscan columns, the house has remained a single family residence with little alteration. Completed by the prosperous grocer George Wagener, the house descended to Wagener's daughter and her Virginia-born husband, Dr. Harrison Randolph, the president of the College of Charleston in its important early-twentieth-century years.

114 SMITH STREET, GUSTAVUS J. LUDEN DWELLING
Constructed 1884–86

Dr. Luden acquired a large tract in the mid-1880s from the Benthem estate. Shortly thereafter he built this house and its neighbors at *112* and *116 Smith Street* in typical Charleston form. These three dwellings of the side-hall plan have front doorways with Italianate bracketed overhangs, side piazzas, front end gables, and Italianate window surrounds. In the 1880s the Paragon Building Association further subdivided these properties with other plots and created Murphy's Court, a complex of small Charleston single houses with side, one-story piazzas.

132 SMITH STREET, JOHN BICKLEY TENEMENT
Constructed circa 1859; altered 1920s

John Bickley, who lived at *64 Vanderhorst Street*, acquired this property as part of a tract purchased in 1824 from Justice Benjamin Faneuil Dunkin. It was covenanted in the conveyance that Bickley would not build on the southwest corner of the property and obstruct the view from Dunkin's house at *89 Warren Street*. After the death of the judge and the filling of the portion of the mill pond bordering the edge of the site, Bickley constructed a two-and-a-half-story plantation style house on a raised basement. In 1861 Theodore Dehon

Wagner, a partner in the blockade-running firm of John Fraser and Company, purchased the dwelling.

The scored and stuccoed brick facade and double-tiered piazzas, as well as important interior features, survive even though the building was converted to apartments in the early-twentieth century. Corner additions, staircases on the piazza, and a cast metal canopy above the entry tend to obscure the house's early character. Vague evidence of the architrave of the building's principal entry, now closed, remains on the Smith Street elevation.

156 SMITH STREET, THOMAS MILLER HOUSE

Constructed circa 1870; rehabilitated 1986

Built for Dr. Thomas E. Miller, this Charleston single house reflects the beginning of the transition from Greek Revival to Italianate architecture that occurred in the early-1870s. Dr. Miller was one of the foremost African American leaders in Reconstruction South Carolina. A member of the fifty-first U.S. Congress, he was the founder and first president of South Carolina State College. The house remained in the Miller family until 1950.

81 ST. PHILIP STREET, SOUTHERN BELL ADMINISTRATION BUILDING

Constructed 1938; various renovations with additions

Philip Trammell Shutze, architect

Several wooden houses were demolished in the late-1930s for the construction of what may be the finest early-twentieth-century office building in Charleston. Atlanta's noted classical architect Philip Trammell Shutze designed several hundred buildings for the Southern Bell Telephone and Telegraph Company. For this commission Shutze studied Savannah and Charleston architecture, particularly the work of William Jay, to design a public building in keeping with local architecture. The original portion of the Southern Bell Building consists of three stories with a rusticated ground floor set above a basement with lunette windows. A Doric-columned portico shelters the entry to the building. Upper-story windows, separated by belt coursing, feature semicircular heads and, on the second story, Greek fret panels beneath the sills. The latter features seem strongly derived from the William Mason Smith House at *26 Meeting Street*, now even more positively attributed to Jay. Later horizontal and vertical additions have severely compromised the integrity of Shutze's design, but its essential beauty remains intact.

5 THOMAS STREET, SARAH BATEMAN TENEMENT
Constructed 1895–99

The widow of Charles D. Bateman, who lived in the late-Federal style house to the south at *64 Vanderhorst Street*, constructed this elaborate Queen Anne style Victorian house on land subdivided from her property. The structure has a hipped roof with lower cross gables in an L-shape and boasts a wraparound porch with gable entry and spindle-work detailing surrounding an octagonal-shaped tower with a conical roof.

6 THOMAS STREET, LEGARE-RHETT HOUSE
L *Constructed 1833; restored mid-1980s*

This house was built by James Legare in 1833 and sold to Robert Barnwell Rhett, a politician best known for his title the "Father of Secession." In 1863 the Rhett family sold the house to George

A. Trenholm of *172 Rutledge Avenue*, the wealthy merchant whose ships were used as blockade runners during the Civil War and who became a Confederate secretary of the treasury. Theodore D. Wagner bought the property in 1866 and quickly resold it in 1867 to Thomas M. Hanckel, a trustee for Mrs. Susan H. Hanckel, for $10,000. The Hanckels owned the property for seventy-five years; they sold the house in 1940 to the Shahid family.

The wooden Greek Revival dwelling with flanking bays and three-story porticoes was built on a high, stuccoed brick basement within brownstone piers. Interesting characteristics of this house are the polygonal bays, which create two large octagonal rooms on each floor.

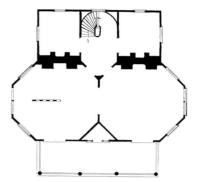

Measured plan of the first floor, 6 Thomas Street

7–11 THOMAS STREET, CHARLESTON IMPROVEMENT CORPORATION HOUSES
Constructed 1905–10

The Charleston Improvement Corporation, better known for its development in lower Charleston, acquired these three lots during the first decade of the twentieth century. All three of the dwellings exhibit the characteristics of the Queen Anne style. The corporation built 7 Thomas Street and 9 Thomas Street as nearly identical two-story, three-bay houses that have front end gable roofs and one-story piazzas with pedimented entries and spindle work. The dwelling at 11 Thomas Street retains its overlapping roof gables, two-story bay, and double-tiered front piazzas, although it has been altered.

12 THOMAS STREET, JAMES LEGARE TENEMENT
Constructed 1837–40

The planter and merchant James Legare, builder of the house at 6 *Thomas Street*,

built this investment dwelling on the northwest corner of his property in the late-1830s. In scale, the house seems reminiscent of similar Greek Revival, side-hall-plan dwellings of the same period, especially the brick version with similar detailing at *72 Anson Street*. The multitiered portico consists of two tiers of Tuscan columns supported on stuccoed piers at the ground level.

13 THOMAS STREET, BENJAMIN F. DUNKIN TENEMENT
Constructed 1823–28

The New England–born chancellor of the Equity Court of Appeals, Justice Benjamin Faneuil Dunkin, built this two-and-a-half-story Charleston single house on a raised foundation a few years after building his own residence on the lot immediately to the west. A late-Neoclassical pedimented architrave with semicircular transom and engaged Tuscan columns provides entry to a piazza with similar columns supporting a wooden arcade. The surviving kitchen building, modified in the late-nineteenth century, remains on the Warren Street elevation.

14 THOMAS STREET, ST. MARK'S EPISCOPAL CHURCH
Constructed 1875–78

St. Mark's Episcopal Church, at the corner of Thomas and Warren Streets, reflects the surviving popularity of Greek Revival style in post–Civil War Charleston. St. Mark's was organized in 1865 largely by families holding free status before the Civil War. The church building, erected by the local architect Louis J. Barbot, has served its Episcopal African American congregation for more than a century. Barbot's design for St. Mark's appears to be a simplified version of the Spring Street Methodist Church, which was designed by Barbot and his partner, John H. Seyle, nearly twenty years earlier. The interior design of the building is somewhat similar to the Church of the Holy Communion, located on Ashley Avenue, and contains a highly ornamented altar of wood and plaster. Dr. Toomer Porter, founder of Porter Military Academy, served both congregations as a rector. St. Mark's is a classic temple-form structure with a heavy pedimented gable end. The portico has four columns topped by Corinthian capitals. These capitals support a full entablature with three fascias in the architrave, a plain frieze, a cornice with dentils, ovolo molding, and a single corona. The cornice is repeated in the pediment. The tympanum, like the body of the structure, is faced with narrow boards. The church has three doors facing Thomas Street, all of which have simple surrounds and molded cornices. Each doorway is folding, consisting of three sunken panels to each leaf. The transom door also consists of four sunken panels. There are ten triple-hung windows of richly ornamented stained glass. Pilasters, without bases or caps, lie between each bay on the front and side facades of the church. The masonry foundation has an arched panel under each of the side windows.

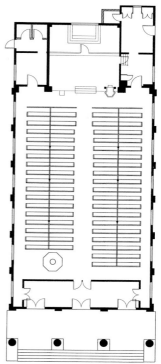

Measured floor plan, St. Mark's Episcopal Church

15 THOMAS STREET, SAMUEL S. MILLS HOUSE

Constructed circa 1840

Samuel Sage Mills, a native of Massachusetts, bought a substantial corner property including this site and 177 feet along Warren Street in 1839. Mills constructed this building while his brother-in-law, Lawrence A. Edmondston, erected a similar dwelling on the western portion of the property at *86 Warren Street*. A single Ionic pilaster survives at the southeast corner of the Mills dwelling, but its match at the northeast corner was removed many years ago. A subsequent

owner also removed the Ionic-columned portico on the south elevation. Architectural historians have generally noted that the external appearance of the building, with its pilasters, dentiled cornice, and Greek Revival recessed doorway, and its internal plan, without a central stair hall, more resemble New England style houses of the period.

8 VANDERHORST STREET, STEELE-KNOBELOCH HOUSE
Constructed 1855–58

A King Street hat merchant built this two-story, late–Greek Revival house soon after he bought the vacant lot from planter William Bell. Bell, who lived on Society Street, had bought the lot from Thomas Radcliffe Shepherd, a nephew of Thomas Radcliffe. Charles H. Simonton, attorney, judge, and Confederate soldier, apparently bought the property with a completed house in 1858. Mrs. Elizabeth Knobeloch bought the dwelling in 1872, and her family lived here until the mid-twentieth century. On both the front and rear elevations French doors open onto the double-tiered piazzas, which have Ionic columns on the first floor and Tower of the Winds Corinthian columns on the second. Although much of this section of the neighborhood lost its character after World War II, particularly with the demolition of the Orphan House and its chapel across the street, the Steele-Knobeloch House has remained a splendidly maintained residence to the present day.

12 VANDERHORST STREET, IRISH VOLUNTEERS ARMORY
Constructed 1888; rehabilitated mid-1980s; rebuilt behind facade 1989–90

The Irish Volunteers, a militia company founded in Charleston in 1798, erected this Gothic style armory six years after buying the property from the city in 1882. The Irish

Volunteers were one of a number of elite companies who served with distinction in the War of 1812, the Seminole War of 1836, and the War Between the States. Bay windows sheathed with diagonally set tongue and groove siding ornament the irregularly shaped front facade. Plaques with the date of construction, "1888," the obscure date "1784," and harps along with shamrocks decorate the face of the building and the crenellated parapet. Although the structure was splendidly rehabilitated as offices by its owners, an architectural firm and an engineering firm, some years before Hurricane Hugo, the 1989 storm's winds or a spawned tornado destroyed all but the front portion of the old armory. The owners again restored the front portion and rebuilt a new wing behind.

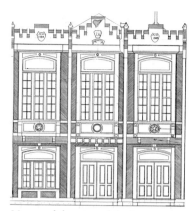

Measured drawing of the front (south) elevation, Irish Volunteers Armory, 12 Vanderhorst Street

37 VANDERHORST STREET, JAMES L. HONOUR HOUSE

Constructed 1859–71

The banker James L. Honour constructed one of the most finely detailed Greek Revival single houses surviving in Radcliffeborough. The weatherboarded building sits on a high masonry foundation. A closed gable roof with tripartite window and three side pedimented dormers surmounts the building, while a double-tiered piazza with Tuscan columns shades the west side of the dwelling. The piazza screen features a Greek Revival architrave framed by engaged Tuscan columns. Honour was a resident owner, an unusual characteristic in this area of Charleston, which was filled with rental properties, and he continued to live in this house until his death in the mid-1880s.

44 VANDERHORST STREET, AARON LORYEA HOUSE

Constructed circa 1863

A Charleston merchant built what may be one of the only houses constructed dur-

ing the War Between the States. Aaron Loryea acquired the lot, carved out of a property to the west, from Robert Mallar. A tall gable roof with tripartite window in its front end and three large pedimented dormers shelters the dwelling and piazza below. Fine wood detailing, including a wide frieze band; a Tuscan-columned piazza with elaborately turned balusters; and a rectilinear piazza screen with large glass transom and sidelights seem the hallmarks of this wartime construction.

64 VANDERHORST STREET, JOHN BICKLEY HOUSE

Constructed 1824–26

A wealthy lumber merchant and Goose Creek rice planter built this two-and-a-half-story, plantation style, brick house in the mid-1820s. Characterized by late-Federal or Regency detailing, the structure has a red sandstone staircase that approaches a double-tiered piazza set on an arcaded foundation. Tuscan columns support a flattened arcade on the first tier of the piazza that forms the foundation for a second tier. A central brick pediment with dogtoothed cornice extends from the roof, matching detailing on the side gables. The Bickley family held the property until 1880, conveying it then to Charles Bateman, a railway freight agent. By this point change through subdivision and differing economic conditions substantially affected the character of the Radcliffeborough district.

Doorway, 64 Vanderhorst Street

72–76 VANDERHORST STREET, JOHN J. MAPPUS TENEMENTS

Constructed circa 1875–78

John J. Mappus purchased the parcel from which these three lots derived at a public auction of John Fraser and Company and its partners in 1875. The auction represented the culmination of the U.S. government's case against the John Fraser Company, which began in 1867, for their blockade running during the Civil War. All three dwellings follow the Charleston single house style with closed gable front ends and side double-tiered piazzas. Each building has undergone some alteration, particularly 76 Vanderhorst Street, which lost its piazza spaces to enclosures in the twentieth century.

64–66 WARREN STREET, JAMES GABEAU HOUSE
Constructed circa 1816; rehabilitated 1980s

64 Warren Street before any rehabilitation in 1980

A cooper and descendant of French Huguenot immigrants became one of the first lot purchasers in Radcliffeborough to build a substantial dwelling in the emerging suburb at 64 Warren Street. A raised basement and brick piers support the main two-and-a-half-story wood, plantation style dwelling, which has a one-story front piazza approached by an original marble staircase with a wrought-iron railing. A pediment with a bull's-eye window projects from the gable roof, along with two pedimented dormers. Gabeau also acquired the lot known as 66 Warren Street, and his estate built a new two-and-a-half-story closed gable single house shortly before conveying the property.

67 WARREN STREET
Constructed circa 1878

66 Warren Street

Although the westernmost houses on the south side of this block of Warren Street, including numbers 61, 63, and 65, date from the antebellum period, Joseph Nelson built a two-story, Queen Anne style dwelling on this lot in 1878–79 under a ten-year lease from Sophia F. S. Marion. The front double-tiered piazza with surmounting pediment and elaborate jigsaw-cut decoration extends into a curvilinear wall that wraps the west side of the building. The northeast corner above the entry terminates in a six-sided tower with a bellcast roof finial.

68 WARREN STREET, JANE MACINTOSH HOUSE
Constructed circa 1874–75

Jane MacIntosh built this simple two-story Charleston single house with double-tiered piazzas right after purchasing this lot for $400 in 1874 from Sophia Frances Shepard Wilson, owner of *57 Radcliffe Street.* Several other single houses on this side of Warren Street follow this same sort of pattern with a mix of late–Greek Revival and Italianate styles. Another single woman, Miss Virginia Webb, built a similar house at *72 Warren Street* in the late-1870s.

86 WARREN STREET, LAWRENCE A. EDMONDSTON HOUSE
Constructed circa 1840; restoration in progress 1970s–90s

The brother-in-law of Samuel Mills, Lawrence A. Edmondston, built this two-story wooden dwelling. Although the original entry faced Smith Street, the present Warren Street elevation retains its original double-tiered piazzas with Ionic columns. Like its neighbor, the building has unusual flush boarded siding and a modillioned cornice over a wide undecorated frieze. Neglected for several decades, 86 Warren has been gradually restored over the last several years by a new owner.

89 WARREN STREET, CHANCELLOR BENJAMIN FANEUIL DUNKIN HOUSE
Constructed circa 1823–24; rehabilitated 1985; restored 1990s

Justice Benjamin F. Dunkin, a native of Massachusetts and descendant of the wealthy Faneuil family of Boston, became chancellor of the Court of Equity of South Carolina and acquired substantial town

Doorway, 89 Warren Street

property as well as ownership of a large plantation, Midway, in All Saints Parish near Georgetown. In 1823 Dunkin purchased six lots in Radcliffeborough from Payton Wood, selling three lots after completing his house and gardens on the other three. The four-story dwelling at 89 Warren Street has a late-Neoclassical style entry with engaged columns on the Warren Street side. Large polygonal bays mark the east and west ends of the dwelling, and two tiers of piazzas on a brick piered foundation face the remnant of the Dunkin House garden. Falling into disrepair after World War II, the building was in a substantial state of deterioration before its initial rehabilitation by an investor in the mid-1980s and ongoing work by a new owner.

GLOSSARY

Acanthus A decorative element based on a plant of the Mediterranean region. Images resembling the plant's thick scalloped leaves commonly appear in Corinthian capitals and in friezes of the Colonial and Greek Revival period.

Acroteria Bases or pedestals topping the peak and lower ends of a pediment or the sculpture on such pedestals.

Allée A garden walkway shaded by trees or bordered by ornamental shrubs arranged in parallel rows.

Anthemion A decorative element found in classical Greek and ancient Roman architecture, based on the flower and leaves of the honeysuckle; extensively used in the Greek Revival period in friezes and ironwork.

Arcade A series of arches supported by columns or piers that create a covered walk or space open at one or both sides. Also called a "loggia."

Architrave The surround, including vertical and horizontal members of a door or window opening. Also the bottom portion of an entablature found beneath the frieze.

Art Deco The fashionable Jazz Age style concurrent with International Modern in the 1920s and the 1930s. The name derives from a Paris exhibition of decorative and industrial art in 1925.

Art Moderne An architectural style generally used 1930–45, characterized by an overall streamlined appearance, asymmetrical facade, smooth wall surfaces with rounded corners, limited ornamentation, flat roof, wraparound windows, and curved canopies over the front door.

Arts and Crafts An early-twentieth-century building style that features low pitched roofs, porches supported with square columns that sometimes rest on large piers, and decorative beams at the cornice line.

Ashlar The patterning of smooth stones laid horizontally with clean vertical joints.

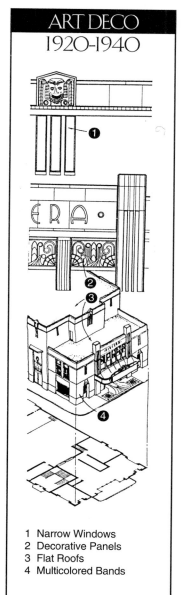

ART DECO
1920–1940

1 Narrow Windows
2 Decorative Panels
3 Flat Roofs
4 Multicolored Bands

Baluster An individual picket or column supporting the rail in a balustrade, on a porch, piazza, or roof parapet.

Balustrade A series of balusters connected at the top by a rail or coping, used on piazzas, porches, or along eaves to hide the roof.

Bargeboard Ornately carved decorative element attached to the ends of the overhanging eaves of a gable roof.

Barracoon An enclosure or group of buildings that formed a compound where enslaved Africans were held after arrival in the Americas or prior to sale.

Bay One unit of a building that consists of several like units, most often defined as a window or door opening. In modern buildings, a bay refers to the space between structural columns or piers.

Bay Window A multisided projecting window.

Beaux Arts A method of design popular at the end of the nineteenth and the beginning of the twentieth centuries which emphasizes the use of symmetrical facades, ornamented wall surfaces, exterior quoins, pilasters, columns, and low (mansard) roofs.

Bellcast Roof Any roof having a curve in its slope at the eaves.

Belt Course A band of wood or masonry projecting or flush across the face of a building that delineates the approximate location of an upper floor in two- and three-story structures.

Bermuda Stone A coquina material mined in Bermuda and some Caribbean islands imported in blocks to colonial Charleston as a building material.

Bolection A projecting molding, usually large and convex, often associated with early paneling.

Boss A circular or oval ornament ordinarily placed at the termination of a molding.

Bowfat Also known as a buffet or beaufet. An interior architectural feature resembling a closet or cupboard and used for the storage and display of tea and tablewares.

Brickwork (Bonds) The repetitive arrangement of bricks into various patterns which are both functional and aesthetic: guaranteeing the structural strength of a masonry wall while also lending the masonry wall surface texture. In Charleston the four most common types of brick bonds are English bond, a pattern consisting of alternating rows of headers (small end) and stretchers (long side); Flemish bond, in which headers and stretchers alternate in each course; American or common bond, a pattern that emerged in the early-nineteenth century consisting of three to five courses of stretchers to each course of headers; and stretcher bond, a pattern of stretchers used most often in modern brick veneer construction.

Bucranium A sculpted ox skull, often seen in classical and Greek Revival architecture in the metopes of a frieze. A series of such figures is known as bucrania.

Bull's-eye Window A round or oval window which may be glazed, opened, or louvered. The term may also refer to a round or oval panel.

Cantilever The horizontal projection of an element without visible support and counter balanced behind the wall, as in a stair beam, bay windows or balcony.

Capital The uppermost part of a column or pilaster, which supports the entablature; visible in the Doric, Tuscan, Corinthian, Ionic, and Composite orders.

Capola A small circular or polygonal structure on a roof usually for decoration and observation; a square or rectangular version for lighting interior spaces is a monitor.

Carpenter Gothic An architectural style derived from the Gothic Revival style characterized with wooden ornamentation such as bargeboards, brackets, and spindle-work porches.

Casement hinged windows that open outward.

Chamfered A beveled surface formed by cutting away the edge of two intersecting flat surfaces.

Channel An early term for the grooving of a column, pilaster, or other elements such as a triglyph.

Chevaux-de-Frise Called commonly in Charleston a "chevaux-de-fres," a security device mounted on gates and fences consisting of an iron band through which project numerous sharp points.

Cistern A receptacle, usually constructed in the form of a vault from brick, used to collect rain water for drinking and household use.

Cladding An external covering or skin applied to a structure for aesthetic or protective purposes.

Clapboard A horizontal wood sheathing consisting of relatively short, narrow boards, often tapering on one side.

Classical Revival An architectural style common from the third quarter of the eighteenth century through the first half of the nineteenth century in which an entry porch (portico) with triangular gable above and supported by columns dominates the front facade. Windows are typically five-ranked and symmetrically balanced with the center door.

Clerestory A large unobstructed window in an upper story of a building.

Coffering Ceiling decoration formed by recessed panels, as coffered ceiling, coffered dome.

Colonial A broad term inclusive of the early American vernacular architecture derived successively from post-medieval, baroque, and early Georgian styles.

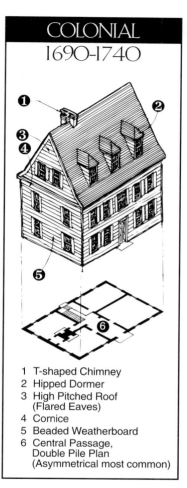

COLONIAL 1690-1740

1 T-shaped Chimney
2 Hipped Dormer
3 High Pitched Roof (Flared Eaves)
4 Cornice
5 Beaded Weatherboard
6 Central Passage, Double Pile Plan (Asymmetrical most common)

Colonial Revival An architectural style based on America's centennial spirit of the 1870s featuring colonial (Georgian) and Federal detailing, especially with multipaned sash windows, columned porticoes, and pedimented door architraves.

Colonette A small or slender column, usually decorative in nature.

Console Bracket Ornamental bracket often in an "S" or scroll-shaped form used to support a door, window, or pediment.

Coping A decorative or projecting cap for a wall or parapet, often used in Charleston to describe low masonry walls topped by wood or iron fencing.

Corbel A projection formed by step courses of brick and often seen in Charleston in parapets, cornices, and chimney caps.

Cornice In classical architecture, the uppermost, or top, projecting section of an entablature; in American buildings, the ornamental molding along the top of a building, wall, or feature.

Corona The projection in the mid or upper portion of a cornice above a bed molding and beneath the crown molding, often incorporating a recessed drop edge.

Cove Ceiling A ceiling with the molding, concave in profile, between the ceiling of a room and the cornice.

Craftsman A style that succeeded the Queen Anne which incorporates details such as large windows with diamond panes, flared wood or brick columns, and wide dormers projecting from gable roofs. Elegant joinery including exposed beams and half-timbering also characterizes the form.

Cupola A domical roof resting on a small circular or polygonal projection at the ridge of a roof commonly used for observation or as a belfry. See also "Lantern."

Curvilinear Gable A gable that has multiple curving sides.

Demilune Half-moon or crescent shaped.

Dentils Small square blocks which form a portion of many cornices, especially those of the Georgian, Federal, Neoclassical, and Colonial Revival styles whose designs were inspired by buildings of antiquity.

Dependency A building which serves a subordinate service function such as a kitchen or stable and ordinarily located at the rear of Charleston lots.

Dogtoothed A decorative cornice treatment in masonry buildings consisting of a row of projecting bricks set at a 45 degree angle. Also called "sawtoothing."

Dormer A gable or shed-roofed window projecting from a sloping roof.

Double-pile A seventeenth- and eighteenth-century building type typified by a rectangular block two rooms deep, the two rows of rooms usually being separated by a passage running the length of the house.

Earthquake Bolts Any of the iron bolts and the decorative washers often used with them that are attached to iron rods inserted laterally through buildings to provide additional structural support. Although this means of supplying additional strength was employed in the early-nineteenth century, earthquake bolts in Charleston are most often associated with repairs made to buildings following the 1886 earthquake. Also called "tie rods."

Eastern Stick Also known as "Eastlake." An architectural style of 1860 to circa 1900 characterized by asymmetry and angularity, stickwork (i.e., narrow boards nailed to the exterior walls so as to repeat and reinforce the structural skeleton), verandas with diagonal braces, steeply pitched intersecting gable roofs, wood siding (usually board and batten or clapboard), and gable trim.

Eaves The projecting overhang at the edge of a roof.

Egg and Dart A decorative molding derived from classical architecture and featuring convex egg shapes interspersed between pointed bands with a dartlike appearance.

Ell A projecting wing placed perpendicularly to the principal structure and forming a right angle.

Entablature The whole of the horizontal part above the columns of classical buildings on the top of any building itself and generally consisting of three parts: cornice, frieze, and architrave.

Fanlight A semicircular or elliptical window with radiating panes most often found over doors.

Fascia The flat, horizontal band in an architrave, often serving as a division.

Federal A term used by Americans for "Neoclassical," this architectural style is typified by a symmetrical facade with semicircular or elliptical fanlights over the front door, which are often incorporated into a more elaborate door surround that commonly includes a decorative crown or small entry porch. Also called "Adamesque."

Fenestration The arrangement of windows on the exterior of a building.

Finial An ornament often spherical or turned and generally placed at the top of a roof or pediment.

Fish-scale Shingle A rounded shingle commonly used in Victorian period and Queen Anne style buildings.

Fleur de Lis A French term for *lily;* originally the royal coat of arms of France; sometimes seen as an architectural detail.

Flute One of the vertical grooves on the shaft of a column or pilaster.

Free-flying Staircase Often cantilevered, a staircase with no visible means of support.

Fretwork A band consisting of an ornamental design composed of a repeating series of interlocking rectangular patterns and often incorporating a Greek key motif.

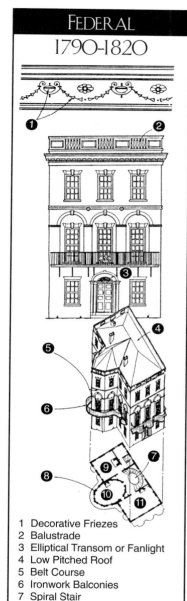

FEDERAL
1790–1820

1 Decorative Friezes
2 Balustrade
3 Elliptical Transom or Fanlight
4 Low Pitched Roof
5 Belt Course
6 Ironwork Balconies
7 Spiral Stair
8 Bowed Projector or End
9, 10, 11 Geometric Rooms

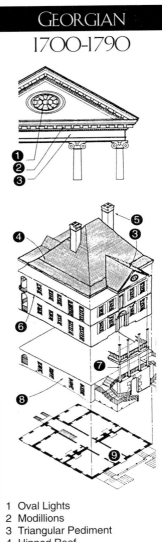

GEORGIAN
1700-1790

1 Oval Lights
2 Modillions
3 Triangular Pediment
4 Hipped Roof
5 Box Chimney
6 Belt Course
7 Columned Portico
8 Raised Foundation or Basement
9 Central Hall Plan

Frieze The middle section of an entablature between the architrave below and the cornice above.

Gable The area at the end of a building formed by simple ridged roof; most often triangular.

Gable Roof A sloping roof that terminates at one or both ends with a gable.

Gambrel Roof A sectioned, two-sided roof with double slopes of unequal size on each side, known in eighteenth-century Charleston as a Dutch roof or curbed roof.

Georgian An architectural style derived from the public architecture of Roman antiquity characterized by symmetrical facades and interior plans and decorative elements such as pedimented door surrounds, multipane sash windows, and cornices.

Gothic Revival An architectural style inspired by the cathedrals and castles of medieval Europe and characterized by steeply pitched roof with cross gables, ornamental bargeboards, hood moldings over doors and windows, lancet windows, and crenellations along eave lines.

Gougework Decorative carving applied to door and window architraves, to capitals of columns or pilasters, and, most often, to interior features such as chimney pieces, friezes, and cornices; effected by a chisel with a partly cylindrical blade having a bevel on either the concave or convex side.

Greek Revival An architectural style generally in use from 1820 to 1875, inspired by the simpler classicism of remnants of Greek buildings in Greece and southern Italy. Characterized by simpler forms and a lack of decoration, it often employs low gable roofs, pediments, plain columns, and simple window and door architraves often embellished with anthemion motifs.

Guilloche Ornament used frequently in entablatures that resembles twisted bands.

Hipped Roof A roof type with sloping rafters rising from two adjacent sides of a building.

Hood Molding Large molding over a window, typical of the Gothic style and originally intended to direct water away from the window opening.

Hyphen A modern term for a small structure connecting two larger buildings.

International A term coined in America in 1932 to refer to the new architectural style of the twentieth century as created before World War I by such architects as Frank Lloyd Wright, Charles Garnier, Adolf Loos, Joseph Hoffman, and Walter Gropius. The style is characterized by asymmetrical composition, cubic general shapes, absence of moldings, and large windows in horizontal bands.

Italianate An architectural style derived from the picturesque movement of the mid-nineteenth century, featuring such details as roof balustrades, bay windows, arched porches (arcades), double bracketed cornices, and polygonally shaped walls.

Jack Arch A straight or flat arch laid in brick that is sometimes rubbed or gauged.

Jacobean The English architectural style associated with the reign of King James I and featuring straight or curved gables and other details influenced by The Netherlands.

Jerkinhead Roof A roof form in which the top of a gable is clipped and slopes inward to form a hip; also called a "clipped gable roof."

Keystone A voussoir set in the middle of an arch made of stone but often mimicked in Charleston in stuccoed brick and wood.

Lancet Window A tall, narrow window with a pointed arch at its top.

Lantern A small, open structure at the top of a roof or dome that provides light to the rooms below; also called a "root monitor."

Lintel A horizontal element, always structural and sometimes decorative over a window or door opening.

Long Room The entertaining room of a tavern or public house; a venue for dinners, balls, plays, or government assembly.

Lunette A semicircular opening, such as a window, or a flat semicircular surface.

Mansard Roof A roof having two slopes on all four sides and most often associated with buildings from the last decades of the nineteenth century.

Merlon A parapet with alternating indentations and raised portions.

Metope In a frieze of Doric portico, the space between the triglyphs sometimes filled with ornamental decoration such as bucrania.

Modillion One of a series of horizontally projecting brackets in the upper part of a cornice under a corona.

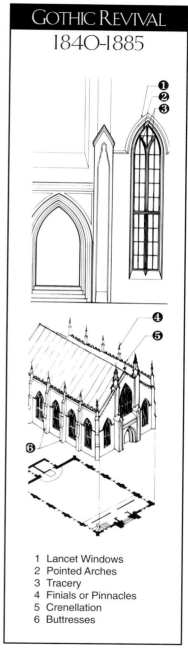

GOTHIC REVIVAL
1840-1885

1 Lancet Windows
2 Pointed Arches
3 Tracery
4 Finials or Pinnacles
5 Crenellation
6 Buttresses

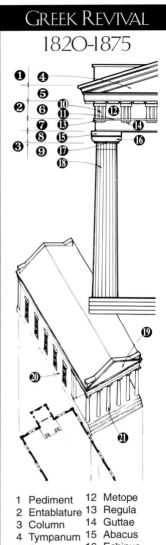

GREEK REVIVAL
1820-1875

❶ ❹
❺
❷ ❻ ⑩
❼ ⑪ ⑫
❽ ⑬ ⑭
❸ ❾ ⑮ ⑯
⑰
⑱

⑲

⑳

㉑

1 Pediment	12 Metope
2 Entablature	13 Regula
3 Column	14 Guttae
4 Tympanum	15 Abacus
5 Cornice	16 Echinus
6 Frieze	17 Annulets
7 Architrave	18 Fluting
8 Capital	19 Pediment
9 Shaft	20 Flat Walls
10 Triglyph	21 Large Heavy
11 Tenia	Columns

Mullion A large vertical stone or wooden bar which separates two casement windows.

Muntins One of the thin strips of wood used for holding panes of glass within a window.

Muquarnas Ceiling ornamentation in Islamic architecture formed by corbelled squinches made of several layers of brick scalloped out to resemble natural stalactites.

Narthex The traverse vestibule in a church either preceding the nave and aisles or preceding the facade of the building.

Neoclassical A period of architecture which began in the 1760s as a reaction against the excesses of the late-Baroque and Rococo periods. Based partly on archaeological discoveries at Pompeii and Herculaneum, the style was popularized in England by William Chambers and Robert Adam. See Federal.

Neoclassical Revival An architectural style generally used 1900–40, characterized by two-story pedimented portico or porch supported by colossal columns (usually with Ionic, Corinthian, or Composite capitals), a centrally located doorway, and symmetrically placed windows.

Newel A vertical post that forms the bottom landing or top termination of a stair balustrade; also the central pillar of a spiral stairwell.

Oculus A circular opening in a wall or at the apex of a dome.

Ovolo A convex molding whose profile is a quadrant of a circle or eclipse. Also known as quarter round.

Palladian Window See Venetian Window.

Pantile Clay roofing tile which is S-shaped in cross section.

Parapet A low wood or masonry wall used to screen the roof and sometimes for decorative features.

Parterre A flat garden space with formal beds arranged in a pattern.

Patera A flat or low relief oval or circular ornament often used for decoration in Neoclassical architecture.

Pavilion A projecting portion of a building, often in the center of the facade and incorporating a varied roof form; also a garden structure or pleasure building.

Pediment The triangular area formed by a horizontal element and two raking, or sloping, elements such as a door, window, or portico.

Peristyle A range of columns surrounding a building or courtyard most often supporting or engaged with the roof.

Piazza A covered open porch or veranda supported by columns or pillars and attached to the outside of a building. In Charleston such porches usually append to the side elevation of single houses and were intended as outdoor living space and a device to shade south or west facing windows from the heat of the sun.

Piazza Screen A one-story wall incorporating a doorway that separates a piazza from the public way.

Pilaster A rectangular column with a base, shaft, and capital engaged, or attached, to a wall often supporting a door pediment or piazza.

Porte Cochere A covered entry, often a portico, through which vehicles can drive.

Portico A large porch, usually with a pedimented roof supported by columns.

Portland Stone A white or grayish limestone extracted from deposits on the Isle of Portland in south central England, notable for its excellent quality for the carving of detailed architectural elements.

Pressed Brick Clay bricks with low water content compressed under high pressure with the result that their edges are sharp and surfaces have a sheen.

Proscenium In a theater, it is the space between the curtain and orchestra, sometimes including the arch and frontispiece facing the auditorium.

Purbeck Stone A buff limestone found on the south coast of England, often polished and used in several major Charleston colonial buildings as paving stones.

Quatrefoil A form denoting four lobe-shaped curves found in Gothic architecture.

Queen Anne A Victorian architectural style derived after the work of the English architect Richard Norman Shaw and featuring an irregular plan and varied elements, including bay windows, cross-gabled roofs, oddly shaped porches, and often jigsaw-cut wood decoration and spindle work.

ITALIANATE
1830-1900

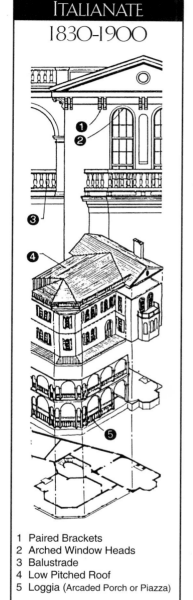

1 Paired Brackets
2 Arched Window Heads
3 Balustrade
4 Low Pitched Roof
5 Loggia (Arcaded Porch or Piazza)

657

QUEEN ANNE
1860–1916

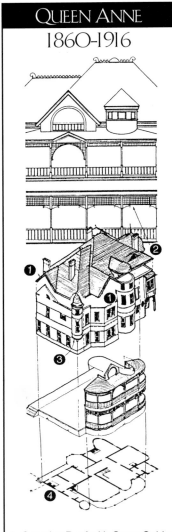

1 Complex Roof with Cross Gables
2 Elaborate Wood Bracket Work
   (Also Spindle Work, Jigsaw-cut
   Decoration)
3 Turrets or Towers
4 Asymmetrical Floor Plan

Quoining See Quoins.

Quoins Stones, rectangular pieces of wood, or brick panels (sometimes stuccoed in Charleston) used to accentuate, and sometimes to strengthen, the corners of buildings.

Rectilinear A shape bounded or formed by straight lines.

Rococo Revival A mid-nineteenth-century architectural style utilizing the heavy, asymmetrical decorative forms popular in mid-eighteenth-century Europe with Chinese and Gothic motifs mingling with C- and S-curves and floral devices.

Romanesque Revival An architectural style popular at the end of the nineteenth century characterized by round arches over door and window openings, asymmetrical facade, towers with conical roofs, and an emphasis on the appearance of strength and durability imparted through the use of stonework. Often referred to as Richardsonian Romanesque because of the work of its most noted practitioner, H. H. Richardson.

Rose Window A circular window, generally found in Gothic Revival churches, formed by individual sections separated by tracery and arranged as in the spokes of a wheel.

Rotunda A circular roof or building often topped by a domed or peaked circular roof.

Rustication Stonework with deep, sunk joints between blocks and most often employed on basements or lower floors or around entrances to suggest strength and solidity. In Charleston, and elsewhere in the South, this effect was sometimes achieved in wood and stuccoed brick.

Second Empire A Victorian architectural style originating in mid-nineteenth-century France featuring mansard or four-sided roofs with bracketed cornices, decorative hoods over windows and doors and classical pediments, balustrades, and paired columns.

Ship Chandlery A warehouse or other building adapted for the sale and storage of maritime supplies.

Single House A single-pile dwelling with a central hall passage and one room on either side; a term used in Charleston to denote a house of this plan with its side end facing the public right-of-way.

Single Pile See above.

Soffit Exposed underside of an arch, cornice, door surround, or beam, as a paneled soffit.

Spandrel A triangular space to the side of an arch. The area between arches in an arcade.

Spatterdash A rough-textured stucco coating, often with swirls and grooves, generally associated with early-twentieth-century architecture.

Spindle Work A balustrade incorporating closely placed turned wooden balusters often used in Queen Anne style building.

Surbase Baseboard; wainscoting or a handrail and the area below.

Tenement Any real property, such as a house, owned by one person and occupied or rented by another.

Terra Cotta A fired clay material, usually unglazed, molded in ornamental forms and applied to the facades of buildings for decoration.

Torchère A tall ornamental lighting device often fitted with candles.

Tower of the Winds Also known as "Temple of the Winds." A simple form of Corinthian columned capital based on those found on the ancient Choragic Monument of Lysikrates, often used in Greek Revival architecture.

Transom A rectangular or arched window over a door or window, often consisting of a series of separate glass panes or lights.

Trefoil A lobe or leaf-shaped curve formed by the cusping of a circle or arch. The number of foils involved is indicated by a prefix, e.g., trefoil, quatrefoil.

Triglyph A block of three raised vertical members formed by chamfered channels and edges, generally found between the metopes in the frieze of a Doric order building.

Tympanum The space formed within the three sides of a pediment; also the space within an arch above a doorway.

Vault An arched ceiling or roof, or an arched passageway. A barrel vault has a semicircular cross section, while a groined vault is formed by the intersection of two barrel vaults, as at the intersection of the transepts of a church.

Venetian Window A three-part window with a large central arched section that is flanked by narrower, square-headed windows. Often called "Palladian windows" after the Italian Renaissance architect for whom they are a hallmark design.

Vergeboard See Bargeboard.

Vernacular Used in architecture to denote the use of regional or local craftsmanship tradition in the design or execution of a building.

Voussoirs One of the wedge-shaped stones, or bricks (sometimes laid and stuccoed in Charleston to appear as stones) that form an arch.

Weatherboard In Charleston, exterior wood sheathing of equal size, lapped to shed water. Early examples feature beaded edges.

The drawings in this glossary are from the poster Architecture Styles of Historic Charleston, *a cooperative education project of Drayton Hall of the National Trust for Historic Preservation and Historic Charleston Foundation.*

FOR FURTHER READING

Although the primary sources mentioned in the front served as the bases for much of the research in this book, the author frequently consulted printed books, including those listed below. Many of these are available around the city for purchase and in libraries.

History: Charleston

Bellows, Barbara. *Benevolence Among Slaveholders*. Baton Rouge: Louisiana State University Press, 1993.

Bland, Sidney. *Preserving Charleston's Past, Shaping Its Future: The Life and Times of Susan Pringle Frost*. Westport, Conn.: Greenwood Press, 1994.

Bull, Kinloch Jr. *The Oligarchs in Colonial and Revolutionary Charleston: Lieutenant Governor William Bull II and His Family*. Columbia: University of South Carolina Press, 1991.

Calhoun, Jeanne, and Martha Zierden. *Charleston's Commercial Landscape, 1803–60*. Charleston: The Charleston Museum, 1984.

Coclanis, Peter A. *The Shadow of a Dream: Economic Life and Death in the South Carolina Low Country, 1670–1920*. New York: Oxford University Press, 1989.

Dalcho, Frederick. *An Historical Account of the Protestant Episcopal Church in South Carolina*. Charleston: E. Thayer, 1820; reprint, New York: Arno, 1972.

Doyle, Don H. *New Men, New Cities, New South*. Chapel Hill & London: University of North Carolina Press, 1990.

Drago, Edmund L., ed., *"Broke by the War": Letters of a Slave Trader*. Columbia: University of South Carolina Press, 1991.

Fraser, Charles. *Charleston, Sketchbook, 1796–1806*. Charleston: Carolina Art Association, Gibbes Art Gallery, 1959.

———. *Reminiscences of Charleston*. Charleston, 1854. Reprint, Charleston: Garnier & Company, 1969.

Fraser, Walter Jr. *Charleston! Charleston!* Columbia: University of South Carolina Press, 1989.

Hagy, James William. *This Happy Land, The Jews of Colonial and Antebellum Charleston*. Tuscaloosa: University of Alabama Press, 1993.

Jaher, Frederick. *The Urban Establishment*. Urbana: University of Illinois Press, 1982.

Johnson, Michael, and James Roark. *No Chariot Let Down: Charleston's Free People of Color on the Eve of the Civil War*. Chapel Hill: University of North Carolina Press, 1984.

Koger, Larry. *Black Slaveowners, Free Black Slave Masters in South Carolina, 1790–1860*. Jefferson, N.C., 1986.

Leiding, Harriette Kershaw. *Charleston, Historic and Romantic*. Philadelphia: J. B. Lippincott, 1931.

Leland, Isabella. *Charleston, Crossroads of History*. Woodland Hills, Calif.: Windsor Publications, 1980.

Lilly, Edward G. *History of the Churches of Charleston*. Charleston: Legerton and Co., 1966.

Mazyck, Arthur, and Gene Waddell. *Charleston in 1883*. Easley, S.C.: Southern Historical Press, 1983.

McCusker, John J., and Russell R. Menard. *The Economy of British America, 1607–1789*. Chapel Hill: University of North Carolina Press, 1985.

O'Brien, Michael, and David Moltke-Hansen, eds. *Intellectual Life in Antebellum Charleston*. Knoxville: University of Tennessee Press, 1986.

Pease, William H., and Jane Pease. *Ladies, Women, and Wenches: Choice and Constraint in Antebellum Charleston and Boston*. Chapel Hill: University of North Carolina Press, 1990.

————. *The Web of Progress*. New York: Oxford University Press, 1985.

Powers, Bernard. *Black Charlestonians, A Social History, 1822–1885*. Fayetteville: University of Arkansas Press, 1994.

Pringle, Elizabeth W. Allston. *Chronicles of Chicora Wood*. New York: Charles Scribner's Sons, 1922.

Ravenel, Harriott H. R. *Charleston, The Place and the People*. New York: Macmillan, 1912.

Ripley, Warren. *Charles Towne, Birth of a City*. Charleston: News & Courier and Evening Post, 1970.

Rogers, George C. Jr. *Charleston in the Age of the Pinckneys*. Reprint, Columbia: University of South Carolina Press, 1980.

Rogers, George C. Jr., and C. James Taylor. *A South Carolina Chronology*. Columbia: University of South Carolina Press, 1994.

Rosen, Robert. *Confederate Charleston: An Illustrated History of the City and the People During the Civil War*. Columbia: University of South Carolina Press, 1994.

————. *A Short History of Charleston*. San Francisco: Lexicos Press, 1982.

Rosengarten, Dale, et al. *Between the Tracks: Charleston's East Side During the Nineteenth Century*. Archaeological Contributions 17. Charleston: The Charleston Museum, 1987.

Spruill, Julia Cherry, and Anne Firor Scott. *Women's Life and Work in the Southern Colonies*. New York: W. W. Norton, 1972.

Wallace, David Duncan. *South Carolina: A Short History, 1520–1948*. Columbia: University of South Carolina Press, 1961.

Walsh, Richard. *Charleston's Sons of Liberty*. Columbia: University of South Carolina Press, 1959.

Way, William. *History of the New England Society of Charleston, South Carolina for One Hundred Years, 1819–1919*. Charleston: New England Society, 1920.

Weir, Robert M. *Colonial South Carolina: A History*. Millwood, N.Y.: KTO Press, 1983.

Diaries, Letters, and Travel Accounts: Charleston and South Carolina

Chesnut, Mary Boykin. *A Diary from Dixie*. Edited by Ben Ames Williams. Cambridge: Harvard University Press, 1980.

Hall, Mrs. Basil. *The Aristocratic Journey*. Reprint, London: G. P. Putnam's Sons, 1931.

Jackson, Donald, and Dorothy Twohig, eds. *The Diaries of George Washington: Volume VI, January 1790–December 1799*. Charlottesville: University Press of Virginia, 1979.

Kemble, Frances Anne. *Journal of a Residence on a Georgia Plantation in 1838–1839*. Edited by John A. Scott. Athens: University of Georgia Press, 1984.

Lambert, John. *Travels through Lower Canada and the United States of America in the Years 1806, 1807, and 1808*. 3 vols. London: Richard Phillips, 1810.

Merrens, H. Roy, ed. *The Colonial South Carolina Scene: Contemporary Views, 1697–1774*. Columbia: University of South Carolina Press, 1977.

Milligen-Johnston, Dr. George. "A Short Description of the Province of South Carolina, with an Account of the Air, Weather, and Diseases, at Charles Town." In *Colonial South Carolina: Two Contemporary Descriptions*, edited by Robert L. Meriweather. Columbia: University of South Carolina Press, 1951.

Pinckney, Eliza Lucas. *The Letterbook of Eliza Lucas Pinckney, 1739–1762*. Edited by Elise Pinckney. Chapel Hill: University of North Carolina Press, 1972.

Rochefoucauld-Liancourt, François, Duc de la. *Travels through the United States of North America 1795, 1796, and 1797*. 4 vols. London: R. Phillips, 1799.

Waring, Thomas, ed. *The Way It Was in Charleston*. Old Greenwich, Conn.: Devin-Adair Company, 1980.

Architecture and Gardens: Charleston and South Carolina

Briggs, Loutrel W. *Charleston Gardens*. Columbia: University of South Carolina Press, 1951.

Bryan, John M., ed. *Robert Mills, Architect*. Washington, D.C.: American Institute of Architects Press, 1989.

Cauthen, Henry F. Jr. *Charleston Interiors*. Charleston: The Preservation Society of Charleston, 1979.

Chamberlain, Samuel, and Narcissa Chamberlain. *Southern Interiors of Charleston, South Carolina*. New York: Hastings House, 1956.

Cothran, James R. *Gardens of Historic Charleston*. Columbia: University of South Carolina Press, 1995.

Davis, Evangeline, and N. Jane Iseley. *Charleston Houses and Gardens*. Charleston: Society of Charleston, 1975.

Kovacik, Charles F., and John J. Winberry. *South Carolina: The Making of a Landscape*. Columbia: University of South Carolina Press, 1987.

Lane, Mills. *Architecture of the Old South: South Carolina*. Savannah: Beehive Press, 1984.

Leiding, Harriette Kershaw. *Historic Houses of South Carolina*. Philadelphia: J. B. Lippincott, 1921.

Lounsbury, Carl R., ed. *An Illustrated Glossary of Southern Architecture and Landscape*. New York: Oxford University Press, 1994.

Peatross, C. Ford, ed., and Alicia Stansin, comp. *Historic America: Buildings, Structures, and Sites*. Washington, D.C.: Library of Congress, 1983.

Preservation Society of Charleston. *The Churches of Charleston and the Lowcountry*. Columbia: University of South Carolina Press, 1994.

Prime, Alfred Coxe. *The Arts & Crafts in Philadelphia, Maryland, and South Carolina*. 2 vols. Reprint of 1929 edition, New York: DeCapo Press, 1969.

Ravenel, Beatrice St. Julien. *Architects of Charleston*. Reprint of 1945 edition, Columbia: University of South Carolina Press, 1992.

Richardson, Emma B. *Charleston Garden Plats*. Leaflet No. 19. Charleston: The Charleston Museum, 1943.

Savage, J. Thomas Jr., with photography by N. Jane Iseley. *The Charleston Interior*. Greensboro, N.C.: Legacy Publications, 1995.

Severens, Kenneth. *Charleston Antebellum Architecture and Civic Destiny*. Knoxville: University of Tennessee Press, 1988.

Simons, Albert, and Samuel Lapham Jr., eds. *Charleston, South Carolina*. The Octagon Library of Early American Architecture, volume 1. New York: American Institute of Architects Press, 1927. Reprinted as *The Early Architecture of Charleston*. Columbia: University of South Carolina Press, 1970.

Smith, Alice Ravenel Huger, and D. E. Huger Smith. *The Dwelling Houses of Charleston, South Carolina*. Philadelphia: J. B. Lippincott, 1917.

Stockton, Robert. *The Great Shock, The Effects of the 1886 Earthquake on the Built Environment of Charleston, South Carolina*. Easley, S.C.: Southern Historical Press, 1986.

Stoney, Samuel Gaillard. *Plantations of the Carolina Low Country*. Charleston: Carolina Art Association, 1938.

———. *This is Charleston: A Survey of the Architectural Heritage of a Unique American City*. Charleston: Carolina Art Association, 1944.

Wells, John, and Robert E. Dalton. *The South Carolina Architects 1885–1935*. Richmond, Va.: New South Architectural Press, 1992.

Whitelaw, Robert N. S., and Alice F. Levkoff. *Charleston, Come Hell or High Water*. Columbia, S.C.: The R. L. Bryan Company, 1975.

Archaeology: Charleston

Calhoun, Jeanne, Elizabeth Paysinger, and Martha Zierden. *A Survey of Economic Activity in Charleston, 1732–1770*. Archaeological Contributions No. 2. Charleston: The Charleston Museum, 1982.

Calhoun, Jeanne A., Elizabeth J. Reitz, Michael B. Trinkley, and Martha A. Zierden. *Meat in Due Season: Preliminary Investigations of Marketing Practices in Colonial Charleston*. Archaeological Contributions No. 9. Charleston: The Charleston Museum, 1984.

Grimes, Kimberly M., and Martha A. Zierden. *A Hub of Human Activity: Archaeological Investigations of the Visitors Reception and Transportation Center Site*. Archaeological Contributions No. 13. Charleston: The Charleston Museum, 1988.

Honerkamp, Nicholas, and Martha Zierden. *Charleston Place: The Archaeology of Urban Life*. Leaflet No. 31. Charleston: The Charleston Museum, 1989.

Joseph, J. W., and Rita Folse Elliott. *Restoration Archeology at the Charleston County Courthouse Site (38CH1498), Charleston, South Carolina*. Stone Mountain, Ga.: South Associates, 1994.

Trinkley, Michael, and Debi Hacker. *Life on Broad Street: Archeological Survey of the Hollings Judicial Center Annex*. Chicora Research Contribution 192. Columbia, South Carolina, 1996.

Zierden, Martha A., *Big House/Back Lot: An Archaeological Study of the Nathaniel Russell House*. Archaeological Contributions No. 25. Charleston: The Charleston Museum, 1996.

———. *The Nathaniel Russell House: Initial Archaeological Testing*. Archaeological Contributions No. 24. Charleston: The Charleston Museum, 1995.

———. *Preliminary Report: Archaeological Investigations at the Powder Magazine*. Charleston: The Charleston Museum, 1994.

————. et al. *An Archaeological Study of the First Trident Site, Charleston South Carolina.* Archaeological Contributions No. 6. Charleston: The Charleston Museum, 1983.

————. *Charleston's First Suburb: Excavations at 66 Society Street.* Archaeological Contributions No. 20. Charleston: The Charleston Museum, 1988.

————. *Exploration of the North Entrance of the Joseph Manigault House.* Archaeological Contributions No. 15. Charleston: The Charleston Museum, 1986.

————. *Georgian Opulence: Archaeological Investigations of the Gibbes House.* Archaeological Contributions No. 12. Charleston: The Charleston Museum, 1987.

————. *Investigating Elite Lifeways Through Archaeology: The John Rutledge House.* Archaeological Contributions No. 21. Charleston: The Charleston Museum, 1989.

Art and Decorative Arts: Charleston

Bayless, Charles. *Charleston Ironwork: A Photographic Survey.* Orangeburg, S.C.: Sandlapper, 1987.

Burton, E. Milby. *Charleston Furniture, 1700–1815.* Second edition, Columbia: University of South Carolina Press, 1950.

Curtis, Elizabeth Gibbon. *Gateways & Doorways of Charleston, South Carolina in the Eighteenth and Nineteenth Centuries.* New York: Architectural Book Publishing Co., 1926.

Deas, Alston. *The Early Ironwork of Charleston.* Columbia, S.C.: Bostick & Thornley, 1941.

Middleton, Margaret Simons. *Henrietta Johnston of Charles Towne, South Carolina, America's First Pastellist.* Columbia: University of South Carolina Press, 1966.

————. *Jeremiah Theus, Colonial Artist of Charleston.* Columbia: University of South Carolina Press, 1953. Reprint, Charleston, 1991.

Rutledge, Anna W. *Artists in the Life of Charleston: Through Colony and State from Restoration to Reconstruction.* Reprint, Columbia: University of South Carolina Press, 1980.

Sanders, Boyd, and Ann McAden. *Alfred Hutty and the Charleston Renaissance.* Orangeburg, S.C.: Sandlapper, 1990.

Severens, Martha R. *Alice Ravenel Huger Smith: An Artist, a Place and a Time.* Charleston: Gibbes Museum of Art, 1993.

Vlach, John Michael. *Charleston Blacksmith: The Work of Philip Simmons.* Revised edition, Columbia: University of South Carolina Press, 1992.

ILLUSTRATION CREDITS

N. Affidzi: p. 625

The Abby Aldrich Folk Art Museum (Colonial Williamsburg Foundation): p. 339

American Institute of Architects (The White Pine Series): p. 585 bottom

Avery Institute for African American History and Culture: p. 505 bottom

Daniel Beaman, AIA (Cummings and McCrady): p. 88 bottom; p. 184 bottom

The Cathedral Church of St. Luke and St. Paul: p. 628 top

Charleston County Register Mesne Conveyance: p. 38; p. 41; p. 53 top; p. 84 bottom; p. 89 top; p. 98 bottom; p. 108 top; p. 132 middle; p. 148; p. 160 middle; p. 180 bottom; p. 183; p. 194 bottom; p. 198 top; p. 245 middle; p. 259 bottom; p. 260 bottom; p. 265 bottom; p. 279 top; p. 293; p. 321 bottom; p. 347 top; p. 392 bottom; p. 412 bottom; p. 426; p. 433 bottom; p. 462 top; p. 479; p. 480 bottom; p. 541 top; p. 586 bottom; p. 618; p. 619 bottom

Charleston Evening Post and The News and Courier: p. 111 bottom (photo by W. A. Jordan); p. 340 bottom (photo by J. Richard Burbage); p. 414 bottom (photo by R. A. Nettles); p. 420 (photo by W. A. Jordan); p. 423 top (photo by J. Richard Burbage); p. 427 (photo by W. A. Jordan); p. 434 (photo by J. Richard Burbage); p. 459 bottom; p. 460 bottom (photo by W. A. Jordan); p. 489 bottom (photo by R. A. Nettles); p. 511 middle; p. 553 top (photo by W. A. Jordan).

Charleston Library Society: p. 56; p. 248 top; p. 355 bottom

The Charleston Museum: p. 29; p. 59 top; p. 63 bottom; p. 79 bottom; p. 86; p. 90 top; p. 109 bottom; p. 119 top; p. 159; p. 182; p. 198 bottom; p. 199; p. 219; p. 225; p. 267 top; p. 272 bottom; p. 332 bottom; p. 336 top; p. 368 top; p. 383 top; p. 397 top; p. 411 bottom; p. 414 top; p. 414 middle; p. 482; p. 517; p. 569 bottom; p. 576 2d from top; p. 591 top; p. 595 bottom; p. 613 top; p. 619 top

Collection of City Hall, Charleston, South Carolina: p. 157 top

Shelley Clark-Glidewell (Evans & Schmidt, Architects): p. 360

Mrs. Richard Coen: p. 160 top

Colonial Williamsburg Foundation: p. 25 top; p. 435 bottom

The Gibbes Museum of Art / Carolina Art Association: *Hovedkirken I* (Meeting Street View) by S. Trier, hand-colored engraving, p. 23 top; *Panorama of Charleston, 1850* by John William Hill, tinted lithograph, p. 27 bottom; *Bedon's Alley, 1921,* by Alfred Hutty, drypoint, p. 54 top; *The Banking House of G. A. Trenholm and Son, Harper's Magazine* 1857, engraving, p. 55 middle; *Rainbow Row, before 1930* by George W. Johnson, print from glass negative, p. 99 top; *Hibernian Hall,* engraving, p. 187; *The Mills House, Charleston, S. C. , 1853,* by Frederick J. Pillner, engraving, p. 189 bottom; *At the Bend in Church Street* by Alice Ravenel Huger Smith, drawing, p. 215; *View of Tradd Street, before 1930* by George W. Johnson, black-and-white print from glass negative, p. 280 top; Detail of *Panorama of Charleston,* by John William Hill, hand-colored lithograph on paper, p. 291; *Magazine Street, Charleston* by Elizabeth O'Neill Verner, etching, p. 341 bottom; *Meeting Street, Charleston,* by Thomas Addison Richards, lithograph, p. 413; *A View Near Charleston, 1802,* by Charles Fraser, watercolor on paper, p. 481; *Interior View of Old St. Luke's Episcopal Church* by William D. Clarke, black-and-white photograph, p. 604; Detail of *View of Charleston, 1846,* by Henry Jackson, oil on canvas, p. 617

William Graham: p. 180 top; p. 435 top; p. 497 bottom; p. 612

Mrs. William O. Hanahan, Jr. : p. 92

Historic American Buildings Survey: p. 70 top; p. 167; p. 171 bottom; p. 173 top; p. 186 bottom; p. 223 middle; p. 267 bottom (photo by Jack Boucher); p. 269 bottom; p. 270 (photo by Jet Lowe); p. 307 bottom; p. 337 bottom (photo by Jack Boucher); p. 345 (photo by Jack Boucher); p. 351 bottom; p. 392 top; p. 395 middle; p. 396; p. 605 middle; p. 605 bottom; p. 606 top; p. 627 (photo by Jack Boucher)

Historic American Engineering Record: p. 389 middle; p. 405 top; p. 405 bottom

Historic Charleston Foundation:

HCF Collection: p. 25 bottom; p. 27 top; p. 28 top; p. 30; p. 31 bottom; p. 33 top; p. 35; p. 37 bottom; p. 39; p. 42; p. 43 top; p. 50; p. 53 bottom; p. 55 bottom; p. 57 top; p. 63 top; p. 68; p. 77; p. 79 top; p. 80 top; p. 83; p. 89 bottom; p. 90 bottom; p. 116 bottom; p. 117 bottom; p. 137; p. 144 top; p. 157 bottom; p. 158; p. 165; p. 171 top; p. 176 bottom; p. 181 top; p. 184 top; p. 188 top; p. 197 top; p. 202 top; p. 203 middle; p. 204; p. 205; p. 207 top; p. 221 top; p. 224 top; p. 228 bottom; p. 223 top; p. 242; p. 243 top; p. 256 bottom; p. 258 top; p. 261 bottom; p. 264 top; p. 271 top; p. 273 top; p. 276 top; p. 278; p. 279 bottom; p. 285; p. 321 top; p. 323 bottom; p. 329 bottom; p. 335; p. 346 bottom; p. 349 middle; p. 350 top; p. 350 bottom; p. 357 top; p. 358 top; p. 366 top; p. 372 top; p. 393; p. 395 top; p. 399 top; p. 402 bottom; p. 409 top; p. 412 top; p. 423 bottom; p. 428 top; p. 431 top; p. 431 bottom; p. 432 bottom; p. 439 bottom; p. 445 top; p. 449 middle; p. 449 bottom; p. 452 bottom; p. 454 bottom; p. 461 top; p. 465 top; p. 466; p. 467 top; p. 473 top; p. 486; p. 492 middle; p. 502 bottom; p. 534 top; p. 585 top; p. 586 top; p. 590 bottom; p. 591 bottom; p. 592 top; p. 595 top; p. 601 top; p. 603 bottom; p. 609 top; p. 629 top; p. 631 bottom; p. 634 top; p. 637 top; p. 645 top; p. 645 middle; p. 646 top

The Sams Collection: p. 115; p. 195 bottom; p. 294 top; p. 294 bottom; p. 295 top; p. 298 bottom; p. 318 bottom; p. 322 top; p. 336 bottom; p. 338 middle; p. 348; p. 369 top; p. 372 bottom; p. 483 top; p. 561 bottom;

From Charleston Illustrated, 1875: p. 166; p. 169; p. 209 top; p. 245 bottom; p. 337 top; p. 349 top; p. 357 bottom; p. 373 top; p. 450; p. 458 bottom; p. 546; p. 610;

From A Walk Around Ye Old Historic Charleston, 1912: p. 70 bottom; p. 119 bottom; p. 193 middle

HCF PHOTOS BY:

Carroll Ann Bowers: p. 54 bottom; p. 67 bottom; p. 73 top; p. 94 top; p. 117 bottom; p. 138 top; p. 139; p. 140 top; p. 144 bottom; p. 145 top; p. 145 bottom; p. 146 bottom; p. 149 bottom; p. 151 top; p. 151 bottom; p. 152; p. 162 top; p. 162 bottom; p. 164 top; p. 174; p. 178 top; p. 178 bottom; p. 190 top; p. 191; p. 210 top; p. 213 top; p. 214 top; p. 264 bottom; p. 271 bottom; p. 273 middle; p. 273 bottom; p. 274 bottom; p. 283 top; p. 284; p. 286 top; p. 286 bottom; p. 310 top; p. 312 top; p. 433 middle; p. 555; p. 562 bottom; p. 579 middle; p. 581 bottom; p. 582 bottom; p. 583 bottom; p. 621 top; p. 621 bottom

Thomas Ford: p. 250 top

C. T. Greene: p. 65

Carter L. Hudgins: p. 484 top; p. 489 middle; p. 490; p. 491 top; p. 492 top; p. 493; p. 495 middle; p. 495 bottom; p. 498 top; p. 500 top; p. 500 bottom; p. 506 top; p. 507 bottom; p. 508 top; p. 513 middle; p. 513 bottom; p. 515 top; p. 518 top; p. 520 top; p. 523 top; p. 523 bottom; p. 525 bottom; p. 527 bottom; p. 530 bottom; p. 532 top; p. 532 bottom; p. 534 bottom; p. 535 top; p. 536 top; p. 538 top; p. 538 middle; p. 543 top; p. 544 top; p. 545 top; p. 545 bottom; p. 548 top; p. 548 bottom; p. 551 top; p. 552 bottom; p. 557 top; p. 557 bottom; p. 559 bottom; p. 560 top; p. 561 middle; p. 562 top; p. 564 top; p. 565 bottom; p. 566 bottom; p. 567 top; p. 569 top; p. 576 middle; p. 579 bottom; p. 580 bottom; 581 top; p. 583 bottom

Carl Julien: p. 233 middle; p. 249 top

Julian Metz: p. 60 bottom; p. 61 bottom; p. 216 top

S. H. Norvell: p. 206

Rick Rhodes: p. 142 bottom; p. 146 middle; p. 175 bottom; p. 177 bottom; p. 226 top; p. 226 bottom; p. 231 bottom; p. 232 middle; p. 233 bottom; p. 239 bottom; p. 245 bottom; p. 282 bottom; p. 287 bottom

Terry Richardson: p. 240 top; p. 287 top; p. 308 middle

Katherine Saunders: p. 61; p. 66; p. 71; p. 72 middle; p. 73 bottom; p. 74 top; p. 74 bottom; p. 75 top; p. 75 bottom; p. 76 bottom; p. 81; p. 82; p. 84 top; p. 93; p. 94 bottom; p. 96 top; p. 98 top; p. 100 top; p. 101; p. 102; p. 104 top; p. 104 bottom; p. 106; p. 107 top; p. 107 bottom; p. 108 bottom; p. 111 top; p. 112; p. 114 bottom; p. 116 top; p. 118; p. 119 middle; p. 120; p. 121; p. 122; p. 125 bottom; p. 126; p. 129 top; p. 130 top; p. 130 middle; p. 132 bottom; p. 133 top; p. 133 bottom; p. 134 top; p. 134 bottom; p. 135 bottom; p. 136; p. 138 bottom; p. 142 top; p. 143 bottom; p. 146; p. 150 top; p. 150 bottom; p. 161 top; p. 168; p. 172 top; p. 173 middle; p. 175 top; p. 176 top; p. 179 top; p. 192; p. 193 top; p. 200 top; p. 200 bottom; p. 201; p. 202 bottom; p. 212 top; p. 213 bottom; p. 217 bottom; p. 223 top; p. 227 top; p. 227 bottom; p. 230; p. 236 middle; p. 238; p. 239 top; p. 244; p. 245 top; p. 247 bottom; p. 252 top; p. 252 bottom; p. 253 bottom; p. 259 top; p. 272 top; p. 275 top; p. 299 bottom; p. 300 top; p. 301 top; p. 302 bottom; p. 303 top; p. 304; p. 305 top; p. 305 bottom; p. 306 top; p. 306 bottom; p. 308 top; p. 309 middle; p. 309 bottom; p. 311 bottom; p. 312 bottom; p. 313 top; p. 314 top; p. 314 bottom; p. 315 top; p. 315 middle; p. 315 bottom; p. 316; p. 317 bottom; p. 318 top; p. 319 top; p. 319 middle; p. 319 bottom; p. 320 top; p. 322 bottom; p. 323 top; p. 324 top; p. 325 top; p. 326 top; p. 326 bottom; p. 327 top; p. 327 bottom; p. 330; p. 332 middle; p. 333; p. 343; p. 346 top; p. 347 bottom; p. 349 bottom; p. 350 middle; p. 352; p. 353 top; p. 353 bottom; p. 354 top; p. 354 bottom; p. 356 top; p. 356 bottom; p. 358 bottom; p. 359 top; p. 359 bottom; p. 361; p. 362 bottom; p. 364; p. 365 top; p. 365 bottom; p. 367 top; p. 369 bottom; p. 371; p. 374; p. 375 right; p. 376 top; p. 376 bottom; p. 378; p. 379 top; p. 379 bottom; p. 381 top; p. 381 bottom; p. 385; p. 387 bottom; p. 388; p. 389 bottom; p. 390 top; p. 390 bottom; p. 391 top; p. 391 middle;

p. 391 bottom; p. 397 middle; p. 398 top; p. 398 bottom; p. 399 bottom; p. 400 top; p. 400 bottom; p. 403; p. 404; p. 406 middle; p. 407 bottom; p. 408 top; p. 408 bottom; p. 409 bottom; p. 416 top; p. 416 middle; p. 416 bottom; p. 417 top; p. 417 bottom; p. 418 top; p. 418 bottom; p. 419 bottom; p. 428 bottom; p. 429 top; p. 429 bottom; p. 433 top; p. 436 bottom; p. 437 top; p. 437 bottom; p. 437 middle; p. 438 top; p. 439 top; p. 440; p. 441 top; p. 442 top; p. 443 top; p. 443 bottom; p. 444 bottom; p. 445 middle; p. 445 bottom; p. 446 bottom; p. 449 top; p. 452; p. 455 bottom; p. 456 top; p. 457 top; p. 457 bottom; p. 458 top; p. 459 top; p. 462 bottom; p. 463 top; p. 463 bottom; p. 464 top; p. 465 middle; p. 465 bottom; p. 468 top; p. 468 bottom; p. 469; p. 470 top; p. 470 bottom; p. 472 top; p. 472 bottom; p. 473 bottom; p. 474 bottom; p. 475 top; p. 476 bottom; p. 488; p. 491 bottom; p. 494 top; p. 494 bottom; p. 495 top; p. 511 bottom; p. 512; p. 513 top; p. 514 top; p. 514 bottom; p. 515 bottom; p. 516 top; p. 516 bottom; p. 518 bottom; p. 526 top; p. 535 middle; p. 535 bottom; p. 549 bottom; p. 550; p. 551 bottom; p. 559 top; p. 560 bottom; p. 563 top; p. 564 bottom; p. 568; p. 570 bottom; p. 571 top; p. 572 top; p. 573; p. 574 top; p. 574 middle; p. 574 bottom; p. 575 top; p. 575 bottom; p. 576 top; p. 577; p. 578 bottom; p. 580 top; p. 587 middle; p. 587 top; p. 587 2d from top; p. 587 bottom; p. 588 top; p. 588 middle; p. 588 bottom; p. 589 top; p. 589 bottom; p. 590 top; p. 592 middle; p. 592 bottom; p. 594 top; p. 594 bottom; p. 595 middle; p. 596 top; p. 596 bottom; p. 597 top; p. 598; p. 599 top; p. 600 top; p. 600 bottom; p. 601 bottom; p. 602 top; p. 602 middle; p. 602 bottom; p. 603 top; p. 606 middle; p. 606 bottom; p. 607 bottom; p. 608 top; p. 608 bottom; p. 609 bottom; p. 611; p. 614; p. 622 top; p. 622 bottom; p. 623; p. 624; p. 628 bottom; p. 629 bottom; p. 630 top; p. 630 bottom; p. 631 top; p. 632 bottom; p. 633 top; p. 633 bottom; p. 636 top; p. 636 bottom; p. 637 bottom; p. 638 top; p. 638 bottom; p. 639 middle; p. 639 bottom; p. 640 top; p. 641 bottom; p. 642; p. 643 bottom; p. 644 top; p. 644 middle; p. 644 bottom; p. 645 bottom; p. 646 middle; p. 646 bottom

Wayne Saunders: p. 189 top; p. 297 top; p. 297 bottom; p. 298 top; p. 299 top; p. 303 bottom; p. 306 middle; p. 307 top; p. 308 bottom; p. 310 bottom; p. 311 top; p. 317 top; p. 320 bottom

Louis Schwartz: p. 52 bottom; p. 72 top; p. 190 bottom; p. 203 top; p. 235 bottom; p. 247 top; p. 261 top; p. 474 top; p. 561 top

Henry Staats: p. 105; p. 258 bottom; p. 497 top; p. 537; p. 593

William Struhs: p. 23 bottom; p. 27 middle; p. 31 top; p. 33 bottom; p. 43 bottom; p. 44 top; p. 44 bottom; p. 48 top; p. 53 middle; p. 55 top; p. 57 bottom; p. 58; p. 62; p. 64 top; p. 72 bottom; p. 76 top; p. 99 bottom; p. 110; p. 124; p. 128 top; p. 128 bottom; p. 129 bottom; p. 130 bottom; p. 131 top; p. 132 top; p. 140 bottom; p. 141; p. 143 top; p. 153; p. 160 bottom; p. 163; p. 164 bottom; p. 177 top; p. 179 bottom; p. 186 top; p. 194 top; p. 197 bottom; p. 203 bottom; p. 207 bottom; p. 208; p. 209 bottom; p. 210 bottom; p. 211 top; p. 211 bottom; p. 212 bottom; p. 218; p. 224 bottom; p. 228 top; p. 229; p. 232 top; p. 232 bottom; p. 240 bottom; p. 243 bottom; p. 246; p. 249; p. 251; p. 253 top; p. 254 top; p. 255 bottom; p. 256 top; p. 257 top; p. 257 middle; p. 257 bottom; p. 263 top; p. 263 bottom; p. 265 top; p. 265 bottom; p. 266 top; p. 266 bottom; p. 270; p. 272 top; p. 273 2d from top; p. 275 bottom; p. 276 bottom; p. 277 bottom; p. 288; p. 289; p. 290; p. 301 bottom; p. 324 bottom; p. 340 top; p. 341 top; p. 351 top; p. 366 bottom; p. 367 bottom; p. 370; p. 373 bottom; p. 375 left; p. 377 bottom; p. 380; p. 383 bottom; p. 387 top; p. 389 top; p. 401 top; p. 401 bottom; p. 402 top; p. 406 bottom; p. 415 top; p. 419 top; p. 421 left; p. 422 top; p. 422 bottom; p. 424 top; p. 424 bottom; p. 425; p. 432 top; p. 432 middle; p. 436 top; p. 438 bottom; p. 444 top; p. 446 top; p. 448; p. 451; p. 452 middle; p. 453 bottom; p. 454 top; p. 456 bottom; p. 458 top; p. 464 bottom; p. 467 bottom; p. 471 top; p. 471 bottom; p. 475 bottom; p. 477; p.

480; p. 483 bottom; p. 484 bottom; p. 485 top; p. 485 bottom; p. 487 top; p. 487 bottom; p. 489 top; p. 492 bottom; p. 496 top; p. 496 bottom; p. 498 bottom; p. 499 bottom; p. 501; p. 502 top; p. 503; p. 504; p. 505 top; p. 506 bottom; p. 507 top; p. 508 bottom; p. 509; p. 510; p. 511 top; p. 516 middle; p. 519 left; p. 519 right; p. 520 bottom; p. 521 top; p. 521 middle; p. 521 bottom; p. 522; p. 523 middle; p. 524; p. 525 top; p. 526 bottom; p. 527 top; p. 528; p. 529 top; p. 529 bottom; p. 530 top; p. 531; p. 533; p. 536 bottom; p. 537 top; p. 539 top; p. 540; p. 541 bottom; p. 542; p. 544 bottom; p. 547; p. 549 top; p. 552 bottom; p. 553 bottom; p. 554 top; p. 554 bottom; p. 556 top; p. 556 middle; p. 556 bottom; p. 558; p. 565 top; p. 566 top; p. 567 bottom; p. 570 top; p. 576 bottom; p. 578 top; p. 582 top; p. 597 bottom; p. 599 bottom; p. 607 top; p. 609 middle; p. 634 middle; p. 635 top; p. 635 bottom; p. 640 bottom; p. 644 2d from top

HCF Measured Drawings: p. 37 top; p. 69; p. 80 bottom; p. 95; p. 146 top; p. 161 bottom; p. 170; p. 173 bottom; p. 185; p. 193 bottom; p. 216 bottom; p. 222; p. 231 top; p. 255 top; p. 258 middle; p. 262; p. 265 middle; p. 280 bottom; p. 283 bottom; p. 296 bottom; p. 319; p. 342; p. 421 right; p. 442 bottom; p. 455 top; p. 499 top; p. 500 middle; p. 538 bottom; p. 620; p. 625; p. 632 top; p. 634 bottom; p. 641 top

Carl Julien: p. 613 bottom

Glenn Keyes, AIA: p. 643 top

Mrs. I. M. Lemacks: p. 543 bottom

Library of Congress: p. 386 bottom; p. 395 bottom

LS3P Architects: p. 362 top

Richard Marks, III: p. 539 bottom; p. 639 top

Massachusetts Commandery Military Order of the Loyal Legion and the U. S. Army Military History Institute: p. 28 bottom

Medical University of South Carolina: p. 621 middle

The Museum of Early Southern Decorative Arts: *A View of Charles-Town, the Capital of South Carolina, 1774,* painted by Thomas Leitch, engraved by Samuel Smith, p. 26

The National Archives, Brady Collection: p. 28 middle; p. 51; p. 123 bottom; p. 302 top; p. 329 top; p. 331; p. 338 top; p. 338 bottom

Louis Nelson: p. 88 top

Mr. and Mrs. Robert Prenner: p. 264 bottom

Preservation Consultants: p. 67 top (drawing by John Laurens); p. 363 (photo by John Laurens); p. 384 (photo by John Laurens); p. 407 top

Collection of Ronald Ramsey: p. 59 bottom; p. 114 top; p. 236 top

Ron Anton Rocz: p. 386 top

St. Andrews Lutheran Church: p. 476 top

P. Sanders: p. 172 bottom

South Carolina Department of Archives and History: p. 109 top

The South Carolina Historical Society: p. 24; p. 125 top; p. 131 bottom; p. 135 top; p. 155 bottom(used with permission of Mrs. Maurice Cohen); p. 156; p. 181 bottom; p. 188 bottom; p. 220 bottom (used with permission of Mitchell, Small & Donahue, Architects); p. 296 top; p. 300 bottom; p. 313 bottom(used with permission of Mitchell, Small & Donahue, Architects); p. 460 top; p. 461 bottom

Mr. and Mrs. Arthur Swanson: p. 282 top

The Valentine Museum, Cook Collection: p. 626; p. 113; p. 260 top; p. 498 middle

Collection of Robert N. S. Whitelaw: p. 332 top (*Artwork of Charleston, 1898)*; p. 579 top (*Artwork of Charleston, 1898*); p. 605 top (*Artwork of Charleston, 1898*); p. 615 top (*Artwork of Charleston, 1898*)

Dr. G. Fraser Wilson: p. 309 top

Yale University Art Gallery: *View along the East Battery* by S. Barnard, Mabel Brady Garvan Collection, p. 91 and p. 221 bottom

GENERAL INDEX

Devereux, John Henry (architect), 168, 269, 297, 366, 369, 386
Dewar, Charles, 282
Dewar-Lee-Pringle House, **282**
Dewees, William, 89, 587
DeWolf, Anne, 269
Dieckhoff, Cordt, House, 588–89, **588**
Dime Savings Bank, 371
Dingle, George, 193; John (city engineer), 330; Olive O., 330
Dingle, George, House, **193**
Dingle House, **330**
Dinkelburg, Frederick P. (architect), 266–67
Divine, Thomas (mason), 491
Dock Street Theater, 126, 179–80, **179, 180,** 440
Don, Alexander, 234
Dorre, Henry (baker), 380
Dorrill, Robert, 131
Dorrill, Robert, House, **131**
Doscher, John H., 121
Doughty, Thomas, 421
Doughty, Thomas, House, **422**
Douxsaint-Macaulay House, 84
Dove, William Pritchard, 135
Dove, William Pritchard, House, 135–36, **135**
Dowd, Martin (bottle dealer), 418
Dowd, Martin, Tenements, **418**
Downie, Robert (tinsmith), 164
Downie, Robert, Buildings, **164**
Drake, Charles, 275; Miles (dry goods merchant), 374
Drake, Charles, House, **275**
Drapers, Ernest, 141
Drayton, Charles, 222, 593; Eliza, 222; John (planter), 235; Rebecca, 506; Sarah, 593; Col. William, 224
Drayton, Charles, House, **222**
Drayton, John, House, 235–36, **236**
Drayton-Girardeau House, **506**
Drayton Hall, **25,** 222, 235
DuBois, W. E. B., 429
Ducat, George (shipbuilder), 147
Ducat, George, House, **147**
Dulles, Allen, 106; John Foster, 106; Joseph, 106
Dulles, Joseph, House, **106**

Duncan, Daniel (laborer), 328; Daniel Z. (fireman), 328; Patrick, 634
Duncan House (Ashley Hall School), 26, 634
Duncan, Daniel Z., House, 327–28, **327**
Duncan, Patrick, Villa, **434**
Duncan Street, 618
Dunham, Mr. and Mrs. Thomas, 105
Dunkin, Alfred Huger, 624; Justice Benjamin Faneuil, 617, 636, 640, 646; Eliza Huger, 624
Dunkin, Benjamin Faneuil, House, 646–47, **646**
Dunkin, Benjamin F., Tenement, **640**
Dupré, Benjamin (tailor), 433; Juliana, 464
Dupré, Benjamin, House, **433**
Dupré, Juliana, Tenements, **463**
Dutarque, Lewis (planter), 106
Dutarque-Guida House, 106–7
Dutch Church Alley, 346
Duvall, Stephen (harbor pilot), 68

Earle, John E., 189
Earthquake of 1886, 56, 60, 107, 108, 141, 149, 167, 182, 190, 198, 210, 220, 235, 248, 252 273, 317, 327, 340, 347, 389, 393, 408, 421, 456, 468, 476, 487, 492, 508, 522, 557, 574, 578, 587, 590, 632
Eason's Boarding House, 524
East Battery, 119, 198, **199,** 217–23, 240, 295, 469
East Bay Street, **35,** 49, **50,** 51, 70, 74, 90–16, 120, 134, 197, 200, 207, 211, 243, 253, 335, 339, 348–50, 357, 367, 381, 424, 425, 430–36, 557, 595, 601
Eberly, John, 127
Eckhard, Jacob (organist), 284–85
Eckhard, Jacob, House, 284–85, **284**
Eckhardt, Mary Elizabeth Burckmeyer Elsworth, 470
Eckhardt-Patrick House, **470**
Eddings, John, 310
Edmonston, Charles (merchant), 102, 119, 221; Lawrence, 617, 641, 646; Lawrence A., **646**
Edmondston-Alston House, 198, 221–22, **221**

Maiden Lane, **455**, 458
Majestic Square, 339, 344, **362**
Mallar, Robert, 644
Manigault, Charles, 224; Charlotte, 613; Gabriel, 26, 32, 111, 139, 157, 158, 166–67, 182, 224, 412, 607, 612; Joseph (planter), 388, 612, 623, 630; Louis, 225
Manigault-Sinkler House, **224**
Manigault, Gabriel, House (demolished), 188
Manigault, Gabriel, Tenement, **111**
Manigault, Joseph, House, 26, 29, 612–13, **612**, **613**, 614
Mansfield, George, 548
Mansion House Hotel, 166, 282
Mansion House Hotel Annex, 164–65
Mappus, John J., 644
Mappus, John J., Tenements, 644–45, **644**
Marine Hospital, 351–52, **351**
Mariner's Church, 397
Marion, Gen. Francis, 83; memorial to, 394; Mary A. S., 83; Sophia F. S., 645
Marion, Francis, Hotel, 384–85, **384**; Hotel Company, 384
Marion Square, 393–94, **393**, 446
Marjenhoff, W. C., 115
Market Hall, 27, **339**, 395–96, **395**, **396**
Market Street, 335, 337, 345, 346, 362, 363, 400, 404
Marks, Francis, 387
Marks, Francis, House, 387–88, **387**
Marlborough Realty Houses, **408**
Marscher, Anna, 484
Marsh, James, 350, 453
Marsh, James, House, **453**
Marshall, Alex, 162; Mary, 493; T. K., 162
Marshall Buildings, **162**
Martelle, Miss Laura, 322
Martelle, Laura, Houses, 322–23, **322**
Martin, Fredericka, 390; James, 514; John C., 56; Robert (cotton trader), 400, 483, 586, 595; Sarah, 320; William, 434; William M., 56;
Martin House, **320**

Martin, Robert, House, **595**, 623
Martindale, James C., 514
Martino, Dr. John, 174
Martschink Building, 347–48, **347**
Martschink Warehouse, 405
Mary Street, 405, 585
Mashburn, Catherine, 491
Mashburn, Catherine, House, **491**
Masonic Temple Building, 369–70, 370
Matthewes, George (planter), 501
Matthewes-Legare House, **501**
Matthews, Anthony (merchant), 44, 71, 215; Gov. John, 554; Maurice, 155; S. J. L., 328
Matthews, George, House, **215**
Matthews, S. J. L., House, 328
Matthews, William, 602
Matthiessen, Johanna, 493; William, 583
Mathiessen, William, Tenement, **583**
Mattson, Alex (draymaster), 407–8
Mattson, Alex, House, 407–8, **408**
Maverick, Samuel, Jr., 386
Maxwell, Nathaniel G., 566
Maxwell, Nathaniel, House, **566**
Maybank, Gov. Burnet Rhett, 242, 613
Mayer, Franz, and Company (Munich), 209, 451
Mayer, John George, 134
Mayer, John George, House, **134**
Mazyck, Alexander, 585; Arthur, 296; Catherine, 343; Charlotte, 165; Isaac, III, 76–77, 165, 287, 336, 342
Mazyck, Benjamin, Tenement, **391**
Mazyckborough, 585, 593, 597, 599, 601
Mazyck, Isaac, House, 76–77, **76**
Mazyck (now Logan) Street, 337
Mazyck's Pasture, 585, 587
Mazyck-Wraggborough, 585–615
McBeth, James, 214
McBride, Patrick (merchant), 361
McBride-Chicco Building, **361**
McCabe, Benjamin, 561–62, 594; Benjamin F., 586
McCabe, Benjamin, Tenements, **594**

Sell, Elizabeth, House, 594–95, **595**
Seminole War, 643
Sessions, T. V. (carpenter), 443
Severens, Ken, 37
Seyle, John, 58; John H. (architect),
58, 641; Samuel, 499
Seyle, Samuel, Building, 404;
Seyle, Samuel, House, **499**
Seymour, Gov. Horatio, 269; Sally,
282
Shaffer, Frederick, 623; Walter L., 398
Shaffer, Frederick, House, **623**
Shamrock Terrace, 91
Shepherd, Sophia Frances Perry, 633;
Thomas Radcliffe, 642
Shepherd-Wilson House, **633**
Sherfesee, Louis, 523
Sherman, Gen. William T., 621
Shingler, William Pinckney (cotton
factor), 56, 198, 308–9
Shingler, William Pinckney, Houses,
308–9, **308, 309**
Shoolbred, James (planter), 539
Short Street, 390
Shubrick, Col. Thomas, 175
Shutze, Philip Trammell (architect), 637
Shrewsbury, Stephen, 432
Shrewsbury, Stephen, House, **432, 433**
Sickles, Gen. Daniel, 598–99
Siegling, Henry, 152; John, 365
Siegling Music House, 365–66, **366**
Simonds, Andrew, 199, 266; Daisy,
266; John C., 223
Simmons, Francis, 243; James, 259;
Philip (ironworker), 34–35, 210,
426, 428, 435
Simmons-Edwards House, 243–44,
243
Simmons, James, House, **259**
Simmons, Philip, Garden, 425
Simms, William Gilmore, 112
Simons, Albert (architect), 69, 74, 81,
88, 91, 93, 103, 106, 122, 177,
185, 188, 210, 220, 278, 307, 324,
325, 439–40, 460, 490, 525, 568,
571; Dr. Benjamin Bonneau, 435;
Caroline, 300; Edward, 486;
Francis, 198; Harriett, 325;
Harriett R., 536; James, 174, 319;
James S., 561; John (merchant),

498; John Hume (planter), 485;
Keating L., 540; Dr. Manning, 321;
Mary Hume Lucas, 485; Maurice,
234, 319; Samuel Wragg, 300;
Thomas Grange, 506, 540; Dr.
Thomas Y., 67; W. Lucas, 81; Wil-
liam Bayard, 541
Simons and Lapham, architects, 313,
324, 345, 511
Simons Center for the Arts, **568**
Simons Houses, **300**
Simons, Harriett Porcher, House, **325**
Simons, Harriett R., House, **536**
Simons-Jager House, **319**
Simons, James S., House, **561**
Simons, John C., House, **498**
Simons, John Hume, House, **485**
Simons, Lapham, Mitchell and Small,
386, 568
Simons, Maurice, House, 234
Simons, Manning, House, 321
Simons Tenements, **266**
Simonton, Charles H. (attorney), 642
Simpson, Jonathan, House, 96–97, **96**
Singer Manufacturing Company, 358
Single house, 26, 37–41
Singuinate, Giovanni B., 416
Sisters of Charity of Our Lady of
Mercy, 262, 469
Sisters of Our Lady of Mercy Orphan-
age, 408
Skirving, James, 248
Slave Mart, **64**; Museum, 101
Small, Jacob, 497
Small, Robert Scott, Library, 515
Smiser, Paul (planter and craftsman), 87
Smith, Agnes, 57; Alexander, 288 (tai-
lor); Alice Ravenel Huger, 72; B.
Pressley, 492; Benjamin (trader),
160, 161; Benjamin (building sup-
ply merchant), 449; Benjamin
(planter), 529, 531; Capt. Ben-
jamin (shipbuilder), 200; Daniel
Elliott Huger, 72; Edwin H. (cabi-
netmaker), 125; Eliza Middleton
Huger (Mrs. William Mason
Smith), 72; Frank M., 538;
Henrietta, 559; Henry Augustus
Middleton, 222; Hugh (architect),
57, 158; Joel, 446; John, 61; Josiah

Ward, James McCall, 286
Ward, James McCall, House, **286**
Warham, Charles, House, 140
Waring, Benjamin, 558; Clarence, 302; Elizabeth Cordes, 599; Dr. and Mrs. Joseph I., 241; Laura Witte, 238; Leila, 200; May, 200; Morton, 207; Thomas R. (editor), 238
Waring House, **238**
Waring, Clarence, House, 302–3, **302**
Waring, May and Lelia, House, **200**
Waring, Morton, House, **207**
Warnecke, John Carl, 404
Warnecke and Partners, 403–4
Warner, Cyrus (draftsman-architect), 450
Warren, Russell, 577
Warren Street, 617, 618, 624, 629, 636, 640, 641, 645–47
Washbee Range, 504
Washington, President George, 78, 148, 195; Col. William, 267
Washington, Col. William, House, 267–68, **268**
Washington Light Infantry, 460
Washington Park, 195
Waterfront Park, 30, 152–53, **153**
Water Street, 149–52, 216
Watt, James (grocer), 213
Watson, John (gardener), 414
Wayne, Daniel G. (architect-builder), 456, 578
Webb, Virginia, 646; Matthew, 39; Walter, 231
Webb, Walter, Store, **231**
Weeks, J. S., and Company Range, 398–99, **398**
Wegman, Catherine, 597
Wegman-Holmes House, 597–98, **597**
Wells, Anna, 150; Edgar (tailor), 60; Dr. Edward, 150; John, 147; Robert, 147; Sabina Elliott, 150
Wells, Edgar, House, **232**
Wentworth Street, 370, 371, 413, 418, 419, 457, 468, 469, 471–77, 485, 491, 501, 522, 543, 553, 555, 562, 567, 569–83
Wentworth Street Baptist Church, 610
Wentworth Street Methodist Protestant Church, 475

Werner, Christopher, 32, 206, 249, 511; Fannie, 310
Werner, Fannie, House, **310**
Wesner, Frederick (architect), 182, 341–42, 393, 450
West, Charles, 103
Westcoat, Sarah, 596
Westcoat, Sarah, House, **596**
West Point Mill, 430, 481
West Street, 409
Whaley, W. Gibbes (attorney), 92; Richard S., 250
Whaley-Lapham House, **250**
Whilden, William, 553
Whilden, Elias, House, **632**
Whilden-Hirsch House, **553**
White, Charles Otto, 634 Dr. Christopher G., 535; Edward Brickell (architect), 27, 56, 85, 88, 193, 339, 348, 385, 395–96, 402, 445–46, 466–67, 477, 496, 510, 513, 571; Elizabeth Smith, 555; George (contractor), 395; James (merchant), 380 John (stonecutter), 186; John B., 248; J. T. H. (planter), 598; W. T., 45
White, Christopher, and Tobias-Lopez Tenement, **535**
White, James, Building, **380**
White, James, House, **555**
White, J. Thomas Hamlin, House, 598–99, **599**
Whitechapel Foundry, 185
Whitelaw, Patti Foos, 135; Robert N. S., 135
Whiteman, William, Tenement, **628**
White Oak Plantation, 612
White Point, 150, 197, 216, 291, 295; Gardens (public pleasure grounds), 219, 227, **291**
White-Williman House, **248**
Whitney, Drennis, Tenement, **237**
Whitney, Theodore, House, **307**
Wickenberg House, **622**
Wickliffe (John Hume Lucas) House, **622**
Wienges, Conrad M. (saddler and harness maker), 63
Wieters, E. F. A., and Sons (wholesale grocers), 114; O. F. (wholesale grocer), 116; O. T. (grocer), 115

INDEX OF STREETS